S0-AIW-296

Problems in Differential Diagnosis:

From DSM-III to DSM-III-R in Clinical Practice

Problems in Differential Diagnosis:

From DSM-III to DSM-III-R in Clinical Practice

Andrew E. Skodol, M.D.
Columbia University
College of Physicians and Surgeons
and the
New York State Psychiatric Institute

1400 K Street, N.W.
Washington, DC 20005

Note: The author has worked to ensure that all information in this book concerning drug dosages, schedules, and routes of administration is accurate as of the time of publication and consistent with standards set by the U.S. Food and Drug Administration and the general medical community. As medical research and practice advance, however, therapeutic standards may change. For this reason and because human and mechanical errors sometimes occur, we recommend that readers follow the advice of a physician who is directly involved in their care or the care of a member of their family.

The case vignettes included in this book are based on the case histories of real patients. Care has been taken, however, to disguise the identities of the patients by altering such details as age, occupation, and locale.

Diagnostic criteria and decision trees in this book are reprinted with permission from the *Diagnostic and Statistical Manual of Mental Disorders, Third Edition, Revised*. Copyright © 1987 American Psychiatric Association.

Books published by the American Psychiatric Press, Inc., represent the views and opinions of the individual authors and do not necessarily represent the policies and opinions of the Press or the American Psychiatric Association.

Manufactured in the United States of America
89 90 91 92 4 3 2 1

The paper used in this publication meets the minimum requirements of the American National Standard for Information Sciences—Permanence of Paper for Printed Library Materials ANSI Z39.48-1984. ∞™

Library of Congress Cataloging-in-Publication Data

Skodol, Andrew E.
Problems in differential diagnosis : from DSM-III to DSM-III-R in clinical practice / Andrew E. Skodol.
p. cm.
Includes bibliographies and index.
ISBN 0-88048-044-0 (alk. paper)
1.Diagnosis, Differential. 2. Mental illness—Diagnosis.
3. Diagnostic and statistical manual of mental disorders.
I. Title.
[DNLM: 1. Mental Disorders—classification. 2. Mental Disorders—diagnosis. WM 141 S628p]
RC473.D54S56 1989
616.89' 075—dc19
DNLM/DLC 89-6
for Library of Congress CIP

Contents

List of Tables *vii*
List of Figures *xi*
Foreword *xiii*
Allen J. Frances, M.D.
Introduction *xv*
Acknowledgments *xix*

1 **Diagnostic Interviewing** 1
2 **Multiaxial Diagnosis** 39
3 **Disturbances with Specific Organic Etiologies** 77
4 **Disturbances Associated with the Use of Psychoactive Substances** 121
5 **Psychotic Features** 161
6 **Mood Disturbances** 221
7 **Anxiety Syndromes** 275
8 **Physical Complaints** 319
9 **Personality Disturbances** 373
10 **Antisocial, Aggressive, or Violent Behavior** 425
11 **Differential Diagnosis in the Elderly** 449
12 **Miscellaneous Syndromes: Common and Uncommon, New and Old** 471
Index *519*

To Laura, Daniel, and Alison
With the heart

List of Tables

1.1 Major Mental Syndromes and Their Defining Features 34

2.1 DSM-III-R Guidelines for Specifying Current Severity of Disorder 51

2.2 DSM-III-R Axis IV Rating Scales 62

2.3 Questions Measuring Marital Dissatisfaction 66

2.4 Questions Measuring Job Dissatisfaction 67

2.5 DSM-III-R Global Assessment of Functioning (GAF) Scale 69

3.1 DSM-III-R Diagnostic Criteria for Delirium 85

3.2 DSM-III-R Diagnostic Criteria for Dementia 88

3.3 DSM-III-R Diagnostic Criteria for Organic Anxiety Syndrome 100

3.4 DSM-III-R Diagnostic Criteria for Organic Personality Syndrome 101

3.5 A Sample of Systemic and Central Nervous System Diseases That Cause Organic Mental Disorders and Their Corresponding Code Numbers in the ICD-9-CM 112

4.1 DSM-III-R Diagnostic Criteria for Psychoactive Substance Dependence 133

4.2 DSM-III-R Diagnostic Criteria for Psychoactive Substance Abuse 140

4.3 Psychoactive Substance-Induced Organic Mental Disorders in DSM-III and DSM-III-R 150

4.4 DSM-III-R Diagnostic Criteria for Posthallucinogen Perception Disorder 152

4.5 Psychoactive Substances, Medications, and Poisons That Can Cause Symptoms of Mood Disturbance or Anxiety 153

5.1 Disorders in the Differential Diagnosis of Psychotic Features 162

5.2 DSM-III-R Diagnostic Criteria for Schizophrenia 182

5.3 DSM-III-R Diagnostic Criteria for Delusional Disorder 186

5.4 DSM-III-R Diagnostic Criteria for Schizophreniform Disorder 198

5.5 DSM-III-R Diagnostic Criteria for Schizoaffective Disorder 209

6.1 Disorders in the Differential Diagnosis of Disturbances in Mood 226

6.2 Identifying Features of DSM-III-R Mood Disorders 227
6.3 DSM-III-R Diagnostic Criteria for Major Depressive Episode 230
6.4 A Comparison of DSM-III and DSM-III-R Definitions of Melancholia 238
6.5 DSM-III-R Diagnostic Criteria for Dysthymia 243
6.6 DSM-III-R Diagnostic Criteria for Manic Episode 259
6.7 DSM-III-R Diagnostic Criteria for Cyclothymia 264
7.1 Disorders in the Differential Diagnosis of Anxiety Syndromes 278
7.2 Characteristic Features of DSM-III-R Anxiety Disorders 280
7.3 DSM-III-R Diagnostic Criteria for Panic Disorder 283
7.4 DSM-III-R Diagnostic Criteria for Panic Disorder with Agoraphobia 290
7.5 DSM-III-R Diagnostic Criteria for Social Phobia 293
7.6 DSM-III-R Diagnostic Criteria for Posttraumatic Stress Disorder 304
7.7 Symptom Clusters in DSM-III-R Generalized Anxiety Disorder 313
7.8 Features of DSM-III-R Anxiety Disorders of Childhood or Adolescence 314
8.1 Disorders in the Differential Diagnosis of Physical Complaints 324
8.2 DSM-III-R Diagnostic Criteria for Somatization Disorder 334
8.3 DSM-III-R Diagnostic Criteria for Somatoform Pain Disorder 343
8.4 DSM-III-R Diagnostic Criteria for Trichotillomania 349
8.5 DSM-III-R Diagnostic Criteria for Insomnia Disorders 359
8.6 DSM-III-R Diagnostic Criteria for Hypersomnia Disorders 360
8.7 DSM-III-R Diagnostic Criteria for Anorexia Nervosa 364
8.8 DSM-III-R Diagnostic Criteria for Bulimia Nervosa 366
9.1 DSM-III vs. DSM-III-R Criteria for Histrionic Personality Disorder 391
9.2 DSM-III vs. DSM-III-R Criteria for Dependent Personality Disorder 392
9.3 DSM-III-R Personality Disorder Clusters, Specific Types, and Their Defining Clinical Features 396
9.4 DSM-III-R Diagnostic Criteria for Narcissistic Personality Disorder 406
9.5 DSM-III-R Diagnostic Criteria for Borderline Personality Disorder 411
9.6 DSM-III-R Diagnostic Criteria for Avoidant Personality Disorder 414

9.7 DSM-III-R Diagnostic Criteria for Self-defeating Personality Disorder 418

9.8 DSM-III-R Diagnostic Criteria for Sadistic Personality Disorder 419

10.1 Disorders in the Differential Diagnosis of Antisocial, Aggressive, or Violent Behavior 430

10.2 Symptoms of DSM-III-R Attention-Deficit Hyperactivity Disorder 437

10.3 Symptoms of DSM-III-R Conduct Disorder 442

11.1 Differential Diagnosis of Mental Disorders in the Elderly 451

12.1 DSM-III-R Diagnostic Criteria for Multiple Personality Disorder 475

12.2 DSM-III-R Paraphilias 481

12.3 A Comparison of DSM-III and DSM-III-R Criteria for Voyeurism 482

12.4 Essential Features of Impulse Control Disorders Not Elsewhere Classified in DSM-III-R 486

12.5 DSM-III-R Diagnostic Criteria for Pathological Gambling 486

12.6 DSM-III-R Diagnostic Criteria for Brief Reactive Psychosis 495

12.7 DSM-III-R Diagnostic Criteria for Late Luteal Phase Dysphoric Disorder 503

12.8 DSM-III-R Diagnostic Criteria for Tourette's Disorder 514

12.9 DSM-III-R Diagnostic Criteria for Induced Psychotic Disorder 515

12.10 Proposed Diagnostic Criteria for Possession/Trance Disorder 516

List of Figures

3.1 DSM-III-R Decision Tree for the Differential Diagnosis of Organic Mental Disorders 82

4.1 Decision Tree for the Differential Diagnosis of Disorders Associated with the Use of Psychoactive Substances 130

5.1 DSM-III-R Decision Tree for the Differential Diagnosis of Psychotic Features 164

5.2 Typical Patterns of Prodromal, Active Psychotic, and Residual Symptoms in Psychotic Disorders 193

5.3 Differential Diagnosis of Schizophrenia, Psychotic Mood Disorders, and Schizoaffective Disorder Based on Relationship of Mood Disturbance to Psychotic Features Over Time 205

6.1 DSM-III-R Decision Tree for the Differential Diagnosis of Mood Disturbances 224

6.2 Examples of Clinical Courses of Major Depressive Episodes with Chronic Depressive Symptoms 250

7.1 DSM-III-R Decision Tree for the Differential Diagnosis of Anxiety Disorders 276

8.1 Decision Tree for the Differential Diagnosis of Physical Complaints 322

8.2 Decision Tree for the Differential Diagnosis of Sexual Dysfunction 351

8.3 Decision Tree for the Differential Diagnosis of Sleep Disturbance 354

10.1 Decision Tree for the Differential Diagnosis of Antisocial, Aggressive, or Violent Behavior 428

Foreword

I began my training as a resident in psychiatry twenty years ago, in the same year as the publication of DSM-II. You may recall that DSM-II was a very thin book that seemed to be of no great interest to anyone but Bob Spitzer and medical records librarians. Most of us realized that psychiatric diagnosis had very little to do with treatment planning, perhaps because our teachers were unable to agree in their methods of making diagnoses and because most patients received more or less the same treatments regardless of the diagnosis.

All of this had changed greatly twelve short years later with the publication of DSM-III. DSM-III was a very fat book that interested almost everyone because it represented and was promoting a radical paradigm shift in psychiatry. Psychiatry had acquired a shared language that allowed diagnoses to be made with very respectable reliability. In the interim between DSMs, it had also become increasingly clear that specific psychiatric diagnoses often led to quite specific treatment recommendations. The availability of a reliable diagnostic system served to further the study of the validity of psychiatric disorders and the development of treatment strategies (both psychopharmacologic and psychotherapeutic) targeted to the specific psychiatric syndromes. The provision of explicit diagnostic criteria and of the multiaxial system in DSM-III was an innovation that thrust psychiatric diagnosis back into a central position in the clinical and research enterprise.

Andy Skodol was a member of the Biometrics Research Department, under the direction of Bob Spitzer, during the exciting years when this group was coordinating the work that culminated in DSM-III. He has an intimate knowledge of the criteria sets for the DSM systems derived from having helped create them and from extensive experience in training others in their use. Dr. Skodol also combines the gifts of an experienced clinician and a dedicated scholar.

It is therefore no surprise to me that Dr. Skodol has written a fascinating and invaluable book, one that will reward careful study and sharpen the diagnostic skills of all who read and use it. Patients in real life are rarely easily recognizable prototypes who conform clearly to the definitions provided by the criteria sets in DSM-III and DSM-

III-R. Diagnostic decisions in clinical practice are often difficult and subtle and require judicious weighing of the evidence. Dr. Skodol's book provides numerous case examples that are true to the complexity of the clinical situation and provide us with a ringside account of how a diagnostic master solves the clinical puzzles we routinely encounter in everyday practice. What gradually emerges beyond the specifics of various diagnostic decision points that are addressed, is Dr. Skodol's method of systematic and logical sorting of clinical data in the application of the criteria-based diagnostic system.

I value this book so highly that we are sending it to all those individuals who are now most closely engaged in preparing DSM-IV. Dr. Skodol's expert exegesis of DSM-III-R is the best starting point I can think of for the discussion and literature reviews that will ultimately result in the next revision of our diagnostic system.

Allen J. Frances, M.D.

Introduction

Dorland's Medical Dictionary defines the word *diagnosis* as "The art of distinguishing one disease from another," or "The determination of the nature of a case of disease." The diagnostic process in medicine is the application of a set of principles about the nature, mechanisms, and causes of illness to an individual case. Differential diagnosis is the process of distinguishing one illness from another.

Before the advent of DSM-III, many clinicians believed that the diagnosis of mental disorders was a practice of dubious value. Psychiatric diagnoses had been demonstrated by a number of studies to be unreliable; two clinicians evaluating the same patient would often disagree on the appropriate diagnosis. The benefit—to either the patient or the clinician—of assigning a diagnosis was uncertain at best. It was commonly thought by both scholars and the public at large that psychiatric "labels" had negative effects on patients because they engendered prejudice and interfered with patients' abilities to function in society—as workers, for example.

National and international efforts to develop improved classification systems for mental disorders continue because a fundamental, first step in the diagnostic enterprise is to classify pathological states according to certain important distinctions among those states. A classification is the systematic arrangement of any similar entities on the basis of differing characteristics. A nomenclature is a classified system of names. Nosology is the specific science of the classification of diseases. The definitions and classification of all illnesses are in a sense arbitrary; the definitions of diseases and illnesses are conventions, constructs, abstractions that do not correspond to anything in nature. They are justified by their usefulness. An agreed-upon language, a classification or nomenclature, is, however, essential for analytic thinking, for reasoning about any subject.

On a practical level, a classification enables users to communicate with each other about disorders in a shorthand fashion that summarizes certain agreed-upon features of categories that would be much more complicated to convey otherwise. A classification ideally also aids the clinician in either preventing the occurrence of a disorder or modifying its course through treatment. Finally, the ultimate purpose of a classification is to further understanding of the causes of disorders and the processes involved in their development and persistence.

In the years since its publication in 1980, DSM-III became widely used in mental health settings of all types, in the United States and throughout the world. Never before has a classification of mental disorders attracted the degree of interest and attention and stimulated as much controversy as has DSM-III. This "high profile" has undoubtedly been due to the belief that in its innovations, particularly diagnosis by specified criteria and the multiaxial evaluation system, DSM-III held great promise for improving psychiatric diagnostic practice, thereby not only facilitating research into the causes and treatments of mental disorders but also, consequently, improving patient care.

The implications for psychiatric education of adopting DSM-III as the official classification of mental disorders in the United States were not anticipated. DSM-III included no organized, integrated, educational component. Following its publication, demands for training were numerous. Both the American Psychiatric Association and the Columbia University Department of Psychiatry organized national symposia and continuing education courses and workshops to teach DSM-III multiaxial diagnosis. Various teaching aids for DSM-III were also developed. The best known are the APA's *DSM-III Institutional Instruction Kit* and the *DSM-III Case Book,* written by my former colleagues in the Biometrics Research Department of the New York State Psychiatric Institute and me.

Over the years, clinicians became familiar with the basics of the DSM-III system. As familiarity increased, so did an appreciation of the complexity of the system. Now a revision of DSM-III has been published. DSM-III-R was motivated by the experiences of clinicians and an "explosion" of research on nosologic issues in psychiatry that indicated that refinements in the classification were necessary. Although initially conceptualized as a "fine-tuning," DSM-III-R includes hundreds of specific changes in the diagnostic criteria that define the disorders and guide the clinician through the process of differential diagnosis.

The idea for *Problems in Differential Diagnosis* came from the DSM-III Advanced Clinical Workshop—a training program that I developed and presented at annual meetings of the American Psychiatric Association from 1981 through 1985. In this workshop, I addressed, with the help of experts in psychiatric diagnosis from across the country, the more difficult aspects of DSM-III differential diagnosis. We focused on those aspects of differential diagnosis that required the most clinical judgment or concerning which the DSM-III approach seemed ambiguous or inadequate or the guidelines presented were most difficult to understand.

I have written this book to aid in the continuing improvement of the diagnostic skills of clinicians who are familiar with the basics of DSM-III and who are making the transition to DSM-III-R. The book assumes a knowledge of the fundamentals of the DSM-III and DSM-III-R classifications and the DSM-III diagnostic criteria and multiaxial system. It focuses on complex or subtle problems, situations, and issues in differential diagnosis that commonly arise in clinical practice. I have emphasized how the Work Group to Revise DSM-III attempted to resolve, in DSM-III-R, some of the problems of DSM-III, although some problems apply equally to both systems. I have also tried to anticipate some new problems introduced by DSM-III-R.

My goals for *Problems in Differential Diagnosis* are threefold: (*1*) to guide clinicians in the application of rigorous principles of differential diagnosis in spite of the complexity or ambiguity of the clinical problem; (*2*) to place the DSM-III and DSM-III-R systems in a clinical context by focusing, as clinicians do, on syndromes of psychopathology from which a diagnosis must be made, and by including many clinical case examples from my own experience; (*3*) to bring together clinical and research traditions in order to emphasize the potential clinical value of differential diagnostic distinctions. Studies of the familial distribution of mental disorders may have relevance in assisting the clinician to identify persons at high risk for a disorder and thus undertake efforts at prevention. Treatment response studies are of value in guiding the clinician from an accurate diagnosis to the selection of appropriate treatment. Follow-up studies allow the clinician to prognosticate about the future course of a patient's condition. These standards for validating a psychiatric diagnostic category are, I believe, closely linked to the clinical purposes of the diagnostic process.

I have organized the book to facilitate refining the reader's skills in differential diagnosis according to DSM-III and DSM-III-R. It begins with a chapter on diagnostic interviewing that describes the elements of an adequate diagnostic interview, obstacles to successful completion of the interview, and strategies for overcoming problems. Then follows a chapter on multiaxial diagnosis. The bulk of the book consists of chapters on problems in differential diagnosis organized by major mental syndrome: psychoactive substance dependence, psychotic features, mood disturbance, anxiety, physical complaints, personality disturbance, and antisocial, aggressive, or violent behavior.

Since all of these syndromes may be associated with or caused by endogenous or exogenous organic factors, these chapters are preceded by one on disturbances with specific organic etiologies. This arrangement of the material mimics the step in the differential diagnostic process of first ruling out an organic mental disorder before considering functional mental disorders and reduces the redundancy that would result from discussing organic factors as potential causes of each of the major syndromes.

Within the major chapters there are clarifications of new or confusing terminology, an overview of the diagnostic possibilities for each syndrome, and discussion of specific problems in arriving at an accurate diagnosis and how best to resolve them. Chapters are frequently subdivided by subsyndrome, so that delirium and dementia are considered separately under disorders with specific organic etiologies, and depressive and bipolar (manic) syndromes, under mood disturbances.

Two chapters are devoted to special problems in differential diagnosis. Chapter 11 presents problems in the differential diagnosis of mental disorders among elderly patients, and the final chapter includes problems in the differential diagnosis of disorders that do not fit neatly into the more common mental disorder syndromes, including some that are not even listed in DSM-III or DSM-III-R or are specific to certain non-Western cultures.

Problems in Differential Diagnosis is meant to be used in conjunction with DSM-III or DSM-III-R. As such, no attempt was made to include the diagnostic criteria sets for all disorders. Instead, diagnostic criteria from DSM-III-R are reproduced for new diagnoses not included in DSM-III, such as organic anxiety syndrome and trichotillomania, and for disorders that have undergone substantial revision from DSM-III to DSM-III-R, such as social phobia and multiple personality disorder.

Decision trees from DSM-III-R are reproduced or, in some cases, modified and expanded to reflect my broader approach to the differential diagnosis of certain syndromes. New decision trees have been developed for areas of differential diagnosis not represented by trees in DSM-III-R. The diagnostic possibilities represented by the logic of the trees are presented in tables, in order to facilitate the clinician's learning a comprehensive differential for each major syndrome.

Problems in Differential Diagnosis is meant to be used by all mental health practitioners and advanced students of psychiatry, psychology, social work, and related disciplines who use DSM-III or DSM-III-R in their clinical work. It is the result of experiences over the past ten years that have shaped my approach to psychiatric diagnosis in clinical practice. I hope it will provide an impetus for the development of sharpened diagnostic acumen in other clinicians, present and future.

Acknowledgments

I am indebted to all those who have taught with me in DSM-III and DSM-III-R courses, from whom I have learned. The list is long and includes the following people: Nancy C. Andreasen, M.D., Dennis P. Cantwell, M.D., Jean Endicott, Ph.D., Allen J. Frances, M.D., Miriam Gibbon, M.S.W., Rachel Gittelman, Ph.D., Frederick Goodwin, M.D., John Greist, M.D., John Gunderson, M.D., Gerard Hogarty, M.S.W., Steven E. Hyler, M.D., Helen S. Kaplan, M.D., Kenneth S. Kendler, M.D., Donald F. Klein, M.D., John Kuehnle, M.D., Michael R. Liebowitz, M.D., Jerrold Maxmen, M.D., J. Craig Nelson, M.D., Michael K. Popkin, M.D., Ronald O. Rieder, M.D., Arthur Rifkin, M.D., Edward Sachar, M.D., David Shaffer, M.D., Lawrence Sharpe, M.D., Michael Sheehy, M.D., Robert L. Spitzer, M.D., Myrna Weissman, Ph.D., Janet B. W. Williams, D.S.W., and Lyman C. Wynne, M.D.

I am also indebted to other experts in psychiatric diagnosis whose work I have followed, and is referenced throughout this volume.

Special thanks go to the colleagues with whom I have co-taught the course on diagnostic interviewing described in Chapter 1: Robert Spitzer, M.D., Chief, Biometrics Research Department, New York State Psychiatric Institute; Ronald Rieder, M.D., Director of Residency Training, New York State Psychiatric Institute; and Michael Sheehy, M.D., Director, Silver Hill Foundation, New Canaan, CT.

Thanks are due also to all of the clinicians, residents, and students whose experiences with patients and challenging questions served as the springboard for this volume.

I am very grateful, needless to say, to my able assistants in the preparation of this manuscript: Harriet Ayers, swift and reliable in her typing of the many drafts of the work; and Betty Appelbaum, diligent and supportive in her editing of my unhewn prose.

Finally, to the patients whose problems have provided the case material for this book, I owe a lasting debt of gratitude for teaching us all.

CHAPTER 1

Diagnostic Interviewing

This chapter is based on my experiences, for the past nine years, in teaching a course on interviewing to psychiatric residents in their second year of postgraduate training and supervising, at first hand, intake evaluations in outpatient and emergency-room settings. The title, "Diagnostic Interviewing," indicates that the major purpose of the interviews I shall be discussing is to establish a working diagnosis that can serve as the basis for an initial plan for treatment. My colleagues and I have sometimes referred to our course content as "the initial interview," but we realize that clinicians may vary widely, depending on their theoretical orientations and consequent approaches to treatment, in what kinds of information they expect to obtain in the first contact with a patient, how long they want to spend with the patient, and by what means they go about gathering the desired information.

In our course and during sit-in supervision, we have usually imposed a time limit of one-half hour on the interviewer. Under ordinary clinical circumstances, such brevity would be necessary only in emergency situations, in which time may actually be even more limited. But since we recognize the need for information beyond a DSM-III or DSM-III-R diagnosis to plan treatment, we conceive of this interview as an essential part of all psychiatric evaluations, even if embedded in an assessment that may last one or more hours, or be spread over several sessions. We have resisted identifying this interview with an interview that might be required in Part II of the specialty examination for certification in psychiatry by the National Board of Medical Examiners, although parallels have been drawn by others because of the similar time restrictions. We believe that the diagnostic interview is of much broader clinical utility.

This chapter will describe an approach to diagnostic interviewing. I shall not attempt to cover the psychiatric interview as a whole; the reader is referred to other treatments of this subject (1-3). Instead,

I shall focus on the techniques we have found most effective in obtaining the information necessary to make a DSM-III or DSM-III-R multiaxial assessment, and shall illustrate, with numerous clinical examples, those techniques and the handling of problems that might be encountered. To some extent, problems in differential diagnosis that will be discussed in subsequent chapters are anticipated, since one source of difficulty in arriving at an accurate diagnosis is inadequate information available on which to base it.

PURPOSES OF A DIAGNOSTIC INTERVIEW

The main purpose of the diagnostic interview is to gather the information necessary for making a DSM-III or DSM-III-R multiaxial diagnostic assessment. As part of this overall goal, it is necessary to form a cooperative alliance with the patient that will facilitate the information-gathering process. It will also be necessary to manage obstacles to the successful completion of the task. Finally, it is desirable that the interview be perceived by the patient as therapeutic, in the sense that he or she feels understood by an empathic interviewer and optimistic about future contacts with that interviewer or other mental health professionals. The interviewer is not considered successful if a diagnosis can be made but the patient becomes less willing to continue or seek treatment.

Basic Assumptions

I shall assume that the information is to be gathered primarily from the patient himself or herself. There are obviously numerous instances in which supplemental or even critical data need to be obtained from a significant other. Some of these include the situation in which the patient is unable to provide information, e.g., in the case of a dementia, is unwilling, e.g., in the case of a paranoid psychosis, or provides an inaccurate assessment of his or her own state of mind, e.g., in the case of a manic episode or a personality disorder. Nevertheless, in each case, attempts are routinely made to get information directly from the patient.

A second basic assumption is that the diagnostic enterprise is a "joint venture," a collaboration between the clinician and the patient. It is very important, in using our technique, that the clinician be comfortable with the basic premise that he or she has expertise in understanding the nature of patients' problems and that even the reluctant patient stands to profit from the evaluation encounter. This holds true even though the patient may have to experience some distress in recounting the difficulties that led to seeking or receiving care. Novice interviewers often have considerable difficulty accepting and feeling comfortable in the role of the expert and consequently approach the patient apologetically, allow the patient to guide the flow of the interview completely, or, conversely, feel that the obligation for a successful interview rests solely on the interviewer. Our technique maintains that the interviewer assumes that the interview will be of mutual benefit and communicates matter-of-factly to the patient the expectation that the patient will be cooperative. Of course, there are many instances in which the patient is not cooperative to some degree; but by having and communicating the expectation of cooperation, the clinician can use certain techniques in dealing with the uncooperative patient. These will be discussed in more detail in the sections on specific problems that follow.

A corollary assumption is that the patient who is suffering wants to talk about it, even if expressing reluctance. Although it is frequently painful, most patients feel better about having told an empathic listener about their problems. Sometimes the patient's overt reluctance is due to a feeling or perception that the interviewer is not genuinely interested in hearing about or attempting to understand his or her troubles. This may be specific to the particular patient and related to character traits, or it may be specific to the particular interview situation and a response to the interviewer's communicating boredom, anxiety about his or her own performance, or the impression that the material is too emotionally charged to listen to or too irrelevant to be of interest. The interviewer is obliged, to the best of his or her ability, to present a concerned, interested, and involved presence to the patient, in order to maximize cooperation. Ultimately, the patient who feels that his or her problems are acceptable and understandable by an expert in human emotions and their disturbances will feel relieved and more inclined to seek further treatment.

Hypothesis-testing Strategies

The structure of the diagnostic interview involves repeatedly formulating and testing hypotheses about the nature of the patient's problems. This is true of all psychiatric interviews, but the theoretical orientation of the interviewer regarding the etiology or pathogenesis of the problem makes the hypotheses that are being tested by a range of clinicians widely divergent. In the diagnostic interview, the hypotheses are concerned largely with the nature of the disorder that could account for the difficulties being described by the patient and, within the context of the DSM-III and DSM-III-R multiaxial system, their relationship to physical factors, psychosocial stressors, and adaptive functioning. Questions, probes, clarifications, and confrontations in the diagnostic interview should be motivated by a particular hypothesis being considered by the clinician that requires active testing.

Clinicians are sometimes unsure of the extent to which their interviews should be structured. Should they be relatively focused, with closed-ended questions, or more free-flowing, with open-ended questions and considerable tolerance for the direction the interview takes? Although members of our department have been much involved in the development of structured interviews for psychiatric research, we usually do not recommend structured interviews for general clinical purposes. Some elements of structured interviewing, however, fit into the strategy of diagnostic interviewing we advocate.

We have observed three types of interviewing style among psychiatric clinicians. Robert Spitzer has dubbed them the "smorgasbord," the "checklist," and the "canine" approaches.

Interviewers using the smorgasbord approach are not guided by specific hypotheses to be tested for the particular patient being interviewed, but instead feel that a variety of areas of importance should be "sampled," such as complaints, stressors, early childhood history, social relations, family history of mental disorder, etc. The interviewer takes a "taste" of each, but devotes himself or herself to none, and frequently is left at the end with a collection of data that lacks coherence and leaves many essential questions unanswered.

In contrast, using the checklist, interviewers approach patients with preconceived notions of what is important for them to know about the patient in detail and ask questions in a set, unvarying, and frequently closed-ended manner, almost disregarding the particular problems or experiences of the patient. Using this approach, the interviewer comes up with a list of signs and symptoms, but frequently fails to make important discriminations among syndromes that have similar complaints. Moreover, patients are "left cold" by the checklist because it is evident that the interviewer is imposing a structure on their problems that barely acknowledges their experiences or distress.

In the final approach, the canine, the interviewer functions like the proverbial dog in search of a bone. The bone in this case, of course, is the diagnostically crucial information. The interviewer "sniffs" around for potentially vital data and, on spotting a suspicious area, "digs" until he or she reaches the "bone" or discovers that he or she has been misled. In the latter case, the interviewer proceeds to another area and "digs" where his clinical sense tells him the "bone" may be discovered.

Some readers may be discouraged by the comparison of the interviewer to a backyard dog, but the point that the interviewer's efforts should be guided by well-formulated hypotheses and their testing is well taken. It is frequently useful to combine elements of the three styles described above. The interviewer may begin with a series of open-ended questions to get an overview of the patient's difficulties and a sense of how the patient views his or her own troubles. When the patient begins to discuss crucial information, the interviewer narrows the focus in order to evaluate the diagnostic significance of the information. A question such as "How has your mood been?" may elicit a welling-up of tears in the patient's eyes. Probing the significance of this tearful response may then uncover the fact that the patient has indeed felt persistently depressed, sad, and pessimistic about the future for several weeks. The interviewer may then shift to a quick but thorough check to see if the patient has also been experiencing associated symptoms of a major depressive syndrome such as loss of appetite, sleep disturbance, loss of energy, and inability to concentrate every day for two weeks or more. Thus, by shifting from one mode of interviewing to another, the interviewer establishes the presence of a major depressive episode. From this point on, the goal of the interviewer may be to proceed with the differential diagnosis of major depressive episodes (see Chapter 6), or he or she may wish to learn more about the circumstances, including psychosocial stressors, that were associated with the current episode.

The hypothesis-testing strategy obviously and appropriately places the interviewer in control of the interview. There is a delicate balance to be struck between exerting this necessary control and being overcontrolling to the degree that the patient is not given a chance to talk and consequently feels that the interviewer is not listening. Most beginning interviewers usually err on the side of allowing the patient too much control of the interview. On the other hand, more experienced interviewers may reach premature closure on the nature of the problem—some studies have shown that diagnoses are commonly made and not changed after the first few minutes with a patient (4,5)—and not be open to hearing the patient out and following new leads.

Structure of the Interview

The diagnostic interview should be structured to yield the information necessary to make a DSM-III or DSM-III-R multiaxial assessment. I follow a format, modeled on a medical examination, that includes a determination of (*1*) identifying information, (*2*) the chief complaint, (*3*) a history of the present illness, (*4*) a history of past mental illness and treatment, (*5*) patterns of personality functioning, (*6*) current and past physical health, (*7*) the occurrence of psychosocial stressors, (*8*) recent and past levels of adaptive functioning, (*9*) optional, potentially relevant information, including family history, developmental history, formal mental status testing, or other information necessary to plan treatment.

Beginning the Interview

Most interviews begin with the interviewer's introducing himself or herself and explaining the purpose of the interview, if it is not self-evident. Explanations may be that the interview is being conducted primarily to teach residents about interviewing or about psychiatric diagnosis, or that it is being conducted at the request of a third party, such as the patient's therapist, or a lawyer, or a representative of a social agency. An alternative approach is to ask the patient whether he or she understands the purpose of the interview first, before providing the explanation. This may give the interviewer a brief glimpse of the patient's cognitive functioning and degree of cooperativeness and help determine the structure of the interview to follow.

Obtaining identifying information. Many interviewers prefer to start an interview by asking a few questions necessary to obtain basic information about the patient—age, marital status, number of children, place of residence, occupation or grade in school, etc. For patients already in the hospital, this may also include the ward or service on which the patient is hospitalized and when the patient was admitted or how long he or she has been in the hospital. This approach has the advantage of serving as an "ice-breaker" and allowing the patient to get accustomed to the interviewer and the interview setting before launching into an examination of the presumably more emotionally charged issues that led to the consultation or evaluation.

Even this is not without pitfalls, however, since sometimes what would ordinarily be straightforward demographic information turns out to be intimately connected to the patient's problems, or to be a sensitive area for other reasons. For instance, a patient consulting a therapist over concerns about homosexuality or who has recently become widowed may be put off, upset, or unexpectedly defensive when asked, "Are you married?" Another disadvantage is that the interviewer may make an initial impression of being too automatic or mechanical, going through certain steps without real interest or concern. Both patient and interviewer know that the "real" questions about the patient's troubles are yet to come.

Whether to obtain this information initially or not seems a matter of personal comfort or preference. Most such information is important to know, but could be obtained at other points in the interview when, far from being a diversion, it may actually have heightened relevance. For example, a single woman complaining that she is feeling upset and desperate about her dwindling chances for marriage or motherhood, or a young person complaining about overly controlling or restrictive parents, would probably find the question "How old *are* you?" appropriate and meaningful.

Eliciting the chief complaint. Interestingly, one of the most difficult parts of the diagnostic interview is the initial question aimed at encouraging the patient to begin telling about his or her problems. Since the initial question frequently sets the tone for the entire interview, how it is phrased is very important. I have found that a specific question cannot be recommended for all interviewers: the phraseology needs to come naturally to the interviewer and be appropriate for the particular patient and the setting. The most common opening question I put to already hospitalized patients goes something like this: "So, tell me how it is that you've come to be in the hospital?" For an outpatient consultation, I may say, "So, tell me about what's been bothering you and how I can help."

Each of these openings is made as matter-of-factly as possible, in keeping with my philosophy that patients want to talk and want my input as a professional into their situations. In addition, neither is phrased completely as a question, but rather as a firm request or gentle demand, conveying both my expectation that the patient will want to respond and my willingness to listen. For me, such questions set the tone for the cooperative enterprise the ideal interview is designed to be and facilitate the exploration to follow.

Other clinicians have a myriad of other opening questions, many undoubtedly effective. There are a few, however, that I have heard while supervising that I think are not as good. One such opening is overly apologetic and passive, e.g., "I wonder if you could just tell me a little bit about . . . " The "wonder" conveys the sense that there is as good a chance that the patient will not as will tell the interviewer about what is troubling him or her, and that the interviewer has little or no expectation of cooperation. "Just" implies that it is really nothing to tell, when in fact it is something. "A little bit" is a mixed message. If the interviewer is truly interested in learning about the patient, and if it is worthwhile for the patient to be speaking to a professional, then one really wants to know "a lot" or "all" or "everything," not just "a little bit."

"Maybe you could tell me . . ." conveys the same sense of uncertainty: the "could" begs the issue of whether or not the patient "would" tell. Most patients, unless they are severely demented, delirious, or disorganized, *can* tell; the question is, *Will* they?

Interviews that begin like this do not inspire confidence and potentially push the patient away. They frequently make the rest of the interview difficult because they set the stage for noncooperation and a lack of self-disclosure on the part of the patient.

Other less than optimal openings include "What were the events or circumstances that led up to your hospitalization?" This question may place too much emphasis on a historical recounting of the chain of events leading to the patient's seeking treatment or being hospitalized and may be inappropriate in many cases. It also points the patient, and possibly the direction of the interview, away from affects or unusual thoughts that may be central to the patient's condition. A question such as "What happened that led to your hospitalization?" presents similar problems.

Other related leads into the patient's chief complaint are, "How do you happen to be in the hospital?"; "What were the problems that brought you to the hospital?"; or "What brought you to the hospital?" The first question implies passivity on the part of the patient, i.e., that he or she played no part in seeking treatment, and could play right into the hands of a manic or paranoid patient who felt that there really was nothing wrong with him, but that he had been "railroaded" into the hospital by others. The second question obviously invites the answer, "I don't have any problems." The following brief exchange between an interviewer and a manic 25-year-old man illustrates this point.

Holy Man

Patient: By the way, before we start, I just wanted to tell you that everything I say, there's no bullshit. It's the truth.
Interviewer: Why don't we begin by your telling me exactly what it was that got you into the hospital?
Patient: I was transferred from City Hospital.
Interviewer: O.K., what got you into that hospital?
Patient: I was pretending to be an undercover cop.
Interviewer: You were pretending to be an undercover cop? How come?
Patient: How come? I had just seen the movie *Serpico*. And I knew I could do a better job.
Interviewer: Was it recently that you saw the film?
Patient: About two months ago.
Interviewer: This had been going on for some time then?
Patient: Yeah.

Interviewer: So, how long has it been since you were last feeling well?
Patient: Last feeling well? Right now!
Interviewer: You've been feeling well, then?
Patient: Oh, yeah. I've been feeling well for the past . . . I've been feeling well for a long time.
Interviewer: However, going into the hospital means that other people are not certain that you're well.
Patient: Of course! That's what I've been dealing with.
Interviewer: Well, then, let's rephrase the question. How long has it been since others have felt that there was something the matter with you?
Patient: That began about three months ago. I was telling my sister that I could take any amount of cyanide or mescaline, or any other drug, and that it wouldn't have any effect on me at all. She didn't believe me.

In this example, the experienced interviewer quickly picked up on the patient's denial of his illness and turned the focus onto how others might have perceived the problem. This led the patient to speak quite candidly about how he had been feeling and what he had been doing and made the interviewer's task of understanding the nature of the problem a relatively easy one.

The last of the questions above, "What brought you to the hospital?", implies passivity and is too concrete. Some patients answer this question literally—"An ambulance."

Some interviewers open their interviews by asking the patient, "How do you feel?" This opening has a certain value in that it obviously conveys to the patient that the interviewer is very interested in finding out about the patient's feelings, which are invariably something that the patient wants and needs to talk about. Such a question can also be extremely facilitating if the patient happens to have some strong feelings, such as embarrassment or anger, about being interviewed. These negative feelings may be especially important if the patient is being evaluated or interviewed involuntarily, as in the case of a forensic or workmen's compensation evaluation.

There are pitfalls to this approach, however. In my experience, interviews that begin with such a here-and-now "feelings" orientation frequently come up short on facts. The patient may experience the invitation to "ventilate" as rewarding, but the interviewer may find himself or herself being somewhat unselective about the affects explored and failing to find out such important facts, from a differential diagnostic point of view, as the time course of a mood disturbance, its persistence, the precipitating events or circumstances, or the role of drugs in its development. The skillful diagnostic interviewer at some point obviously has to introduce the question of how the patient is or was feeling, especially if the patient does not spontaneously mention it.

Actually, whether or not a patient begins to talk about events, relationships to others, feelings, or other matters, in response to a less directive opening question, such as the ones I previously suggested, he or she may reveal some important features of his or her personality. Also, the experienced interviewer should be able to spot the patient who is reluctant or resistant because of feelings about the interview situation or the interviewer and address these feelings as a way of overcoming an obstacle to collecting needed information. In this case, the observation is "I am not getting much information." The hypothesis to be tested might be "This patient may be embarrassed by the group interview situation," which could be tested by a question: "You seem to be having trouble answering my questions. Is there something about being here that bothers you?"

A final, frequently nonproductive opening question is, "Why did you come to the hospital?" Although it is often very important to gauge a patient's insight into his or her problems, the "why" questions sometimes imply that the interviewer expects a relatively high level of understanding of the problem by the patient. This can then put off the patient who understands very little about why he or she is feeling what he or she is feeling or thinking what he or she is thinking. It seems much better to begin with eliciting a description of *what* it is the patient is feeling or thinking and only later introduce the question of why.

Data Gathering

Once the chief complaint has been elicited, the clinician then aims for expansion on the part of the patient that will lead to thorough understanding of the nature of the problem and raise possible hypotheses regarding the actual diagnosis. This requires an elaboration of the presenting problem on the part of the patient. Some patients will spontaneously go into detail about what they have been feeling, experiencing, or doing in relationship to the chief complaint. For example, a patient who says "I've been having anxiety attacks" may immediately launch into a description of what kinds of symptoms he or she has been experiencing, when they occur, when and how they began, and how severe or disabling they have become. Some patients may require minimal prompting, as the following interview excerpt demonstrates.

Anxiety Attacks

Patient: I've been having these "seizures" of anxiety.
Interviewer: Seizures of anxiety? What are they like?
Patient: Well, I get these attacks of anxiety that come on me when I'm driving or in a crowded place. I feel my heart start to pound and I get all short of breath. I can't concentrate, I feel nauseous, and all of my body goes tight.

Other patients will need considerably more structured probing:

More Anxiety Attacks

Patient: Well, I just feel anxious inside, you know?
Interviewer: What do you mean, anxious?
Patient: I don't know, just anxious.
Interviewer: Are there physical symptoms involved?
Patient: Well, yes, my heart pounds real hard and fast and I feel like I can't get my breath.
Interviewer: Anything else?
Patient: What do you mean?
Interviewer: Well, do you get chest pains . . . , do you sweat . . . , ?
Patient: Yes. In fact, there was one time when I thought I was actually having a heart attack!

Some clinicians prompt with mere repetition of what the patient has said, sometimes with a questioning inflection—"Anxiety attacks?"—or with a general probe, such as "Tell me about that."

Certain patients provide more than enough information in describing their reasons for coming to the hospital or clinic. For them, the chief complaint is only one aspect of what might be a complex tale of events, circumstances, times, places, and interactions with others that led to the clinical contact. Under these conditions, the clinician must make a choice about the kind of information that is expected to be most relevant and direct the flow of the interview accordingly. For the purpose of making a diagnosis, the clinician will usually want to focus the patient on the syndrome or syndromes that, on the basis of initial impressions, seem likely to be present. For example, a manic syndrome may be suspected in a patient who has pressured speech and appears overactive, or the syndrome of panic anxiety may seem a likely diagnosis for someone who reports extreme anxiety or severely restricted activities.

Using an interviewing strategy that focuses attention on symptoms and syndromes often means that certain interesting and perhaps important data, such as quality of interpersonal relations or degree of social functioning, will be passed over, at least initially. It is a temptation for a novice interviewer or one not used to making diagnoses as part of the initial interview to conduct a social history-taking interview that will end up lacking the specific information necessary for a diagnostic formulation. Of course, this is not to say that the interviewer should appear uninterested in dramatic or poignant revelations on the part of the patient, such as the recent death of a close family member, or a history of being sexually abused as a child. An unresponsive interviewer will obviously alienate the patient; thus, appropriate, empathic acknowledgment of what the patient has related is desirable. An in-depth exploration of the issue, however, should probably be postponed until the interviewer better understands the nature of the present disturbance.

History of the present illness. After obtaining a clear picture of the patient's presenting complaints, the interviewer focuses on the development of the problem. Usually, attention is first devoted to the current episode, which may turn out to be a recurrence or may have been preceded by an episode of another mental disorder. Aspects of the clinical course of a patient's problems have come to receive considerable emphasis in modern psychiatric diagnosis, in that features of a disturbance such as its duration or frequency of occurrence have been incorporated into the diagnostic criteria of psychotic, mood, and anxiety disorders, among others.

The history of the present illness should begin with documentation of the onset of the present episode. Documenting episode onset has recently become an area of interest for clinicians and researchers as strategies for early intervention and prevention of episodes of disorder have been developed (6-8). Determining when a person was last his or her "usual self" or when an episode began is not easy, however, since the clinician is focusing on subtle changes that are hard to distinguish from ordinary fluctuations in a person's sense of well-being that may occur from day to day, or on the development of a new problem within the context of some other, more chronic difficulties. At a minimum, the clinician tries to document: (*1*) the onset of the first noticed sign, symptom, or behavior change that is part of the current syndrome, and (2) the time at which the full symptom picture became apparent. These two points in time are often helpful in trying to understand the interaction between events or situations and psychopathology. For example, did a negative event, such as a marital separation or being fired from a job, lead to an episode or exacerbation of a disorder, or was the former a consequence of the latter? Until more is known about the interplay of potentially pathogenic factors and mental disorders, diagnosis and treatment planning are best served by avoiding premature etiologic speculations.

After determining probable onset, the clinician attempts to elicit the course of development of the syndrome. This frequently leads to determining a point at which the syndrome reached its worst or was most severe. In many diagnostic interviews, it is this worst period that should become the focus of more intensive cross-examination about specific symptoms, especially in cases in which there is some ambiguity. Thus, a patient who reports ideas of reference that are not clearly delusional can have his or her reality testing explored with reference to the time when the thoughts were most intense. Similarly, a person with depressed mood can be assessed for the symptoms of a full depressive syndrome, needed for the diagnosis of major depression, at the height of the episode.

If a patient does not meet the criteria for a particular disorder at the most severe point in its course, then the disturbance is below threshold for the diagnosis in question, and another, potential diagnosis or no diagnosis should be considered (see also the discussion of adjustment disorder in Chapter 6 and the discussion of V codes in Chapter 12). The value of focusing on the worst period is greatest if this period has occurred within the past six months. Recent research has shown that reports about mental disorders occurring in the distant past are subject to memory effects and other sources of unreliability (9,10).

Past psychiatric history. Although the details of previous episodes of psychopathology may be somewhat unreliable, there remains a need to determine certain aspects of past psychiatic history. The earliest age at which a person had an episode of mental disorder may have diagnostic or prognostic significance. For a patient with a current psychotic disorder, previous episodes of psychotic mood disorders may establish the diagnosis. The occurrence of two different syndromes, such as depression and physical complaints or substance use and psychosis, will result in different diagnostic judgments depending on the relationship between the two syndromes over time. These situations will be discussed in detail in the chapters dealing with each of the major areas of differential diagnosis.

Previous treatment, especially psychotropic drug treatment and hospitalizations, are important details of the past psychiatric history. In determining differential diagnosis, clinicians sometimes tend to overstate the significance of response to medication, however. Although response to psychotropic medication has become a standard for validating psychiatric diagnoses in research studies, there is still too much individual variation in patients' responses to medications for those responses to be used as guides to differential diagnosis. Previous treatment with and response to medication can nevertheless be useful as confirmatory data once a diagnosis based on phenomenology has been determined. Prior hospitalizations usually indicate a malignant process, which occasionally may go undetected in the history of the present illness because of the patient's defenses or oversight on the part of an unsuspecting clinician.

Personality functioning. Following the multiaxial format of DSM-III and DSM-III-R, the area for assessment after the principal clinical syndrome or syndromes have been diagnosed is that of personality functioning. The major pitfalls in personality assessment and diagnosis according to DSM-III and DSM-III-R are discussed in detail in Chapter 9. In this chapter I shall consider (*1*) eliciting information relevant to personality functioning, and (2) distinguishing disturbances in personality functioning from Axis I conditions already established.

According to DSM-III and DSM-III-R, personality disorder invariably disturbs social and/or occupational functioning. Eliciting information, for example, about the extent, closeness, and quality of relationships with friends and the capacity for a sustained, reciprocal relationship with a close other person is important. Some of this information will come spontaneously in the course of the patient's description of the present illness, but some of it may require specific questions. Job attainment, job stability, educational level and performance, and relationships with bosses and co-workers are also important in assessing personality.

Once the clinician has gained an idea about personality functioning through general questions, he or she may pursue a specific personality disorder with direct questions. An impulsive, self-destructive, moody person may not spontaneously describe the boredom, conflict over values, or a volatile temper that would indicate borderline personality disorder; the clinician may need to pose direct, relevant questions. Although, traditionally, people have not been thought to be good direct evaluators of their own personality traits, some recent research has used direct questions (11,12) and even self-reports (13,14) to assess personality functioning.

A major caveat in assessing personality disorders in the initial interview is that what appears to be a trait phenomenon, i.e., an enduring personality characteristic, may in fact be state dependent, that is, a function of the person's Axis I psychopathology. Clinicians may attempt to circumvent this obstacle by asking a question such as, "Other than when you are depressed, as you told me about a few minutes ago, do you tend to be a very emotional, reactive kind of person, or cool-headed and in control?" This is much more easily done if the Axis I disorder is a fairly recent and discrete episode than if it is a long-standing, pervasive disorder; in the latter case, the separation of the Axis I disorder from a personality disorder is both artificial and practically impossible.

Physical status. DSM-III and DSM-III-R include an axis for noting the presence of physical disorders or conditions that may be relevant to understanding or managing the treatment of the patient. The presence (or absence) of known physical disorders has diagnostic significance for a number of Axis I disorders and conditions, as described in Chapters 3 and 8. A few selected questions about a person's overall physical health, the presence of any chronic physical problems that require treatment, whether the person sees a medical doctor with regularity, and whether any medications have been taken in the relevant past are indicated in an initial diagnostic interview. The period of interest is most often that spanning the current illness and any past episodes of diagnostic significance.

Stressors. In DSM-III and DSM-III-R multiaxial diagnosis, the presence of psychosocial stressors that may have led to the development or exacerbation of the mental disorder is indicated on Axis IV. At some point, if it is not readily apparent, the clinician should inquire whether anything stressful occurred just before onset of the earliest symptoms of the disorder. Exploration of the role of subtle stressors is held for the later portions of the interview, so as not to detract from an adequate exploration of the psychopathology.

Adaptive functioning. DSM-III and DSM-III-R also include an axis, number V, for noting level of functioning. In DSM-III this was for rating the highest level of adaptive functioning during the year preceding the clinical evaluation. This axis was made a part of the multiaxial system of DSM-III in the belief that adaptive functioning has considerable prognostic value, independent of the Axis I or II disorder. Most clinicians routinely collect data about a person's quantity and quality of social relationships and ability to function on a job or in school. Sometimes these areas of functioning are affected by the present illness, but in other situations they need to be probed in their own right. As I shall discuss in Chapter 2, Multiaxial Diagnosis, the concept of functioning rated on Axis V has been changed in DSM-III-R, and both the highest level during the past year and the current level are rated. Social and occupational functioning continue to influence the ratings.

Optional areas of assessment. The above-discussed phases of the diagnostic interview data-gathering process are considered essential to a DSM-III or DSM-III-R multiaxial evaluation. There are several other areas that many clinicians think are also relevant, such as family history of mental disorder and developmental history.

Eliciting a family history of mental disorder among the first-degree relatives of patients undergoing evaluation is a common part of many initial interviews. Many clinicians attempt to use family history information to guide their differential diagnosis in confusing cases. There are several problems with this approach. First, the frequency with which a positive family history can be elicited, even among the relatives of people with major mental disorders such as schizophrenia or major depression, is relatively low. In the Danish Adoption Study of Schizophrenia (15,16), probands' family histories have been scrutinized by numerous investigators (17-20), and the frequency of schizophrenia among the biological relatives of adoptees with schizophrenia is less than 10%. Including people with so-called schizophrenic-spectrum disorders, defined in a number of different ways, increases the percentage to up to 25%. The figures for affective disorder in relatives of people with affective disorders generally range from approximately 15% to 35% (21,22). These estimates are based on rigorous family-history and family study methodologies that are known to uncover a higher rate of disorder in relatives than the routine questions asked about family history by clinicians (23). Therefore, the clinician is more likely than not to elicit a negative family history.

Moreover, even with regard to the major mental disorders, family history does not appear to be diagnostically specific. In recent studies by Gershon and associates (24) and Andreasen and co-workers (25), unipolar depression was the most common diagnosis among the first-degree relatives of probands with bipolar I, bipolar II, unipolar affective, and schizoaffective disorders (defined by RDC criteria). Published studies of a familial loading for schizophrenia have recently used a mentally ill comparison group that would allow for a test of the specificity of the schizophrenic-spectrum disorders for schizophrenia, as opposed to serious mental disorders in general, and the initial results fail to support the specificity hypothesis (26,27). Thus, the clinician would be at a loss to assign a specific diagnosis on the basis of an accurately reported illness in a close family member.

There have been virtually no tests of the ability of the unstandardized family-history reports that clinicians typically elicit to distinguish patients with mental disorders from controls and no evidence that these are useful in making a differential diagnosis. There is evidence, however, that the more certain a positive family history, in terms of the nature of the disorder and its being treated, the more valid is the diagnosis of the *proband* in terms of a positive dexamethasone suppression test (28). Therefore, clinicians who have solid evidence of a particular disorder in a relative could legitimately use this information to *confirm* a diagnostic impression of a patient that was based on phenomenology or course.

Psychodynamically oriented clinicians, in particular, believe that a developmental history is an essential diagnostic tool. DSM-III has been criticized for its paucity of psychodynamically relevant material (29,30). Most clinicians who are not psychodynamically oriented find that a lack of systematization makes assessments of this kind unreliable, and that there are few indications that most developmental occurrences are diagnostically specific.

There are a few notable exceptions, particularly relevant to child psychiatry. Delays in developmental milestones such as walking, talking, controlling elimination, etc., can be indicative of subtle brain abnormalities that can later lead to problems with attention, hyperactive behavior, or learning disabilities. Gross deficits in language and social development indicate a pervasive developmental disorder. Problems with separation during latency or adolescence are sometimes found in the histories of adults with anxiety disorders (31). With the exception of certain specific problem areas, however, developmental history does not usually prove to be diagnostically helpful.

Because a psychiatric diagnosis, even one based on a multiaxial approach, is usually inadequate for formulating a complete treatment plan, other data must be elicited in an initial evaluation. The nature of these data will commonly be determined by the treatment orientation of the particular clinician. For example, a behaviorist will be interested in the pattern of behavioral responses that reinforces the symptom expression; a psychoanalytically oriented therapist will explore conflicts, defenses, ego functions, and object relations; a family therapist will concentrate on an analysis of family functioning in terms of leadership, boundaries, affectivity, communication, and task orientation.

At various times, additional axes for inclusion in DSM-III have been proposed for many of these areas of assessment (32,33); but, in general, their lack of standardization and the resulting increase in complexity that adding more axes to the multiaxial diagnostic process would entail have deterred their adoption. It seems best to accept the fact that a diagnosis cannot provide all treatment-relevant information and that "nondiagnostic" information is necessary for effective treatment-planning, regardless of the treatment being considered. The reader is referred to other texts for a more complete discussion of planning treatment (34-36).

POTENTIAL PROBLEMS

Numerous problems that interfere with efficient data collection and arriving at the best possible diagnostic understanding of the patient may be encountered in conducting a diagnostic interview. These may be considered patient problems or interviewer problems.

Patient Problems

Obviously, the interviewing strategy described in this chapter requires that the patient be somewhat verbal and, for the most part, cooperative. An initial obstacle can be a patient who does not speak. With silent patients, a judgment must be made concerning whether the patient is actually mute, as in catatonic schizophrenia, or is deliberately not speaking because he or she is distrustful or generally uncooperative. If the patient is mute, attempts should be made to establish whether there is impairment in level of consciousness suggestive of an organic brain syndrome. Standard neurological texts, such as that by Plum and Posner (37), include guidelines for distinguishing catatonic stupor from organic stupor and coma. If the patient has no organic problem, it is in the interests of the interviewer to explain the purposes of the interview to the patient and to take the opportunity to observe the patient in detail. Such patients are unlikely to respond by cooperating, but some diagnostically relevant information can be obtained by observation alone, e.g., from the patient's general appearance and gross motor activity, if there is any. When the patient appears rigid, without spontaneous movements, the interviewer, having described this procedure in advance, can move the patient's limbs passively to test for waxy flexibility. The interviewer can also observe the patient's apparent degree of attentiveness and can sometimes make a judgment about his or her affective state, particularly if the patient is extremely fearful or anxious.

If the patient appears negativistic, he or she is probably suspicious or distrustful of the interviewer. Wary patients do not usually appear rigid, may sometimes turn their heads away from the interviewer, and may give nonverbal signs of annoyance, impatience, or disgust, such as deep sighs or audible noises. When eye contact can be made, the distrustful patient appears visibly anxious and threatened. Since the diagnostic interview is conceived as an essentially nonconfrontational and mutually cooperative enterprise, an explanation to this effect and of the purpose of the interview can sometimes gain the cooperation of the distrustful patient. Although the information obtained is very likely to be incomplete or inaccurate, gaining enough trust to allow the patient to speak will enable the interviewer to observe the thought processes, for evaluating formal thought disorder, and the content, for assessing delusions.

Another problem patient is the one who speaks, but does not provide adequate information. A range of psychopathology may account for this behavior. A hostile, argumentative patient may refuse to answer some or all of the interviewer's questions, may ridicule the interview or the interview process, and/or may verbally berate or actually threaten the interviewer. The management of the hostile and threatening patient is beyond the scope of this chapter, and is covered adequately in various textbooks on emergency psychiatry (38-40). The main reason for mentioning this problem here is to point out that interviewers frequently neglect to "reflect back" to the patient the apparent affect that is impeding the conduct of the interview (e.g., "You sound very angry"; "It sounds as if you're here unwillingly"; "I don't understand why you're so mad at me"). This maneuver, coupled with an attempt to point out the potential usefulness of a cooperative alliance between the patient and the interviewer, sometimes enables the interviewer to proceed. Furthermore, if the patient is nonpsychotic, an effort by the clinician to get him or her to see the irrationality of at least the anger directed against the interviewer can have diagnostic significance and facilitate the evaluation process.

Labels

A 21-year-old, single woman was interviewed on videotape. The tape was the second she had made; both were intended for use in teaching a class on diagnostic interviewing.

The young lady was dressed all in white. She had long, wavy, brown hair that obscured some of her face. She was barefoot and smoked a cigarette. Upon entering the studio, she sat down in a swivel chair and spun around, full circle.

Interviewer: So, how old are you, Margaret?

Patient: 21.

Interviewer: How long have you been here in the hospital?

Patient: Since Saturday.

Interviewer: How is it that you're in the hospital?

Patient: Oh no, not again! I'm not going to answer the same questions. I

already spoke to Barbara Lake, and she told me that I would not have to answer the same questions over and over. You've heard this before!
Interviewer: I haven't.
Patient: Well, go look at the videotape.
Interviewer: Look, I know it's difficult to talk about some of these things, but one of the ways that we can get to know you better and maybe be of some help is to go over the same story many times. Each of us might be able to understand a little bit more.
Patient: Well, if these are the same questions, and I'm going to have the same answers, and this is the same room and the same videotape, you can go check out the other film. I won't answer the same questions.
Interviewer: Well, you know, I must say, when you signed the consent form, you said that you agreed to talk about certain things—things I wouldn't understand or that no one could ever understand.
Patient: That's right.
Interviewer: So why get so angry at me? Why not tell me about that?
Patient: Well, O.K. You see, you keep asking me questions that I have no answers to. Something in my imagination has opened up—inside of me. O.K.? If it's opened up inside of me, there's no possible way I could put it in words, to translate it to you. Now, in my imagination, it's silent. It has no words. If I put it into words, you'll hear something that you'll understand, but you won't understand my silence. In my mind I see pictures and images, but how can I put a picture or an image into words so that you can see it—unless I talk in colors.
Interviewer: Is this something new that's been happening to you?
Patient: No, it's been happening since I was born.
Interviewer: Didn't you say that there was an "opening up" of your imagination? To me that implied a change of some kind.
Patient: OK. A child's imagination is open. It's not confined to the physical life—yet. Until the child is sent to school, and thoughts are put into its head, like "One and one is two" and "This is green, and this is blue," a child does not see like that. All right? A child doesn't need to see like that. Nobody needs to see like that. If someone tells me that "Two plus two equals four," I'll hear it, but I don't have to believe it. I finally came to realize that everything that society tries to put into your head is just because somebody made it up.
Interviewer: When did you come to that realization?
Patient: About three years ago. I always knew it. But I was so involved in being sent to school and having to do what somebody else told me to do. I just said, "Hey, wait a minute; this is my life, I'm not going to spend it anybody else's way."
Interviewer: Is there anything that happened that was associated with that change?
Patient: No, nothing I could put in words. It was internal.
Interviewer: Did you change your behavior in some way as a result?
Patient: Oh, sure. I stopped damning everything in sight by putting a label on it. I accepted everything for what it was. Now, I see something on that table. You might call it a book. But I just see something there. I could see the table, but to me it's not a table, it's just something that I see. I need no labels for anything. If somebody asks me my name, I just tell them that I am, and that's all that matters. Now who are you? I mean, can you answer that question, "Who are you?" Does your name tell me that? Does your age tell me that?

Interviewer: I guess it's identifying information.
Patient: Right, labels.

The interviewer proceeded to investigate the possibility of a psychotic disorder. The final diagnosis was an identity disorder.

Inadequate information may also be a manifestation of psychotic thinking. An extremely psychotic person who is cooperative may be too confused in his or her thinking to organize material meaningfully; may have poverty of content of thought, so that little of substance is expressed; may have such extreme loosening of associations as to be incoherent; or may be so delusional that all factual material has been distorted. Although these signs are of obvious diagnostic significance for the presence of psychosis, they may make determination of certain historical facts necessary for a differential diagnosis impossible. For example, a history of recent drug ingestion or of a preceding period of elevated mood and hyperactive behavior may not be elicited from the patient and may have to be confirmed by other sources. With psychotic patients it is usually valuable to interact with the person even if the reliability of the content of the information is suspect, since most of the mental status examination can be done on the basis of observation and listening alone.

The patient with an organic brain syndrome generally also provides inadequate information. This may be due to the patient's impaired level of consciousness, which makes him or her unable to attend to, and thus respond appropriately to, the interviewer's questions. The patient's answers may appear to be *non sequiturs*. Memory loss, leading to confabulation or interference with immediate recall of the questions asked, also severely limits the usefulness of the facts elicited. It is advisable to attempt to have the organically impaired patient focus attention to the extent possible, on questions or commands that are expressed as simply as will permit the elicitation of accurate answers. Examples would be orientation questions, simple facts, or instructions to follow simple directions, in order to discover the extent of impairment. Memory loss is frequently mentioned as a chief complaint; when it is not, it may be suspected from inconsistent answers, and investigated more formally in the mental status examination.

In the following case vignette, a neurologic disorder interferes with a man's ability to answer questions coherently. Excerpts taken from an evaluation interview illustrate how the clinician gradually adjusts his approach and appropriately judges the nature of the disturbance despite the paucity of the information available.

I Gotta Get Out of Here

Interviewer: Good morning Mr. Morgan. I'm Dr. Clay. I'll be taking care of you while you are in the hospital.
Patient: Good morning, Mr. Mor . . . , I mean . . . . Oh, boy, I gotta get out of here.
Interviewer: Is something the matter, Mr. Morgan?
Patient: Is something the matter? I gotta get out of here.

So began an evaluation interview by Dr. Clay, a senior resident rotating on the neuropsychiatric service of a large, general hospital in a midwestern city, with Mr. Jack Morgan, a 59-year-old, retired, high-school chemistry teacher. After several other unsuccessful forays into history taking, Dr. Clay tried a different tack.

Interviewer: O.K., Mr. Morgan; I can see that you're having a hard time right now. Let me ask you a few basic questions. Do you know the name of this place?
Patient: Midwestern General Hospital.
Interviewer: And today's date?
Patient: July 22, 1985.
Interviewer: Tell me your name?
Patient: Jack Morgan.
Interviewer: O.K. Who's the President?
Patient: Ronald Reagan.
Interviewer: And who was President before him?
Patient: Jimmy Carter.
Interviewer: I'd like you to remember three words for me: "dog," "green," and "truth." Can you repeat those?
Patient: Dog, green, and truth.
Interviewer: O.K. Please remember those words. I'm going to ask you what they were again in a few minutes.

From these questions, the resident concluded at least that Mr. Morgan was oriented, was able to attend to and understand simple questions and commands, and could recall certain well-known facts. Then Dr. Clay became more ambitious in his questions once again.

Interviewer: Mr. Morgan, what do you do for a living?
Patient: Thirty-five years of physics, biology, chemistry (referring to how long he had been a teacher and what subjects he taught).

And again:

Interviewer: Can you tell me why you came to the hospital?
Patient: I came from the school. I came from the hospital, . . . no, to the hospital because I wanted a job, I mean I wanted to get well. Oh, boy. I can't get the words out right.

And, again:

Interviewer: We're going to stop soon, but can you define the word *fabric* for me?
Patient: Fabric, fabric turns out to have a sweater, sheets, blankets, clothing.
Interviewer: Can you recall those three words that I asked you a few minutes ago?
Patient: Those three words?

Dr. Clay correctly recognized Mr. Morgan's severe word-finding difficulty—an expressive aphasia—and deficits in delayed recall. He arranged for a complete dementia workup. A history taken from Mr. Morgan's wife revealed that he had experienced cognitive decline over a three-year period, forcing an early retirement. He had become increasingly unsure of himself, indecisive, distressed, and depressed. Following a neuropsychiatric evaluation, diagnoses of major depression (Axis I) and transcortical fluent aphasia (Axis III) were made.

Finally, information obtained may be inadequate because the patient may be deliberately misleading. This may occur with antisocial personality disorder, malingering, factitious disorder, or certain other conditions. When the clinician is aware that he is being misled or lied to, confrontation can facilitate the interviewing process by promoting respect for the clinician in the eyes of the patient. This usually has to be done in as nonjudgmental or nonauthoritarian way as possible. Exceptions to this approach are warranted in special situations, or in the case of specially trained personnel, such as peer-group counselors in a narcotics rehabilitation program, who may be able to be very confrontational.

The patient's behavior may also disrupt the interview. The patient may be hyperactive and need to get up from the chair to pace the room or examine its contents (books, pictures, etc.). I believe it is best to maintain a degree of behavioral control of disruptive patients. This does not have to be done rigidly: I will allow the agitated or anxious patient to stand up, but I will not allow him or her to wander about; and I will suggest that we cannot accomplish what is necessary in the interview unless the patient remains seated. Once again, picking up on the patient's apparent affect may help (e.g., "You look very nervous to me"). Obviously, one cannot, and would not want to, force the patient to be seated; and in some instances, the interview may have to be terminated.

An actually threatening or menacing patient cannot be interviewed in the way outlined in this chapter. Behavioral limits are required—both verbal and, if necessary, pharmacologic. The clinician cannot do his or her job while feeling in physical danger, and permitting uncontrolled behavior is not in the interests of the patient. Again, emergency psychiatry texts offer more detailed advice (41,42).

Some patients experience powerful emotions during an interview, e.g., depression or anxiety, which, although more apt to arouse the interviewer's empathy than hostility or anger, can also present difficulties from the point of view of completing an adequate diagnostic interview. A patient may cry uncontrollably, or may experience such high levels of anxiety that he or she does not wish to remain in the interview situation or cannot concentrate on the questions asked. Obviously, these affective signs are very revealing; but in and of themselves, they are not diagnostic.

A skilled interviewer must express verbally to the patient an appreciation of the degree of distress that he or she is experiencing and allow the patient some moments to experience the affect, but not to be overwhelmed by it. Such responses on the part of the interviewer assume that he or she is able to sit with a person who is in severe emotional distress and tolerate open expression of these emotions. Generally, supportive psychotherapy techniques will help the patient in severe emotional distress. If these fail, the interviewer can give an explicit instruction to the patient: "This is very hard for you, obviously. I think you need to try to pull yourself together now, so that we can go on. Take a few minutes to get hold of yourself. Try hard; it will be better for you."

In rare instances, no interviewer intervention will suffice. I have never had the experience of a patient's not being able to continue because of uncontrolled crying, although I have had patients with overwhelming anxiety who have been unable to continue with any interaction other than one focused on describing their fear and somatic sensations.

In this list of patient disruptions, which is not by any means meant to be exhaustive, one further situation warrants mention. This is the case of a patient, perhaps with erotomania, who displays superseductive or uncontrolled sexual behavior. Such a patient may wish to disrobe, touch or kiss the interviewer, or sit on his or her lap. I mention this kind of patient because, although the behavior may not be physically dangerous to the interviewer, it is often very threatening. It is also another example of unrestrained expression of impulses; and it is not in the interests of the patient to permit such behavior to go uncontrolled. Therefore, the clinician needs to assert the same degree of limit setting as he or she would in the case of the overly aggressive patient who is losing control.

Interviewer Problems

Obviously, inadequate interviewing technique, from the point of view of any of the preceding discussion, constitutes an interviewer problem. In this section, in order not to be redundant, I shall discuss several other interviewer issues important for the conduct of an adequate diagnostic interview.

The central purpose of the initial interview, as stated above under basic assumptions, is to make a psychiatric diagnosis. An adequate psychiatric diagnosis is one that is reliable. Reliability refers to the replicability of discriminations made among things by certain procedures (43); reliability is applicable to psychiatric diagnoses made on the basis of data about emotional problems, or to medical diagnoses made on the basis of a chest X-ray or an electrocardiogram.

Sources of diagnostic unreliability. The reliability of psychiatric diagnosis has been a concern among researchers since the early 1960s. Traditionally, psychiatric diagnoses have not been particularly reliable, even for broad discriminations such as among psychosis, neurosis, or personality disorder (44). A 1962 study described the sources of diagnostic unreliability or error variance (45). Error variance refers to the unreliability of measurements due to inadequacies of the measurement procedures rather than to true differences among the things being measured. The sources of error variance are now referred to as information variance, interpretation variance, and criterion variance.

Much of the innovative research in the area of psychiatric diagnosis in the past two decades has involved the development of methods for reducing these sources of variance. Structured interviews with standardized question formats (46), such as the Present State Examination (PSE) (47), the Schedule for Affective Disorders and Schizophrenia (SADS) (48), the Diagnostic Interview Schedule (DIS) (49), and the Structured Clinical Interview for DSM-III-R (SCID) (50), have been developed in order to reduce diagnostic unreliability due to differences in the amounts, kinds, and sources of information available to two clinicians about a particular patient that might lead them to different diagnostic judgments. Specified diagnostic criteria, which outline the essential features and common associated features of the various mental disorders and important ways to discriminate among disorders that might closely resemble one another, were developed, first, for use in research studies (51,52) and then, with DSM-III, eventually for general clinical use (53). Diagnostic criteria ensure that two clinicians with the same information will summarize this information according to the same rules in making a diagnostic determination. Structured interviews and explicit diagnostic criteria have been demonstrated, in numerous studies, to improve the reliability of psychiatric diagnosis (54-58).

Still remaining is interpretation variance, which is due to differences in how clinicians interpret what they observe or what is told to them. When a person's affective expression is judged to be flat, when a discursive speech pattern indicates loose associations, or when self-referential ideas are delusional are all matters of clinical judgment. This important step between the collection of data in the interview and its distillation into a diagnostic formulation has, for the most part, eluded methodological innovation. Generally, adequate training in the recognition and interpretation of psychopathological signs and symptoms is the recognized approach to reducing interpretation variance; but since most clinicians receive their training in one or two programs or settings, they are limited by the approaches to interpreting psychopathology and the biases of their teachers and supervisors. Standardized glossaries of definitions of signs and symptoms, such as those found in DSM-III and DSM-III-R, are helpful but rely on the clinician's translation of written descriptions into visual, auditory, and emotional stimuli.

What is needed in this area is a complete course in modern psychopathology, presented in videotape format, that has been prepared by a large and diverse group of expert clinicians. To date, small collections of videotaped patient interviews are available in several training packages (59,60), but psychiatry has yet to invest in a complete instructional course.

Error variance and the clinical interview. Each of the above-noted sources of variance has relevance as an interviewer problem in the routine clinical diagnostic interview as discussed in this chapter. There are a few principles of interviewing that can help eliminate these problems.

Interviewers frequently lack sufficient information for a diagnosis following a routine clinical interview (61). This is especially true in the era of DSM-III, when specific kinds of information are necessary to establish that a clinical problem meets the criteria for a particular disorder. The problem of inadequate information from the clinical interview stems from three sources: (*1*) lack of knowledge of the relevant clinical syndromes in the differential diagnosis of a problem area and the kinds of information necessary to rule out or include the various possibilities; (2) failure to pursue clues that suggest diagnostic possibilities; and (3) failure to explore each diagnostic possibility fully.

In the first situation, the clinician must know, for example, that schizophreniform disorder is relevant in the differential diagnosis of recurrent psychotic episodes and that the clinical course of each episode must be less than six months, including prodromal and residual symptoms, for the diagnosis to be made. If the interviewer does not have this diagnosis in mind, then he or she will not know to explore the onset and recovery phases of each episode as part of the diagnostic interview. The major remedy for this problem is thorough study and practice, using the principles of differential diagnosis represented now by the DSM-III-R decision trees (62).

The second problem arises if the clinician is not aware of or sensitive to the patient's expressing a somewhat bizarre idea or displaying depressed affect, which, if noted and pursued with gentle probing, may yield evidence of a delusional system or a full depressive syndrome. Inexperienced clinicians, in particular, frequently shy away from the emotionally charged material that usually is the most revealing diagnostically. In this case, experience, supervision, and in some cases, perhaps, personal therapy may assist in developing better interviewing skills.

The final case is one in which the clinician is aware of the problem area, and perhaps even of the information necessary for establishing a diagnosis, but fails to ask enough questions to determine, or fully clarify in his or her own mind, that a symptom is present or absent. For example, in the case of a depression following a stressful life event, the clinician may not establish whether a full depressive syndrome was present or whether the patient's erratic sleeping patterns correspond to a new sleep disturbance ushered in by the onset of depressed mood. The checklist approach described earlier in this chapter is essential when a particular diagnosis requires that a complex of symptoms be present. But in conducting the examination, it makes no sense to move from one symptom to another without having a firm idea about the presence or absence of each.

In my experience (61), inadequacies of information are the leading causes of diagnostic inaccuracies in the DSM-III era. Although certain researchers have suggested the use of structured interviews for general clinical purposes (63), I believe that interviewers can be trained to incorporate the advantages of the structured interview in their routine diagnostic assessments. The possibilities of establishing emotional rapport with the patient are doubtless greater when a structured questionnaire is not used.

Problems in interpreting psychopathology are frequent, as mentioned previously. One pitfall in interviewing in the DSM-III era is the abuse of the checklist approach, so that the interview becomes an attempt at eliciting "yes" or "no" answers to a series of questions. A simple "yes" rarely suffices as evidence of the presence of a symptom; the interviewer is obliged to elicit examples of the experience or behavior in question. I instruct interviewers to get as detailed a picture as possible of the person's experience in order to be able to have an almost visual image of the person during the time he or she reports being symptomatic. When an interviewer makes such detailed attempts at depicting the subject's symptoms, ambiguity is frequently reduced. If still uncertain, I find it helpful to repeat to the patient, in summary fashion, what I understand he or she has told me, to clarify whether I am understanding it correctly or am somehow off the mark.

In the following vignette, a patient presents a vague and confusing history, replete with psychiatric jargon that obscures the nature of her problems. The interviewer is persistent. He begins with the patient's words, but insists that she give more specific examples of her behavior, focuses on a particular point in time, and feeds back to the patient the limits of his understanding. Eventually, he arrives at the core problem that led to the young woman's hospitalization.

Shell Thick, Verbiage Slick

Interviewer: How long have you been on 9 South?
Patient: About three months.
Interviewer: How was it that you got hospitalized?
Patient: I was in a situation . . . there was a lot of pressure on me. I didn't have the defense mechanisms. I was losing control—going into a situational depression due to anxiety.
Interviewer: When did this all begin?
Patient: I was in a residence for four months. Since March. I never got my foot off the ground. I was in a bad day program. It wasn't built on sincere motives.
Interviewer: I gather you've had problems before. Have you ever been hospitalized before this?
Patient: Yeah, for one month in 1984. At St. Francis.
Interviewer: You said that you were under pressure.
Patient: Yeah, I couldn't face the reality that this program was not operating under sincere motives. There was no support.
Interviewer: What was it like to be under pressure?
Patient: Trapped, helpless. I turned toward this guy—it wasn't a healthy attraction—it culminated in a disaster. I lost complete control; I became completely vulnerable.
Interviewer: How did you lose control?
Patient: Yelling, screaming—complete disorientation.
Interviewer: How were you feeling?
Patient: It brought out my vulnerabilities—my weaker side. If you can remove yourself from situations that are small, you won't get to large scale situations. It started small.
Interviewer: How did it start?
Patient: If someone insulted you—if you had a situation—you'd get flustered.
Interviewer: Do you remember a particular instance?
Patient: One time somebody criticized me in public for not doing a chore and suggested that I be thrown out. I was very angry.
Interviewer: How angry did you get?
Patient: I said, "I think you're schizophrenic." I put the other person down. If you build a house, it's bound to fall. Inside, I felt trapped.
Interviewer: You said you felt depressed and anxious.
Patient: It's hard to remember, I don't remember. It was so bad.
Interviewer: What do you mean by depressed?
Patient: Hopeless, very dependent on this man. He was unreliable. He had a very shaky sense of himself. We were fighting every day—it was a bomb that kept blowing up.

Interviewer: What other feelings were you having?
Patient: It was a situation of anxiety. From anxiety comes depression, not the other way. Whenever I had anxiety, I would get depressed.
Interviewer: What sort of thoughts were you having?
Patient: Oh, I would fantasize about suicide, but I wouldn't plan it. I once made a gesture. I took a towel and put it around my neck. It was kind of staged for Bob. Is the purpose of this meeting to determine the presence of inner anxiety?
Interviewer: How often did you feel this anxiety?
Patient: It was free-floating anxiety. At the time it was more externalized. It came out as aggression—crying, screaming, verbally abusing someone. Depression was from the anxiety.
Interviewer: Were you having trouble sleeping?
Patient: No.
Interviewer: How was your appetite?
Patient: It fluctuates. Last December I weighed 125 lbs. I was laying in bed, doing nothing. I had been at school, I couldn't hold on, I went home. I was on Anafranil and Parnate. I gained 90 lbs. to 210. I ate all the time at the halfway house.
Interviewer: I'd like to get back to how you were feeling. Why do you think it's so hard for you to remember?
Patient: I want to forget. I was so confused. It was very hurtful to be rejected. It was another failure—there have been so many. My constant failure over losing control—over and over. The staff was getting to me. I was losing strength.
Interviewer: You mentioned the hospitalization four years ago, in 1984. What was that for?
Patient: Anxiety.
Interviewer: How were you between then and now?
Patient: First I had agoraphobia, then obsessive-compulsive disorder. I had an obsession about a teacher—it was a dependence that was of delusional intensity.
Interviewer: What do you mean, "delusional intensity"?
Patient: I was constantly worrying that this teacher was not my friend, didn't like me, didn't think a lot about me.
Interviewer: Give me an example.
Patient: I would ask my mother to reassure me over and over again about aspects of conversations. It was a verbalization ritual.
Interviewer: You know, I'm still unclear about the period leading up to this hospitalization. You've told me that you lost control, that you got very angry, and that you yelled and screamed. What isn't clear to me is just how far out of control you were. Did you feel that you had lost control of your thinking?
Patient: I felt trapped. I was very scared. I wanted to even the score. I felt I was being treated unfairly. My thoughts were racing—overwhelming thoughts. I kept saying, "You're unfair, you can't do this to me!"
Interviewer: Did you feel that people were deliberately trying to hurt you?
Patient: I was afraid of them. They were constantly on me. They put this guy in charge of my group doing chores. It's antagonizing—to put people in charge of other people. They were using negative reinforcement on me. They called me fat. "You don't understand," I said to them. "You put this guy over me purposely to get to me. You set me up

to fail!" I tried to call my parents. I was in a panic. I really felt that they were out to get me.

Interviewer mistakes involving diagnostic criteria, providing he or she has thorough knowledge of them, are limited to instances when it is difficult to understand the meaning of particular criteria or to appreciate the nuances implied by them. An example would be the appropriate use of the DSM-III hierarchical exclusion criteria for making the most parsimonious diagnostic assessment warranted by the patient's condition. In fact, there are numerous subtleties in the DSM-III and DSM-III-R systems on which accurate, reliable diagnosis rests. These key points will be emphasized in the subsequent chapters of this book.

MENTAL STATUS EXAMINATION

There are several excellent texts (3,64) that provide detailed descriptions of the psychiatric mental status examination. In this chapter, I shall briefly make points about the traditional mental status examination that are relevant to DSM-III or DSM-III-R diagnosis and to the diagnostic interview approach presented here. In general, I believe that most of a patient's mental status can be assessed, without special questions, in the course of eliciting the chief complaint, the history of the present illness, and the other diagnostically relevant information discussed above.

Sections of Mental Status Examination

I divide the mental status examination into ten components: (*1*) appearance, (2) behavior, (3) mood, (4) affect, (5) thought process, (6) thought content, (*7*) orientation, (*8*) memory, (*9*) judgment, (*10*) insight.

Appearance. Many clues to the nature of the patient's condition are provided by his or her appearance. This source of information is sometimes so obvious that it is overlooked. Under this category I include the person's personal hygiene and grooming, manner of dress, and any striking or unusual aspects of appearance. These become sources of hypotheses from the moment the patient is first observed. Are poor grooming and shabby dress indicative of mental or physical disorder, or of extreme poverty or recent exposure to extreme circumstances? Why does the patient wear sunglasses indoors—is he suspicious, or is there an ophthalmologic or pharmacologic reason for photosensitivity?

Behavior. Behavior includes the patient's overall demeanor and degree of cooperativeness, congeniality, etc., plus motor behavior, such as agitation, retardation, or handwringing. Behavior is observed throughout the interview; changes in attitude, posture, or motor behavior at certain times during the interview may indicate a sensitive or emotionally upsetting topic.

Mood. Mood is the sustained or pervasive emotional state of the person. Moods may be described as depressed, anxious, elated, or angry. Any unpleasant mood is referred to as dysphoric. Persons with normal mood are said to be euthymic. A person may tell an interviewer what his or her mood is like, or it may be inferred from what the person says or does. When a dysphoric mood is severe, it can affect the person's state of mind and functioning and constitute a disorder of mood (see Chapter 6).

Affect. Affect, in contrast to mood, is more immediately expressed or observed emotion. A patient may express sadness, hostility, or happiness, but these may be transitory or associated with a particular subject or person. Other important aspects of emotional expression in the interview are range, appropriateness, and stability. If a patient does not have a normal range of affect, it may be constricted by feelings of depression or may be blunted or flat, that is, severely reduced in intensity to the point of showing no signs of emotional expressivity, because of a pervasive psychotic disorder, such as schizophrenia.

Generally, the interviewer expects that when a patient talks about an upsetting topic, his or her emotions will also tend to be upset. When this is not the case, e.g., if the patient giggles when describing hallucinations, then the affect is said to be inappropriate to the content of the patient's speech, cognition, or perceptions. Although affects may change during the course of an interview, a certain evenness in the change indicates a degree of stability. If affects change dramatically from one minute to the next, this is called labile affect, and suggests severe, often organic, mental disorder. Affect is assessed primarily by observation during the diagnostic interview.

Thought processes. A person's thought processes are assessed through his or her speech. Here an assumption is made that the flow of a person's spontaneous speech is a direct reflection of his or her cognitive processes. Thus, if it is difficult to follow a patient's speech because he or she shifts from one topic to another with only the remotest connection between them, the thought processes are said to be characterized by loosening of associations. Milder versions of associative loosening include (*1*) circumstantiality, in which the person provides a wealth of irrelevant detail before getting to the point of the question, and (*2*) tangentiality, in which the person goes off on a tangent, from which he or she may not return. Severe loosening of associations leads to incoherence. Rapid shifts from one topic to another, which in and of themselves may make sense, coupled with accelerated speech, is called flight of ideas.

If present, these kinds of formal thought disorder are invariably evident in any substantial amount of conversation elicited from the patient. It is rarely necessary, therefore, to resort to interpretation of proverbs in order to detect formal thought disorder. Interpretation of proverbs is determined as much by intellectual and educational level as by mental illness.

Thought content. Thought content includes the themes and preoccupations expressed by the patient. Delusional ideas, hallucinatory experiences, obsessions, phobias, and suicidal ideation may all be topics on which the interview will focus. The patient's cognitive and perceptual experiences are obviously relevant to DSM-III and DSM-III-R differential diagnosis.

Orientation. A patient who is fully alert, with intact attention, who participates meaningfully and consistently in a diagnostic interview rarely fools a clinician by turning out to be disoriented. Exceptions might be in the case of certain dementias in which the patient's ability to confabulate is so smooth as not to raise the suspicions of the interviewer. Disorientation to time is the most sensitive indicator and the first to become impaired by organic brain processes. Disorientation to place follows, and disorientation to person appears last. Actually, a noncomatose patient is virtually never unaware of who he or she is; a more sensitive indicator of disorientation to person is whether the patient knows who the clinician is.

Memory. Memory impairment can be tested by formal questions, but short-term memory loss is almost always evident from the patient's spontaneous speech. Typically, a patient will forget the line of questioning or what he or she was in the process of saying. Only confabulation about remote past situations and events is observed to be coherent, and this material is usually introduced inappropriately in response to questions about the recent past or quickly becomes apparent if the person's experience is not structured by the clinician.

Although I may ask a patient to remember three objects for five minutes, a much better indicator of functional impairment due to memory loss may he telling me what he or she had for breakfast, his or her room number in the hospital, or the name of his or her nurse.

Judgment. If a patient believes that thoughts are being placed in his or her head by invisible laser beams or has spent half-a-year's salary on a new car, judgment is impaired. This is true regardless of what he or she would do if he or she found a stamped envelope on the street. In this instance, contrived questions tell us less than common sense.

Insight. Insight, for diagnostic purposes, does not refer to an understanding of the underlying conscious or unconscious motivations for behavior: insight in this context refers to the ability to view one's behavior objectively, from the point of view of another, and to see its possible basis in faulty logic or to recognize its unreasonable excess. Capacity for insight becomes important in evaluating the reality testing of someone who expresses unusual beliefs or in assessing the ego-syntonic vs. the ego-dystonic nature of obsessions or phobias. It may make the difference, for example, in a diagnosis of schizotypal personality disorder vs. schizophrenia.

The role of formal mental status questions. Although all elements of the mental status examination can be derived from observations made in the course of a general diagnostic interview, for the purpose of clarifying ambiguous memory impairment or other cognitive deficits more formal questioning may be needed. This should never be introduced as a series of "silly" questions, but rather as a "special" set of questions designed to help the interviewer arrive at a diagnosis. The purpose of the questions may even be explained. Since it is frequently difficult to interpret a moderate number of mistakes on the basis of a few questions, I recommend the use of the 30-item Mini-Mental State Examination (65) because of its standard format and its scoring and interpretive guidelines.

Differential Diagnosis

The first step in differential diagnosis is to identify a major syndrome corresponding to the patient's complaints or problems. Syndromes usually fall into one of five basic problem areas: (*1*) emotions, e.g., depression, anxiety; (2) thinking and perception, e.g., delusions, hallucinations, cognitive impairment; (3) problems of living, e.g., social relationships, work functioning; (4) physical complaints, e.g., unexplained pain, fear of having a disease; (5) behavior, e.g., uncontrolled use of psychoactive substances, violence.

Table 1.1 lists the major mental syndromes and their defining features. Each syndrome is represented by a chapter in this book. A

Table 1.1 Major Mental Syndromes and Their Defining Features*

Syndrome	Features
Disturbances with specific organic etiologies	Symptoms of memory impairment, disturbance of attention, disorganized thinking, delusions, hallucinations, mood disturbance, anxiety, or marked personality change due to a specific organic factor other than psychoactive substances.
Disturbances associated with psychoactive substances	Maladaptive behaviors indicative of impaired control over use of psychoactive substances or the mental symptoms and maladaptive behavior associated with the toxic effects of psychoactive substances on the central nervous system.
Psychotic features	Gross impairment in reality testing as evidenced by delusions, hallucinations, incoherence, or marked loosening of associations, catatonic stupor or excitement, or grossly disorganized behavior.
Mood disturbances	Persistently depressed, elevated, expansive, or irritable mood.
Anxiety syndromes	Symptoms of irrational and excessive anxiety or worry, avoidance behavior, or increased arousal not attributed to a psychotic disorder.
Physical complaints	Symptoms of physical disorders adversely affected by psychological factors, physical complaints or irrational anxiety about illness, disturbances in physical functioning with psychological etiology.
Personality disturbances	Behaviors or traits characteristic of recent and long-term functioning that cause impairment in social or occupational functioning.
Antisocial, aggressive, or violent behavior	Anger, agitation, rage attacks, violence, assault, or antisocial behavior.
Other syndromes	Dissociative states, paraphilias, gender identity problems, disturbances of impulse control, etc.

* These syndromes and their defining features correspond, in part, to those represented by the DSM-III-R decision trees. In this book, several areas of differential diagnosis are expanded beyond the DSM-III-R trees, and areas not represented by trees are also discussed.

definitive diagnosis may be evident upon completion of an initial interview, or more information may be necessary; sometimes, extensive evaluation may be needed to reach a final diagnostic judgment. Problems in arriving at a "best possible" diagnosis of a mental disorder, given the "state of the art" represented by DSM-III and DSM-III-R, are discussed in the chapters that follow.

SUMMARY

This chapter reviews principles of diagnostic interviewing to be followed in making a DSM-III or DSM-III-R multiaxial assessment. The diagnostic interview is conceived of as an enterprise of mutual cooperation between an expert clinician actively testing hypotheses and a patient in distress who stands to benefit from the clinician's expertise. The elements of an adequate diagnostic interview are described, with special reference to the particular data needed by the DSM-III systems. Obstacles to the successful completion of the interview are discussed, and strategies to circumvent them are presented.

REFERENCES

1. Sullivan HS: The Psychiatric Interview. London, Tavistock Publications, 1954
2. MacKinnon RA, Michels R: The Psychiatric Interview in Clinical Practice. Philadelphia, WB Saunders, 1971
3. MacKinnon RA, Yudofsky SC: The Psychiatric Evaluation in Clinical Practice. Philadelphia, JB Lippincott, 1986
4. Gauron EF, Dickinson JK: Diagnostic decision making in psychiatry. I. Information usage. Arch Gen Psychiatry 14:225–232, 1966
5. Sandifer MG, Hordern A, Green LM: The psychiatric interview: the impact of the first three minutes. Am J Psychiatry 126:968–973, 1970
6. Herz MI, Melville C: Relapse in schizophrenia. Am J Psychiatry 137:801–805, 1980
7. Heinrichs DW, Carpenter WT Jr: Prospective study of prodromal symptoms in schizophrenic relapse. Am J Psychiatry 142:371–373, 1985
8. Rabiner CJ, Wegner JT, Kane JM: Outcome study of first-episode psychosis. I. Relapse rates after one year. Am J Psychiatry 143:1155–1158, 1986
9. Pulver AE, Carpenter WT Jr: Lifetime psychotic symptoms assessed with the DIS. Schizophr Bull 9:377–382, 1983
10. Bromet EJ, Dunn LO, Connell MM, Dew MA, Schulberg HC: Long-term reliability of diagnosing lifetime major depression in a community sample. Arch Gen Psychiatry 43:435–440, 1986
11. Stangl D, Pfohl B, Zimmerman M, Bowers W, Corenthal C: A structured interview for the DSM-III personality disorders. A preliminary report. Arch Gen Psychiatry 42:591–596, 1985
12. Loranger AW, Susman V, Oldham J, Russakoff L: The Personality Disorder Examination: a preliminary report. J Personality Disord 1:1–13, 1987

13. Hurt SW, Hyler SE, Frances A, Clarkin JF, Brent R: Assessing borderline personality disorder with self-report, clinical interview, or semistructured interview. Am J Psychiatry 141:1228–1231, 1984
14. Millon T: The MCMI provides a good assessment of DSM-III disorders: the MCMI-II will prove even better. J Pers Assess 49:379–391, 1985
15. Kety SS, Rosenthal D, Wender PH, Schulsinger F: The types and prevalence of mental illness in the biological and adoptive families of adopted schizophrenics. J Psychiatr Res 6:345–362, 1968
16. Kety SS, Rosenthal D, Wender PH, Schulsinger F, Jacobsen B: Mental illness in the biological and adoptive families of adopted individuals who have become schizophrenic: A preliminary report based on psychiatric interview, in Genetic Research in Psychiatry. Edited by Fieve R, Rosenthal D, Brill H. Baltimore, Johns Hopkins Press, 1975, pp 147–165
17. Spitzer RL, Endicott J, Gibbon M: Crossing the border into borderline personality and borderline schizophrenia. The development of criteria. Arch Gen Psychiatry 36:17–24, 1979
18. Lowing PA, Mirsky AF, Pereira R: The inheritance of schizophrenia spectrum disorders: a reanalysis of the Danish adoptee study data. Am J Psychiatry 140:1167–1171, 1983
19. Kendler KS, Gruenberg AM: An independent analysis of the Danish adoption study of schizophrenia. VI. The relationship between psychiatric disorders as defined by DSM-III in the relatives and adoptees. Arch Gen Psychiatry 41:555–564, 1984
20. Siever LJ, Gunderson JG: Genetic determinants of borderline conditions. Schizophr Bull 5:59–86, 1979
21. Coryell W, Winokur G, Andreasen NC: Effect of case definition on affective disorder rates. Am J Psychiatry 138:1106–1109, 1981
22. Weissman MM, Kidd KK, Prusoff BA: Variability in rates of affective disorders in relatives of depressed and normal probands. Arch Gen Psychiatry 39:1397–1403, 1982
23. Weissman MM, Merikangas KR, John K, Wickramaratne P, Prusoff BA, Kidd KK: Family-genetic studies of psychiatric disorders. Arch Gen Psychiatry 43:1104–1116, 1986
24. Gershon ES, Hamovit J, Guroff JJ, Dibble E, Leckman JF, Sceery W, Targum SD, Nurnberger JI, Goldin LR, Bunney WE: A family study of schizoaffective bipolar I, bipolar II, unipolar, and normal control probands. Arch Gen Psychiatry 39:1157–1167, 1982
25. Andreasen NC, Rice J, Endicott J, Coryell W, Grove WM, Reich T: Familial rates of affective disorder: a report from the National Institute of Mental Health Collaborative Study. Arch Gen Psychiatry 44:461–469, 1987.
26. Coryell W, Zimmerman M: The heritability of schizophrenia and schizoaffective disorder: a family study. Arch Gen Psychiatry 45:323–327, 1988
27. Squires-Wheeler E, Skodol AE, Friedman D, Erlenmeyer-Kimling L: A preliminary report of the specificity of DSM-III schizotypal personality traits. Psychol Med 18:757–765, 1988
28. Zimmerman M, Coryell W, Pfohl BM: Importance of diagnostic thresholds in familial classification: dexamethasone suppression test and familial subtypes of depression. Arch Gen Psychiatry 42:300–304, 1985
29. Cooper AM, Michels R: DSM-III: An American view (book forum). Am J Psychiatry 138:128–129, 1981
30. Frances A, Cooper AM: Descriptive and dynamic psychiatry: a perspective on DSM-III. Am J Psychiatry 138:1198–1202, 1981

31. Raskin M, Peeke HV, Dickman W, Pinsker H: Panic and generalized anxiety disorders. Developmental antecedents and precipitants. Arch Gen Psychiatry 39:687–689, 1982
32. Karasu TB, Skodol AE: VIth axis for DSM-III: psychodynamic evaluation. Am J Psychiatry 137:607–610, 1980
33. Fleck S: A holistic approach to family typology and the axes of DSM-II. Arch Gen Psychiatry 40:901–906, 1983
34. Lewis JM, Usdin G (eds): Treatment Planning in Psychiatry. Washington, DC, American Psychiatric Association, 1982
35. Greist JH, Jefferson JW, Spitzer RL (eds): Treatment of Mental Disorders. New York, Oxford University Press, 1982
36. Perry S, Frances A, Clarkin J: A DSM-III Casebook of Differential Therapeutics. New York, Brunner/Mazel, 1985
37. Plum F, Posner JB: The Diagnosis of Stupor and Coma. Philadelphia, F.A. Davis, 1966
38. Bassuk EL, Birk AW: Emergency Psychiatry: Concepts, Methods, and Practices. New York, Plenum Press, 1984
39. Slaby AE, Lieb J, Tancredi LR: Handbook of Psychiatric Emergencies, Second Edition. New York, Medical Examination Publishing, 1981
40. Glick RA, Meyerson AT, Robbins E, Talbott JA (eds): Psychiatric Emergencies. New York, Grune and Stratton, 1976
41. Bassuk EL, Skodol AE: The first few minutes: identifying and managing life-threatening emergencies, in Emergency Psychiatry: Concepts, Methods, and Practices. Edited by Bassuk EL, Birk AW. New York, Plenum Press, 1984
42. Skodol AE: Emergency management of potentially violent patients, in Emergency Psychiatry: Concepts, Methods, and Practices. Edited by Bassuk EL, Birk AW. New York, Plenum Press, 1984
43. Fleiss JL: Statistical Methods for Rates and Proportions, Second Edition. New York, John Wiley, 1981
44. Spitzer RL, Fleiss JL: A re-analysis of the reliability of psychiatric diagnosis. Br J Psychiatry 125:341–347, 1974
45. Ward CH, Beck AT, Mendelson M, Mock JE, Erbaugh JK: The psychiatric nomenclature. Arch Gen Psychiatry 7:198–205, 1962
46. Hasin DS, Skodol AE: Standardized diagnostic interviews for psychiatric research, in The Implements of Psychiatric Research. Edited by Thompson C. Chichester, England, John Wiley, in press
47. Wing JK, Birley JLT, Cooper JE, Graham P, Isaacs AD: Reliability of a procedure for measuring and classifying 'Present Psychiatric State'. Br J Psychiatry 113:499–515, 1967
48. Endicott J, Spitzer RL: A diagnostic interview: the Schedule for Affective Disorders and Schizophrenia. Arch Gen Psychiatry 35:837–844, 1978
49. Robins LN, Helzer JE, Croughan J, Ratcliff KS: National Institute of Mental Health Diagnostic Interview Schedule. Arch Gen Psychiatry 38:381–389, 1981
50. Spitzer RL, Williams JBW, Gibbon M: The Structured Clinical Interview for DSM-III-R (SCID). New York, Biometrics Research Department, 1987
51. Feighner JP, Robins E, Guze SB, Woodruff RA Jr, Winokur G, Munoz R: Diagnostic criteria for use in psychiatric research. Arch Gen Psychiatry 26:57–63, 1972
52. Spitzer RL, Endicott J, Robins E: Research Diagnostic Criteria: rationale and reliability Arch Gen Psychiatry 35:773–782, 1978
53. Spitzer RL, Endicott J, Robins E: Clinical criteria for psychiatric diagnosis

and DSM-III. Am J Psychiatry 132:1187–1192, 1975

54. Helzer JE, Robins LN, Taibleson M, Woodruff RA, Reich T, Wish ED: Reliability of psychiatric diagnoses: I. A methodological review. Arch Gen Psychiatry 34:129–133, 1977
55. Helzer JE, Clayton PJ, Pambakian R, Reich T, Woodruff AR Jr, Reveley MA: Reliability of psychiatric diagnosis. II. The test-retest reliability of diagnostic classification. Arch Gen Psychiatry 34:136–141, 1977
56. Spitzer RL, Forman JBW, Nee J: DSM-III field trials. I. Initial interrater diagnostic reliability. Am J Psychiatry 138:815–817, 1979
57. Grove WM, Andreasen NC, McDonald-Scott P, Keller MB, Shapiro RW: Reliability studies of psychiatric diagnosis: theory and practice. Arch Gen Psychiatry 38:408–413, 1981
58. Shrout PE, Spitzer RL, Fleiss JL: Quantification of agreement in psychiatric diagnosis revisited. Arch Gen Psychiatry 44:172–177, 1987
59. American Psychiatric Association: The DSM-III Institutional Instruction Kit. Washington, DC, American Psychiatric Association, 1981
60. Webb LJ, DiClemente CC, Johnstone EE, Sanders JL, Perley RA: DSM-III Training Guide. New York, Brunner/Mazel, 1981
61. Spitzer RL, Skodol A, Williams JBW, Gibbon M, Kass F: Supervising intake diagnosis. A psychiatric "Rashomon." Arch Gen Psychiatry 39:1299–1305, 1982
62. American Psychiatric Association: Diagnostic and Statistical Manual of Mental Disorders, Third Edition, Revised. Washington, DC, American Psychiatric Association, 1987
63. Helzer JE: The use of a structured diagnostic interview for routine psychiatric evaluations. J Nerv Ment Dis 169:45–49, 1981
64. Maxmen JS: Essential Psychopathology. New York, WW Norton, 1986
65. Folstein MF, Folstein SW, McHugh PR: Mini-Mental State: A practical method of grading the cognitive state of patients for the clinician. J Psychiatr Res 12:189–198, 1975

CHAPTER 2

Multiaxial Diagnosis

The concept of multiaxial diagnosis was first introduced in psychiatry by Essen-Möller and Wohlfahrt in 1947 (1) and was briefly used in Denmark as part of a national classification of mental disorders. Although several multiaxial schemas have been proposed since then, none attracted widespread attention or achieved official sanction until DSM-III's multiaxial system was introduced. The DSM-III multiaxial approach has been regarded as a major advance in psychiatric nosology (2-6), is widely taught in training programs in the United States (7,8), and has been accepted internationally (9-13); but thus far, it appears to be used clinically only on a relatively limited basis, and it has generated surprisingly few research studies (14).

Likely reasons for the disappointing practical impact include:

1. Of the innovative features of DSM-III (including diagnostic criteria), multiaxial diagnosis was probably the most foreign in nature to the majority of mental health professionals.
2. Because of its novelty, knowledge of how to use the multiaxial system appropriately has been slow to develop in most clinicians.
3. Even if used appropriately, clinicians are not sure of the value of the multiaxial system.

This chapter will attempt to rectify this situation by better explaining the rationale for multiaxial diagnosis, reviewing the conventions for the use of the various axes, with emphasis on the ambiguities in the instructions given in the DSM-III manual, and describing the clinical value of the information collected on each axis. A description of the changes made in DSM-III-R in the multiaxial system, to make it more used and useful in clinical settings, will complete the discussion of each axis.

RATIONALE FOR MULTIAXIAL DIAGNOSIS

It has been recognized for a long time that the salient clinical features of mental disorders can be so complex as to be difficult to capture with single diagnostic concepts (15). Throughout the evolution of psychiatric nosology, aspects of the disorders, such as their hypothesized etiologies, their impact on individuals' functioning, and their prognostic implications, in addition to their signs and symptoms, have been recognized as clinically important and have been incorporated at various times into diagnostic labels. For example, DSM-I (16) included the schizophrenic reaction, emphasizing the Meyerian notion that these illnesses occurred in response to stressful life circumstances; and DSM-II (17) listed transient situational disturbances at various stages of life, emphasizing not only the reactive aspect but the time-limited nature of such disorders. It makes intuitive sense that such features as severity, duration, and potential causes—whether physical or psychosocial—are of great interest in assessing any mental disorder: this information helps the clinician in planning treatment or in determining prognosis.

The two important ways in which multiaxial diagnosis reduces clinical complexity are by ensuring that all patients are considered from diverse points of view and by making these assessments relatively independent of the symptom picture and of each other, thus promoting their reliability. An "axis" is nothing more than a "clinical perspective," and the number of axes that are chosen for inclusion in a multiaxial evaluation system is limited only by the feasibility of collecting the necessary information as part of a routine clinical examination and by the potential rewards for the effort.

In the multiaxial systems that have been proposed in different parts of the world, the axes generally have covered clinical phenomenology, etiological factors, duration and course, level of functioning, and severity of illness (18). The axes incorporated into DSM-III were as follows: Axis I—clinical syndromes and conditions; Axis II—personality disorders and specific developmental disorders; Axis III—physical disorders; Axis IV—severity of psychosocial stressors; and Axis V—highest level of adaptive functioning in the past year. Each of these axes was selected for its potential clinical value.

CONCEPTUAL PROBLEMS WITH THE DSM-III MULTIAXIAL SYSTEM

The initial general problem with the DSM-III multiaxial system was its lack of conceptual consistency. The official name for Axis I—clinical syndromes—is unfortunate because Axis II is also a clinical axis, in the traditional sense. The rationale for dividing Axis I and Axis II conditions from each other was to ensure "that consideration is given to the possible presence of disorders that are frequently overlooked when attention is directed to the usually more florid Axis I disorder" (19, p. 23). Personality disorders in adults and specific developmental disorders (learning disabilities) in children were the disorders designated for Axis II in DSM-III. The conceptual difference between the two axes, therefore, was between disorders with more florid symptoms and a more fluctuating, if not episodic, course (Axis I) versus disorders with usually more subtle symptoms (there are clearly some exceptions) and a more stable and chronic course (Axis II).

Critics of the DSM-III multiaxial approach (20-22) were quick to point out that for children there were two categories of disorders, mental retardation and pervasive developmental disorders, that, although not meeting the subtle symptoms standard, certainly possessed the enduring stable pattern of disturbance that characterized Axis II disorders. In DSM-III-R, Axis I still refers to clinical syndromes and V codes, but Axis II now covers developmental disorders and personality disorders. The developmental disorders are divided into mental retardation, pervasive developmental disorders, specific developmental disorders, and other developmental disorders. The Axis II disorders have in common an onset early in life and a generally stable, persistent course, without remissions and exacerbations, into adult life. This combination of features is thought to be uncharacteristic of most Axis I disorders, for which the course can be either progressive or potentially reversible.

The change toward more of a conceptual distinction between the two axes may satisfy some, but still leaves much to be desired. Axes I and II remain mixtures of phenomenology and descriptions of aspects of clinical course. A system in which clinical signs and symptoms were listed on one axis and features of course such as age at onset, persistence, and duration were listed on another axis would have greater conceptual consistency than the current systems, which for numerous disorders mix symptoms and features of course together in the diagnostic criteria. Unfortunately, however, such an approach would be even more difficult for most clinicians trained in traditional categorical diagnosis to assimilate.

The conceptual basis of Axis III physical disorders has also been questioned (20,23). Axis III in DSM-III was for noting physical disorders "potentially relevant to the understanding or management" (19, p. 26) of a person with a mental disorder. DSM-III went on to say that the physical disorder might be etiologic for the mental disorder, as in the case of a neurological disorder associated with a dementia, or simply important enough for the clinician to be aware of in treating the patient. Thus, Axis III is in part an etiologic axis with respect to an Axis I disorder and in part an axis for assessing a person's physical status. Its etiologic aspects it shares with Axis IV—severity of psychosocial stressors—and it has been suggested that a more consistent system might have included *all* etiologic factors on one axis and none mixed in with Axis I diagnoses, as is currently the case in DSM-III and DSM-III-R organic mental disorders, psychoactive substance use disorders, and adjustment disorders. A convention for noting an etiologic relationship between Axis III and Axis I disorders was considered for DSM-III-R (24), but was dropped because of the added complexity the convention introduced. Other specific problems with the use of Axis III will be discussed later in this chapter.

On Axis IV, clinicians were to note the presence and severity of psychosocial stressors that contributed to the development or exacerbation of the current disorder. Axis IV was, and is, a completely etiologic or pathogenic axis, but is limited to noting the effects of stressors. The above discussion of the conceptual appeal of a single etiologic axis applies to Axis IV as well as to Axis III.

Another major conceptual criticism of Axis IV has been the implicit assumption that acutely stressful events and chronically stressful life circumstances exert the same effect on a person's mental functioning. Most data on the subject of stress do not support this conclusion (21,22), and most continuing research on the life stress process conceptually separates stressful events from ongoing social situations. Their mode of interaction with each other and with factors characteristic of the person (e.g., personality attributes or a family history positive for mental disorder) in the production of mental disorders is a subject of current investigation (25,26).

Furthermore, in one of the few empirical studies of the use of Axis IV in clinical settings (27), a colleague, Dr. Patrick Shrout, and I found that the DSM-III definition of a psychosocial stressor led to such a broad definition of stressor that certain nonstressors, such as mental symptoms, became confounded with the Axis IV rating. In an attempt to rectify the overly broad and excessively general reference to psychosocial stressors in DSM-III, DSM-III-R includes a new convention for specifying whether the stressors are predominantly acute events, with a duration of less than six months, or predominantly enduring circumstances, with a duration of greater than six months. The examples of each scale point in the new, abbreviated six-point scale of severity (the scale point for noting minimal stress was eliminated) have been revised in DSM-III-R so that what was an almost exclusively event-oriented list of examples in DSM-III now includes separate examples of both kinds of stressors for adult patients and for children and adolescents.

The Axis V concept of highest level of adaptive functioning past year reflected the assumption that the year before evaluation of the patient or his or her entry into clinical care was the most relevant for determining a person's prognosis. Axis V was included in DSM-III because it was anticipated that a person who fully recovered from an episode of a mental disorder would be expected to return to his or her recent best level of functioning, and that the degree of recovery could, in cases of partial remission, be estimated partly from how closely to this level a person did return. Critics (21,22) have pointed out that this is a rather simplistic notion and that in more chronic disorders, such as schizophrenia or an irreversible dementia, the highest level of functioning in the past year would have far different clinical and prognostic implications than it would in acute disorders, such as an episode of major depression.

The DSM-III Axis V rating was based largely on a person's social and occupational functioning, with no reference to psychological functioning. Studies using the Global Assessment Scale (28) and the Children's Global Assessment Scale (29) have shown that overall severity of disturbance ratings are reliable and are related to treatment. Since the degree of use and the documented usefulness of the DSM-III Axis V ratings have been disappointing, the Work Group to Revise DSM-III replaced Axis V with a 90-point scale assessing combined psychological, social, and occupational functioning on a continuum, the Global Assessment of Functioning (GAF) Scale. This was done with the expectation that clinicians would find the rating more useful and be more likely to include it in routine practice.

However, two new problems have been introduced by inclusion of this concept of functioning.

The first problem is that the independence of the Axis V rating from the Axis I and II diagnosis is now severely compromised, since psychological functioning, i.e., symptoms, has become a part of the rating. This will severely restrict the prognostic utility of the Axis V rating, because the nature of a person's disorder will directly help determine the rating (30). Thus, the Work Group changed the utility of Axis V from a prognostic one to one associated with treatment. This may disappoint some clinicians, and the increased circularity of the rating and further confounding of the axes of the multiaxial system will probably arouse more criticism.

The second problem inherent in the new scale is the added number of factors needed for the rating. The scanty research evidence available on the use of DSM-III's Axis V indicates that the ratings were not based broadly on aspects of social and occupational factors, but on a relatively narrow set of components of functioning (31). The introduction of a third set of factors, psychological, might be expected to further reduce the significance of the other two for making the ratings, especially since the psychological factors might be expected to influence the ratings most heavily. This problem will be discussed in more detail in the section below on difficulties with Axis V conventions.

DIFFICULTIES WITH MULTIAXIAL CONVENTIONS

The instructions for the use of the DSM-III multiaxial system were rather skimpy and confined, for the most part, to the eight-plus pages of the book on the use of the manual. This made the introduction of the multiaxial system into clinical work on a widespread basis very difficult, since most American mental health practitioners were totally unfamiliar with any system of multiaxial diagnosis. The guidelines for the use of the DSM-III multiaxial system were a series of conventions, usually limited to an instruction conveyed by a sentence to a paragraph of text, perhaps accompanied by an example or two. The conventions were arrived at by consensus, among the members of the original DSM-III multiaxial subcommittee, about the purposes of each axis. They were arbitrary in the sense that they were not based primarily on any research data indicating their appropriateness for their stated purposes.

Extensive experience in teaching, supervising, and studying the use of the multiaxial system in clinical practice has made it clear that interpretation of these conventions has led to many problems in the accurate and appropriate use of the system, which, in turn, has probably discouraged many clinicians from using it. This past experience suggests that there will also be problems with new DSM-III-R conventions.

Axis I

Most of the difficulties involving Axis I categories will be discussed in the chapters covering differential diagnosis of various problem areas, such as psychotic features or disturbances in mood. There are, however, a few specific conventions with regard to Axis I that have applicability across a wide range of diagnostic categories and therefore are best dealt with in this chapter on multiaxial diagnosis. These are *(1)* the principle of diagnostic parsimony, (*2*) diagnostic hierarchies, (*3*) exclusion criteria, and (*4*) ratings of severity in DSM-III-R.

Principle of diagnostic parsimony. DSM-I and DSM-II instructed clinicians to make a single diagnosis that best captured the nature of a patient's psychopathology. DSM-III was the first American Psychiatric Association classification that explicitly encouraged making multiple diagnoses, if warranted. It is self-evident that a person with an anxiety disorder might also have developed substance abuse, perhaps as a consequence of self-medicating the primary condition. Similarly, a person with alcohol dependence might very well develop the syndrome of alcohol withdrawal delirium upon abrupt cessation of drinking. These mixed clinical syndromes occur commonly, and can justify the use of more than one diagnosis, since often two distinct approaches to treatment will be indicated, one for each disorder. The phobic patient who abuses antianxiety agents or alcohol may best have the phobia treated with behavior therapy, but may also require drug detoxification and/or a special treatment program, such as Alcoholics Anonymous, for the substance use disorder. Delirium tremens is an acute medical emergency requiring sedation, hydration, fluid and electrolyte balancing, etc.; alcohol dependence requires detoxification and rehabilitation.

There are limits to the number of multiple diagnoses that seem appropriate, however. Since many mental disorders are admixtures of various kinds of symptoms, it is not intuitive to split syndromes so that each aspect is diagnosed separately, unless there is some clinical motive for doing so. This principle of parsimony in assigning diagnoses applied to DSM-III Axis I disorders.

DSM-III-R still emphasizes such parsimony, but not to the same extent as did DSM-III. There are fewer exclusion criteria in DSM-III-R (see below under *Diagnostic hierarchies*), but there continue to be diagnoses that subsume others. A patient with schizophrenia is very likely to experience extreme anxiety as a result of threatening delusions or hallucinations. Since anxiety is so ubiquitous in schizophrenia, even though it is not one of the criteria for that disorder, there is little justification for making a separate diagnosis of anxiety disorder; the anxiety is expected to remit following effective treatment of the primary psychopathology with antipsychotic medication. In DSM-III-R a diagnosis of generalized anxiety disorder (GAD) should be made for a person with schizophrenia only if the anxiety is unrelated to the problems inherent in schizophrenia. Such an occurrence would be extremely rare.

Diagnostic hierarchies. DSM-III did not include the primary-secondary distinction of certain other nosologic schemas because it was principally an atheoretical diagnostic system. The disorders in the classification were arranged according to a roughly hierarchical structure, however, so that disorders higher in the classification were assumed to have features of disorders lower in the classification, but the reverse was not true. Thus, organic mental disorders may present with virtually any type of psychopathology, but no other disorders have all the essential features of the organic mental disorders. The clinical picture of schizophrenia may include depression, anxiety, or hypochondriacal concerns, but only certain types of major depression, and none of the anxiety or somatoform disorders, have psychotic symptoms.

The concept embodied by diagnostic hierarchies has its critics, who assert that hierarchies impose premature etiological closure on the diagnostic system, and that the clinician should diagnose major syndromes independently in order to determine whether the additional disorder (or disorders) makes any clinical difference, rather than assume that it does not (32). Certain diagnostic hierarchies have come under scrutiny by psychiatric researchers. In particular, a group of Yale investigators has studied the hierarchical relationship in DSM-III between affective and anxiety disorders (33,34). In DSM-III, affective diagnoses generally excluded diagnoses of anxiety disorder. In the Yale studies, however, it was demonstrated that people who had both affective and anxiety syndromes more frequently had first-degree relatives with anxiety disorders than did people with affective syndromes alone. This suggested that there was an independently inherited vulnerability to anxiety disorder, even among patients who had affective illnesses. Such a potent clinical factor should not go unrecognized because the anxiety syndrome was excluded by a hierarchical principle. Other clinically significant data can be recaptured when certain hierarchies are disassembled. These will be discussed in subsequent chapters.

DSM-III-R is much more judicious in its use of diagnostic hierarchies, including them only when an additional diagnosis would be literally redundant or when an organic etiology is evident. Spitzer (35) has generalized the principles as follows:

> 1. When an organic mental disorder can account for the symptoms, it preempts the diagnosis of any other disorder that could produce the same symptoms. . . .
>
> 2. When a more pervasive disorder, such as schizophrenia, commonly has associated symptoms that are the defining symptoms of a less pervasive disorder, such as dysthymia, only the more pervasive disorder is diagnosed if both its defining symptoms *and* associated symptoms are present. . . .

Thus, in DSM-III-R the diagnoses of panic disorder and generalized anxiety disorder are not made in the face of evidence that a psychoactive substance intoxication, such as amphetamine intoxication, which has anxiety symptoms prominent in its criteria, is the cause of the problem (see also Chapter 4, Disturbances Associated with the Use of Psychoactive Substances). Nor would the symptoms of social withdrawal characteristic of schizoid personality disorder be diagnosed separately if a person had schizophrenia.

Exclusion criteria. Diagnostic hierarchies are operationalized by means of exclusion criteria. Exclusion criteria are to be distinguished from inclusion criteria, which are the hallmark clinical features of each disorder. Exclusion criteria help the clinician distinguish between closely related disorders, e.g., the exclusion criteria in the diagnostic criteria for schizophrenia and for the mood disorders help the clinician distinguish between schizophrenia with a superimposed (postpsychotic) depression and a major depressive episode with mood-incongruent psychotic features. In DSM-III the exclusion criterion that determined the diagnostic hierarchies in which the symptoms of one kind of syndrome, e.g., anxiety, were subsumed by a more pervasive disorder, e.g., major depression, was phrased "not due to another mental disorder, such as. . . ."

This phrase was a source of major misunderstanding among users of DSM-III because of the ambiguity of the expression "due to," which could refer to a causal relationship between two syndromes, a temporal sequence in their development, or some other association. After careful consideration of the intent of the "not due to" criterion, the Work Group to Revise DSM-III recognized that the criterion referred to several different relationships between syndromes, depending upon which classes of disorders were involved. Hence, in DSM-III-R the criterion more explicitly describes the relationship in one of several ways.

First, there is the case of the basic rule that the symptoms of one disorder may indeed be a part of the manifestations of another, more pervasive disturbance. Thus, the symptoms of uncomplicated alcohol withdrawal are still subsumed by the more pervasive disturbance alcohol withdrawal delirium, and the exclusion criterion states, ". . . not due to any physical or other mental disorder, such as Alcohol Withdrawal Delirium" (36, p. 130).

Next, there is the case in which a disorder is, in the strict sense, responsible for the symptoms of another particular syndrome. In this case the "primary" disorder would be a necessary and sufficient condition for the excluded disorder. For example, a manic syndrome might be the clinical picture of a cocaine intoxication. In such cases (e.g., manic episode) the exclusion criterion in DSM-III-R reads, "It cannot be established that an organic factor initiated and maintained the disturbance" (36, p. 217).

Finally, in the case of syndromes that develop during the course of another mental disorder in which the symptoms are a variant of the features of the primary disorder, the DSM-III-R criteria read "Not occurring only during the course of. . . ." An example would be the reduced sexual desire that commonly is associated with a major depression. The relevant DSM-III-R exclusion criterion for hypoactive sexual desire disorder, reads, "Not occurring only during the course of another Axis I disorder (other than a Sexual Dysfunction), such as Major Depression" (36, p. 293).

Exclusion criteria play an integral part in differential diagnosis by the DSM-III and DSM-III-R systems. The specific exclusion criteria for each disorder will be discussed in detail in subsequent chapters of this book.

A Man of Many Moods

A 35-year-old, single insurance salesman was referred for psychiatric consultation by his internist, to whom he went complaining of loss of energy. Physical examination was unremarkable, and laboratory tests failed to indicate a cause for his fatigue. The man admitted to feeling depressed for several months and agreed to the referral.

The history revealed that the patient had a long-standing pattern of fluctuating moods. Since college graduation he had been experiencing periods of several weeks at a time in which he felt very good about himself, was very outgoing, had boundless energy, and was extremely productive in terms of clients contacted and sales made. At other times he found every aspect of his life "boring" or "too difficult," felt like staying in bed all day, and convinced himself that his lucrative business was over. Once before, in his mid-20s he had become so depressed that he could not go to work; at that time he saw a psychotherapist for a year, and the severe depression remitted.

Eight months before the current consultation, the patient's father had died suddenly of a myocardial infarction. Initially the patient was surprised that he experienced no strong feelings of grief, although he realized, from his previous treatment, that his feelings about his father, who was stern and demanding, were ambivalent. For the past four months, however, he had had increasingly severe depression. He was very critical of his occupation—"We're all just parasites, selling people stuff they don't even need"—could not find anything (including sex) to interest him, and was so fatigued that he couldn't "even move in the morning" and routinely slept till noon. He could not decide what to do first each day, and wondered whether he should "go on disability." When questioned about the role of his father's death, he reported that he sometimes thought of his father, but more often was preoccupied with himself.

When alone in his apartment, the patient frequently felt panicky: there was a sense that he would never feel normal again; his heart suddenly began to race, he became sweaty, his chest became tight, and he felt dizzy and had tingling sensations in his extremities. He does not recall having had anxiety attacks like these before the recent development of depression.

> To try to bolster his mood, the patient had begun to use cocaine more or less regularly. His "highs" made him feel good enough to go out at night to a bar to try to meet women, but the "highs" were short-lived. When the effects of the drug wore off, he felt "worse than ever." The anxiety attacks were unrelated to the cocaine use.

This salesman's condition raises many possibilities for Axis I diagnosis. His chronic pattern of alternating hypomanic and depressed moods for many years suggests a diagnosis of cyclothymia. His current depressive syndrome is more severe than that observed in uncomplicated bereavement, first developed several years after cyclothymia, and thus warrants the additional diagnosis of major depression, recurrent (a second episode). The patient would be expected to return to a cyclothymic pattern after recovery from major depression unless additional treatment interventions (i.e., with lithium carbonate) were undertaken. The panic attacks occurring during the depressive episode would have been excluded by DSM-III criteria for major depressive episode, but, according to DSM-III-R, would warrant a third diagnosis, panic disorder, of potential etiologic and treatment significance (see also below and Chapter 7).

Since this man appears to be trying to alleviate his depression with cocaine, a drug that probably aggravates his mood disturbance over the long run, a third diagnosis would be cocaine abuse (there is no clear evidence of the more pervasive syndrome of dependence—see Chapter 4). The clinician may wonder whether a diagnosis of cocaine intoxication or cocaine withdrawal is justified. The cocaine appears to counterbalance the depressed mood, but there is no clear indication that it leads to maladaptive behavior. If the clinician were evaluating the man in an emergency room following a fight resulting from cocaine use, then the additional diagnosis of cocaine intoxication would be in order. Withdrawal from cocaine leads to dysphoric mood and symptoms such as fatigue and hypersomnia, but in light of the patient's preexisting depression, there seems no need to diagnose withdrawal.

Hypoactive sexual desire disorder would not be diagnosed since it is excluded when it occurs only during the course of a major depressive episode, as noted previously. Hypersomnia related to another mental disorder, a disorder in the new DSM-III-R class of sleep disorders, is a possibility, however, provided the patient was getting adequate amounts of sleep, had a hard time awakening, and the oversleeping occurred every day for at least a month (see also Chapter 8).

This case illustrates the complexity of a clinical syndrome that can be conveyed by multiple diagnoses and the compromise between heterogeneity and redundancy that Axis I represents.

DSM-III-R severity ratings. A new Axis I convention has been introduced with the DSM-III-R system: a severity rating, which can be made for all Axis I disorders, of mild, moderate, severe, in partial remission (or residual state), or in complete remission. This convention was introduced because of recognition that the same disorder often varies considerably in terms of severity of the symptoms and that symptoms themselves vary over time. A person with major depression may have four symptoms for two weeks and just meet the criteria for the diagnosis or may have all the symptoms of the disorder for six months; he or she may have lost 10 lbs in one instance and 30 lbs in another. The remission states are included because diagnoses for patients are frequently made or required at various stages in the course of an illness and its treatment. DSM-III was not very clear in delineating the time frame to which its diagnoses applied; this was particularly a problem when a patient who was being evaluated no longer actually met the criteria for the disorder that was responsible for his or her first seeking treatment.

Two important points about the severity rating need to be emphasized. The first is that the mild, moderate, or severe ratings refer to the *current* severity of the symptoms and the amount of impairment that results. The clinician is instructed to take into account the number, intensity, and duration of the signs and symptoms of the disorder in making the rating. In the cases of the above hypothetical patients with major depression, in the first instance the disorder would be rated as mild, and in the second, as severe. The second point to be emphasized is that a distinction is implied in cases that present some symptoms of a disorder, but no longer meet the relevant criteria: the clinician must decide whether to classify it as "in partial remission" or "residual state." "In partial remission" is to be used when the clinician anticipates that the patient will recover completely, and "residual state," when there is little expectation that the patient will recover within the next few years. Examples of the latter would be cases of autistic disorder or attention-deficit hyperactivity disorder.

The following nine disorders have specific levels of severity included as part of the DSM-III-R criteria: attention-deficit hyperactivity disorder, conduct disorder, oppositional defiant disorder, dementia, psychoactive substance dependence, manic episode, major depressive episode, panic disorder with agoraphobia, and the paraphilias. For all other disorders, Table 2.1 reproduces the general guidelines for rating severity.

TABLE 2.1 DSM-III-R Guidelines for Specifying Current Severity of Disorder

Mild: Few, if any, symptoms in excess of those required to make the diagnosis **and** symptoms result in only minor impairment in occupational functioning or in usual social activities or relationships with others.

Moderate: Symptoms or functional impairment between "mild" and "severe."

Severe: Several symptoms in excess of those required to make the diagnosis and symptoms markedly interfere with occupational functioning or with usual social activities or relationships with others.

In Partial Remission or **Residual State:** The full criteria for the disorder were previously met, but currently only some of the symptoms or signs of the illness are present. *In partial remission* should be used when there is the expectation that the person will completely recover (or have a complete remission) within the next few years, as, for example, in the case of a major depressive episode. *Residual state* should be used when there is little expectation of a complete remission or recovery within the next few years, as, for example, in the case of autistic disorder or attention-deficit hyperactivity disorder. (*Residual state* should not be used with schizophrenia, since by tradition there is a specific residual type of schizophrenia.) In some cases the distinction between *in partial remission* and *residual state* will be difficult to make.

In Full Remission: There are no longer any symptoms or signs of the disorder. The differentiation of *in full remission* from recovered (no current mental disorder) requires consideration of the length of time since the last period of disturbance, the total duration of the disturbance, and the need for continued evaluation or prophylactic treatment.

Axis II

The major problems with Axis II conventions have had to do with the thresholds for making DSM-III personality disorder diagnoses and the difficulties inherent in a system of diagnosis that uses categories to describe phenomena that often seem better characterized by dimensions of personality functioning. A full discussion of the theoretical and practical problems associated with diagnosing personality disorder according to DSM-III and DSM-III-R can be found in Chapter 9.

Axis III

Problems with the Axis III conventions have been encountered in the clinician's decision about whether a disorder is relevant to "the understanding and management" of the patient, and therefore should be listed, or whether it is not. In a psychiatric outpatient clinic, my associates and I found that approximately 50% of patients had some physical disorder listed on Axis III (37). This figure is encouraging since Axis III was included in the DSM-III multiaxial system because physical disorders in patients attending psychiatric clinics have typically been overlooked (38,39). In our clinic, inexperienced clinicians still tend to underestimate the significance of physical disorders in patients with mental disorders.

Recent research on risk factors in major depression and schizophrenia indicates that the occurrence of physical illness or injury in the year preceding onset of these disorders constitutes a strong risk factor (25,26). Moreover, many physical conditions, even if they are not illnesses (e.g., pregnancy or menopause), have implications for clinical management, especially drug therapy. The only published study on the impact of Axis III on clinical practice found that the axis did not appear to convey accurately the documented physical problems of a group of patients in a state hospital (40). It is probably better to err on the side of being overinclusive rather than underinclusive in the use of Axis III.

Lilliputian Legacy

A 39-year-old, single, black male was admitted to the psychiatric service of a large municipal hospital after members of a community outreach team convinced him that he needed help. "It's all a question of how you treat the small ones," he said. "The small ones must be treated with dignity, when they come out."

The patient had a 15-year psychiatric history, and had been known to the team for over five years. He had the persistent belief that during his first psychiatric hospitalization, he had involuntarily had "internal, reconstructive, orthopedic" surgery, during which nurses had surreptitiously put several hundred "small persons" in place of his bone marrow. Some of these were good, helping to hold his body together; but others, "the disruptive ones," were "troublesome and unruly." "They argue and fight and use these little electrical cattle prods to injure me," he explained. The patient was convinced that only a special magnetic machine would be able to safely deliver the little people from his body so that the good ones would not be harmed.

The patient was notoriously poor at complying with antipsychotic drug treatment. He believed the medications might poison the good people with the bad. When in a psychotic episode, he was known to drink heavily—usually wine and beer. He had had to be detoxified from alcohol on two previous hospitalizations and once had gone into withdrawal delirium while hospitalized.

The admitting multiaxial diagnosis listed schizophrenia, chronic, with acute exacerbation and alcohol dependence on Axis I. Axis III had no diagnosis listed.

Routine admission blood tests revealed elevated liver enzymes. A medical consultant examined the patient and found a palpable liver, peripheral edema, and jaundiced sclera. A diagnosis of cirrhosis of the liver was made.

If Axis III is intended to correct the long-standing problem of neglect of adequate assessments of the physical status of psychiatric patients, especially targeted should be those with chronic mental disorders. Previous studies (38,39) have shown that in fewer than half of the cases in a variety of treatment settings was the mental health clinician aware of an important physical illness. In the patient with a so-called "dual diagnosis," i.e., one with a chronic psychotic disorder and a substance use disorder, the psychiatrist should be alert to the possible presence of serious physical illness. In the case above, not only is the illness serious but it has obvious implications for the management of the patient's psychosis with antipsychotic drugs.

Use of Axis III by nonmedical mental health professionals. One thorny obstacle to effective application of Axis III has been the reluctance of mental health professionals who are not psychiatrists to make judgments about the physical status of their patients (41). Psychologists, psychiatric social workers, and others have been concerned that they may even be guilty of malpractice if they list illnesses on Axis III. However, Axis III was not intended to indicate that a particular physical disorder was actually diagnosed by the person recording the multiaxial evaluation. This is true even of psychiatrists who, for instance, may have had a patient with a known physical disorder referred from a medical clinic or by a private physician, and would then list that physical disorder on Axis III. There is no implication that the psychiatrist made the latter diagnosis.

The suggestion has been made that nonmedical clinicians may wish to indicate the source of their information on Axis III, e.g., "hypertension—from medical chart," or "hypothyroidism—per Dr. Smith."

Relationship to Axis IV. A third question raised about the use of Axis III is whether a physical illness that is important primarily as a psychosocial stressor should be listed on Axis IV only, or on both Axis III and Axis IV. An illness that compromises a person's livelihood, ushers in a new phase of life, results in severe financial hardship, or poses a threat to survival certainly would be important in the overall management of the patient, but also would be redundant in terms of an Axis IV assessment.

I generally have recommended that clinicians list the illness on both axes, although the instructions in DSM-III are not clear in this regard. In my experience, clinicians tend to list acute illnesses on both Axis III and Axis IV and chronic illnesses on Axis III only. This is the case despite the fact that Axis IV can be used for both acute and chronic psychosocial stressors. Clinicians tend to use Axis IV more for life-event stress and less for ongoing burdens and handicaps (see below). I have also observed that patients with more chronic mental disorders, such as schizophrenia, are more likely to have a physical illness listed on Axis III only than are patients with episodic disorders such as major depression, who usually have the illness listed on both axes.

Axis IV

The brief instructions for the use of Axis IV found on pages 26-28 in DSM-III contain a series of conventions each of which presents certain problems when implemented in clinical practice. They have also been identified each as potential sources of unreliability of, or disagreement about, appropriate Axis IV ratings (42-44). The key conventions are the following:

1. The clinician rates only those stressors judged to have contributed significantly to the development or exacerbation of the current disorder.
2. The rating is based on the amount of stress an "average" person would experience under similar circumstances, not on the severity of the person's response to the stressor or his or her particular vulnerability to it.
3. The rating is to be based on the number of stressors, whether they were desirable or not or under the person's control, and the amount of change resulting from the stressors.
4. The stressor usually has occurred within the year preceding the current episode of illness.
5. The stressor may either be a precipitating event or result from the person's psychopathology.

Each of these conventions has considerable significance, in the opinion of researchers studying the life-stress process, and has been the focus of some of the criticism of Axis IV. The following sections consider each convention separately, discuss the problem from a theoretical point of view, and illustrate the practical problems with examples from clinical practice.

Etiologic role of the stressors. The decision to list and rate only etiologically relevant stressors was based on a desire to give the Axis IV rating predictive validity. The assumption was that a particular disorder would have a better prognosis if it occurred as a result of a severe psychosocial stressor rather than a mild stressor, or if there were no stressor at all.

Although the attempt to link the occurrence of psychosocial stressors to the development or exacerbation of a mental disorder has a theoretical basis, it also is the source of a number of practical problems. First, the requirement of etiologic relevance makes the clinician very selective in his or her choice of stressors to be listed and rated. Previous research has shown that when two raters follow a fairly standardized procedure in identifying what stressors may have occurred in a person's life, there can be relatively good agreement, i.e., reliability (45). If the clinician's job is to determine both whether a stressor occurred *and* whether it was etiologically relevant, this is likely to be a source of disagreement or unreliability.

In general, a tool that cannot be used reliably has little usefulness (validity). In a comparison of Axis IV as used clinically in an outpatient clinic and on an inpatient ward, we found that many fewer events were listed and rated on Axis IV than were revealed by a standardized life-events interview (27). In examining why stressful events such as going to jail or getting a divorce had not been listed by clinicians on Axis IV, we discovered that, most often, these "events" had been judged to be consequences of the patients' illness rather than causes or precipitants. Sometimes they were judged not to have had a significant effect on the patients' clinical state. Patients whose stressors were not rated on Axis IV tended to have more chronic mental illnesses, such as schizophrenia (see also below).

In a study of the supervision of residents and psychology interns in making multiaxial diagnoses (37), we found two common errors related to this convention: *(1)* a stressor was rated that had caused no change in the patient's condition, *(2)* a stressor and a change in the patient's condition were noted, but the two were actually rather clearly unrelated. An example of the first error would be a patient with chronic schizophrenia who had lost his place of residence; he might then be hospitalized, even though there was no exacerbation of the disorder, because no other disposition was currently possible. In this case a rating of 5-Severe would be inconsistent with the DSM-III system, not because the loss of residence was not a severe stressor, but because the stressor rating was not applicable since there was no change in the patient's condition. Using Axis IV as intended in DSM-III, the clinician should give a rating of 0.

The problem with this convention as applied in this clinical situation is that it can lead to a systematic bias against rating and listing stressors in chronic mental illnesses such as schizophrenia. In another study of the use of Axis IV (46), we found a lower mean rating for schizophrenia compared with more episodic disorders, such as major depression (even with "0's" excluded), and many fewer events listed. We also found that clinicians were very inconsistent in their use of ratings "0" versus "1—None" for indicating that a stressor was not relevant because the patient's condition had not changed. Some patients with ratings of 0 had no diagnosis or diagnosis deferred on Axis I; this clearly indicated that the rating was not made because no disorder was involved. Many had schizophrenia, and most of these had "no change in condition" appended to the Axis IV rating. For others, however, it was not clear whether the 0 was being used because of a lack of adequate information, because there was no change in the patient's condition, or because the stressor that was present was judged not relevant.

The other error involved this judgment of relevancy. For example, a patient with a clear exacerbation of schizophrenia was picked up by the police for disturbing passers-by in a park. This stressor might be rated as of moderate severity, except that it had nothing to do with the exacerbation of illness. Again a rating of "0—Not applicable" would be in line with the DSM-III convention. In our Axis IV study, of those patients who received a "1—None" rating on Axis IV, many had schizophrenia with acute exacerbations or schizophreniform disorder. It is likely that at least some of these ratings reflected the clinician's judgment that stressors, even if present, were not relevant to the exacerbation of a psychotic illness.

Thus, the conventions governing the etiologic relationship lead to errors in the use of Axis IV and to biases that may cause underestimation of the role stress may be playing in a patient's current situation. Furthermore, once a stressor is judged not applicable and is not listed, it is lost from the record, and the discovery of a future relationship to a disorder that is not at first apparent (47-49) is no longer possible.

In DSM-III-R the definitions of scale points 1 and 0 have been changed to reduce ambiguity. The point "1—None" now reads "No acute events (No enduring circumstances) that may be relevant to the disorder" (36, p. 27). instead of "No apparent psychosocial stressor" (19, p. 27). Point 0 now refers to "Inadequate information, or no change in condition" (36, p. 11) instead of "No information or not applicable" (19, p. 27). Information loss and bias still seem likely because of the etiologic relevance issue even in the new system.

As a possible solution to this problem, I suggest that the circumstances in which the 0 or 1 rating should be given be clearly indicated as follows: "0—inadequate information available" or "no change in patient's condition"; "1—not relevant to change in patient's condition" or, to the best of the clinician's ability to judge on the basis of adequate data, "no relevant stressors." Since the listing of stressors is separate from the rating, those that occurred, but were rated 0 because of lack of a relationship to a changed condition or 1 because they were, at least initially, presumed irrelevant to a change, can be listed and thus be part of the record for future reference.

Unless the etiological relationship can be demonstrated to have predictive validity, it may eventually be removed from the system. Other investigators have reported difficulties among clinicians attempting to make the etiologic judgment and have used Axis IV without this requirement (50). Patients with psychotic affective disorders were still found to have experienced more stress than patients with nonaffective psychoses. Even without the intended predictive validity, the presence of psychosocial stressors has important implications as a focus of treatment. Clinicians who want to ensure comprehensive assessment of psychosocial stressors should use a standardized life events assessment technique (45,51-53). The alternative would be to employ a relatively short list of severe stressors likely to account for most serious psychopathology (54).

Estimating the theoretically average response. Rating the severity of the stressors according to an estimate of the response of an "average" person under similar circumstances has met with widespread criticism (23,55). The rationale for this convention was that the average severity rating would ensure that Axis IV would not be redundant in terms of Axis I, on which the severity of the patient's response is indicated by the nature of the psychiatric diagnosis itself. Thus, if two patients lose their jobs and one develops an adjustment disorder with depressed mood whereas the other suffers a full-blown major depressive episode, the difference in reaction to the same event indicates that, for reasons that may have clinical import, the second patient was more vulnerable than the first. An alternative way of rating the severity of the stressor would be based on the person's idiosyncratic response; some have argued that it is this peculiar vulnerability or the person's way of viewing and interpreting the stressor that has the most clinical relevance (55).

Clinicians in practice have had trouble keeping the convention of the average person's response in mind and frequently rate a patient's overreaction to a stressor. An example would be a lawyer with compulsive personality disorder who developed a major depression with suicidal ideation after losing a trial. A rating of "5—Severe" or "6—Extreme," because of the severity of the depression itself, would be incorrect according to the DSM-III convention; "4—Moderate" for such a setback would be more appropriate.

Traditionally there have been two approaches to measuring life-event stress. The first, similar to the DSM-III approach, is to use a life-event checklist with a scale of objective severity that assigns a "weight" based on ratings made by a series of judges. This approach is typified by the work of Holmes and Rahe (56). In juxtaposition to this approach has been the contextual threat measure used in the work of Brown and Harris (52), which recognizes that events are differentially stressful depending upon potentially mitigating factors, such as the presence or absence of social supports. This approach has been criticized for confounding aspects of the life stress process, i.e., life events and social support, which should be measured independently of one another. Although the DSM-III "average" rating is supposed to be made taking into account persons in "similar circumstances and with similar sociocultural values," the scale according to which clinicians make severity ratings in DSM-III contains as examples of the scale points events that fairly closely reflect the severity ratings of an objectively derived life-events rating scale, the Psychiatric Epidemiology Research Interview (PERI) Life-Events Inventory (51). Since only 15 specific events with ratings as examples for adults and 14 for children are given in DSM-III, without extensive instructions on how to take "circumstances" into account, it seems very likely that clinicians will simply rate most stressors according to their own conceptualizations of theoretically average response.

Assessing qualitative characteristics of the stressors. DSM-III states that judgment of the severity of the stressors involves consideration of "the amount of change in the individual's life caused by the stressor, the degree to which the event is desired and under the individual's control, and the number of stressors" (19, p. 26). This convention reflects a growing appreciation, among investigators of the effects of life events on health, that there is considerable variability within life-event categories, and that aspects of that variability, such as consequent major life changes, extremely negative in results, or unanticipated, lead to the worst health outcomes (45,56-61). Unfortunately, DSM-III gives no further instructions on how to take variability into account in making ratings. With respect to the "summed effect of all the psychosocial stressors that are listed" (19, p. 27), if a patient experiences both a marital separation and a serious physical illness (two events with "5—Severe" ratings according to DSM-III), should the rating be 5, or be increased to 6, or even to 7?

In our study of 362 patients, my colleague and I found that 69.3%

had at least one event listed on Axis IV, 22.4% had two events, and 7.5%, three (27). Mezzich and co-workers (62) have also reported a high frequency of listing of multiple stressors. An analysis of the severity ratings indicated that only the stressfulness of the first listed event made a significant contribution to the Axis IV rating (46), thus confirming that clinicians are at a loss as to how to rate multiple stressors. There are systems for rating the variability of life events that interested clinicians might learn (45,56-61), but they would undoubtedly be considered too complex for inclusion in the DSM-III multiaxial system at this point.

One change that might improve the reliability of the Axis IV ratings by standardizing the "summing" convention would be to make it explicit that the severity rating should be based on the first-listed, presumably most severe stressor, but that when more than one stressor is present, all should be listed, because of their importance in focusing treatment. DSM-III-R has incorporated this suggestion to some extent in new instructions: "When more than one stressor is present, the severity rating will generally be that of the most severe stressor. However, in the case of multiple severe or extreme stressors, a higher rating should be considered" (36, p. 19).

Determining the time frame. The DSM-III convention is that most stressors will have occurred within a year before the current disorder, but that there are circumstances or disorders for which the stressor will have occurred in the more distant past. DSM-III also allows that the stressor may be an anticipated future event, e.g., retirement. In my opinion, if one is to preserve a link between a stressor and a disorder that is not trivial or coincidental, clinicians should rate only extreme or catastrophic stressors, such as rape, death of a child, war combat, or concentration camp experience, that occur outside the one-year time frame. This is generally the convention in research that focuses on the effects of remote versus recent events. Similarly, anticipated events should be rated only if they are of some consequence.

Distinguishing cause and effect. DSM-III states that the stressor "frequently plays a precipitating role in a disorder" but may also be a consequence of the individual's psychopathology (19, pp. 26-27). Although it conforms to clinical experience, this convention tends to blur a very important distinction in the relationship of the stressor to the disorder. Independent or fateful negative events, such as the death of a close relative or friend or being the victim of an assault, have been shown to be powerful risk factors for the development of major depression (25,26). In the specific example given in DSM-III—

alcohol dependence leading to marital problems and divorce, which in turn led to a major depression—if there is any prognostic significance to the occurrence of the extreme stressor (i.e., the divorce), it is certainly limited to the prognosis of the mood disorder. In fact, it is more likely that the prognostic value of the presence of the stressor is completely obviated by the fact that the divorce was in no way a fateful loss event. If clinicians list and rate such events, they should realize that the prognostic significance of such nonindependent events is undoubtedly much less than the treatment planning significance.

Swept Away

"When they lowered the coffin into the ground," she said, "I knew that my life was over." So concluded a 33-year-old housewife as she related the story of the accidental drowning of her 5-year-old daughter and the subsequent disintegration of her marriage over the preceding 15 months to the psychiatric resident evaluating her for outpatient treatment.

The resident described the case to her supervisor as follows. The woman had been "reasonably" happily married for six years to a man she considered "a good provider," though "not emotionally demonstrative." They had one child, named Jennifer, who was the pride of both of their lives. Discussions of future children became bogged down in debates about whether or not the husband would become more involved in the child-care responsibilities and whether the wife was a good mother.

Then disaster struck. Jennifer was playing one early spring afternoon in the woods behind her house with a friend when she accidentally slipped on the soft mud into a large stream, swollen from a recent rain and melting snow from the mountains that ran behind the property. The current swept her quickly downstream. She apparently struck her head on a rock and lost consciousness. The friend ran home for help. The mother called the fire department. The body of the dead girl was found, a short time later, about three-quarters of a mile below the place where she fell into the stream.

The couple reacted with shock and disbelief. At first the husband tried to be comforting to his wife; but as the months passed, he became more and more blaming: "How could you let her go out there by herself? What were you doing, watching T.V.?" The mother indeed felt responsible and guilty, and her grief turned into morbid depression. She found herself unable to shop for food or cook dinner; she slept as much as she could. She had nightmares of her daughter being swept away in the stream. She started to substitute herself for her daughter in the images. Then one day her husband came home to find his wife had taken an overdose of sedatives.

The woman refused follow-up referral for psychiatric care offered by the emergency-room physician, but she continued to be depressed.

> After six months, the husband could not stand it anymore and announced that he wanted a divorce. Another suicide attempt ensued, followed by a three-month hospitalization. At the time of her present evaluation, the patient was almost, but not completely, recovered. Her life in shambles, she asked the resident, "Can you really help me?"

In reviewing the multiaxial diagnostic assessment of this patient, the supervisor noted that the resident had given a rating of "6—Extreme" on Axis IV and listed "death of a child" and "poor relationship with husband" as the specific stressors. In the ensuing discussion it was pointed out to the resident that it was not clear that the poor relationship with the husband was a stressor or a symptom, or even whose symptom it was. When asked why "divorce" was not listed, the resident replied that the patient was already depressed. Technically, a worsening of the depression at the point a desire for the divorce was announced justifies listing divorce as well as death of a child as stressors for the major depression, which is currently "in partial remission."

Rating acute vs. chronic stressors. A number of critiques have been made about DSM-III's decision to rate both acute, discrete, life-event stressors and chronic, ongoing stressful life circumstances on the same scale and to combine them in the same rating (21,22). The effects of these different types of stressors are most certainly different; and, as has been mentioned before, they are generally considered separately in models of the life-stress process. In fact, DSM-III reflected some apparent ambivalence about whether to include both kinds of stressors. It is clear that the intention in the manual is for both types to be rated. On page 28 (19), under "Types of psychosocial stressors to be considered," there are many examples of chronic stressors: conjugal discord, discordant relationship with boss, unemployment, persecution, single parent, foster family, institutional rearing, etc. In the scale of severity ratings itself, however, on page 27 (19), all the examples for adults and all for children and adolescents except two are stressors with a discrete onset that can be determined and thus can be rated as individually occurring life events. The lack of examples illustrating the stressfulness of ongoing situations may reflect the greater difficulty in quantifying their impact.

In the previously mentioned study on the use of Axis IV in clinical practice (27), we found that many events listed on Axis IV could not be confirmed by an independent life-events interview, particularly if they were rated as mild or less in severity, as opposed to catastrophic or extreme. Researchers studying Axis IV ratings on adolescents have reported a similar finding (43). In our experience, one of the most common reasons for the discrepancy was that Axis IV stressors of lesser severity were often more like chronic strains (e.g., being a single mother, or chronically unemployed) than life events.

Because of the criticism of this DSM-III convention and the confusion engendered by intermingling two distinct types of stressors, the revised DSM-III includes a statement that the specific stressors should be characterized as *(1)* predominantly acute events with a duration of less than six months, or *(2)* predominantly enduring circumstances with a duration of more than six months. Table 2.2 shows the revised Axis IV severity-rating format with new examples of both events and ongoing circumstances illustrating scale points.

Validity of Axis IV. The validity of Axis IV was supported by the results of a study of Axis IV ratings of 130 depressed inpatients (53).

TABLE 2.2 DSM-III-R Axis IV Rating Scales

Severity of Psychosocial Stressors Scale: Adults

Code	Term	Examples of stressors	
		Acute events	**Enduring circumstances**
1	**None**	No acute events that may be relevant to the disorder	No enduring circumstances that may be relevant to the disorder
2	**Mild**	Broke up with boyfriend or girlfriend; started or graduated from school; child left home	Family arguments; job dissatisfaction; residence in high-crime neighborhood
3	**Moderate**	Marriage; marital separation; loss of job; retirement; miscarriage	Marital discord; serious financial problems; trouble with boss; being a single parent
4	**Severe**	Divorce; birth of first child	Unemployment; poverty
5	**Extreme**	Death of spouse; serious physical illness diagnosed; victim of rape	Serious chronic illness in self or child; ongoing physical or sexual abuse
6	**Catastrophic**	Death of child; suicide of spouse; devastating natural disaster	Captivity as hostage; concentration camp experience
0	**Inadequate information, or no change in condition**		

Severity of Psychosocial Stressors Scale: Children and Adolescents

Code	Term	Examples of Stressors	
		Acute events	**Enduring circumstances**
1	**None**	No acute events that may be relevant to the disorder	No enduring circumstances that may be relevant to the disorder
2	**Mild**	Broke up with boyfriend or girlfriend; change of school	Overcrowded living quarters; family arguments
3	**Moderate**	Expelled from school; birth of sibling	Chronic disabling illness in parent; chronic parental discord
4	**Severe**	Divorce of parents; unwanted pregnancy; arrest	Harsh or rejecting parents; chronic life-threatening illness in parent; multiple foster home placements
5	**Extreme**	Sexual or physical abuse; death of a parent	Recurrent sexual or physical abuse
6	**Catastrophic**	Death of both parents	Chronic life-threatening illness
0	**Inadequate information, or no change in condition**		

Axis IV scores were more highly correlated with undesirable than desirable events, exits (i.e., losses) than entrances, and discrete and time-limited events than ongoing circumstances. Higher Axis IV ratings were also associated with a lower rate of abnormal dexamethasone suppression test results, a higher rate of risk for alcoholism, a greater likelihood of co-morbid personality disorders, and a greater frequency of attempted suicide during the index episode.

The ability of Axis IV severity ratings to predict patient prognosis, however, remains an open question. Thus far, Axis IV ratings have been found by Mezzich and his associates (63) to have a modest but significant correlation with the decision to admit a patient from a walk-in clinic to inpatient hospital care. And Gordon and associates (64,65) have found that a measure, which they call the "strain ratio," derived by dividing Axis IV ratings by inverted (8 minus the Axis V score) Axis V ratings, is related to length of hospital stay. The higher the strain ratio, that is, the greater the degree of psychosocial stress associated with the disorder compared with the level of adaptive functioning, the longer patients needed to be hospitalized. Only one study, by Zimmerman and his co-workers (66), has compared outcomes between two groups of patients with the same or similar disorders, one of which rated high on the Axis IV scale and the other, low. They failed to find the predicted relationship between high severity-of-stressor ratings and good prognosis in a sample of depressed inpatients.

The absence of clear-cut predictive validity for Axis IV led the Multiaxial Advisory Committee to the Work Group to Revise DSM-III to consider recommending that the Axis IV severity rating be dropped from DSM-III-R. The usefulness of the listing of stressors for treatment planning mitigated against a radical dismantling of the Axis IV, which, it was agreed, would effectively end its use in clinical or research settings. Thus, the jury remains out on Axis IV until at least preparation of DSM-IV.

Axis V

DSM-III instructed clinicians to base Axis V ratings on their composite assessment of three major areas of adaptive functioning: social relations, occupational functioning, and use of leisure time. It went on to say that "social relations should be given greater weight because of their particularly great prognostic significance" (19, p. 28). Leisure time was expected to play a role only when other areas of functioning were intact or the opportunity for occupational functioning was limited because of circumstances such as physical handicap or retirement.

The major overall problem that I have encountered in the use of Axis V has been the tendency for clinicians to overrate adaptive functioning because they individualize the rating to a particular patient, or patient group, rather than compare the patient with a hypothetical population of all people. For example, a patient with primary degenerative dementia was given a rating for highest level of adaptive functioning during the past year of "4—Fair" because she had been functioning "well for her," instead of "6—Very Poor," which was indicated because she was extremely socially isolated and needed assistance in all aspects of living except simple self-care tasks. Another example I have encountered was an adolescent with mental retardation whom a trainee regarded as "functioning better than most" and rated "3—Good," instead of "6—Very Poor." This adolescent was totally dependent on the institution in which he lived for all of life's necessities. Again, in my opinion, the instructions for rating social and occupational functioning in DSM-III were scanty and ambiguous.

The following sections review these conventions, problems clinicians have had in interpreting them, and some data on the use of Axis V in a clinical setting that illustrate the problems and offer some clarifications. Finally, I shall discuss the evidence that Axis V has lived up to its promise of predictive validity.

Assessing social relations. Social relations according to DSM-III "include all relations with people, with particular emphasis on family and friends. The breadth and quality of interpersonal relationships should be considered" (19, p. 28). These instructions are broad and leave much to the individual clinician's discretion. Is being married important? Having many friends or a few close ones? Being in multiple social roles and situations, or feeling satisfaction from them? And how much should these or other aspects of social functioning "count" relative to one another?

My colleagues in the Social Psychiatry Research Unit at Columbia University and I have studied some of these questions as part of an exploration of risk factors for the major mental disorders (25). We recruited over 350 patients from the outpatient psychiatric clinic at Columbia Presbyterian Medical Center and an inpatient ward at the New York State Psychiatric Institute. All these patients had carefully supervised multiaxial diagnoses according to DSM-III. They then also received an independent interview (in some cases, two independent interviews) that assessed, in some detail, aspects of their social functioning (31).

In particular, we determined whether a patient was married (not counting those who were unmarried and under 30 years old) and "measured" his or her degree of marital satisfaction (if married) by means of eight questions. If single, we determined the patient's satisfaction with being single by means of six questions. Examples of these questions can be found in Table 2.3. We also found out whether or not a patient had someone to help him or her, i.e., had a social network, in nine areas of activity: taking care of the house while he or she was out of town, discussing decisions at work, helping with household tasks, engaging in recreational activities, looking after children, dating, discussing personal worries, getting advice on important decisions, and borrowing money. We then constructed several variables that described aspects of the patient's social network, including how many individuals were in the network, how many would be considered close confidants, how many were social companions, etc. By means of multivariate regression analyses, we demonstrated, to our surprise, that neither marital status or satisfaction nor satisfaction with being single and dating played a significant part in determining clinicians' Axis V ratings. We found that certain of the characteristics of the social network made a small contribution to the Axis V ratings. No aspect of social functioning had as much impact on clinicians' ratings of adaptive functioning as did aspects of occupational functioning (see below).

Our findings suggest that clinicians must systematically inquire about various social roles that a person may be in and his or her degree of satisfaction in that role if they are to capture the dimension of social relations on Axis V. It is suggested from the examples of levels of functioning given in the Axis V table on page 29 of DSM-III (19) that both attainment of a role and satisfaction with it are important.

Assessing occupational functioning. Occupational functioning refers broadly to functioning as a worker, student, or homemaker. The DSM-III convention is to include in the rating "The amount, complexity, and quality of the work accomplished" (19, p. 28). High occupational productivity is given the highest ratings of adaptive functioning only when it "is not associated with a high level of subjective discomfort" (19, p. 29).

TABLE 2.3 Questions Measuring Marital Dissatisfaction[1]

1. During the past (year/month), how often have you felt uncomfortable with your (husband/wife/mate)?

2. Sometimes (husbands and wives/people in a relationship) have differences of opinion about showing love. During the past (year/month), how often has this been a problem for you in your (marriage/relationship)?

3. During the past (year/month), how often have you felt affectionate toward your (husband/wife/mate)?

4. During the past (year/month), how often has the thought come to your mind that your (husband/wife/mate) doesn't really love you?

5. When it comes to sexual relations, about how often during the past (year/month) have you and your (husband/wife/mate) had sex, on the average?

6. During the past (year/month), how have you felt about sexual relations?

7. During the past (year/month), how satisfied have you been with your (marriage/relationship)?

8. During the past (year/month), how satisfied has your (husband/wife/mate) been with your (marriage/relationship)?

[1] Taken from the Psychiatric Epidemiology Research Interview (PERI). Questions are scored on a scale of 0 to 4, with a high score indicating dissatisfaction.

Our investigation of Axis V ratings included several measures of "occupational" functioning in the workplace and in the home. We assessed how much of the time the person was employed and at what occupation. We recorded the income earned over the preceding year. We also measured, with four items, the amount of satisfaction the person experienced in his or her job. Then we focused on how well those who had responsibility for at least half of the housework actually performed that work (seven questions). Finally, if he or she had children, we asked seven questions about how much satisfaction the person expressed about functioning as a parent. Examples of the questions are given in Table 2.4.

As noted above, occupational factors generally had a much higher bearing on Axis V ratings than did social factors. Not being employed during the period assessed counted heavily against high levels of adaptive functioning (as strong an association as having been in jail), and neglect of housework was also a significant determinant of poorer ratings. Interestingly, and contrary to explicit DSM-III instructions, reporting dissatisfaction with one's job did not affect clinicians' ratings of patients on Axis V. No association was found with parental satisfaction or dissatisfaction. Finally, a person's earnings had a strong effect on better ratings of adaptive functioning, regardless of the person's job satisfaction.

Assessing use of leisure time. I have not had a great deal of experience with clinicians' attempts to integrate leisure-time activities into Axis V ratings, nor am I aware of any studies that would be of

TABLE 2.4 Questions Measuring Job Dissatisfaction[1]

1. During the past (year/month), how satisfied have you been with the kind of work you do?

2. During the past (year/month), how satisfied have you been with your wage or salary level?

3. During the past (year/month), how satisfied have you been with your future in this job?

4. During the past (year/month), in general, how interested have you been in the work that you were doing?

[1] Taken from the Psychiatric Epidemiology Research Interview (PERI). Questions are scored on a scale of 0 to 4, with a high score indicating dissatisfaction.

help. Leisure-time activities might have most bearing in a retired population, and therefore might best be studied in the elderly. Extrapolating from the occupational functioning experience, I should anticipate that the extent to which a person was involved in leisure activities and how much satisfaction he or she derived from them would be the relevant variables, but that the latter would typically tend to carry less weight.

Separate ratings for DSM-III-R? It has been pointed out (67) that adaptive functioning is frequently not uniform across the two main dimensions of social and occupational functioning. Some people may have very positive interpersonal relations with family and friends, but low occupational attainment or satisfaction; conversely, other people may be very successful in their work and derive great personal satisfaction therefrom, but have very poor social relations, even within the nuclear family. In factoring both of these dimensions of functioning into one rating, the clinician loses this variability in ratings of mediocre adaptive functioning such as "4—Fair"—variability that may have considerable significance in focusing treatment. Therefore, a suggestion was made that DSM-III-R should have separate ratings for social functioning and occupational functioning.

Our experience with Axis V would support this proposal. Our data suggest that, without a complex set of instructions explaining the relative weights to be given to social factors and occupational factors (which in themselves are multifaceted), the Axis V ratings may be made based on the most visible and objective data available. In most cases this seems to be the nature of a person's occupation and how much money he or she makes. Social factors tend to be neglected, perhaps because they are more subtle or difficult to assess. The independent ratings would ensure that attention was paid to each aspect of adaptive functioning, no matter how good, or bad, the other.

The final version of DSM-III-R has an approach to assessing functioning very different from that of DSM-III. A new 90-point scale replaces the 7-point one and incorporates symptom severity as well as levels of social and occupational functioning. The new Axis V, called the Global Assessment of Functioning (GAF) Scale (Table 2.5), was adapted from the Global Assessment Scales for adults and children that have proven reliable and useful as measures of change. The GAF Scale, by including psychological symptoms, will, I believe, further reduce the importance of the other components of functioning (30). I think that to continue to conceptualize the social and occupational factors in this global rating of functioning as separate will help to combat the tendency for one dimension to dominate the others.

TABLE 2.5 DSM-III-R Global Assessment of Functioning Scale (GAF) Scale

Consider psychological, social, and occupational functioning on a hypothetical continuum of mental health-illness. Do not include impairment in functioning due to physical (or environmental) limitations.

Note: Use intermediate codes when appropriate, e.g., 45, 68, 72.

Code	
90 81	**Absent or minimal symptoms** (e.g., mild anxiety before an exam), **good functioning in all areas, interested and involved in a wide range of activities, socially effective, generally satisfied with life, no more than everyday problems or concerns** (e.g., an occasional argument with family members).
80 71	**If symptoms are present, they are transient and expectable reactions to psychosocial stressors** (e.g., difficulty concentrating after family argument); **no more than slight impariment in social, occupational, or school functioning** (e.g., temporarily falling behind in schoolwork).
70 61	**Some mild symptoms** (e.g., depressed mood and mild insomnia); **OR some difficulty in social, occupational, or school functioning** (e.g., occasional truancy, or theft within the household), **but generally functioning pretty well, has some meaningful interpersonal relationships.**
60 51	**Moderate symptoms** (e.g., flat affect and circumstantial speech, occasional panic attacks) **OR moderate difficulty in social, occupation, or school functioning** (e.g., few friends, conflicts with co-workers).
50 41	**Serious symptoms** (e.g., suicidal ideation, severe obsessional rituals, frequent shoplifting) **OR any serious impairment in social, occupational, or school functioning** (e.g., few friends, conflicts with co-workers).
40 31	**Some impairment in reality testing or communication** (e.g., speech is at times illogical, obscure, or irrelevant) **OR major impairment in several areas, such as work or school, family relations, judgment, thinking, or mood** (e.g., depressed man avoids friends, neglects family, and is unable to work; child frequently beats up younger children, is defiant at home, and is failing in school).
30 21	**Behavior is considerably influenced by delusions or hallucinations OR serious impairment in communication or judgment** (e.g., sometimes incoherent, acts grossly inappropriately, suicidal preoccupation) **OR inability to function in almost all areas** (e.g., stays in bed all day; no job, home, or friends).
20 11	**Some danger of hurting self or others** (e.g., suicide attempts without clear expectation of death, frequently violent, manic excitement) **OR occasionally fails to maintain minimal personal hygiene** (e.g., smears feces) **OR gross impairment in communication** (e.g., largely incoherent or mute).
1	**Persistent danger of severely hurting self or others** (e.g., recurrent violence) **OR persistent inability to maintain minimal personal hygiene OR serious suicidal act with clear expectation of death.**
0	**Inadequate information.**

Listless Litigator

A 45-year-old litigator in a large midwestern law firm consulted a psychiatrist at the suggestion of one of his partners. An extremely capable and highly successful expert in contract law, the man had been having unusual difficulty over the past six months. He was uncharacteristically late for appointments, disinterested in his work, easily distractible, and disinclined to accept invitations to dinner or to a game of squash. He admitted to his colleague that he had become increasingly depressed since he had lost a $250,000 investment in an aborted shopping center venture.

The psychiatrist confirmed that the attorney had indeed been suffering from a major depressive episode for the preceding four months. The lawyer felt almost constantly depressed and listless and claimed to have lost "all zest for life." He had lost 20 pounds, was waking up at 4:00 A.M., and was unable to return to sleep, could concentrate only with great difficulty, and had begun to question the direction and purpose of his life.

In spite of these symptoms and the difficulties with his work that his partners had noticed, he was at work every day, met with clients, carried his caseload, made court appearances, and had even tried a case within the past two weeks. He was staying at work late with the more junior lawyers in order to make up for his deficits, sometimes not arriving home until 10:00 or 11:00 P.M., when he would have two or three Scotches, in order to fall asleep, anticipating his early morning awakening.

The past personal history of the lawyer revealed that he was twice divorced and had one child by his first marriage. He was a graduate of a prestigious Eastern law school and had been a "workaholic since day one." He had risen quickly in his firm, and was making a six-figure salary by the time he was 30.

Although he was handsome and charming and very appealing to women, he found he could invest very little of himself in intimate relationships with them. The needs of his two wives had been too much for him to handle. "I came home at night exhausted. All I wanted to do was eat and stare at the T.V. awhile. My first wife wanted to talk about her day, about the baby. She wanted my opinion about this or my advice about that. I could hardly listen." His second wife had her own business. This, he thought, would "guarantee her independence," but often she wanted to meet for a drink after work or go to a gym together. All he wanted was to be left alone. Since his second divorce, he had dated a number of attractive and successful women but had made sure "it was on my terms." He had numerous male friends who apparently liked and respected him, but he saw them only sporadically.

The lawyer in this case vignette has some marked discrepancies in his levels of adaptive functioning. In the year preceding his consultation, his highest level of occupational functioning would warrant a superior rating by DSM-III standards, but only a fair rating on social relations—possibly even poor with respect to close, intimate relationships with women. Averaging these two levels to a rating of "good" does justice to neither, and in fact indicates "slight impairment" in both. The vignette argues for separate ratings.

A GAF rating according to DSM-III-R further complicates the picture. The highest level, past-year rating would have to be near 50 because of social impairment, and the current level would also be near 50. Now, however, the patient has some moderately severe symptoms as well. The change in his condition is not reflected in a change in the ratings and the discrepancy between his ability to function on the job and his being quite depressed is not evident.

Individual ratings on a GAF-type scale of symptoms and social and occupational functioning in the past year might be 90, 50, and 90, respectively; current individual ratings might be 55, 50, and 75. Such individual ratings would capture the complexities involved in assessing this patient's functioning, the discrepancies between his social and occupational functioning, the relative independence of functioning and symptoms, and the recent change in his condition.

The validity of Axis V. The two studies of the value of Axis V ratings are those multiaxial studies mentioned before, by Mezzich and associates (63) and Gordon and colleagues (64,65). In the Mezzich study, Axis V ratings were more closely related to admission decisions than were Axis IV ratings of severity of psychosocial stressors. And when the concept of adaptive functioning was changed from highest level in the past year to current level, the relationship was greatest of all the "nondiagnostic" multiaxial variables. From the start, although Axes IV and V were officially in DSM-III for use in special clinical and research settings, many clinician/administrators in very mainstream psychiatric settings, e.g., state hospitals, recognized the value of Axis V ratings, and have routinely required them. Admission and discharge decisions are being made daily on groups of patients whose serious underlying mental disorders (e.g., schizophrenia) have changed little on Axis I, II, or III. This experience has been documented by the Mezzich group.

Although our Axis V study (31) did not indicate great differences depending on whether the time frame for functioning referred to the past year or to the past month, certain clinical decisions would naturally be based on the most recently demonstrated ability to function. A longer-range view of functioning would possibly bear a greater relationship to prognosis, however. The GAF Scale in DSM-III-R therefore includes a provision for rating both highest levels of adaptive functioning during the past year and current levels. More meaningful for prognosis than highest level during the past year might be highest premorbid level (21,22). However, the longer the period since onset of the illness, the harder it is to evaluate premorbid functioning; and the more chronic the disorder, the less prognostically relevant is such functioning (19).

In the Gordon and co-workers study of Axis V ratings (64), better adaptive functioning tended to offset highly stressful precipitating events or circumstances in predicting length of inpatient hospital stay. The strain ratio measure makes intuitive sense in that (*1*) highly stressful circumstances would be expected to lengthen the period until recovery or until reaching a new level of adaptation, and (*2*) the better the person's previously demonstrated capacity to adapt, the more rapidly the process might be expected to proceed, regardless of the degree of stress. These findings have also recently been extended to length of outpatient treatment (65).

The ultimate prognostic utility of Axis V, like that of Axis IV, remains to be determined by empirical study. The DSM-III-R shift to a Global Assessment of Functioning Scale can certainly be expected to be related to treatment needs and utilization. The prognostic value of the new Axis V seems no more certain than that of the old, and may even be less, owing to the greater confounding of Axis I diagnosis (symptoms) and resultant functioning.

SUMMARY

This chapter describes both conceptual and practical problems with one of the most novel features of DSM-III and DSM-III-R classifications, the multiaxial evaluation system. On the basis of practical experience in teaching and supervising multiaxial diagnosis, theoretical critiques that have appeared in the literature, and a handful of empirical studies, the concepts and conventions of the DSM-III five axes system are reviewed in order to clarify ambiguities and to suggest approaches to more reliable and valid multiaxial assessments. The changes in the system included in DSM-III-R are described, and attempts are made to anticipate future difficulties.

REFERENCES

1. Essen-Möller E, Wohlfahrt S: Suggestions for the amendment of the official Swedish classification of mental disorders. Acta Psychiatr Scand Suppl 47:551–555, 1947
2. Frances A: The DSM-III personality disorders section: a commentary. Am J Psychiatry 137:1050–1054, 1980
3. Mackenzie TB, Popkin MK, Callies AL: Clinical applications of DSM-III in

consultation-liaison psychiatry. Hosp Community Psychiatry 34:628–631, 1983

4. Berner P, Katschnig H, Lenz G: DSM-III in German-speaking countries, in International Perspectives on DSM-III. Edited by Spitzer RL, Williams JBW, Skodol AE. Washington, DC, American Psychiatric Press, 1983, pp 109–125
5. Retterstøl N, Dahl AA: Scandinavian perspectives on DSM-III, in International Perspectives on DSM-III. Edited by Spitzer RL, Williams JBW, Skodol AE. Washington, DC, American Psychiatric Press, 1983, pp 217–234
6. Williams JBW: The multiaxial system of DSM-III: Where did it come from and where should it go? I. Its origins and critiques. Arch Gen Psychiatry 42:175–180, 1985
7. Williams JBW, Spitzer RL, Skodol AE: DSM-III in residency training: results of a national survey. Am J Psychiatry 142:755–758, 1985
8. Williams JBW, Spitzer RL, Skodol AE: DSM-III in the training of psychiatric residents and medical students: a national survey. J Psych Educ 120:75–86, 1986
9. Engles ML, Ghadirian AM, Dongier M: DSM-III in Canada: the viewpoint of academic psychiatrists, in International Perspectives on DSM-III. Edited by Spitzer RL, Williams JBW, Skodol AE. Washington, DC, American Psychiatric Press, 1983, pp 135–143
10. Hanada K, Takahashi S: Multi-institutional collaborative studies of diagnostic reliability of DSM-III and ICD-9 in Japan, in International Perspectives on DSM-III. Edited by Spitzer RL, Williams JBW, Skodol AE. Washington, DC, American Psychiatric Press, 1983, pp 273–290
11. Mezzich JE, Fabrega H Jr, Mezzich AC, Coffman GA: International experience with DSM-III. J Nerv Ment Dis 173:738–741, 1985
12. Rey JM, Andrews W: Towards ICD-10: the attitudes of Australian and New Zealand psychiatrists. Aust N Z J Psychiatry 19:422–426, 1985
13. Malt UF: Clinical experiences with the DSM-III system of classification. Five years of experience with the DSM-III system in clinical work and research: some concluding remarks. Acta Psychiatr Scand 73, Suppl 328:76–84, 1986
14. Williams JBW: The multiaxial system of DSM-III: where did it come from and where should it go? II. Empirical studies, innovations, and recommendations. Arch Gen Psychiatry 42:181–186, 1985
15. Strauss JS: A comprehensive approach to psychiatric diagnosis. Am J Psychiatry 132:1193–1197, 1975
16. American Psychiatric Association: Diagnostic and Statistical Manual of Mental Disorders. Washington, DC, American Psychiatric Association, 1952
17. American Psychiatric Association: Diagnostic and Statistical Manual of Mental Disorders, Second Edition. Washington, DC, American Psychiatric Association, 1968
18. Mezzich JE: Patterns and issues in multiaxial psychiatric diagnosis. Psychol Med 9:125–137, 1979
19. American Psychiatric Association: Diagnostic and Statistical Manual of Mental Disorders, Third Edition. Washington, DC, American Psychiatric Association, 1980
20. Kendell RE: DSM-III: a British perspective (book forum). Am J Psychiatry 137:1630–1631, 1980
21. Rutter M, Shaffer D: DSM-III. A step forward or back in terms of the

classification of child psychiatric disorders? J Am Acad Child Psychiatry 19:371–394, 1980
22. Kendell RE: DSM-III: a major advance in psychiatric nosology, in International Perspectives on DSM-III. Edited by Spitzer RL, Williams JBW, Skodol AE. Washington, DC, American Psychiatric Press, 1983, pp 55–68
23. Roth Sir M: The achievements and limitations of DSM-III, in International Perspectives on DSM-III. Edited by Spitzer RL, Williams JBW, Skodol AE. Washington, DC, American Psychiatric Press, 1983, pp 91–105
24. Williams JBW: Multiaxial diagnosis, in An Annotated Bibliography of DSM-III. Edited by Skodol AE, Spitzer RL. Washington, DC, American Psychiatric Press, 1987, pp 31–36
25. Dohrenwend BP, Shrout PE, Link B, Martin JL, Skodol AE: Overview and initial results from a risk factor study of depression and schizophrenia, in Mental Disorders in the Community: Progress and Challenge. Edited by Barrett JE, Rose RM. New York, Guilford Press, 1986, pp 184–215
26. Dohrenwend BP, Levav I, Shrout PE, Link BG, Skodol AE, Martin JL: Life stress and psychopathology: progress on research begun with Barbara Snell Dohrenwend. Am J Community Psychol 15:677–715, 1987
27. Skodol AE, Shrout PE: The use of DSM-III Axis IV in clinical practice: rating etiologically significant stressors. Am J Psychiatry 146:61–66, 1989
28. Endicott J, Spitzer RL, Fleiss J, Cohen J: The Global Assessment Scale: a procedure for measuring overall severity of psychiatric disturbance. Arch Gen Psychiatry 33:766–771, 1976
29. Shaffer D, Gould MS, Brasic J, Ambrosini P, Fisher P, Bird H, Aluwahlia S: A children's global assessment scale (CGAS). Arch Gen Psychiatry 40:1228–1231, 1983
30. Skodol AE, Link BG, Shrout PE, Horwath E: The revision of Axis V in DSM-III-R: should symptoms have been included? Am J Psychiatry 145:825–829, 1988
31. Skodol AE, Link BG, Shrout PE, Horwath E: Toward construct validity for DSM-III Axis V. Psychiatry Res 24:13–23, 1988
32. Boyd JH, Burke JD Jr, Gruenberg E, Holzer CE 3d, Rae DS, George LK, Karno M, Stoltzman R, McEvoy L, Nestadt G: Exclusion criteria of DSM-III: a study of co-occurrence of hierarchy-free syndromes. Arch Gen Psychiatry 41:983–989, 1984
33. Leckman JF, Merikangas KR, Pauls DL, Prusoff BA, Weissman MM: Anxiety disorders and depression: contradictions between family study data and DSM-III conventions. Am J Psychiatry 140:880–882, 1983
34. Leckman JF, Weissman MM, Merikangas KR, Pauls DL, Prusoff BA: Panic disorder and major depression. Increased risk of depression, alcoholism, panic, and phobic disorders in families of depressed probands with panic disorder. Arch Gen Psychiatry 40:1055–1060, 1983
35. Spitzer RL: Nosology, in An Annotated Bibliography of DSM-III. Edited by Skodol AE, Spitzer RL. Washington, DC, American Psychiatric Press, 1987, pp 3–12
36. American Psychiatric Association. Diagnostic and Statistical Manual of Mental Disorders, Third Edition, Revised. Washington, DC, American Psychiatric Association, 1987
37. Skodol AE, Williams JBW, Spitzer RL, Gibbon M, Kass F: Identifying common errors in the use of DSM-III through diagnostic supervision. Hosp Community Psychiatry 35:251–255, 1984
38. Barnes RF, Mason JC, Greer C, Ray FT: Chronic medical problems in the

chronic mentally ill. Medical illness in chronic psychiatric outpatients. Gen Hosp Psychiatry 5:191–195, 1983
39. Koranyi, EK: Morbidity and rate of undiagnosed physical illnesses in a psychiatric clinic population. Arch Gen Psychiatry 36:414–419, 1979
40. Maricle R, Leung P, Bloom JD: The use of DSM-III Axis III in recording physical illness in psychiatric patients. Am J Psychiatry 144:1484–1486, 1987
41. Williams JBW, Spitzer RL: Focusing on DSM-III's multiaxial system. Hosp Community Psychiatry 33:891–892, 1982
42. Rey JM, Stewart GW, Plapp JM, Bashir MR, Richards IN: DSM-III axis IV revisited. Am J Psychiatry 145:286–292, 1988
43. Rey JM, Stewart GW, Plapp JM, Bashir MR, Richards IN: Sources of unreliability of DSM-III axis IV. Aust NZ J Psychiatry 21:75–80, 1987
44. Rey JM, Plapp JM, Stewart GW, Richards IN, Bashir MR: Reliability of the psychosocial axes of the DSM-III in an adolescent population. Br J Psychiatry 150:228–234, 1987
45. Paykel ES: Methodological aspects of life event research. J Psychosom Res 27:341–352, 1983
46. Skodol AE, Shrout PE: The use of DSM-III Axis IV in clinical practice: rating the severity of the stressors. Unpublished manuscript
47. Lloyd C: Life events and depressive disorder reviewed, II: Events as precipitating factors. Arch Gen Psychiatry 37:541–548, 1980
48. Tennant C: Life events and psychological morbidity: the evidence from prospective studies. Psychol Med 13:483–486, 1983
49. Depue RA, Monroe SM: Conceptualization and measurement of human disorder in life stress research: the problem of chronic disturbance. Psychol Bull 99:36–51, 1986
50. Schrader G, Gordon M, Harcourt R: The usefulness of DSM-III axis IV and axis V assessments. Am J Psychiatry 143:904–907, 1986
51. Dohrenwend BS, Krasnoff L, Askenasy AR, Dohrenwend BP: Exemplification of a method for scaling life events: the PERI life events scale. J Health Soc Behav 19:205–229, 1978
52. Brown GW, Harris T: The Social Origins of Depression. London, Tavitock Publications, 1978
53. Zimmerman M, Pfohl B, Stangl D, Coryell W: The validity of DSM-III axis IV (severity of psychosocial stressors). Am J Psychiatry 142:1437–1441, 1985
54. Brugha T, Bebbington P, Tennant C, Hurry J: The list of threatening experiences: a subset of 12 life event categories with considerable long-term contextual threat. Psychol Med 15:189–194, 1985
55. Frances A, Cooper AM: Descriptive and dynamic psychiatry: a perspective on DSM-III. Am J Psychiatry 138:1198–1202, 1981
56. Holmes TH, Rahe RH: The social readjustment rating scale. J Psychosom Res 11:213–218, 1967
57. Paykel ES, Myers JK, Dienelt MN, Klerman GL, Lindenthal JJ, Pepper MP: Life events and depression: a controlled study. Arch Gen Psychiatry 21:753–760, 1969
58. Finlay-Jones R, Brown GW: Types of stressful life events and the onset of anxiety and depressive disorders. Psychol Med 11:803–815, 1981
59. Henderson S, Byrne DG, Duncan-Jones P: Neurosis and the Social Environment. London, Academic Press, 1982
60. Isherwood J, Adam KS, Hornblow AR: Readjustment, desirability, expec-

tedness, mastery and outcome dimensions of life stress, suicide and auto-accident. J Human Stress 8:11–18, 1982
61. Shrout PE, Link BG, Dohrenwend BP, Skodol AE: Characterizing life events as risk factors for depression. Unpublished manuscript
62. Mezzich JE, Coffman GA, Goodpastor SM: A format for DSM-III diagnostic formulation: experience with 1,111 consecutive patients. Am J Psychiatry 139:591–596, 1982
63. Mezzich JE, Evanczuk KJ, Mathias RJ, Coffman GA: Admission decisions and multiaxial diagnosis. Arch Gen Psychiatry 41:1001–1004, 1984
64. Gordon RE, Jardiolin P, Gordon KK: Predicting length of hospital stay of psychiatric patients. Am J Psychiatry 142:235–237, 1983
65. Gordon RE, Vijay J, Sloate SG, Burket R, Gordon KK: Aggravating stress and functional level as predictors of length of psychiatric hospitalization. Hosp Community Psychiatry 36:773–774, 1985
66. Zimmerman M, Pfohl B, Coryell W, Stangl D: The prognostic validity of DSM-III axis IV in depressed inpatients. Am J Psychiatry 144:102–106, 1987
67. Linn L, Spitzer RL: DSM-III. Implications for liaison psychiatry and psychosomatic medicine. JAMA 247:3207–3209, 1982

CHAPTER 3

Disturbances with Specific Organic Etiologies

The classification and diagnosis of mental disorders with specific organic etiologies is complicated in DSM-III and DSM-III-R because of several factors: (*1*) the organization of the classification into sections, in compliance with the conventions of the International Classification of Diseases, 9th Revision, Clinical Modification (ICD-9-CM) (1); (*2*) the definitions of terms used; (*3*) the revision of certain key diagnostic concepts and the introduction of new diagnostic categories; and (*4*) the assessment of the role of organic factors in the production of the disorders. Certain refinements have been introduced into the DSM-III-R system, but much of the classification and the principles for its use remain the same as in DSM-III.

Organization

As the title of this chapter indicates, the unifying diagnostic feature for certain mental disorders is the presence of an organic factor that is etiologically responsible for the disturbance. Although many additional mental disorders, such as schizophrenia or affective disorders, may eventually be shown to have organic causes, traditionally, and currently, only those disorders for which the organic factor can be specified are considered organic mental disorders.

The DSM-III class "organic mental disorders" was divided into two sections: section 1 was designated "Organic mental disorders whose etiology or pathophysiological process is listed below (taken from the mental disorders section of ICD-9-CM)"; section 2 was called

"Organic brain syndromes whose etiology or pathophysiological process is either noted as an additional diagnosis from outside the mental disorders section of ICD-9-CM or is unknown." This cryptic division into sections was, as noted above, in keeping with the ICD-9-CM (CM = Clinical Modification, officially in use in general medicine in the United States), which considered a few organic mental disorders to have etiologies that were integral to their classification as mental disorders and most others to be secondary to another physical disorder or condition that would be listed under another appropriate section in the ICD-9-CM. An example of the second case might be a dementia associated with hypothyroidism; the hypothyroidism is listed under endocrine, nutritional, and metabolic diseases and immunity disorders in ICD-9-CM, with a code of 244.X (fourth-digit X refers to subtypes). On an admittedly arbitrary basis, the two etiological processes that are considered themselves to be integral to mental disorders are the aging process, which can lead to dementia, and the ingestion of certain substances or drugs. Thus, section 1 in DSM-III was further subdivided in two parts, the first being "Dementias arising in the senium and presenium," and the second, "Substance-induced organic mental disorders." All other organic mental disorders were assigned codes from section 2.

The Work Group to Revise DSM-III considered making a major departure from this convention by listing the substance-induced organic mental disorders in another class, the psychoactive substance use disorders, along with the diagnoses of substance dependence and substance abuse. (See Chapter 4, Disturbances Associated with the Use of Psychoactive Substances.) The advisory committees on organic and substance use disorders working on DSM-III-R debated whether it was a more unifying principle to cluster together disorders that were associated with substances rather than those that had specific organic etiologies. In terms of clinical differential diagnosis, it is useful to distinguish between the toxic direct effects of a drug on the central nervous system and the other problems and consequences of illicit drug use. Frequently, different treatment approaches are required, e.g., acute sedation and detoxification for a person with barbiturate withdrawal and drug rehabilitation for the underlying barbiturate dependence. Ultimately, this logic prevailed. The same three groups of organic mental disorders are classified in DSM-III-R as in DSM-III; the division into sections 1 and 2 was considered unnecessary and was dropped.

TERMINOLOGY

DSM-III referred to both organic brain syndromes and organic mental disorders. "Organic brain syndromes" described the hallmark clinical features, i.e., behaviors, emotions, and cognitions that resulted from organic factors, without reference to a specific etiology. They constituted the "building blocks" of the classification. "Organic mental disorders" referred to these basic syndromes when they were coupled with a specific etiology. The organic brain syndromes in DSM-III were delirium, dementia, amnestic syndrome, delusional syndrome, hallucinosis, affective syndrome, personality syndrome, intoxication, and withdrawal. In DSM-III, a primary degenerative dementia or an alcohol withdrawal delirium were considered organic mental disorders because the etiologic factors, brain tissue degeneration and alcohol cessation, respectively, are named.

DSM-III-R has simplified matters slightly by dropping the term *brain* and referring only to organic mental syndromes and disorders. The difference between *syndrome* and *disorder* remains: whether or not a specific etiology is mentioned. A new organic mental syndrome, organic anxiety syndrome, has been added to the group in DSM-III-R. Several of the other organic mental syndromes have been redefined, in particular, organic personality syndrome. Each will be discussed in separate sections below.

Conceptual Revisions

The DSM-III descriptions of organic mental disorders (OMDs) appeared strange to many seasoned psychiatrists because they did not include a number of time-honored distinctions among OMDs, and they reflected revised concepts underlying several familiar diagnostic terms. DSM-III also introduced a number of new diagnostic entities that formerly were not thought of as disturbances with organic etiologies.

Psychotic vs. Nonpsychotic OMDs

DSM-III did not use a psychotic/nonpsychotic distinction between organic mental disorders as a basis for classification. This change was motivated by the fact that the term *psychotic* had come to be used loosely with reference to organic mental disorders. In DSM-II (2), for example, it could refer to a degree of *severity* that caused a person to be unable to meet the demands of everyday living. A severe, incapacitating dementia could be classified as psychotic. DSM-III included a very clear-cut definition of the term *psychotic* in its glossary of technical terms (3, pp. 367-368) that required defects in the person's ability to test reality as evidenced by the presence of delusions or hallucinations. Clearly, not all severe organic mental disorders are accompanied by delusions or hallucinations. For those that are, DSM-III had as potential diagnoses specific organic brain syndromes—organic delusional syndrome or organic hallucinosis—or subclasses of the dementias arising in the senium and presenium.

Acute vs. Chronic OMDs

A second broad change in DSM-III was that the organic mental disorders were no longer referred to as acute or chronic brain syndromes. This change was necessitated by recognition of the potentially deleterious consequences that might result from equating "acute" with "reversible" and "chronic" with "irreversible" OMDs, as was the case in DSM-II. Confounding notions of onset and clinical course with outcome could lead clinicians to assume that any OMD with an abrupt onset could be reversed and, more dangerously, that any slowly or insidiously developing OMD was, by definition, irreversible. There are numerous clinical examples of situations in which neither is the case. Dementias can occur suddenly following major brain trauma and be totally irreversible; others can develop with the slow progression of an endocrinopathy, such as hypothyroidism, and have a dramatic remission following adequate treatment of the underlying disorder.

In DSM-III and DSM-III-R, any of the OMDs can be considered acute or chronic on the basis of their onset and/or duration, but the question of reversibility or treatability depends entirely on the nature of the underlying etiologic process.

Global vs. Partial Symptoms

The third major conceptual revision in the DSM-III approach to the organic mental disorders that was important in differential diagnosis was recognition of organic mental syndromes with partial or selective areas of impairment or symptomatology. According to DSM-III, it was no longer necessary that there be a global reduction in cognitive capacities or performance in order for the diagnosis of an organic mental disorder to be made. Lipowski (4-6) has cogently argued that many systemic and cerebral diseases lead directly to changes in central nervous system (CNS) functioning that are limited predominantly to one sphere of cognition or perception, or to regulation of mood or general personality functioning, and that have few, or even none, of the signs traditionally associated with "organicity."

This revision leads to a much wider cast net of syndromes to be considered in the differential diagnosis of mental symptoms that may prove to have an organic etiology. These will be discussed in the following sections on global organic mental syndromes and partial organic mental syndromes. The unifying feature of all the OMDs in the DSM-III and DSM-III-R systems remains the presence of an organic factor etiologically responsible for the syndrome.

Overview of Differential Diagnosis

Figure 3.1 reproduces the DSM-III-R (7) decision tree for the differential diagnosis of organic mental disorders. The clinician "enters" the tree once there is "evidence . . . of a specific organic factor that is judged to be etiologically related to the disturbance . . . ." (9, p. 382). This tree is of limited value to the diagnostician because the logic of patient assessment and differential diagnosis proceeds from eliciting a symptom or observing a sign, to establishing the presence of a syndrome, to making a specific diagnosis (see also Chapter 1): the step of considering possible organic etiologies usually comes *after* syndrome identification, unless the patient presents with a known physical illness that causes mental symptoms. The most common symptoms that lead a clinician to consideration of organic etiologies are disturbances or impairments of attention, memory, or cognition; these symptoms are found lower in the decision tree, after the organic etiology has been established, but in fact can have either organic or nonorganic (functional) etiologies.

In the sections that follow, I shall consider problems in the differential diagnosis of the individual organic mental syndromes as *syndromes*, i.e., as if the organic etiology is not yet established. This approach seems to me to be a closer approximation of actual clinical practice.

Global Organic Mental Syndromes

The two organic mental syndromes that are characterized by global impairment of cognitive functioning traditionally associated with "organicity" are delirium and dementia. Delirium corresponds roughly to the concept of an acute brain syndrome, and dementia, to a chronic brain syndrome, if the terms *acute* and *chronic* refer to the clinical course and, particularly, to the onset of the disorders. Although these two syndromes share the feature that multiple higher cortical functions are impaired, there are important features that distinguish them. Differential diagnosis can have life-saving consequences to patients with these disturbances.

Delirium

The hallmark clinical feature of delirium in DSM-III was clouding of consciousness, "with reduced capacity to shift, focus, and sustain

Figure 3.1 DSM-III-R Decison Tree for the Differential Diagnosis of Organic Mental Disorders

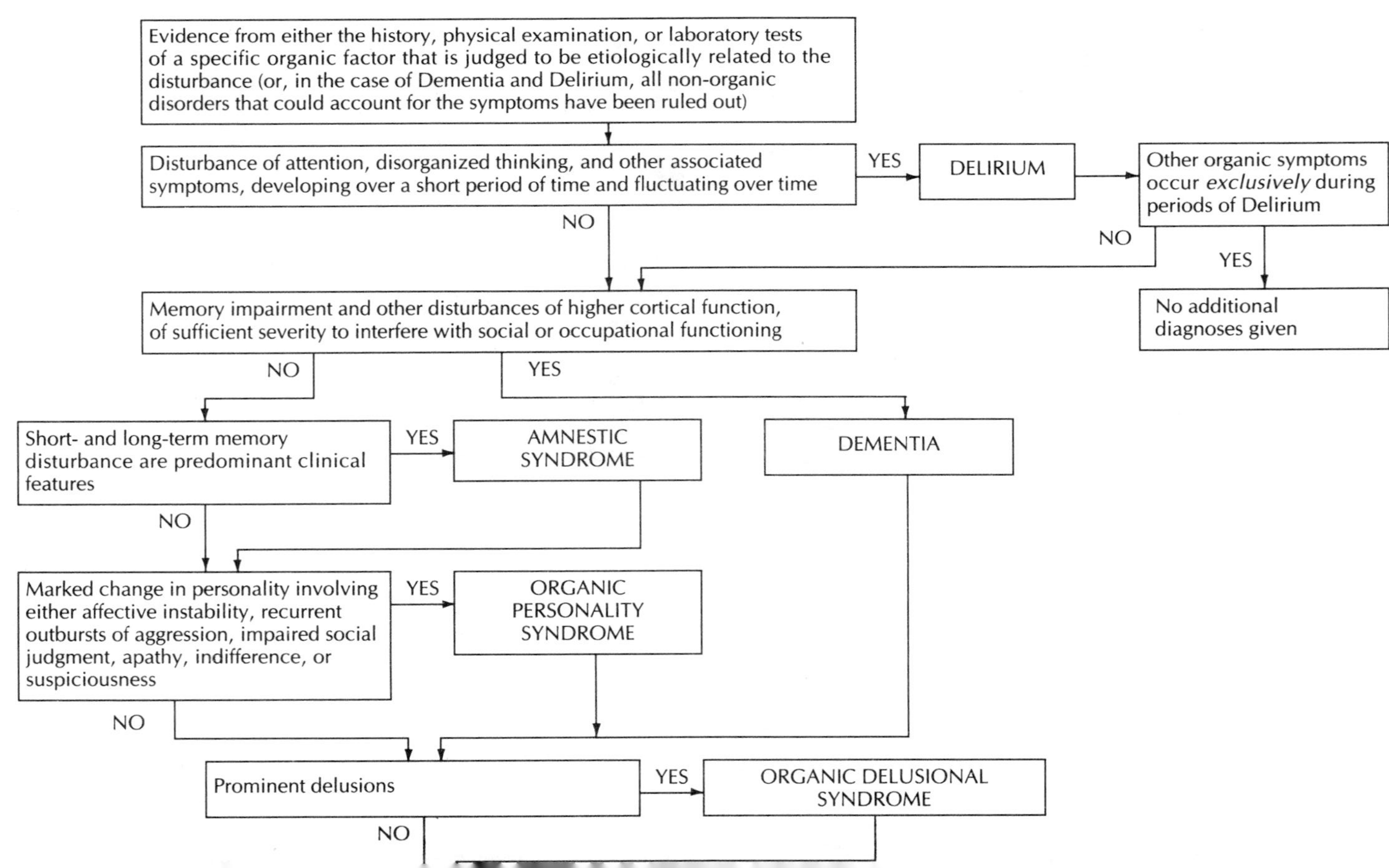

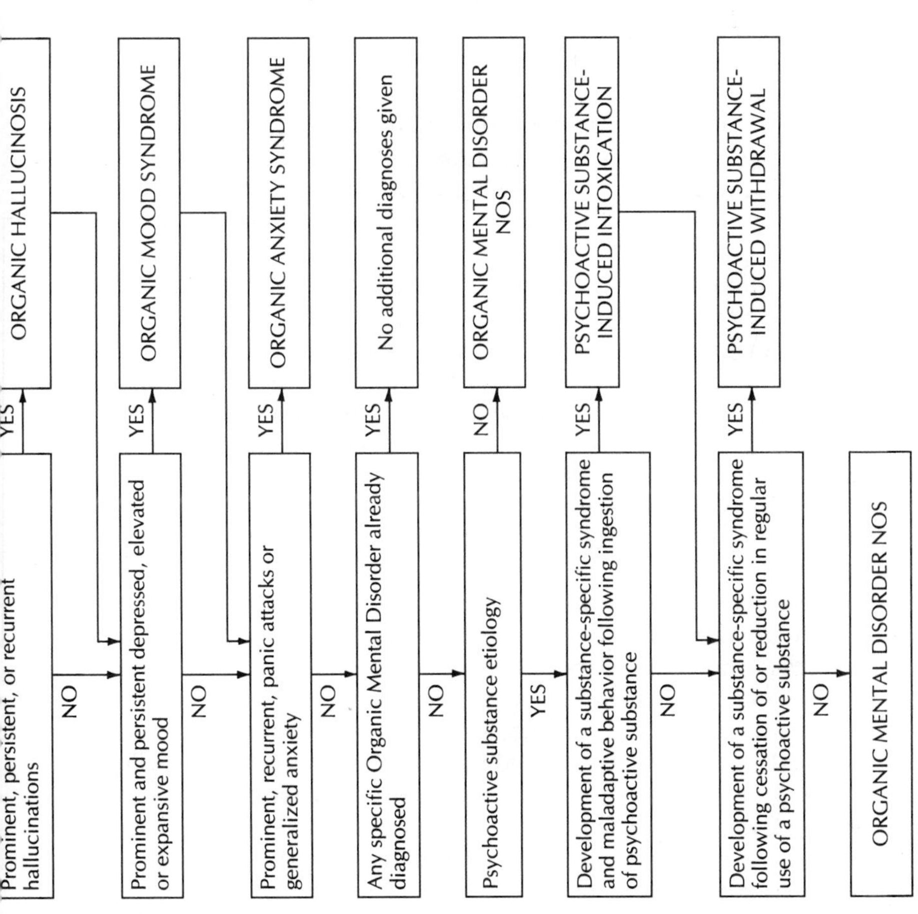

Prominent, persistent, or recurrent hallucinations
YES
ORGANIC HALLUCINOSIS
NO
Prominent and persistent depressed, elevated or expansive mood
YES
ORGANIC MOOD SYNDROME
NO
Prominent, recurrent, panic attacks or generalized anxiety
YES
ORGANIC ANXIETY SYNDROME
NO
Any specific Organic Mental Disorder already diagnosed
YES
No additional diagnoses given
NO
Psychoactive substance etiology
NO
ORGANIC MENTAL DISORDER NOS
YES
Development of a substance-specific syndrome and maladaptive behavior following ingestion of psychoactive substance
YES
PSYCHOACTIVE SUBSTANCE-INDUCED INTOXICATION
NO
Development of a substance-specific syndrome following cessation of or reduction in regular use of a psychoactive substance
YES
PSYCHOACTIVE SUBSTANCE-INDUCED WITHDRAWAL
NO
ORGANIC MENTAL DISORDER NOS

attention to environmental stimuli" (3, p. 107). Some critics objected to the expression *clouding of consciousness* as too vague, but agreed that disturbances of attention and wakefulness were central to delirium (4,8). The patient with a delirium is not alert or is hyperalert, but under either circumstance cannot respond selectively to stimuli or direct attention appropriately.

DSM-III also required disorientation and memory impairment for the diagnosis. Typically, the delirious patient is disoriented to time, at least, and, in more severe cases, is disoriented to place and to person (others), but does not lose the sense of personal identity. In the memory sphere, immediate recall is impaired because of reduced capacity to attend to new stimuli; recent memory is more impaired than remote.

Other symptoms typical of delirium, including perceptual disturbances (misinterpretations, illusions, hallucinations), incoherent speech (due to disorganized thinking), disturbance of the sleep/wakefulness cycle (insomnia or daytime drowsiness), and increased or decreased psychomotor activity, were grouped together in DSM-III, and two of four of them were expected to be present for a diagnosis to be made. In fact, all are usually present.

The diagnostic criteria have been changed in DSM-III-R; the revised criteria are reproduced in Table 3.1. The essential features no longer refer to "clouding of consciousness," but continue to focus on the ability to maintain and shift attention. Disorientation and memory impairment have been added to the list of common features. Only two of *six* symptoms are now required, and disorganized thinking is essential for the diagnosis to be made.

Delirium vs. functional disorder. Eliminating disorientation and memory impairment as cardinal features (i.e., required by criteria in every case) may make the differential diagnosis between organic delirium and certain functional cognitive disorders more difficult. For instance, the differential diagnosis of an acute psychotic syndrome (see also Chapter 5) characterized by incoherent speech with hallucinations and psychomotor agitation, two of the symptoms under criterion C for delirium in DSM-III-R, rests on the determination of the capacity to attend to external stimuli and identification of the specific organic etiology, criterion E.

A further change in criterion E complicates the situation in DSM-III-R in that a statement parallel to that found in criterion E for dementia (see below) has been added (see Tables 3.1 and 3.2). The rationale for the second provision in criterion E for dementia is that primary degenerative dementia (Alzheimer's disease) is a diagnosis

Table 3.1 DSM-III-R Diagnostic Criteria for Delirium

A. Reduced ability to maintain attention to external stimuli (e.g., questions must be repeated because attention wanders) and to appropriately shift attention to new external stimuli (e.g., perseverates answer to a previous question).

B. Disorganized thinking, as indicated by rambling, irrelevant, or incoherent speech.

C. At least two of the following:

   (1) reduced level of consciousness, e.g., difficulty keeping awake during examination
   (2) perceptual disturbances: misinterpretations, illusions, or hallucinations
   (3) disturbances of sleep-wake cycle with insomnia or daytime sleepiness
   (4) increased or decreased psychomotor activity
   (5) disorientation to time, place, or person
   (6) memory impairment, e.g., inability to learn new material, such as the names of several unrelated objects after five minutes, or to remember past events, such as history of current episode of illness

D. Clinical features develop over a short period of time (usually hours to days) and tend to fluctuate over the course of a day.

E. Either (1) or (2):

   (1) evidence from the history, physical examination, or laboratory tests of a specific organic factor (or factors) judged to be etiologically related to the disturbance
   (2) in the absence of such evidence, an etiologic organic factor can be presumed if the disturbance cannot be accounted for by any nonorganic mental disorder, e.g., manic episode accounting for agitation and sleep disturbance

that can be confirmed by laboratory tests, in many cases performed only on postmortem pathology specimens (see below). Since DSM-III is a clinical diagnostic system, the very typical symptom constellation and progression of primary degenerative dementia warrant the diagnosis if all other causes of dementia have been ruled out. It is difficult to imagine the parallel for delirium. The revised criterion E in DSM-III-R introduces a circularity into the differential diagnostic process. With an acutely psychotic patient, if the clinician cannot find an organic etiology, he or she usually assumes functional illness. According to DSM-III-R, the clinician could be ruling out the functional illness (How?) in order to assume an organic cause.

Since distractibility can accompany acute psychotic and acute manic syndromes and make the distinction from delirium difficult, the clinician would be advised to rely on the requirement of evidence from the history, physical examination, or laboratory tests of a specific organic factor judged to be etiologically related to the disturbance, even using the DSM-III-R system, and to look for signs of the other typical symptoms of delirium such as disorientation, memory loss, and disturbances of sleep/wakefulness. The diagnosis of delirium can usually be confirmed by an electroencephalogram (EEG). The most typical EEG abnormality in delirium is generalized slowing of background activity (9). In cases in which the patient is agitated and hyperactive, there may also be superimposed fast activity. This is especially common in drug-related deliria (10). Because the clinical state in delirium typically fluctuates, more than one EEG (serial EEGs) may be indicated. A normal EEG may be observed when the patient is less impaired (11).

Once the clinical diagnosis of delirium has been confirmed by EEG, the clinician proceeds to identify the underlying etiology, if it is not already known. Usually the EEG and additional laboratory testing are all done simultaneously as part of a delirium work-up. The most common causes of delirium are (*1*) drug intoxication and withdrawal; (*2*) systemic disorders, including endocrine, nutritional, neoplastic, metabolic, vascular, and infectious disorders and poisonings; and (*3*) diffuse diseases of the central nervous system, including inflammation, tumor, trauma, and vascular disease. Intoxication and withdrawal, which are considered separate mental disorders in DSM-III-R, are discussed in Chapter 4. Table 3.5 lists some common diseases that may cause delirium (see below).

Another differential diagnostic problem made more difficult with the revised DSM-III-R system is the distinction between delirium and acute functional confusional states in the elderly (8). This problem will be discussed in the chapter on Differential Diagnosis in the Elderly (Chapter 11).

Delirium vs. Other OMDs. Delirium, as a global syndrome, takes diagnostic precedence over organic mental disorders with more limited features. Thus, a delusional syndrome would be an appropriate diagnosis for an organic disturbance limited to delusions; but if attentional problems and disorganized thinking develop or are also present and the delusions occur exclusively during periods of delirium, delirium *only* is the appropriate diagnosis. Patients with dementia may be especially vulnerable to developing delirium. The two diagnoses may be made conjointly since the manifestations of the dementia preceded the development of delirium (see also below).

Dementia

Dementia is becoming an increasingly prevalent mental disorder in the United States as the proportion of the elderly in the population rises. Roughly 5% of people over 65 and between 20% and 35% of those over 85 suffer from a dementia. Approximately 50% of these patients have primary degenerative dementia of the Alzheimer type (PDDAT) (Alzheimer's disease) (12), the remaining cases being caused by other illnesses such as infection, neoplasm, endocrinopathy, or cerebral infarction. An estimated 10%–20% of patients with dementia have treatable disorders (13).

In DSM-III the diagnosis of dementia depended upon determination of extensive loss of intellectual abilities of sufficient severity to interfere with social or occupational functioning, memory impairment, and some other signs of cognitive or other higher cortical function disturbance, such as impaired abstract thinking, impaired judgment, aphasia, apraxia, agnosia, constructional difficulty, or personality change, i.e., alteration or accentuation of premorbid traits. In a dementia uncomplicated by delirium, attentional capacity is not impaired. The criteria of DSM-III explicitly stated, however, that delirium (or intoxication) might be superimposed on a dementia. In fact, aging processes and other causes of brain damage or disease, particularly vascular and degenerative, facilitate cognitive disorganization in response to physical illness and thus appear to predispose people to delirium. This joint diagnosis is particularly significant in the elderly (see Chapter 11), since in as many as 25%–50% of cases, delirium precedes death in the hospitalized elderly (14).

The DSM-III-R criteria for dementia (see Table 3.2) are similar to those in DSM-III with a few exceptions. The cardinal feature is now impairment in short- and long-term memory. Evidence of memory impairment must now be objective, not limited to the patient's subjective complaint of reduced memory. Such impairment can be demonstrated, for example, by a Mini Mental State Examination (15,16) or more extensive neuropsychological tests, such as the Wechsler Memory Scale (17) or the Luria-Nebraska neuropsychological battery. Research has shown that subjective reports of memory problems and objective performance on memory tests are not closely related (18). "Loss" of memory or other functions no longer needs to be documented, since demonstrating loss would actually imply having assessments made at two points in time; demonstrating impairment is now sufficient.

Some other evidence of disturbance of higher cortical function and resulting functional impairment continues to be required. In order to clarify the relationship to delirium, criterion D now indicates

Table 3.2 DSM-III-R Diagnostic Criteria for Dementia

A. Demonstrable evidence of impairment in short- and long-term memory. Impairment in short-term memory (inability to learn new information) may be indicated by inability to remember three objects after five minutes. Long-term memory impairment (inability to remember information that was known in the past) may be indicated by inability to remember past personal information (e.g., what happened yesterday, birthplace, occupation) or facts of common knowledge (e.g., past Presidents, well-known dates).

B. At least one of the following:
   (1) impairment in abstract thinking, as indicated by inability to find similarities and differences between related words, difficulty in defining words and concepts, and other similar tasks
   (2) impaired judgment, as indicated by inability to make reasonable plans to deal with interpersonal, family, and job-related problems and issues
   (3) other disturbances of higher cortical function, such as aphasia (disorder of language), apraxia (inability to carry out motor activities despite intact comprehension and motor function), agnosia (failure to recognize or identify objects despite intact sensory function), and "constructional difficulty" (e.g., inability to copy three-dimensional figures, assemble blocks, or arrange sticks in specific designs)
   (4) personality change, i.e., alteration or accentuation of premorbid traits

C. The disturbance in A and B significantly interferes with work or usual social activities or relationships with others.

D. Not occurring exclusively during the course of delirium.

E. Either (1) or (2):
   (1) there is evidence from the history, physical examination, or laboratory tests of a specific organic factor (or factors) judged to be etiologically related to the disturbance.
   (2) in the absence of such evidence, an etiologic organic factor can be presumed if the disturbance cannot be accounted for by any nonorganic mental disorder, e.g., major depression accounting for cognitive impairment.

Criteria for severity of dementia:

Mild: Although work or social activities are significantly impaired, the capacity for independent living remains, with adequate personal hygiene and relatively intact judgment.

Moderate: Independent living is hazardous, and some degree of supervision is necessary.

Severe: Activities of daily living are so impaired that continual supervision is required, e.g., unable to maintain minimal personal hygiene; largely incoherent or mute.

that the disturbance should not be limited to periods of delirium, but allows for a diagnosis of delirium to be superimposed on an already existing dementia. Part (2) of criterion E, the diagnostic criterion requiring a specific organic factor, appears to contradict the hierarchical principle that is operative in the system and represented in the DSM-III decision tree. The principle is that organic mental disorders, those with demonstrable organic etiologies or, in the case of PDDAT, presumed organic etiologies take precedence over functional disorders. The only exception to the requirement for evidence of a specific organic etiology should be in the case of primary degenerative dementia, in which other organic causes of dementia have been ruled out. If excluding a functional disorder is equivalent to evidence of an organic mental disorder, then, again, the system becomes circular, i.e., the absence of an organic etiology indicates a functional mental disorder, and the absence of a functional disorder indicates one that is organic.

There are investigators, however, who advocate dropping the requirement of an organic factor completely in the diagnostic criteria for dementia (19). They argue that dementia, like depression or psychosis, is a syndrome that in some cases may have an organic etiology and in others may be caused by a functional disturbance. This approach to diagnosis would be closer to a true multiaxial system (see Chapter 2) in which the clinical syndrome would be recorded on one axis and all potential etiologic factors listed on a separate axis.

Dementia vs. pseudodementia. A most compelling clinical problem lending itself to this kind of multiaxial approach is the syndrome of pseudodementia. This syndrome of apparent dementia resulting from a functional mental illness is important because of its treatment implications. A relatively small but significant proportion of patients with the clinical picture of dementia responds to the appropriate treatment of an underlying mental illness. The majority of these patients, roughly 60%, have an underlying affective disorder (20). The remainder have another disorder, most commonly a conversion disorder or histrionic personality disorder. The former group is older, and a proportion includes people with both an affective disorder and another source of cognitive impairment, such as primary degenerative dementia.

The differential diagnosis of pseudodementia is difficult; currently there are no valid diagnostic criteria. In its section on differential diagnosis of dementia (3, p. 111), DSM-III stated that in affective disorder, cognitive impairment was "secondary to the disturbed affect," which was primary. In an organic dementia, abnormalities of mood were "less pervasive than in depression." DSM-III went on to state that the patient with pseudodementia, if sufficiently motivated, could be shown to have intact intellectual functioning. Furthermore, the onset of the cognitive dysfunction was more abrupt, the symptoms progressed more rapidly, and frequently there was a history of previous mental illness. DSM-III concluded that "In the absence of evidence of a specific organic etiologic factor, if the features suggesting major depressive episode are at least as prominent as those suggesting dementia, it is best to diagnose major depressive episode and to assume that the features suggesting dementia are secondary to the depression." A trial of antidepressant medication or electroconvulsive therapy might help to clarify the diagnosis.

In his review of pseudodementia, McAllister (20) adds a few more helpful suggestions for differential diagnosis but points out that the problem is even more complicated because of the proportion of patients who have both an affective disorder and another source of dementia. It does appear helpful to separate out those patients with a dementia due to mental illnesses other than depression. These patients present with a "caricature or burlesque of dementia," exaggerated complaints of the severity of impairment, and other manifestations of histrionic behavior, according to McAllister. Some of them may qualify for a diagnosis of factitious disorder with psychological symptoms. For the other group, whom he believes to have a true "depression-induced organic mental disorder," McAllister suggests new terminology, such as "depressive dementia" or "dementia syndrome of depression" (21). The usual indicators of CNS dysfunction, such as an abnormal EEG and computed tomography (CT) scan, may not be conclusive, especially if obtained only cross-sectionally; and the results of an amytal interview may be ambiguous. In elderly patients with a history of affective disorder, McAllister recommends a course of somatic treatment, for both therapeutic and differential diagnostic purposes. The differential diagnosis of dementia versus pseudodementia in the elderly is discussed further in Chapter 11.

On Becoming Unglued

The 78-year-old pastor of St. Ignatius Church confided to his assistant that he feared he was losing his mind. At the pulpit the previous Sunday, he had felt confused during the delivery of his sermon. He reported difficulty "comprehending" his own words, was unsure of the points he was trying to make and what exactly he had already said. "It was like my mind had lost its glue; there was just a jumble of disconnected thoughts," he lamented. Although the younger priest assured him that the sermon had been clear "for the most part," the pastor was despondent since his reputation for eloquent and inspiring sermons had always been his greatest source of pride.

Over the next three weeks, Father O. gave no sermons, deferring to Father S. He became increasingly preoccupied with his problem as he began to forget appointments, found that he could not concentrate during meetings with parishioners, and could not remember their names. His mood became more depressed. He felt no enthusiasm and had no goals, no sense of a positive future. He had difficulty falling asleep, woke up several times during the night, and ended the night awake watching the sun rise. His appetite remained normal. He felt anxious, at times, as he pondered about what was happening to him.

Father S. finally convinced Father O. to see his doctor, Dr. P., the internist in town. After eliciting the history and performing a physical examination, which revealed no changes from the previous one six months earlier (the patient had mild aortic stenosis and elevated blood pressure, but was otherwise in good health), Dr. P. ordered a battery of blood and other laboratory tests. That weekend, Dr. P. discussed Father O's case with his son-in-law, a psychiatrist, over dinner. The possibility of a major depressive episode causing progressive cognitive impairment was raised.

When the tests failed to reveal any significant organic etiology for the mental symptoms, Dr. P. called Father O. back to his office. A closer history revealed that although Father O. had no history of prior depression, a younger brother had suffered from both depression and a drinking problem. In fact, his brother had been hospitalized for failing health about six weeks before, and the news had reached Father O. shortly before his problems seemed to begin. Dr. P. prescribed a tricyclic antidepressant.

Six weeks later Father O. was back at the pulpit, feeling his usual self.

Differentiating near-threshold cases. As with many diagnoses, recognizing the prototypic case with a fullblown picture of dementia is not as problematic as recognizing mild cases with symptoms near the threshold of qualifying for a diagnosis. As Jorm and Henderson (22) have contended, dementia has a dimensional nature and ranges from mild to severe. This observation is supported by data from community surveys that show a continuous distribution of signs of cognitive impairment with no "hump" in scores at the lower end to suggest that dementia is a discrete entity (23).

In discussing possible improvements in DSM-III criteria for dementia to help identify mild cases (24), Jorm and Henderson (22) propose "anchor points" for rating the severity of the intellectual impairment *and* of the associated functional impairment, which may vary somewhat independently of the intellectual loss, depending both on the person's premorbid intelligence level and the demands imposed by the person's particular environment. In this schema, derived from work done by Hughes and colleagues (25), "mild" dementia would be characterized by moderate memory loss, more for new learning; "moderate" dementia would be more severe, with only well-learned new material retained, but rapidly lost; and in "severe" dementia, only memory fragments would remain. The effect of mild dementia on functioning would be almost imperceptible: the person would be able to complete his or her usual tasks independently, e.g., at work and in financial affairs, social groups, and complicated chores or hobbies. Moderate dementia would result in no effective functioning outside the home and in only simple chores, hobbies, or interests at home. In severe dementia there would be no functioning outside the person's own room. DSM-III-R now includes a similar grading of the severity of functional impairment resulting from dementia (see Table 3.2).

Jorm and Henderson regard the index of criterion C symptoms to be a measure of diagnostic certainty in assessing a person for dementia or as an aid in identifying dementias with particular etiologies, especially Huntington's disease, senile dementia of the Alzheimer type, and multi-infarct dementia (see also below). All of these guidelines seem worthy of consideration by the clinician evaluating a "near-threshold" or potential case of mild dementia. Other investigators have also offered or studied instruments and methods for rating the severity of dementia (16, 26-29). These can be employed by the clinician as ancillary tools in case of uncertainty.

PARTIAL OR SELECTIVE MENTAL SYNDROMES

Partial or selective organic mental syndromes are, in contradistinction to delirium and dementia, characterized by discrete and limited clinical manifestations, often not those traditionally associated with the concept of organicity. As mentioned previously, DSM-III listed organic amnestic syndrome, organic delusional syndrome, organic hallucinosis, organic affective syndrome, organic personality syndrome, and atypical or mixed organic brain syndrome. It also included in this group intoxication and withdrawal as additional organic brain syndromes caused by substances. DSM-III-R has added organic anxiety syndrome to the basic list.

The overriding difficulty of diagnosing these organic mental syndromes is the unfamiliarity of many clinicians with the idea that an organic mental syndrome can be present in the absence of cognitive or intellectual deficits. Once the clinician has accepted the fact that any mental syndrome may have an organic cause, making these diagnoses comes more easily. The following sections briefly outline the most common difficulties in diagnosing partial syndromes.

Organic Amnestic Syndrome

Organic amnestic syndrome is diagnosed when cognitive deficits due to organic causes are limited to short-term and/or long-term memory impairment. Attention and degree of alertness are normal, distinguishing the syndrome from delirium; and other cognitive functions are not affected, distinguishing it from dementia. Amnestic syndrome may result from head trauma, surgery, infarction, or infection affecting diencephalic and medial temporal structures of the brain, including the mammillary bodies, fornix, and hippocampus. Psychiatrists are quite familiar with the most common cause of amnestic syndrome—thiamine deficiency resulting from chronic alcoholism, otherwise known as Korsakoff's syndrome. The following case illustrates an instance of amnestic syndrome as a step in the progression of primary degenerative dementia.

Backstage with Rosie

A 70-year-old woman was brought by her niece to an evaluation and treatment center specializing in problems of the elderly. The niece, who lived in a rural community 75 miles away, had become concerned after a regular monthly visit to her aunt's apartment in the city. On the visit the niece noticed that her aunt's supply of food was unusually low. The few fruits and vegetables in the refrigerator were rotten, and unopened mail was piling up. When she asked her aunt about these, the elderly woman looked surprised and said, "Well, I guess I just didn't get around to my chores this week!"; otherwise, she seemed her usual self.

In fact, the niece had been becoming increasingly uneasy about her aunt's living situation over the past year. Her aunt, whose name was Rosie, had no children of her own and, since her husband's death five years before, had been living alone in an apartment she had inhabited for 35 years. The niece, as the closest living family member, had assumed the responsibility of a monthly drive into the city to visit and check on Rosie's well-being.

In earlier years, Rosie had had a weekly routine that she always followed, going Mondays to the grocery store, Tuesdays doing her laundry, and so forth. But for a year, Rosie's schedule seemed to have become disrupted. She seemed also to be constantly misplacing things in her apartment and repeating stories and details of her daily life that she had told her niece on previous visits.

When the psychiatrist interviewed Rosie, he found that she was a woman with a rich and exciting past. Both she and her husband had been in the theater; her husband had been a manager and she, a wardrobe designer. Her eyes lit up as she spoke of shows like *South Pacific* and *My Fair Lady* and shared some ancient gossip about romantic liaisons between actors and actresses who starred in movies and were on the covers of magazines when the psychiatrist was a child. "Even what's-his-name," she said. "You know, the one who's the President. You should have seen him flirting with all the young girls. Of course, that was before he got married."

But no matter how hard she tried, Rosie could not remember the President's name. In addition, many other common current facts and events eluded Rosie's recall. She would look up at the ceiling, then back at the psychiatrist, shaking her head, "I knew that, you know; I just can't seem to think of it right now." As for her reason for coming to the hospital, she said, "Well, I was due for a checkup. A friend of the family is an internist, and he insisted that I come over."

Rosie was unable to remember any of three objects a few minutes after she had repeated them; she struggled, but performed the serial 7's task with only two mistakes. She was able to repeat six numbers, find similarities between objects, and, except for some difficulty with word- and name-finding, showed no marked aphasia, apraxia, agnosia, or constructional difficulties. She admitted that her forgetfulness was "getting to be a problem" and agreed to let the psychiatrist and her niece arrange for some home assistance.

A work-up for dementia was negative, except for the beginning signs of cortical atrophy on a CT scan.

Organic Delusional Syndrome

Organic delusional syndrome is diagnosed when delusions are the major clinical feature. For this diagnosis to apply, the disturbance should not occur exclusively during the course of delirium. The occurrence of psychotic symptoms in a person with abnormalities of attention and arousal suggests delirium (see also Chapters 5 and 11). Certain dementias may present with persecutory or other delusions. If delusions of organic etiology also occur, according to DSM-III-R both organic delusional disorder and dementia may be diagnosed. This departs from DSM-III practice, according to which only patients with PPD and delusions could be unambiguously diagnosed. For the latter patients the diagnosis of PDD with delusions would be made by either system (290.20 or 290.12, depending on age at onset, see additional discussion of PDD below).

Organic delusional syndrome vs. functional psychotic disorder. Organic delusional syndrome is included in the differential diagnosis of psychotic features. DSM-III-R suggests that a first episode of a psychotic disorder after age 35 should suggest an organic etiology. The most difficult cases involve instances in which an organic etiology, such as a drug, may be regarded either as a precipitant of a psychotic disorder or as a cause in and of itself. This situation will be discussed in the section on psychoactive substance-induced organic mental disorders in Chapter 4.

As indicated in the chapter on the differential diagnosis of psychotic features (Chapter 5), many patients with schizophrenia have clinical/historical features or laboratory findings suggestive of organic factors. Examples are a history of childhood head trauma or adolescent drug abuse, cognitive deficits in neuropsychological testing, and abnormally large cerebral ventricles on CT scan. Were these nonspecific suggestions of organic mental syndromes used to exclude the diagnosis of schizophrenia, many chronically hospitalized mental patients would receive a diagnosis of an organic mental disorder. Although at least some causes of the schizophrenic syndrome are organic, as yet no specific etiologies that would account for a large proportion of cases of schizophrenia have been discovered. In individual cases, when a specific organic etiology can be identified, the diagnosis of organic delusional syndrome is more appropriate. Sometimes, even in the presence of a known neurologic illness, the appropriate diagnosis is difficult to assign.

Paranoid or Parinaud's?

The patient is a 24-year-old single, male student at a large university in the northwestern United States with a three-and-a-half-year history of mental problems who was referred to a medical center by his private psychiatrist for diagnostic evaluation.

The illness began during the patient's freshman year in college, when he had a brief episode of agitation and paranoid ideation requiring a two-day hospitalization. The following year he was again hospitalized, this time for two weeks, after an altercation with another male student in his dorm who frequently made fun of him. Several punches were thrown, the other student urinated on his door, and the patient poured lighter fluid on his own door and was about to set it on fire when the resident advisor interceded. The patient admits to hearing voices of girls he was interested in during this period, and occasionally he responded vocally to the voices.

After the second admission, the patient left school and returned home to take classes at a local community college. He was followed as an outpatient, and functioned adequately except for occasional brief episodes during which he would become paranoid and exhibit inappropriate laughter. Approximately a year and a half before the present admission, his functioning had begun to deteriorate; he stopped bathing and attending classes regularly and became more withdrawn and lethargic. He was hospitalized for 11 months in a private psychiatric hospital, where he was treated with phenothiazines and psychotherapy and showed some improvement. Soon after discharge, symptoms such as those of the preceding year recurred. He was admitted to a local community hospital, two months prior to his current medical center admission, with severe social isolation, poverty of thought, autism, paranoid ideation, and inability to take care of himself.

While hospitalized at the private hospital, the patient had begun to complain of bitemporal headaches and vertical diplopia. An EEG was normal, and a neurological examination revealed "no significant findings." A chart note indicated some abnormal motor movements, which were attributed to anxiety. Episodes of dizziness accompanied by buckling knees and falls to the ground without unconsciousness began at that time.

While at the community hospital, the patient's falls became more frequent, he developed urinary incontinence and vomiting, and had difficulty with near vision. An EEG revealed moderately diffuse cerebral slowing, and a CT scan showed considerable dilation of the lateral and third ventricles, with possible aqueductal stenosis. The patient was transferred for further diagnostic evaluation and treatment.

Admission mental status exam revealed a markedly withdrawn, apathetic, unkempt, and slow-moving man with poverty of speech, but no delusions, hallucinations, or loose associations. He had a moderately severe dementia. Physical examination was remarkable for restricted upgaze of the eyes, pupils that reacted to accommodation, but not to light, blurred nasal disk margins on fundoscopic exam, retraction and convergence nystagmus, increased muscle tone, spastic gait, and bilateral hyperreflexia, ankle clonus, and Babinski's reflex.

A repeat CT scan with contrast demonstrated 3+ hydrocephalus and a midline posterior third ventricle mass near the pineal. A ventriculo-peritoneal shunt was performed, and the patient's mental status and physical symptoms improved dramatically.

The differential diagnostic process is challenged by a case such as this one. Initially, the enlarged cerebral ventricles on CT scan were interpreted as consistent with a diagnosis of chronic schizophrenia, and attempts were made to explain all other physical signs and symptoms on this basis of psychological processes (urinary incontinence secondary to regression, for example). In fact, the grossly enlarged ventricles found in this case were much larger than the one-to-two standard deviations above the normal mean for a ventricular-brain ratio that have been reported for a proportion of patients with schizophrenia (30,31)—an enlargement just visible to the eye. Bilateral long-tract signs confirmed the medical center psychiatrist's view that the patient had hydrocephalus, which explained the vomiting, falls, and incontinence. The classic eye signs of restricted, voluntary upward gaze of the eyes (Parinaud's syndrome), pupils not reactive to light but to accommodation, convergence spasm, and retractory nystagmus alerted the neurologist to the diagnosis of a pineal region tumor.

The mental disorder at the time of admission to the medical center was a dementia, secondary to hydrocephalus. But could the original presentation as schizophrenia be attributed to early growth of the tumor? Although there are a few cases of schizophrenialike syndromes associated with hydrocephalus due to long-standing, congenital stenosis of the aqueduct of Sylvius (32), pineal tumors rarely, if ever, present initially with psychotic symptoms.

In this case we should postulate two processes: a schizophrenic or schizophreniform disorder, possibly with a relatively good prognosis, with a subsequent change toward a much more malignant course accounted for by the growing tumor and resulting hydrocephalus. This formulation (rather than an either/or functional vs. organic disorder distinction), which I prefer, suggests that an abrupt or unexpected change in the clinical course of a patient's mental disorder should alert clinicians to the possibility of a superimposed physical disorder.

Organic Hallucinosis

In organic hallucinosis, hallucinations predominate. The most common causes are drugs and alcohol; blindness, deafness, and seizure foci in the occipital and temporal lobes can also cause hallucinosis. The same exclusion applies for ruling out delirium as with organic delusional syndrome. In order to distinguish the two organic psychotic syndromes, DSM-III told the clinician to base the diagnosis on the predominant symptoms. Most clinicians would find that organic psychoses frequently included both delusions and hallucinations.

My reading of the intent of DSM-III in such cases was to consider the delusional syndrome the more pervasive diagnosis, i.e., the diagnosis to apply in most cases with delusions and hallucinations. Hallucinosis was more for those special cases in which the psychopathology was typically limited to hallucinations, such as in alcohol hallucinosis. In DSM-III-R a forced choice is not necessary: both diagnoses may be given.

Organic Mood Syndrome

Recognition of organic mood syndromes is a step forward in differential diagnosis. Organic mood syndromes are frequently caused by drugs, such as antihypertensives, but also by endocrine disturbances, such as hyper- or hypothyroidism, or carcinoma of the pancreas. It is important to recognize that both depressive and manic syndromes may be due to organic causes. The concept of secondary mania has received increased attention in recent years (33). DSM-III-R instructs the clinician to specify either manic, depressed, or mixed when making the diagnosis of an organic mood disorder. The following case is one of an organic mood syndrome caused by a stroke.

The Loquacious Librarian

A 43-year-old white, divorced female was referred for psychiatric consultation during an admission to the neurology service of a university hospital. Six weeks earlier she had sustained an intracerebral hemorrhage involving the right temporal area. Treated initially for influenza, the patient had next sought an ophthalmologic evaluation, complaining of decreased vision. The ophthalmologist noted a left homonymous hemianopsia. A subsequent CT scan showed hemorrhage without evidence of associated tumor or A-V malformation. The patient's behavioral difficulties following the hemorrhage prompted an outreach physician to advise referral to the university for full neurologic and psychiatric evaluation.

In the university hospital, the patient proved a challenge for the nursing staff, who found it difficult to "corral" her. She was hyperactive, seldom remained in her room, and wandered throughout the hospital. On one occasion she barged into the hospital chapel and quizzed the only occupant regarding the content of his prayers. She made multiple demands of the nurses, who grew increasingly irate with her. She was up all night and expected middle-of-the-night therapy sessions. When limits were set, she reacted with anger. "Fucking nurse" (or aide or doctor), she was frequently heard to mutter as she paced the halls. During her psychometric testing, she made sexual advances to the psychologist.

In meetings with her doctor, she spoke rapidly and shifted from topic to topic. First, she would tell the psychiatrist about her vegetable garden, then about a "crush" she had on a boy in high school, and then about her views on "Reaganomics." The psychiatrist could barely get a word in. Though complaining of "something wrong in my head," she denied feeling a change in mood or speech. She noted some difficulty with concentration and memory.

A librarian, the patient was described by her mother as "quiet and serious" before the hemorrhage and markedly "nervous" after it. The patient observed that she had always been a hard worker, "the best they've ever had," and expressed great pride in her ability to support her parents and her son on $153 a week.

Mania following stroke is somewhat unusual (34). Most of the work on organic mood disorder secondary to stroke has focused on depression (35, 36). The problem of a physical affective disorder, i.e., the differential diagnosis of functional affective disorder precipitated by physical illness vs. organic mood disorder caused by physical illness, is currently a subject of considerable nosologic interest. In Chapter 11, Differential Diagnosis in the Elderly, a summary of current guidelines for this differential diagnosis is presented. DSM-III-R is limited in this regard, in that its only recommendation is that the presence of a previous history of mood disorder in the person or a positive family history favors mood disorder over organic mood syndrome. To illustrate, in a recently reported series of patients with Cushing's disease (37), 85% of those who were found to have a lifetime major depressive syndrome had the initial onset of depression either during the year in which medical signs and symptoms of Cushing's disease developed or at sometime after. The patients with Cushing's disease also had a significantly lower rate of familial major affective disorder than that found among a control group of outpatients with major depression. These findings would be consistent with the notion that the depression seen in Cushing's disease is most often an organic mood syndrome.

Organic Anxiety Syndrome

Organic anxiety syndrome is a new diagnosis in DSM-III-R. Mackenzie and Popkin (38) correctly observed that DSM-III included no organic equivalent of anxiety disorders, even though there are many physical illnesses in which anxiety is the principal behavioral symptom. The most common causes of organic anxiety syndromes are substance ingestion (stimulants) and withdrawal (sedatives) and endocrine disorders such a pheochromocytoma, hyperthyroidism, hypoglycemia, and hypercortisolism. Brain tumors in the vicinity of the third ventricle and seizure foci near the diencephalon (temporal lobe) are other known etiologies.

Organic anxiety syndrome vs. functional anxiety disorder. The differential diagnosis of organic anxiety syndromes caused by the direct effects of physical illness on the CNS from physical disorders that cause anxiety mediated through their psychological meaning for the person is comparable with the parallel differential for mood syndromes. Mackenzie and Popkin (38) point out that persuasive evidence that the anxiety is organically caused would be the production of symptoms in a patient who was exposed to an agent such as excessive thyroxine in the course of treatment, or the observation that a CNS dysfunction, such as the spike-wave EEG phenomena of temporal lobe epilepsy, and the anxiety symptoms covaried over time. If the patient's age at onset is greater than 35, or if the family history is negative for anxiety disorder, suspicion of an organic anxi-

Table 3.3 DSM-III-R Diagnostic Criteria for Organic Anxiety Syndrome

A. Prominent, recurrent, panic attacks (criteria A, C, and D of panic disorder) or generalized anxiety (criterion D of generalized anxiety disorder).

B. There is evidence from the history, physical examination, or laboratory tests of a specific organic factor (or factors) judged to be etiologically related to the disturbance.

C. Not occurring exclusively during the course of delirium.

ety syndrome should be raised when symptoms appear to be unrelated in onset to the patient's having received any threatening information or to any discernible significant psychological conflict. A history of substance use or a family history of an illness known to cause organic anxiety, such as hyperthyroidism, would also increase the possibility of organic anxiety syndrome.

The occurrence of organic anxiety syndrome, rather than an organic mood syndrome, in a person who has a disease such as Cushing's disease, which may cause either, may indicate a genetic or developmental vulnerability to anxiety symptoms. There is evidence that people with anxiety disorders (39) or, more specifically, panic disorder (40) are susceptible to developing anxiety following intravenous infusion with sodium lactate.

Table 3.3 displays the DSM-III-R criteria for organic anxiety syndrome.

Organic Personality Syndrome

Organic personality syndrome is the diagnosis that applies when a person has a marked personality disturbance stemming from organic factors. The causes of organic personality syndrome usually involve structural damage to the brain; neoplasms, head trauma, and vascular disease head the list. Temporal lobe epilepsy, multiple sclerosis, and Huntington's disease also produce the syndrome.

The criteria for organic personality syndrome have been revised somewhat in DSM-III-R. The new criteria are presented in Table 3.4. A subtle change has been introduced into the basic description of the hallmark feature in criterion A; the characteristic pattern of behavior may either be *lifelong* or represent a *change* (as in DSM-III) or an accentuation. This new description recognizes that a person may

Table 3.4 DSM-III-R Diagnostic Criteria for Organic Personality Syndrome

A. A persistent personality disturbance, either lifelong or representing a change or accentuation of a previously characteristic trait, involving at least one of the following:
   (1) affective instability, e.g., marked shifts from normal mood to depression, irritability, or anxiety
   (2) recurrent outbursts of aggression or rage that are grossly out of proportion to any precipitating psychosocial stressors
   (3) markedly impaired social judgment, e.g., sexual indiscretions
   (4) marked apathy and indifference
   (5) suspiciousness or paranoid ideation

B. There is evidence from the history, physical examination, or laboratory tests of a specific organic factor (or factors) judged to be etiologically related to the disturbance.

C. This diagnosis is not given to a child or adolescent if the clinical picture is limited to the features that characterize attention-deficit hyperactivity disorder.

D. Not occuring exclusively during the course of delirium, and does not meet the criteria for dementia.

Specify explosive type if outbursts of aggression or rage are the predominant feature.

either be born with or may incur organic insults at a very early age that determine certain characteristics of his or her behavior, e.g., a tendency toward aggressive behavior, for the rest of his or her life. This person's disorder is best characterized as an organic personality syndrome when the specific organic factors are known.

The signs and symptoms of organic personality syndrome according to DSM-III-R are: (*1*) affective instability, (*2*) recurrent outbursts of aggression or rage, (*3*) markedly impaired social judgment, (*4*) apathy and indifference, (*5*) suspiciousness or paranoid ideation. DSM-III included an item for emotional lability; this has been split in DSM-III-R into an affective component and an aggressiveness component. At one point a diagnosis of organic aggressive syndrome was suggested for DSM-III-R. The combined changes of allowing that the personality pattern be lifelong and that the major manifestation of the disturbed behavior be aggressiveness made DSM-III-R organic personality syndrome an adequate and sufficient diagnosis for these cases. DSM-III-R instructs clinicians to specify when the organic personality syndrome is the "explosive" type. In light of this change in the items describing the behaviors associated with organic personality syndrome, the DSM-III item referring to impaired impulse control now refers only to the more narrow feature of impaired social judgment.

At a preliminary phase of its development, the DSM-III-R criteria for organic personality included a reference to evidence of "an abnormality in brain function or structure," instead of "organic factors," as determined by *neuropsychological* and laboratory tests, and cited such examples of abnormalities as a history of head trauma, neurological "soft signs," or an abnormal EEG. This wording was an attempt to be more specific about the "organic factors" needed for the diagnosis of an OMD. As such, it may be an improvement over comparable criteria for the other organic mental syndromes. On the other hand, organic personality syndrome almost always results from an illness intrinsic to the brain, whereas the other OMSs may more commonly occur as a result of the effects of a systemic illness on the CNS. Although certainly an "abnormality in brain functioning" exists in these cases, the criterion worded in this way could lead to excessively narrow interpretations of the illnesses that may be involved. Ideally, the organic etiology criterion should be uniform across the organic mental syndromes so that reference to evidence of "the effects of systemic illnesses on the CNS" or "abnormality in brain functioning or structure" could have been included.

The nature of the behavioral problems in a particular patient with organic personality disorder will depend on the localization of the pathological process in the brain (e.g., frontal vs. temporal lobes), the nature of the disturbance itself (e.g., discrete and focal vs. more diffuse), and the person's premorbid personality characteristics. Disturbances involving principally the frontal lobes are characterized either by (*1*) emotional lability with aggressiveness, temper outbursts, and poor social judgment, or by (*2*) apathy and indifference. It is a common clinical observation that disease processes in the brain frequently accentuate premorbid personality traits, so that, for example, a person who has been generally "closed," guarded, and unfriendly in life becomes frankly suspicious or paranoid.

Organic personality syndrome vs. other mental disorders. Important disorders in the differential diagnosis of organic personality syndrome are dementia, attention-deficit hyperactivity disorder, intermittent explosive disorder, and schizophrenia and the related psychotic disorders. Deterioration in aspects of a person's personality functioning frequently accompanies, or often precedes, the intellectual decline of dementing processes. Organic personality disorder may therefore be a diagnosis given at the early stages of a progressively dementing illness. When memory impairment is also significant, the diagnosis of dementia takes precedence.

Attention-deficit hyperactivity disorder, with its inattention, impulsivity, and hyperactivity, may conceptually resemble organic personality syndrome (especially in DSM-III-R) when associated with diagnosable neurological illness or with neurological soft signs indicative of perinatal physical difficulties. In DSM-III and DSM-III-R, the diagnosis of attention-deficit hyperactivity disorder would be sufficient so long as the clinical features were limited to those of that disorder.

Intermittent explosive disorder is characterized by outbursts of rage. By DSM-III-R guidelines, this diagnosis is made only in the absence of specific organic factors etiologically related to the aggression (see also Chapter 10, Antisocial, Aggressive, or Violent Behavior). For differentiating organic personality syndrome from the psychotic disorders, it is once again the absence of a specific organic factor that helps to distinguish between the prodromal and residual phases of schizophrenia and this disorder. Of course, when psychotic symptoms are prominent, a diagnosis of a psychotic disorder, organic or functional, is necessary.

The following case vignette illustrates a differential diagnostic problem.

A Bitter Pill To Swallow

A 43-year-old woman was admitted to a medical-psychiatric unit of a university hospital in the Midwest. Her family reported a three-week history of increasing irritability and agitation that culminated in a fit of rage in which she screamed at the top of her lungs and threw kitchen utensils at her teenage daughter, who had come home a half-hour later than expected from a high school dance.

The woman had been diagnosed as having multiple sclerosis (MS) three years before. Symptoms of the illness had actually begun several years before that. The woman experienced periodic weakness in her legs, which occasionally made her knees buckle; decreased hearing first in one, then the other, ear; and, finally, double vision, which caused her to consult a neurologist who made the diagnosis.

At about the same time as the physical symptoms began, the patient also became depressed because of problems she was having with her husband. Over the ensuing six years she had several severe episodes of depression in which she cried all day, couldn't get out of bed, ate very little, had no interests, and could barely function in her roles of housewife and mother. During these periods she felt as if "God must be punishing me" by having given her MS. At other times she was able to use considerable denial and carry on as if nothing were wrong.

In the past year the symptoms of the MS had required increasing doses of steroids. About six weeks before the current hospitalization, the dose of prednisone was raised to 90 mg/day. The patient started to call her friends at all hours of the day and night, signed up for adult education courses for every night of the week, and bought several expensive dresses, "just in case." She also felt generally irritable with surges of anger. No one seemed to be able to do anything right. "I felt like I hated my husband and my children, I actually felt like I could kill them." The patient's affect rapidly changed as she described the incidents; at one moment she was in tears, and the next she was chattering matter-of-factly, as if describing a movie or a book she had read.

The treating psychiatrist elicited a long history of emotional instability with long-standing problems with anger. The patient had formed very strong attachments with others throughout her life, but these relationships were very troubled. She had been in and out of therapy since a teenager. Marital problems had existed for 15 years, but the couple coped because the children were young. Now, however, her husband was threatening to leave her. Although she had had periods of several days of depression, until five years ago she had never had an episode for as long as two weeks when she felt depressed every day. Now she felt that without antidepressants, she would constantly be depressed. Lithium carbonate had also been previously prescribed, after she had asked her psychiatrist, "Isn't there a pill for anger?"

The coincident onset of symptoms of serious depression and early signs of MS, in the absence of previous major depressive episodes, makes the diagnosis of organic mood syndrome likely in this case. The mood disorder required specific pharmacologic intervention, over and above the treatment for the underlying illness. MS can cause symptoms of the manic syndrome as well. In this patient's case, however, it seems that the steroids may have been responsible for her mood disorder—a psychoactive substance-induced organic mood syndrome (see Chapter 4). Some clinicians might consider an additional diagnosis of organic personality syndrome warranted in this case: premorbid personality traits of emotional instability, interpersonal difficulties, and poor control of anger appear to have been exaggerated by the central effects of the MS.

Organic Mental Syndrome NOS

In keeping with the shift away from the use of the term *atypical* to refer to residual diagnostic categories in DSM-III-R, organic mental syndromes that do not meet the *descriptive* criteria for any of the specified types are called OMS not otherwise specified (NOS). All such syndromes do, of course, meet the organic etiology criterion for an OMS, the defining characteristic of this group of disorders. Also, in the revision of DSM-III, examples of the residual classes are more numerous. In the case of OMS NOS, DSM-III-R indicates that the diagnosis may apply to the neurasthenic picture associated with early Addison's disease or unusual pre- or postictal behavioral or consciousness disturbances associated with epilepsy.

Dementias Arising in the Senium and Presenium

The dementias that arise in the senium (after 65) and presenium (before 65) were divided in DSM-III into primary degenerative dementia (PDD) and multi-infarct dementia (MID). In DSM-III-R, categories of senile and presenile dementias not otherwise specified (NOS) have been added to the classification.

Differentiating Major Types

Primary degenerative dementia (PDD) corresponds to the clinical entity of Alzheimer's disease (AD) or to senile dementia of the Alzheimer's type (SDAT) if its age at onset is after 65 (see section on *Subtypes by age at onset* below). The specific diagnosis is now called primary degenerative dementia of the Alzheimer's type (PDDAT) in DSM-III-R. PDDAT is a diagnosis by exclusion; it is the presumed diagnosis in cases for which the criteria for dementia are met and all other causes of dementia have been ruled out. The term *primary* in the PDDAT classification means not secondary to any other physical illness. Therefore, distinguishing PDDAT from other causes of dementia, especially multi-infarct dementia, is critical. Research evidence and clinical experience indicate that this is not always a straightforward task.

Alzheimer's disease is a clinicopathological diagnosis that depends on postmortem findings of typical degenerative changes in the brains of people who have died from it. There are neurofibrillary tangles, senile plaques, and granulovacuolar bodies. Although these changes are neither perfectly sensitive to or specific for Alzheimer's disease (41), the diagnosis of primary degenerative dementia is an attempt to define a clinical diagnosis that can be used by psychiatrists to describe the organic mental disorders of living patients whose brains would show these classic degenerative processes on autopsy.

PDDAT vs. other causes of dementia. The criteria for primary degenerative dementia of the Alzheimer's type in the DSM-III systems are: (*1*) the presence of a dementia (see page 88 above), (*2*) an insidious onset with a generally progressive, deteriorating course, and (*3*) the exclusion of all other specific causes of dementia by history, physical examination, and laboratory tests. Alzheimer's disease is coded (331.00) on Axis III.

In its section on the differential diagnosis of PDD, DSM-III-R mentions the following causes of dementia that should be ruled out: subdural hematoma, normal-pressure hydrocephalus, cerebral neoplasm, Parkinson's disease, vitamin B_{12} deficiency, hypothyroidism, and psychoactive substance intoxication. Tuberculosis or encephalitis might be added to the list, so that the following accepted general categories of dementia-causing physical illnesses would be represented: (*1*) toxic, (*2*) nutritional, (*3*) infectious, (*4*) endocrine, (*5*) neoplastic, (*6*) vascular, and (*7*) other cerebral conditions.

All patients being evaluated for dementia should have a complete physical, including neurological, examination. DSM-III-R does not give suggestions for the laboratory work-up that might be sufficient for ruling out alternate causes of dementia, but other authors (42,43) have suggested that serum enzymes and electrolytes, CBC, urinalysis, chest X-ray, EKG, serological test for syphilis (VDRL) and fluorescent treponemal antibody (FTA) test, thyroid function test, vitamin B_{12} and folate levels, Pap smear, stool examination for occult blood, EEG, and CT scans of the brain will screen for most of the reversible causes of dementia. This screening battery would be followed by more specific studies such as a lumbar puncture, heavy metal screening of the urine, or other tests (sigmoidoscopy, barium enema, bone scan, arteriography) to pin down a specific etiology if none has been detected but one is still suspected on clinical grounds. Not only is this process useful for establishing a correct diagnosis, but in this particular case the correct diagnosis, i.e., a secondary dementia, has vital treatment significance.

There is some evidence (44) that use of Roth's modified criteria (45), which correspond well to DSM-III criteria, to diagnose primary degenerative dementia in the living enables clinicians to identify cases with classic degenerative findings of Alzheimer's on autopsy, but no major vascular lesions, with approximately 80% accuracy; 20% of cases were found to be of another type of degenerative encephalopathy. In this study, clinical means of ruling out vascular illnesses and stroke were used.

PDDAT vs. MID. The differential diagnosis between PDDAT and multi-infarct dementia (MID), however, presents a number of problems. The criteria for MID include: (*1*) the presence of a dementia; (2) a stepwise deteriorating course (i.e., not uniformly progressive), with patchy distribution of deficits early in the clinical course; (3) focal neurological signs and symptoms, such as hyperactive deep tendon reflexes, positive Babinski signs, weakness of an extremity, or difficulty walking; and (4) evidence from the history, physical examination, or laboratory tests of significant cerebrovascular disease that is judged to be etiologically related to the disturbance.

In its discussions of the diagnosis of PDDAT vs. MID, DSM-III emphasized the differences in course (progressively uniform deterioration vs. patchy, stepwise deterioration), in neurological signs and symptoms (absent vs. present), and in evidence of cerebrovascular disease (absent vs. present). In their very complete reviews of the clinical differentiation of primary degenerative and multi-infarct dementia, Liston and LaRue (46,47) raise doubt that current criteria are adequate for differentiating clearly between the two disorders.

All three of the above proposed differences between PDD and MID have a long history in the psychiatric and neurological literature. DSM-III criteria for MID rely heavily on the work of Slater and Roth (48) and Hachinski and colleagues (49), who introduced the term *multi-infarct dementia* and associated its differentiation from PDD with a score on a scale, the Ischemic Score (IS). The IS assigns points for each of the following 13 clinical features thought to be associated with cerebrovascular dementia: abrupt onset (2 points), stepwise deterioration (1 point), fluctuating course (2), nocturnal confusion (1), relative preservation of personality (1), depression (1), somatic complaints (1), emotional incontinence (1), history of hypertension (1), history of strokes (2), evidence of associated atherosclerosis (1), focal neurological symptoms (2), and focal neurological signs (2). A score of 7 or higher is traditionally thought to indicate MID, whereas a score of 4 or less is associated with PDD.

Numerous studies have failed to corroborate fully the original association between IS scores and clinical diagnosis of PDD or MID. Not all of the features of the IS have been found to discriminate the two types of dementia; even the most distinctive features, such as abrupt onset, history of stroke, and focal symptoms, have been found in only about 50 of MID cases, and are present in some PDD patients. Even CT evidence of infarcts is absent in 50% of clinically diagnosed MID patients. Electroencephalograms (EEG), regional cerebral blood flow (rCBF), and angiography have provided even more tenuous evidence. Liston and LaRue (46,47) also question the reliability of ascertaining such clinical features as abruptness of onset and fluctuating course and conclude that "the margin of error associated with the antemortem diagnosis of MID is unacceptably high."

In their review of correlations with postmortem findings, Liston and LaRue (46,47) indicate that although there are some cases of dementing illness in which the brain pathology is primarily vascular as opposed to degenerative, there is considerable doubt about the ability of clinical criteria to distinguish them reliably and validly. They point out that there is frequent overlap between the etiologies and pathologies of degenerative and vascular dementias. Small strokes occur fairly often in the course of steadily progressive dementias of the senile type, although the evidence for the strokes is not always associated with a worsening of the dementia. In other patients with mixed pathology, a clinical dementia may become evident in unrecognized early PDD with the occurrence of one or more small strokes. The association with sudden onset, stepwise deterioration, and neurological signs might erroneously lead to the conclusion that the patient has MID only. The best features of the IS appear to be abrupt onset, stepwise deterioration, history of stroke, and focal neurological signs and symptoms; at best, when absent these can help rule out ischemia as a cause of progressive dementia and thus contribute to a diagnosis of PDD by exclusion. DSM-III-R states that both illnesses may coexist, and recommends that both diagnoses be made in such cases. Perhaps in a future revision of the DSM, a category for mixed dementia (MIX) will be added.

Distinguishing Subtypes

Primary degenerative dementia of the Alzheimer type may be subtyped by age at onset and presence of complicating symptoms. Multi-infarct dementia may be subtyped by accompanying symptoms only.

Subtypes by age at onset. It is commonly believed that PDD beginning before or after age 65 has no clinically differentiating features; thus, DSM-III dropped the terms *senile* and *presenile dementia* and relegated the distinction to subtyping. Recently, however, a study has appeared that indicates heterogeneity between early- and late-onset PDD. Specifically, Selzer and Sherwin (50) have found a greater frequency of language disturbance (speech, verbal comprehension, object naming, etc.) and left-handedness and a much shorter relative survival time in PDD with a presenile onset. Whether an earlier age at onset simply worsens the clinical features of the disease or there is a fundamental difference between early and later onset is still an open question.

A second study (51,52) has shown that patients with PDD who have language disturbance are more likely to have a family history of dementia than those who do not, suggesting a genetic component in a heightened vulnerability of the left hemisphere in patients with PDD of presenile onset. From the point of view of differential diagnosis,

PDD with presenile onset is probably easier to recognize than PDD with senile onset because of the more obvious deviations in intellectual functions from the norm. With advancing age, the differential between the beginning of a true dementia and the forgetfulness that sometimes accompanies older age becomes more difficult. This latter condition, sometimes termed *benign senescent forgetfulness* because it does not progress into the more advanced stages of PDD, is characterized by an inability to recall details of an experience, but preservation of the memory of the experience itself. This relatively stable condition does not lead to functional impairment or have a higher than normal mortality rate. If it advances to include other cognitive functions, such as orientation, concentration, or naming of objects, or severe recent memory deficits, the progression indicates what has been referred to as phase II, the confusional phase, of Alzheimer's disease (41).

Subtyping by complicating psychopathology. DSM-III and DSM-III-R provide for subtypes of PDD with either senile or presenile onset and of multi-infarct dementia according to the presence of complicating psychopathology. Earlier in this chapter, the complications of delirium and depression co-occurring with dementia were discussed. In cases of PDD complicated by a superimposed delirium, the codes 290.30 (senile onset) or 290.11 (presenile onset) are used. If a patient is deemed to have PDD with depression as a secondary phenomenon (as opposed to a pseudodementia secondary to an affective disorder), then the code 290.21 (senile onset) or 290.13 (presenile onset) is employed.

In the previous discussion of organic delusional syndrome, it was stated that global cognitive impairment is absent; some cases of PDD, however, may have delusions as a complication. In these cases, the codes 290.20 and 290.12 apply to PDD with senile and with presenile onset, respectively. Comparable (but different) codes are provided to indicate MID complicated by delirium, delusions, or depression, or uncomplicated.

Senile and Presenile Dementias NOS

All dementias arising in the senium or presenium that cannot be classified as a specific dementia (i.e., from the mental disorders diagnoses) are classified in DSM-III-R as either senile dementia NOS or presenile dementia NOS. Examples of the latter include Pick's disease or Jakob-Creutzfeldt disease. The etiologic factor or illness is noted on Axis III.

This addition to DSM-III-R has, unfortunately, introduced a conflict between the categories of senile dementia NOS (290.00) and presenile dementia NOS (290.10) and the more general diagnosis of dementia (294.10), from the section of the classification on organic mental disorders associated with Axis III physical disorders or conditions, or whose etiology is unknown. For example, a dementia associated with a brain tumor is given as an example of both senile or presenile dementia NOS (p. 119) and of dementia itself (p. 162) in DSM-III-R (7).

The intent of the residual senile or presenile dementia categories was to cover dementias resulting from processes related to the aging of the brain (i.e., degenerative and vascular disease) or to ingestion of psychoactive substances. Therefore, the clinician should reserve use of these diagnoses for conditions that do not meet criteria for a specific DSM-III-R diagnosis from among these two groups of disorders—for example, degenerative dementia resulting from Pick's disease (frontal lobes affected only), which would now be conceptually distinct from PDDAT. The general diagnosis of dementia would be used for all other situations in which a dementia resulted from another systemic or CNS disease.

In the following case vignette, a complicated clinical problem taxes the clinician's ability to assign an accurate DSM-III-R diagnosis.

Uninvited Guests

The psychiatrist pulled up to the modest brick house on tree-lined Oak Street, number 219, got out of his car, and made his way up the concrete walk to the front porch. There, an elderly, white-haired man was sweeping the steps. "Oh, you must be the doctor!" he said congenially. "Come in! Come in! Can I get you something to drink?"

The psychiatrist had been asked by a friend to make a "house call"on his 71-year-old mother, who lived in a small town 40 miles from the medical center. The friend had explained that for the past six weeks his mother had been very upset because she thought neighborhood children who lived on the block had singled her out for harassment. She believed the children had "a stakeout" on her house; and she, in turn, spent much of the day spying back from behind closed window shades. "For every window (in the house) there's a pair of eyes looking in," she told several members of her family.

In addition, the woman had lost her usually good appetite, resulting in a 23-lb. weight loss over the summer, was having trouble sleeping, was subject to frequent crying spells, and was generally agitated. She stated that she was not interested in visiting with friends, that she felt easily fatigued, and that "this whole thing is probably all my fault anyway." The son also described a two-year history of memory problems—she repeated stories or items of news as many as eight to ten times in the course of an evening visit—and distractibility.

The psychiatrist found Mrs. C. to be a thin woman with loose-fitting clothing. She smiled faintly when they shook hands, but for the most part looked frightened and preoccupied. She became tearful when she tried to explain her predicament. Administering the Mini Mental State Exam, the psychiatrist noted a score of 20. As they sat conversing at the kitchen table, he also noted mild tremors of Mrs. C.'s hands when she reached for the tea she was drinking and a rhythmic tremor of her right leg under the table. He asked to rotate her wrists and noted prominent cogwheel rigidity.

General medical and neurological consultations were arranged. A screening battery of tests for dementia was negative. The neurologist diagnosed mild Parkinson's disease, for which he prescribed Sinemet, and ordered a CT scan, which revealed mild cortical atrophy, but no other abnormalities. Tricyclic antidepressants and a small dose of antipsychotic medication were prescribed by the psychiatrist. There was a dramatic improvement in the patient's mood, and the paranoid ideation disappeared over the ensuing three months.

Periodic visits over the next few years found Mrs. C. usually in better spirits, but with increasing loss of cognitive capacities. The Parkinson's disease was well controlled. The first time the psychiatrist attempted to withdraw the antipsychotic medication, Mrs. C. greeted him at the door with "There's someone living in the basement—I think they want to buy the house." She said she could hear voices conversing and saw faces in the dark. "I set six places at the table for dinner, but John (her husband) couldn't see them."

In this case the patient's earliest change in her usual self was the beginning of memory loss. Mild signs of Parkinson's disease were probably developing, but were not noticed. She came into treatment for a major depression with psychotic features. Parkinson's disease can be a cause of both dementia and depression (53); however, the medications for the neuromuscular symptoms seemed to have no effect on the mental symptoms. In addition, cortical atrophy consistent with a degenerative brain process was found. There was no history of previous major depressive episodes or a family history positive for mood disorders. A diagnosis of primary degenerative dementia with depression *and* delusions, complicated or contributed to by Parkinson's disease, seemed best to capture this woman's complex clinical picture.

Other Organic Mental Disorders

All organic mental disorders that are not substance induced and are not of the three types of dementia associated with aging, primary degenerative dementia, multi-infarct dementia, or senile or presenile dementia NOS are coded in the DSM-III-R system according to the last section of the organic mental disorders classification. The section

Table 3.5 A Sample of Systemic and Central Nervous System Diseases That Cause Organic Mental Disorders and Their Corresponding Code Numbers in the ICD-9-CM

Disease or Illness Class	Specific Type	ICD-9-CM[1] Code	Associated Organic Mental Syndrome							
			Delirium	Dementia	Amnestic	Delusional	Hallucinosis	Mood	Anxiety	Personality
Infectious	Typhoid fever	002.0	•							
	Botulism	005.1	•							
	Tuberculous meningitis	013.0	•	•						
	Brucellosis	023 [1]	•						•	
	Meningococcal meningitis	036.0	•	•						
	Septicemia	038 [2]	•							
	Jakob-Creutzfeldt	046.1		•						
	Spotted fevers	082.0	•							
	General paresis	094.1		•						
	Late effects of viral encephalitis	139.0		•						
Neoplasms	Malignant neoplasm of pancreas	157						•		
	Malignant neoplasm of brain	191	•	•					•	•
	Secondary malignant neoplasm of brain	198.3	•	•						•
	Benign neoplasm of brain	225.0	•	•						•

Endocrine	Thyrotoxicosis	242	•					•	•	
	Acquired hypothyroidism	244		•				•	•	•
	Hypoglycemia NOS	251.2	•						•	
	Hyperparathyroidism	252.0	•							
	Cushing's syndrome	255.0						•	•	•
	Corticoadrenal insufficiency	255.4						•		•
Nutritional	Thiamine deficiency	265	•		•					
	Other B-complex (folic acid) deficiency	266.2		•						
Metabolic	Disorders of fluid, electrolyte, and acid-base balance	276	•							
Blood	Pernicious anemia	281.0		•					•	
Nervous System	Bacterial meningitis	320	•			•				
	Encephalitis	323	•			•				
	Intracranial abscess	324	•							
	Alzheimer's disease	331.0		•						
	Obstructive hydrocephalus	331.4	•	•						
	Parkinson's disease	332		•				•		
	Huntington's chorea	333.4		•		•				•
	Multiple sclerosis	340		•					•	•
	Epilepsy	345	•			•	•		•	•
	Anoxic brain damage	348.1	•	•	•					

Table 3.5 A Sample of Systemic and Central Nervous System Diseases That Cause Organic Mental Disorders and Their Corresponding Code Numbers in the ICD-9-CM (*cont.*)

Disease or Illness Class	Specific Type	ICD-9-CM[1] Code	Associated Organic Mental Syndrome							
			Delirium	Dementia	Amnestic	Delusional	Hallucinosis	Mood	Anxiety	Personality
Circulatory	Essential hypertension	401	•	•						
	Acute myocardial infarction	410	•							
	Pulmonary embolism	415.1	•						•	
	Heart failure	428	•							
	Subarachnoid hemorrhage	430	•							
	Late effects of cerebrovascular disease	438		•	•			•		•
Respiratory	Viral pneumonia	480	•							
	Emphysema	492	•						•	
Digestive	Acute necrosis of liver	570	•							
	Alcoholic cirrhosis of liver	571.2	•							
Genito-urinary	Chronic renal failure	585	•							

Musculo-skeletal and Connective Tissue	Systemic lupus erythematosus	710.0	•					•	•	•
Injuries	Closed fracture of skull with hemorrhage	800.2	•		•					
	Concussion	850	•							
	Subarachnoid, subdural, or extradural hemorrhage following injury	852	•	•	•					•
	Burns classified according to extent of body surface involved	948	•							
Poisonings	Bromine compounds	967.3	•	•					•	
	Antidepressants	969.0	•							
	Toxic effect of carbon monoxide	986	•							

[1]Code numbers taken from: Commission on Professional and Hospital Activities: The International Classification of Diseases, 9th Revision, Clinical Modification. Ann Arbor, MI, Commission on Professional and Hospital Activities, 1978.

[2]Three-digit codes are frequently followed by subtypes indicated in a fourth digit.

for organic mental disorders associated with Axis III physical disorders or conditions or whose etiology is unknown may increase clinician coding errors as noted above in the case of brain tumor, but presents only one other hurdle in the appropriate use of DSM-III-R. The organic mental disorder diagnoses themselves are defined by the criteria previously discussed and are identical regardless of the underlying physical illness. All such etiologic illnesses, however, are listed on Axis III of DSM-III-R's multiaxial system (see also Chapter 2, Multiaxial Diagnosis).

The etiologic relationship of the physical disorder to the organic mental disorder is usually self-evident. Diagnostic codes for all clinically recognized physical illnesses can be found in the International Classification of Diseases, 9th Revision, Clinical Modification (ICD-9-CM) (1). Table 3.5 gives the list of organic mental syndromes and an array of physical disorders, with the corresponding ICD-9-CM code, that may cause them.

SUMMARY

In this chapter problems in the differential diagnosis of mental disorders with known nonsubstance-induced organic etiologies are discussed. This area of differential diagnosis has undergone considerable conceptual revision in the DSM-III and DSM-III-R systems, and thus presents challenges, especially for those trained according to more traditional concepts. Differentiation of global and partial organic mental syndromes is reviewed, with special emphasis on assessment of the "evidence" for an organic etiology, recognition of delirium, and differentiation of pseudo- from true dementia. The new DSM-III-R diagnoses of organic anxiety syndrome and of the revised organic personality syndrome are presented. An in-depth discussion of the limits to the differential diagnosis of primary degenerative dementia from multi-infarct dementia is given. Further clinical discussion and examples of difficult differential diagnoses of organic mental disorders will be found in Chapter 11, Differential Diagnosis in the Elderly.

REFERENCES

1. Commission on Professional and Hospital Activities: The International Classification of Diseases, 9th Revision, Clinical Modification. Ann Arbor, MI, Commission on Professional and Hospital Activities, 1978
2. American Psychiatric Association: Diagnostic and Statistical Manual of Mental Disorders, Second Edition. Washington, DC, American Psychiatric Association, 1968
3. American Psychiatric Association: Diagnostic and Statistical Manual of

Mental Disorders, Third Edition. Washington, DC, American Psychiatric Association, 1980
4. Lipowski ZJ: A new look at organic brain syndromes. Am J Psychiatry 137:674–678, 1980
5. Lipowski ZJ: Organic brain syndromes: new classification, concepts and prospects. Can J Psychiatry 29:198–204, 1984
6. Lipowski ZJ: Organic mental disorders—an American perspective. Br J Psychiatry 144:542–546, 1984
7. American Psychiatric Association: Diagnostic and Statistical Manual of Mental Disorders, Third Edition, Revised. Washington, DC, American Psychiatric Association, 1987
8. Lipowski ZJ: Transient cognitive disorders (delirium, acute confusional states) in the elderly. Am J Psychiatry 140:1426–1436, 1983
9. Engel GL, Romano J: Delirium: a syndrome of cerebral insufficiency. J Chronic Dis 9:260–277, 1959
10. Pro JD, Wells CE: The use of the electroencephalogram in the diagnosis of delirium. Dis Nerv System 38:804–808, 1977
11. Devaul RA, Guynn RW: Delirium, in Difficult Diagnosis. Edited by Taylor RB. Philadelphia, WB Saunders Co, 1985, pp 84–90
12. Wells CE: Chronic brain diseases: an overview. Am J Psychiatry 135:1–21, 1978
13. Smith JS, Kiloh LG: The investigation of dementia: results in 200 consecutive admissions. Lancet 1:824–827, 1981
14. Rabins PV, Folstein MF: Delirium and dementia: diagnostic criteria and fatality rates. Br J Psychiatry 140:149–153, 1982
15. Folstein MF, Folstein SE, McHugh PR: "Mini-Mental State." A practical method for grading the cognitive state of patients for the clinician. J Psychiatr Res 12:189–198, 1975
16. Anthony JC, LeResche L, Niaz V, Von Korff MR, Folstein MF: Limits of the "Mini Mental State" as a screening test for dementia and delirium among hospital patients. Psychol Med 12:397–408, 1982
17. Wechsler D: A standardized memory scale for clinical use. J Psychol 19:87–95, 1945
18. Kahn RI, Zarif SH, Hilburt NM, Niederehe EG: Memory complaint and impairment in the aged. Arch Gen Psychiatry 32:1569–1573, 1975
19. Small GW, Jarvik LF: DSM-III diagnosis of dementia (letter). Am J Psychiatry 140:948, 1983
20. McAllister TW: Overview: pseudodementia. Am J Psychiatry 140:528–533, 1983
21. Folstein MF, McHugh PR: Dementia syndrome of depression, in Alzheimer's Disease: Senile Dementia and Related Disorders. Edited by Katzman R, Terry RD, Bick KL. New York, Raven Press, 1978, pp 87–93
22. Jorm AF, Henderson AS: Possible improvements to the diagnostic criteria for dementia in DSM-III. Br J Psychiatry 147:394–399, 1985
23. Kay DWK, Henderson AS, Scott R, Wilson J, Rickwood D, Grayson DA: The prevalence of dementia and depression among the elderly living in the Hobart community: a comparison of the data obtained using different diagnostic criteria. Psychol Med 15:771–788, 1985
24. Henderson AS: The coming epidemic of dementia. Aust N Z J Psychiatry 17:117–127, 1983
25. Hughes CP, Berg I, Danziger WI, Corbin IA, Martin RI: A new clinical state for the staging of dementia. Br J Psychiatry 140:566–572, 1982
26. Coughlan AK, Hollows SE: Use of memory tests in differentiating organic

disorder from depression. Br J Psychiatry 145:164–167, 1984
27. Reisberg B, London E, Ferris SH, Borenstein BA, Scheier L, DeLeon MJ: The Brief Cognitive Rating Scale: language, motoric, and mood concomitants in primary degenerative dementia. Psychopharmacol Bull 19:702–708, 1983
28. Reisberg B, Ferris SH, Anand R, DeLeon MJ, Schneck MK, Buttinger L, Borenstein J: Functional staging of dementia of the Alzheimer's type. Annals NY Acad Sci 435:481–483, 1984
29. Reisberg B, Ferris SH, Franssen E: An ordinal functional assessment tool for Alzheimer's-type dementia. Hosp Community Psychiatry 36:593–661, 1985
30. Andreasen NC, Smith MR, Jacoby CG, Dennert JW, Olsen SA: Ventricular enlargement in schizophrenia: definition and prevalence. Am J Psychiatry 139:292–295, 1982
31. Nasrallah HA, Jacoby CG, McCalley-Whitters M, Kuperman S: Cerebral ventricular enlargement in subtypes of chronic schizophrenia. Arch Gen Psychiatry 39:774–777, 1982
32. Reveley AM, Reveley MA: Aqueduct stenosis and schizophrenia. J Neurol Neurosurg Psychiatry 46:18–22, 1983
33. Krauthammer C, Klerman GL: Secondary mania. Arch Gen Psychiatry 35:1333–1339, 1978
34. Robinson RG, Boston JD, Starkstein SE, Price TR: Comparison of mania and depression after brain injury: causal factors. Am J Psychiatry 145:172–178, 1988
35. Robinson RG, Lipsey JR, Price TR: Diagnosis and clinical management of post-stroke depression. Psychosomatics 26:769–772; 775–778, 1985
36. Robinson RG, Starr LB, Price TR: A two year longitudinal study of mood disorders following stroke: prevalence and duration at six months follow-up. Br J Psychiatry 144:256–262, 1984
37. Hudson JI, Hudson MS, Griffing GT, Melby JC, Pope HG Jr: Phenomenology and family history of affective disorder in Cushing's disease. Am J Psychiatry 144:951–953, 1987
38. Mackenzie TB, Popkin MK: Organic anxiety syndrome. Am J Psychiatry 140:342–344, 1983
39. Pitts FN, McClure JN: Lactate metabolism in anxiety neuroses. N Engl J Med 227:1329–1336, 1967
40. Liebowitz MR, Fyer AJ, Gorman JM, Dillon D, Appleby IL, Levy G, Anderson S, Levitt M, Palij M, Davies SO, Klein DF: Lactate provocation of panic attacks. I. Clinical and behavioral findings. Arch Gen Psychiatry 41:764–770, 1984
41. Schneck MK, Reisberg B, Ferris SH: An overview of current concepts of Alzheimer's disease. Am J Psychiatry 139:165–173, 1982
42. Wells CE: Management of dementias, in Congenital and Acquired Cognitive Disorders. Edited by Katzman R. New York, Raven Press, 1979, pp 281–292
43. Lippmann SB: Dementia, in Difficult Diagnosis. Edited by Taylor RB. Philadelphia, WB Saunders Co, 1985, pp 90–103
44. Sulkava R, Haltia M, Paetau A, Wikstrom J, Palo J: Accuracy of clinical diagnosis in primary degenerative dementia: correlation with neuropathological findings. J Neurol Neurosurg Psychiatry 46:9–13, 1983
45. Roth M: The natural history of mental disorders in old age. J Ment Sci 101:281–301, 1955
46. Liston EH, LaRue A: Clinical differentiation of primary degenerative and

multi-infarct dementia: a critical review of the evidence. Part I. Clinical studies. Biol Psychiatry 18:1451–1465, 1983

47. Liston EH, LaRue A: Clinical differentiation of primary degenerative and multi-infarct dementia: a critical review of the evidence. Part II. Pathological studies. Biol Psychiatry 18:1467–1484, 1983
48. Slater E, Roth M: Clinical Psychiatry, 3rd ed. Baltimore, Williams & Wilkins, 1969, pp 593–596
49. Hachinski VC, Lassen NA, Marshall J: Multi infarct dementia: a cause of mental deterioration in the elderly. Lancet 2:207–210, 1974
50. Seltzer B, Sherwin I: A comparison of clinical features in early and late-onset primary degenerative dementia. One entity or two? Arch Neurol 40:143–146, 1983
51. Folstein MF, Breitner JCS: Language disorder predicts familial Alzheimer's disease. Johns Hopkins Med J 149:145–147, 1981
52. Breitner JCS, Folstein MF: Familial Alzheimer dementia: a prevalent disorder with specific clinical features. Psychol Med 14:63–80, 1984
53. Mayeux R, Stern Y, Williams JBW, Cote L, Frantz A, Dyrenfurth I: Clinical and biochemical features of depression in Parkinson's disease. Am J Psychiatry 143:756–759, 1986

CHAPTER 4

Disturbances Associated with the Use of Psychoactive Substances

The clinical problems in differential diagnosis discussed in this chapter have in common their relationship to the use of psychoactive substances. Psychoactive substances are drugs or chemicals that alter ordinary states of consciousness, including mood, cognition, and behavior; they are generally self-administered. In some cases the relationship is etiologic: the disturbance is a direct consequence of drug ingestion. In other cases a pattern of pathological behaviors develop (some of which are physiologically mediated) in association with repeated self-administration of these substances, which cause distress and functional disability. These conditions are usually referred to as drug abuse, or addiction, or dependence. In addition, psychoactive substances sometimes serve as the precipitant of another major functional mental disorder, such as an episode of schizophrenia or mania.

In each of these cases, differential diagnosis can present thorny problems. In general, in my experience (1), in spite of the widespread use and abuse of psychoactive substances among psychiatric patients, the mental disorders associated with such substances often are unrecognized in general clinical practice.

Classification and Terminology

A significant reorganization of disorders associated with psychoactive substances was considered for DSM-III-R. In DSM-III the organic mental syndromes that were the direct consequence of the effects of drugs on the central nervous system were included in section 1 of the description of organic mental disorders (see Chapter 3). In the revised manual, DSM-III substance-induced organic mental disorders were to be included with DSM-III substance use disorders as two subclasses in the renamed class "Psychoactive Substance Use Disorders." (The term *psychoactive* precedes *substance* for greater specificity of meaning.)

The rationale for classifying the substance-induced syndromes among the organic mental disorders was that they shared a necessary and sufficient organic etiology. Furthermore, it was thought that the treatment implications of an acute organic mental syndrome caused by acute drug ingestion were very different from those of a long-standing pattern of maladaptive behavior that developed with substance abuse. In other words, an acute LSD-induced (hallucinogen) hallucinosis often required emergency intervention with talking-down and sometimes antianxiety or antipsychotic medication, whereas heroin (opioid) dependence required long-term residential rehabilitation or methadone maintenance.

The DSM-III-R advisory committee on psychoactive substance use disorders urged that the two types of syndrome be combined into one class because the people most likely to develop substance-induced organic mental disorders would be those with ongoing substance dependence disorders. Because of the considerable likelihood of co-occurrence of these disorders, it was hoped that unification of a class of psychoactive substance use disorders would promote recognition of both types of disorder. In treatment settings, recognition of a substance-induced organic mental disorder would arouse a clinician's suspicion of an underlying substance dependence disorder; and in patients with evident or known substance dependence, an acute panic reaction or psychotic episode would suggest that a disorder with a substance-induced etiology should be high on the list of differential diagnoses.

Since neither substance-induced organic mental disorders nor substance use disorders were diagnosed as frequently as they should have been in general clinical settings using DSM-III, the change in DSM-III-R may have been warranted. In the end, the decision was to leave the substance-induced organic mental disorders in the class of organic mental disorders in DSM-III-R. Whether or not a revision would have led to heightened clinician sensitivity to these disorders cannot be known.

In this chapter, I shall discuss problems in diagnosing disorders associated with psychoactive substances and a number of clinical situations in which psychoactive substance use disorders should be diagnosed but generally have not been.

PROBLEMS IN DSM-III CONCEPTS OF SUBSTANCE USE DISORDER

DSM-III divided substance use disorders into two general syndromes: substance abuse and substance dependence. Experts in the diagnosis and treatment of drug addiction have taken issue with this division of substance use disorders into abuse and dependence syndromes (2-4). They have been concerned that the distinctions were arbitrary, inconsistently applied, and gave inadequate coverage in the classification itself to the psychopathology encountered in clinical practice. These observations have led to the rather extensive revision of the concept of psychoactive substance use disorder in DSM-III-R.

Substance Abuse in DSM-III

Substance abuse, in general terms, was defined in DSM-III as a pathological pattern of substance use and associated impairment in social or occupational functioning of at least one month's duration. Clinicians frequently thought of DSM-III substance abuse as synonymous with "psychological drug addiction" or "psychological dependence."

Evidence of a pathological pattern of use could be intoxication throughout the day, inability to cut down or stop use, repeated (unsuccessful) efforts to control use, use of a substance in spite of the existence of a physical problem that the person knows is exacerbated by the substance, need for daily use for adequate functioning, and episodes of complications of substance intoxication, such as blackouts, overdoses, or the development of substance-induced organic mental syndromes. Social impairment meant a breakdown in relations with family and friends due to the irresponsible, erratic, impulsive, or aggressive behavior often displayed by drug-abusing people. Repeated legal difficulties due to substance use were also included. Occupational impairment resulted when a person was absent from work or school because of substance use, was functioning ineffectively on the job or in school because of actual intoxication, hangover, etc. The duration of one month was stipulated to ensure a clinically significant syndrome, and referred to a pattern of maladaptive use that did not necessarily have to be continuous. Several drinking binges causing family disruption over a one-month period is given in DSM-III as an example of a pattern sufficient to meet the duration criterion.

Substance Dependence in DSM-III

DSM-III substance dependence corresponded to physiological drug addiction. The evidence for physiological dependence was either tolerance to the substance—that is, increased amounts were necessary to achieve the desired effect or there was a reduced effect of a standard dose—or withdrawal, defined as the development of a substance-specific organic mental syndrome following cessation or reduction in the intake of a substance that was regularly used.

Although drug withdrawal is universally accepted as indicating physiological habituation to a substance and thus physical dependency, use of tolerance as an indication of physical dependency is much more controversial. First, tolerance to substances such as alcohol or cocaine (5) may be more innate than acquired. Alcohol-naive people, for example, may differ greatly from each other in their capacities to drink alcohol without becoming impaired, and some may show much more tolerance to alcohol than other people develop after heavy and prolonged alcohol consumption. Second, in many people a certain degree of tolerance to alcohol develops relatively easily: it does not necessarily require heavy drinking, nor does it necessarily progress. Tolerance in this case does not seem sufficient to warrant a diagnosis of dependence. Thus, although with respect to many drugs certain people appear able to consume many times an average dose, the exact mechanisms and significance of this phenomenon are not fully understood.

Inconsistencies in DSM-III Criteria

In general, in DSM-III substance dependence assumed the presence of substance abuse. A frequent error in the use of DSM-III diagnoses of substance use disorders was recording both abuse and dependence diagnoses when a person had developed dependence as a result of abuse: a dependence diagnosis was sufficient. An acute episode of substance *withdrawal* that constituted the evidence for substance dependence would, however, warrant an additional diagnosis because of its potential relevance for treatment, as noted above. The following case illustrates these principles.

August Days

"Hello?"
"Hello, is this Dr. Sharkey?"

"Yes."

"This is Mrs. Smith; I'm a patient of Dr. Black's. He said you were covering for him while he was on vacation."

"Yes. What can I do for you?"

So began a telephone consultation with a 55-year-old divorced schoolteacher and a young psychiatrist one August morning. The teacher had recently, against medical advice, signed herself out of a psychiatric unit of a general hospital where she had gone to be evaluated for anxiety and to be detoxified from a benzodiazepine drug.

Mrs. Smith had a five-year history of mouth pain, which she said had been alternately diagnosed as trigeminal neuralgia or temporomandibular joint (TMJ) dysfunction. For this she had taken Percocet and Valium. The drugs relieved the symptoms somewhat; but the beneficial effects would gradually wear off, necessitating an increase in the dose. She had seen numerous internists, neurologists, and psychiatrists, some of whom were reluctant to prescribe medications indefinitely. Attempts to treat the pain with Tegretol and Elavil had been short-lived because of side effects she said were "horrendous."

Nine months earlier, Mrs. Smith's husband had died suddenly of a myocardial infarction. During the ensuing months, the pain in her mouth had become worse, and anxiety had developed. Her Valium dose rose to 90 mg/day, but she still complained of feeling shaky, weak, having difficulty falling asleep, and waking up at 3:00 A.M. and being unable to fall back to sleep without taking at least 15-20 mg of Valium. She was increasingly absent from work, feeling either "hung over" or "exhausted" in the morning. Depressed mood and vegetative signs of depression were not prominent. She described one acute attack that sounded like a panic attack, for which she had seen a cardiologist, who said that her heart was normal.

She had signed out of the hospital because she could not stand the anxiety and pain that developed as the Valium was reduced. She had obtained Dr. Black's name from a friend; he had seen her once. She had pleaded with him to allow her to try being detoxified from Valium as an outpatient. He had suggested that she might profit from a trial of imipramine or lithium.

When she called Dr. Sharkey, Mrs. Smith had exhausted the supply of Valium she was to use while reducing the dose. She had been unable to reduce her intake by more than 10 mg/day and had had only enough to take 15 mg for the past 2 days, and none in the past 24 hours. She reported a rapid heartbeat, sweating, weakness in her knees, shaking hands, nausea, anxiety, and insomnia.

Mrs. Smith has a problem with Valium: she needed larger and larger doses to control facial pain and "anxiety." By DSM-III criteria, she exhibited a pathological pattern of use, evidenced by her inability to cut down or stop use and ingestion of more than 60 mg of diazepam a day. She had been unable to go to work regularly because of symptoms related to heavy use of the drug. Since this had been going on for more than one month, she met the criteria for diazepam abuse. She also had developed tolerance, and her "anxiety" seemed likely to be a symptom of withdrawal. Therefore, the diagnosis of diazepam dependence takes precedence. The syndrome Mrs. Smith described to the covering psychiatrist over the telephone sounds like an episode of diazepam withdrawal. Thus, this additional organic mental disorder diagnosis is warranted because treatment may be necessary to prevent the development of seizures or withdrawal delirium.

As will be seen in the sections of this chapter that follow, this patient's Valium use meets DSM-III-R criteria for diazepam (sedative, hypnotic, or anxiolytic) dependence (moderate). The principle of also diagnosing the superimposed uncomplicated diazepam (sedative, hypnotic, or anxiolytic) withdrawal still applies, according to DSM-III-R.

In DSM-III, two classes of substances, alcohol and cannabis, required explicit evidence of one or the other aspect of substance abuse for a dependence diagnosis—either a pathological pattern of use or social or occupational impairment. These qualifications were introduced because of the widespread, socially sanctioned, recreational use of these two classes of substances. Since tolerance, for example, to alcohol was relatively easily developed, unless there was evidence of pathological use or impairment, too many false-positive diagnoses of dependence could be made.

Clinicians encounter other circumstances in which dependence to a substance may develop, but there was no abuse. Examples would be iatrogenic dependence on analgesic opioids (mentioned in DSM-III) or on sedative/hypnotics prescribed by physicians. An argument may be made that the consequences and risks inherent in barbiturate dependence are the same whether the dependence is self-induced or iatrogenically induced; on the other hand, if the dependence diagnosis incorporates the abuse concept, then in iatrogenic cases it would mistakenly signal a problem that ordinarily has long-term treatment implications for the affected person.

In the case of cannabis dependence, in addition to one sign of maladaptive use or impairment, tolerance was required. This is because no withdrawal syndrome to cannabis was recognized in the DSM-III substance-induced organic mental disorders. Some clinicians think that tolerance to cannabis is uncertain; some people who smoke the substance regularly report that it becomes easier rather than harder to get "high."

Tobacco dependence was another idiosyncratically defined disorder. The criteria called for continuous use for at least one month and one of three specific problems related to smoking: unsuccessful attempts to stop or cut down on smoking, the development of tobacco withdrawal, or continued smoking in spite of a serious physical disorder, such as emphysema or coronary artery disease, that the person knows is exacerbated by tobacco. Hughes and co-workers (6) found that DSM-III criteria for tobacco dependence were overinclusive in that they identified nearly all middle-aged male smokers in a general population sample as dependent. These authors also suggested that such a broad definition of tobacco dependence might not be clinically useful.

Besides these conceptual inconsistencies, there were others in DSM-III within the subdivisions of pattern of pathological use and impairment in social and occupational functioning. Rounsaville and colleagues (3) have pointed out that although inability to stop or reduce use, intoxication throughout the day, and evidence of complications (i.e., substance-induced OMDs, overdoses) are listed in the diagnostic criteria for each of the eight (not including tobacco) specific classes of substances of abuse, other general criteria for a pathological pattern appear in some classes, but not others. For instance, the specifications regarding alcohol and barbiturates (and similarly acting sedatives and hypnotics) include approximate doses of the drugs that might be considered pathological; for the other drugs, there are none. The criteria for opioid, amphetamine, and cannabis abuse refer to daily use for at least one month; those for the other classes do not. In the case of cannabis abuse and dependence, the features that are said to characterize a pathological pattern of use that constitutes abuse are not identical with those that are said to characterize a pathological pattern of use for dependence. Criteria for social and occupational impairment are considerably more consistent, except that alcohol abuse is the only category that mentions family difficulties, and cannabis is the only one to specify loss of interest in usual activities.

Some of these inconsistencies were not as crucial for clinicians using DSM-III criteria as they were for researchers. Clinicians could use the criteria more flexibly and recognize the underlying concept behind a pathological pattern. Researchers, on the other hand, would find such inconsistencies problematic in terms of identifying homogeneous patient groups. Rounsaville (4) believes that these inconsistencies have contributed to the relative infrequency of references to DSM-III substance use disorders in research studies.

Inadequate Categories

DSM-III included abuse categories for eight classes of substances: alcohol, barbiturates or similarly acting sedatives or hypnotics, opioids, cocaine, amphetamines or similarly acting sympathomimetics, phencyclidine or similarly acting arylcyclohexylamines, hallucinogens, and cannabis. There were dependence diagnoses for only five of these eight: alcohol, barbiturates, opioids, amphetamines, and cannabis. In addition, there was a diagnosis of tobacco dependence (see above), but no abuse.

The reason for not including dependence diagnoses for cocaine, phencyclidine, and hallucinogens was that, in the opinion of the DSM-III advisory committee on substance use disorders, there was no evidence that syndromes of tolerance or withdrawal existed for these substances (7,8). This view is now regarded with considerable skepticism by clinicians and researchers, especially in light of the explosion of cocaine use and abuse in recent years (9). Although traditionally cocaine has been thought to be associated with reverse tolerance or kindling (10), at least in cases of cocaine-induced psychosis, the fact that some people can consume 50 times a normal dose of cocaine suggests that tolerance does exist. Furthermore, a withdrawal syndrome characterized by dysphoria, depression, and drug craving has been described (11). The similarities between cocaine and amphetamine, for which there is a dependence syndrome in DSM-III, also suggest that exclusion of a syndrome of cocaine dependence from DSM-III was premature.

Among frequent cocaine users, a substantial group reports tolerance and some withdrawal (9). According to DSM-III criteria, these people can be diagnosed only as cocaine abusers, even though they meet the general, conceptual criteria for dependence. A story common among people coming today for cocaine treatment follows.

The Unnatural

A 25-year-old former minor-league pitcher was admitted to the hospital for treatment of cocaine "abuse." He had been bingeing on "freebase" off and on for the previous year, had been dropped by his team, and had been fired from two other jobs. Although he had resolved on many occasions to stop using cocaine, just as many times he found himself driving to that part of town where he could find his "connections," and another binge would begin. He now felt totally out of control: "I've been smoking so much that sometimes I think I'm about to die."

In fact, just one week before the hospitalization, the man awoke from a sleep feeling that his left arm was "dead." He rushed to the emergency room of the local hospital, where a neurological exam revealed unequal palpebral fissures, asymmetric palate, dysarthria, mild left hemiparesis, and left-sided sensory impairment. An EEG and CT scan were normal, and an acute brain-stem encephalopathy was diagnosed. The condition resolved spontaneously within 24 hours, but so frightened the man that he agreed to psychiatric hospitalization.

The young man had been introduced to cocaine three years earlier by a teammate while the two were having a few beers after a game.

Although he was tall, handsome, and in very good physical condition, he found it difficult to meet women. The idea of walking up to a strange woman and starting a conversation intimidated him. He was even uncomfortable when girls tried to pick him up, as frequently happened. He was not nervous playing in front of crowds of people, however. He found that being high on cocaine enabled him to feel much more at ease socially, to be "on top of things," and "the life of the party."

Initially, he "snorted" cocaine only on weekends and only in social situations. After about two years, however, he found that his desire to use cocaine had begun to increase in frequency and intensity. His actual use, as measured by the amount of money he was spending on the drug, began to increase "geometrically," until he could spend up to $300 a night for several nights in a row for "freebase."

His performance on the field first became erratic, with one good outing followed by one in which he would not be able to complete a single inning. Then he started to miss the team bus, and showed up late for games, or not at all. He stole money from his roommate's wallet on several occasions when he was "short on cash." Finally, near the end of the last season, about three months earlier, he had been dropped from the team following a "shoving match" with his manager when he was told he was being demoted to a lower-level minor-league team. He took a job as a short-order cook, then one pumping gas, in order to make money, but lost each job when he could not get to work.

As his fortunes turned for the worse, his binges grew progressively more severe. When he wasn't bingeing, he lay in bed, exhausted. Then he began to feel increasing depression, irritability, and agitation. Another binge would follow.

The mechanism for progressive, uncontrolled cocaine use is not clearly understood. A diagnosis of cocaine dependence certainly seems warranted in the case of "The Unnatural."

The absence of a category of cocaine dependence in DSM-III may have contributed to perpetuating the myth, common even in medical circles, that cocaine is a safe drug.

Overview of Differential Diagnosis

DSM-III-R includes no decision tree for the differential diagnosis of disturbances associated with the use of psychoactive substances. Such substances, however, qualify as an organic etiologic factor and therefore enter into the decision-making process in the differential diagnostic logic of the organic mental disorders decision tree (see Chapter 3).

Figure 4.1 presents a simplified version of the decision-making steps the clinician takes in evaluating a patient with a problem related to psychoactive substances. Virtually any psychological sign or symptom or type of maladaptive behavior can be due to psychoactive

Figure 4.1. Decision Tree for the Differential Diagnosis of Disorders Associated with the Use of Psychoactive Substances

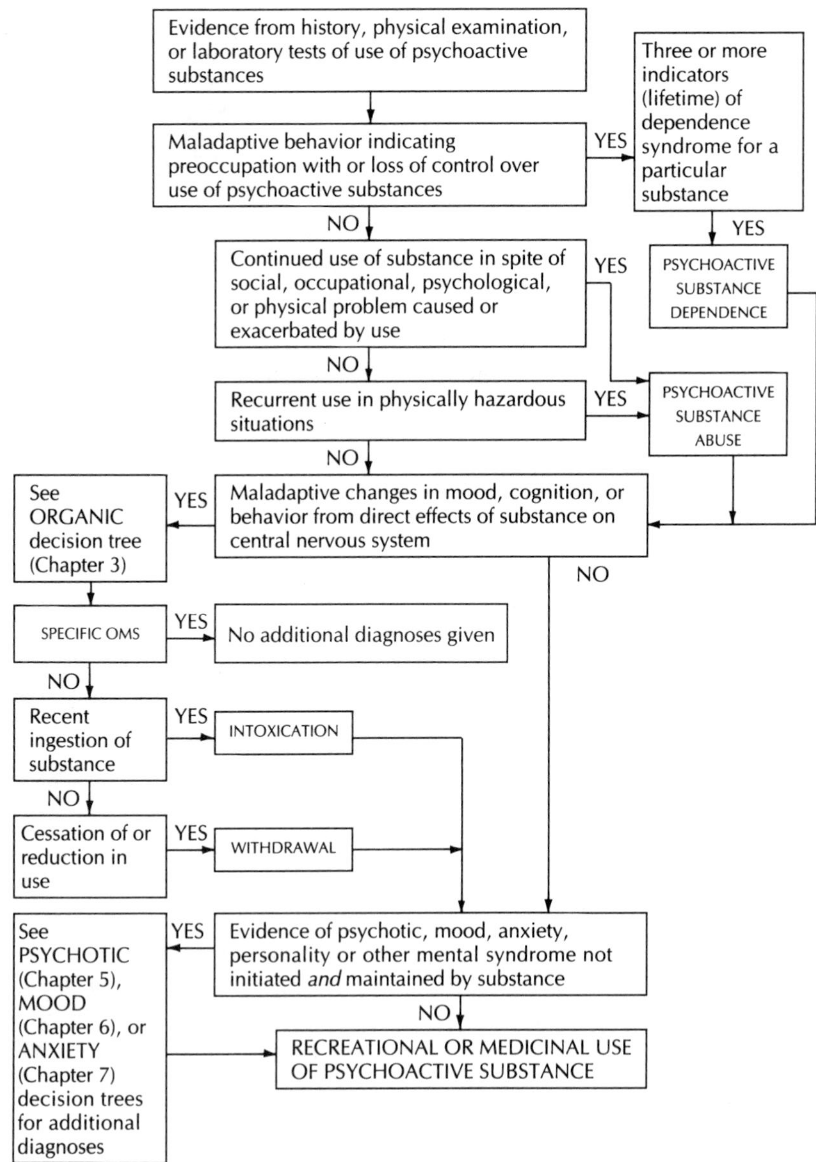

substances. A reliable history of substance use, physical evidence such as substance-related physical illnesses or conditions, results of screening tests of the urine, or blood levels of a substance can lead the clinician with increasing certainty toward a diagnosis of a psychoactive substance-related disorder.

As has already been mentioned, the direct toxic effects of a psychoactive substance on the central nervous system need to be differentiated from maladaptive behaviors that develop when a person loses control over substance use. A wide range of behaviors might characterize a dependence syndrome. In order to make a complete DSM-III-R diagnostic assessment, the clinician needs to determine whether dependence is, or ever has been, present for the substance in question; how severe the problem with substances is currently; whether the person's problems are accounted for solely by the substance use or there is another, or more than one other, associated mental disorder; and the exact substance, or substances, being used. Multiple diagnoses are possible.

Because of the inconsistencies and inadequacies of the DSM-III categories, the advisory committee on psychoactive substance use disorders to the Work Group to Revise DSM-III recommended substantial revisions for DSM-III-R. These changes included: *(1)* the collapse of the DSM-III categories of abuse and dependence into one DSM-III-R category, psychoactive substance dependence; *(2)* use of the category of psychoactive substance abuse as a diagnosis for people with problems with psychoactive substances that do not meet the criteria for dependence; and *(3)* a switch from a monothetic to a polythetic approach to diagnosis.

General Problems in Differential Diagnosis

Many clinicians criticized DSM-III criteria for substance use disorders because they relied largely on a history of substance use from the patient or an informant to alert the clinician to a possible problem with drugs. The first difficulty in differential diagnosis is that people with substance use disorders are notoriously inaccurate or even deceptive in their reports of patterns of substance use. Second, they frequently use multiple substances, making the DSM-III system of specifying each individual substance by name in its diagnostic labels a sham, or even an impossibility. Third, many of the drugs subject to abuse are sold in impure, adulterated forms, and the substances added to "cut" them may themselves be toxic.

The role of the physical examination. A thorough physical examination can provide the first clues to a substance use problem that the patient may be denying. Needle marks, tachycardia, elevated blood pressure, pupillary dilation (from amphetamines, cocaine, hallucinogens) or constriction (from opioids), nystagmus, or the physical signs of potentially substance-related physical conditions such as cirrhosis or perforated nasal septum are usually obvious giveaways.

The most dangerous situations not to be overlooked by the clinician are dependencies that are likely to lead to severe withdrawal syndromes, such as alcohol dependence or dependence on barbiturates. Physical signs of intoxication, such as slurred speech, incoordination, or unsteady gait, should be evident following a challenge with a test dose of 200 mg of pentobarbital or significant tolerance to sedative/hypnotic drugs is present and a withdrawal syndrome likely unless preventive treatment is instituted. Intoxication states and complications arising from them enter into the differential diagnosis of many functional disorders.

The use of toxicologic analyses. The DSM-III systems are primarily classifications based on signs and symptoms of psychopathology and, with the exception of the organic mental disorders, do not include the results of laboratory tests in the diagnostic criteria for disorders. Even for OMDs, laboratory documentation of organic factors is not necessary. In DSM-III-R, however, a section has been added on the use of laboratory tests as aids in the diagnosis of psychoactive substance use disorders and psychoactive substance-induced organic mental disorders.

The ways in which DSM-III-R recommends that toxicologic tests can be helpful include the following:

1. The use of highly sensitive urine screening tests (such as thin-layer chromatography (TLC) or enzyme immunoassay (EIA) for psychoactive substances in cases in which substances are being considered etiologic for mental symptoms (see section below on psychoactive substance-induced OMDs);
2. The use of screening tests when a history of substance use or abuse is suspected by the clinician, but is being denied by the patient;
3. The use of highly specific tests, such as gas chromatography/mass spectrometry, for preparation of testimony or reports in courts of law;
4. The use of urine or blood tests to distinguish between specific substances that may cause similar clinical signs and symptoms of intoxication;
5. The use of urine tests to distinguish substances from which a person might be having withdrawal when an accurate history is not available or multiple substances may be involved; and

6. The use of blood levels to determine whether a person is tolerant to a psychoactive substance.

Recognizing the Dependence Syndrome

The opinion of the Psychoactive Substance Use Disorders Advisory Committee working on DSM-III-R was that the division of substance-related problems into abuse and dependence in DSM-III was arbitrary and artificial. The categories failed to reflect the theoretical and empirical developments in research on drug dependence, particularly work on the alcohol dependence syndrome (12-14). A World Health Organization memorandum on the nomenclature and classification of drug- and alcohol-related problems described the dependence syndrome as a continuum, "a quantitative phenomenon that exists in different degrees" and included cognitive, behavioral, and physiological aspects (13). The essential feature was thought to be that a behavioral pattern developed "in which the use of a given psychoactive drug, or class of drugs, is given a much higher priority than other behaviors that once had higher value." The compulsive nature of drug-taking or impaired control over drug use was a facet of drug dependence that many experts thought was missing from both of the DSM-III diagnoses.

The DSM-III-R criteria for psychoactive substance dependence are listed in Table 4.1. This category combines those features of DSM-III abuse and dependence that were not problematic, and adds

Table 4.1 DSM-III-R Diagnostic Criteria for Psychoactive Substance Dependence

A. At least three of the following:

(1) substance often taken in larger amounts or over a longer period than the person intended
(2) persistent desire or one or more unsuccessful efforts to cut down or control substance use
(3) a great deal of time spent in activities necessary to get the substance (e.g., theft), taking the substance (e.g., chain smoking), or recovering from its effects
(4) frequent intoxication or withdrawal symptoms when expected to fulfill major role obligations at work, school, or home (e.g., does not go to work because hung over, goes to school or work "high," intoxicated while taking care of his or her children), or when substance use is physically hazardous (e.g., drives when intoxicated)
(5) important social, occupational, or recreational activities given up or reduced because of substance use

(6) continued substance use despite knowledge of having a persistent or recurrent social, psychological, or physical problem that is caused or exacerbated by the use of the substance (e.g., keeps using heroin despite family arguments about it, cocaine-induced depression, or having an ulcer made worse by drinking)
(7) marked tolerance: need for markedly increased amounts of the substance (i.e., at least a 50% increase) in order to achieve intoxication or desired effect, or markedly diminished effect with continued use of the same amount

Note: The following items may not apply to cannabis, hallucinogens, or phencyclidine (PCP):

(8) characteristic withdrawal symptoms (see specific withdrawal syndromes under psychoactive substance-induced organic mental disorders)
(9) substance often taken to relieve or avoid withdrawal symptoms

B. Some symptoms of the disturbance have persisted for at least one month, or have occurred repeatedly over a longer period of time.

Criteria for Severity of Psychoactive Substance Dependence:

Mild: Few, if any, symptoms in excess of those required to make the diagnosis, and the symptoms result in no more than mild impairment in occupational functioning or in usual social activities or relationships with others.

Moderate: Symptoms or functional impairment between "mild" and "severe."

Severe: Many symptoms in excess of those required to make the diagnosis, and the symptoms markedly interfere with occupational functioning or with usual social activities or relationships with others.*

In Partial Remission: During the past six months, some use of the substance and some symptoms of dependence.

In Full Remission: During the past six months, either no use of the substance, or use of the substance and no symptoms of dependence.

---

*Because of the availability of cigarettes and other nicotine-containing substances and the absence of a clinically significant nicotine intoxication syndrome, impairment in occupational or social functioning is not necessary for a rating of severe nicotine dependence.

several new items to capture dimensions of drug dependence missing from DSM-III. Tolerance and withdrawal are still in the criteria set, but neither is required for a diagnosis of dependence in DSM-III-R. Relief drug use, that is, taking a drug to relieve withdrawal symptoms, is added to bridge the gap between behavior and physiology.

Impairment in social and occupational functioning has been recast in terms of three criteria: *(1)* the person's being intoxicated or impaired, when expected to fulfill a social or occupational role; *(2)* the person's giving up activities in favor of substance use; and *(3)* the person's continuation of use despite significant consequent exacerbation of social, psychological, or physical problems. These three criteria attempt to add the "driven" quality of the drug-taking behavior, or impaired control, and extend the kinds of impairment resulting from drug use into the physical sphere, beyond the substance-induced OMDs mentioned in DSM-III. Instead of a pathological pattern of use as described in DSM-III, the criteria in its revision specify that if a person spends a disproportionate amount of time taking drugs or arranging to get them, this in itself is pathological, regardless of the amounts taken or the amount of time spent actually intoxicated. Another typical behavior of the dependent person is inability to gauge the amount of drug desired and frequent overshooting of the mark. Finally, as was mentioned in several DSM-III categories of abuse, a persistent desire and repeated unsuccessful attempts to cut down on the use of a substance usually indicates a problem.

DSM-III-R includes specific categories of dependence for each of the classes of psychoactive substances that are in DSM-III, two being renamed: alcohol; sedatives, hypnotics, or anxiolytics; opioids; cocaine; amphetamine or similarly acting sympathomimetics; phencyclidine or similarly acting arylcyclohexylamines; hallucinogens; cannabis; and nicotine. In addition, a category of inhalant dependence has been added to cover dependent sniffing of glue and other inhaled substances that can induce euphoria.

Distinguishing Degrees of Severity

The alcohol dependence syndrome has been described in the literature as graded in intensity rather than an all or nothing phenomenon (14). The literature on personality disturbance (see Chapter 9) suggests that when this is the case, polythetic rather than monothetic categories are more appropriate. A polythetic diagnostic category specifies a number of features that characterize a disorder, some specific number of which, but no single feature, is required for making the diagnosis. Thus, of the nine DSM-III-R criteria for substance dependence, *any* three are sufficient. In essence, a prototypic clinical picture is described to which a particular case may correspond to a greater or lesser extent.

The new DSM-III-R category of substance dependence is likely to characterize a relatively mild dependence syndrome at its threshold for diagnosis. More severely dependent people are likely to have five, six, or more features. The clinician may specify the degree of severity, following the diagnosis, according to criteria that differ only slightly from the DSM-III-R convention that applies to all diagnostic categories. Some clinicians may have difficulty recognizing the milder forms of dependence. For example, a college student who smokes marijuana nearly every day, often goes to class high, and has given up his scholarship job or position on the school newspaper to smoke with his friends could be diagnosed as having cannabis dependence. Another problem that the polythetic categorization introduces is that two people with the same dependence diagnosis can present very different clinical pictures and in fact have no features in common. These differences may require or suggest quite different treatment approaches.

The following two case vignettes of alcohol dependence illustrate these problems.

The Wine Aficionado

A 38-year-old investment banker and his wife sought treatment from a couples' therapist for problems in their ten-year marriage. The wife complained that "his work always comes first," that he was "too self-centered," and that he criticized her—and just about everyone else they knew—incessantly. He, in turn, felt that she was primarily interested in spending money and in getting her hair and nails done. He found their sex life uninteresting and too infrequent. "Once a week, whether we need it or not," was how he put it.

The major arguments the couple had were usually on weekends, driving home from dinner or a party, or as they were getting ready for bed. The quarrels usually began with the husband "picking on" something that the wife had said and then making generalized disparaging comments about her "narrowness" or "naiveté." A detailed history taken by the therapist revealed that the banker frequently had two or three cocktails and two or three glasses of wine on these occasions and, although not feeling "drunk" when they went home, nonetheless felt somewhat intoxicated.

The husband had been "a moderate social drinker" all of his adult life. He was a wine aficionado who subscribed to several wine newsletters, attended wine-tasting classes regularly, and went out once a week to shop for a wine cellar in his basement that contained about 500 bottles of classified Bordeaux and better Burgundies plus a couple of cases of "everyday wine." He routinely had wine with dinner, sometimes preceded by a cocktail or two. Occasionally, he felt "a little high," having had "one too many" during the week, which he regretted because he then would not be able to do work that he had intended to do at home that evening. He always paid attention to how much he was drinking and often resolved to "cut down." Over the ten years of his marriage, however, he had probably increased, rather than decreased, his alcohol intake. He never drank during the day, and was never absent from work because of a hangover (although he admitted to a "queasy" Sunday morning every couple of months). He had frequently driven his car while still feeling the effects of alcohol, but up to this point had never had an accident or received a ticket for driving while intoxicated.

The Wine Aficionado has a pattern of alcohol use that is not uncommon in American society and that meets criteria for alcohol dependence. He often has "one drink too many," and has long recognized the need to control or cut down on his alcohol intake. He spends a fair amount of time on wine-related activities that have become a kind of hobby. He has used alcohol under hazardous circumstances, and alcohol intoxication disinhibits aggressive impulses that lead to criticism of, and arguments with, his wife. He may have developed tolerance over the years and occasionally has mild withdrawal symptoms. The severity of his alcohol dependence would probably be classified as mild or moderate.

This case contrasts markedly with the next one, "The Panhandler."

The Panhandler

A 35-year-old man was picked up by police from a street corner after he was observed by numerous passersby walking down the middle of a busy avenue shouting at no one in particular and waving his arms around his head as if to ward off some kind of attack. The police found the man dirty and disheveled, with torn clothes, no socks, and wearing one sneaker and one brown oxford shoe. He smelled of alcohol. He looked warily at the officers when they asked him his address. "Gracie Mansion" was his answer.

The man was taken to an emergency room, where he had to be strapped to a wheelchair and put in a quiet room. He continued to scream and rocked violently in the chair. The intern called to examine him noted marked diaphoresis, a pulse of 135, and blood pressure, as best as he could determine it, of at least 150/110. The man looked frightened and continued to shout curses and warnings amidst incoherent mumbling. The intern diagnosed alcohol withdrawal delirium (delirium tremens) and administered 50 mg of Librium intramuscularly.

The man was admitted to the hospital and detoxified over a seven-day period. Abdominal pain and vomiting led to a diagnosis of pancreatitis, which was treated.

A social worker was able to obtain the name and address of a brother who lived upstate and who supplied a history. The patient had been an insurance salesman who developed a severe drinking problem in his mid-20s. Both his mother and father had been alcoholics, and both had died of alcohol-related illnesses before age 60. The patient had been married for three years, but his drinking made him verbally and physically abusive to his wife, who divorced him when he was 30. Afterward, the drinking became even worse. Over the course of one year, he lost four jobs because of absences from work due to drinking binges. When he could no longer afford an apartment, he moved into a single-room occupancy hotel and went on welfare. He lived thus for several years, but his brother recalled that an altercation with the hotel manager had led to his losing his room. The brother had heard nothing from the patient for two years and had assumed he was dead.

The patient reported that he had been sleeping on park benches, in doorways, and over subway gratings. He sifted garbage for food and panhandled money from motorists at stoplights. With the money he bought $0.99 bottles of wine and an occasional pint of whiskey or rum. He was not sure what had happened to bring him to the hospital this time, but acknowledged that he had been in hospitals before.

"The Panhandler" has severe alcohol dependence with almost total preoccupation with alcohol, episodes of alcohol withdrawal delirium, functional impairment, and an alcohol-related physical disorder.

These two cases illustrate the broad spectrum of psychopathology subsumed by the DSM-III-R criteria for dependence.

The polythetic approach of DSM-III-R to diagnosing substance dependence resolves some of the problems with the DSM-III categories of abuse and dependence while begging the issue on others. It is now possible, for example, to diagnose cocaine dependence and hallucinogen dependence in cases in which the drug-taking behavior has become compulsive and out of control, whether or not tolerance or withdrawal is present. On the other hand, the inclusion of tolerance and withdrawal in the diagnostic prototypes for dependence on these drugs may be interpreted as a shift of 180 degrees on the issue of whether such physiologically mediated concomitants of taking these drugs actually occur. Furthermore, evidence on the existence of tolerance or withdrawal is not what motivated the change; rather, it is the result of an overall broadening of the concept of the disorders that stems from a shift from a more classic category to the prototype. The controversy about the significance of tolerance in the diagnosis of alcoholism remains unresolved, as does differentiation of iatrogenic or inadvertent substance dependence.

The decisions to formulate the prototypic category as a list of 9 features (during original discussions, it was a list of 12) and to require 3 for the diagnosis have been evaluated in a small field trial assessing the significance of various different numbers of criteria that might serve as cut-points, i.e., the minimum number of features for diagnosis (15). This study demonstrated that a diagnostic threshold set at three or more DSM-III-R criteria yielded better levels of agreement between a DSM-III diagnosis of a substance use disorder, either dependence or abuse, and a DSM-III-R diagnosis of psychoactive substance dependence for all classes of substances except hallucinogens. Either increasing or decreasing the cut-point by one criterion lessened the agreement. DSM-III-R criteria diagnosed slightly more people as having a disorder related to the use of psychoactive substances than did DSM-III. In cases in which a diagnosis could be made by DSM-III, but not by DSM-III-R, the most common reason was that the DSM-III diagnosis of dependence was made solely on the basis of tolerance to the substance.

It has been shown, in general, that the most efficient diagnostic criteria depend on the rate at which the disorder is occurring in the population (base rate), and on the intended use of the diagnosis (16). With regard to substance use disorders, research has shown that it is easier to recognize a disorder in a clinical population in which the phenomenon is more common and more severe (17-20) than in a community sample in which cases are more rare and frequently milder (21-23).

A limitation of the field trial of DSM-III-R criteria is that it was conducted using only subjects recruited from two treatment settings. The authors of the field trial believe that the new definition of dependence will enable clinicians to make a diagnosis earlier in the course of a disorder, before social consequences are evident, because social consequences are no longer required for the diagnosis. This, presumably, would facilitate early intervention and, perhaps, prevention of the development of more severe disorders.

Research in substance dependence has yet to face adequately the need for external validation of alternative concepts of dependence (4). Shifts in concept like the one introduced in DSM-III-R need to be shown to define a population that has a maximally positive family history or maximal evidence of other known risk factors, suggests a particular treatment approach, or has a more uniform prognosis or short- or long-term outcome. Until such time as that is achieved, the concepts remain the products of strong opinions of certain professionals, but are of unknown scientific significance.

Dependence vs. Abuse

As was mentioned above, there was no strong theoretical support for the DSM-III distinction between substance abuse and substance dependence. Furthermore, in one of the few empirical studies testing the validity of the DSM-III division, Schuckit and his colleagues (24) found that the presenting clinical characteristics and course over a one-year follow-up period failed to distinguish people who met criteria for DSM-III alcohol abuse from those who met criteria for alcohol dependence.

Table 4.2 DSM-III-R Diagnostic Criteria for Psychoactive Substance Abuse

A. A maladaptive pattern of psychoactive substance use indicated by at least one of the following:

(1) continued use despite knowledge of having a persistent or recurrent social, occupational, psychological, or physical problem that is caused or exacerbated by use of the psychoactive substance
(2) recurrent use in situations in which use is physically hazardous (e.g., driving while intoxicated)

B. Some symptoms of the disturbance have persisted for at least one month, or have occurred repeatedly over a longer period of time.

C. Never met the criteria for psychoactive substance dependence for this substance.

In DSM-III-R, the category of psychoactive substance abuse is used as a residual category for diagnosing maladaptive patterns of psychoactive substance use that do not meet, and have never met, the criteria for dependence for that particular substance. Table 4.2 depicts the DSM-III-R diagnostic criteria for psychoactive substance abuse. If the person's problem has met criteria for dependence in the past, but now is beneath the threshold for the diagnosis or has been completely resolved, the diagnosis of dependence can be specified as "in partial remission" or "in full remission," according to the severity subtypes listed in Table 4.1.

RELATIONSHIP OF PSYCHOACTIVE SUBSTANCE USE DISORDERS TO OTHER MENTAL DISORDERS

The remaining major problems in differential diagnosis of psychoactive substance dependence have to do with the relationship of dependence diagnoses to other Axis I and II disorders and to each other when multiple substances are involved. Examples of the former problem are cases of schizophrenia, anxiety disorder, personality disorder, or psychoactive substance-induced organic mental disorders. Examples of the latter would include people who use alcohol, cannabis, and cocaine and/or other combinations of substances. Discussion of all of these situations, except the relationship of substance dependence to substance-induced organic mental disorders (discussed on page 146), follows in this section.

As mentioned previously, my experience indicates that clinicians underutilized DSM-III substance use disorders categories. This phenomenon occurs most often when the problem with psychoactive substances is not the presenting problem or reason for seeking treatment and when it is associated with another mental disorder (25-28). Patients undoubtedly tend to minimize difficulties associated with the use of such substances, but clinicians also appear to operate according to different "thresholds" for diagnosis, depending on the nature of the other psychopathology. It is easier, for example, for a clinician to recognize alcoholism or Valium dependence in a patient who has been self-medicating for an affective (mood) disorder or an anxiety disorder than in a patient with schizophrenia or with borderline personality disorder.

Many studies (29-33) have shown that people with primary diagnoses of substance use disorders have a wide range of other Axis I and II disorders as well. Most common are depressive disorders, antisocial personality disorder, and substance use disorders other than the principal diagnosis. Coexisting mental disorders may influence the prognosis of the substance use disorder (34-39) or indicate potentially beneficial treatment approaches (40,41).

For example, Schuckit (33), in a study of DSM-III alcohol dependence, found major prognostic differences among people with alcoholism depending on the presence and nature of other diagnosable disorders. Compared with patients with a primary diagnosis of alcoholism, *(1)* patients with alcoholism secondary to antisocial personality disorder had a poor prognosis for alcohol, drug, and social problems; *(2)* those with primary diagnoses of other substance use disorder had a greater likelihood of continued drug and social problems, although not as great as that for the patients with primary antisocial personality; and *(3)* patients with a primary mood disorder were more likely to abstain from use of alcohol following treatment, but were also more likely to have significant continuing depression. In primary alcoholism, depression tended to abate within days to weeks of abstinence.

In a substance dependence treatment setting, other major psychopathology may not always be recognized and therefore may go untreated. Treece (42) has proposed a special multiaxial format for dealing with this problem that designates separate axes for the substance use problem, other Axis I disorders, and Axis II disorders.

Substance Dependence and Mood Disorders

The DSM-III and DSM-III-R approaches encourage multiple diagnoses in cases in which this is warranted. In several different areas of psychiatric diagnosis, such as of the mood disorders, a primary-secondary distinction has been made when more than one diagnosis is applicable. The primary-secondary distinction traditionally has referred to the temporal relationships between syndromes, so that a substance dependence disorder that developed in a person with a recurrent or chronic affective disorder would be considered "secondary" to the "primary" mood disturbance. The primary-secondary distinction among the mood disorders has been shown to have significance with respect to external validators of diagnostic groups, such as family history, and to biological homogeneity. Much less is known about the significance of such a distinction in the case of substance use disorders, although there are some intriguing possibilities, with treatment relevance.

DSM-III and DSM-III-R do not use the primary-secondary distinction, but instead suggest that the clinician indicate which of the multiple diagnoses is to be considered the principal diagnosis, defined as the one currently requiring attention or treatment. Since substance dependence problems frequently require specialized treatment approaches [e.g., Alcoholics Anonymous (AA), Narcotics Anonymous (NA), or methadone maintenance], the diagnosis that is considered principal may depend on the point of view of the treating clinician. A general psychiatrist treating a patient with alcoholism superimposed on a recurrent major depression may regard the mood disorder as the principal diagnosis from the point of view of his or her decision to treat the patient with antidepressant medication, but the alcoholism counselor to whom the psychiatrist refers the patient may view the substance dependence as his or her principal focus of treatment when recommending AA.

In the case "A Man of Many Moods" in Chapter 2, the diagnosis of cocaine dependence could be viewed as a secondary complication of the mood disorder, cyclothymia. The development of cocaine dependence in relationship to preexisting affective disorder has received increasing attention as severe cocaine addiction has been on the rise. It has been reported that 20%-50% of people with cocaine dependence have underlying affective disturbances, including major depression, dysthymic and cyclothymic disorders, and bipolar disorder (43,44). Although it may be at first counterintuitive that a disorder that can cause mood elevation could lead to use of a euphoria-inducing drug, this patient's description and the prevalence of cocaine use among the successful and well-to-do make cocaine use in relation to these states more understandable. Similarly, it is doubtful that many professional athletes, another apparently high-risk group, are depressed; they are likely to be very active, energetic, self-assured. Sometimes, this personality style may be present in the extreme. In at least one publicized case, the athlete was described as buying and selling 16 cars in one year and endorsing three brands of tennis shoes simultaneously.

The relationship of cocaine dependence to mood disorder has led to one line of reasoning that suggests treatment approaches with medications therapeutic for the underlying condition, i.e., antidepressants and lithium (45). The observation that cocaine "crashes" are associated with intensely dysphoric affective states among chronic abusers has also suggested the usefulness of using antidepressant medication to treat cocaine dependence. Cocaine dependence leads to other differential diagnostic problems as well, since states of intoxication or withdrawal may be confused with manifestations of an underlying affective disorder.

The differential diagnosis of substance-induced organic mood syndrome will be discussed in a later section.

Substance Dependence and Personality Disorder

The next case illustrates a psychoactive substance use disorder in combination with a personality disorder. In a private practice setting, the treatment focus on the personality psychopathology may obscure the substance problem, especially when the diagnostic criteria include use of a psychoactive substance as one of the signs of the personality disorder.

The Showgirl

A 40-year-old former chorus-line dancer entered treatment following a bitterly contested divorce. She had been working as a receptionist for a large clothing manufacturer on 7th Avenue, but was having increasing difficulty getting to work.

Although her marriage had been fraught with difficulties—her husband openly cheated on her and was verbally cruel—once the divorce was finalized, the patient began to feel very anxious. She began to appear regularly at her internist's office with a variety of physical complaints, including dizziness, stomach pain, difficulty falling asleep, and feeling shaky. He started her on Valium, 2 mg BID. Over the course of a year, he gradually increased the dose to 5 mg QID, but the patient herself used even more. In addition, each evening the woman drank four or five cocktails or a bottle of wine, and frequently felt so "hung over" the next morning that she could not get out of bed. Occasionally she also had "one too many" at lunch, to rid herself of the "shakes." The internist finally referred her for psychiatric consultation.

The patient was a very attractive, though heavily made up, woman, looking slightly overweight, but still with long, thin, muscular dancer's legs, which were eye-catching beneath her short, above-the-knees, red satin dress. She related her story with considerable animation and emotion, sobbing uncontrollably at times and at other times beseeching the psychiatrist, "You look like such a nice man. You will help me, won't you?"

The patient's behavior during her marriage had been fairly unstable. At first she had been very enamored of her former husband, who was a young, but very successful, surgeon. She reluctantly admitted that later she became very jealous of his professional success, and was very "sulky" when he came home late or needed to be away at a meeting. She said she needed more of his attention. She actually began her heavy bouts of drinking while they were still married; often her husband would come home and find her "passed out" on the couch. Sometimes she took a few sleeping pills as well.

These incidents provoked numerous arguments in which there was "lots of yelling and throwing things" on her part and resulting cold hostility from him. On a couple of occasions, she superficially scratched her arms with a knife or a "pop-top" from a beer can. The more incidents there were, the further the husband withdrew from her and the more desperate the patient became.

When divorce was first discussed, the patient refused, fearing that she would not be able to "exist" on her own. Then the husband started to see other women and allowed them to call him at home, making no effort to conceal his extramarital affairs from his wife. Finally, with a comfortable financial settlement, she agreed to the divorce.

Regarding her symptoms of anxiety, the patient added that she was "frightened of everybody and everything." Most men she thought were going to attack her, and so she was constantly wary on the street or even in the office. She frequently "went blank" at work, or would shake so hard she couldn't hold a pencil. In addition to the Valium that she got from her internist, she had other supplies from her gynecologist and from a friend who was a doctor. At several times in the past year, she admitted, she had been taking 60-70 mg/day. Attempts to reduce the amount made her "too nervous."

In this case the patient clearly meets criteria for alcohol dependence. There is frequent preoccupation with alcohol use, frequent drinking of greater amounts than intended and being intoxicated and hung over at work, and impairment in social relationships because of alcohol. In addition, there is Valium dependence, because the patient exhibits tolerance, unsuccessful attempts to reduce Valium use, and withdrawal symptoms upon attempting to reduce the dosage. This syndrome is also an example of the iatrogenic or inadvertent psychoactive substance dependence syndrome, in that it was at least contributed to by the internist's attempts to treat the frequent anxiety states that accompanied her personality disorder with benzodiazepines. The patient, at the point when she sought psychiatric consultation, was maintaining an active role in the perpetuation of the dependence, and the syndrome was no longer purely "iatrogenic."

The Showgirl's Axis II disorder is best characterized as histrionic personality disorder with borderline traits. Although borderline personality traits (see Chapter 9) include impulsivity in at least two potentially self-damaging areas and substance use is an example, when the substance use leads to the dependence syndrome, additional diagnoses should be made, and the dependence syndrome undoubtedly will require treatment.

Dependence on Multiple Substances

DSM-III included an odd assortment of diagnoses for people who abused or were dependent on more than one substance. "Other, mixed, or unspecified substance abuse" could be used when the substances abused were from more than one nonalcoholic category, but this categorization was to be used only when the specific substances could not be identified or the abuse involved so many substances that the clinician preferred to note the combination rather than each specific substance. If the person had a dependence syndrome, then dependence on a combination of opioid and other nonalcoholic substances or dependence on a combination of substances excluding opioids and alcohol was the diagnostic choice.

The same rules of usage applied to these dependence diagnoses as to mixed substance abuse. These combination diagnoses resulted in a hierarchy that meant that alcohol abuse and dependence would be noted in all cases as separate diagnoses and that opioid dependence would be specifically noted in all cases in which it was present. Beyond these guidelines, however, there was no indication how many individual abuse or dependence diagnoses should be made; the threshold for the combination diagnoses was left up to the clinician.

The corresponding categories in DSM-III-R are polysubstance dependence and psychoactive substance dependence not otherwise specified (NOS). The former category is for a person who has, for a period of at least six months, "repeatedly used at least three categories of psychoactive substances (not including nicotine and caffeine), but no single psychoactive substance has predominated" (46, p. 185). The person may, during this period, have met the criteria for dependence on psychoactive substances as a group, but not for any one particular substance. Psychoactive substance dependence NOS is for a dependence on a substance that cannot be classified in the specific categories; anticholinergics are given as an example. It may also be used as an initial diagnosis when dependence is present, but the specific substance is not yet known.

These combination diagnoses are more helpful clinically than those of DSM-III. Individual dependence diagnoses are no longer left to the clinician's discretion; if the person's condition meets criteria for dependence on more than one psychoactive substance, multiple diagnoses are to be made.

One of the rationales for the increased specificity of diagnosis in the area of substance use in DSM-III over previous classifications (i.e., the classification by ten drug classes and the specification within the diagnostic class of the individual drug used) was to add information that might be helpful in planning treatment, e.g., barbiturate detoxification. Use of the combination dependence categories in DSM-III obscured the individual drugs involved and dissuaded the clinician from actively attempting to identify the individual drugs. In cases in which neuroadaptation had occurred, this had deleterious effects on the patient, who was at risk for a serious withdrawal syndrome, without the clinician's being aware of this. Now, thorough efforts to evaluate the clinical features associated with each drug used regularly and listing of individual diagnoses for every dependence syndrome known to be associated with significant neuroadaptation are required.

Finally, however, with regard to psychoactive substance dependence NOS, it is difficult, given the criteria, to imagine making a substance dependence diagnosis without knowledge of what the substance is. How, for example, can a person be preoccupied with taking a substance, develop tolerance to it, use it at times when he or she is expected to fulfill a social or occupational obligation, and not know what the substance is? In practice, the clinician may in some cases *suspect* substance dependence, because of certain situations or symptoms (e.g., missing work or therapy sessions, having slurred speech, having severe financial problems) that the patient *denies* are related to substance use; since in such cases the criteria for substance dependence are seldom actually met, the best diagnosis the clinician can make is a *provisional* one of psychoactive substance dependence NOS.

PSYCHOACTIVE SUBSTANCE-INDUCED ORGANIC MENTAL DISORDERS

In DSM-III and DSM-III-R the psychoactive substance-induced organic mental disorders are grouped with other organic mental disorders in order to emphasize the difference between the central nervous system effects and the behavioral/cognitive effects of psychoactive substance use. In this book these disturbances are discussed here with psychoactive substance dependence in order to emphasize the frequency with which they occur in people who abuse drugs or are drug dependent. Since the treatment of a number of the substance-induced organic mental disorders constitutes a psychiatric and/or medical emergency, their recognition has great clinical importance.

Problems with DSM-III Categories

The DSM-III diagnoses of substance-induced organic mental disorders consisted of the basic organic mental syndromes (see Chapter 3), plus intoxication and withdrawal, combined with the DSM-III classes of substances of abuse and dependence with which the syndromes were believed to occur. The only exception was that there was a syndrome of caffeine intoxication, but no caffeine abuse or dependence. Caffeine use does not seem to lead to social or occupational impairment, and caffeine withdrawal was considered clinically insignificant. For certain classes of drugs, a wide array of syndromes was described—e.g., for alcohol, seven, and for barbiturates, four. For others, only one or two syndromes were described—e.g., for opioids, intoxication and withdrawal, and for cocaine, intoxication only. Each of these syndromes was described by criteria referring to the particular physiological, psychological, and behavioral changes that were observed to be the direct effects of use, or reduction in use, of each substance on the brain.

A hierarchy existed within several of the syndromes described for each drug. For example, the acute ingestion of amphetamine might result in intoxication; a more severe reaction resulting in a delirium would take diagnostic precedence, although many features of intoxication might also be present. Similarly, "alcohol withdrawal" described the basic syndrome that resulted from cessation or reduction in use of alcohol in a person who had a neuroadaptation to alcohol. If the withdrawal syndrome was severe, i.e., produced delirium tremens, then the diagnosis of alcohol withdrawal delirium would apply. This system of hierarchies has been a source of confusion to some clinicians who are unfamiliar with the various categories within the drug subclasses.

Another problem with the DSM-III system was that clinicians began to find that the range of diagnoses available was inadequate to describe the syndromes encountered in practice. With the increasing numbers of patients coming for treatment of cocaine abuse, for example, clinicians encountered two syndromes characterized by severely dysphoric affect, one associated with heavy and progressive cocaine use, which seemed most like a substance-induced organic affective syndrome, and one associated with attempts to go without cocaine, which appeared to be a form of cocaine withdrawal. Neither of these syndromes was recognized by DSM-III. There was no diagnosis for a cocaine-induced psychosis, nor was there any residual syndrome under cocaine-induced OMDs for classifying these states. The next vignette describes one such clinical problem, which has become increasingly common in the 1980s.

A Specious Drug

"What is this? You tell me what this is!" the man shouted.

"What's *what?*" the girl replied, incredulously.

"This!" he said, pointing to some small pieces of lint that he had picked from behind the cushions of the couch. "Are you trying to tell me this isn't the drug? You're lying, you know that? You're lying!"

For the past two months the young man and his girlfriend had been having arguments over whether she was "stealing" his cocaine. The couple had been regular users during their two-year relationship, but lately the young man had become increasingly preoccupied with the notion that his girlfriend was seeing other men, and sharing his cocaine with them to boot. It all began gradually as he started to notice that his supply of the drug seemed smaller, each time he went back to use it, than he remembered it was from the previous time. He began repeatedly checking the drawer where he kept it, more and more often, until at the peak of his suspicion he sometimes opened the drawer 20 to 30 times in the course of a single hour.

Then he started noticing bits and pieces of what he decided was cocaine on the rug or between the couch pillows or in the kitchen cabinets where the dishes were kept. He fingered, smelled, and sometimes tasted cat hairs, lint, bread crumbs, scraps of paper, dust balls—every imaginable speck of white he saw—thinking that they were remnants of the cocaine powder that his girlfriend was using behind his back. Next, he began to peel back the edges of wallpaper at the seams—"Aha, here's some!" he would shout as he examined the pieces of paint or dust that adhered to the sticky surface. Finally, he dismantled the entire bathroom medicine cabinet, pulling it from the wall, wild-eyed as he was showered by bits of white plaster crumbling from the wall. "Now, I've got you!"

An organic delusional syndrome can develop following use of cocaine, particularly in heavy users. In the absence of this man's having a preexisting history of a functional psychotic disturbance (and any evidence that his girlfriend was cheating on him or stealing the substance), a diagnosis of cocaine-induced organic delusional disorder would be most likely, given the history of heavy use of cocaine. Toxicologic testing could be helpful if the patient were being evaluated within 48 hours of use. Resolution of the syndrome after a period of drug-free observation would confirm the diagnosis, although in cocaine- and amphetamine-induced delusional disorders, the clinical course can be protracted (up to a year).

Other examples of conditions that clinicians encountered, but for which there was no adequate DSM-III diagnosis, were the dementia associated with chronic heavy use of barbiturates, psychosis following PCP ingestion, and flashbacks from hallucinogen use. These and other inadequacies of clinical coverage led to some expansion of the categories of psychoactive substance-induced syndromes in DSM-III-R.

Expanded DSM-III-R Categories

There are ten new specific syndromes for substance-induced organic mental disorders in DSM-III-R. Table 4.3 summarizes the new substance-induced categories and compares the new schema with DSM-III. Recognition that additional types of drugs can cause delirium and mood and delusional disorders and introduction of a new syndrome of posthallucinogen perception disorder make for many additional differential diagnostic considerations in the difficult area of substance-induced vs. functional disorders.

Substance-Induced OMDs vs. Functional Disorders

DSM-III-R substance-induced organic mental disorders figure in the differential diagnoses of psychotic disorders, mood and anxiety disorders, dissociative disorders, and personality disorders. These problems are also addressed in the primary chapters in this book on the differential diagnosis of each of these syndromes.

Substance-induced disorders vs. psychotic disorders. Since many psychoactive substances can cause delusions and hallucinations and, in fact, have psychotomimetic effects that have been used as models of functional psychotic illness, the differential diagnosis between a psychotic syndrome due to a substance vs. a primary psychotic illness in a person who uses a psychoactive substance is a common one in many emergency and inpatient settings. In fact, it has been estimated that as many as one-third of patients admitted to psychiatric hospitals have a history of drug abuse (47).

In some cases the relative onsets of the drug use and the psychotic illness allow the clinician to determine that the person has a primary functional illness and that the substance abuse is important, but secondary. Exacerbations of psychosis in such people would usually not be thought of as substance induced. For a person without a previous history of a psychotic disorder who has used amphetamines, cannabis, or hallucinogens, for example, and presents with

Table 4.3 Psychoactive Substance-Induced Organic Mental Disorders in DSM-III and DSM-III-R

Class of Psychoactive Substance	Syndrome											
	Intoxi-cation	Idiosyn-cratic intoxi-cation	With-drawal	With-drawal delirium	Amnestic disorder	Dementia	Delirium	Delu-sional disorder	Halluci-nosis	Mood disorder	Per-ception disorder[1]	Mixed or other
Alcohol	o •	o •	o •	o •	o •	o •			o •			
Sedative/hypnotics	o •		o •	o •	o •							
Opioids	o •		o •									
Cocaine	o •		•				•	•				
Amphetamines	o •		o •				o •	o •				
Phencyclidine	o •						o •	•		•		o •
Hallucinogen								o •	o •	o •	•	
Cannabis	o •							o •				
Nicotine (tobacco)			o •									
Caffeine	o •											
Inhalant	•											
Other or unspecified	o •		•		o •	o •	o •	o •	o •	o •		o •[2]

Key: DSM-III = o; DSM-III-R = •.

[1]Full name is posthallucinogen perception disorder.

[2]In DSM-III there were separate categories for other or unspecified substance-induced atypical or mixed organic mental disorder and personality disorder. In DSM-III-R there are separate categories for Other or unspecified psychoactive substance-induced organic mental disorder NOS, personality disorder, and anxiety disorder.

delusions or hallucinations that persist beyond the expected duration of the drug action, the question of whether the drug has caused this syndrome or merely served as a precipitant of a first episode of an underlying, primary psychotic disorder is critical. Although acute treatment, i.e., antipsychotic pharmacotherapy, may be indicated in either case, decision on planning long-term treatment, in terms of maintenance antipsychotic medication or rehabilitative measures, will vary depending on how the basic disturbance is understood.

A number of investigators have addressed this problem over the years (48-51). Problems in study design have made conclusions about the role of drugs in the onset and course of psychotic disturbances difficult to draw. However, several recent studies present consistent findings that may help the clinician in differential diagnosis.

Tsuang and his colleagues (47) report that drug-abusing patients with psychoses of short duration had better premorbid functioning than either those with psychoses of longer duration associated with drug abuse or those with schizophrenic illnesses without a history of drug abuse. The patients who had been ill longer had poorer insight, more disorganized thoughts, flat or inappropriate affect, more delusions, and more Schneiderian first-rank symptoms. The presence of depression, auditory or visual hallucinations, disorientation, or memory deficit did not distinguish between the two groups. A positive family history for schizophrenia or for affective disorder characterized the longer duration reactions compared with those of the shorter duration.

The conclusion that might be drawn is that the longer the psychosis lasts, the less relative importance the drug use itself may have for the disturbance: personality and constitutional (genetic) factors become more important, and the disturbance resembles a functional illness, the drug reaction serving the role of a precipitant. In Tsuang's terms (47), the longer duration drug-related syndromes were more like atypical schizophrenia, which is closer to the DSM-III concepts of schizophreniform disorder or of bipolar disorder, manic, with mood-incongruent features, than to schizophrenia itself. Thus, the ultimate differential diagnosis might require a period of follow-up of six months or more. For all patients with pictures of psychotic features apparently induced by drugs, periodic diagnostic and prognostic reassessments are sound clinical practice.

LSD-induced psychoses have been the focus of recent study. Vardy and Kay (52) found on follow-up of a series of patients with LSD-induced psychoses that they were fundamentally similar to patients with schizophrenia in terms of symptoms, family history, and course of illness. This study is consistent with the interpretation that when an apparent drug-induced psychotic syndrome persists beyond

Table 4.4 DSM-III-R Diagnostic Criteria for Posthallucinogen Perception Disorder

A. The reexperiencing, following cessation of use of a hallucinogen, of one or more of the perceptual symptoms that were experienced while intoxicated with the hallucinogen, e.g., geometric hallucinations, false perceptions of movement in the peripheral visual fields, flashes of color, intensified colors, trails of images from moving objects, positive afterimages, halos around objects, macropsia, and micropsia.

B. The disturbance in A causes marked distress.

C. Other causes of the symptoms, such as anatomic lesions and infections of the brain, delirium, dementia, sensory (visual) epilepsies, schizophrenia, entoptic imagery, and hypnopompic hallucinations, have been ruled out.

the duration of the drug action, the role of the drug is best considered a precipitant of, but not etiologically responsible for, the psychosis.

Posthallucinogen perception disorder (PHPD) is yet another diagnosis that must be distinguished from others with psychotic features. The criteria for this disorder (see Table 4.4) include flashbacks. Flashbacks are transient, spontaneous recurrences of an hallucinogen's acute effects appearing after a period during which the person has not been using the substance (53). Less is known about the relationship of other underlying psychopathology to the occurrence of flashbacks (54) than to other substance-induced psychotic syndromes. Perhaps the best guidelines for distinguishing flashback phenomena from hallucinations of functional psychotic illness, in the absence of a clear history concerning past hallucinogen use, are the phenomena themselves. Few psychotic syndromes are so restricted in their manifestations. Also, people with flashbacks are almost always aware that they are pathologic. Clinicians should be wary about interpreting too diverse a clinical picture as a flashback.

Substance-induced disorders vs. mood disorders. Numerous substances are known to induce mood disturbances, both depression and mania, and anxiety symptoms. Drugs, medications, and poisons that should be considered in the differential diagnosis of patients with affective and anxiety symptoms are listed in Table 4.5. DSM-III and DSM-III-R include a diagnosis "other or unspecified psychoactive substance mood disorder," and DSM-III-R has added a comparable diagnosis for anxiety disorder for medications or poisons that induce organic mental disorders. Not to be forgotten, however, are the

Table 4.5 Psychoactive Substances, Medications, and Poisons That Can Cause Symptoms of Mood Disturbance or Anxiety

Substance	Depression/dysphoria	Euphoria/irritability	Anxiety/nervousness
Alcohol	•	•	•
Amphetamines	•	•	•
Antipsychotics	•		
Barbiturates and other sedative/hypnotics	•	•	•
Bromides and heavy metals	•		
Caffeine			•
Cannabis		•	•
Carbon disulfide	•		
Carbon monoxide	•		
Cocaine	•	•	•
Digitalis	•		
Hallucinogens	•		•
Inhalants		•	
Lead poisoning	•		
Methyldopa	•		
Nicotine		•	•
Opioids	•	•	
Oral contraceptives	•		
Phencyclidine	•		•
Propranolol	•		
Reserpine	•		
Steroids	•	•	•

intoxication or withdrawal states of the major psychoactive drugs. Alcohol and barbiturate intoxication list mood change among the definitional items; opioid, cocaine, amphetamine, and cannabis intoxication mention euphoria or grandiosity (opioid intoxication also includes dysphoria) and other symptoms associated with the manic syndrome. Alcohol, amphetamine, and barbiturate withdrawal include depressed mood or irritability. Invariably, the differential diagnosis must be made on the basis of the presence of physical symptoms, the history of drug ingestion, and/or toxicologic studies.

A mood syndrome that is still not well covered by the DSM-III-R substance-induced group is the dysphoria that accompanies progressive cocaine use. Many patients present to cocaine abuse treatment facilities with a history of weeks or months of symptoms of the full depressive syndrome at virtually all times other than when acutely intoxicated. The syndrome coincides in time with a period of escalating cocaine use, may or may not be associated with preexisting mood disorder, and appears to play a role in "driving" the user to increasingly larger quantities in order to relieve the symptoms. The syndrome can be considered to be the acute effects of cocaine withdrawal (DSM-III criteria describe depressed mood, fatigue, and disturbed sleep); but there is some evidence that cocaine itself, at times of maximal use, depletes the store of neurotransmitters associated with depression, and that this might actually be a cocaine-induced affective disturbance. Until the nature of cocaine effects and the syndromes associated with it are better understood, clinicians using DSM-III-R will diagnose this condition as cocaine withdrawal.

The longer the period of abstinence before the evaluation, the less likely it is that the persistence of a dysphoric mood represents the effects of cocaine withdrawal. Although the course of cocaine withdrawal depression has not been thoroughly studied, experienced clinicians expect this depression to show signs of resolving within one week of the patient's being drug free (55,56).

One recently completed study sheds some light on the symptomatology of the abstinence period following a cocaine binge and its temporal progression. Gawin and Kleber (11) describe a triphasic course for symptoms occurring in the period following cessation of cocaine use. In the first phase, lasting from several hours up to six days, patients reported typical crash symptoms consisting of depression, anhedonia, insomnia, irritability, anxiety, confusion, suicidal ideation, paranoia, and gradually diminishing cocaine craving. These syndromes were sometimes severe enough to meet DSM-III criteria for major depression except that they were of short duration and related to organic factors. At the end of the phase, patients were hypersomnolent. In the second phase, termed "the withdrawal phase" by these authors, mood began to be euthymic; but as time went by, anhedonia, mild dysphoria, anergia, anxiety, and irritability returned. These symptoms recurred after one to five days of normal mood, and could persist for up to ten weeks if the person resisted cocaine use, for it was during this period that craving for the euphoric effects of cocaine reemerged and frequently led to relapse bingeing. If abstinence could be sustained, then a third phase ensued, with normal mood and episodic cocaine craving that was precipitated by environmental cues. Gawin and Kleber believe that it is inappropriate to refer to the cocaine crash as withdrawal because it is not during this period that the maximum risk of resuming cocaine abuse occurs. Rather, they believe that the middle of phase two is associated with the greatest likelihood of relapse. If a neuroendocrine basis for phase-two symptoms can be established (57), the process might better be termed *neuroadaptation* rather than withdrawal.

When the depression associated with cocaine abstinence does not remit, the clinician should suspect a nonorganic disorder. Since cocaine abuse can have many negative effects on a patient's marital, occupational, financial, and family life, it is possible that peristent depression represents a stressor-induced disorder. If the symptoms are relatively mild or of brief duration, they may represent an adjustment disorder with depressed mood. If there is a significant, serious depressive episode, it may be major depression, and the severity of the psychosocial stressors should be recorded on Axis IV of the multiaxial system. Whether the episode should be considered a first one or a recurrence of an underlying disorder precipitated by stress depends on the assessment of the past history.

Substance-induced disorders vs. anxiety disorders. With respect to anxiety symptoms, anxiety and nervousness are mentioned in the diagnostic criteria for alcohol withdrawal, barbiturate withdrawal, alcohol hallucinosis, cocaine delusional disorder, amphetamine delusional disorder, PCP intoxication, and caffeine intoxication. The absence of psychotic symptoms rules out delusional disorders and hallucinosis. PCP is associated with physiological and other psychological changes. Caffeinism is a cause of anxiety symptoms in a general medical setting, and unsuspected alcohol or other sedative withdrawal is probably a very common cause of anxiety in medical and psychiatric clinics and hospitals. Since the consequences of acute sedative or hypnotic withdrawal can be physically serious, it is often better to diagnose these syndromes provisionally when there is a reasonable suspicion of their presence and to treat the patient prophylactically with a detoxification regimen.

Posthallucinogen perception disorder may be confused with the intrusive recollections of past highly traumatic experiences that characterize the anxiety disorder posttraumatic stress disorder (PTSD). This can be a particularly difficult differential diagnosis to make in a person, such as a Vietnam War veteran, with a history of past hallucinogen experience and exposure to high stress. The distinction may be even less clear using DSM-III-R criteria for PTSD, which mention hallucinations and flashbacks as possible ways in which the traumatic event is reexperienced (see Chapter 7). The intrusive thoughts in PTSD are classically of the trauma itself, for example, reliving an episode of being under heavy fire or witnessing the death of fellow soldiers; flashback phenomena do not usually have a content that is thematically consistent or repetitive, or that is well-formed. PTSD patients may also have other symptoms of the disorder, including other forms of reexperiencing the trauma (e.g., dreams, reliving experiences), avoidance behavior or numbing (e.g., avoidance of thoughts and activities associated with the trauma, markedly diminished interest), and symptoms of increased arousal (e.g., insomnia, irritability, hypervigilance). If both disorders are present, both diagnoses can be given.

Substance-induced disorders vs. personality disorders. Periods of intoxication accompanied by mood lability, irritability, and aggressive behavior may suggest the presence of a personality disorder characterized by poor impulse control, such as borderline or antisocial personality disorder. Obviously, these disorders include other characteristic behaviors as well (see Chapter 9, Personality Disturbances). Because of the high frequency of drug use among certain personality types (30,32,58,59), substance-induced organic mental disorder diagnoses may often be made as additional diagnoses for people with an Axis II disturbance. If a particular symptom of suspected personality disturbance is limited to periods of intoxication, it should be considered a state-dependent phenomenon, not a personality trait. For example, if a person has a volatile temper only when intoxicated, this will not meet the borderline criterion for inappropriate, intense anger. Multiaxial diagnosis helps the clinician conceptualize the problems of patients with diagnoses of both psychoactive substance-induced organic mental disorder and personality disorder.

SUMMARY

This chapter examines difficulties in differential diagnosis presented by the DSM-III classification of substance use disorders and substance-induced organic mental disorders and the proposed solutions of DSM-III-R. Highlights of the new system include a uniform category of dependence emphasizing impairment in control over drug use, a polythetic diagnostic approach indicating a gradient of severity for psychoactive substance dependence, and the introduction of several new categories of substance-induced organic mental disorder. Problems with the revised system are anticipated, and clarifications are offered.

REFERENCES

1. Skodol AE, Williams JBW, Spitzer RL, Gibbon M, Kass F: Identifying common errors in the use of DSM-III through diagnostic supervision. Hosp Comunity Psychiatry 35:251–255, 1984
2. Caetano R: Two versions of dependence: DSM-III and the alcohol dependence syndrome. Drug Alcohol Depend 15(1–2):81–103, 1985
3. Rounsaville BJ, Spitzer RL, Williams JBW: Proposed changes in DSM-III

substance use disorders: description and rationale. Am J Psychiatry 143:463–468, 1986

4. Rounsaville BJ: Substance use disorders, in An Annotated Bibliography of DSM-III. Edited by Skodol AE, Spitzer RL. Washington, DC, American Psychiatric Press, 1987, pp 77–83
5. Brechner EM: Licit and Illicit Drugs. Mount Vernon, NY, Consumers Union, 1972
6. Hughes JR, Gust SW, Pechacek TF: Prevalence of tobacco dependence and withdrawal. Am J Psychiatry 144:205–207, 1987
7. Spitzer RL, Williams JBW, Skodol AE: DSM-III: the major achievements and an overview. Am J Psychiatry 137:151–164, 1980
8. Kuehnle J, Spitzer R: DSM-III classification of substance use disorders, in Substance Abuse: Clinical Problems and Perspectives. Edited by Lowinson JH. Baltimore, Williams & Wilkins, 1981, pp 19–23
9. Skodol AE: Diagnostic issues in cocaine abuse, in Cocaine Abuse: New Directions in Treatment and Research. Edited by Spitz HI, Rosecan JS. New York, Brunner/Mazel, 1987, pp 119–137
10. Post RM, Kopanda RT: Cocaine, kindling, and psychosis. Am J Psychiatry 133:627–632, 1976
11. Gawin FH, Kleber HD: Abstinence symptomatology and psychiatric diagnosis in cocaine abusers: clinical observations. Arch Gen Psychiatry 43:107–113, 1986
12. Edwards G, Gross MM: Alcohol dependence: provisional description of a clinical syndrome. Br Med J 1:1058–1061, 1976
13. Edwards G, Arif A, Hodgson R: Nomenclature and classification of drug and alcohol related problems. Bull WHO 59:225–242, 1981
14. Edwards G: The alcohol dependence syndrome: a concept as stimulus to inquiry. Br J Addict 81:171–183, 1986
15. Rounsaville BJ, Kosten TR, Williams JBW, Spitzer RL: A field trial of DSM-III-R psychoactive substance dependence disorders. Am J Psychiatry 144:351–355, 1987
16. Finn SE: Base rates, utilities, and DSM-III: shortcomings of fixed-rule systems of psychodiagnosis. J Abnorm Psychol 91:294–302, 1982
17. Singerman B, Stoltzman RK, Robins LN, Helzer JE, Croughan JL: Diagnostic concordance between DSM-III, Feighner, and RDC. J Clin Psychiatry 42:422–426, 1981
18. Craig TJ, Goodman AB, Haugland G: Impact of DSM-III on clinical practice. Am J Psychiatry 139:922–925, 1982
19. Hesselbrock V, Stabenau J, Hesselbrock M, Mirkin P, Meyer R: A comparison of two interview schedules: the Schedule for Affective Disorders and Schizophrenia–Lifetime and the National Institute for Mental Health Diagnostic Interview Schedule. Arch Gen Psychiatry 39:674–677, 1982
20. Boyd JH, Derr K, Grossman B, Lee C, Sturgeon S, Lacock DD, Bruder CI: Different definitions of alcoholism, II: A pilot study of 10 definitions in a treatment setting. Am J Psychiatry 140:1314–1317, 1983
21. Rounsaville BJ, Rosenberger P, Wilber CS, Weissman MM, Kleber HD: A comparison of the SADS/RDC and the DSM-III. Diagnosing drug abusers. J Nerv Ment Dis 168:90–97, 1980
22. Boyd JH, Weissman MM, Thompson WD, Myers JK: Different definitions of alcoholism, I: Impact of seven definitions on prevalence rates in a community survey. Am J Psychiatry 149:1309–1313, 1983
23. Leonard KE, Bromet EJ, Parkinson DK, Day N: Agreement among

Feighner, RDC and DSM-III criteria for alcoholism. Addict Behav 9:319–322, 1984

24. Schuckit MA, Zisook S, Mortola J: Clinical implications of DSM-III diagnoses of alcohol abuse and alcohol dependence. Am J Psychiatry 142:1403–1408, 1985
25. Crowley T, Chesluk O, Dilts S, Hart R: Drug and alcohol abuse among psychiatric admissions: a multidrug clinical toxicologic study. Arch Gen Psychiatry 30:13–20, 1974
26. Fischer DE, Halikas JA, Baker JW, Smith JB: Frequency and patterns of drug abuse in psychiatric patients. Dis Nerv System 36:550–553, 1975
27. Reichler BD, Clement JL, Dunner DL: Chart review of alcohol problems in adolescent psychiatric patients in an emergency room. J Clin Psychiatry 44:338–339, 1983
28. Hasin D, Endicott J, Lewis C: Alcohol and drug abuse in patients with affective syndromes. Compr Psychiatry 26:283–295, 1985
29. Kosten TR, Rounsaville BJ, Kleber HD: DSM-III personality disorders in opiate addicts. Compr Psychiatry 23:572–581, 1982
30. Hesselbrock MN, Meyer RE, Keener JJ: Psychopathology in hospitalized alcoholics. Arch Gen Psychiatry 42:1050–1055, 1985
31. Khantzian EJ, Treece C: DSM-III psychiatric diagnosis of narcotic addicts. Recent findings. Arch Gen Psychiatry 42:1067–1071, 1985
32. Powell BJ, Penick EC, Othmer E, Bingham SF, Rice AS: Prevalence of additional psychiatric syndromes among male alcoholics. J Clin Psychiatry 43:404–407, 1982
33. Schuckit MA: The clinical implications of primary diagnostic groups among alcoholics. Arch Gen Psychiatry 42:1043–1049, 1985
34. Rounsaville BJ, Tierney T, Crits-Christoph K, Weissman MM, Kleber HD: Predictors of treatment outcome in opiate addicts: evidence for the multidimensionality of addicts' problems. Compr Psychiatry 23:462–478, 1982
35. Rounsaville BJ, Weissman MM, Wilber CH, Crits-Christoph K, Kleber HD: Diagnosis and symptoms of depression in opiate addicts: course and relationship to treatment outcome. Arch Gen Psychiatry 39:151–156, 1982
36. McLellan AT, Luborsky L, Woody GE, O'Brien CP, Droler K: Predicting response to alcohol and drug abuse treatments: role of psychiatric severity. Arch Gen Psychiatry 40:620–625, 1983
37. Kosten TR, Rounsaville BJ, Kleber HD: A 2.5-year follow-up of depression, life crises, and treatment effects on abstinence among opioid addicts. Arch Gen Psychiatry 43:733–739, 1986
38. Rounsaville BJ, Kosten TR, Weissman MM, Kleber HD: Prognostic significance of psychopathology in treated opiate addicts. A 2.5 year followup study. Arch Gen Psychiatry 43:739–745, 1986
39. Rounsaville BJ, Dolinsky ZS, Babor TF, Meyer RE: Psychopathology as a predictor of treatment outcome in alcoholics. Arch Gen Psychiatry 44:505–513, 1987
40. Woody GE, McLellan AT, Luborsky L, O'Brien CP: Psychiatric severity as a predictor of benefits from psychotherapy: The Penn-VA study. Am J Psychiatry 141:1172–1177, 1984
41. Woody GE, McLellan AT, Luborsky L, O'Brien CP: Sociopathy and psychotherapy outcome. Arch Gen Psychiatry 42:1081–1086, 1985
42. Treece C: DSM-III as a research tool. Am J Psychiatry 139:577–583, 1982
43. Weiss RD, Mirin SM, Michael JL: Psychopathology in chronic cocaine abusers. Presented at the 136th Annual Meeting of the American Psychiatric Association, New York, May 4, 1983

44. Gawin FH, Kleber HD: Cocaine abuse treatment: open clinical trial with desipramine and lithium carbonate. Arch Gen Psychiatry 41:903–909, 1984
45. Rosecan JS, Nunes EV: Pharmacological management of cocaine abuse, in Cocaine Abuse: New Directions in Treatment and Research. Edited by Spitz HI, Rosecan JS. New York, Brunner/Mazel, 1987, pp 255–270
46. American Psychiatric Association: Diagnostic and Statistical Manual of Mental Disorders, Third Edition, Revised. Washington, DC, American Psychiatric Association, 1987
47. Tsuang MT, Simpson JC, Kronfol Z: Subtypes of drug abuse with psychosis: demographic characters, clinical features, and family history. Arch Gen Psychiatry 39:141–147, 1982
48. Bowers MB Jr: Acute psychosis induced by psychotomimetic drug abuse: I. Clinical findings. Arch Gen Psychiatry 27:437–440, 1972
49. Bowers MB Jr: Psychoses precipitated by psychotomimetic drugs: a follow-up study. Arch Gen Psychiatry 34:832–835, 1977
50. Young B: A phenomenological comparison of LSD and schizophrenic states. Br J Psychiatry 124:64–74, 1974
51. Erard R, Luisada PV, Peale R: The PCP psychosis: prolonged intoxication or drug-induced functional illness? J Psychedelic Drugs 12:235–251, 1980
52. Vardy MM, Kay SR: LSD psychosis or LSD-induced schizophrenia? A multimethod inquiry. Arch Gen Psychiatry 40:877–883, 1983
53. Strassman RJ: Adverse reaction to psychedelic drugs. A review of the literature. J Nerv Ment Dis 172:577–595, 1984
54. Alarcon RD, Dickinson WA, Dohn HH: Flashback phenomena: clinical and diagnostic dilemmas. J Nerv Ment Dis 170:217–223, 1982
55. Siegal RK: Cocaine smoking. J Psychoactive Drugs 14:321–337, 1982
56. Smith DE: Diagnostic treatment and aftercare approaches to cocaine abuse. J Substance Abuse Treat 1:5–9, 1984
57. Gawin FH, Kleber HD: Neuroendocrine findings in chronic cocaine abusers: a preliminary report. Br J Psychiatry 147:569–573, 1985
58. Grande TP, Wolf AW, Schubert DSP, Patterson MB, Brocco K: Associations among alcoholism, drug abuse, and antisocial personality: a review of literature. Psychol Rep 55:455–474, 1984
59. Treece C, Nicholson B: DSM-III personality type and dose levels in methadone maintenance patients. J Nerv Ment Dis 168:621–628, 1980

CHAPTER 5

Psychotic Features

The DSM-III approach to the classification and diagnosis of disorders with prominent psychotic features represented a radical departure from DSM-II and other traditional approaches. Central to the controversial approach taken by DSM-III was the considerable narrowing of the concept of schizophrenia. Requiring an active phase of psychosis, functional deterioration, six months' duration of illness, and no prominent or persistent affective syndrome concurrent with the psychosis all excluded patients who, in other diagnostic systems, would have been diagnosed as having schizophrenia and assigned them to different diagnostic categories—other psychotic disorders, mood disorders, or even personality disorders. The goal was to define a category of schizophrenia that was more homogeneous with respect to important clinical variables and more typical of the severe mental disorder originally described by Kraepelin as dementia praecox.

DSM-III schizophrenia and other psychotic disorders have been the subjects of a substantial number of empirical studies. Many of these have supported the validity of DSM-III distinctions in terms of clinical usefulness, and others have suggested that some new or additional distinctions among the disorders be made. In DSM-III-R, the practice of dividing the psychotic disorders into smaller, more clinically meaningful groups is maintained and the multiple distinctions that therefore need to be made make the differential diagnosis of psychotic features particularly difficult.

Overview of Differential Diagnosis

The differential diagnosis of a mental disorder characterized by psychotic features proceeds according to a logic based on the following sequence of questions:

1. Are the patient's symptoms, in fact, indicative of psychosis?
2. Is an organic factor etiologically related to the disturbance?

3. Are the psychotic symptoms typical of schizophrenia?

4. Has there been a deterioration in functioning?

5. Has there been a period during which there were continuous signs of disturbance for at least six months?

6. Did the psychosis develop in reaction to a severely stressful life event?

7. Are there also symptoms of a mood disturbance and, if so, how are these related in time to the development of the psychotic symptoms?

8. What was the age at onset of the disorder?

These questions form the basis of the revised decision tree for the differential diagnosis of psychotic features included in DSM-III-R (see Figure 5.1). Although the revision represents an improvement (1) in the guidelines to this particularly difficult area of differential diagnosis over those included in DSM-III, each question involves considerations and determinations that are not trivial. The diagnoses represented by the decision tree are summarized in Table 5.1.

What Is Psychosis?

Before the advent of DSM-III, the meanings of the terms *psychosis* and *psychotic disorder* were confusing. Some clinicians used *psychosis* to refer to particular modes of thinking, usually termed *primary process*

Table 5.1 Disorders in the Differential Diagnosis of Psychotic Features

ORGANIC MENTAL DISORDERS
- Delirium
- Dementia
- Organic delusional syndrome
- Organic hallucinosis

SCHIZOPHRENIA

MOOD DISORDERS
- Major depression with psychotic features
- Bipolar disorder with psychotic features

DELUSIONAL (PARANOID DISORDER)

PSYCHOTIC DISORDERS NOT ELSEWHERE CLASSIFIED
- Brief reactive psychosis
- Schizophreniform disorder
- Schizoaffective disorder
- Induced psychotic disorder
- Psychotic disorder not otherwise specified

thinking, while others referred to certain observable signs or symptoms. The former definition was abstract in nature, involved relatively high levels of inference on the part of the clinician, and was, therefore, unreliable. The latter definition was complicated by the confounding of certain *types* of symptoms with the *severity* of a wide variety of symptoms. Severity was a criterion for psychosis in the DSM-II and ICD-9 classifications of mental disorders, the specification being that "the individual is unable to meet the ordinary demands of life."

These misleading and ambiguous variations in the meaning of the term *psychosis* undoubtedly contributed to the mediocre levels of diagnostic reliability for the general diagnosis of "psychosis" reported by Spitzer and Fleiss (2) in their review of reliability studies of psychiatric diagnosis in the prediagnostic criteria era.

Determining the Presence of Psychotic Features

The glossary definition of *psychotic* in DSM-III required that the clinician find evidence of a gross deficit in reality testing, usually indicated by the presence of delusions or hallucinations. According to DSM-III and DSM-III-R, use of the term *psychotic* may also be appropriate "when a person's behavior is so grossly disorganized that a reasonable inference can be made that reality testing is markedly impaired" (3, p. 404). Markedly incoherent speech without awareness by the person that the speech is not understandable would be included.

The definitions of delusions in DSM-III and DSM-III-R require that the clinician make two additional judgments: (*1*) that the false beliefs are not understandable in relation to the person's subcultural group, and (*2*) that they are firmly held. Hallucinations are indicative of psychosis only when the person experiencing them has no insight into their pathological nature. These judgments require the clinician's interpretation that a person's thoughts, perceptions, speech, or behavior deviate significantly from hypothesized norms before any criterion referring to the presence of psychotic features can be met. Such judgments are among the most difficult that mental health professionals have to make, and often are of obviously great consequence to patients since they may be the basis for determining a particular course of treatment and/or whether a person may be involuntarily hospitalized, or be held responsible for criminal acts.

Assessing Subcultural Relativity

In the case of delusions, a common difficulty is distinguishing an unusual belief, or set of beliefs, not shared by many people from a

Figure 5.1 DSM-III-R Decision Tree for the Differential Diagnosis of Psychotic Features

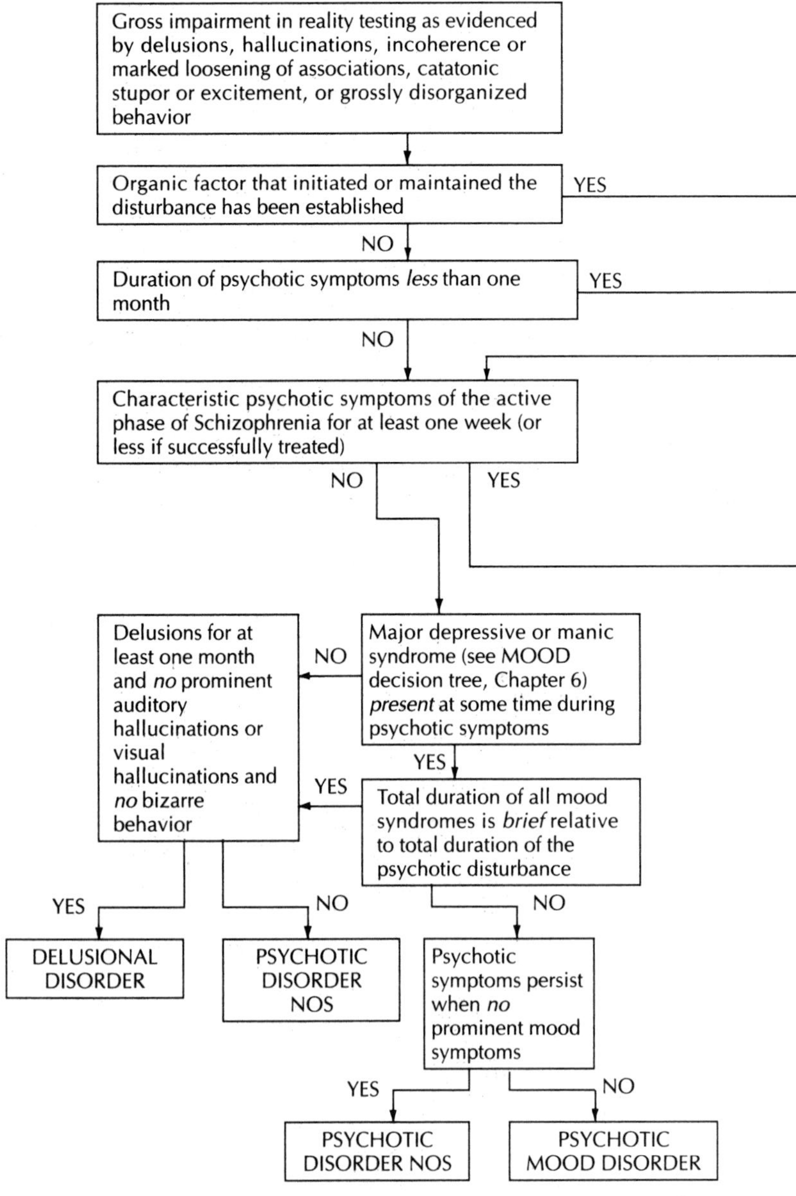

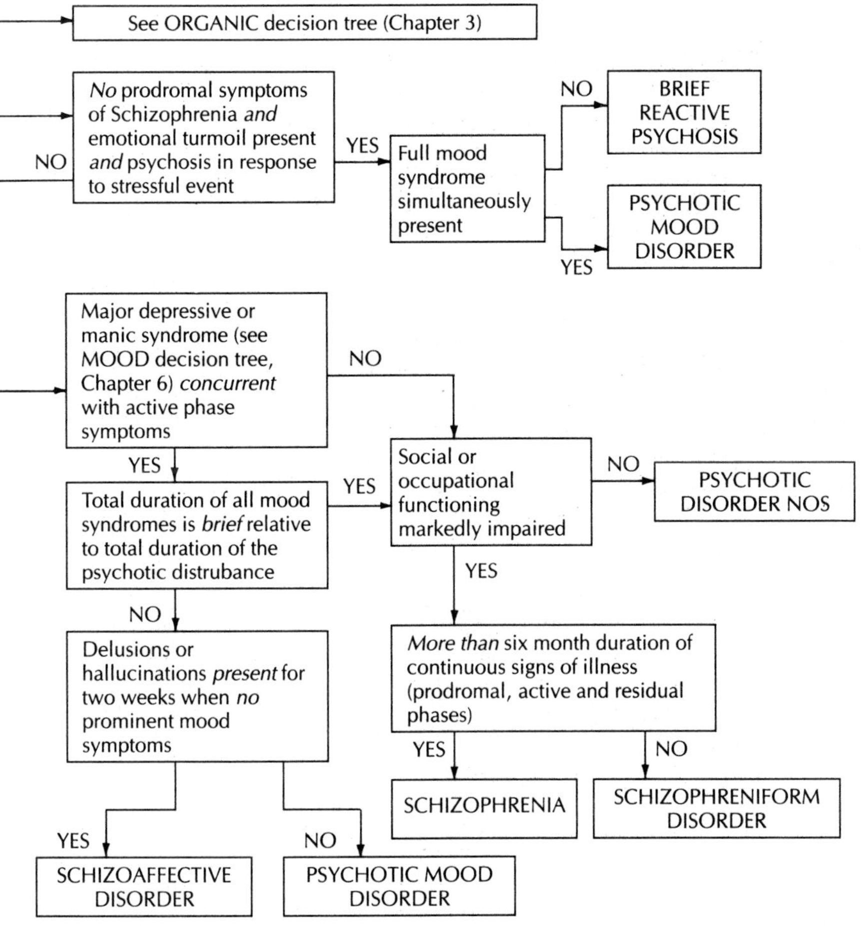
See ORGANIC decision tree (Chapter 3)
No prodromal symptoms of Schizophrenia *and* emotional turmoil present *and* psychosis in response to stressful event
NO
YES
Full mood syndrome simultaneously present
NO
BRIEF REACTIVE PSYCHOSIS
YES
PSYCHOTIC MOOD DISORDER
Major depressive or manic syndrome (see MOOD decision tree, Chapter 6) *concurrent* with active phase symptoms
NO
YES
Total duration of all mood syndromes is *brief* relative to total duration of the psychotic distrubance
YES
Social or occupational functioning markedly impaired
NO
PSYCHOTIC DISORDER NOS
YES
More than six month duration of continuous signs of illness (prodromal, active and residual phases)
YES
SCHIZOPHRENIA
NO
SCHIZOPHRENIFORM DISORDER
NO
Delusions or hallucinations *present* for two weeks when *no* prominent mood symptoms
YES
SCHIZOAFFECTIVE DISORDER
NO
PSYCHOTIC MOOD DISORDER

completely idiosyncratic belief that has no support from a subcultural group. A prototype of the problem follows. The patient being evaluated believes in animism, i.e., in spiritual beings.

Espíritu Errante[1]

A 25-year-old, recently widowed Puerto Rican mother of two was brought to the psychiatric emergency department of a large municipal hospital in New York City by three of her neighbors. The women had just come from a *misa,* a gathering of *espiriteros,* or mediums, of the Hispanic *espiritismo,* or spiritualism, belief.

The woman had asked for the help of one of her neighbors who was known to be a medium because her two children were having problems. The older, a boy aged nine, had become very rebellious at home and had been caught stealing the week before. The younger, a girl aged seven, was having nightmares and was refusing to go to school. Their mother feared that they might be possessed by an *espíritu errante,* or evil spirit, that was influencing their behavior negatively. The children's father, a grocery clerk, had been killed in a robbery of the store one month before.

The *misa* was attended by a number of the woman's neighbors who possessed the *facultades,* or abilities, to contact the spirit world. When it came time for the woman herself to go into a trance so that her spirits might be contacted, a problem developed. During the ritualistic chanting of prayers, the woman appeared to become more and more agitated. The most powerful of the mediums attempted a *despojo,* or exorcism of an evil spirit, which she thought might, in fact, be possessing the woman; but instead of responding, the woman turned on the medium and attempted to strangle her. At the same time, she claimed that she was the Devil, was more powerful than all the others in attendance, and had been instructed to kill them. When the group realized that she was not responding to their prayers, they grabbed her, put her in a car, and drove her to the hospital.

When examined by the psychiatrist, the woman was at first calmer. She appeared, however, to be having conversations with multiple other people who were not in the room, and her eyes periodically darted from one corner of the ceiling to another, as if she were responding to calls or other auditory stimuli. She would not answer the psychiatrist's questions; instead, she rambled on in a mixture of Spanish and English. Twice she suddenly jumped up from her chair and ran to the door to leave the interviewing room, looking panicked. Security was called to make sure she did not run away.

In an attempt to understand the patient's monologue, the psychiatrist called in the principal *espiritista,* who had come with the group to act as interpreter. The medium said the woman was talking about being the Devil and having supernatural powers and confirmed the apparent conversations with other *entidades,* or spirits, but also admitted that there was much the woman was saying that did not make sense. Concerning the relationship of the woman's current behavior and speech to the *espiritismo* meeting that evening, the medium shook her head and said, "Doctor, the *misa* is over."

In this case, the patient is a member of a cultural group that practices *espiritismo,* a belief system that would be unfamiliar to many non-Hispanic clinicians (4). It is a group that believes that a person can be possessed by good and bad spirits that are as much a part of that person as his or her intelligence, musical ability, or physical strength. The fact that the spirits can exist outside of the body, however, means that the "ego" of the person is not delimited by the skin. When the patient in "Espíritu Errante" begins to speak of the devil possessing her and making her do things outside her control, it is not altogether evident that this is "crazy" from the perspective of the group. It is against the group norm, however, that the beliefs must be contrasted. This is greatly facilitated when another group member, perhaps even an authority, such as the medium in the above case, indicates that the person is deviant, even from the subcultural perspective. When this sort of aid is not available, the clinician can ask questions designed to uncover idiosyncrasy in the belief or some central position of the person in the belief system.

The fact that our patient, who had gone for help from spiritualists, should herself end up possessing the most power, and the persistence of the possession state, with apparent hallucinations long after the ritual was over, both argue against her beliefs' being shared by the larger group. Since those beliefs go "beyond the pale" of the subcultural belief system, they are highly suggestive of psychosis, provisionally, a brief reactive psychosis, in light of her recent stressors (see also Chapter 12).

Other examples of religious belief systems that might be unfamiliar to many clinicians and therefore require particular care in evaluating a patient with unusual beliefs might be extreme Fundamentalist, Christian Scientist, or Theosophist beliefs or the messianic beliefs of ultraconservative Hassidic Jews.

Similar considerations about the person's subculture are relevant when evaluating the reported experience of seeing visions or hearing voices. Seeing visions or hearing voices as part of a religious experience is called *eidetic imagery.* It is common in certain religious groups, and therefore can present problems in the diagnosis of a psychotic disorder among members of these sects. In the case "Heavenly Vision" (see Chapter 12), the patient reports that, for 20 years, she had been having "different levels of visionary states" during which she both saw and heard God. In response to such a vision, she said, "I felt I had been instructed to step out of the car and remove my clothes as a sort of shocking, attention-getting episode depicting the stripping that this nation is to be going through soon." Although this patient's perceptual experiences were apparently common among members of her religious group, and were in fact the subject of a book written by a leader of that group, my colleagues and I argued in an article (5) that idiosyncratic aspects of her beliefs and the bizarreness of her behavior indicated that she had been at least briefly psychotic. Thus, although we could not be certain that the visions she described were extraordinary in relation to her group, we were convinced that she had a psychotic disorder (the reader is referred to the article for complete justification of our DSM-III diagnosis of atypical psychosis).

The Ability to Test Reality

Since DSM-III and DSM-III-R define psychosis as a gross impairment in a person's ability to test reality, the clinician must test all erroneous and inaccurate beliefs expressed by the patient and perceptions reported for the degree to which the patient is aware of the deviance and unreality of the experiences. When beliefs are discordant with reality, but are basically a matter of judgment, the clinician would not interpret this as indicative of a delusion. Thus, a narcissistic and grandiose person who feels that his work is more praiseworthy than his supervisor does, or a chronically depressed patient who feels he is doomed to failure, are not considered to be psychotic simply because their judgments are not necessarily accurate or true. In their extreme form, however, these exaggerated beliefs may become delusions—for example, if the grandiose person developed a full-blown manic episode and believed he was due to receive the Nobel Prize.

Once a person has described a belief that, by its extremity or unusual nature, suggests a delusion, the clinician needs to confront the patient with the extreme or unusual nature of the beliefs. (See also section on interviewing the psychotic patient under Patient Problems in Chapter 1.) Some patients will be reasonably able to see the unreality of what they have stated; to recognize it as an exaggeration or the expression of a fear, wish, or desire; or to indicate that what was said was meant as a metaphor, to communicate more vividly a feeling rather than something actually believed. Others will insist what was said was true and persist in repeating their belief or reporting their experiences despite the clinician's skepticism or even concrete evidence to the contrary.

Not all delusions need to be so fantastic or unusual as to immediately defy credulity. In fact, DSM-III introduced a distinction between bizarre delusions that are "patently absurd" and have "no possible basis in fact" from other delusions that by definition are false beliefs, but could possibly, under some circumstances, be true. Examples of the former would be some of the Schneiderian first-rank delusions of passivity and control, such as thought broadcasting, insertion, or withdrawal; examples of the latter might be grandiose, persecutory, or somatic delusions.

Bizarre delusions (see below) are of particular significance for the diagnosis of schizophrenia. Nonbizarre delusions may sometimes contain "a kernel of truth" that may cause the clinician to fail to recognize the delusional nature of a particular belief. Thus, if a patient, following a period of increasing marital discord, develops a belief that his wife is having multiple affairs with his neighbors, the fact that she may be fed up with the relationship, thinking about divorce, and even beginning to "look around" does not preclude the possibility that the patient is delusional. Neither does the wife's denial of the affairs preclude the possibility that she is indeed being unfaithful. In this case, the clinician's tactic in assessing the possible delusional nature of the beliefs might be to inquire about the evidence for the patient's belief, how he came to this conclusion. Frequently, a patient's evidence is flimsy, circumstantial, and disjointed. The husband may report that his wife bought a new lipstick, said "Hello" to the next-door neighbor while they were grocery shopping, and seemed more tired than usual, and on the basis of this had drawn his conclusion. On the other hand, the evidence may be more substantial and compelling, in which case one would need other signs of a psychotic disorder before making a diagnosis.

Determining the Tenacity of False Beliefs

Since a delusion must also be "firmly sustained" in the face of contrary evidence or proof, the clinician may need other signs in addition to the patient's not having insight into the unreality of his belief. This evidence may be actions or activities in which the patient engages as a result of his or her "delusion." What the patient is led to do as a result of the beliefs is often helpful in distinguishing ideas of reference, i.e., overvalued ideas held with less than delusional intensity, from delusions of reference. For instance, in the first case, a person who feels that two people walking behind him may be laughing about how he is dressed may simply hasten, somewhat uncomfortably, on his way, whereas in the second, he may stop, turn around, and punch one of the people, or go home and barricade himself in his room.

In the following vignette, a clinician examines the ability of a patient to test reality concerning her unusual beliefs and the degree of conviction with which she holds them.

Bad News

A 30-year-old former secretary is being interviewed during her fourth psychiatric hospitalization in four years. She tells the interviewer that her problems began five years before when her employer and several co-workers decided to undertake a "campaign" to help her to work out her problems, which she says included depression, anger, passivity, dependency, and fear of people. The help of her parents, brothers and sisters, and several friends was enlisted; but, according to the patient, the program failed. "I feel damaged inside—disconnected. I can't see things clearly; it all looks like total darkness to me. My personality is dead . . . it's like pieces of my personality have been chopped off."

The interviewer proceeds.

Interviewer: I'm not sure I know what you mean by your personality is dead or pieces of it have been chopped off.

Patient: I have no feelings left inside; something snapped.

Interviewer: How did this happen?

Patient: This program they put me on.

Interviewer: Tell me about the program.

Patient: Well, I can't be too coherent about it . . . it's hard sometimes to comprehend. I've been involved in this program for the past five years. It seems that everything that people say to me has a message in it—a message that's intended to help me, or help me to help myself.

Interviewer: Yes?

Patient: Then I started to feel that even when I was by myself, I'd be getting these messages—especially from the television—ABC News was a part of it.

Interviewer: What were these messages?

Patient: They were like instructions—do this, or don't do that. Be like this, don't be like that.

Interviewer: Were you hearing the messages?

Patient: No, they were indirect, like by implication.

Interviewer: Is it going on now?

Patient: Yes, even here in the hospital.

Interviewer: Give me an example. How does it work?

Patient: Well, I'll be watching the news, and a commercial will come on for a detergent or something. There is this beautiful, wholesome-looking young woman, a mother I guess. And I'll decide they are telling me to stop screwing around with different men, get married, stop drinking, you know—clean up my act. Pretty soon, all the shows are geared up toward giving me information.

Interviewer: Who's behind it?

Patient: I'm not sure; I think my ex-boss.

Interviewer: Have you told the doctors about it?

Patient: Oh, yes.

Interviewer: What do they say?

Patient: They say I'm delusional.

Interviewer: Could that be?

Patient: No, not this. I get paranoid about things—distortions are part of my illness. But this is real.

Interviewer: How can you tell?

Patient: The experience is so real. I know my perceptions.

Interviewer: Why would ABC News care about you in particular—of all other people?

Patient: After a while, I became a problem. I've become very outspoken on this; people listen to me. I started to drive my co-workers crazy. I told them about mind control that was going on in America with kids. Even the airplanes that roar overhead are part of it. I know they were trying to help me, but it's the wrong kind of help.

Interviewer: What about losing parts of your personality?

Patient: Well, after I started to call people, like at the network, to complain, then the program got even more intensive. My apartment was bugged; everything I said went back to ABC. They started to use this machine to stimulate parts of my brain; this was supposed to finish up the program. But it's gone too far; something snapped; my brain has changed.

Interviewer: When this is going on, how do you feel?

Patient: I'm insane with anxiety and fear.

Interviewer: What else have you done to stop it, in addition to calling the network?

Patient: Sometimes, I just stand in the middle of the street screaming at people—the whole community can get in on it.

Interviewer: How do people react?

Patient: I think I frighten them. But I want this to stop.

Identifying Other Symptoms of Psychosis

Several other symptoms indicative of psychosis present special problems for accurate diagnosis. These include formal thought disorder, flat or inappropriate affect, and the negative symptoms of schizophrenia.

Formal thought disorder. A disorder in the formal aspects of thought, as opposed to the content of thought (delusions), is inferred from certain characteristics of the patient's speech, including its coherence and comprehensibility. The most commonly described disorder of thought is loosening of associations. Traditionally, however, judgments about the presence of loose associations in a patient's speech have been relatively unreliable. Loosening of associations has been demonstrated in the speech of normal people, and is often hard to distinguish from flight of ideas, which is more characteristic of mania.

Andreasen (6,7) has tackled the problem of unreliable ratings of thought disorder by defining a number of different terms to describe the qualitative differences detectable among thought-disordered patients. Examples of her definitions are *derailment* (a term she thinks is more descriptively accurate than loose associations), defined as "a pattern of spontaneous speech in which the ideas slip off the track onto one that is completely unrelated" (6, p. 1319) and *tangentiality*, defined as "replying to a question in an oblique, tangential, or even irrelevant manner" (6, p. 1318). Andreasen considers flight of ideas "a derailment that occurs rapidly in the context of pressured speech" (6, p. 1319). Using these definitions, Andreasen has demonstrated substantially more reliable judgments on the part of clinicians about the presence and each type of thought disorder in a given patient.

Although these definitions include some terms that might be unfamiliar to clinicians, they should be learned, since they reduce variance in the diagnostic process stemming from clinician differences in their interpretations of the disorder in a patient's thought. Even with more reliable definitions, however, some controversy exists regarding the diagnostic significance of thought disorder, which, although traditionally associated with schizophrenia, has also been demonstrated to occur frequently in mania (8-10).

Flat or inappropriate affect. Disturbances in affect have also traditionally been unreliably diagnosed. The problem begins with confusion of the definition of *affect* as opposed to *mood* (11). Affect is defined in DSM-III as "an immediately expressed and observed emotion" and is distinguished from mood, a pervasive and sustained emotion, as weather is distinguished from climate. In DSM-III-R, affect is defined as "A pattern of observable behaviors that is the expression of a subjectively experienced feeling state (emotion) (3, p. 391). Several degrees of disturbance in affect can be observed: restricted affect involves a reduction in the range and intensity of emotional expression; blunted affect is a more severe reduction in the intensity of affective expression; and flat affect is a virtual lack of signs of affective expression. In DSM-III-R inappropriate affect is described as being "clearly discordant with the content of the person's speech or ideation" (3, p. 391).

Ratings of affective disturbance have been demonstrated to be more reliable if based on precise definitions and measurement, as in the case of Taylor and Abrams's Scale for Emotional Blunting (12). Again, however, even when judgments about affective blunting or flatness are reliable, their diagnostic significance is controversial. Boeringa and Castellani (13) found that flat affect was not particularly diagnostic of schizophrenia, and was very rare in affective disorders. They agreed with Taylor and Abrams that the absence of broad affect may be more useful in ruling out affective disorders than in diagnosing schizophrenia.

DSM-III and DSM-III-R have handled the unreliability of judgments of formal thought disorder and flat or inappropriate affect and the controversy surrounding their diagnostic significance by reducing the "weight" each has in making a diagnosis of schizophrenia (see below the discussion of criterion A for schizophrenia under Establishing the Presence of Certain Psychotic Symptoms).

Negative symptoms. It has recently been suggested that negative symptoms and the so-called "deficit syndrome" (or state) are more indicative of true or nuclear schizophrenia, or of a particular subgroup of schizophrenia associated with poor prognosis, than positive symptoms, the delusions and hallucinations that seem to be, for the most part, not specific for the diagnosis of schizophrenia. The best-known conceptualization of negative symptoms is that of Andreasen (14,15), and of the related, but not coextensive, deficit state, those of Heinrichs et al. (16) and Carpenter et al. (17). Andreasen's list of negative symptoms includes alogia, affective flattening, avolition-apathy, anhedonia-asociality, and attentional impairment. She has been able to demonstrate their reliability and validity in a small group of schizophrenics. Heinrichs' and Carpenter's definition of the deficit state includes enduring defects in a person's capacity for a sense of purpose, motivation, curiosity, and empathy and an inability to experience pleasure and to interact with others emotionally. Defects in these areas result in impairments in interpersonal relationships (e.g., avoidance, withdrawal), role functioning (e.g., as worker, parent), and participation in day-to-day community life.

In DSM-III, many negative symptoms were included among the residual symptoms that were described as often being present following the acute psychotic phase of the illness. Since the presence of residual symptoms generally meant that the six-month minimum duration criterion was met (see below), and since DSM-III schizophrenia has been demonstrated, with one exception (18,19), to be associated with poor outcome (20-24), DSM-III schizophrenia, residual type, actually corresponded fairly closely to the deficit state. Because additional evidence had accumulated since DSM-III's publication that the negative symptom subtyping had predictive validity, it was decided to add to the list of DSM-III-R residual symptoms "marked lack of initiative, interests, or energy" (3, p. 195), the only item in Andreasen's list without a DSM-III counterpart.

Special Problems in Assessing Psychotic Features

Several special problems confronting the clinician assessing a patient for the presence of psychotic features have recently received some attention in the research literature.

The effect of retrospective history-taking. Frequently, characteristics of prior episodes of illness may have particular diagnostic and treatment significance. This situation may arise in an outpatient setting following a hospitalization concerning which the clinician does not have access to hospital records or has reasons to question their accuracy, or in the case of a patient who shows some impairment (residual symptoms) currently, but has no history suggestive of acute psychosis, except in the distant past. Documenting a psychotic episode in the latter case would be important for making a differential diagnosis between schizophrenia and schizotypal personality disorder. Also, in some patients with current affective episodes with psychotic features, the presence of such features in the past without an affective syndrome would help to distinguish among schizophrenia, schizoaffective disorder, and a major mood disorder with psychotic features.

The difficulties in retrospectively diagnosing psychotic episodes have been described in Endicott and associates' (25) family history study of psychotic disorders and in Pulver and Carpenter's study (26) of the effectiveness of the NIMH epidemiological assessment instrument, the Diagnostic Interview Schedule (DIS), in discerning psychotic episodes in patients known previously to have had documented psychoses. In the former study, the investigators found among 1,084 first-degree relatives of 298 probands with Research Diagnostic Criteria (RDC) diagnoses of affective disorders or schizoaffective disorders only 28 who recalled ever having been psychotic. Although associated with the presence or absence of psychosis in probands, this rate was considered a sizable underestimation of the true prevalence. These relatives were evaluated using the most advanced research techniques available, including structured interviews; hence, the average clinical evaluation would be expected to be even less successful at detecting lifetime psychosis.

The effect of recovery: "sealing over." The Pulver and Carpenter study found that at least one-third of patients judged to have had schizophrenia or manic-depressive illness at the time of hospitalization 11 years previously were not identified by the DIS as having a history of psychotic illness. The authors conclude that these results may be attributable to the highly structured format of the DIS or to the ineffectiveness of lay interviewers for whom the instrument was designed. They also note, however, that:

1. Episodes of psychosis are often accompanied by lack of insight, and thus may not be remembered as illness at all.
2. Bizarre experiences are not easily discussed with other people, especially strangers.

3. Suppression, repression, blocking, and denial, which would interfere with a person's ability to describe past experiences accurately, are apt to be most prominent when the experiences are ego-alien, as many psychotic experiences are.

4. The social stigma associated with psychotic illnesses is likely to contribute to deliberate withholding of information about such illnesses, especially schizophrenia.

All of these processes are apt to be operative in the standard clinical evaluation. The clinician is in an advantaged position if he or she has access to information provided by a parent, spouse, or other person closely associated with the patient. Of course, no information source should be considered infallible, and memory lapses and psychological motivations must be considered in evaluating the veracity of all informants. As in the rest of medicine, when the history is scanty or questionably accurate, more reliance must be placed on clinical observation and examination.

Ruling Out an Organic Factor

Once the presence of a psychotic syndrome has been established, the first consideration in differential diagnosis is ruling out an organic etiology for the syndrome. The decision tree for the differential diagnosis of psychotic features makes the decision about whether or not a known organic feature is responsible for the clinical picture the first step in differential diagnosis. The DSM-III diagnostic criteria for schizophrenic disorder, paranoid disorder, and all of the specific diagnostic categories within the psychotic disorders not elsewhere classified group included a criterion stating "not due to an organic mental disorder," or an equivalent thereof. In DSM-III-R, the equivalent criterion reads "It cannot be established that an organic factor initiated and maintained the disturbance."

The purpose of including such exclusionary criteria is to eliminate one source of heterogeneity in the historically broad American concept of schizophrenia. Schizophrenia had sometimes been diagnosed in certain cases when the classic symptoms were present even though there was either an obviously or strongly suspected organic cause for them, such as the ingestion of hallucinogenic drugs. In the early and mid-seventies, researchers and clinicians (27,28) pointed out that classically schizophreniclike symptoms could have organic causes, but that these illnesses had different treatment and prognostic implications and should not be thought of as schizophrenic disorders. DSM-III adopted the stance that illnesses with known organic etiologies should be excluded from schizophrenia; the "not due to" statement was made to ensure this distinction. The evidence for an organic etiology could come from history, physical examination, or laboratory tests, in keeping with the DSM-III definition of an organic brain syndrome (see also Chapter 3).

For many clinicians and researchers, the "not due to" criterion became a source of ambiguity in the DSM-III principles of differential diagnosis. Although the intent of the criterion was to separate out psychotic illnesses in which the organic factor was a necessary and sufficient cause of the syndrome, numerous instances were encountered in which an organic factor, known or suspected, was a contributing cause. In many psychotic people, acute episodes and hospitalizations were often associated with periods of increased substance abuse, e.g., of amphetamines or phencyclidine. In other institutionalized, chronically psychotic patients, a possible organic influence could often be documented by history (e.g., of early head trauma), by physical examination (e.g., detection of "soft" neurological signs), or by laboratory tests (e.g., revealing enlarged cerebral ventricles). Should evidence of an organic "factor" of this kind be used to rule out a diagnosis of schizophrenia? The following case vignette illustrates the problem.

The Devil's Bride

A 24-year-old single woman was hospitalized for the eighth time in five years. She had been living in a group home for the mentally ill when she suffered one of her "anxiety attacks."

"It's like a seizure," she said. "I go into another world. I can hear people talking but I can't talk back. They started when I was 19.

"It's scary. It can happen every few weeks and last a few hours or a few days. I wake up dirty. I feel scared, lost. Lights flash, and I see tough-looking men. Then I see Jesus, God, and the Devil. I see my mother, who committed suicide; it's like she's alive again. I see little balloons out there, like two beach balls.

"At the group home, they told me I got very agitated. I felt possessed. I felt that a demon was trying to come into my body. I felt that tricks were being played on me in my room. The devil went up inside of me—raped me. I know this sounds weird. My mother was standing there watching it. I heard God talking—He said that I was a slut, that I had married the devil. I thought I was pregnant, I thought I was going to have the devil's baby. I guess I was screaming and yelling.

"I was adopted when I was two years old. I'm mentally retarded. I've always been in special education classes. When I was little, the other kids used to call me names—like 'reject' or 'retard.' I was very retarded in high school. My mother had to tell me when to bathe and when to shave my underarms.

"Sometimes I get very angry and upset. I break things or try to hurt myself. I stabbed myself when my aunt died.

"I've been here two weeks. I'm starting to heal again."

Examination by a neurologist revealed mild cognitive impairment, difficulty with balance, and slight gait ataxia. A CT scan showed mild enlargement of the lateral cerebral ventricles. No specific neurologic disorder was diagnosed.

In the above case, the diagnosis of schizophrenia is warranted, since an organic factor is not both necessary and sufficient (the DSM-III-R principle). Some researchers have found that more than half of DSM-III schizophrenics have abnormalities on neurological examination suggesting organic contributing factors (29,30); and although ancillary treatment for attacks of violence, with propranolol, for example, may be indicated, the clinical course and treatment response are consistent with those of chronic schizophrenia.

Organic Delusional Syndrome and Organic Hallucinosis

The most common organic causes of psychotic syndromes are drugs. DSM-III included in its section on substance-induced organic mental disorders (see also Chapter 4, Disturbances Associated with the Use of Psychoactive Substances) categories for delusional syndromes caused by amphetamines, hallucinogens, and cannabis, and hallucinosis caused by alcohol and hallucinogens. In addition, the criteria for phencyclidine mixed organic mental disorder indicate that an organic delusion syndrome may occur in the progression from one type of organic brain syndrome to another. In DSM-III-R, a delusional syndrome has been added for cocaine and phencyclidine, and a posthallucinogen perception disorder has also been included.

In some cases differentiation of a drug-induced psychotic syndrome from a "functional" disorder is relatively clear, e.g., when a relatively healthy person takes a drug such as cannabis, suddenly develops a paranoid delusion that lasts for several hours, but disappears as the drug is metabolized, and then returns to his or her usual mental state. Evidence of more serious preexisting psychopathology complicates matters, however. The role of the drug as a causal agent for the psychosis blends into its role as a precipitant in the case of a highly vulnerable person. The persistence of a delusion beyond the expected time is also confusing. There are reports that with drugs such as amphetamines, the delusions may persist for up to one year following chronic heavy use and still be considered organically caused.

In spite of the fact that several researchers have studied drug-induced psychoses (31,32), the guidelines for differential diagnosis remain uncertain. DSM-III-R recommends that if there is persistent disorientation or memory impairment, an organic etiology should be suspected, even though confusion sometimes accompanies the acute onset of a functional psychotic episode. For further discussion, the reader is referred to Chapter 4.

Other physical causes for an organic delusional syndrome include temporal lobe epilepsy, Huntington's disease, and various neoplastic and vascular lesions of the cerebral cortex, especially of the nondominant hemisphere. Other causes of organic hallucinosis include blindness, deafness, and seizure disorders. Distinguishing such conditions from a "functional" psychotic disorder usually depends on discovery of the underlying physical illness. In DSM-III and DSM-III-R, the physical illness is noted on Axis III. Onset of a psychotic syndrome in the second half of life in a previously healthy person should cause a clinician to suspect an organic etiology.

Dementias Associated with Delusions

The other major specific organic causes for psychoses included in DSM-III and DSM-III-R are the primary degenerative and multi-infarct dementias. Since these may be complicated by the development of delusions, a notation of subclassification "with delusions" is included for these disorders. The distinction from a functional psychotic disorder depends on the presence of impairment in memory and other cognitive functions characteristic of dementia (see also Chapter 3).

RULING OUT FACTITIOUS SYMPTOMATOLOGY AND MALINGERING

The next important step in the differential diagnostic decision tree for psychotic syndromes, according to DSM-III, was to rule out factitious symptoms or malingering. Actually, as a revised decision tree by Spitzer and associates (1) reflected, this step is logically the first, since if the symptoms are in some way being faked, then the clinician is not dealing with a true psychotic syndrome at all. The decision that a patient has a factitious disorder rests on the clinician's judgment that the symptoms, in this case the psychosis, are under voluntary control. The term *factitious* means not real, with the implication that the dissembling is purposefully hidden from the observer. In this way, the term *factitious* differs from *fictitious*, which also means not real, but which does not convey an attempt to hide the unreality.

Factitious disorders are distinguished from malingering in that in the former, the person voluntarily produces symptoms for reasons that are not totally apparent from the situation. In the case of a factitious psychosis, the person might be attempting to remain a patient in a mental hospital rather than be discharged into the community, to have responsibility for children taken over by a social agency, or to receive punishment by the administration of unnecessary psychotropic medications. In contrast, malingering is a situation in which the goal of faking an illness is readily apparent, e.g., avoiding military duty or collecting disability insurance. Admittedly, there are gray areas between the extremes, but usually a more in-depth consideration of a person's psychology is necessary to understand the reasons for feigning illness in factitious disorder.

The diagnosis for a factitious psychosis in DSM-III and DSM-III-R is factitious disorder with psychological symptoms (300.16). Its recognition hinges on determination that the symptoms are under voluntary control. Unfortunately, defining exactly what is meant by the concept of voluntary control has not been easy, and there remains a good deal of ambiguity about differential diagnoses between real and factitious illnesses (see also Chapter 8). DSM-III says that an indication of factitious disorder is a clinical picture that does not correspond to any recognizable mental disorder. An example is the syndrome of "pseudologica fantastica," in which a person makes up what seem to him or her to be bizarre responses to questions, but that would, in fact, be quite rare for a person with a true psychotic illness. Another clue to the diagnosis might be temporal inconsistencies, i.e., the person may act normally at certain times but at other times, such as when being examined or observed, produce dramatic symptoms.

Factitious psychosis may correspond in some cases to the older concept of hysterical psychosis, a term that, although having multiple meanings and usages (33), has historically conveyed the notion of a psychosis that is in some way not real or is feigned in order to achieve a particular effect (see also Chapter 12). In clinical practice, these diagnoses are often made with uncertainty, and are always based on judgments and inferences that may be wrong.

In DSM-III and DSM-III-R, malingering is not defined as a mental disorder: it is listed as a V code for conditions not attributable to a mental disorder that are a focus of attention or treatment. A person may try to act or talk as if psychotic. Many of the same features of the presentation that suggested factitious illness may lead the clinician to suspect malingering. The mimicking of psychotic symptoms is called malingering, according to DSM-III, when the objective of the person feigning the illness is "obviously recognizable with an understanding of the individual's circumstances rather than of his or her individual psychology" (34, p. 331). Thus, a person who pretends to be crazy in order to escape prosecution for criminal acts would be considered to be malingering, in the absence of other information suggesting motives more unusual or idiosyncratic than simply to avoid going to jail.

One of the best-known examples in the recent psychiatric literature of malingering that included psychotic symptomatology is the famous paper, by David Rosenhan, "On Being Sane in Insane Places" (35). In this study, a number of psychologists reported feigned hallucinations in order to be admitted to psychiatric hospitals. Their goal, obviously, was not to become patients in order to be taken care of, but rather to attempt to prove that mental health professionals cannot distinguish real from feigned mental illness and, therefore, that psychiatric diagnosis is an invalid exercise. In his rebuttal, Robert Spitzer (36) cogently argued that the study really had no bearing on the issue of the validity of psychiatric diagnosis, but rather was an illustration of how hard it is to rule out malingering in clinical situations in which the motive is hard to discern or the patient does not present a great deal of "pseudopsychopathology."

Another interesting clinical situation is one in which a patient with a real psychotic disorder sometimes exaggerates or feigns symptoms in order to achieve some gain. In *Psychopathology: A Case Book* (37), my colleagues and I described a man with a diagnosis of schizophrenia who sometimes feigned an exacerbation of his illness in order not to be discharged from the hospital. Given the staff's knowledge of this patient and his fears of having to live independently outside the protection of the institution, diagnoses of both schizophrenia and factitious disorder seemed warranted. A similar situation might exist if, for example, a patient with schizophrenia lost his welfare check and appeared at an emergency room for admission in order to get food. In this case, of course, the clinician would need to decide whether the stress of being temporarily without an obvious source of funds was enough to cause a real exacerbation of the illness or if the patient realized that by acting crazy, he increased his chances of being admitted and thus taken care of.

Sometimes the clinician may have to accede to a patient's desires and evaluate the impact of his or her decision on the patient's condition. True exacerbations of a psychotic illness, even if precipitated by psychosocial stressors, do not usually immediately remit when environmental changes are made that alleviate the stress.

MAKING THE DIAGNOSIS OF SCHIZOPHRENIA

Once organic etiologies and feigned illness have been ruled out, the diagnosis of schizophrenia, according to DSM-III and DSM-III-R, involves several other discrete steps, including *(1)* establishing the presence of certain psychotic symptoms, *(2)* finding evidence of a deterioration in functioning, *(3)* assessing the duration of signs of the illness, and *(4)* determining the relationship in time of the development and course of psychotic symptoms and mood disturbances in patients who present with both.

The DSM-III concept of schizophrenia, defined by the inclusion and exclusion criteria corresponding to these steps in differential diagnosis, was motivated by a need to correct an American clinical practice of diagnosing schizophrenia for a wider range of patients than clinicians did in other parts of the world. Evidence of the use of a broad concept of schizophrenia in the United States came primarily from a series of comparisons between American psychiatrists and psychiatrists from the United Kingdom (38,39). The change was initiated not merely in the interests of international diagnostic conformity but also in response to valid criticisms that the broad American concept of schizophrenia had little predictive validity in terms of what it conveyed about potential treatment response, future course of illness, or possible etiologic influences such as a positive family history. Although clinicians have been somewhat slow to adopt the revised concept of schizophrenia (40,41), since the publication of DSM-III, evidence has begun to accumulate that the narrower definition (20,42) has greater validity than any other conceptualizations currently in use (43).

Establishing the Presence of Certain Psychotic Symptoms

Criterion A for schizophrenia in DSM-III required that certain, specific psychotic symptoms be present. The list included bizarre delusions; delusions other than those with a persecutory or jealous content unless these were accompanied by hallucinations; particular auditory hallucinations, such as a voice making a running commentary on a person's thoughts or behavior, two voices conversing with each other, or mood-incongruent (see also Chapter 6) auditory hallucinations on several occasions; formal thought disorder characterized by incoherence, loose associations, illogical thinking, or poverty of content of speech if associated with either blunted, flat, or inappropriate affect, delusions or hallucinations, or catatonic or other grossly disorganized behavior. This list contained redundancies and implied more variations than were actually the case (44). It has been simplified in DSM-III-R (see Table 5.2), but, with a few notable exceptions (see below), continues to convey the same ideas about which kinds of psychotic symptoms are indicative of schizophrenia and which either are not or are not as useful in making a differential diagnosis.

The DSM-III criterion A for schizophrenia appeared to emphasize the first-rank symptoms (FRSs) postulated by Kurt Schneider to be

Table 5.2 DSM-III-R Diagnostic Criteria for Schizophrenia

A. Presence of characteristic psychotic symptoms in the active phase: either (1), (2), or (3) for at least one week (unless the symptoms are successfully treated):

(1) two of the following:

(*a*) delusions
(*b*) prominent hallucinations (throughout the day for several days or several times a week for several weeks, each hallucinatory experience not being limited to a few brief moments)
(*c*) incoherence or marked loosening of associations
(*d*) catatonic behavior
(*e*) flat or grossly inappropriate affect

(2) bizarre delusions (i.e., involving a phenomenon that the person's culture would regard as totally implausible, e.g., thought broadcasting, being controlled by a dead person)

(3) prominent hallucinations (as defined in (1) (*b*) above) of a voice with content having no apparent relation to depression or elation, or a voice keeping up a running commentary on the person's behavior or thoughts, or two or more voices conversing with each other.

B. During the course of the disturbance, functioning in such areas as work, social relations, and self-care is markedly below the highest level achieved before onset of the disturbance (or, when the onset is in childhood or adolescence, failure to achieve expected level of social development).

C. Schizoaffective disorder and mood disorder with psychotic features have been ruled out, i.e., if a major depressive or manic syndrome has ever been present during an active phase of the disturbance, the total duration of all episodes of a mood syndrome has been brief relative to the total duration of the active and residual phases of the disturbance.

D. Continuous signs of the disturbance for at least six months. The six-month period must include an active phase (of at least one week, or less if symptoms have been successfully treated) during which there were psychotic symptoms characteristic of schizophrenia (symptoms in A), with or without a prodromal or residual phase, as defined below.

Prodromal phase: A clear deterioration in functioning before the active phase of the disturbance that is not due to a disturbance in mood or to a psychoactive substance use disorder and that involves at least two of the symptoms listed below.

Residual phase: Following the active phase of the disturbance, persistence of at least two of the symptoms noted below, these not being due to a disturbance in mood or to a psychoactive substance use disorder.

Prodomal or residual symptoms:

(1) marked social isolation or withdrawal
(2) marked impairment in role functioning as wage-earner, student, or homemaker
(3) markedly peculiar behavior (e.g., collecting garbage, talking to self in public, hoarding food)
(4) marked impairment in personal hygiene and grooming
(5) blunted or inappropriate affect
(6) digressive, vague, overelaborate, or circumstantial speech, or poverty of speech, or poverty of content of speech
(7) odd beliefs or magical thinking, influencing behavior and inconsistent with cultural norms, e.g., superstitiousness, belief in clairvoyance, telepathy, "sixth sense," "others can feel my feelings," overvalued ideas, ideas of reference
(8) unusual perceptual experiences, e.g., recurrent illusions, sensing the presence of a force or person not actually present
(9) marked lack of initiative, interests, or energy

Examples: Six months of prodromal symptoms with one week of symptoms from A; no prodromal symptoms with six months of symptoms from A; no prodromal symptoms with one week of symptoms from A and six months of residual symptoms.

E. It cannot be established that an organic factor initiated and maintained the disturbance.

F. If there is a history of autistic disorder, the additional diagnosis of schizophrenia is made only if prominent delusions or hallucinations are also present.

Classification of course. The course of the disturbance is coded in the fifth digit:

1-Subchronic. The time from the beginning of the disturbance, when the person first began to show signs of the disturbance (including prodromal, active, and residual phases) more or less continuously, is less than two years, but at least six months.

2-Chronic. Same as above, but more than two years.

3-Subchronic with acute exacerbation. Reemergence of prominent psychotic symptoms in a person with a subchronic course who has been in the residual phase of the disturbance.

4-Chronic with acute exacerbation. Reemergence of prominent psychotic symptoms in a person with a chronic course who has been in the residual phase of the disturbance.

5-In remission. When a person with a history of schizophrenia is free of all signs of the disturbance (whether or not on medication), "in remission" should be coded. Differentiating schizophrenia in remission from no mental disorder requires consideration of overall level of functioning, length of time since the last episode of disturbance, total duration of the disturbance, and whether prophylactic treatment is being given.

0-Unspecified.

pathognomonic of the disorder. The examples given for bizarre delusions, "being controlled, thought broadcasting, thought insertion, or thought withdrawal" (34, p. 188), plus several of the specific types of auditory hallucinations mentioned above, are considered by Schneider to be FRSs. As is evident from the list, however, other psychotic symptoms may also indicate schizophrenia; and, what is more, the subsequent criteria for schizophrenia and the criteria for major mood disorders should make it clear that the DSM-III systems do not regard FRSs as pathognomonic of schizophrenia.

The significance of bizarre vs. nonbizarre delusions. The most difficult concept in the symptom criteria for schizophrenia in DSM-III was that of bizarre delusions. Bizarre, with reference to delusions, was defined in DSM-III as delusions in which the "content is patently absurd and has no possible basis in fact" (34, p. 356). The Schneiderian delusions of passivity and control are generally not possible under any circumstances; in contrast, the experience of being watched by the CIA or of having one's phone tapped by the FBI, although possibly having no basis in reality in the particular situation, can in fact happen. The concept of bizarre delusions has assumed new and greater diagnostic significance in DSM-III-R because of changes in the concepts defining paranoid disorders (see below).

Ruling out a delusional (paranoid) disorder by DSM-III-R. In DSM-III, the only delusions that were not indicative of schizophrenia were persecutory delusions or delusions of jealousy in the absence of prominent hallucinations. These delusions defined the DSM-III concept of paranoid disorders. Other features of DSM-III paranoid disorders, according to the diagnostic criteria, were emotion and behavior appropriate to the content of the delusional system and a duration of at least one week. Exclusion criteria ruled out bizarre delusions, the formal thinking disorder of schizophrenia, hallucinations, psychotic symptoms limited to periods when the patient was in a full affective syndrome, and organic etiologies.

Following the appearance of DSM-III, Kendler and associates published several studies (45,46) and literature reviews (47,48) that raised serious questions about the validity of the DSM-III concept of paranoid disorders. Kendler pointed out that, historically, the evidence favored the existence of a group of psychotic disorders characterized principally by nonbizarre, nonaffective, nonorganic delusions in the absence of formal thought disorder, with or without hallucinations. He referred to these disorders as delusional disorders, following the practice of Winokur (49), or as simple delusional disorders when hallucinations were not present. He went on to show that this broader definition of delusional disorder involved a relative sparing of functional capacities (usually associated with the traditional concept of paranoid disorders), diagnostic consistency over time, and familial association (43).

The Work Group to Revise DSM-III and its Ad Hoc Advisory Committee on Schizophrenia and Other Psychotic Disorders regarded this evidence as substantial and replaced DSM-III paranoid disorders with delusional disorder in DSM-III-R. The diagnosis of delusional disorder therefore now allows for other types of delusions, such as somatic, grandiose, and erotic as well as persecutory and jealous. What are still excluded are bizarre delusions. Since these then become critical in the differential diagnosis between schizophrenia and delusional disorder, DSM-III-R has attempted to redefine "bizarre delusions" more clearly as follows:

> A false belief that involves a phenomenon that the person's culture would regard as totally implausible. Example: A man believed that when his adenoids had been removed in childhood, a box had been inserted into his head, and that wires had been placed in his head so that the voice he heard was that of the governor. (3, p. 395)

There are no subtypes of acute or chronic delusional disorder in DSM-III-R corresponding to acute paranoid disorder and paranoia in DSM-III. The minimum duration required for a diagnosis of delusional disorder is now one month. Induced psychotic disorder, corresponding to shared paranoid disorder, is now included in the class of psychotic disorders not elsewhere classified. There did not seem to be evidence that this unusual disorder, in which one person's delusion is adopted by an intimate other, was necessarily related to the more common types of delusional disorder studied by Kendler.

DSM-III-R still maintains that prominent hallucinations are not part of the classic picture of delusional disorder. Table 5.3 presents the diagnostic criteria for the new DSM-III-R class of delusional (paranoid) disorder.

The diagnostic significance of hallucinations. The main problem in using hallucinations as a criterion in diagnosing, in addition to those mentioned previously, is difficulty in assessing the presence of true hallucinations. Patients sometimes report hallucinations when their experience is not really perceptual, but rather cognitive, i.e., is a delusion. The following brief vignette illustrates this point.

Pigeons

A 31-year-old British woman moved to the United States following a divorce. Shortly after her arrival she reported that she began to

Table 5.3 DSM-III-R Diagnostic Criteria for Delusional Disorder

A. Nonbizzare delusion(s) (i.e., involving situations that occur in real life, such as being followed, poisoned, infected, loved at a distance, having a disease, being deceived by one's spouse or lover) of at least one month's duration.

B. Auditory or visual hallucinations, if present, are not prominent (as defined in schizophrenia, A(1) (*b*)).

C. Apart from the delusion(s) or its ramifications, behavior is not obviously odd or bizarre.

D. If a major depressive or manic syndrome has been present during the delusional disturbance, the total duration of all episodes of the mood syndrome has been brief relative to the total duration of the delusional disturbance.

E. Has never met criterion A for schizophrenia, and it cannot be established that an organic factor initiated and maintained the disturbance.

Specify type: The following types are based on the predominant delusional theme. If no single delusional theme predominates, specify as **unspecified type.**

Erotomanic type
Delusional disorder in which the predominant theme of the delusion(s) is that a person, usually of higher status, is in love with the subject.

Grandiose type
Delusional disorder in which the predominant theme of the delusion(s) is one of inflated worth, power, knowledge, identity, or special relationship to a deity or famous person.

Jealous type
Delusional disorder in which the predominant theme of the delusion(s) is that one's sexual partner is unfaithful.

Persecutory type
Delusional disorder in which the predominant theme of the delusion(s) is that one (or someone to whom one is close) is being malevolently treated in some way. People with this type of delusional disorder may repeatedly take their complaints of being mistreated to legal authorities.

Somatic type
Delusional disorder in which the predominant theme of the delusion(s) is that the person has some physical defect, disorder, or disease.

Unspecified type
Delusional disorder that does not fit any of the previous categories, e.g., persecutory and grandiose themes without a predominance of either; delusions of reference without malevolent content.

"receive messages" from pigeons that she saw in the street. She stated that she could "read these messages through their eyes." On close questioning, she denied that she heard the pigeons say anything or heard any voices or audible sounds other than their ordinary warbling.

Initially, many clinicians might interpret this symptom as a hallucination, when in fact there is no auditory perceptual experience, but rather a delusional (false) conviction.

Also confusing are misinterpretations of actual perceptual experiences that lead to falsely reported perceptions. These are referred to as illusions, and are to be distinguished from hallucinations. An example would be a conversation in a hallway outside an apartment that is overheard by a paranoid person as a conversation that includes several derogatory or threatening references to himself. Sometimes people report hearing voices talking, or seeing things in a darkened room, when they are either falling asleep or awakening. The former are known as hypnogogic, and the latter, as hypnopompic hallucinations. Although true hallucinations, neither is considered characteristic of schizophrenic psychoses.

The ambiguities in the interpretation of perceptual experiences as hallucinations led the DSM-III Task Force to include detailed definitions of hallucinations, as contrasted to illusions, in the glossary of technical terms. DSM-III criteria for schizophrenia also emphasized the hallucinations that are most characteristic of schizophrenia—those referred to as first-rank symptoms by Schneider—i.e., a voice making a running commentary on a person's thoughts or behavior, or two voices conversing with each other. An example of both types in one patient would be the voices that said of a 46-year-old woman with schizophrenia, "There she goes, the ugly pig, look at her, look at her. Yes, now she's touching her filthy body; you know she's thinking filthy thoughts; now see, she's going to try to leave." Complex, nonaffective hallucinations of other types on multiple occasions may also meet the criteria for active, psychotic symptoms of schizophrenia, as would hallucinations in the presence of a marked formal thought disorder.

Other psychotic symptoms in schizophrenia. Primarily because of the unreliability noted previously, other symptoms traditionally considered characteristic of schizophrenia, such as incoherence, loose associations, or illogical thinking and flat, blunted, or inappropriate affect, receive less emphasis in the DSM-III and DSM-III-R criteria for schizophrenia. These meet criterion A only if they occur together or if they are accompanied by some evidence of either delusions or hallucinations or catatonic behavior. A combination of symptoms would be expected to be a more reliable indicator of active psychosis than any of the symptoms alone. In DSM-III-R these symptoms remain in combination.

Assessing Deterioration in Functioning.

DSM-III criterion B for schizophrenia required "deterioration from a previous level of functioning in such areas as work, social relations, and self-care" (34, p. 189). Endicott and her group (50), in a study of the reliability of the individual criteria of DSM-III, found low reliability for this item (kappa = 0.19), and many clinicians have found the criterion ambiguous.

The first point of confusion has been whether the deterioration in functioning can be limited to the episode of acute psychosis itself or whether the deterioration should be evident even after resolution of the acute episode, i.e., when the patient is in a residual phase. Since Kraepelin, "core," "nuclear," or "true" schizophrenia has traditionally been associated with a progressive, downward course, reflected, in part, by deterioration in the person's functional capacities. DSM-III schizophrenia was defined narrowly and purposely to correspond to a core syndrome of schizophrenia that would have a relatively poor prognosis. One measure of this validity was predicted to be recurrence and deterioration in social and occupational functioning (34, p. 181). Did this mean that DSM-III criterion B *required* progressive deterioration without the possibility of complete remission?

Actually, the intent of criterion B was to distinguish the schizophrenic disorders in which psychotic symptoms almost invariably interfere with a person's functioning from paranoid disorders in which a person can be extremely delusional and yet the psychosis appear as if compartmentalized, in the sense that most areas of functioning are not impaired. The following case vignette is an example of a delusional (paranoid) disorder in which there is no evidence of a deterioration in functioning.

Girl in White

"Excuse me, I'm looking for Dr. Stein," said a 24-year-old, third-year medical student through the open door to a young psychiatrist as he sat at his desk opening the mail.

"I haven't seen him today," replied the psychiatrist. "Actually, I think he's on vacation."

The young woman stood at the door.

"Is there something the matter? Can I help?" asked the doctor.

The young woman began to cry. She entered the office and proceeded to tell the following story. Since the beginning of the current academic year, her first involving clinical clerkships, the young woman had been becoming increasingly anxious. She was convinced that all of her classmates and the attending and house staff on the services through which she had rotated were talking about her. Apparently, at the end of the preceding year, shortly before her final exams, she had gone to bed with one of her instructors, a married man 15 years her senior. It had been a one time affair, an impulsive act on both their parts, and both vowed not to mention it to anyone.

When school resumed, however, the patient began to notice classmates whispering when she entered the room, giving her strange smiles, and making cryptic remarks, which she interpreted as allusions to the fact that they knew of her escapade. When asked to give an example of the kinds of remarks made, she said, "Somebody asked me if I was glad to be out of the basic sciences. I felt he was baiting me—I thought he meant that I wouldn't have passed the last semester if I hadn't slept with Dr. M." She began to feel that all of the medical school believed she had fraudulently entered the clerkship year and that the administration was allowing her to continue because they feared that she would have a "nervous breakdown" if she were exposed. She managed to complete the first two four-week clerkships, receiving good marks and comments on her performance, by keeping to herself and concentrating on work with the patients. She was constantly embarrassed, becoming flushed and having difficulty talking whenever she had to present at rounds or in a conference, but somehow she struggled through.

In the past four weeks, however, she had been experiencing an increasing sense of panic, since she now felt that people that she knew from outside the school, or even that she was meeting for the first time, somehow had learned about her behavior and were indirectly commenting on it. She was unconvinced by the psychiatrist's suggestion that she might be reading into people's comments notions based on her own feelings about what she had done.

The woman denied hallucinations, and there was no history of drug or alcohol use. Although she had been crying and having some trouble sleeping at night because of her constant replaying of conversations and exchanges with people from the previous day, there was no evidence of a full depressive syndrome.

In this case, the absence of a deterioration in functioning is actually redundant in ruling out schizophrenia because the psychotic symptoms are limited to nonbizarre, persecutory delusions, which alone do not meet criterion A for schizophrenia.

DSM-III also stated, with regard to the prognosis of schizophrenia: "A complete return to premorbid functioning is unusual—so rare, in fact, that some clinicians would question the diagnosis" (34, p. 185). Technically speaking, however, it was possible to meet the deterioration requirement on the basis of impairment in functioning during the acute episode itself. Hospitalization, with its obvious connotations of inability of the person to care adequately for himself or herself or to control his or her behavior so that others would not be endangered is usually sufficient evidence of deterioration. Particular circumstances surrounding a hospitalization, e.g., for the purpose of receiving special tests, would not necessarily indicate deterioration in functioning. Even if their condition does not necessitate hospitalization, most patients with schizophrenia will exhibit gross disruption in their relationships with others, becoming withdrawn and detached, and will be unable to function adequately in their major roles, as either worker or student.

Ambiguity with regard to the deterioration determination also arose when the clinician considered the diagnosis of schizophrenia in children. Although specific diagnoses for gross disturbances in the development of children are included in the DSM-III and DSM-III-R sections on disorders usually first evident in infancy, childhood, or adolescence, it is also possible to make the diagnosis of schizophrenia in children under the age of 12. It is frequently hard to document the required deterioration in functioning in a developing child who has as yet not reached his or her full capacity. What one sees more frequently is an arrest in development and a failure to progress.

The DSM-III-R criterion for schizophrenia that requires functional impairment has been reworded in an attempt to reduce ambiguity (see Table 5.2).

DETERMINING THE DURATION OF SYMPTOMS

One of the most controversial aspects of the DSM-III definition of schizophrenia was the inclusion of a criterion requiring a minimum duration of disturbance of at least six months. This was motivated by the desire to define a group of patients who were somewhat homogeneous with respect to treatment-response, prognostic, and family-history variables. Specifically, treatment with psychotropic drugs would ordinarily be indicated; the prognosis, as mentioned above, would be poor; and the family history would frequently be positive for schizophrenia, suggesting that familial and possibly genetic factors were important in the etiology. Data available before publication of DSM-III (51,52) suggested that the desired homogeneity of these external correlates of the schizophrenic diagnosis could not be achieved on the basis of a cross-sectional picture of symptoms. These earlier "good prognosis/poor prognosis schizophrenia" studies, however, also suggested that some minimum-duration requirement was necessary to achieve greater predictive validity. Primarily because of data from the International Pilot Study of Schizophrenia (52) and the Iowa 500 (51), the Task Force selected a six-month duration.

Studies in recent years, by Helzer and colleagues (20) and Stephens and associates (21), have confirmed the validity of the DSM-III definition, compared with those in the RDC, Feighner criteria, and CATEGO, in terms of predicting a poor overall prognosis, as measured by time spent hospitalized, persistence of symptoms, and impairment in social and occupational functioning. The former group also concluded that the six-month duration criterion made a contribution to this predictive validity, but was not solely responsible for it (53). The Feighner criteria for schizophrenia, although specifying somewhat different characteristic symptoms, also require six months' duration and, interestingly, are the closest to DSM-III with respect to predicting a poor prognosis.

The six-month duration requirement has presented several problems. The first, and most common, clinical question has been whether the six months' duration refers to the duration of the active psychotic symptoms. DSM-III was explicit in stating that this was not the case. The requirement was "Continuous signs of the illness for at least six months at some time during the person's life, with some signs of the illness at present. The six-month period must include an active phase during which there were symptoms from (criterion) A, with or without a prodromal or residual phase, as defined below" (34, p. 189).

DSM-III-R schizophrenia continues to require a duration of six months. Table 5.2 includes the DSM-III-R symptoms characteristic of a prodromal or residual phase. At least two of the nine are necessary; and deterioration in functioning should not be due to a disturbance in mood or to a substance use disorder. As can be seen, the symptoms overlap considerably with the concepts of negative symptoms of schizophrenia and the deficit syndrome.

Establishing the onset of a prodromal phase of illness is not easy when the symptoms are somewhat subtle and/or are being assessed retrospectively, as is frequently the case. Endicott and her co-workers (50) found that most of the individual items in the DSM-III list of prodromal symptoms could be assessed in patients with schizophrenia with average reliability (median kappa = 0.51; range from −0.02 for vague speech and unusual perceptions to 0.73 for peculiar behavior and impairment in hygiene). Spring (54) has noted the ambiguous nature of the onset of schizophrenia as it pertains to the possibility that stressful life events may contribute to the etiology or precipitate episodes of the illness. Brockington and Meltzer (55) have underscored the importance of using multiple informants and multiple sources of information for documenting episodes of illness in research studies.

Several groups of investigators are currently studying the onset of episodes of schizophrenia, because of the clinical importance of early detection of onset. Docherty and his group (56) have reported on "stages of onset" of schizophrenia. Herz and Melville (57) and Heinrichs and Carpenter (58) have developed criteria for predicting relapse from early signs for use in their studies of the effects of minimum maintenance drug therapy and of early pharmacologic intervention in decreasing morbidity due to schizophrenia. Interestingly, some of the symptoms specified are relatively nonspecific changes suggestive of prodromal symptoms, and some are actually acute symptoms of psychosis. Although prodromal symptoms may be uncertain signs of relapse, if the clinician waits for psychotic symptoms to appear, early intervention for prevention of acute episodes may be a moot point.

Identifying Patterns of Schizophrenic Illness

The patterns of illness the clinician most frequently encounters that meet the duration requirement for schizophrenia are depicted in Figure 5.2

Illustration A is of a patient who has a relatively typical, gradual deterioration in functioning that might be characterized by progressive social withdrawal, disregard for personal hygiene, peculiar behavior, and dropping out of school or quitting a job. This period, which might last from several months to several years, then culminates in an episode of acute psychotic symptoms. If these symptoms are among those that DSM-III or DSM-III-R considers indicative of schizophrenia, the diagnosis is made (point E_1). DSM-III does not state explicitly how long the person must be psychotic to meet DSM-III criteria following a long prodromal period. Is one hour enough? Generally, it was to be understood that this active phase of psychosis should have lasted at least a few days or, more usually, a week. In the examples of typical courses of symptoms in schizophrenia, one week was mentioned. In order to avoid this ambiguity, DSM-III-R states that the active psychotic phase should have lasted at least one week, unless treatment has been initiated so quickly and been so successful that the psychosis resolves in less time.

A major difficulty is how the clinician should diagnose patients during a prodromal phase of an illness that he or she strongly suspects is incipient schizophrenia when the person has never been frankly psychotic (point E_2). Since many of the symptoms of prodromal schizophrenia are comparable with many of those in the criteria for schizotypal personality disorder, the latter diagnosis is a possibility. DSM-III offered this diagnosis as the most likely for patients who

Figure 5.2 Typical Patterns of Prodromal, Active Psychotic, and Residual Symptoms in Psychotic Disorders

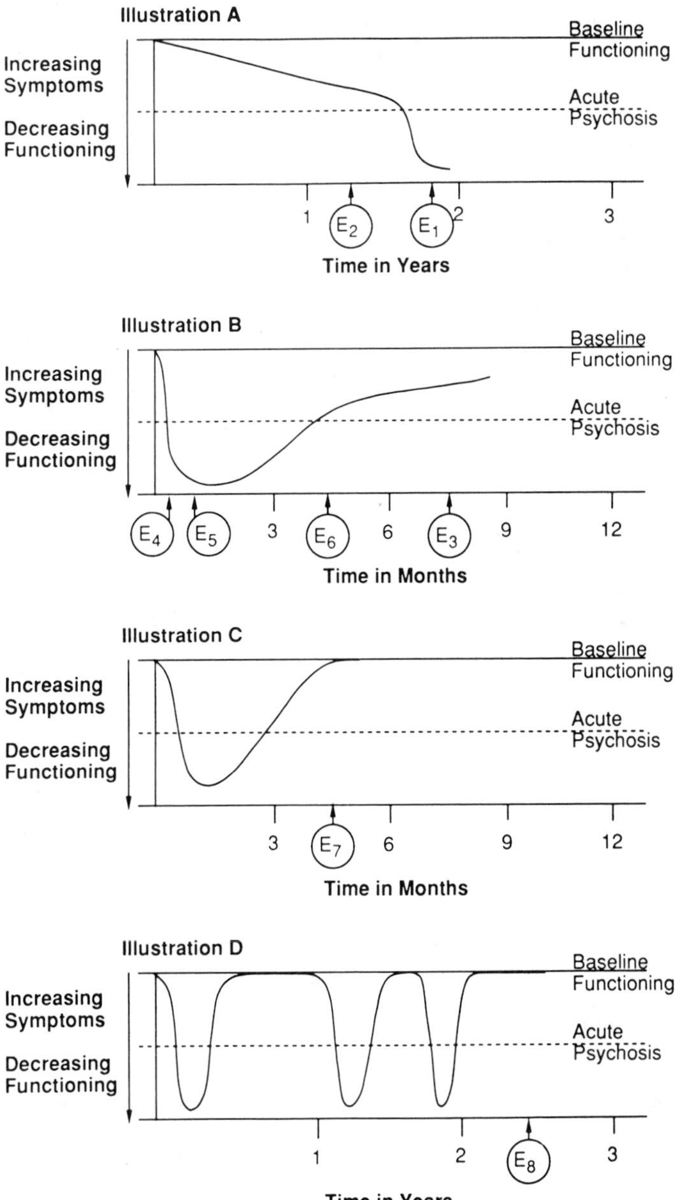

would have formerly, by DSM-II, been diagnosed as having simple or latent schizophrenia, but who would be excluded from the DSM-III diagnosis since they never, by definition, develop the necessary active psychotic phase. The notions of simple and latent schizophrenia and the concept of personality disorder in DSM-III imply a stable clinical picture, however, so many clinicians would feel uncomfortable about using the diagnosis of schizotypal personality disorder in a clinical situation in which the picture is one of evolving, progressively worsening symptoms.

Another possibility is to use, as we did in Case #139, the "Minister's Daughter," in the *DSM-III Casebook* (59), the diagnosis of unspecified mental disorder, nonpsychotic. This diagnosis conveys the clinician's judgment that the person clearly suffers from a mental disorder, but that disorder does not (as yet) correspond to one of the specified disorders in DSM-III or DSM-III-R. This option is unsatisfying, however, because clinicians may already have a rather strong suspicion that the underlying process and the eventual diagnosis will be schizophrenia, a psychotic disorder.

The third option is to list the diagnosis as "deferred." Although acceptable, this designation fails to discriminate between a situation in which the clinician is uncertain whether the person has a mental disorder and one in which a mental disorder is apparent but does not meet any specific criteria.

The following vignette describes a patient whose initial presentation eludes a definitive diagnosis, but who, in retrospect, could readily be recognized as having been in a prodromal phase of schizophrenia.

Going No Place Fast

A 22-year-old man was brought for psychiatric consultation by his parents, who were concerned that he was "going no place fast." The young man had been spending most of his time alone in his room, apparently listening to music, or just "daydreaming." His few friends had stopped calling, since he had turned down all of their recent invitations to go out. He avoided his parents, except to come out of his room for meals or to give laundry to his mother. When his parents asked what was the matter, he either said "Nothing" or talked in very abstract, philosophical terms about things he felt were wrong with society.

The patient had been shy since high-school days. His grades had been fair, and he had had a few friends with whom he socialized. He had never dated until college. He had attended a local community college, but had dropped out after two years, citing too much pressure and claiming that "Everyone there is a jerk."

The patient hung around for several months; then his father, who was in the construction business, insisted that he work for him. After a few months of working as a laborer, he quit because, he said, the boss was "picking on me." He got a job as a cashier in a hardware store, then one delivering pizzas, but quit each because of arguments with bosses and co-workers.

The consultation was prompted when his mother noted that he was not bathing or shaving regularly and was "smiling a lot to himself" at the dining table. When examined by the psychiatrist, the patient initially denied any bizarre, persecutory, or other unusual beliefs or experiences. "My parents and I just see things differently," he said. "They do things their way, and they just want me to do the same." When asked where "his way" was leading, he said, "I just have to find myself; I do a lot of thinking. I'll be O.K.; everybody should just leave me alone." Other than smoking some marijuana, the patient denied drug or alcohol use.

The psychiatrist explained to the family that he was unable to determine the exact nature of the young man's problems, but that they should meet several more times for further evaluation. He did not hear from the family for about eight months.

Then, the psychiatrist received a call saying that the patient had been acting increasingly strangely for two weeks. He had painted religious sayings on the walls of his room, was playing his music so loudly that the neighbors complained, and told his mother that "The KKK wants to kill all Christian Jews."

When examined at this time, the young man spoke very loosely about the Pope, Nazis, Jews, Lutherans, and mass transportation. "The Russians killed Kennedy. Christians and Jews both believe in ground burials. There are differences from the Moslems—pyramids—It's interesting that the Greeks believed the earth was a woman . . . two busts . . . rotational. It might be considered a Seder plate. The issue was never life after death."

Illustration B in Figure 5.2 depicts the course of a psychotic illness in which the person experiences relatively rapid decompensation and development of an acute psychosis. This rapid deterioration may occur over only a couple of weeks to a month. Commonly, the person is treated pharmacologically for the acute symptoms, which may then remit over several weeks. In some patients, however, once the acute psychosis is resolved, symptoms of a residual phase of illness persist, e.g., the patient may remain withdrawn socially, as his or her affect continues to be blunted or flat.

If this residual phase persists, so that the length of time from the beginning of the deterioration to the point at which at least two residual symptoms remain exceeds six months, then the diagnosis of schizophrenia is made (E_3). The onset of a more dramatic change in the patient's behavior as was the case in illustration B is usually easier to date, at least by family members, than is the slow deterioration in the preceding illustration.

This clinical course nonetheless presents certain difficulties for differential diagnosis. If the patient who eventually develops this picture is seen early in the course of the illness, for example, to treat an acute psychosis (E_4), then, obviously, the diagnosis of schizophrenia cannot be made. (This is the case for first episodes; see below for an explanation of the significance of recurrences.) DSM-III provided several other diagnostic possibilities for this patient at this time. If the patient had actually been psychotic for at least a day or two at the time of the evaluation and the possibility of an organic etiology and an affective disorder (see also below) had been ruled out, the diagnosis of atypical psychosis would be made. This diagnosis was equivalent to the commonly used diagnosis of "acute psychotic episode," which, however, has never had a place in the official nomenclature.

"Atypical psychosis" was used in DSM-III as a residual category indicating that a psychotic picture was present—and could be treated—but that a more definitive diagnosis could not be made, in this case because it was too early in the clinical course. Some have objected to the use of the term *atypical* because, in fact, many of these conditions are very "typical" psychotic syndromes. "Atypical" was used throughout DSM-III for lack of a better term to designate residual cases of disorder that did not meet criteria for more specific diagnoses from a particular diagnostic class. Atypical psychosis was the diagnosis unless or until evidence accumulated that the psychosis had lasted at least two weeks.

At that point (E_5), according to DSM-III criteria, the diagnosis of schizophreniform disorder applied. Schizophreniform disorder corresponds to the DSM-II and ICD-9-CM diagnoses of acute schizophrenia. According to DSM-III, any combination of prodromal, acute, and residual psychotic symptoms that lasted at least two weeks but less than six months (and were nonorganic, nonaffective) warranted the diagnosis of schizophreniform disorder. For instance, if the clinician evaluated the patient in illustration B four months into the clinical course (E_6), at an aftercare clinic following a hospitalization, and the patient was no longer psychotic, but still had residual symptoms, schizophreniform disorder would be the diagnosis—even though, in a substantial number of patients, the residual symptoms might be quite persistent, and two months later the diagnosis would have to be changed to schizophrenia.

According to DSM-III-R, schizophreniform disorder has no minimum duration, so that at points E_4, E_5, and E_6, in illustration B, this diagnosis applies. Atypical psychosis is now termed "psychotic disorder not otherwise specified," which is still a residual diagnosis for disorders that do not meet criteria for diagnosis of a more specific psychotic disorder. This diagnosis will not be as frequently used as atypical psychosis was in DSM-III, however, because the range of phenomena covered by schizophreniform, delusional, and schizoaffective (see below) disorders has been expanded in DSM-III-R.

Some clinicians and researchers (60) have objected to the DSM-III system because it meant that a particular patient might receive three different diagnoses (i.e., first atypical psychosis, then schizophreniform disorder, and finally schizophrenia) for the same illness within a six-month period. The DSM-III rationale was that since it is impossible to predict outcome on the basis of the cross-sectional pattern of psychotic symptoms, these diagnoses indicated increasing degrees of certainty about the nature of a psychotic disorder as the patient's clinical course evolved and did or did not become chronic. The system gave the patient a kind of "prognostic benefit of the doubt," reserving the diagnosis with the most ominous prognostic implications, schizophrenia, for patients who already showed a minimal degree of chronicity. This was expected to have not only social implications, in that the often stigmatizing label of schizophrenia (61) would be much less loosely used, but also important clinical implications, in that patients with schizophreniform disorder would not be prematurely committed to long-term maintenance antipsychotic medication regimens, with their inherent risks of tardive dyskinesia (62), or assumed to require expensive, and sometimes chronicity-provoking, sheltered, long-term, rehabilitative care.

DSM-III-R, by maintaining the six months' duration requirement separating schizophrenia from schizophreniform disorder, preserves some of this stepwise progression toward the diagnosis of schizophrenia earlier in the course of a psychotic illness. In order to make a distinction, however, between patients who were receiving the diagnosis of schizophreniform disorder early in the course of a psychotic disturbance that might, or might not, progress to schizophrenia from patients with the diagnosis who were, in fact, *expected* to have a good prognosis, DSM-III-R instructs the clinician to specify "with" or "without good prognostic features." The revised diagnostic criteria for schizophreniform disorder (see Table 5.4) require two from a list of four features: acute onset, good premorbid functioning, absence of blunted affect, and symptoms of confusion, disorientation, or perplexity at the height of the psychotic episode.

Establishing a relationship to stress. In some cases, psychotic symptoms appear following a severe psychosocial stressor. If the disturbance lasted less than two weeks, then, according to DSM-III, a diagnosis of brief reactive psychosis was warranted. In DSM-III-R, the

Table 5.4 DSM-III-R Diagnostic Criteria for Schizophreniform Disorder

A. Meets criteria A and C of schizophrenia

B. An episode of the disturbance (including prodromal, active, and residual phases) lasts less than six months. (When the diagnosis must be made without waiting for recovery, it should be qualified as "provisional.")

C. Does not meet the criteria for brief reactive psychosis, and it cannot be established that an organic factor initiated and maintained the disturbance.

Specify: without **good prognostic features** or **with good prognostic features,** i.e., with at least two of the following:

(1) onset of prominent psychotic symptoms within four weeks of first noticeable change in usual behavior or functioning
(2) confusion, disorientation, or perplexity at the height of the psychotic episode
(3) good premorbid social and occupational functioning
(4) absence of blunted or flat affect

maximum duration of a brief reactive psychosis has been extended to one month (see also Chapter 12). Patients with brief reactive psychosis usually exhibit a great deal of emotional turmoil, but no period of increasing psychopathology immediately preceding the stressor. DSM-III-R criteria indicate that there should be no prodromal signs of schizophrenia and that the patient should not meet criteria for schizotypal personality disorder. Unfortunately, schizotypal personality disorder is listed among the predisposing factors for brief reactive psychosis in DSM-III-R. Clinicians should ignore this statement.

An additional important point here is that the stressor cannot be trivial. DSM-III stated that the stressor must be severe enough so that it "would evoke significant symptoms of distress in almost anyone" (34, p. 201). Examples given included the loss of a loved one (by death) or the psychological trauma of combat. DSM-III-R criteria state that the psychotic symptoms appear shortly after, and in response to, "one or more events that, singly or together, would be markedly stressful to almost anyone in similar circumstances in the person's culture" (3, p. 207). The prognosis of brief reactive psychosis is, by definition, good: people with the disorder are expected to recover completely within one month, and to have no residual symptoms. Occasionally, an illness following a severe stressor will not remit, and the diagnosis will have to be changed.

There are several other important points in differential diagnosis in cases of psychotic syndromes of brief duration. Clinicians sometimes have asked, What is the minimum duration of psychotic symptoms necessary to make the diagnosis of atypical psychosis (now schizophreniform disorder)? They are usually referring to patients with borderline personality disorder (BPD) who, many think, typically exhibit very brief, transient, "micropsychotic" episodes, lasting from minutes to hours, but not days. Whether or not these are characteristic of patients with BPD (see also Chapter 9), I believe an additional diagnosis of psychotic disorder is warranted when the occurrence of the symptoms indicates some special steps in the treatment. A patient may require small doses of antipsychotic medication to alleviate severe anxiety that leads to a brief period of defective reality testing (63), or special measures may be taken in psychotherapy to deal with the development of episodes of psychotic transference. Of course, there has never been a designation for "atypical psychosis in remission," so one might wonder under what circumstances a clinician would be making a diagnosis of a condition that lasted only a few hours. The most likely occasion would be to convey a "lifetime" diagnosis of a patient in treatment, such as "borderline personality disorder with frequent episodes of a psychotic disorder."

Subtyping schizophrenia along its course. Another problem area as the clinician follows the longitudinal course of a psychotic disorder arises from the DSM-III subclassifications of schizophrenic disorders. DSM-III and DSM-III-R apply two types of subclassification simultaneously: a phenomenologic one, and a subtype by type of course.

The phenomenologic subtype is coded in the fourth digit as disorganized, catatonic, paranoid, undifferentiated, or residual. With the exception of the paranoid subtype, these are of questionable clinical significance, though relatively easily recognized. The paranoid subtype as described in DSM-III-R has been shown to have a better prognosis in terms of better occupational functioning and a greater capacity for independent living than the other subtypes, particularly if "stable" over time, that is, if all episodes, past and present, have been paranoid (64). Use of the term *paranoid* to describe this subtype is somewhat idiosyncratic, however, and will surprise some clinicians. The paranoid subtype of DSM-III-R schizophrenia is defined by *(1)* preoccupation with one or more systematized delusions or with frequent auditory hallucinations related to a single theme, and *(2)* absence of incoherence, marked loosening of associations, flat or grossly inappropriate affect, catatonic behavior, or grossly disorganized behavior. "Paranoid," meaning persecutory, delusions are *not* required.

Furthermore, the residual type refers more to a *phase* of the illness than to a specific phenomenological subtype, as usually conceived.

DSM-III criteria stated that there had to have been at least one episode of schizophrenia previously, but that the clinical picture occasioning the current evaluation or admission to clinical care was without prominent psychotic symptoms. The residual symptoms required were taken from the list in the diagnostic criteria for schizophrenia, but no specific number was required. Presumably, at least two were required, for consistency with the six months' duration criterion for schizophrenia. In DSM-III-R, the criteria describe a state with no prominent psychotic symptoms and two residual symptoms from the list in criterion D for schizophrenia. This type necessitates a change in phenomenologic subtype from what it had been in an acute episode to "residual" when the patient is no longer actively psychotic, with a resultant loss of information. Paradoxically, DSM-III instructed the clinician to go back to the phenomenologic type that described the last acute episode, i.e., paranoid or catatonic, if the patient further recovered and was to be noted as "in remission."

The mixing of phenomenologic subtype with aspects of clinical course leads to a second source of confusion about the subclassification of schizophrenia. In the fifth digit, the course of the illness is coded according to five subclasses: subchronic (total continuous duration of all phases of illness less than two years, but greater than six months); chronic (total duration greater than two years); subchronic with acute exacerbation (reemergence of active psychotic symptoms in a person with a subchronic course who has been in a residual phase); chronic with acute exacerbation (same as subchronic with exacerbation except course has been chronic), and in remission (free of all signs of the illness whether or not on medication).

In DSM-III these course subclassifications were set off in the diagnostic manual as if they applied only to the residual type of schizophrenia. This was obviously a production error, and contradicted the preceding definition of residual subtype (cannot be residual with prominent active symptoms). The course subtypes were intended to refer to all phenomenologic types, and are now listed in DSM-III-R with the diagnostic criteria (see Table 5.2). It is useful to note, however, that

1. The subchronic and chronic subtypes are the only course designations consistent with the residual type of illness.
2. "Subchronic" and "chronic" can also apply to patients who remain actively psychotic with prominent symptoms throughout most of their clinical courses.
3. The "with acute exacerbation" subtypes imply that the person has been in a residual phase and has now decompensated again.

Another question that has been asked is, How long should a symptom-free person have his or her illness referred to as "in remission" before the "diagnosis" should be changed to "no mental disorder?" For many disorders, such as schizophrenia, psychoactive substance use disorders, and major mood disorders, remission is often achieved by use of medications and other active treatments, and there is often a high likelihood of relapse, especially when treatments are prematurely withdrawn or interrupted. This is not to say that all major depressive episodes are going to be recurrent or all psychoactive substance use disorders lifelong; but certainly if, in the clinician's judgment, the patient's symptom-free state is more aptly described as "in remission" because of the effects of prophylactic treatment, rather than "no mental disorder," the former should be designated. It may be more uncommon to achieve a completely symptom-free state in schizophrenia than in major depression, but the effectiveness of maintenance antipsychotic medications (65-67) and certain psychosocial treatments (68,69) in preventing relapse are well known; therefore, "in remission" might be commonly used even though the patients remain in treatment.

Figure 5.2 depicts several clinical situations that do not meet the six-month duration criterion. Illustration C in this figure is of the course of a hypothetical patient who has a relatively acute decompensation into psychosis, is treated, and recovers completely, all within a six-month period. There are no residual symptoms, and the patient returns, in all respects, to his or her previous level of functioning (E_7). This "acute schizophrenic" picture was called schizophreniform disorder in DSM-III and was intended to correspond to what has been referred to in the literature as good prognosis schizophrenia (see also discussion above). People with this disorder have been expected to have a more benign clinical course and to respond to treatments, such as lithium carbonate, that are ordinarily used for affective disorders (70,71).

Since the publication of DSM-III, there have been several studies concerning the validity of the diagnosis of schizophreniform disorder. Helzer and associates (20) found that the outcome of patients with this disorder was significantly better than that for DSM-III schizophrenia in terms of a variety of parameters. Coryell and Tsuang (72,73) also found a better outcome for patients whose schizophreniclike illness lasted less than six months, but the critical duration of illness that distinguished the better from the worse prognostic groups in their study was only about two months, rather than DSM-III's six. Some questions have been raised about the limited definition of symptoms that were considered as prodromal in their study (74). Fogelson and his colleagues (75) found that the clinical histories, family histories, treatment responses, and outcomes of patients with DSM-III schizophreniform disorder were so similar to bipolar disorder that they considered schizophreniform disorder to be a variant of affective disorder. From the six case histories presented, however, I believe these patients probably warranted a DSM-III diagnosis of schizoaffective disorder, which may explain why they closely resembled major affective disorders in external validating characteristics.

Some clinicians have questioned the role of medications in suppressing symptoms in schizophreniform disorder. In other words, if the duration is less than six months because of antipsychotic medication, is this still schizophreniform disorder? That the antipsychotics will alleviate acute psychotic symptoms is beyond question; the effect that they have on residual, negative, or deficit symptoms is more controversial (76). In true schizophrenia, in my opinion, the expectation is that *some* residual symptoms will persist in spite of effective antipsychotic therapy, and that these symptoms will extend the clinical course beyond the six-month limit. Since the medications are not particularly effective against residual symptoms, a case in which medications result in complete symptom remission should be diagnosed as schizophreniform.

A more problematic question is what to do if the patient has complete remission, but is still on medication at the end of six months. In DSM-III there was no diagnosis for schizophreniform disorder in remission, so one cannot make a parallel argument to the above for schizophrenia in remission. Technically speaking, the diagnosis of such a case has to be schizophreniform disorder because there are no residual symptoms. Some clinicians might feel uncomfortable using the diagnosis of schizophreniform disorder to refer to patients for whom the possibility of relapse is high and psychotic symptoms would persist, without much chance of spontaneous remission, unless intervention with antipsychotics was continued. To deal with this ambiguity, I suggest keeping in mind the intent of the schizophreniform diagnosis to define a group with a better prognosis until proven otherwise. In cases in which the remission is totally dependent on maintenance medication, I suspect there will be future relapses, one or more of which will last longer than six months or leave the patient with some residual symptoms and thus meet the criteria for schizophrenia. Using DSM-III-R, the clinician can note schizophreniform disorder, in remission, using the general severity criteria on page 24 of the manual.

Another question about medications and the duration of symptoms criteria is how to distinguish some of the side effects that can occur from antipsychotic medications from the residual symptoms of schizophrenia. Antipsychotic medications, because of their sedative properties, make patients appear less emotionally expressive and slow them down physically and mentally. These side effects may be misconstrued as blunted or flat affect and may interfere with normal role functioning. Obviously, doses of medication should be titrated to their lowest effective level in the prophylaxis of recurrent psychoses in order to minimize side effects. At lower doses, improvement in affect or functioning may occur, confirming the role of the drugs in producing these signs. The clinician should also look for evidence of other residual symptoms, such as digressive or vague speech or social isolation, when it remains unclear whether the patient is experiencing significant drug side effects.

Illustration D in Figure 5.2 shows the course of a patient with recurrent schizophreniform episodes. In none of these episodes, considered alone, do the symptoms last six months or longer. Added together, however, the total duration (E_8) is well over six months. DSM-III and DSM-III-R state that the signs of the illness need to be continuous for the six-month duration to be met; therefore, this illustration does not apply to schizophrenia, but should be diagnosed at each episode as schizophreniform disorder. The long-term course of recurrent schizophreniform episodes with consistent return to baseline levels of functioning has not been well documented, and some clinicians may doubt the syndrome's existence.

One general criticism of the inclusion of a duration criterion in the definition of schizophrenia deserves mention. Kendell (77) has suggested that it decides a priori what ought to be determined empirically, that is, that patients with schizophrenia have a worse prognosis than other psychotic patients. Expressed another way, Fenton and his associates (78) have referred to the logic of the duration requirement as tautologic, that is, that chronicity breeds chronicity, and all that is being found is what was required in the first place. I think, however, in considering the outcome studies of Helzer's group (20,53), that the six-month duration can be a useful and even potentially powerful clinical tool if the clinician, by eliciting a comprehensive history or observing a patient over a relatively brief period of time (six months), can make prognostic judgments and estimations about treatment needs for ten times that length of time into the future. Estimating prognosis and determining the need for treatment are, after all, among the major clinical uses of diagnosis in medicine in general.

An alternative classification approach would be to note duration separately, on an axis for clinical course, as has been proposed by Strauss et al. (79). This approach has the advantage of allowing durations of illness of different lengths to be compared for their prognostic utility and of noting the durations of other syndromes, such as depression or anxiety, in order to investigate their prognostic significance.

DETERMINING THE RELATIONSHIP OF PSYCHOTIC SYMPTOMS TO AFFECTIVE SYNDROMES

A major way in which the DSM-III concept of schizophrenia was narrowed was by the diagnostic importance given to the relationship between the time of occurrence of psychotic symptoms and affective, manic, or depressive syndromes. The change paralleled a growing awareness in American psychiatry that affective syndromes were often powerful predictors of treatment response and outcome, even when schizophreniclike symptoms were present. This research began in the United States principally with the work of Abrams and Taylor (80-83) and was summarized persuasively in a major review article by Pope and Lipinski (84) that was published in 1978, during the period between the second and final drafts of DSM-III. The evidence mustered by Pope and Lipinski convinced the Task Force to change the DSM-III concept of schizophrenia from that of the Research Diagnostic Criteria (85) to that which eventually appeared in the manual.

Criterion D for schizophrenia in DSM-III and criterion C for manic and major depressive episodes (see Chapter 6) indicated the principles of differential diagnosis to be followed in the case of a patient who had both psychotic and full affective syndromes. These two criteria in DSM-III were among the most difficult for clinicians to interpret. Figure 5.3 is a schematic diagram, taken from Williams and Spitzer (86), that our group has used extensively in teaching this difficult differential.

In illustration A, a brief period of affective symptoms precedes the development of a psychotic syndrome, which in turn lasts longer than six months. In this case, criterion D for schizophrenia allowed the diagnosis to be made, since the full affective syndrome was "brief in duration relative to the duration of the psychotic symptoms." In fact, a relatively common presentation of schizophrenia is one following a period of affective symptoms as a prodrome. This, in my experience, is more often depression than mania, although the acute excitement that sometimes accompanies an acute psychotic episode can be confused with a manic episode in an illness that later is more typically schizophrenic. The final diagnosis in illustration A can be made only six months into the course, when the duration criteria for schizophrenia have been met, or at a sufficiently far-advanced point in the course of schizophreniform disorder to allow the clinician to judge that the psychosis is persisting and prominent whereas the affective symptoms have essentially disappeared.

Figure 5.3 Differential Diagnosis of Schizophrenia, Psychotic Mood Disorders, and Schizoaffective Disorder Based on Relationship of Mood Disturbance to Psychotic Features Over Time

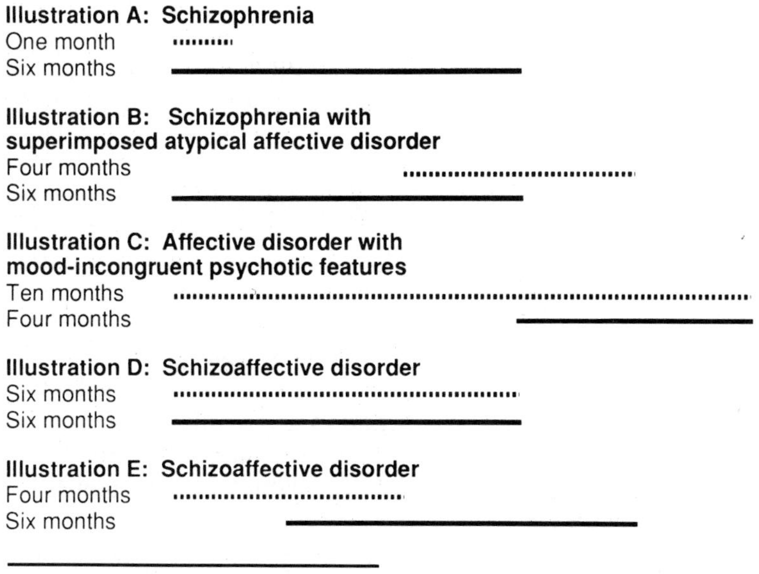

Illustration A: Schizophrenia
One month
Six months

Illustration B: Schizophrenia with superimposed atypical affective disorder
Four months
Six months

Illustration C: Affective disorder with mood-incongruent psychotic features
Ten months
Four months

Illustration D: Schizoaffective disorder
Six months
Six months

Illustration E: Schizoaffective disorder
Four months
Six months

Broken lines indicate a full affective syndrome (depressed or manic). Dotted lines indicate schizophreniclike psychotic symptoms. The number of months are the duration of the symptoms, the position of the "affective" line shows the relative time of onset and end of the affective syndrome in relation to the psychotic symptoms.

In illustration B, the schizophrenic psychotic symptoms developed first and persisted for over six months. Several months into the psychosis, an affective syndrome developed, and persisted even beyond the resolution of the psychosis. In practice, this most commonly occurs as the psychotic symptoms begin to subside. The affective syndrome that is seen is usually a depression that results as the patient begins to appreciate the serious nature of his or her illness, to realize that certain firmly held beliefs were actually delusions, that he or she is in a psychiatric hospital, or some other demoralizing aspect of the situation. Clinicians recognize this phenomenon as a postpsychotic depression (87,88).

The treatment implications of this syndrome are controversial, but some advocate the use of antidepressant medications (89) and/or stress the increased risk of suicide during this phase of the illness. Therefore, according to DSM-III, a significant depression at this stage would warrant an additional diagnosis of an atypical affective disorder superimposed on schizophrenia. The atypical category was used to distinguish this syndrome from a major affective disorder, since it is doubtful that the implications of this syndrome in the presence of schizophrenia are the same as in major depression—in terms of familial pattern, for example. Although a manic syndrome could, according to DSM-III, be the affective syndrome in illustration B, this would seem to be a much rarer occurrence in actual clinical practice.

The patient in illustration C had a prominent and persistent full affective syndrome, already of six months' duration, before the development of psychotic symptoms. Since the affective syndrome in this case was neither brief nor subsequent to the psychotic symptoms, exclusion criterion D ruled out schizophrenia. And since the psychotic symptoms resolved along with the affective syndrome, they did not dominate the clinical picture before the affective syndrome began or after it remitted, and diagnostic criterion C for either a major depressive episode or a manic episode is met. This case represented a very significant shift in diagnostic practice. It meant that no psychotic symptom, regardless of how bizarre, was inconsistent with the diagnosis of a major affective disorder so long as the psychosis is temporally confined to the period during which the patient had the full affective syndrome.

Since the publication of DSM-III, a number of significant studies have confirmed the wisdom of its approach, especially with regard to mania. The research groups of Rosenthal (90), Pope (91), Brockington (92), and Abrams and Taylor (93) have all concurred in finding that bizarre, first-rank, or other schizophreniclike psychotic symptoms occurring in the context of a manic episode have no implications insofar as familial pattern, differential treatment response, or long-term outcome is concerned. With or without the psychotic symptoms, the illnesses show a familial relationship to affective disorders, respond to lithium treatment, and exhibit a better long-term outcome.

Although DSM-III treated depression in a parallel fashion in terms of its exclusion criteria, the validity of this decision cannot be so well supported. There are suggestions that depressed patients with schizophreniclike psychotic symptoms have less clear-cut treatment responses and outcomes, falling somewhere between those expected for schizophrenia and those for affective disorders (94-96). A more detailed discussion of this subject appears in Chapter 6, Mood Disturbances.

Making a Diagnosis of Schizoaffective Disorder According to DSM-III

The final two illustrations in Figure 5.3 are of clinical situations not clearly resolvable by the use of DSM-III exclusion criteria. In the first, it is not possible to determine which of the two syndromes developed first, and both appear to persist for an equally long time. Under these circumstances, the clinician would not be able to make the differential diagnosis between schizophrenia with a superimposed atypical affective disorder and a major affective disorder with mood incongruent psychotic features. This situation was one of the examples given in DSM-III of appropriate use of the diagnosis of schizoaffective disorder. Schizoaffective disorder was the only diagnosis in DSM-III without specified criteria and was treated as a residual category. Before publication of DSM-III, there were several current conceptualizations of schizoaffective disorder, which overlapped to only a modest degree; none of them had compelling support in terms of validity (97,98). Initially, drafts of DSM-III used the RDC (85) for schizoaffective disorder, manic or depressed. But part of the effect of allowing for mood-incongruent psychotic features in the picture of major affective disorders (see above) was that a large proportion of the cases that would have met RDC for schizoaffective disorder became psychotic affective disorders according to DSM-III.

The final example in Figure 5.3, illustration E, depicts a patient who initially had an episode of a full affective syndrome and then developed mood-incongruent psychotic features. But, in contrast to the course expected in a psychotic affective disorder, the affective features remit, but the psychotic features persist. Since the psychotic features were not confined to the period during which there was a full affective syndrome, major affective disorder is ruled out by criterion C for a major depressive or manic episode. Since the affective syndrome preceded the psychotic symptoms and was not brief, DSM-III schizophrenia is ruled out by criterion D. Thus, unable to make a differential diagnosis, the clinician again must resort to the use of the schizoaffective category. This was the other example of schizoaffective disorder given in the DSM-III manual.

Although it is mood-incongruent psychotic features that are mentioned in these examples, if the delusions or hallucinations, for instance, in illustration E, were mood-congruent, would the diagnosis change? Coryell and Tsuang (96) investigated the significance of mood-incongruence in patients with psychotic affective disorders and found some differences in the direction of a poorer outcome compared with mood-congruent delusional depressives, but their patients would not, in most cases, have been diagnosed as schizoaffective disorder.

My opinion is that schizoaffective disorder is appropriate in situations in which the psychotic and mood syndromes are not contemporaneous whether the psychotic features are mood-incongruent or mood-congruent. If, however, there are no delusions or hallucinations, but only loose associations, incoherence, catatonic symptoms, or flat affect overlapping with a prominent and persistent mood syndrome, then diagnoses of both psychotic disorder NOS and depressive or bipolar disorder NOS should be made.

The decision not to include criteria for DSM-III schizoaffective disorder has met with considerable criticism. Some have argued that the lack of criteria impedes research (99) or implies that schizoaffective disorder no longer exists (100). Still others have argued that since most studies have shown that affective disorders with mood-incongruent psychotic features strongly resemble major affective disorders on indices of validity, there is no need for a schizoaffective disorder category (91).

Making a Diagnosis of Schizoaffective Disorder Using DSM-III-R

The Ad Hoc Advisory Committee on Psychotic Disorders to the Work Group to Revise DSM-III recognized that the DSM-III schizoaffective category could become an amorphous grouping with little clinical or research meaning. They therefore committed themselves to devising criteria. The group was also committed, however, not to interfere with the criteria that defined psychotic affective disorders with mood-incongruent features because it was agreed that the bulk of the evidence since DSM-III's publication (at least for mania) supported the wisdom of such a decision. A preliminary review of the use of DSM-III schizoaffective disorder in clinical practice (Williams, personal communication) suggested that the two illustrations of a diagnosis of schizoaffective disorder given in DSM-III described most of the instances in which that diagnosis would be made.

In recent research on schizoaffective disorder, it is difficult to interpret the findings because translation of the criteria used by different investigators into DSM-III criteria is by no means straightforward. Evidence has continued to accumulate, however, that, in spite of the previously discussed data on major affective disorders with mood-incongruent psychotic features, there is a group of patients who, in terms of a number of external validating characteristics, resemble neither schizophrenia nor affective disorder (101). These patients appear most often to typify the first use of the diagnosis of schizoaffective disorder described in DSM-III, that is, they have periods of major affective and schizophreniclike symptoms, but these symptoms do not always coexist in time over the course of the disorder. Interestingly, this example of schizoaffective disorder is very close to the RDC subtype schizoaffective disorder, mainly schizophrenic. The other RDC subtype of schizoaffective disorder, mainly affective, is very close to what was in DSM-III major affective disorder with mood-incongruent psychotic features.

It was decided, therefore, to specify by diagnostic criteria the first example of the use of the schizoaffective diagnosis in DSM-III and to make these the diagnostic criteria for DSM-III-R schizoaffective disorder (Table 5.5), a category compatible with RDC schizoaffective, mainly schizophrenic, subtype. It is expected that these patients will have more of a genetic relationship to schizophrenia than other "schizoaffective" patients and that their treatment responses and symptomatic and functional outcomes will be intermediate between those for schizophrenia and major mood disorders (102). There was even discussion of including this category under the diagnostic class of schizophrenic disorders, to clearly separate them from their "schizoaffective" counterparts classified as major mood disorders; but on reconsideration, it was thought preferable to leave the category within the class of psychotic disorders not elsewhere classified.

Those who worked on revising DSM-III believed that the important differential diagnostic principles based on the relationship of psychotic and mood syndromes to each other over time were clinically

Table 5.5 DSM-III-R Diagnostic Criteria for Schizoaffective Disorder

A. A disturbance during which, at some time, there is either a major depressive or a manic syndrome concurrent with symptoms that meet the A criterion of schizophrenia.

B. During an episode of the disturbance, there have been delusions or hallucinatons for at least two weeks, but no prominent mood symptoms.

C. Schizophrenia has been ruled out, i.e., the duration of all episodes of a mood syndrome has not been brief relative to the total duration of the psychotic disturbance.

D. It cannot be established that an organic factor initiated and maintained the disturbance.

Specify: **bipolar type** (current or previous manic syndrome) or
depressive type (no current or previous manic syndrome)

valid, although hard to apply in practice. Hence, the categories of major depression and bipolar disorder with mood-incongruent psychotic features, corresponding to RDC schizoaffective, mainly affective, disorder, remain intact in DSM-III-R, reflecting the evidence of their similarity to major mood disorders. The question of whether it makes a difference if the affective syndrome is mania or depression is still not resolved: therefore, the criteria for both kinds of syndrome continue to be formulated in parallel fashion.

In an attempt to make the criteria that guide clinicians in the differential diagnosis of mixed disturbances of mood and psychotic features more useful, the relevant diagnostic criteria have been rewritten. Criterion C for DSM-III-R schizophrenia (see Table 5.2) now states that schizoaffective disorder and mood disorder with psychotic features must be ruled out, which would be the case if a major depressive or manic syndrome had ever been present during an active phase and the total duration of all episodes of mood disturbance had been brief relative to total duration of active and residual phases of the disturbance. The fact that the residual phase is specifically included allows for schizophrenia to be the principal diagnosis even when there is a long period of postpsychotic depression. In DSM-III-R terminology, the postpsychotic depression would be classified as depressive disorder NOS.

The other DSM-III example of schizoaffective disorder, in which the timing of the development and persistence of the syndromes are not clear—because of inadequate information, for instance—is listed in DSM-III-R, along with several other, more specific ones, as psychotic disorder NOS. Since this diagnosis is recognized as a residual category conveying limited information, and since inadequacy of information was given as the reason for being unable to make a more precise diagnosis than schizoaffective disorder in certain instances, it was thought that a nonspecific category would be more appropriate for use in such cases. Further research is necessary to determine if other meaningful subgroups of schizoaffective disorder could be teased out of what is still probably a heterogeneous grouping (103,104).

A dramatic psychiatric case history appeared in *The New Yorker* in a series of articles entitled "The Patient," by journalist Susan Sheehan (105-108). "The Case of Sylvia Frumkin: Misdiagnosis or Misfortune?" was published as a DSM-III case study in *Hospital & Community Psychiatry* (109). Sylvia Frumkin's story is a poignant portrayal of the career of the chronic mental patient and an uncomfortable reminder of how difficult the diagnostic process is and how ineffective our interventions can sometimes be.

Sylvia Frumkin

Sylvia Frumkin, a 34-year-old single woman, has spent nearly 10 of her past 18 years in a psychiatric hospital. The most detailed presentation of her history describes a 7-month hospitalization when she was 30 years old. Ms. Frumkin had been discharged from the hospital just two weeks earlier, and was living in a hospital-supervised apartment. She slipped in a bathtub while washing her hair with mouthwash and was taken to a medical emergency room, where she became agitated and accused the doctor of incompetence.

After being hospitalized, Ms. Frumkin spent long periods of time singing, talking to herself, disrobing, and covering her face with lipstick. With hospital staff and patients she was verbally abusive, hypercritical, provocative, unkind, and abrupt.

Her mood was labile—at times cheerful, at others, angry, hostile, or threatening. Her affect was often inappropriate to her circumstances and to the content of her thought. Her speech and thought processes were circumstantial, fragmented, and illogical, with loose associations and flight of ideas. Throughout, her sensorium was clear.

Ms. Frumkin was the younger of two daughters born to Russian immigrant parents. As a little girl she had had difficulty making friends and had had several imaginary companions. She was a good student (her IQ was 138) and was in advanced classes. She was, however, physically clumsy, and not very attractive.

Psychological problems began when she was 14, shortly after her sister became engaged to a medical student. Ms. Frumkin became restless, overtalkative, emotionally shallow, anxious, easily angered, sexually confused, and dirty and made a suicide gesture; she began to receive outpatient treatment. After several months, she was hit by a car, and suffered a concussion and contusions. Shortly thereafter she became increasingly anxious and had periods of inexplicable giggling; she began to say that she was Cinderella, that her therapist was her fairy godmother, and that she would marry Paul McCartney, her Prince Charming. She was hospitalized for the first time when she began to believe that she wasn't her parents' daughter and that her name was Linette.

There followed, over the ensuing 18 years, a series of 24 hospitalizations. Her symptoms included agitated, aggressive, and bizarre behavior; hyperactivity; assaultiveness; command hallucinations; bizarre delusions (for instance, turning into a cat); grandiose and erotomanic delusions; rambling, incoherent speech, with loose associations; and poor judgment. In all, her hospitalizations totaled 118 months, including one continuous period of 31 months and another of 22 months.

Ms. Frumkin received the gamut of psychiatric somatotherapies. Antipsychotic medications included chlorpromazine, trifluoperazine, thioridazine, chlorprothixene, haloperidol, perphenazine, and molindone—sometimes in combinations. Doses ranged from the obviously subtherapeutic to usually effective doses equivalent to 1,500–2,500 mg of chlorpromazine; on one occasion, Ms. Frumkin received as much as

300 mg per day of haloperidol. Chlordiazepoxide, diazepam, imipramine, lithium, and megavitamins were also tried. The patient had several courses of electroconvulsive therapy and a 40-treatment course of insulin coma. There was no clear pattern of response or nonresponse to the various treatments.

Between hospitalizations, Ms. Frumkin functioned at a marginal level, was unkempt and socially isolated, gained great amounts of weight, and was very abusive to others, especially her family. She lived at home, in hotel wards, at halfway houses, and in community rehabilitation facilities. She attended various sheltered workshops, vocational and rehabilitation programs, and resocialization clubs, and on several occasions was housed by religious groups. Nothing worked very well. (109, pp. 807-808, Reprinted with permission)

According to DSM-III criteria, if one assumes that a full affective syndrome was present in this case, the critical question for differential diagnosis is whether it was present at all times when Ms. Frumkin was psychotic. If one is unable to determine the relative onsets, durations, and resolutions of affective and psychotic syndromes, according to DSM-III a diagnosis of schizoaffective disorder should be made. According to DSM-III-R, however, ambiguous cases are diagnosed as psychotic disorder NOS. DSM-III-R schizoaffective disorder indicates the distinctive pattern of some episodes of psychotic mood disturbances and others of psychotic symptoms without mood disturbance. Personally, I have never been convinced that major mood syndromes were a prominent feature of Ms. Frumkin's psychopathology, let alone that the psychotic symptoms she experienced always occurred in the context of a major mood syndrome. Therefore, using DSM-III criteria, I made a diagnosis of schizophrenia, undifferentiated or disorganized subtype, chronic with acute exacerbations, and using DSM-III-R, this would still be my diagnosis of choice.

THE DIAGNOSTIC SIGNIFICANCE OF AGE AT ONSET

DSM-III criterion E for schizophrenia stipulated that the onset of the prodromal or active phase of the illness must be prior to age 45. This decision was based on the opinion that a person who functions normally, perhaps even at a superior level, for a large portion of life, without even beginning to have difficulties, and then develops a schizophreniclike psychosis must have a fundamentally different illness from someone who deteriorates into psychosis with severe functional impairment in late adolescence or early adult life. According to DSM-III, patients with late onset were given a diagnosis of atypical psychosis.

Since publication of DSM-III, critics (110-112) of this age restriction on schizophrenia have spoken out, citing clinical examples of late-onset schizophrenia, research data on the phenomenon, and a tradition, particularly in the European literature, of diagnosing a condition called paraphrenia, or late paraphrenia, that was deemed related to true schizophrenia. Paraphrenia, they argue, had an onset late in life, but was otherwise indistinguishable from schizophrenia in terms of symptoms, functional impairment, and chronicity, and was different on these dimensions from so-called paranoid disorders.

The Ad Hoc Advisory Committee on Psychotic Disorders to the Work Group to Revise DSM-III evaluated this evidence and found it sufficient to warrant some change in the way late-onset cases were handled. The reader is referred to Chapter 11, Differential Diagnosis in the Elderly, for a more detailed discussion of this subject. A compromise decision was made to introduce a subcategory specification of late onset (age at onset after 45) for schizophrenia, corresponding to paraphrenia. This change allows for a distinction to be made, for clinical and research purposes, between early- and late-onset cases. It is expected that before DSM-IV is published, research evidence will have accumulated to document the significance of age at onset in schizophrenia.

Is There a Minimum Age at Onset for Schizophrenia?

Although there is no minimum age at onset in the diagnostic criteria for schizophrenia, the diagnostic decision tree for psychotic features in DSM-III directed the clinician evaluating a child less than 12 years of age to rule out the pervasive developmental disorders, infantile autism, and child onset pervasive developmental disorder or atypical pervasive developmental disorder. Some researchers, most notably Cantor and co-workers (113), have taken exception to this apparent exclusion of children under 12 from a diagnosis of schizophrenia, describing a group of children who clearly meet criteria for schizophrenia, not for the pervasive developmental disorders. In the initially revised decision tree (1), clinicians were directed to consider pervasive developmental disorders first, implying that if they were not present, a diagnosis of schizophrenia could be considered for a child.

Although it was thought important to separate infantile autism and childhood-onset pervasive developmental disorder (without delusions, hallucinations, incoherence, or marked loosening of associations) from schizophrenia and other psychoses of adult life, because of the uncertain relationship of the former to the latter, it was clearly the intention of the DSM-III Task Force to allow schizophrenia to be diagnosed in childhood. The differential diagnosis of infantile autism (34, p. 89) mentions schizophrenia occurring in childhood, but with hallucinations, delusions, incoherence, and loose associations.

In DSM-III-R, the relationship of autistic disorder of childhood to childhood schizophrenia has been further clarified. DSM-III-R criterion F for schizophrenia states that if there is a history of autistic disorder, the additional diagnosis of schizophrenia is made only if prominent delusions or hallucinations are also present. Schizophrenia occurring in a child also "preempts the residual diagnosis of pervasive developmental disorder NOS" (3, p. 193).

SUMMARY

This chapter describes difficult problems in the differential diagnosis of patients with psychotic features. It begins with a discussion of pitfalls in the recognition of psychosis by the clinician, including how to determine whether the patient can test reality, whether delusional beliefs are firmly held, and whether beliefs are or are not part of a subcultural belief system. The chapter then details some of the difficulties in interpreting less reliable symptoms of psychosis, such as formal thought disorder and flat affect. Some special problems in assessing psychotic features such as the effect of recovery on recall are considered.

The chapter then follows the logic of the decision tree for the differential diagnosis of psychotic features in discussing difficulties in ruling out organic etiologies and factitious symptoms and malingering. The specific symptoms required for a diagnosis of DSM-III and DSM-III-R schizophrenia are covered, including the new boundaries between schizophrenia and the revised concept of delusional (paranoid) disorder in DSM-III-R. Difficulties and controversies in determining the other symptoms required for a diagnosis of schizophrenia —deterioration in functioning, duration of symptoms, relationship in time of psychotic and mood syndromes, and age at onset—complete the chapter.

NOTE

1. This vignette was prepared with the assistance of Lourdes Dominguez, M.D., PGY-3 resident at the New York State Psychiatric Institute.

References

1. Spitzer RL, Williams JBW, Wynne, LC: A revised decision tree for the DSM-III differential diagnosis of psychotic patients. Hosp Community Psychiatry 34:631–633, 1983
2. Spitzer RL, Fleiss JL: A re-analysis of the reliability of psychiatric diagnosis. Br J Psychiatry 125:341–347, 1974
3. American Psychiatric Association: Diagnostic and Statistical Manual of Mental Disorders, Third Edition, Revised. Washington, DC, American Psychiatric Association, 1987
4. Bird HR, Canino I: The sociopsychiatry of *Espiritismo:* findings of a study in psychiatric populations of Puerto Rican and other Hispanic children. J Am Acad Child Psychiatry 20:725–740, 1981
5. Spitzer RL, Gibbon M, Skodol A, Williams JBW, Hyler S: The heavenly vision of a poor woman: a down-to-earth discussion of the DSM-III differential diagnosis. J Operational Psychiatry 11:169–172, 1980
6. Andreasen NC: Thought, language, and communication disorders. I. Clinical assessment, definition of terms and evaluation of their reliability. Arch Gen Psychiatry 36:1315–1321, 1979
7. Andreasen NC: Thought, language, and communication disorders. II. Diagnostic significance. Arch Gen Psychiatry 36:1325–1330, 1979
8. Harrow M, Grossman LS, Silverstein ML, Meltzer HY: Thought pathology in manic and schizophrenic patients. Arch Gen Psychiatry 39:665–671, 1982
9. Harrow M, Silverstein M, Marengo J: Disordered thinking: does it identify nuclear schizophrenia? Arch Gen Psychiatry 40:765–771, 1983
10. Solovay MR, Shenton ME, Holzman PS: Comparative studies of thought disorders. I. Mania and schizophrenia. Arch Gen Psychiatry 44:13–20, 1987
11. Owens H, Maxmen JS: Mood and affect: a semantic confusion. Am J Psychiatry 136:97–99, 1979
12. Abrams R, Taylor MA: A rating scale for emotional blunting. Am J Psychiatry 135:226–229, 1978
13. Boeringa JA, Castellani S: Reliability and validity of emotional blunting as a criterion for diagnosis of schizophrenia. Am J Psychiatry 139:1131–1135, 1982
14. Andreasen NC: Negative symptoms in schizophrenia: definition and reliability. Arch Gen Psychiatry 39:784–788, 1982
15. Andreasen NC: Positive vs. negative schizophrenia: a critical evaluation. Schizophr Bull 11:380–389, 1985
16. Heinrichs DW, Hanlon TE, Carpenter WT Jr: The quality of life scale: an instrument for rating the schizophrenic deficit syndrome. Schizophr Bull 10:388–398, 1984
17. Carpenter WT Jr, Heinrichs DW, Wagman AMI: Deficit and nondeficit forms of schizophrenia: the concept. Am J Psychiatry 145:578–583, 1988
18. Harding CM, Brooks GW, Ashikaga T, Strauss JS, Breier A: The Vermont longitudinal study of persons with severe mental illness: I. Methodology, study sample, and overall status 32 years later. Am J Psychiatry 144:718–726, 1987
19. Harding CM, Brooks GW, Ashikaga T, Strauss JS, Breier A: The Vermont longitudinal study: II. Long-term outcome of subjects who retrospec-

tively met DSM-III criteria for schizophrenia. Am J Psychiatry 144:727–735, 1987
20. Helzer JE, Brockington IF, Kendell RE: Predictive validity of DSM-III and Feighner definitions of schizophrenia: a comparison with Research Diagnostic Criteria and CATEGO. Arch Gen Psychiatry 38:791–797, 1981
21. Stephens JH, Astrup C, Carpenter WT Jr, Shaffer JW, Goldberg J: A comparison of nine systems to diagnose schizophrenia. Psychiatry Res 6:127–143, 1982
22. Westermeyer JF, Harrow M: Prognosis and outcome using broad (DSM-II) and narrow (DSM-III) concepts of schizophrenia. Schizophr Bull 10:624–637, 1984
23. McGlashan TH: Testing four diagnostic systems for schizophrenia. Arch Gen Psychiatry 41:141–144, 1984
24. Endicott J, Nee J, Cohen J, Fleiss JL, Simon R: Diagnosis of schizophrenia: prediction of short-term outcome. Arch Gen Psychiatry 43:13–19, 1986
25. Endicott J, Nee J, Coryell W, Keller M, Andreasen N, Croughan J: Schizoaffective, psychotic, and nonpsychotic depression: differential familial association. Compr Psychiatry 27:1–13, 1986
26. Pulver AD, Carpenter WT Jr: Lifetime psychotic symptoms assessed with the DIS. Schizophr Bull 9:377–382, 1983
27. Ollerenshaw DP: The classification of the functional psychoses. Br J Psychiatry 122:517–530, 1973
28. Skodol A, Buckley P, Salamon I: The ubiquitous symptoms of schizophrenia. Compr Psychiatry 17:511–516, 1976
29. Woods BT, Kinney DK, Yurgelun-Todd D: Neurologic abnormalities in schizophrenic patients and their families. I. Comparison of schizophrenic, bipolar, and substance abuse patients and normal controls. Arch Gen Psychiatry 43:657–663, 1986
30. Heinrichs DW, Buchanan RW: Significance and meaning of neurological signs in schizophrenia. Am J Psychiatry 145:11–18, 1988
31. Tsuang MT, Simpson JC, Kronfol Z: Subtypes of drug abuse with psychosis: demographic characteristics, clinical features, and family history. Arch Gen Psychiatry 39:141–147, 1982
32. Bowers MB Jr: Acute psychosis induced by psychotomimetic drug abuse: I. Clinical findings. Arch Gen Psychiatry 27:437–440, 1972
33. Bishop ER Jr, Holt AR: Pseudopsychosis: a reexamination of the concept of hysterical psychosis. Compr Psychiatry 21:150–161, 1980
34. American Psychiatric Association: Diagnostic and Statistical Manual of Mental Disorders, Third Edition. Washington, DC, American Psychiatric Association, 1980
35. Rosenhan DL: On being sane in insane places. Science 179:250–258, 1973
36. Spitzer RL: More on pseudoscience in science and the case for psychiatric diagnosis: a critique of DL Rosenhan's "On being sane in insane places" and "The contextual nature of psychiatric diagnosis." Arch Gen Psychiatry 33:459–470, 1976
37. Spitzer RL, Skodol AE, Gibbon M, Williams JBW: Psychopathology: A Case Book. New York, McGraw-Hill, 1983
38. Copeland JRM, Cooper JE, Kendell RE, Gourlay AJ: Differences in usage of diagnostic labels amongst psychiatrists in the British Isles. Br J Psychiatry 118:629–640, 1971
39. Kendell RE, Cooper JE, Gourlay AJ, Copeland JRM, Sharpe L, Gurland

BJ: Diagnostic criteria of American and British psychiatrists. Arch Gen Psychiatry 25:123–130, 1971

40. Lipkowitz MH, Idupuganti S: Diagnosing schizophrenia in 1980: a survey of U.S. psychiatrists. Am J Psychiatry 140:52–55, 1983
41. Lipkowitz MH, Idupuganti S: Diagnosing schizophrenia in 1982: the effect of DSM-III. Am J Psychiatry 142:634–637, 1985
42. Kendell RE, Brockington IF, Leff JP: Prognostic implications of six alternative definitions of schizophrenia. Arch Gen Psychiatry 36:25–34, 1979
43. Kendler KS: Schizophrenia and other psychotic disorders, in An Annotated Bibiography of DSM-III. Edited by Skodol AE, Spitzer RL. Washington, DC, American Psychiatric Press, 1987, pp 85–93
44. Kendler KS, Spitzer RL, Williams JBW: Psychotic disorders in DSM-III-R. Unpublished manuscript
45. Kendler KS: Demography of paranoid psychosis (delusional disorder): a review and comparison with schizophrenia and affective illness. Arch Gen Psychiatry 39:890–902, 1982
46. Kendler KS, Masterson CC, Davis KL: Psychiatric illness in first degree relatives of patients with paranoid psychosis, schizophrenia and medical illness. Br J Psychiatry 147:524–531, 1985
47. Kendler KS: Are there delusions specific for paranoid disorders vs. schizophrenia? Schizophr Bull 6:1–3, 1980
48. Kendler KS: The nosologic validity of paranoia (simple delusional disorder). Arch Gen Psychiatry 37:699–706, 1980
49. Winokur G: Delusional disorder (paranoia). Compr Psychiatry 18:511–521, 1977
50. Endicott J, Nee J, Fleiss J, Cohen J, Williams JBW, Simon R: Diagnostic criteria for schizophrenia: reliabilities and agreement between systems. Arch Gen Psychiatry 39:884–889, 1982
51. Tsuang MT, Dempsey GM, Rauscher FL: A study of atypical schizophrenia. Arch Gen Psychiatry 33:1157–1160, 1976
52. Sartorius N, Jablensky A, Shapiro R: Cross-cultural differences in the short term prognosis of schizophrenic psychoses. Schizophr Bull 4:102–113, 1978
53. Helzer JE, Kendell RE, Brockington IF: Contribution of the six-month criterion to the predictive validity of the DSM-III definition of schizophrenia. Arch Gen Psychiatry 40:1277–1280, 1983
54. Spring B: Stress and schizophrenia: some definitional issues. Schizophr Bull 7:24–33, 1981
55. Brockington IF, Meltzer HY: Documenting an episode of psychiatric illness: need for multiple information sources, multiple raters, and narrative. Schizophr Bull 8:485–492, 1982
56. Docherty JP, van Kammen DP, Siris SG, Marder SR: Stages of onset of schizophrenic psychosis. Am J Psychiatry 135:420–426, 1978
57. Herz MI, Melville C: Relapse in schizophrenia. Am J Psychiatry 137:801–805, 1980
58. Heinrichs DW, Carpenter WT Jr: Prospective study of prodromal symptoms in schizophrenic relapse. Am J Psychiatry 142:371–373, 1985
59. Spitzer RL, Skodol AE, Gibbon M, Williams JBW: DSM-III Casebook. Washington, DC, American Psychiatric Association, 1981
60. Beiser M, Fleming JAE, Iacono WG, Lin T-Y: Refining the diagnosis of schizophreniform disorder. Am J Psychiatry 145:695–700, 1988
61. Link BG, Cullen FT, Frank J, Wozniak JF: The social rejection of former

mental patients: understanding why labels matter. Am J Sociology 92:1461–1500, 1987

62. Kane JM, Smith JM: Tardive dyskinesia: prevalence and risk factors 1959–79. Arch Gen Psychiatry 39:473–481, 1982
63. Goldberg SC, Schultz SC, Schultz PM, Resnick RJ, Hamer RM, Friedel RO: Borderline and schizotypal personality disorders treated with low-dose thiothixene vs placebo. Arch Gen Psychiatry 43:680–686, 1986
64. Kendler KS, Gruenberg AM, Tsuang MT: Subtype stability in schizophrenia. Am J Psychiatry 142:827–832, 1985
65. Hogarty GE, Schooler NR, Ulrich RF, Mussare F, Herron E, Ferro P: Fluphenazine and social therapy in the aftercare of schizophrenic patients: relapse analyses of a two-year controlled study of fluphenazine decanoate and fluphenazine hydrochloride. Arch Gen Psychiatry 361:1283–1294, 1979
66. Schooler NR, Levine J, Severe JB, Brauzer B, DiMascio A, Klerman GL, Tuason VB: Prevention of relapse in schizophrenia: an evaluation of fluphenazine decanoate. Arch Gen Psychiatry 37:16–24, 1980
67. Falloon I, Watt DC, Shepperd M: A comparative controlled trial of pimozide and fluphenazine decanoate in the continuation therapy of schizophrenia. Psychol Med 8:59–70, 1978
68. Falloon IRH, Boyd JL, McGill CW, Razoni J, Moss HB, Gilderman HA: Family management in the prevention of exacerbations of schizophrenia. N Engl J Med 306:1437–1444, 1982
69. Leff J, Kuipers L, Berkowitz R, Eberlein-Vries R, Sturgeon D: A controlled trial of social intervention in the families of schizophrenic patients. Br J Psychiatry 141:121–134, 1982
70. Prien RF, Caffey EM, Klett CJ: A comparison of lithium carbonate and chlorpromazine in the treatment of excited schizoaffectives. Arch Gen Psychiatry 27:182–189, 1972
71. Maj M: Effectiveness of lithium prophylaxis in schizoaffective psychoses: application of a polydiagnostic approach. Acta Psychiatr Scand 70:228–234, 1984
72. Coryell W, Tsuang MT: DSM-III schizophreniform disorder: comparisons with schizophrenia and affective disorder. Arch Gen Psychiatry 39:66–69, 1982
73. Coryell W, Tsuang MT: Outcome after 40 years in DSM-III schizophreniform disorder. Arch Gen Psychiatry 43:324–328, 1986
74. Gibbon M, Spitzer RL: DSM-III schizophreniform disorder (letter). Arch Gen Psychiatry 40:1255–1256, 1983
75. Fogelson DL, Cohen BM, Pope HG: A study of DSM-III schizophreniform disorder. Am J Psychiatry 139:1281–1285, 1982
76. Breier A, Wolkowitz OM, Doran AR, Roy A, Boronow J, Hommer DW, Pickar D: Neuroleptic responsivity of negative and positive symptoms in schizophrenia. Am J Psychiatry 144:1549–1555, 1987
77. Kendell RE: DSM-III: a British perspective (book forum). Am J Psychiatry 137:1630–1631, 1980
78. Fenton WS, Mosher LR, Matthews SM: Diagnosis of schizophrenia: a critical review of current diagnostic systems. Schizophr Bull 7:452–476, 1981
79. Strauss JS, Hafez H, Lieberman P, Harding CM: The course of psychiatric disorder, III: Longitudinal principles. Am J Psychiatry 142:289–296, 1985

80. Taylor MA, Abrams R: The phenomenology of mania: a new look at some old patients. Arch Gen Psychiatry 29:520–522, 1973
81. Taylor MA, Gaztanaga P, Abrams R: Manic-depressive illness and acute schizophrenia: a clinical, family history, and treatment-response study. Am J Psychiatry 131:678–682, 1974
82. Abrams R, Taylor MA, Gaztanaga P: Manic-depressive illness and paranoid schizophrenia: a phenomenologic, family history, and treatment-response study. Arch Gen Psychiatry 31:640–642, 1974
83. Taylor MA, Abrams R: Manic-depressive illness and "good prognosis" schizophrenia. Am J Psychiatry 132:741–742, 1975
84. Pope HG Jr, Lipinski J: Diagnosis in schizophrenia and manic-depressive illness: a reassessment of the specificity of "schizophrenic" symptoms in the light of current research. Arch Gen Psychiatry 35:811–828, 1978
85. Spitzer RL, Endicott J, Robins E: Research Diagnostic Criteria: rationale and reliability. Arch Gen Psychiatry 35:773–789, 1978
86. Williams JBW, Spitzer RL: DSM-III forum: diagnosing psychotic disorders and affective disorders with psychotic features. Hosp Community Psychiatry 34:595–596, 1983
87. Siris SG, Rifkin A, Reardon GT, Doddi SR, Strahan A, Hall KS: Stability of the postpsychotic depression syndrome. J Clin Psychiatry 47:86–88, 1986
88. Siris SG, Rifkin A, Reardon GT, Endicott J, Pereira DH, Hayes R, Casey E: Course-related depressive syndromes in schizophrenia. Am J Psychiatry 141:1254–1257, 1984
89. Siris SG, Morgan V, Fagerstrom R, Rifkin A, Cooper TB: Adjunctive imipramine in the treatment of postpsychotic depression. Arch Gen Psychiatry 44:533–539, 1987
90. Rosenthal NE, Rosenthal LN, Stallone F, Dunner DL, Fieve RR: Toward the validation of RDC schizoaffective disorder. Arch Gen Psychiatry 37:804–810, 1980
91. Pope HG Jr, Lipinski JF, Cohen BM, Axelrod DT: "Schizoaffective disorder": an invalid diagnosis? A comparison of schizoaffective disorder, schizophrenia, and affective disorder. Am J Psychiatry 137:921–927, 1980
92. Brockington IF, Wainwright S, Kendell RE: Manic patients with schizophrenic or paranoid symptoms. Psychol Med 10:73–83, 1980
93. Abrams R, Taylor MA: Importance of schizophrenic symptoms in the diagnosis of mania. Am J Psychiatry 138:658–661, 1981
94. Brockington IF, Kendell RE, Wainwright S: Depressed patients with schizophrenic or paranoid symptoms. Psychol Med 10:665–675, 1980
95. Brockington IF, Helzer JE, Hillier VF, Francis AF: Definitions of depression: concordance and prediction of outcome. Am J Psychiatry 139:1022–1027, 1982
96. Coryell W, Tsuang MT: Major depression with mood-congruent or mood-incongruent psychotic features: outcome after 40 years. Am J Psychiatry 142:479–482, 1985
97. Procci WR: Schizo-affective psychosis: fact or fiction? A survey of the literature. Arch Gen Psychiatry 33:1167–1178, 1976
98. Brockington IF, Leff JP: Schizoaffective psychosis: definitions and incidence. Psychol Med 9:91–99, 1979
99. Meltzer HY, Arora RC, Metz J: Biological studies of schizoaffective disorders. Schizophr Bull 10:49–70, 1984
100. Meltzer HY: Schizoaffective disorder: is the news of its nonexistence

premature? Schizophr Bull 10:11–13, 1984
101. Himmelhoch JM, Fuchs CZ, May SJ, Symons BJ, Neil JF: When a schizoaffective diagnosis has meaning. J Nerv Ment Dis 169:277–282, 1981
102. Levinson DF, Levitt MEM: Schizoaffective mania reconsidered. Am J Psychiatry 144:415–425, 1987
103. Brockington IF, Meltzer HY: The nosology of schizoaffective psychosis. Psychiatr Dev 4:317–338, 1983
104. Levitt JJ, Tsuang MT: The heterogeneity of schizoaffective disorder: implications for treatment. Am J Psychiatry 145:926–936, 1988
105. Sheehan S: The patient, I: Creedmoor Psychiatric Center. The New Yorker, May 25, 1981, pp 49–111
106. Sheehan S: The patient, II: Disappearing incidents. The New Yorker, June 1, 1981, pp 53–123
107. Sheehan S: The patient, III: Is there no place on earth for me? The New Yorker, June 8, 1981, pp 50–128
108. Sheehan S: The patient, IV: The air is too still. The New Yorker, June 15, 1981, pp 46–124
109. Frances A, Skodol AE: The case of Sylvia Frumkin: misdiagnosis or misfortune? Hosp Community Psychiatry 33:807–808, 1982
110. Grahame PS: Schizophrenia in old age (late paraphrenia). Br J Psychiatry 145:493–495, 1984
111. Rabins P, Pauker S, Thomas J: Can schizophrenia begin after age 44? Compr Psychiatry 25:290–293, 1984
112. Volavka J: Late-onset schizophrenia: a review. Compr Psychiatry 26:148–156, 1985
113. Cantor S, Evans J, Pearce J, Pezzot-Pearce T: Childhood schizophrenia: present but not accounted for. Am J Psychiatry 139:758–762, 1982

CHAPTER 6

Mood Disturbances

Most clinically significant disturbances in mood were classified as affective disorders in DSM-III. Those in which a physical disease or exogenous agent known to cause a mood abnormality could be identified were called organic affective disorders and were classified with the organic mental disorders. Although research evidence has been accumulating that biological factors underlie many of the psychopathological conditions referred to as affective disorders, these factors are as yet not well enough identified or specified to conceptualize such disorders as "organic" in the sense in which that term is used in DSM-III.

Minor disturbances in mood that are reactions to psychosocial stress are called adjustment disorders. Some disturbances in mood, e.g., that following the death of a person one cares about, are considered normal or even adaptive. These normal grief reactions are called uncomplicated bereavement in the DSM-III and DSM-III-R systems, and are classified as V codes, conditions not attributable to a mental disorder that are a focus of attention or treatment. Differential diagnosis of *nonorganic* mood disturbances is the subject of the present chapter.

Revised Terminology and Reorganization of the DSM-III Class

Communication about emotions has typically suffered from semantic confusion regarding the meaning of the terms *mood* and *affect* (1). As noted in Chapter 1, the DSM-III distinction is drawn on the basis of the pervasiveness and persistence of the disturbance. Mood is like climate, and affect is like weather: the former is more lasting, whereas the latter is transitory and changing. Moods are described as depressed, euphoric, irritable, or dysphoric; normal mood is called euthymic. Affects include sadness and elation, but also anxiety and anger. Disturbances characterized by anxiety have not, traditionally, been called affective disorders, but are grouped in their own diagnostic class.

Disturbances with anger as a prominent feature have no unified class, but are scattered throughout the classification, e.g., as conduct disorders, organic mental disorders, psychotic disorders, or personality disorders. As yet there does not appear to be a disorder whose essential feature (meaning most predominant clinical feature) is anger. Chapter 10 in this book, Antisocial, Aggressive, or Violent Behavior, examines in detail the more extreme situations in which anger may play an important part.

Because of the mood/affect confusion and the self-evident conclusion that significant disturbances of feelings and emotions along the depression/euphoria continuum are disturbances of mood, not affect, DSM-III-R has changed the name of the pertinent class of disorders from affective disorders to mood disorders. It is hoped that this will further more uniform use of terminology in this area.

The second most obvious change in DSM-III-R from DSM-III in this segment of the classification has been a reorganization of the major diagnostic categories. In DSM-III, the affective disorders were subdivided into major, "other specific," and atypical affective disorders. The major affective disorders, major depression (unipolar affective disorder) and bipolar disorder, were the most severe in terms of symptoms. The "other specific," dysthymic disorder and cyclothymic disorder, were symptomatically less severe, but more chronic. The "other specific" category was an awkward concession to critics who argued that the original draft term *chronic minor* would create problems by implying that these disorders were either not severe enough or likely enough to respond to treatment to justify their being treated at all.

The atypical affective disorders in DSM-III were simply residual categories for patients with significant mood disturbances that did not meet the criteria for one of the four specified diagnoses. "Atypical" was used throughout DSM-III to indicate this type of residual diagnosis in each diagnostic class; with reference to the affective disorders, however, this term was particularly unfortunate and caused considerable confusion and consternation. "Atypical depression" had been proposed during the course of DSM-III's development as a term referring to a syndrome with a particular set of signs and symptoms that possibly predicted a selective response to monoamine oxidase (MAO) inhibitor antidepressants (2), but this was not the concept embodied in the DSM-III diagnosis of atypical affective disorder.

DSM-III-R Terms and Classification

In DSM-III-R the mood disorders are divided into bipolar disorders and depressive disorders. This division preserves the DSM-III separation of mood disorders into a unipolar type, in which the patient has only depressive episodes (one or more), and a bipolar type, in which the patient has both manic and depressive episodes (3,4). It also recognizes accumulating evidence of the similarity—on phenomenological, biological, and genetic grounds—of the milder, chronic forms of mood disorders to their major counterparts (5-10). Therefore, dysthymia (chronic, mild depression) and cyclothymia (a chronic pattern of alternating highs and lows) are classified as depressive disorders and bipolar disorders respectively. The minor changes in the names of these disorders reflect current usage.

Within each major subgroup of the mood disorders is a residual category; in keeping with the terminological overhaul throughout DSM-III-R for these residual categories, they are called "bipolar disorder not otherwise specified (NOS)" and "depressive disorder not otherwise specified (NOS)." An effort has been made to expand the definitions of these residual categories in DSM-III-R and to provide more examples. These will be discussed below in the sections on differential diagnosis.

Overview of Differential Diagnosis

Figure 6.1 illustrates the DSM-III-R diagnostic decision tree for the differential diagnosis of mood disturbances.

The clinician considers the differential diagnostic logic represented by this tree once a persistently depressed, elevated, expansive, or irritable mood is considered the predominant clinical problem. Table 6.1 summarizes the diagnostic possibilities represented by the decision tree.

Mood Disturbance and Physical Illness

Both depressed and elated mood disturbances may result from physical illness, various medications, and substances of abuse. Differentiating delirium and dementia and organic mood syndromes from functional mood disorders is discussed in Chapter 3. Mood abnormalities that result from the use of psychoactive substances are considered in Chapter 4. In Chapter 11, the differential diagnosis of major depression in the presence of physical illness is discussed.

Figure 6.1 DSM-III-R Decision Tree for the Differential Diagnosis of Mood Disturbances

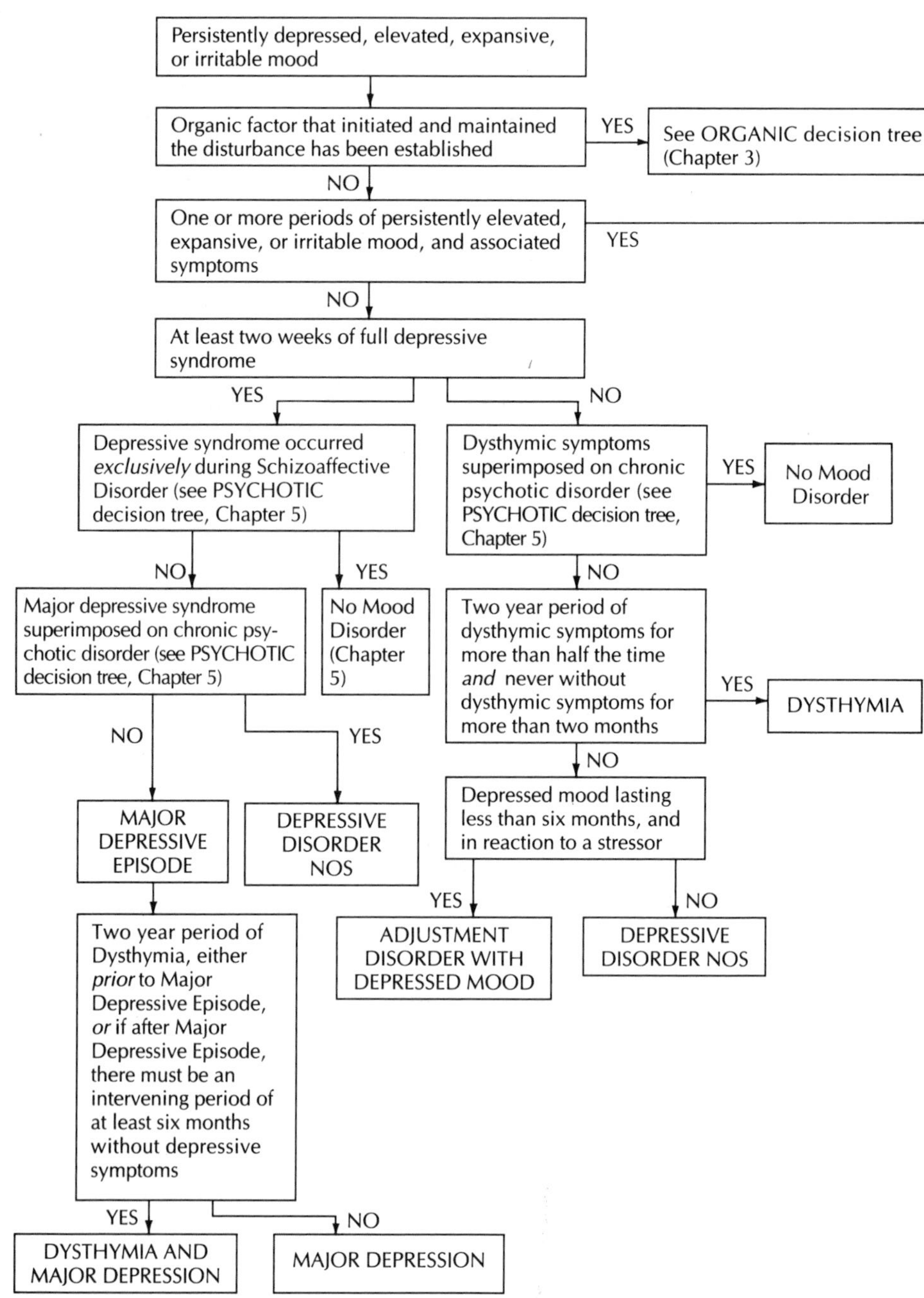

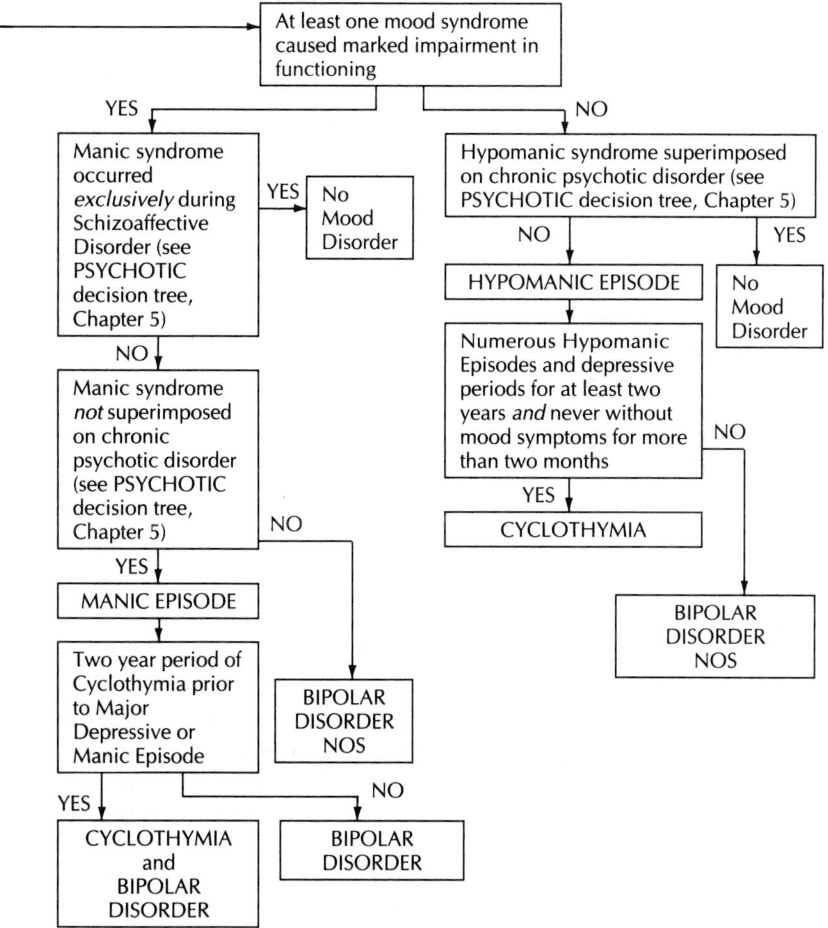
At least one mood syndrome caused marked impairment in functioning
YES
NO
Manic syndrome occurred *exclusively* during Schizoaffective Disorder (see PSYCHOTIC decision tree, Chapter 5)
YES
No Mood Disorder
NO
Manic syndrome *not* superimposed on chronic psychotic disorder (see PSYCHOTIC decision tree, Chapter 5)
YES
NO
MANIC EPISODE
Two year period of Cyclothymia prior to Major Depressive or Manic Episode
YES
NO
CYCLOTHYMIA and BIPOLAR DISORDER
BIPOLAR DISORDER
BIPOLAR DISORDER NOS
Hypomanic syndrome superimposed on chronic psychotic disorder (see PSYCHOTIC decision tree, Chapter 5)
NO
YES
HYPOMANIC EPISODE
No Mood Disorder
Numerous Hypomanic Episodes and depressive periods for at least two years *and* never without mood symptoms for more than two months
YES
NO
CYCLOTHYMIA
BIPOLAR DISORDER NOS

Table 6.1 Disorders in the Differential Diagnosis of Disturbances in Mood

ORGANIC MENTAL DISORDERS
- Delirium
- Dementia
- Organic mood syndrome
- Psychoactive substance-induced intoxication
- Psychoactive substance-induced withdrawal

PSYCHOTIC DISORDERS
- Schizophrenia or other psychotic disorder with superimposed mood disorder
- Schizoaffective disorder

MOOD DISORDERS
- Depressive disorders
  - Major depression
  - Dysthymia
  - Depressive disorder NOS
- Bipolar disorders
  - Bipolar disorder
  - Cyclothymia
  - Bipolar disorder NOS

ADJUSTMENT DISORDER
- Adjustment disorder with depressed mood
- Adjustment disorder with mixed emotional features

Mood Disturbances in Psychotic Disorders

Differentiating mood disorders with psychotic features from psychotic disorders with associated abnormalities in mood depends on the relative durations of the two types of disturbance and on the relationship of the syndromes to each other over time. This differential diagnostic problem is discussed in Chapter 5 in terms of cases in which psychotic features constitute the predominant syndrome, whereas in this chapter the emphasis is on the mood disturbances.

If an organic mental disorder (including those that are induced by psychoactive substances) and psychotic disorders other than psychotic mood disorders have been ruled out, the clinician considers next the mood disorders themselves. The individual DSM-III-R mood disorders and their key identifying features are summarized in Table 6.2.

Table 6.2 Identifying Features of DSM-III-R Mood Disorders

Disorder	Symptom Picture	Severity	Duration
Major depression	Depressive episode(s) only	5 of 9 symptoms every day	Minimum 2 weeks
Bipolar disorder	Manic and depressive episodes, or manic episode(s) only	3 or 4* of 7 symptoms; impairment or hospitalization	No minimum
Dysthymia	Depressed mood	2 of 6 symptoms	Minimum 2 years
Cyclothymia	Hypomanic episodes alternating with depressed mood	No marked impairment or hospitalization	Minimum 2 years
Depressive disorder NOS	Depressive features	Below threshold for major depression	Less than 2 weeks if severe; less than two years or not sustained if mild
Bipolar disorder NOS	Manic or hypomanic features	Below threshold for bipolar disorder	Less than 2 years or not sustained

*Four of seven associated symptoms of mania are needed if the mood disturbance is limited to irritability.

Depressive Disorders: Major Depression

The mood disorders in general, and the depressive disorders in particular, have generated more research and clinical interest in the past 15 years than any other area of psychopathology. Interestingly, there are still many questions concerning the validity of the diagnostic distinctions drawn among various subtypes of mood disorders and between mood disorders and other mental disorders. The difficulties in making these distinctions and their importance will be discussed in the following sections.

Some of the more difficult and confusing aspects of the diagnosis of DSM-III major depression have been (*1*) its threshold for clinical significance, (*2*) its relationship to other related diagnostic concepts of depression, (*3*) the differentiation and clinical utility of its subtypes, and (4) its differential diagnosis from other mental disorders and conditions, including other mood disorders, organic mental disorders, psychotic disorders, anxiety disorders, personality disorders, and normal grief reactions.

Determining the Threshold for Clinical Significance

DSM-III (and DSM-III-R) criteria define major depressive episodes. The same kind of episode may occur in either major depression or bipolar disorder. The threshold for clinical significance of a major depressive episode is set by the requirements of the presence of a depressed mood or loss of interest or pleasure nearly every day for two weeks or more plus at least four more of eight commonly associated symptoms every day during the same two weeks. These symptoms include the familiar sleep disturbance, weight disturbance, psychomotor changes, suicidal ideation, etc.

Some clinicians and investigators have objected that these criteria are too easily met and that depressions of marginal significance are therefore wrongly identified (11). The closest diagnostic concept to DSM-III major depression is the Research Diagnostic Criteria (RDC) definition, which requires evidence of significant impairment in social or occupational functioning and five of a comparable list of eight associated symptoms (12).

Most clinicians and researchers are looking for the diagnosis of major depression to identify a patient group that will be homogeneous with respect to pathogenesis, treatment response, and outcome. DSM-III major depression is clearly a more heterogeneous category than is ideal. It can include cases that vary widely in severity, from some mild enough to have been diagnosed as neurotic depression (10) in past systems to others that have the pervasiveness and persistence of a biological disturbance. DSM-III major depression can also subsume relatively severe reactions to psychosocial stress (recorded and coded on axis IV) that are currently being referred to as situational depressions (13,14).

DSM-III-R major depression continues to be inclusive in terms of severity, but the format of the criteria has been changed, because of an inadvertent weakening of DSM-III criteria. DSM-III recognized that certain patients with serious depression did not complain about depressed mood per se, but rather mentioned a pervasive loss of interest in usual activities and an inability to experience pleasure. Therefore, criterion A for the essential feature of a major depressive episode (MDE) referred to either of these two possibilities. Loss of interest or pleasure also appeared, however, in the index of symptoms in criterion B. Thus, a patient with loss of interest or pleasure as the principal manifestation of his or her mood disturbance could have this symptom counted twice, once in A and once in B, and meet criteria for a full depressive syndrome with only three other associated symptoms. In order to eliminate the redundancy, criteria A and B for DSM-III MDE have been combined in DSM-III-R into a single nine item A criterion specifying that "At least five of the following symptoms have been present during the same two-week period and represent a change from previous functioning; at least one of the symptoms is either (1) depressed mood, or (2) loss of interest or pleasure" (15, p. 222). The other seven symptoms in the list continue to refer to the same associated symptoms as in DSM-III. The DSM-III-R diagnostic criteria for a major depressive episode are reproduced in Table 6.3.

Two other changes have been made in the symptom criteria for MDEs that affect judgments of clinical significance. The first addresses clinical situations in which another mental or physical disorder may directly cause a symptom resembling one of those in the MDE list. Examples would be active delusions or hallucinations that make a person unable to sleep at night (#4, insomnia), formal thought disorder that diminishes a person's capacity to think or concentrate (#8), or a medical illness, such as cancer, that causes anorexia and weight loss. DSM-III-R criterion A includes the statement: "Do not include symptoms that are clearly due to a physical condition, mood-incongruent delusions, or hallucinations, incoherence, or marked loosening of associations" (15, p. 222). Differentiating major depression from certain psychotic disorders or from depression stemming from physical illness (see below) is difficult enough without further confusing the issue by misinterpreting the diagnostic significance of a particular symptom.

The other modification of the symptom list for MDE that assists clinical judgments of significance is that objective evidence is emphasized in addition to a patient's subjective report. Thus, the clinician's or a relative's observation that the patient looks sad or depressed, apathetic or uninterested, and cannot think clearly or concentrate has been added to the criterion items. Psychomotor agitation or retardation continues to be judged only on the basis of objective observation, not subjective feelings, as was the intention in DSM-III.

Furthermore, in DSM-III-R, major depressive episodes can be subclassified in terms of their severity, in the 5th digit of the diagnostic code, as mild; moderate; or severe, without psychotic features. Cases subtyped as mild have few symptoms in excess of those required to make the diagnosis *and* only minor impairment in occupational or social functioning. Moderate major depression would have symptoms or functional impairment more serious than those in

Table 6.3 DSM-III-R Diagnostic Criteria for Major Depressive Episode

Note: A "Major Depressive Syndrome" is defined as criterion A below.

A. At least five of the following symptoms have been present during the same two-week period and represent a change from previous functioning; at least one of the symptoms is either (1) depressed mood, or (2) loss of interest or pleasure. (Do not include symptoms that are clearly due to a physical condition, mood-incongruent delusions or hallucinations, incoherence, or marked loosening of associations.)

   (1) depressed mood (or can be irritable mood in children and adolescents) most of the day, nearly every day, as indicated either by subjective account or observation by others
   (2) markedly diminished interest or pleasure in all, or almost all, activities most of the day, nearly every day (as indicated either by subjective account or observation by others of apathy most of the time)
   (3) significant weight loss or weight gain when not dieting (e.g., more than 5% of body weight in a month), or decrease or increase in appetite nearly every day (in children, consider failure to make expected weight gains)
   (4) insomnia or hypersomnia nearly every day
   (5) psychomotor agitation or retardation nearly every day (observable by others, not merely subjective feelings of restlessness or being slowed down)
   (6) fatigue or loss of energy nearly every day
   (7) feelings of worthlessness or excessive or inappropriate guilt (which may be delusional) nearly every day (not merely self-reproach or guilt about being sick)
   (8) diminished ability to think or concentrate, or indecisiveness, nearly every day (either by subjective account or as observed by others)
   (9) recurrent thoughts of death (not just fear of dying), recurrent suicidal ideation without a specific plan, or a suicide attempt or a specific plan for committing suicide

B. (1) It cannot be established that an organic factor initiated and maintained the disturbance.
   (2) The disturbance is not a normal reaction to the death of a loved one (uncomplicated bereavement).

   Note: Morbid preoccupation with worthlessness, suicidal ideation, marked functional impairment or psychomotor retardation, or prolonged duration suggest bereavement complicated by major depression.

C. At no time during the disturbance have there been delusions or hallucinations for as long as two weeks in the absence of prominent mood symptoms (i.e., before the mood symptoms developed or after they have remitted).

D. Not superimposed on schizophrenia, schizophreniform disorder, delusional disorder, or psychotic disorder NOS.

Specify chronic if current episode has lasted two consecutive years without a period of two months or longer during which there were no significant depressive symptoms.

Specify if current episode is **melancholic type.**

Diagnostic criteria for melancholic type

The presence of at least five of the following:

(1) loss of interest or pleasure in all, or almost all, activities
(2) lack of reactivity to usually pleasurable stimuli (does not feel much better, even temporarily, when something good happens)
(3) depression regularly worse in the morning
(4) early morning awakening (at least two hours before usual time of awakening)
(5) psychomotor retardation or agitation (not merely subjective complaints)
(6) significant anorexia or weight loss (e.g., more than 5% of body weight in a month)
(7) no significant personality disturbance before first major depressive episode
(8) one or more previous major depressive episodes followed by complete, or nearly complete, recovery
(9) previous good response to specific and adequate somatic antidepressant therapy, e.g., tricyclics, ECT, MAOI, lithium

Diagnostic criteria for seasonal pattern

A. There has been a regular temporal relationship between the onset of an episode of bipolar disorder (including bipolar disorder NOS) or recurrent major depression (including depressive disorder NOS) and a particular 60-day period of the year (e.g., regular appearance of depression between the beginning of October and the end of November).

   Note: Do not include cases in which there is an obvious effect of seasonally related psychosocial stressors, e.g., regularly being unemployed every winter.

B. Full remissions (or a change from depression to mania or hypomania) also occured within a particular 60-day period of the year (e.g., depression disappears from mid-February to mid-April).

C. There have been at least three episodes of mood disturbance in three separate years that demonstrated the temporal seasonal relationship defined in A and B; at least two of the years were consecutive.

D. Seasonal episodes of mood disturbance, as described above, outnumbered any nonseasonal episodes of such disturbance that may have occurred by more than three to one.

"mild," but less than those in "severe" depression. Cases of severe major depression have several symptoms in excess of those required for the diagnosis and marked resulting interference with occupational functioning or relationships with others. This subcategory includes no psychotic symptoms, however; these are indicated in another 5th-digit code (see below).

Thresholds for clinical significance are important in differentiating major depressive episodes from chronic dysthymia and from the affective instability of certain personality disorders, and will be discussed below under relevant, specific, differential diagnoses.

Major depression vs. adjustment disorder. If a depressive disturbance fails to meet criterion A because it is not severe enough, then there are two diagnostic possibilities.

Depression resulting from a psychosocial stressor may be diagnosed as an adjustment disorder with depressed mood or with mixed emotional features. The core concepts of an adjustment disorder in DSM-III-R are virtually the same as those in DSM-III and require: (*1*) a psychosocial stressor occurring within the three months before onset of the disturbance, (2) a maladaptive reaction on the part of the patient that is either socially or occupationally impairing or consists of symptoms in excess of a normal or expectable reaction to the stressor, and (*3*) exclusion of the possibility that the disturbance is an instance of a pattern of overreaction to stress or an exacerbation of a more pervasive mental disorder. The three-month time limit represents an effort to ensure that a reaction is traceable to a particular event or set of circumstances, since almost everyone experiences stressors at one time or another. The association should not be spurious: stressors cause problems of some kind in almost everyone; thus evidence of a maladaptive response is required in order to diagnose even this mild mental disorder. If the disturbance is normal and expectable and does not cause impairment, then a V code, such as phase-of-life problem or other life-circumstance problem, marital problem, other specified family circumstances, or other interpersonal problem, may be the appropriate designation.

Clinical judgment is obviously crucial in this distinction. Since certain personality disorders (e.g., the borderline and histrionic) are characterized by unstable affect and overreaction, it is important to differentiate adjustment disorders from these behavior patterns. DSM-III and DSM-III-R state that diagnosis of an adjustment disorder is not made when *characteristic* features of a personality disorder are exacerbated by stress. However, if *new* symptoms are observed in reaction to a stressor, adjustment disorder may be an additional diagnosis.

Rough Times

"I've been having a very rough time," said a 35-year-old woman to the psychiatrist, as she wiped away her tears. The patient, a beautiful, vivacious, and successful fashion model, had been referred for consultation by a friend after she had broken down in tears for the second time in a week while modeling for a magazine feature.

Two weeks earlier the patient's boyfriend of three years had decided to break off their relationship. He claimed that she was "too needy" and did not allow him enough "space." "I was in a state of shock for two days," the woman related; "I couldn't even get out of bed." Subsequently, however, she pulled herself together, with the support of her friends, and tried to follow through on her modeling commitments. She found herself preoccupied with thoughts of the boyfriend and unable to focus on the photographer's directions. She had to take frequent breaks because she felt constantly on the verge of tears. The photographer and the client expressed annoyance that she had to leave the sessions.

The patient reported that she had some difficulty falling asleep but that her appetite was unchanged. She could not understand what she had done to drive her boyfriend away. She was concerned that it was because she was beginning to "show my age." Her worst times were when she thought about the prospect of being alone. Talking with her friends cheered her up.

On further questioning, it became apparent that the patient frequently needed statements and expressions of approval. She worried if her boyfriend did not call at his usual time; and if he was out of town, she worried that he would meet another, more attractive woman. Physical appearance, she believed, was always her major attraction, but lately the beginnings of lines in her face made her use more makeup and think that perhaps she should see a plastic surgeon. Although she described herself as a very emotional person who expressed joy with exuberance and disappointment with tears, only once before—also after a love affair ended—had she felt so bad that it interfered with her work.

When the psychiatrist offered to help her talk through her loss, she broke down again, entreating, "It hurts too much, Doctor. Can't you give me a pill that will take it all away?"

In this case, the woman described has evident histrionic personality traits that include emotional overreaction, but not to the degree experienced after the breakup with her boyfriend. Symptomatically, the depression is not severe enough for a diagnosis of major depression; but because it is affecting her functioning, a diagnosis of adjustment disorder with depressed mood is warranted.

One change in the DSM-III-R criteria for adjustment disorder appears in criterion D. In DSM-III this criterion referred to the duration that an adjustment disorder might have in terms that were too general for practical application. DSM-III stated that when a discrete stressor ceased, the disturbance should remit. If a stressor were ongoing, a person with adjustment disorder would be expected to adapt, with symptom resolution. The question arises, How long can a disturbance last and still be considered an adjustment disorder? DSM-III-R answers this question specifically, in criterion D: "The maladaptive reaction has persisted for no longer than six months." In the 10/15/86 draft of DSM-III-R criterion D, the six month maximum duration was to begin after the stressor (and its environmental consequences) had ceased.

Certain stressful events, such as a divorce, may appear to be discrete, but they may have residual effects that are themselves stressful, such as continued haggling over visitation rights for children. This makes possible the diagnosis of a chronic adjustment disorder. Since reference to "environmental" consequences was deleted in the final draft of DSM-III-R, clinicians will have to change a patient's diagnosis if the symptoms persist more than six months after the stressor unless the sequelae of the stressor are themselves considered new stressors. A concept of "linked" stressors has been described in the life-events literature (16).

Andreasen and her colleagues (17,18) have shown that adjustment disorders as defined in DSM-III have diagnostic validity; specifically, the expectation that the disorders would remit after the precipitating factors ceased was supported. Moreover, their data indicated the existence of a pattern of chronic symptoms in a minority of cases, which suggests that including chronic adjustment disorders in DSM-III-R may have been warranted. Recently, Fabrega and associates (19) found that people with adjustment disorder had higher levels of psychopathology than those receiving a V code, but lower levels than those receiving other DSM-III diagnoses. Patients with an adjustment disorder had experienced more stress, but functioned better, than those with other diagnoses; and they were more stressed, but functioned at a lower level, than those receiving V codes. These results also tended to validate the DSM-III and DSM-III-R use of the category of adjustment disorder as a marginal or transitional category of illness, a condition falling between the various specific diagnostic categories and the "not ill" (V codes) categories.

Other investigators have looked at the validity of stress-related depressions in a different way. Rather than make the diagnostic distinction in terms of severity, as the DSM-III systems do, they base it on the presence of a precipitating event. Depressions developing as a result of a psychosocial stressor they call "situational depressions."

The data on the validity of this diagnostic distinction are mixed.

Hirschfeld et al. (14) found that the presence of stressors did not distinguish depressive episodes from one another in terms of pattern of symptoms, life events, social supports, premorbid personality traits, recovery rates, or familial psychopathology. Zimmerman and co-workers (20) found that depressed inpatients with high ratings of stress on axis IV had poorer hospital outcomes and a trend toward poorer outcome at follow-up six months after discharge. Others have suggested that the category "neurotic" or "reactive" depression may have validity if emphasis is placed on coexisting personality problems (21). (The relationship of depression to personality disturbance will be discussed later in this chapter.) At present, the data at least suggest that symptom severity (adjustment disorder vs. major depression) exerts more of an effect on the prognosis of depressions precipitated by stress than does the presence of stressors themselves.

The second possibility if a depression is not severe enough to be classified as an MDE, and there is no stressor present, is a diagnosis of depressive disorder NOS. This is, in fact, one of the three specific examples of the use of the residual diagnosis given in DSM-III-R. The absence in DSM-III of a more specific diagnosis for milder depressions that are neither chronic nor stress-related has been the source of some criticism (21). Such a diagnosis would be the counterpart of RDC minor depression. The clinical significance of minor depression, however, is not known.

Relating the DSM to Other Diagnostic Systems

One of the most difficult tasks for the clinician is to interpret the significance of research data for clinical practice. This is particularly true in the area of affective or mood disorders, in which so much information has accumulated, but so many different diagnostic terms are in use. The relationship of DSM-III major depression to RDC major depressive disorder has already been mentioned, and is discussed in detail by Williams and Spitzer (22). The RDC are among the most extensively studied sets of criteria for the affective disorders because of the use of the Schedule for Affective Disorders and Schizophrenia (SADS)-RDC system in the NIMH-sponsored Collaborative Study of the Psychobiology of Depression (23).

Other important diagnostic concepts of depression are the primary-secondary affective disorders described by Winokur and coworkers (4) and what are known as the Feighner criteria for primary depression (24). The principal differences between the Feighner criteria and DSM-III and DSM-III-R are the following:

1. The Feighner criteria require evidence of a dysphoric mood,

and not just loss of interest or pleasure.

2. One additional associated symptom is needed (appetite and weight changes are limited to loss–increase is not included; otherwise, the symptoms are identical).

3. A one-month rather than a two-week duration is required.

4. There can be no prior history of significant mental disorder or any serious physical illness preceding or coinciding with the depression.

5. There can be no major psychotic symptoms.

A direct translation of DSM-III major depressions into the primary-secondary types is not possible since, with the exception of certain diagnostic hierarchies, DSM-III allows for multiple diagnoses to be made without any official notation of the temporal priority of the disturbances. Thus, depression occurring during the course of alcoholism is secondary according to the Winokur or Feighner systems, whereas in DSM-III, if major depression and alcohol dependence coexist, the principal diagnosis is the one that is currently the focus of treatment rather than the one that developed first. As was explained in Chapter 2, Multiaxial Diagnosis, the principal diagnosis can be one or the other at any particular time depending upon the treatment focus of the clinician. In the above example, for the psychiatrist prescribing antidepressants, major depression is the principal diagnosis, but for the AA counselor, it is alcohol dependence.

Differentiation and Clinical Utility

Major depressive episodes could, according to DSM-III, be divided into three types: (*1*) with melancholia, (*2*) with psychotic features, and (*3*) without melancholia. These were hypothesized to have clinical validity, especially melancholia, which, like Klein's older concept of endogenomorphic depression, was expected to identify major depressions that would be most responsive to somatic treatments. DSM-III major depressive subtypes have been examined in several research studies and, partly as a consequence, have been revised in DSM-III-R.

Melancholic major depression. The possibility of defining a major depressive subtype that predicts treatment response has great appeal to clinicians, particularly since DSM-III major depression undoubtedly identifies a heterogeneous group of patients. Davidson and associates (25) have compared several different definitions of the melancholic or endogenous subtype of major depression, which is hypothesized to have biologic and familial correlates and to respond to somatic treatment, and found that DSM-III criteria were representative in that they included the most common symptoms of the other major definitions, but were relatively narrow in that they did not identify as many patients as several of the other systems. Restrictiveness, by itself, is no liability if the few patients identified are more homogeneous with respect to the important variables that are associated with the diagnosis. Unfortunately, DSM-III melancholia has met with mixed reviews insofar as its relationship to biological indicators or treatment response is concerned.

If DSM-III melancholia identified a biological disorder, it might be expected that melancholic major depression would be less likely to be associated with psychosocial risk factors than nonmelancholic major depression and more likely to be associated with a family history of affective disorder. Of the six studies that have addressed the question of psychosocial factors, two found lower rates of relevant life events in melancholic depressives (26,27), one found that depressions precipitated by stressors were as likely to be melancholic as nonmelancholic (14). Two studies reported fewer personality disorders among melancholics than nonmelancholics (28,29), but another study failed to confirm this finding (27). Four studies found no significant differences in the morbidity risk for major depression among the first-degree relatives of melancholic compared with nonmelancholic probands (27,30-32).

If DSM-III melancholia distinguished patients with an abnormal dexamethasone suppression test, this would be suggestive of a relationship of the syndrome to biological abnormality. Only two studies report this finding (27,33); the majority do not (34-36).

Finally, no study of antidepressant medication or electroconvulsive therapy has supported DSM-III's suggestion that "melancholics are particularly responsive to somatic treatment" (25,37-47). It is conceivable, however, that both melancholic and nonmelancholic major depression respond to somatic treatments, but that patients with melancholia are unresponsive to nonsomatic, psychosocial treatments. Although factors in the design and conduct of these studies may have affected the results of relevant studies so that the findings cannot be considered conclusive (48), most experts on mood disorders were not impressed with DSM-III melancholia and recommended revisions in DSM-III-R.

The DSM-III-R criteria for melancholia have been recast in a polythetic format. Pervasive loss of interest or pleasure and lack of reactivity (autonomy of mood) are now no longer required, but are two of a list of nine items constituting the new definition. A comparison of DSM-III and DSM-III-R melancholia is displayed in Table 6.4. Six symptoms remain essentially unchanged: loss of interest or pleasure, lack of responsiveness to usually pleasurable stimuli, diurnal mood variation, early morning awakening, psychomotor change, and significant anorexia or weight loss (now specified to be at least 5% of body weight over a one-month period). No single symptom is required. Three new criteria that are not symptoms appear: (*1*) absence of significant premorbid personality disturbance, (2) one or more previous major depressive episodes with recovery, (3) known prior good response to a specific and adequate course of somatic treatment. Distinct quality of mood, a difficult symptom to elicit, and excessive guilt have been eliminated. Five of the nine items are required in DSM-III-R. "Melancholic type" is also now a description to "specify" rather than a distinct subtype of MDE.

The new melancholic syndrome incorporates some features of clinical course (rather than just symptoms) similar to those in the Newcastle scale for endogenous depression, which has been shown to correlate with more validators of endogenous depression in the predicted direction than DSM-III melancholia (27). Loss of interest, lack of reactivity, anorexia, and early morning awakening have been demonstrated to be drug-response symptoms (49).

The DSM-III-R description will tend to be applied to recurrent major depressive episodes. However, since only five of nine items are needed, it is possible to meet the criteria on symptom features alone,

Table 6.4 A Comparison of DSM-III and DSM-III-R Definitions of Melancholia

DSM-III	DSM-III-R
Loss of pleasure	Loss of interest or pleasure
Lack of mood reactivity	Lack of mood reactivity
• **Both are required**	Diurnal variation (worse in A.M.)
	Early morning awakening
Distinct quality of mood	Psychomotor retardation or agitation
Diurnal variation (worse in A.M.)	Significant anorexia or weight loss
Early morning awakening	No premorbid personality disturbance
Psychomotor retardation or agitation	Previous episode with recovery
Significant anorexia or weight loss	Previous good response to somatic treatment
Excessive or inappropriate guilt	
• **At least 3 are required**	• **At least 3 are required**

without any of the three historical items. The polythetic approach opens up the possibility of conceptualizing the melancholic syndrome on a continuum, but also allows a heterogeneity that may continue to be an obstacle to demonstrating validity.

Major depression with psychotic features. Psychotic or delusional depressions have been demonstrated to have a different treatment response pattern than nonpsychotic major depressive episodes (50-52). In brief, psychotic depressions usually do not respond as well to antidepressant medication alone as they do to a combination of antidepressant and antipsychotic drugs or to electroconvulsive therapy.

Technically, DSM-III major depression with psychotic features and the concept of delusional depression are not directly comparable, since the DSM-III definition includes hallucinations and depressive stupor (the patient is mute and unresponsive). Depressive stupor has been removed from the DSM-III-R definition. DSM-III and DSM-III-R classify psychotic features occurring during the course of major depressive episodes as mood-congruent and mood-incongruent. Mood-congruent psychotic features are "delusions or hallucinations whose content is entirely consistent with . . . themes of either personal inadequacy, guilt, disease, death, nihilism, or deserved punishment" (15, pp. 401-402); mood-incongruent psychotic features are those that do not involve such themes. Included under mood-incongruent psychotic features would be persecutory delusions or delusions of passivity or control, such as Schneiderian first-rank delusions that have no relationship to depressive themes. Occasionally, a patient will present with a persecutory delusion related to a depressive theme, e.g., a patient may believe that he or she is the object of scorn, ridicule, or harassment because of having committed some unconscionable act or having had unacceptably evil thoughts. The following case illustrates such a delusion.

My Face Is Black

A 20-year-old woman was admitted to the hospital with a three-month history of incapacitating "depression." About six months earlier she had broken up with her boyfriend. She became increasingly sad and morose, not wanting to get out of bed in the morning, eat meals, or see friends. After about a month, she quit her job, and for two months simply slept and stared at the television.

About one month before admission, the patient's mother noticed a change in her demeanor. The young woman looked frightened and more agitated, paced through the apartment and frequently looked out the windows, under the shades that she insisted be kept drawn, at the street in front of her building. "Mommy, do you think they are going to kill me?" she asked. "Don't let them kill me!" The mother, who had previously taken her daughter to the family doctor, who had given the patient Valium, insisted that they go to the hospital emergency room.

The psychiatrist on call discovered that the patient was convinced that the Mafia was plotting to kill her. This, she believed, was because she had given up her religion, at age 18, when she stopped going to church every Sunday. She now felt "marked" because her face had been gradually turning black "like a werewolf's." She was now in a panic because she felt her murder was imminent. "It's true, isn't it?" she asked. "My face *is* black; they're going to kill me, aren't they? It's true!"

This is an apparently mood-congruent delusion, a punishment by death for having committed an unpardonable sin. In the context of, and limited to, a major depressive episode, this delusion would be fairly typical of psychotic depression. It could also appear in schizoaffective disorder, or even schizophrenia (as was the case in "My Face Is Black") if it persisted beyond the depressive episode or if the depression was brief in duration relative to the duration of the psychotic symptoms (see below and Chapter 5).

Some additional evidence has accumulated on the prognostic significance of DSM-III major depression with psychotic features and its subtypes. Several studies have employed DSM-III criteria directly; several others have used other criteria that can be translated into DSM-III terminology. In a 40-year follow-up study of the Iowa 500 cohort, rediagnosed by DSM-III criteria, Coryell and Tsuang (53) found that outcome in a group of depressed patients with mood-congruent psychotic features resembled that of patients with nonpsychotic major depression; both groups had better outcomes than patients with mood-incongruent features. Patients with major depression with mood-incongruent psychotic features had a better prognosis, however, than did patients with schizophrenia. These findings have confirmed earlier similar findings on short-term outcome (54).

Other data come from the Collaborative Study of the Psychobiology of Depression, which uses RDC criteria, and the follow-up studies of the United States–United Kingdom Diagnostic Study. RDC criteria include only mood-congruent psychotic features in the definition of psychotic major depressive episode. The presence of mood-incongruent features would place a patient in the schizoaffective category. Patients with mood-incongruent psychotic features occurring only during the course of an affective episode (DSM-III major depression with mood-incongruent psychotic features) would be given the diagnosis of schizoaffective disorder, mainly affective, by RDC. The British group uses the term *schizodepressive* to refer to patients with major depressive episodes accompanied by "schizophrenialike" symptoms, which are the Schneiderian first-rank symptoms that also make up the majority of DSM-III mood-incongruent psychotic features. Since their assessments are cross-sectional, they identify patients with coexisting depressive and psychotic syndromes, most of whom are likely to be classified as having major depression with mood-incongruent psychotic features by DSM-III criteria.

The results of these studies are relatively consistent. In terms of RDC, prospectively determined short-term outcome, expressed as persistence of symptoms, proportion recovered, social and occupational impairment, and overall adjustment during a 6-month to 24-month follow-up, shows nonpsychotic depression to have the best outcome, psychotic depression, somewhat worse, and schizoaffective depression, worst of all (55). Although outcome differences between schizoaffective and nonpsychotic depression remain stable over time, mood-congruent psychotic features become less significant. Typical depressive delusions have more of an effect on the outcome of individual depressive episodes than on the lifelong prognosis of major depression. In the British studies (56,57), schizodepressives had an outcome, measured in similar ways, intermediate between that of nonpsychotic depressives and that of patients with schizophrenia.

Taken together, these studies suggest that the diagnosis of major depression with psychotic features has treatment and outcome implications and that the distinction between mood-congruent and mood-incongruent psychotic features may have further significance in predicting a more ominous prognosis among patients with psychotic depression. These distinctions continue to be made in the subcoding of major depressive episodes in the 5th digit in DSM-III-R. The data also suggest that the diagnosis of patients with syndromes of depression and psychosis who do not meet DSM-III and DSM-III-R criteria for major depression with psychotic features may also be important for treatment selection and prognosis. Such patients may, according to DSM-III and DSM-III-R, be diagnosed as either schizoaffective or schizophrenic with a superimposed depressive disorder. These distinctions will be discussed below in the sections on differential diagnosis, and were also considered in Chapter 5.

Major depression with a seasonal pattern. A new subtype of major depressive episode can be specified in DSM-III-R. "Seasonal pattern" can be indicated if there has been a regular relationship between the onset of episodes and a particular 60-day period of the year (usually in the fall) and the occurrence of full remissions also during a particular 60-day period (usually in late winter or early spring). Seasonal affective disorder (58) may be responsive to treatment with light therapy (59). DSM-III-R specifies that there must be at least three episodes of mood disturbance with a temporal seasonal relationship in three separate (two consecutive) years and seasonal episodes outnumbering nonseasonal episodes by more than three to one for criteria of a seasonal pattern to be met.

DEPRESSIVE DISORDERS: DYSTHYMIA

Dysthymic disorder, renamed dysthymia in DSM-III-R, is a chronic, mildly depressive disorder defined by the occurrence of depressive symptoms, of less severity than in major depression, over the course of at least two years. The symptoms are expected to be persistent, in that periods of normal mood, if they occur, do not last more than a few months at a time. Dysthymia is, by definition, a nonpsychotic disorder without delusions, hallucinations, or incoherence.

One of the problems in the differential diagnosis of dysthymia is that the symptom list includes many of the same items that make up the list of symptoms of the full syndrome of major depression. Therefore, distinguishing between dysthymia alone and dysthymic disorder with a superimposed major depressive episode (so-called double depression, see also below) can be difficult. Although there are no guidelines, the intent in DSM-III and DSM-III-R is that the symptoms of dysthymia are less severe.

The diagnostic criteria for dysthymia in DSM-III-R (see Table 6.5) have been revised to simplify them and to eliminate some of the ambiguities. The criteria now state that subjective symptoms *or* objective signs of depression must be present for "most of the day more days than not" (15, p. 232) for at least two years without a symptom-free interval of more than two months at a time. The duration is reduced to one year for children or adolescents. Only two of six associated symptoms of depression need be present. The disorder can no longer begin with a major depressive episode. It is not sustained by a specific organic factor or a psychoactive substance. The diagnosis can be made "secondary" to other mental disorders or physical disorders such as an anxiety disorder or asthma, or can be "primary," but it should be recognized that the coexistence of other disorders introduces heterogeneity to the diagnosis.

Recognizing Heterogeneous Clinical Subtypes

The heterogeneity of dysthymic disorder has been a problem for clinicians and researchers alike. Originally, in DSM-III the disorder

Table 6.5 DSM-III-R Diagnostic Criteria for Dysthymia

A. Depressed mood (or can be irritable mood in children and adolescents) for most of the day, more days than not, as indicated either by subjective account or observation by others, for at least two years (one year for children and adolescents).

B. Presence, while depressed, of at least two of the following:

   (1) poor appetite or overeating
   (2) insomnia or hypersomnia
   (3) low energy or fatigue
   (4) low self-esteem
   (5) poor concentration or difficulty making decisions
   (6) feelings of hopelessness

C. During a two-year period (one year for children and adolescents) of the disturbance, never without the symptoms in A for more than two months at a time.

D. No evidence of an unequivocal major depressive episode during the first two years (one year for children and adolescents) of the disturbance.

   Note: There may have been a previous major depressive episode, provided there was a full remission (no significant signs or symptoms for six months) before development of the dysthymia. In addition, after these two years (one year in children or adolescents) of dysthymia, there may be superimposed episodes of major depression, in which case both diagnoses are given.

E. Has never had a manic episode or an unequivocal hypomanic episode.

F. Not superimposed on a chronic psychotic disorder, such as schizophrenia or delusional disorder.

G. It cannot be established that an organic factor initiated and maintained the disturbance, e.g., prolonged administration of an antihypertensive medication.

Specify primary or **secondary type:**

Primary type: the mood disturbance is not related to a preexisting, chronic, nonmood, Axis I or Axis III disorder, e.g., anorexia nervosa, somatization disorder, a psychoactive substance dependence disorder, an anxiety disorder, or a rheumatoid arthritis.

Secondary type: the mood disturbance is apparently related to a preexisting, chronic, nonmood Axis I or Axis III disorder.

Specify early onset or **late onset:**

Early onset: onset of the disturbance before age 21.
Late onset: onset of the disturbance at age 21 or later.

was intended to correspond roughly to the diagnosis of depressive personality.

Akiskal (60), in a comprehensive review, pointed out at least three different clinical presentations to which the diagnosis of dysthymia could apply: (*1*) primary major depressions with residual chronicity, (*2*) chronic secondary dysphorias, and (*3*) characterological depressions, which he divided into (*a*) character spectrum disorders and (*b*) subaffective dysthymic disorders. The primary depressions with residual chronicity are described as usually of late onset and beginning with a major depressive episode; the patient has not suffered chronic, minor depression, but may have a history of previous major depressive episodes. The chronic secondary dysphorias may occur at any age, and are superimposed on preexisting incapacitating, nonaffective disorders. These other disorders may be physical, e.g., neurologic or rheumatologic diseases, or mental, e.g., chronic somatoform or anxiety disorders. The characterological depressions begin early in life, and may have superimposed major episodes. In Akiskal's experience, some of these, in the character-spectrum group, included depressive episodes without melancholic features and tended to have poor response to antidepressant drugs, results on biological measures (e.g., REM latency) that were not characteristic of affective disorders, associated drug and alcohol abuse, family histories positive for alcoholism and personality disorders, and other symptoms of personality disturbance. Early-onset dysthymic disorder has also been found, by Roy and colleagues (61), to have distinctive, more "neurotic," character traits. The subaffective dysthymic disorders, on the other hand, had depressive episodes with more melancholic features, positive responses to antidepressant therapy, shortened REM latencies, and family histories positive for affective disorders.

The revisions in DSM-III-R reduce some, but not all, of this clinical heterogeneity by classifying several of the clinical types differently (62). The specific effects of the changes will be discussed later in this chapter in the sections on differential diagnosis.

Differential Diagnosis

The following problems in the differential diagnosis of the depressive disorders will be discussed: (*1*) typical vs. atypical depression, (*2*) MD recurrent vs. bipolar disorder, (*3*) MD vs. dysthymia, (*4*) MD with psychotic features vs. schizoaffective disorder, (*5*) depressive disorders vs. anxiety disorders, and (*6*) depressive disorders vs. personality disorders. Two other important problems, MD vs. uncomplicated bereavement and MD vs. physical disorder, will be discussed in Chapter 11, Differential Diagnosis in the Elderly.

Typical vs. atypical depression. In recent years a research literature has developed that suggests that certain patients with significant depressions exhibit "atypical" features that may have special treatment significance. There have been various conceptualizations of the atypical syndrome, but most can be divided into two subtypes: (*1*) anxious depression and (*2*) nonanxious depression with atypical vegetative symptoms, i.e., increased appetite and weight gain, increased sleep, initial insomnia, and reversed diurnal variation in mood (worse in the evenings) (2). As previously mentioned, the DSM-III residual diagnosis of atypical depression had neither of these connotations.

Atypical depressions tend to have an early age at onset. The anxious type is chronic, the vegetative type, recurrent. Most affected people are women, and most are encountered in outpatient, rather than inpatient, settings. Several treatment studies have suggested that certain atypical depressions may respond preferentially to MAO inhibitor antidepressants (63,64). Among the features thought to be predictive are the following: (*1*) increased appetite, weight gain, or sleep; mood reactivity; or anergia; (*2*) chronic agoraphobia with secondary depression; (*3*) primary depression with pain or somatic complaints as prominent features, or psychogenic pain or hypochondriasis with secondary depression. The following vignette illustrates a typical case of atypical depression.

It's Typical

Settling into the chair in the psychiatrist's office, the young woman sighed and said, "I don't know what's going on, I just don't know." For the past two months, the patient, a 25-year-old single art student, had been struggling with feelings of depression and inadequacy. The depression started when the man she had been seeing, a 42-year-old divorced general contractor, told her that he wanted to "slow down" their relationship, which she had assumed was heading for marriage.

The patient found herself crying frequently, not wanting to get out of bed in the mornings, missing classes, fatigued—feeling as though a lead weight had been placed on her shoulders, and constantly eating, "especially anything chocolate." She had gained 15 pounds, making her noticeably plump compared with her usual thin and lithe figure. She was also experiencing anxiety attacks, which on several occasions had led her to turn around on the subway platform and go home rather than go to school.

The patient was convinced that her boyfriend was the only man for her. In the ensuing months, her mood fluctuated with his ambivalence. Whenever she interpreted his behavior or something he said as a sign that they might still work things out, her spirits were buoyed. But, alternatively, when he was distant or critical, she crashed into despair and self-deprecation. She was unable to separate her mood or her thoughts about her ultimate future from his day-to-day attitude toward her.

In "It's Typical," the patient displays the so-called reversed vegetative symptoms, leaden paralysis, and mood reactivity. The sustained nature of the symptoms over the weeks, however, is consistent with a major depressive episode, mild or moderate. The patient also has anxiety attacks, suggesting panic and leading to some agoraphobic avoidance (see below and Chapter 7).

In DSM-III and DSM-III-R, major depression encompasses both typical and atypical features. A patient may, for example, have either decreased or increased appetite, weight loss or weight gain, decreased or increased sleep. A proposal to include atypical depression, as defined by Quitkin and associates (65), as a subtype of major depression was presented to the Mood Disorders Advisory Committee of the Work Group to Revise DSM-III. The proposal was not accepted because the research evidence was considered too preliminary. Since atypical depressions have "reversed" vegetative symptoms and mood reactivity, those that meet criteria for major depression are going, almost always, not to be the melancholic type. If the patient also has a coexisting personality disorder, e.g., histrionic or borderline (so-called "hysteroid dysphoria"), the DSM-III-R criteria for melancholic type will not be met if all the symptoms of atypical depression are present. A patient with atypical depression that is chronic, but milder than in a major depressive episode, may meet the criteria for dysthymia.

Other DSM-III diagnoses that may apply to atypical depression include the anxiety disorders and the somatoform disorders. According to DSM-III, when major depression was present, diagnoses of anxiety disorders and certain somatoform disorders (psychogenic pain and hypochondriasis) were not made if these other disturbances were thought to be due to the major depression. This usually meant that the excluded disturbance was limited in time to periods when the person was depressed. In DSM-III-R, many of the hierarchies between the mood disorders and the anxiety disorders or somatoform disorders have been dismantled, for reasons that will be discussed below.

Although DSM-III mentions only the anxiety disorder obsessive compulsive disorder explicitly, it intended to allow the diagnosis of major depression superimposed on a chronic anxiety disorder, the latter being one that obviously antedated the development of depression by some time. Major depression could also be diagnosed if superimposed on somatization disorder, which suggests that a secondary depression could be diagnosed in the presence of other somatoform disorders as well. Dysthymic disorder could be diagnosed, according to DSM-III, if superimposed on a chronic mental disorder, e.g., an anxiety disorder. DSM-III explicitly ruled out dysthymic disorder in the presence of somatization disorder, however, because mild depressive symptoms were thought to be ubiquitous in this condition. It was unclear whether the same exclusion applied to the other somatoform disorders. When dysthymia was primary, generalized anxiety disorder (GAD), but not the other anxiety disorders, was explicitly excluded; among the somatoform disorders, diagnoses of hypochondriasis and psychogenic pain were not made. The clinician who attempted to apply these complex rules of differential diagnosis to patients with atypical depression was likely to sink into a morass of confusion and apathy.

The Work Group to Revise DSM-III responded to these inconsistencies and to the empirical evidence concerning the potential importance of the co-occurrence of anxiety disorders and depressive disorders by reducing and simplifying the exclusion criteria that make differential diagnosis of mood disorders and these other disorders possible. Among the somatoform disorders, only the new, undifferentiated somatoform disorder (see Chapter 8, Physical Complaints) is excluded by a mood disorder if it occurs exclusively during the course of a mood disorder. Since physical complaints are common components of mood disorders, it would be diagnostically redundant to make additional diagnoses when these symptoms were clearly a part of a depressive syndrome. The relationship of mood and anxiety disorders in DSM-III-R will be discussed later in this chapter and in Chapter 7.

In spite of an increase in the clinician's ability to capture the complex features of atypical depression through using DSM-III-R, many may still miss an official diagnostic category of atypical depression that would suggest MAO inhibitor therapy as the treatment of choice.

Major depression, recurrent vs. bipolar disorder. The distinction between major depression, recurrent, and bipolar disorder rests on whether or not the patient has ever had a manic episode (see also below under Bipolar Disorder). This is not a difficult differential except under a few particular sets of circumstances. The most common cause of mistaken diagnoses of MD, recurrent, is that the clinician confronting a profoundly depressed patient fails to inquire whether there has ever been a manic period. The second common pitfall is that the severely depressed patient is unable to report accurately about other times when he or she was not depressed, i.e., the mood disturbance itself colors recall, so that the history of a manic episode is obscured by the patient's depressive state. In both of these instances, thorough history-taking that includes questioning a third-party (family member or friend) informant is the clinician's best bet.

A third difficult case involves the patient who has milder and shorter hypomanic periods between major depressive episodes. This disorder is classfied as bipolar, not unipolar, and is known to researchers and clinicians as bipolar II (66-70). In DSM-III-R, bipolar II is an example of a bipolar disorder NOS. Thus, a shift from one major diagnostic category to another depends on differentiating hypomanic mood and behavior from a good mood that would be considered normal. This distinction will be taken up in more detail under bipolar disorders.

Major depression vs. dysthymia. Major depression is distinguished from dysthymia in DSM-III and DSM-III-R on the basis of symptom severity and course. Major depression is characterized by severe and pervasive dysphoria or loss of interest or pleasure and associated symptoms every day for at least two weeks and is episodic in that typically it occurs, then remits completely, but may recur. Dysthymia has milder versions of many of the same symptoms, but a much more chronic course—by definition occurring more days than not over a two-year period.

An interesting and clinically useful body of data describing the mood disturbance known as "double depression" has been developed by Keller and associates (71,72) from the Collaborative Study of the Psychobiology of Depression. This disturbance consists of major depressive episodes superimposed on chronic, less severe depression. Keller and associates (72) have shown, in longitudinal studies, that the prognosis of a major depressive episode in patients with double depression is less favorable than that of major depression alone since, as would be expected, resolution of the MDE in the former case brings the patient back only to his or her preexisting baseline, i.e., a state of mild, chronic depression. To the clinician unaware of the usual premorbid mood of the patient, it may appear that the major depressive episodes have had an incomplete response to treatment or have not yet run their full course. DSM-III and DSM-III-R allow for the diagnosis of double depression in that both systems encourage the clinician to diagnose major depression superimposed on dysthymia in patients whose chronic depression worsens periodically and meets the criteria for major depressive episodes. The section on differential diagnosis in DSM-III-R (15, p. 232) states: "it is likely that the person will continue to have Dysthymia after he or she has recovered from the Major Depression."

Keller and co-workers (73) and others (74) have also shown that major depressive episodes without preexisting dysthymia often run a more chronic course than has traditionally been thought. Incomplete remissions and residual symptoms are frequent, occurring in from 20% to 40% of cases. Such cases are diagnostic dilemmas for many clinicians. Occasionally the patient will meet the full criteria for a major depressive episode for the entire two-year period, in which case the diagnosis of major depression would suffice; but more likely the patient will have some, but not all, MDE symptoms during the follow-up period, i.e., be in partial remission. Concerning the differential diagnosis of dysthymic disorder, discussed in DSM-III on page 222, it is stated: "When a Major Depression is in partial remission for a period of two years, Dysthymic Disorder should be considered as an alternative diagnosis to Major Depression in Remission" (75). Most clinicians and researchers consider the implications of this clinical situation to be different from those of the double depression described above (see also the section on dysthymia). Therefore, in DSM-III-R, criterion D for dysthymia states that for the first two years of the disturbance, there was no evidence of an unequivocal major depressive episode. This requirement means that the dysthymic period will have to have been established totally independently of an episode of major depression for both diagnoses to apply.

DSM-III-R now instructs the clinician to specify a major depressive episode as "chronic" if the current episode has gone on for "two consecutive years without a period of two months or longer during which there were no significant depressive symptoms" (15, p. 224). Since the new DSM-III-R convention for indicating the severity of a diagnosis includes "in partial remission," this designation can be used for patients who do not meet DSM-III-R's definition of chronic.

Figure 6.2 gives examples of several of the more common clinical courses of major depressive episodes with chronic depressive symptoms and the corresponding DSM-III-R diagnosis(es).

The following case illustrates the new diagnostic principles, as a case of major depression is followed over many years.

No Relief

A 45-year-old married housewife was interviewed during her sixth psychiatric hospitalization. She was admitted following a suicide attempt in which she put her head in her oven and turned on the gas.

Figure 6.2 Examples of Clinical Courses of Major Depressive Episodes with Chronic Depressive Symptoms

A. **Diagnosis: Major depression, in partial remission**

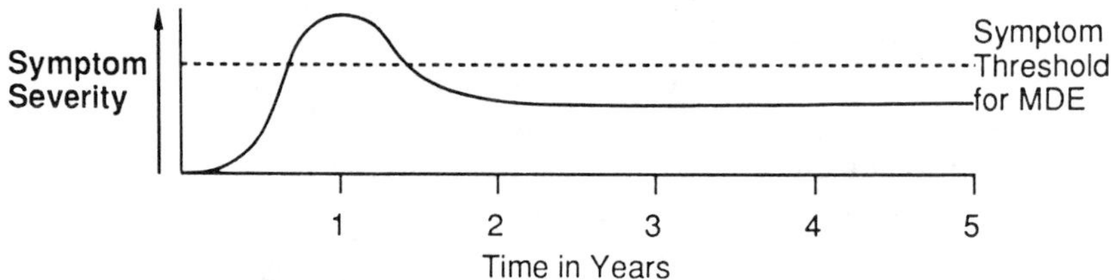

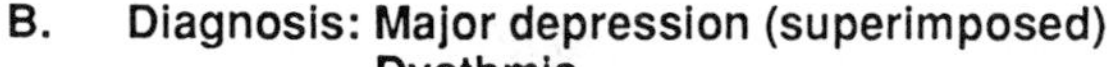
B. **Diagnosis: Major depression (superimposed)**
Dysthmia

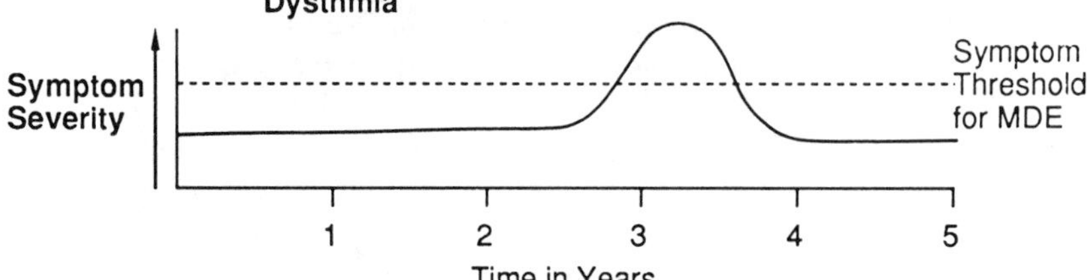

C. **Diagnosis: Major depression, in full remission**
Dysthymia

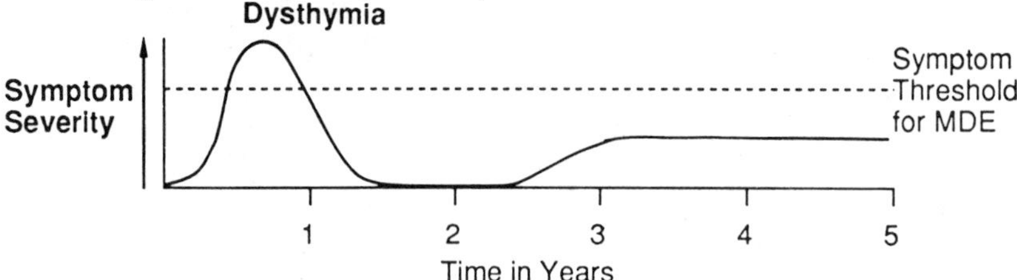

D. **Diagnosis: Major depression, chronic**

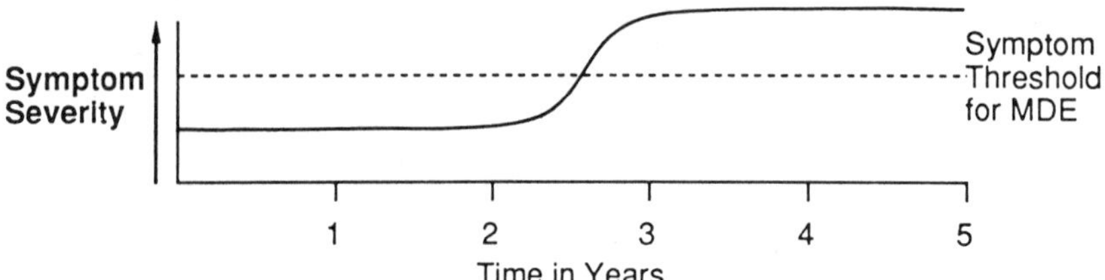

Note: MDE = Major Depressive Episode

One of her teenage children found her and called the police.

The patient reported low self-esteem "for as long as I can remember." She stated that she felt inferior to other children in elementary school because she was poor, overweight, and ugly. She was the fourth of five children; she remembers her mother as constantly overwhelmed, and her father as working all the time or, when home, drunk.

She married the only boy she ever dated shortly after graduating from high school. Within a year they had a child. The patient suffered her first severe depression following the birth and was admitted to a psychiatric ward of a hospital, where she received a course of electroconvulsive (ECT) therapy. The depression responded; in fact, for the next two years she felt almost as good as she could ever remember. She reared her child and worked part time, typing for a semi-retired lawyer.

Then she had another child—and another serious depression necessitating ECT. During the first hospitalization, she had required 10 treatments; this time, 16 were given. The woman reported that although she felt better when she was discharged, she did not feel as well as after the first episode. She did not return to work.

Over the next ten years, she reared her children and took care of the house; for pleasure she played bingo once in a while or had coffee with a neighbor. She described her mood as "usually down in the dumps," but not as bad as after the deliveries of her children. Then she accidentally became pregnant again and, predictably, had a third episode of depression necessitating hospitalization following the birth. This time she received 20 ECT treatments, but continued to feel depressed. She was placed on tricyclic antidepressant medication, which helped to some degree.

Over the ensuing 14 years the patient has had three more serious episodes of depression requiring hospitalization. Treatment has shifted primarily to antidepressant medications. She has received numerous trials of heterocyclic drugs and monoamine oxidase inhibitors, but none has seemed to bring much relief. She now suffers from nearly relentless depression with insomnia, anhedonia, psychomotor retardation, fatigue, extreme feelings that her life has been a waste, and persistent wishes that she were dead.

This unfortunate woman's mood disturbance began as dysthymia in childhood. Her earliest superimposed major depressive episode came after the birth of her first child. Somewhat uncharacteristically, this episode may have gone into full remission after treatment, with few signs of the dysthymia evident. Soon, however, the major depression recurred, leaving her with increased residual symptoms. Given the history of dysthymia, most clinicians would use this diagnosis to describe the chronic, less severe symptoms, even though there was a period when the patient may have been relatively symptom-free. Had there been no dysthymia, then major depressive episode, in partial remission, would have been the appropriate designation after the second episode. In the later years, when the full syndrome of major depression had become constant, the major depression would, according to DSM-III-R typology, be specified as "chronic."

Major depression with psychotic features vs. schizoaffective disorder. As mentioned earlier, in the discussion of the psychotic subtype of major depression, the clinician evaluating a patient with a full depressive syndrome and mood-incongruent psychotic features must consider schizoaffective disorder in the differential diagnosis. In DSM-III and DSM-III-R, the differential between MD with psychotic features and schizoaffective disorder is determined by criterion C for major depressive episode.

Criterion C was a source of confusion for clinicians in the initial printing of DSM-III and underwent a revision between printings. The original wording said: "Neither of the following dominates the clinical picture when an affective syndrome is absent (i.e., symptoms in criteria A and B above): 1) preoccupation with a mood-incongruent delusion or hallucination (see definition below); 2) bizarre behavior." Clinicians wondered why they would even be considering a diagnosis of a major depressive episode if no affective syndrome were present. The criterion was meant to convey the idea that, for patients who had, or had had, the full depressive syndrome and symptoms suggesting schizophrenia, the diagnosis of MDE applied only if those psychotic symptoms occurred solely within the context of the depressive syndrome, not at other times. Thus, it attempted to specify complete temporal overlap of the two syndromes as a requirement for an MDE with psychotic features. In a subsequent reprinting of DSM-III, criterion C was changed slightly to read as follows: "Neither of the following dominate the clinical picture when an affective syndrome (i.e., criteria A and B above) is not present, that is, *before it developed or after it has remitted:* 1) preoccupation with a mood-incongruent delusion or hallucination (see definition below); 2) bizarre behavior."

As has been mentioned previously in this chapter and in Chapter 5, the distinction between major depression with mood-incongruent features and a syndrome with depression and schizophrenialike psychotic features that do not completely overlap in time may have prognostic significance, in that patients with the latter condition may have a clinical course closely resembling schizophrenia (76). This clinical picture is, in fact, one of the two instances in which the DSM-III diagnosis of schizoaffective disorder, the only DSM-III category without specified criteria, might have applied. Even with the clarification made in criterion C, important clinical questions remained. For example, what if the psychotic symptoms that preceded or followed the MDE were mood-congruent? Would the differential diagnostic implications be any different? And given the imprecise nature of retrospective dating of the onset and offset of psychopathological symptoms, by how much time should the psychotic symptoms precede or how long persist before the clinician can be reasonably certain that the two syndromes are not overlapping?

These questions have led to a further revision of criterion C in DSM-III-R. Most experts in this area believe that it does not matter whether the psychotic symptoms are mood-congruent or mood-incongruent; the temporal relationship should take precedence in making a diagnosis. Therefore, DSM-III-R states: "At no time during the illness have there been delusions or hallucinations for as long as two weeks in the absence of prominent mood symptoms (i.e., before the affective symptoms developed or after they have remitted)" (15, p. 223). There is no definition of "prominent," but the clinician can assume that a full depressive syndrome is required.

The criteria for schizoaffective disorder (SA) in DSM-III-R, depicted in Table 5.5 in Chapter 5, now define a group of patients with nonoverlapping affective and psychotic syndromes. In essence, the first example of the possible use of the schizoaffective diagnosis in DSM-III has become the definition of schizoaffective disorder in DSM-III-R. The other example to which the diagnosis of SA disorder in DSM-III applies is the case in which the clinician is unable, because of inadequate information, to determine the relative onsets and offsets of the affective and psychotic syndromes and thus cannot clearly apply the diagnostic criteria of DSM-III to make a differential diagnosis between MDE with psychotic features and schizophrenia or schizophreniform disorder with a superimposed atypical affective disorder. This situation, according to DSM-III-R, would be classified by the residual category of "psychotic disorders not otherwise specified (NOS)." Inadequate information is given as a rationale for using this diagnosis in DSM-III-R.

The other situation in which the clinician may encounter both mood disturbance and psychotic symptoms together is that in which a patient with schizophrenia develops depression at some time during the course of the illness. In most instances these are postpsychotic depressive syndromes; they are of interest to researchers and clinicians for their potential treatment implications (77-79). They usually occur following the acute phase of the illness, and have been thought to be related to the patient's coming to grips with the nature and severity of his or her recent psychotic illness. In DSM-III and DSM-III-R, criterion D rules out the diagnosis of a major depressive episode in these cases, in the revision reading "Not superimposed on either Schizophrenia, Schizophreniform Disorder, Delusional Disorder or Psychotic Disorder NOS" (15, p. 223). The intent of criterion D is to disallow the diagnosis of major depression *and* schizophrenia for a particular episode of illness. With MDE ruled out, the mood disturbance falls into the residual mood disorder category in both systems —"depressive disorder NOS" in DSM-III-R. It is given as example #1 of this diagnostic category.

Depressive disorders vs. anxiety disorders. At the time of preparation of DSM-III, anxiety symptoms of all types were believed to occur frequently as part of a major depressive episode. Although not considered essential features, anxiety, panic attacks, and phobias were listed among the commonly associated features. The criteria for agoraphobia, social phobia, panic disorder, GAD, and obsessive compulsive disorder all explicitly ruled out major depression (any depressive disorder, in the case of GAD) as a cause of the anxiety symptoms by a criterion that stated said "Not due to another mental disorder, such as . . . ." As was mentioned in the discussion of atypical depression, several studies from the Epidemiologic Catchment Area (ECA) Study and other centers (80-83) have indicated that the co-occurrence, or co-morbidity, of major depression and at least several of the anxiety disorders has important etiologic and treatment implications. This will be discussed in detail in the following chapter, Anxiety Syndromes.

For now, it is important to note that, in DSM-III-R, only the criteria for generalized anxiety disorder make the clinician rule out major depression (and other mood disorders), and this exclusion is limited to cases in which the anxiety disturbance occurs only during the course of the mood disorder. Thus, clinicians evaluating patients with mixed depressive and anxious symptoms must consider each syndrome independently to determine if it meets criteria for a DSM-III-R mood or anxiety disorder. Clinicians can now diagnose major depression and dysthymia with and without co-morbid anxiety disorders, and thus track a potentially important diagnostic distinction.

Depressive disorders vs. personality disorders. There has been a great deal of interest in recent years in the relationship of mood disorders to personality disorders (84,85). The relationship has been hypothesized to be one or more of the following nonmutually exclusive possibilities:

1. Personality disorders may be the result of long-standing difficulties with mood disorders, which, because of their severity or chronicity, have adverse effects on a person's overall outlook and ability to cope.
2. Personality disorders of certain kinds may be *formes frustes* of

mood disorders that will become evident with longitudinal follow-up.

3. Personality disorders may constitute a risk factor for mood disorders in the sense that they predispose or make a person vulnerable to their development.

4. Personality disorders and mood disorders may coexist either by chance or as a result of an interaction in which having one disturbance apparently increases the chances of having the other.

There is no reason why the relationship between personality disorders and mood disorders should be the same for each personality disorder or each mood disorder. Therefore, any of the above possibilities could be true in particular cases. The most thoroughly studied relationship, thus far, has been between borderline personality disorder (BPD) and major depression. In their recent review of the literature, Gunderson and Elliot (85) conclude that the higher than expected joint prevalence of mood disorder and BPD results from a shared biophysiological vulnerability to psychological impairment in early development. Multiple innate and environmental factors then interact to produce depression, chronic dysphoria, or borderline behavior—alone or in any combination. The various types and combinations of the disturbances may have particular etiologic, treatment, and prognostic implications.

As a practical matter, the differential diagnosis of mood and personality disorders would appear to be simplified by the DSM-III and DSM-III-R multiaxial systems. Mood disorders are diagnosed on Axis I and personality disorders on Axis II. There are several obstacles to accurate diagnosis, however. The clinician accustomed to searching for the single best diagnosis with which to summarize a patient's condition (as recommended in DSM-I) may look to either Axis I or Axis II for a diagnosis. In fact, the Axis I-II separation was designed specifically to counterbalance this tendency and to encourage clinicians to consider the diagnostic possibilities on both axes independently for all patients. On a more subtle level, the Axis I-II division may suggest a discontinuity between mood and certain personality disorders that is artificial rather than real. It is important, therefore, to remember that the DSM-III and DSM-III-R systems are phenomenologically oriented and largely atheoretical with respect to etiology. Thus, the classification of disorders according to Axis I and Axis II can be seen as a way to note diagnostic heterogeneity on a phenomenologic level—for example, mood disorder alone, mood disorder with one or more personality disorders, or personality disorder alone. Rather than reifying etiologic differences between the disorders, this approach can permit subcategorization that may identify more homogeneous groups of patients for treatment or research purposes.

A third level of diagnostic difficulty in this area results from the fact that patients with both mood and personality disorders are frequently evaluated during an episode of mood disturbance. Because of the way in which depression influences one's ability to assess one's personal attributes and life situation accurately, what might appear as symptoms of a personality disturbance, for example, of a dependent or self-defeating nature, may actually be reflections of a depressed mood. The phenomenon of the dependence of personality traits on mood has been described as a major issue in the diagnosis of personality disorder by Frances (86) and Hirschfeld (87) and associates. It will be discussed in more detail in Chapter 9, along with various strategies that have been developed—for example, in the conduct of diagnostic interviews—for attempting to alleviate the problem.

From the perspective of diagnosing the mood disorder, the question often is: When is the mood disturbance severe enough to warrant a separate diagnosis? This question comes up particularly when the criteria for the personality disorder include items that refer to mood symptoms. In DSM-III, borderline personality disorder had an item for affective instability, avoidant personality disorder described low self-esteem, and dependent personality disorder included lack of self-confidence. In DSM-III-R, the depressive components of dependent and avoidant personality disorders have been removed (see Chapter 9), but the new self-defeating personality disorder has a number of aspects that appear depressive. The answer to the above question is actually straightforward. If the mood disturbance is severe and sustained enough for the diagnosis of a mood disorder, then both diagnoses should be made. The depressive disorder will usually have additional treatment implications.

The clinical significance of the joint diagnosis of depressive disorders and certain personality disorders is becoming increasingly clear. At least two studies have shown the effects of the presence of BPD on major depression. In McGlashan's 15-year follow-up study at Chestnut Lodge (88,89), patients with major depression and borderline personality disorder had a significantly poorer outcome in terms of periods of hospitalization, work, social activity, symptoms, and global functioning than patients with MD alone. In a four- to seven-year follow-up, Pope and associates (90) found that borderline patients with an affective disorder had a prognosis intermediate between that of schizophrenic and bipolar affective disorder comparison groups. Thus, personality disorder appears to worsen the prognosis for major affective disorders.

Winokur (91) has found that people with "neurotic-reactive" depressions display stormy life-styles, specific symptoms, personality abnormalities, more stressful life events before the depression, and a family history of alcoholism. Defining neurotic depression as a disorder that occurs at a younger age, and is associated with a personality disorder, high stress, marital separation, blaming of others, and a nonserious suicide attempt, Zimmerman and his colleagues (92) reported an increased family history of alcoholism, decreased frequency of abnormal dexamethasone-suppression test results, and poorer outcome for persons with neurotic vs. nonneurotic depression. A depression occurring within the context of personality psychopathology may therefore have different clinical significance in terms of the role of predisposing or precipitating factors, treatment approach, or outcome, than depressions in persons without significant premorbid personality problems.

Bipolar Disorders

DSM-III-R groups bipolar disorder, cyclothymia, and bipolar disorder NOS together as bipolar disorders within the class of mood disorders. This regrouping emphasizes the differences between unipolar and bipolar mood disorders. Studies of rates in the community (93) and of phenomenology (94) continue to support this distinction, although some family-study data suggest that, from a familial perspective, the two types of disorder are not so distinct (95).

Bipolar Disorder

The essential feature of bipolar disorder is the occurrence of one or more manic episodes, whether or not there is a history of a major depressive episode. There was some evidence available at the time of preparation of DSM-III that unipolar mania did not exist as a clinical entity (96), evidence that has continued to accumulate (97,98) and support this basic contention. Earlier reports on patients who had only manic episodes were probably due to the relatively short histories of the disturbances. Although bipolar disorder may typically begin with a manic episode and the patient may even have several manic recurrences early on, longitudinal follow-up reveals that depressive episodes eventually occur, a pattern conforming to the more typical "bipolar" course.

Determining the threshold for clinical significance. The major general problem in differential diagnosis of bipolar disorder, as in major depression, has been the threshold for making the diagnosis. Distinguishing abnormally elevated or expansive mood from normal periods of "feeling good" can be a thorny interpretive issue. The major change introduced by DSM-III-R in the criteria for a manic episode (see Table 6.6) is the addition of an impairment criterion (C) that requires "Mood disturbance sufficiently severe to cause marked impairment in occupational functioning or in usual social activities or relationships with others, or to necessitate hospitalization to prevent harm to self or others" (15, p. 217). Manic episode is now no longer an exact counterpart of major depressive episode, since the latter continues to have no impairment criterion, despite similar threshold problems. The other criteria for bipolar disorder in DSM-III-R have been slightly rearranged, and minor changes in content from DSM-III have been made.

One such change involves criterion A. Many clinicians found it difficult to understand DSM-III's qualification of its duration requirement of one week for the diagnosis of a manic episode by adding "or any duration if hospitalization is necessary." The qualification was meant to convey the notion that although duration was a measure of severity, hospitalization certainly indicated a severe syndrome and therefore could supersede the duration requirement. This should circumvent the potential problem in differential diagnosis that would arise if a patient were hospitalized for a manic episode three days after it began and, following another day or two of treatment with antipsychotic medication, no longer had enough of the associated symptoms of mania to meet the full criteria. The initial severity would suffice for the diagnosis. The new criterion A eliminates the one week's duration requirement and focuses attention on the impairment that results from the mood disturbance or the need for hospitalization as an aid to the clinician in assessing clinical significance.

The inclusion of irritable mood in the manic-syndrome concept in both DSM-III and DSM-III-R is a reflection of the broader concept of bipolar disorder that has been developing in the United States since the early 1970s. (See also below, under *Bipolar disorder vs. schizoaffective disorder*.) This has made distinguishing clinically between irritable, manic patients and hostile, agitated patients with schizophrenia more difficult. To aid in making this distinction, the number of manic symptoms required in the presence of an irritable mood is four instead of three; however, since decreased need for sleep, flight of ideas, distractibility, and hyperactivity can be comparable with certain signs of schizophrenia, correct interpretation of these symptoms is necessary for accurate diagnosis. To some psychiatrists it appears almost as if schizophrenia has disappeared, particularly among the caseloads of psychiatric residents, as the desire to "see" mania has increased.

Among the pitfalls in interpreting the symptoms of the manic syndrome are the following:

1. Decreased need for sleep is not the equivalent of decreased

Table 6.6 DSM-III-R Diagnostic Criteria for Manic Episode

Note: A "manic syndrome" is defined as including criteria A, B, and C below. A "hypomanic syndrome" is defined as including criteria A and B, but not C, i.e., no marked impairment.

A. A distinct period of abnormally and persistently elevated, expansive, or irritable mood.

B. During the period of mood disturbance, at least three of the following symptoms have persisted (four if the mood is only irritable) and have been present to a significant degree:
   (1) inflated self-esteem or grandiosity
   (2) decreased need for sleep, e.g., feels rested after only three hours of sleep
   (3) more talkative than usual or pressure to keep talking
   (4) flight of ideas or subjective experience that thoughts are racing
   (5) distractibility, i.e., attention too easily drawn to unimportant or irrelevant external stimuli
   (6) increase in goal-directed activity (either socially, at work or school, or sexually) or psychomotor agitation
   (7) excessive involvement in pleasurable activities that have a high potential for painful consequences, e.g., the person engages in unrestrained buying sprees, sexual indiscretions, or foolish business investments

C. Mood disturbance sufficiently severe to cause marked impairment in occupational functioning or in usual social activities or relationships with others, or to necessitate hospitalization to prevent harm to self or others.

D. At no time during the disturbance have there been delusions or hallucinations for as long as two weeks in the absence of prominent mood symptoms (i.e., before the mood symptoms developed or after they have remitted).

E. Not superimposed on schizophrenia, schizophreniform disorder, delusional disorder, or psychotic disorder NOS.

F. It cannot be established that an organic factor initiated and maintained the disturbance. **Note:** Somatic antidepressant treatment (e.g., drugs, ECT) that apparently precipitates a mood disturbance should not be considered an etiologic organic factor.

sleep, i.e., insomnia. Any patient with severe psychotic symptoms may have trouble sleeping. Therefore, the emphasis should be on the *need* for sleep; manic patients are able to go with little sleep for several consecutive nights without feeling tired.

2. Flight of ideas and loosening of association are likely to be on a continuum of disorganization of thought processes. Researchers who

have studied thought pathology in mania have observed many of the same disturbances that are found in schizophrenia (99-101), particularly when the episode is severe. It is useful to keep in mind that classic flight of ideas takes the form of rapid stream of speech, and is not expressed simply by speech that shifts from one topic to another. In cases in which thought disorder is not characteristic of either of the two ends of the continuum, i.e., classic flight of ideas or gross incoherence, the symptom is not very helpful in differential diagnosis.

3. Distractibility can appear to be present in a patient who is actively hallucinating or acutely paranoid. It is important to note that manic distractibility is a reaction to *external,* not internal, stimuli and that the stimuli are real, not imagined.

4. Hyperactivity in mania classically appears organized and apparently purposeful. In severe mania the activity becomes disorganized, and then can be hard to distinguish from catatonic excitement. DSM-III and DSM-III-R also allow physical restlessness or psychomotor agitation as a sign, but these are as common in schizophrenia as in mania. Most mistaken diagnoses of manic episodes result from clinicians' forgetting that these are disturbances in *mood.* Focusing on the associated symptoms in the absence of a clear-cut mood abnormality is an error. When the mood is irritable, to avoid false-positive diagnoses, I suggest looking for one or more classic symptoms associated with mania, especially grandiosity and evidence of poor judgment such as spending sprees and other indiscretions. Although most clinicians believe that a diagnosis of bipolar is preferable to one of schizophrenia or schizoaffective disorder, mistaken diagnoses in either direction can have negative consequences.

Great Expectations

A 20-year-old college freshman entered a day program following his third psychiatric admission in 18 months. His illness began during the fall of his first year at an Ivy League university. The initial episode followed a two-week period of increased activity during which he joined several extracurricular groups, including the newspaper, the drama club, and the orchestra, and visited four women's colleges on four consecutive nights. His roommates had called the campus police because he had barricaded himself in his dormitory room and could be heard shouting loudly and incoherently at no one they could discern.

The patient was hospitalized at the university hospital for three weeks, then transferred to a hospital in his home state for an additional three-week stay. His diagnosis was bipolar disorder, manic, with psychotic features. He was placed on lithium carbonate, 1,800 mg/day, to achieve a blood level of 1.2 mEq/l. One physician noted that, for a bipolar patient, he had surprisingly disorganized thinking, to the point of virtual incoherence. The patient also exhibited fragmented religious and persecutory delusions, and appeared very infantile and helpless (e.g., he fell out of his chair, and needed assistance to walk). This psychiatrist thought a diagnosis of schizoaffective disorder might be appropriate.

The patient, however, had been a high-achieving only son in a high-achieving family. His father was a physician, a graduate of a rival Ivy school, and his mother was a writer. Both parents were very involved in their son's future and wrote many letters to the college dean to ensure that he would be readmitted the following semester.

The patient was readmitted to the school, but within two months suffered a relapse and was rehospitalized. He had fallen far behind in his work. In the hospital, an antipsychotic was added to the treatment regimen; within four weeks, the patient was again discharged.

Undaunted, the patient took remedial summer classes in preparation for a third try at school. His performance was poor, however: his thinking was slow, and his comprehension was limited. He spent most of his time alone, listening to music and writing trite poetry. His psychiatrist switched him from the antipsychotic to carbamazepam, at the boy's parents' request, in hope that his thinking would become less retarded.

Arrangements were made for the patient to reenter college when, suddenly, his parents called the doctor: "I think he's having another episode." The young man had painted black stripes on the walls of his bedroom and had smashed his sister's record collection. During the psychiatrist's examination, he paced the office; he appeared perplexed and fearful. He spoke incoherently about Jesus and the Devil, and intermittently laughed without reason.

Although this young man had one psychotic episode that occurred within the context of a full manic syndrome, subsequent episodes had fewer and fewer manic symptoms. Standard and even newer treatments for mania did not appear adequate in his case, and his parents' expectations of rapid and full recovery may have contributed to his early relapses. More emphasis on rehabilitation, with a more gradual resumption of his usual activities, plus administration of antipsychotic medications, might have benefited the patient more.

Differentiating subtypes of bipolar disorder. Manic episodes with psychotic features may be noted as either mood-congruent or mood-incongruent psychotic features. In the case of mania, mood-congruent features are defined as delusions or hallucinations whose content is entirely consistent with the themes of inflated worth, power, knowledge, identity, or special relationship to a deity or famous person. Mood-incongruent psychotic features include schizophrenialike symptoms, e.g., thought broadcasting or delusions of being controlled, and catatonic symptoms such as stupor, mutism, negativism, or posturing.

Recognition that mania may be accompanied by schizophrenia-like psychotic symptoms has been largely responsible for the major shift in diagnostic practice in the United States in the last 15 years from making diagnoses of schizophrenia to making diagnoses of bipolar disorder in cases of patients with mixed psychotic and manic syndromes. American psychiatrists employed a very broad definition of schizophrenia in the 1950s and '60s, documented by the U.S.-U.K. comparative diagnostic study (102), that labeled virtually all patients with delusions or hallucinations as schizophrenic. In the early 1970s, studies by Taylor and Abrams (103-106) suggested that certain schizophrenic patients rediagnosed as manic exhibited clinical courses, treatment responses, and outcomes much better than those in typical schizophrenia and indistinguishable from those in typical manic-depressive illness. There then appeared a host of studies (summarized in a well-known review by Pope and Lipinski [107]) supporting the idea that an affective syndrome had more diagnostic significance in terms of treatment and prognosis than particular psychotic symptoms. The idea that certain psychotic symptoms were pathognomonic of schizophrenia, i.e., Schneiderian first-rank symptoms, began to fade. DSM-III included this resetting of the boundary between schizophrenia and affective disorders in its criteria for major depressive and manic episodes.

The differential diagnosis was made in exactly the same way for major depression (as described previously) and mania. In summary, the psychotic symptoms had to occur always within the context of a mood disturbance for the diagnosis of a manic episode to be made. Since DSM-III was published, many studies have appeared that document the clinical similarities between, indeed the virtual identity of, bipolar disorder with mood-incongruent psychotic features and nonpsychotic bipolar disorder. In fact, the continuing studies of manic patients by Taylor and Abrams (108,109), Pope and his colleagues (110), Rosenthal and associates (111), and the group led by Brockington (112,113) are much more consistent in their results than are the parallel studies done with patients with depression. Although DSM-III treats depression and mania identically in terms of the presence of psychotic features, it is possible that some of those features exert a different effect on treatment and outcome when the mood disturbance is depression (see above) as opposed to mania.

Bipolar disorder has three subtypes related to course: mixed, manic, or depressed. These subtypes refer to the phenomenology of the current episode. The mixed subtype describes a current (or most recent) episode with the full symptom picture of both manic and major depressive episodes intermixed or rapidly alternating every few days. Some clinicians have objected to the use of the "mixed" subtype to refer to rapid cyclers, since these two patterns seem distinct and have different treatment implications (114,115). The manic subtype means that the current or most recent episode is manic, and the depressed subtype that it is a major depressive episode in a patient with one or more known previous manic episodes. A seasonal pattern can be specified for bipolar disorder according to the same guidelines as for major depression.

Cyclothymia

According to DSM-III-R, cyclothymia is diagnosed when a patient has had at least a two-year period punctuated by numerous hypomanic and mild depressive periods. Hypomania is elevated, expansive, or irritable mood that is subthreshold for a manic episode because of the absence of marked impairment in functioning, and mild depression refers to depression that does not fully meet criterion A for a major depressive episode. The criteria for cyclothymia require that there be no more than two continuous months in the two previous years of euthymic mood, that there is no clear evidence of a major depressive episode or a manic episode in the first two years, that the cyclothymia is not superimposed on a chronic psychotic disorder, and that the mood abnormalities are not sustained by organic factors or drugs (Table 6.7).

A major change from DSM-III has been the deletion of a symptom list to define the hypomanic periods and the mild depressive periods. It is enough to establish that the patient has had hypomanic episodes and periods of mild depression without further specification. Hypomanic episodes are defined as manic syndromes that meet criteria A and B, but not C, of the manic syndrome.

Difficulties in diagnosing cyclothymia are several. Possibly the hardest problem is distinguishing hypomania from a normal "good" or "upbeat" mood. The symptom list in DSM-III included having more energy, being more productive, thinking especially creatively, and being overly optimistic. Such traits may characterize many successful people—some of whom may actually be cyclothymic. In order to avoid many false-positive diagnoses, the clinician must go to great pains to establish that the good days are really too good.

The DSM-III-R symptoms of hypomania are stronger and facilitate differentiation. However, typically there are some negative consequences as a result of the "up" periods, although impairment is now specifically excluded by the criteria. The person with hypomania usually irritates or alienates other people and makes bad judgments as a result of his or her grandiose plans or expectations. Such defeats then frequently lead to "down" periods. Cyclothymic patients may have superimposed manic episodes, in which case both diagnoses are made.

The absence of a depressive symptom list creates a problem for characterizing the depressed periods. Patients who like or enjoy themselves better when "high" may report euthymic periods as being depressed. In my opinion, the clinician therefore needs some signs of clinical depression, not just a report of dysphoria or loss of interest. Patients with recurrent periods of hypomania or chronic hypomania are diagnosed as having bipolar disorder NOS if there is no evidence of depression and no history of a full-blown manic episode. At the other extreme, a patient whose depressions actually meet the criteria for major depressive episodes might also be better diagnosed as having bipolar disorder NOS, i.e., be classified as a so-called "bipolar II" patient.

Cyclothymia is a particularly difficult diagnosis to make in a patient with a history of use of certain psychoactive substances. The highs and lows associated with cocaine intoxication and withdrawal, for example, are difficult to distinguish from cyclothymia in a chronic user. Interestingly, there are suggestions that cyclothymia may pre-

Table 6.7 DSM-III-R Diagnostic Criteria for Cyclothymia

A. For at least two years (one year for children and adolescents), presence of numerous hypomanic episodes (all of the criteria for a manic episode, except criterion C, which indicates marked impairment) and numerous periods with depressed mood or loss of interest or pleasure that did not meet criterion A of major depressive episode.

B. During a two-year period (one year in children and adolescents) of the disturbance, never without hypomanic or depressive symptoms for more than two months at a time.

C. No clear evidence of a major depressive episode or manic episode during the first two years of the disturbance (or one year in children and adolescents).

   Note: After this minimum period of cyclothymia, there may be superimposed manic or major depressive episodes, in which case the additional diagnosis of bipolar disorder or bipolar disorder NOS should be given.

D. Not superimposed on a chronic psychotic disorder, such as schizophrenia or delusional disorder.

E. It cannot be established that an organic factor initiated and maintained the disturbance, e.g., repeated intoxication from drugs or alcohol.

dispose to cocaine abuse, as the person pharmacologically manipulates his or her own natural mood fluctuations. The clinician should attempt to establish that cyclothymia temporally preceded the cocaine problem before making both diagnoses.

Differential Diagnosis

The following are several of the more subtle distinctions in the differential diagnosis of bipolar disorders.

Bipolar disorder vs. cyclothymia. According to DSM-III the distinction between bipolar disorder and cyclothymia was a matter of degree. Many of the same symptoms appeared in the lists for both disorders, but the implication was that each symptom should be viewed on a continuum of severity. Both included inflated self-esteem, but bipolar disorder mentioned grandiosity and possible delusions of grandeur. Both noted that patients were more talkative than usual, but bipolar disorder also noted that speech was pressured.

Now, in DSM-III-R, the distinction is made on the grounds that manic episodes cause impairment, and cyclothymia does not. As was mentioned above, however, what is gained at the border with bipolar disorder is lost at the border with normalcy, unless one considers some kind of evidence of impairment in deciding what constitutes mood that is "too good." Again, impairment is a matter of degree. A cyclothymic patient may make a foolish investment, but is unlikely to squander a fortune.

Cyclothymia vs. dysthymia. The distinction between cyclothymia and dysthymia depends on the clinician's judgment that during periods when the patient was not depressed, his or her mood was in fact, too good, or a little "high," not simply normal. On superficial questioning, many dysthymic patients who have some nondepressed periods will refer to these periods as "up" periods. If the clinician follows up with questions designed to elicit a clear picture of how the person felt and behaved during these periods, a substantial proportion of these patients will turn out to be initial false positives. Cyclothymic patients' "up" periods are usually more frequent than the breaks in dysphoric mood experienced by dysthymic patients, so the alternation in mood is more evident. As already mentioned, the hypomanic periods of cyclothymic patients as diagnosed by DSM-III-R are now more symptomatically severe, but are purported to cause no interpersonal or occupational difficulties.

Cyclothymia vs. personality disorder. Several aspects of cyclothymia might be confused with elements of a personality disorder. One is that cyclothymia can be a life-long disturbance, similar to personality disorders. In DSM-II cyclothymic personality was, in fact, classified as a personality disorder; but similarities in phenomenology, biology, and treatment response led to classifying cyclothymia as an affective disorder in DSM-III.

The shifts in mood might suggest the affective instability of borderline personality disorder. In the latter disorder, the shifts in mood are typically for a matter of hours, but can last for a few days, bringing them closer to the duration of the mood swings of cyclothymic disorder. Rarely, however, will the patient with BPD alone report symptoms such as racing thoughts or decreased need for sleep. Inflated self-esteem may be confused with the grandiose sense of self-importance of narcissistic personality disorder; gregariousness, with the attention-seeking behaviors in histrionic personality disorder; and poor judgment, with the purposefully self-serving behavior of the antisocial personality disorder. In general, the more pervasive nature of the personality disorders, i.e., a broad pattern of thought, feeling, and behavior in a variety of contexts, as compared with the more narrow mood disturbance of cyclothymia, will enable the clinician to determine the difference. Sometimes patients will meet criteria for both cyclothymia and a personality disorder. On the other hand, the clinician must be careful not to equate symptoms or behaviors secondary to affective disturbance with manifestations of a personality disorder. Another instance of state dependence, this differential will be considered more fully in Chapter 9.

Notorious Indiscretions

A 30-year-old man signed himself into a hospital after his wife threatened to leave him. The man had been caught, for the third time in the couple's three-year marriage, having an affair with another woman.

The patient was a very successful, if somewhat erratic, businessman. He had started as a salesman, but had made so much money and impressed certain clients to such a degree that he left his company and went into business by himself. He had the reputation of a maverick, however, as there were times when he would cancel business meetings for days on end and other times when he was so abrasive that potential customers walked out on him.

His relationship with his wife was pleasant, though not passionate. She also was successful, as a fashion designer, and was much more consistent—"the glue that holds us together," the patient would say. As noted above, since his marriage the man had had three extramarital affairs. They had been with women he met spontaneously, usually "just picking them up" in a store or on a street corner, going to bed with them, and then having brief but torrid romances before discovery by his wife brought them to a close.

Discovery was easy, however, since the patient was notoriously indiscreet. He left telltale signs of dates, such as restaurant matchbook covers, on his bureau with his change. He charged gifts to credit cards for which his wife paid the bills. He would come home hours later than scheduled without an alibi or even a lame excuse. He gave his home phone number to the women, and eventually they would call.

At first, the patient was diagnosed as having a mixed personality disorder with borderline and narcissistic features. On close questioning, however, a cyclic pattern of mood fluctuations dating back to college emerged. The patient had always had some very bad periods, lasting several days to a week, when he would not get out of bed. School and work performance suffered, but he could compensate for this during "up" periods, in which he was extremely energetic, productive, and gregarious. These "ups" sometimes lasted for several months at a time, and usually ended with the patient exhausted and irritable. It was during these expansive periods that he picked up women and carried on the affairs.

After being caught, the man was contrite. It became clear that there were also some stable times during which he was neither up nor down. These periods were usually limited to several weeks at a time. The patient had many good friends of long duration.

Bipolar disorder vs. schizoaffective disorder. The differential diagnosis between bipolar disorder with psychotic features and schizoaffective disorder, manic, is made in exactly the same way as that discussed previously for psychotic major depression and schizoaffective disorder, depressed. The evidence that mood-incongruent delusions occurring within the context of a manic episode makes little clinical difference compared with mood-congruent delusions is even stronger for mania than for depression. The clinical importance of the temporal relationship of the mood and the psychotic syndromes has not been as well documented as for depression, however. Fogelson and his associates (116) reported a small series of what he called schizophreniform patients who had had prior affective episodes and a family history, treatment response, and course of illness similar to those in affective disorders. These patients would probably be diagnosed schizoaffective disorder in DSM-III-R terms because of the nonoverlapping mood and schizophrenialike disturbances. This would support the importance of the temporal course criterion for psychotic mania as well.

SUMMARY

This chapter describes problems in differential diagnosis of patients with mood disturbances. The mood disorders have been well studied in recent years, and subtypes have been examined for clinical utility. Guiding the clinician in taking into account the important aspects of the clinical heterogeneity of patients with mood disorders has been a major focus of this chapter. The importance of psychotic features in mood disorders, the relationship of episodic to more chronic, low-grade disturbances, and the relationship of mood disturbances to other disorders have been among the principal subjects covered. Adjustment disorders have also been discussed, since a diagnosis of the subtype adjustment disorder with depressed mood is commonly made, and can thus serve as a prototype for the others.

REFERENCES

1. Owens H, Maxmen JS: Mood and affect: a semantic confusion. Am J Psychiatry 136:97–99, 1979
2. Davidson JRT, Miller RD, Turnbull CD, Sullivan JL: Atypical depression. Arch Gen Psychiatry 39:527–534, 1982
3. Perris C: A study of bipolar (manic depressive) and unipolar recurrent depressive psychosis. Acta Psychiatr Scand, Supplement 194, 1966, pp 9–188
4. Winokur G, Clayton P, Reich T: Manic Depressive Illness. St Louis, CV Mosby Co, 1969
5. Akiskal HS, Djenderedjian AH, Rosenthal RH, Khani MK. Cyclothymic disorder: validating criteria for inclusion in the bipolar affective group. Am J Psychiatry 134:1227–1233, 1977
6. Akiskal HS: Subaffective disorders: dysthymic, cyclothymic, and bipolar II disorders in the "borderline" realm. Psychiatr Clin North Am 4:25–46, 1981
7. Akiskal HS, Rosenthal TL, Haykal RF, Lemmi H, Rosenthal RH, Scott-Strauss A: Characterological depressions—clinical and sleep EEG findings separating "subaffective dysthymias" from "character-spectrum" disorders. Arch Gen Psychiatry 37:777–783, 1980
8. Akiskal HS, Bitar AH, Puzantian VR, Rosenthal TL, Walker PW: The nosological status of neurotic depression: a prospective 3–4 year follow-up examination in the light of the primary–secondary and the unipolar-bipolar dichotomies. Arch Gen Psychiatry 35:756–766, 1978
9. Klerman GL, Endicott J, Spitzer R, Hirschfeld RMA: Neurotic depressions: a systematic analysis of multiple criteria and meanings. Am J Psychiatry 136:57–61, 1979
10. Akiskal HS: Diagnosis and classification of affective disorders: new insights from clinical and laboratory approaches. Psychiatr Dev 2:123–160, 1983
11. Mattes J: DSM-III criteria for major depressive episode (letter). Arch Gen Psychiatry 38:1068–1069, 1981
12. Spitzer RL, Endicott J, Robins E: Clinical criteria for psychiatric diagnosis and DSM-III. Am J Psychiatry 132:1187–1192, 1975
13. Hirschfeld RMA: Situational depression: validity of the concept. Br J Psychiatry 139:297–305, 1981
14. Hirschfeld RM, Klerman GL, Andreasen NC, Clayton PJ, Keller MB: Situational major depressive disorder. Arch Gen Psychiatry 42:1109–1114, 1985

15. American Psychiatric Association: Diagnostic and Statistical Manual of Mental Disorders, Third Edition, Revised. Washington, DC, American Psychiatric Association, 1987
16. Benjaminsen S: Stressful life events preceding the onset of neurotic depression. Psychol Med 11:369–378, 1981
17. Andreasen NC, Wasek P: Adjustment disorders in adolescents and adults. Arch Gen Psychiatry 37:1166–1170, 1980
18. Andreasen NC, Hoenk PR: The predictive value of adjustment disorders: a follow-up study. Am J Psychiatry 139:584–590, 1982
19. Fabrega H Jr, Mezzich JE, Mezzich AC: Marginal and transitional categories of illness and DSM-III. Arch Gen Psychiatry 44:567–572, 1987
20. Zimmerman M, Pfohl B, Coryell W, Stangl D: The prognostic validity of DSM-III axis IV in depressed inpatients. Am J Psychiatry 144:102–106, 1987
21. van Praag HM: A transatlantic view of the diagnosis of depressions according to the DSM-III: II. Did the DSM-III solve the problem of depression diagnosis? Compr Psychiatry 23:330–338, 1982
22. Williams JBW, Spitzer RL: Research Diagnostic Criteria and DSM-III: an annotated comparison. Arch Gen Psychiatry 39:1283–1289, 1982
23. Katz MM, Secunda SK, Hirschfeld RMA, Koslow S: NIMH Clinical Research Branch Collaborative Program on the Psychobiology of Depression. Arch Gen Psychiatry 36:765–771, 1979
24. Feighner JP, Robins E, Guze SB, Woodruff RA, Winokur G, Munoz R: Diagnostic criteria for use in psychiatric research. Arch Gen Psychiatry 26:57–63, 1972
25. Davidson J, Turnbull C, Strickland R, Belyea M: Comparative diagnostic criteria for melancholia and endogenous depression. Arch Gen Psychiatry 41:506–511, 1984
26. Roy A, Breier A, Doran AR, Pickar D: Life events in depression: relationship to subtypes. J Affective Disord 9:143–148, 1985
27. Zimmerman M, Coryell W, Pfohl B, Stangl D: The validity of four definitions of endogenous depression: II. Clinical, demographic, familial, and psychosocial correlates. Arch Gen Psychiatry, 43:234–244, 1986
28. Charney DS, Nelson JC: Delusional and nondelusional unipolar depression: further evidence for distinct subtypes. Am J Psychiatry 138:328–331, 1981
29. Davidson J, Miller R, Strickland R: Neuroticism and personality disorder in depression. J Affective Disord 8:177–182, 1985
30. Leckman JF, Weissman MM, Prusoff BA, Caruso KA, Merikangas KR, Pauls DL, Kidd KK: Subtypes of depression: family study perspective. Arch Gen Psychiatry 41:833–838, 1984
31. Price LH, Nelson JC, Charney DS, Quinlan DM: The clinical utility of family history for the diagnosis of melancholia. J Nerv Ment Dis 172:5–11, 1984
32. Andreasen NC, Scheftner W, Reich T, Hirschfeld RM, Endicott J, Keller MB: The validation of the concept of endogenous depression: a family study approach. Arch Gen Psychiatry 43:246–251, 1986
33. Jaffe K, Barnshaw HD, Kennedy ME: The dexamethasone suppression test in depressed outpatients with and without melancholia. Am J Psychiatry 140:492–493, 1983
34. Arana GW, Barreira PJ, Cohen BM, Lipinski JF, Fogelson D: The dexamethasone suppression test in psychotic disorders. Am J Psychiatry 140:1521–1523, 1983

35. Beeber AR, Kline MD, Pies RW, Manring JM Jr: Dexamethasone suppression test in hospitalized depressed patients with borderline personality disorder. J Nerv Ment Dis 172:301–303, 1984
36. Davidson J, Lipper S, Zung WW, Strickland R, Krishnan R, Mahorney S: Validation of four definitions of melancholia by the dexamethasone suppression test. Am J Psychiatry 141:1220–1223, 1984
37. Prusoff BA, Weissman MM, Klerman GL, Rounsaville BJ: Research Diagnostic Criteria subtypes of depression: their roles as predictors of differential response to psychotherapy and drug treatment. Arch Gen Psychiatry 37:796–801, 1980
38. Kupfer DJ, Spiker DG: Refractory depression: prediction of nonresponse by clinical indicators. J Clin Psychiatry 42:307–312, 1981
39. Paykel ES, Rowan PR, Parker RR, Bhat AV: Response to phenelzine and amitriptyline in subtypes of outpatient depression. Arch Gen Psychiatry 39:1041–1049, 1982
40. Davidson J, Turnbull C: Isocarboxazid: efficacy and tolerance. J Affective Disord 5:183–189, 1983
41. Razani J, White KL, White, J, Simpson G, Sloane RB, Rebal R, Palmer R: The safety and efficacy of combined amitriptyline and tranylcypromine antidepressant treatment: a controlled trial. Arch Gen Psychiatry 40:657–661, 1983
42. Stewart JW, Quitkin FM, Liebowitz MR, McGrath PJ, Harrison WM, Klein DF: Efficacy of desipramine in depressed outpatients: response according to Research Diagnostic Criteria diagnosis and severity of illness. Arch Gen Psychiatry 40:202–207, 1983
43. Coryell W, Zimmerman M: Outcome following ECT for primary unipolar depression: a test of newly proposed response predictors. Am J Psychiatry 142:862–867, 1984
44. Rich CL, Spiker DG, Jewel SW, Neil JF: DSM-III, RDC, and ECT: depressive subtypes and immediate response. J Clin Psychiatry 45:14–18, 1984
45. Rickels K, Feighner JP, Smith WT: Alprazolam, amitriptyline, doxepin, and placebo in the treatment of depression. Arch Gen Psychiatry 42:134–141, 1985
46. Zimmerman M, Coryell W, Pfohl B: The treatment validity of DSM-III melancholic subtyping. Psychiatry Res 16:37–43, 1985
47. Coryell W, Turner RD: Outcome with desipramine therapy in subtypes of nonpsychotic major depression. J Affective Disord, in press.
48. Skodol AE, Zimmerman M, Hirschfeld RMA: Affective and adjustment disorders, in An Annotated Bibliography of DSM-III. Edited by Skodol AE, Spitzer RL. Washington, DC, American Psychiatric Press, 1987, pp 95–109
49. Nelson JC, Mazure C, Quinlan DM, Jatlow PI: Drug-responsive symptoms in melancholia. Arch Gen Psychiatry 41:663–668, 1984
50. Charney DS, Nelson JC, Quinlan DM: Personality traits and disorder in depression. Am J Psychiatry 138:1601–1604, 1981
51. Frances A, Brown RP, Kocsis JH, Mann JJ: Psychotic depression: a separate entity? AM J Psychiatry 138:831–833, 1981
52. Nelson WH, Kahn A, Orr WW Jr: Delusional depression: phenomenology, neuroendocrine function, and tricyclic antidepressant response. J Affective Disord 6:297–306, 1984
53. Coryell W, Tsuang MT: Major depression with mood-congruent or mood-incongruent psychotic features: outcome after 40 years. Am J Psychiatry 142:479–482, 1985

54. Coryell W, Tsuang M, McDaniel J: Psychotic features in major depression: is mood congruence important? J Affective Disord 4:227–236, 1982
55. Coryell W, Pfohl B, Zimmerman M: The clinical and neuroendocrine features of psychotic depression. J Nerv Ment Dis 172:521–528, 1984
56. Brockington IF, Kendell RE, Wainwright S: Depressed patients with schizophrenic or paranoid symptoms. Psychol Med 10:665–675, 1980
57. Brockington IF, Helzer JE, Hillier VF, Francis AF: Definitions of depression: concordance and prediction of outcome. Am J Psychiatry 139:1022–1027, 1982
58. Rosenthal NE, Sack DA, Gillin JC, Lewy AJ, Goodwin FK, Davenport Y, Mueller PS, Newsome DA, Wehr TA: Seasonal affective disorder: a description of the syndrome and preliminary findings with light therapy. Arch Gen Psychiatry 41:72–80, 1984
59. Wehr TA, Jacobsen FM, Sack DA, Arendt J, Tamarkin L, Rosenthal NE: Phototherapy of seasonal affective disorder. Arch Gen Psychiatry 43:870–875, 1986
60. Akiskal HS: Dysthymic disorder: psychopathology of proposed chronic depressive subtypes. Am J Psychiatry 140:11–20, 1983
61. Roy A, Sutton M, Pickar D: Neuroendocrine and personality variables in dysthymic disorder. Am J Psychiatry 142:94–97, 1985
62. Kocsis JH, Frances AJ: A critical discussion of DSM-III dysthymic disorder. Am J Psychiatry 144:1534–1542, 1987
63. Liebowitz MR, Quitkin FM, Stewart JW, McGrath PJ, Harrison WM, Markowitz JS, Rabkin JG, Tricamo E, Goetz DM, Klein DF: Antidepressant specificity in atypical depression. Arch Gen Psychiatry 45:129–137, 1988
64. Quitkin FM, Stewart JW, McGrath PJ, Liebowitz MR, Harrison WM, Tricamo E, Klein DF, Rabkin JG, Markowitz JS, Wager SG: Phenelzine versus imipramine in the treatment of probable atypical depression: defining syndrome boundaries of selective MAOI responders. Am J Psychiatry 145:306–311, 1988
65. Quitkin F, Rifkin A, Klein DF: Monoamine oxidase inhibitors: a review of antidepressant effectiveness. Arch Gen Psychiatry 36:749–760, 1979
66. Klerman GL: The spectrum of mania. Compr Psychiatry 22:11–20, 1981
67. Dunner DL: Subtypes of bipolar affective disorder with particular regard to bipolar II. Psychiatr Dev 1:75–86, 1983
68. Coryell W, Endicott J, Reich T, Andreasen N, Keller M: A family study of bipolar II disorder. Br J Psychiatry 145:49–54, 1984
69. Coryell W, Endicott J, Andreasen N, Keller M: Bipolar I, bipolar II, and nonbipolar major depression among the relatives of affectively ill probands. Am J Psychiatry 142:817–821, 1985
70. Endicott J, Nee J, Andreasen N, Clayton P, Keller M, Coryell W: Bipolar II. Combine or keep separate? J Affective Disord 8:17–28, 1985
71. Keller MB, Shapiro RW: "Double depression": superimposition of acute depressive episodes on chronic depressive disorders. Am J Psychiatry 139:438–442, 1982
72. Keller MB, Lavori PW, Endicott J, Coryell W, Klerman GL: "Double depression": two-year follow-up. Am J Psychiatry 140:689–694, 1983
73. Keller MB, Lavori PW, Rice J, Coryell W, Hirschfield RM: The persistent risk of chronicity in recurrent episodes of nonbipolar major depressive disorder: a prospective follow-up. Am J Psychiatry 143:24–28, 1986
74. Berti Ceroni G, Neri C, Pezzoli A: Chronicity in major depression. A naturalistic prospective study. J Affective Disord 7:123–132, 1984

75. American Psychiatric Association: Diagnostic and Statistical Manual of Mental Disorders, Third Edition. Washington, DC, American Psychiatric Association, 1980
76. Himmelhoch JM, Fuchs CZ, May SJ, Symons BJ, Neil JF: When a schizo-affective diagnosis has meaning. J Nerv Ment Dis 169:277–282, 1981
77. Siris SG, Rifkin A, Reardon GT, Endicott J, Pereira DH, Hayes R, Casey E: Course-related depressive syndromes in schizophrenia. Am J Psychiatry 141:1254–1257, 1984
78. Siris SG, Rifkin A, Reardon GT, Doddi SR, Strahan A, Hall KS: Stability of the postpsychotic depression syndrome. J Clin Psychiatry 47:86–88, 1986
79. Siris SG, Morgan V, Fagerstrom R, Rifkin A, Cooper TB: Adjunctive imipramine in the treatment of postpsychotic depression. Arch Gen Psychiatry 44:533–539, 1987
80. Boyd JH, Burke JD Jr, Gruenberg E, Holzer CE 3d, Rae DS, George LK, Karno M, Stoltzman R, McEvoy L, Nestadt G: Exclusion criteria of DSM-III: a study of co-occurrence of hierarchy-free syndromes. Arch Gen Psychiatry 41:983–989, 1984
81. Leckman JF, Merikangas KR, Pauls DL, Prusoff BA, Weissman MM: Anxiety disorders and depression: contradictions between family study data and DSM-III conventions. Am J Psychiatry 140:880–882, 1983
82. Weissman MM, Merikangas KR, Wickramaratne P, Kidd KK, Prusoff BA, Leckman JF, Pauls DL: Understanding the clinical heterogeneity of major depression using family data. Arch Gen Psychiatry 43:430–434, 1986
83. Stewart JW, McGrath PJ, Liebowitz MR, Harrison W, Quitkin F, Rabkin JG: Treatment outcome validation of DSM-III depressive subtypes: clinical usefulness in outpatients with mild to moderate depression. Arch Gen Psychiatry 42:1148–1153, 1985
84. Akiskal HS, Hirshfeld MA, Yerevanian BF: The relationship of personality to affective disorders. Arch Gen Psychiatry 40:801–810, 1983
85. Gunderson JG, Elliot GR: The interface between borderline personality disorder and affective disorder. Am J Psychiatry 142:277–288, 1985
86. Frances A: The DSM-III personality disorders section: a commentary. Am J Psychiatry 137:1050–1054, 1980
87. Hirschfeld RMA, Klerman GL, Clayton PJ, Keller MB, McDonald-Scott P, Larkin BH: Assessing personality: effects of the depressive state on trait measurement. Am J Psychiatry 140:695–699, 1983
88. McGlashan TH: The borderline syndrome. II. Is it a variant of schizophrenia or affective disorder? Arch Gen Psychiatry 409:1319–1323, 1983
89. McGlashan TH: The Chestnut Lodge follow-up study: III. Long-term outcome of borderline personalities. Arch Gen Psychiatry 43:20–30, 1986
90. Pope HG Jr, Jonas JM, Hudson JI, Cohen BM, Gunderson JG: The validity of DSM-III borderline personality disorder. A phenomenologic, family history, treatment response, and long-term follow-up study. Arch Gen Psychiatry 40:23–30, 1983
91. Winokur G: The validity of neurotic-reactive depression. New data and reappraisal. Arch Gen Psychiatry 2:1116–1122, 1985
92. Zimmerman M, Coryell W, Stangl D, Pfohl B: Validity of an operational definition for neurotic unipolar major depression. J Affective Disord, in press
93. Boyd JH, Weissman MM: Epidemiology of affective disorders: a reexami-

nation and future directions. Arch Gen Psychiatry 38:1039–1046, 1981
94. Andreasen NC, Grove WM: The classification of depression: traditional versus mathematical approaches. Am J Psychiatry 139:45–52, 1982
95. Gershon ES, Hamovit J, Guroff JJ, Dibble E, Leckman JF, Sceery W, Targum SD, Nurnberger JI, Goldin LR, Bunney WE: A family study of schizoaffective, bipolar I, bipolar II, unipolar, and normal control probands. Arch Gen Psychiatry 39:1157–1167, 1982
96. Nurnberger J, Roose SP, Dunner DL, Fieve RR: Unipolar mania: a distinct clinical entity? Am J Psychiatry 136:1420–1423, 1979
97. Pfohl B, Vasquez N, Nasrallah H: The mathematical case against unipolar mania. J Psychiatr Res 16:259–265, 1981
98. Pfohl B, Vasquez N, Nasrallah H: Unipolar vs. bipolar mania: a review of 247 patients. Br J Psychiatry 141:453–458, 1982
99. Harrow M, Grossman BS, Silverstein ML, Meltzer HY: Thought pathology in manic and schizophrenic patients. Arch Gen Psychiatry 39:665–671, 1982
100. Harrow M, Silverstein M, Marengo J: Disordered thinking: does it identify nuclear schizophrenia? Arch Gen Psychiatry 40:765–771, 1983
101. Harrow M, Grossman LS, Silverstein ML, Meltzer HY, Kettering RL: A longitudinal study of thought disorder in manic patients. Arch Gen Psychiatry 43:781–785, 1986
102. Kendell RE, Cooper JE, Gourlay AJ, Copeland JRM, Sharpe L, Gurland BJ: Diagnostic criteria of American and British psychiatrists. Arch Gen Psychiatry 25:123–130, 1971
103. Taylor MA, Abrams R: The phenomenology of mania: a new look at some old patients. Arch Gen Psychiatry 29:520–522, 1973
104. Taylor MA, Gaztanaga P, Abrams R: Manic-depressive illness and acute schizophrenia: a clinical, family history, and treatment-response study. Am J Psychiatry 131:678–682, 1974
105. Abrams R, Taylor MA, Gaztanaga P: Manic-depressive illness and paranoid schizophrenia: a phenomenologic, family history, and treatment-response study. Arch Gen Psychiatry 31:640–642, 1974
106. Taylor MA, Abrams R: Manic-depressive illness and "good prognosis" schizophrenia. Am J Psychiatry 132:741–742, 1975
107. Pope HG Jr, Lipinski J: Diagnosis in schizophrenia and manic-depressive illness: a reassessment of the specificity of schizophrenic symptoms in the light of current research. Arch Gen Psychiatry 35:811–828, 1978
108. Abrams R, Taylor MA: Importance of schizophrenic symptoms in the diagnosis of mania. Am J Psychiatry 138:658–661, 1981
109. Taylor MA, Abrams R: Schizo-affective disorder, manic type: a clinical, laboratory, and genetic study. Psychiatr Clin (Basel) 16:234–244, 1983
110. Pope HG Jr, Lipinski JF, Cohen BM, Axelrod DT: "Schizoaffective disorder": an invalid diagnosis? A comparison of schizoaffective disorder, schizophrenia, and affective disorder. Am J Psychiatry 137:921–927, 1980
111. Rosenthal NE, Rosenthal LN, Stallone F, Dunner DL, Fieve RR: Toward the validation of RDC schizoaffective disorder. Arch Gen Psychiatry 37:804–810, 1980
112. Brockington IF, Wainwright S, Kendell RE: Manic patients with schizophrenic or paranoid symptoms. Psychol Med 10:73–83, 1980
113. Brockington IF, Hillier VF, Francis AF, Helzer JE, Wainwright S: Definitions of mania: concordance and prediction of outcome. Am J Psychiatry 140:435–439, 1983

114. Secunda SK, Swann A, Katz MM, Koslow SH, Croughan J, Chang S: Diagnosis and treatment of mixed mania. Am J Psychiatry 144:96–98, 1987
115. Wehr TA, Sack DA, Rosenthal NE, Cowdry RW: Rapid cycling affective disorder: contributing factors and treatment responses in 51 patients. Am J Psychiatry 145:179–184, 1988
116. Fogelson, DL, Cohen BM, Pope HG: A study of DSM-III schizophreniform disorder. Am J Psychiatry139:1281–1285, 1982

CHAPTER 7

Anxiety Syndromes

If affective disorders were, in terms of clinical and research interest, the mental disorders of the '70s, then surely anxiety disorders have been the disorders of the '80s. This may be due, in large part, to the extensive subdividing of DSM-II anxiety and phobic neuroses within the DSM-III classification of anxiety disorders and their definition by specified diagnostic criteria. In the past eight years, anxiety disorders have been the subject of numerous phenomenologic, family, treatment, and biological marker studies.

Specialty clinics for the treatment of anxiety disorders by behavioral, cognitive, pharmacologic, and other therapies have sprung up in almost every major medical center. When I first began lecturing about the then new DSM-III classification at various hospitals and mental health centers across the country in 1980, the preferential response of panic disorder to the tricyclic (TCA) antidepressants as an important reason for distinguishing panic from generalized anxiety disorder seemed to be news to many clinicians. Now, psychiatrists routinely prescribe the TCAs for panic attacks, and many, if not most, recognize the usefulness of the MAO inhibitors as well. Antidepressant therapy has also been recommended for use in the anxiety disorders social phobia (1,2) and obsessive compulsive disorder (3-5) and the first phase of a major cross-national study of the use of a new benzodiazepine, alprazolam, for the treatment of agoraphobia with panic attacks has recently been completed (6,7).

In psychiatry, whenever so much attention is devoted to a particular area of diagnosis, existing classification schemes are likely to be found wanting, and so it has been with DSM-III—such is the price of progress. Because of the heightened interest in DSM-III anxiety disorders, clinical experience and empirical data have accumulated to suggest revisions that have been incorporated in DSM-III-R.

Overview of Differential Diagnosis

DSM-III defined anxiety as "Apprehension, tension, or uneasiness that stems from the anticipation of danger . . . ." (8, p. 392).

Figure 7.1 DSM-III-R Decision Tree for the Differential Diagnosis of Anxiety Disorders

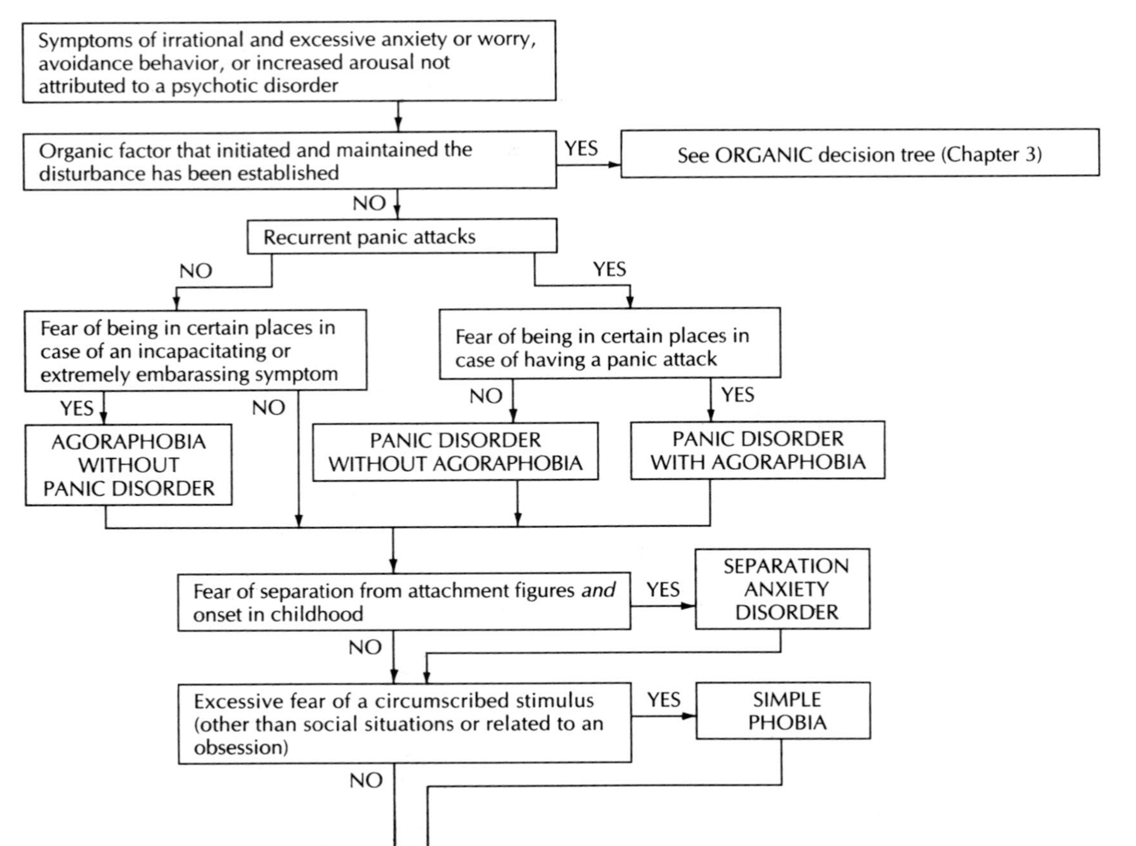

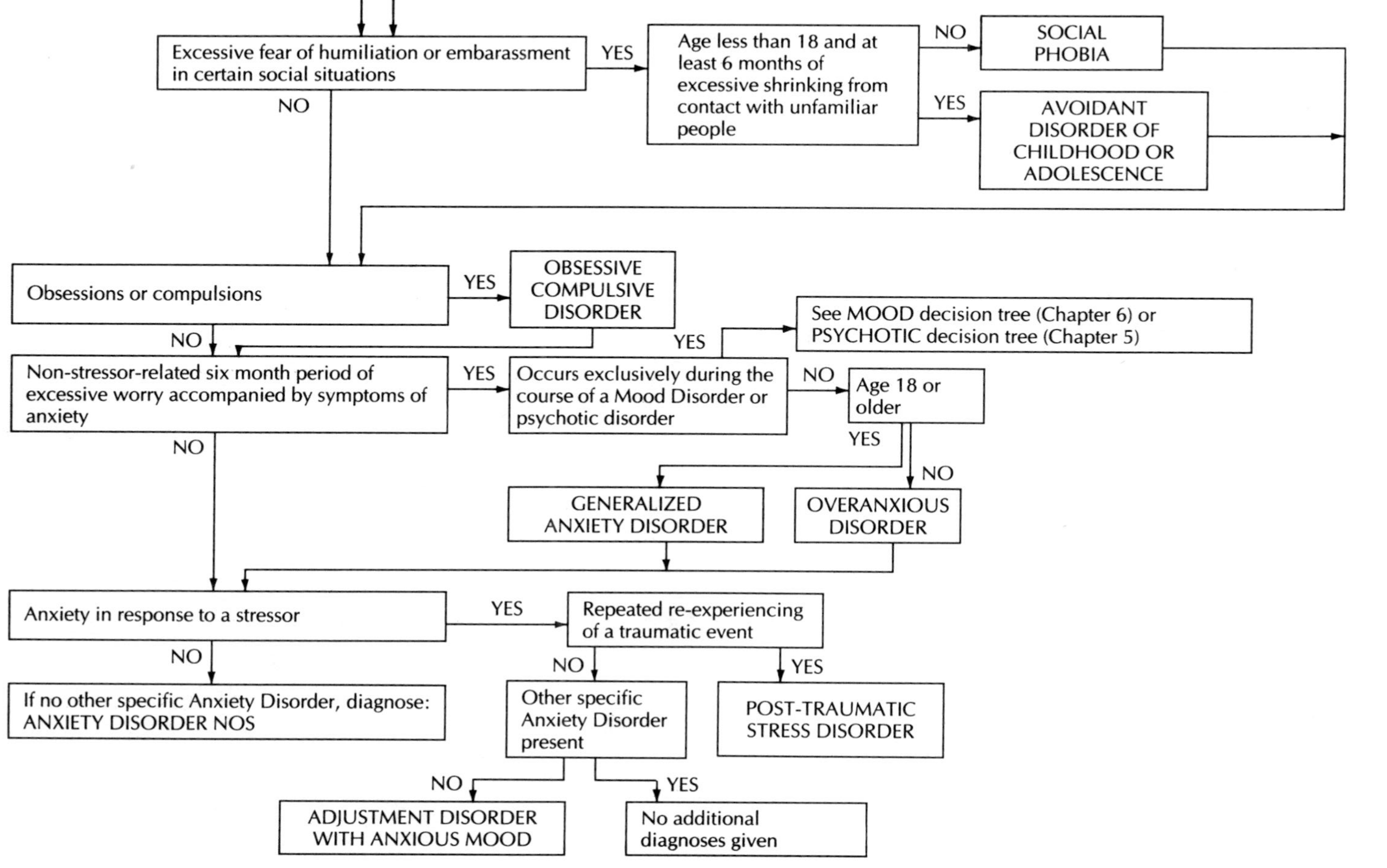
Excessive fear of humiliation or embarassment in certain social situations
YES
Age less than 18 and at least 6 months of excessive shrinking from contact with unfamiliar people
NO
SOCIAL PHOBIA
YES
AVOIDANT DISORDER OF CHILDHOOD OR ADOLESCENCE
NO
Obsessions or compulsions
YES
OBSESSIVE COMPULSIVE DISORDER
NO
Non-stressor-related six month period of excessive worry accompanied by symptoms of anxiety
YES
Occurs exclusively during the course of a Mood Disorder or psychotic disorder
YES
See MOOD decision tree (Chapter 6) or PSYCHOTIC decision tree (Chapter 5)
NO
Age 18 or older
YES
GENERALIZED ANXIETY DISORDER
NO
OVERANXIOUS DISORDER
NO
Anxiety in response to a stressor
YES
Repeated re-experiencing of a traumatic event
YES
POST-TRAUMATIC STRESS DISORDER
NO
Other specific Anxiety Disorder present
YES
No additional diagnoses given
NO
ADJUSTMENT DISORDER WITH ANXIOUS MOOD
NO
If no other specific Anxiety Disorder, diagnose: ANXIETY DISORDER NOS

Anxiety is a ubiquitous human emotion, and excessive, extreme, or impairing anxiety is associated with many mental disorders. Once the clinician has decided that symptoms of irrational or excessive anxiety constitute the major syndrome presented by a patient, he or she proceeds to consider various diagnostic possibilities.

Figure 7.1 reproduces the DSM-III-R Decision Tree for the Differential Diagnosis of Anxiety Disorders. This tree contains some changes in terminology and principles of differential diagnosis from the one in DSM-III. These will be discussed in this chapter. Table 7.1 summarizes the diagnostic possibilities represented by the DSM-III-R decision tree.

TABLE 7.1 Disorders in the Differential Diagnosis of Anxiety Syndromes

ORGANIC MENTAL DISORDERS
- Delirium
- Dementia
- Organic anxiety syndrome
- Psychoactive substance-induced intoxication
- Psychoactive substance-induced withdrawal

PSYCHOTIC DISORDERS

MOOD DISORDERS

ANXIETY DISORDERS
- Panic disorder with agoraphobia
- Panic disorder without agoraphobia
- Agoraphobia without panic disorder
- Social phobia
- Simple phobia
- Obsessive compulsive disorder
- Posttraumatic stress disorder
- Generalized anxiety disorder
- Anxiety disorder NOS

CHILDHOOD OR ADOLESCENT ONSET DISORDERS
- Separation anxiety disorder
- Avoidant disorder of childhood
- Overanxious disorder

ADJUSTMENT DISORDER
- Adjustment disorder with anxious mood
- Adjustment disorder with mixed emotional features

Anxiety and Physical Illness

Increasingly, anxiety has been recognized as a manifestation of many physical illnesses. Included are both anxiety in its general form and panic attacks. The recognition of anxiety due to physical illness has been facilitated in DSM-III-R by the inclusion of a new category, organic anxiety syndrome (9). The discussions of differential diagnosis that follow assume that the clinician has ruled out physical illness as a cause of an anxiety syndrome. A full discussion of organic anxiety syndrome and a table listing a range of physical illnesses that are associated with anxiety can be found in Chapter 3.

Anxiety and Psychoactive Substances

Anxiety can also result from the ingestion of certain psychoactive substances, such as caffeine, or withdrawal from substances, such as sedatives or hypnotics. These syndromes are discussed in detail in Chapter 4.

Ruling Out a Psychotic Disorder

The process of ruling out a psychotic disorder is represented in the decision tree as the initial step, but most clinicians would investigate organic etiologies first in any case. Physical illness or exogenous substances may cause psychotic symptoms, and organic mental disorders therefore take diagnostic precedence.

Fear or extreme anxiety is a common symptom of psychotic disorders such as schizophrenia. Delusions, hallucinations, or grossly disorganized behavior is usually evident to point toward a differential diagnosis of psychosis (see Chapter 5).

DSM-III-R Anxiety Disorders: Revised Criteria and Terminology

Although all of the DSM-III anxiety disorders—except, perhaps, generalized anxiety disorder (GAD)—can be reliably diagnosed (10), thanks to diagnostic criteria, questions have been raised about the validity of some of the disorders as defined in DSM-III and of the distinctions drawn among them. Thus, in DSM-III-R there are rather extensive revisions of the criteria of most of the anxiety disorders, and consequent changes in terminology. This chapter is organized around the DSM-III disorders and problems in the differential diagnosis of each disorder, so as to inform the clinician of the rationale for the derivation of the new DSM-III-R categories from the old.

The discussion begins with panic disorder, the first anxiety dis-

TABLE 7.2 Characteristic Features of DSM-III-R Anxiety Disorders

Disorder	Key Identifying Features
Panic disorder without agoraphobia	Discrete, unexpected panic attacks
Panic disorder with agoraphobia	Unexpected panic attacks, travel restrictions
Agoraphobia without panic disorder	Fear of places from which escape is not possible
Social phobia	Fear of scrutiny, humiliation, embarrassment
Simple phobia	Fear of object or situation
Obsessive compulsive disorder	Intrusive, senseless thoughts or images; stereotyped, ritualistic behaviors
Posttraumatic stress disorder	Unusually traumatic experience, reexperiencing, avoidance or numbing, arousal
Generalized anxiety disorder	Excessive worry or apprehension
Anxiety disorder NOS	Other anxiety or phobic avoidance

order considered in the DSM-III-R decision tree for the anxiety disorders. The key identifying features of panic disorder and the other DSM-III-R anxiety disorders are summarized in Table 7.2

PANIC DISORDER

The recognition of panic disorder (PD) as a separate diagnostic entity within the rubric of anxiety disorder has been one of the most useful of DSM-III's innovations. Panic disorder, as distinguished from generalized anxiety disorder, now almost invariably indicates the use of antidepressant medication to psychiatrists who prescribe psychopharmacologic agents (11). Morever, the presence of panic attacks in patients with atypical depression (see Chapter 6) appears to be one of the key features of the latter disorder, which helps to predict the frequently observed specificity of treatment response to MAO-inhibitor antidepressants (12). Because of its usefulness as a diagnostic category, panic disorder has come under close scrutiny, and problems in its differential diagnosis have been identified.

Distinguishing Panic Disorder from Heightened Anxiety

Panic disorder consists of the frequent occurrence of panic attacks. Panic attacks, as the words imply, are states of very intense anxiety. All anxiety feelings are likely to wax and wane, but not all states of heightened anxiety are synonymous with panic. Adding to the complexity is the observation that not all panic attacks are equally severe: there are "major" attacks, accompanied by a multitude of symptoms, and there are "minor" attacks, with fewer symptoms. The following case vignette illustrates the difficulty in discriminating panic attacks from heightened anxiety.

High Anxiety

During a hospitalization for anorexia and self-mutilation, a 29-year-old single, female, schoolteacher described "anxiety attacks" that caused her to act impulsively. When experiencing such anxiety, she would make superficial cuts on her arms and legs or burn her skin with cigarettes.

A clinician, attempting to rule out a variety of Axis I disorders co-occurring with a personality disorder, inquired about the anxiety.

Interviewer: Tell me about the anxiety you were feeling. What's that like?

Patient: It's very uncomfortable. *(Pause)* Anxiety is a difficult term to define.

Interviewer: What exactly do you feel?

Patient: Tingling, impatient, like I can't sit still—although I do. I can't concentrate, I feel like throwing something, tearing something, doing something destructive.

Interviewer: Is this a chronic tension level that slowly builds, or does it come upon you suddenly?

Patient: Either, both. It's been rather constant this past week.

Interviewer: Do you ever get struck by waves of high anxiety that come from the blue?

Patient: On rare occasions—when I can't say where they come from, consciously. Usually I know.

Interviewer: Can the anxiety build up to, you know, panic proportions? I mean, is it extremely intense?

Patient: I'd have to say, 'Yes.' I have heart palpitations, choking sensations . . .

Interviewer: Hot or cold flashes?

Patient: No.

Interviewer: Faintness or dizziness?

Patient: Um . . . lightheadedness.

Interviewer: Nausea or diarrhea?

Patient: Both.

Interviewer: Pain in the chest?

Patient: Mild, when my heart is going crazy.

Interviewer: Are you afraid you might die or go crazy?

Patient: No, as much as I hate it, I know it will go away.

Interviewer: How long does the anxiety stay at its peak?

Patient: Actually, I was at that state almost the entire weekend.
Interviewer: It didn't come and go?
Patient: No, it was just there all the time.
Few or no overt signs of anxiety were observed. The patient sat calmly and answered questions slowly, after some reflection.

One very important aspect of panic attacks that helps to distinguish them from other states of high anxiety is their sudden onset. Although the DSM-III criteria for panic referred to discrete periods of fear, implying sudden onset, they were ambiguous in this regard. This ambiguity has been rectified in DSM-III-R by the addition of a new criterion, (D), which requires that in some of the attacks, the classic arousal symptoms (criterion C) developed within 10 minutes of the beginning of the first "C" symptom noticed in the attack. (See Table 7.3, DSM-III-R Criteria for Panic Disorder.) This crescendo pattern of onset of a panic attack is critical for the diagnosis.

A number of research groups have studied the differences between panic disorder and generalized anxiety disorder. From a phenomenologic perspective, most studies have found that patients with panic disorder had anxiety characterized by autonomic symptoms—particularly cardiovascular (13,14) of more sudden onset (14) and of generally shorter duration (15) than those in patients with GAD (hence, the colloquial term *cardiac neurosis*). Panic disorder and GAD appear to run separately in families (16,17).

Further complicating the differential diagnosis of PD from GAD is the finding that patients who have had a few panic attacks typically come to fear the possibility of having another. This "anticipatory anxiety" can be symptomatically identical with GAD, but is actually an aspect of PD, and therefore does not warrant a separate diagnosis. Anticipatory anxiety has become a part of the DSM-III-R criteria for panic disorder, which now state (criterion B) that either four attacks have occurred within a four-week period or "one or more attacks have been followed by a period of at least a month of persistent fear of having another attack" (18, p. 238). In addition, the criteria for GAD have been clarified in that the characteristic persistent worry or apprehension needs to be about "two or more life circumstances" (18, p. 252). Persistent worry about having a panic attack would fall below the threshold for this criterion and, furthermore, is specifically ruled out by a new criterion, B, which states that the focus of the anxiety is unrelated to another Axis I disorder, if present.

In evaluating the cardiovascular and respiratory symptoms of panic criterion C, it is important to remember that their occurrence should not be limited to periods of physical exercise. Intense physical exercise can lead to shortness of breath or chest discomfort, which in

Table 7.3 DSM-III-R Diagnostic Criteria for Panic Disorder

A. At some time during the disturbance, one or more panic attacks (discrete periods of intense fear or discomfort) have occurred that were (1) unexpected, i.e., did not occur immediately before or on exposure to a situation that almost always caused anxiety, and (2) not triggered by situations in which the person was the focus of others' attention.

B. Either four attacks, as defined in criterion **A,** have occurred within a four-week period, or one or more attacks have been followed by a period of at least a month of persistent fear of having another attack.

C. At least four of the following symptoms developed during at least one of the attacks:

(1) shortness of breath (dyspnea) or smothering sensations
(2) dizziness, unsteady feelings, or faintness
(3) palpitations or accelerated heart rate (tachycardia)
(4) trembling or shaking
(5) sweating
(6) choking
(7) nausea or abdominal distress
(8) depersonalization or derealization
(9) numbness or tingling sensations (paresthesias)
(10) flushes (hot flashes) or chills
(11) chest pain or discomfort
(12) fear of dying
(13) fear of going crazy or of doing something uncontrolled

Note: Attacks involving four or more symptoms are panic attacks; attacks involving fewer than four symptoms are limited symptom attacks (see agoraphobia without history of panic disorder).

D. During at least some of the attacks, at least four of the **C** symptoms developed suddenly and increased in intensity within ten minutes of the beginning of the first **C** symptom noticed in the attack.

E. It cannot be established that an organic factor initiated and maintained the disturbance, e.g., amphetamine or caffeine intoxication, hyperthyroidism.

Note: Mitral valve prolapse may be an associated condition, but does not preclude a diagnosis of panic disorder.

turn can cause anxiety and fear of a heart attack. The relationship between the physical symptoms and the anxiety is obviously reversed. I have encountered a patient whose symptoms began while doing strenuous cycling, but who later went on to have panic attacks when not exercising.

Frequency as a Measure of Clinical Significance

A patient may present to an internist or a cardiologist following a single panic attack if the symptoms were particularly severe and frightening. Once a cardiac etiology for the symptoms has been ruled out, the patient may be referred for psychiatric consultation.

Is the occurrence of a single panic attack sufficient evidence of psychopathology to institute treatment or close follow-up? In an attempt to deal with the need for a threshold of clinical significance, DSM-III instituted a requirement that three panic attacks occur within a three-week period for a diagnosis of panic disorder to be made. The frequency requirement has been raised in DSM-III-R to four attacks in a four-week period. These are admittedly arbitrary frequency criteria, and it was expected that clinicians would invoke the "criteria as guides" option given to them in DSM-III (8, p. 8) to make the diagnosis and institute treatment when necessary. Thus, a patient who has had one or two major panic attacks a month for the past six months and is developing certain avoidance behaviors, but has never had three (or four) in a four-week period could, and should, be treated. Nonetheless, the frequency criterion does present some problems for differential diagnosis when rigorously diagnosed patients are needed (e.g., in research studies) and in cases of patients close to the borders of clinically significant pathology.

The concepts of "major" and "minor" attacks, described by the Sheehans (19), are important for evaluating frequency. Patients usually have no trouble describing major attacks, and some patients have enough significant major attacks for the diagnosis to be certain. Patients who have a preponderance of minor attacks that do not stand out because of the limited number or severity of symptoms are more difficult to diagnose. In fact, the Sheehans believe that minor attacks may characterize the early course of panic disorder, major attacks developing later. Early recognition and intervention when the attacks are at the minor level may therefore be clinically useful. Moreover, as will be discussed later in this chapter, some patients begin to develop rather significant patterns of avoidance behavior after only one or two major panic attacks. Hence, a rather significant syndrome in terms of disability can exist even when the "four in four weeks" criterion is not met. Three different approaches to assessing the frequency pattern are useful, depending on the circumstances.

The first approach is to focus the questions concerning the occurrence of symptoms on minor attacks if they are frequent. Many patients' minor attacks have enough symptoms (four) and are frequent enough (four in four weeks) to meet the specified criteria. The symptom list in DSM-III-R has been expanded to 13 symptoms by the addition of nausea or abdominal distress; separation of fear of dying, or going crazy, or doing something uncontrolled into two items; and the combination of dizziness, unsteady feelings, and faintness into one item. Other changes in the symptoms are the addition of tachycardia to palpitations and specifying smothering sensations with shortness of breath rather than with choking.

A second approach is also possible with the DSM-III-R revised criteria. This approach documents the necessary symptoms in one major, recent attack and focuses the assessment on whether the person now has a persistent fear (of one month's minimum duration) of having another attack. A history of agoraphobic (see below) avoidance behavior should be a clue to the advisability of taking this perspective, since such avoidance is thought to be typically based on this fear (20). With this approach, the nature of minor attacks becomes irrelevant (providing there has been at least one major attack at some time) since the patient can meet criteria B and C without having had four attacks in four weeks.

Finally, if the Sheehans' views are correct, minor symptom attacks, even if they do not have enough symptoms to meet criterion C, should be counted. Technically, however, according to DSM-III-R the diagnosis of panic disorder would be made only if a patient had one major attack and additional minor attacks meeting the four in four weeks criterion or followed by a month of persistent anticipatory fear. The best policy may be to take a conservative approach, early in the course of the disorder, by requiring at least one major attack before instituting treatment.

Panic vs. Phobic Fears

Patients with phobias experience intense, autonomic, "fight or flight" symptoms associated with fear when exposed to a phobic stimulus. These symptoms can be indistinguishable from those of panic disorder. The difference is that panic attacks are spontaneous, and are not provoked by situations or objects. The spontaneity can be difficult to assess as the course of the disorder progresses since, as has been mentioned, avoidance behavior develops as a result of the person's coming to associate certain places or situations with occurrence of the attacks. The association is spurious in panic disorder, but it is certainly hard for the patient to believe this.

DSM-III includes the qualification that the attacks not be precipitated "only by exposure to a circumscribed phobic stimulus" (8, p. 231). DSM-III-R has the more accurate and clinically helpful phrasing, in criterion A, that "*At some time* during the disturbance" (emphasis added) one or more panic attacks were unexpected (18, p. 237).

Thus, for panic disorder the fear is not always caused by a situation known to precipitate anxiety (agoraphobia or a simple phobia) or in which the person is the focus of others' attention (social phobia). These alternative diagnoses will be discussed later in the chapter. It is conceivable that a person with panic disorder could have an unrelated simple or social phobia, in which case both diagnoses would be made.

Relationship of Organic Factors

As mentioned previously, many physical illnesses and some exogenous substances can cause the symptoms of panic attacks; these are excluded by the diagnostic criteria of DSM-III and DSM-III-R. There is, however, one physical condition not excluded by the latter criteria—mitral valve prolapse. Formerly thought to cause panic symptoms, this condition, which is estimated to occur in 35% of patients with panic disorder (compared with about 5% of the general population) (21), is now thought to be an associated physical factor, but not to be etiologically responsible for the symptoms (22).

Diagnosis of Subthreshold Cases

Clinicians encounter patients who have never had full-blown panic attacks, but many who have had numerous less severe attacks, which also can lead to phobic behavior. In their conceptualization of panic anxiety, Sheehan and Sheehan (19) refer to these as "minor" attacks. DSM-III-R calls attacks involving fewer than four symptoms from criterion C "limited symptom attacks." The notion of a continuum of panic attacks ranging from mild and sporadic to severe and recurrent appears to be supported by recent epidemiologic data from the Epidemiologic Catchment Area (ECA) study (23). Moreover, even if patients receive treatment, they may nonetheless experience panic symptoms, but of reduced severity.

How, then, should such patients' subthreshold panic attacks be diagnosed? One ambiguity in DSM-III has been rectified in its revision. DSM-III-R makes it clear that panic disorder is a "lifetime" diagnosis: if a patient has ever met the criteria for panic disorder, the diagnosis is warranted. If he or she has not had any anxiety attacks in the last six months, this can be specified by the qualification "in full remission." If a patient has had recurrent, limited symptom attacks or no more than one full-blown panic attack in the past month, the DSM-III-R designation for current severity is "mild." "In partial remission" can be used for conditions that fall between "mild" and "in full remission." If a person has recurrent, limited symptom attacks with agoraphobic behavior, then the diagnosis becomes agoraphobia (see below).

Suspension of Hierarchies with Mood Disorders

As has been discussed in the chapter on mood disturbances (Chapter 6), a major shift in thinking regarding the relationship of anxiety disorders and affective disorders has occurred since publication of DSM-III. Because anxiety of all types seemed to be a very common phenomenon in patients with mood disorders, attaching separate DSM-III labels to the anxiety components was believed to be diagnostically redundant. Therefore, DSM-III included criteria to exclude diagnoses of anxiety disorder when affective disorders were present—the so-called "not due to" criteria.

In the last several years a series of studies has concluded that the DSM-III hierarchies between affective and anxiety disorders obscure some significant differences among patients. First, Boyd and associates (24) found, through epidemiologic data, that the presence of major depression (MD) constituted a "risk factor" for panic disorders in that the odds of having panic disorder in a major depressive episode (MDE) were 19 times greater than when not associated with MD. Leckman and colleagues (25,26) showed, in a family study of community subjects with major depression, that compared with the relatives of controls or of depressed persons without an anxiety disorder, the additional presence of an anxiety disorder in a depressed person greatly elevated the risk for first-degree relatives of major depression, panic disorder, and GAD. These findings held true whether the anxiety disorder occurred solely during the course of a major depressive episode or at completely separate times. Weissman and colleagues (27) found a higher rate of risk of major depression in family members of depressed probands with co-occurring anxiety disorders than among relatives of persons with major depression subtyped by other common schemata. These data suggest that depressed and anxious patients may share some etiologically significant features that distinguish them from nonanxious depressed patients. Recent trials of MAO inhibitors in patients with "atypical depression" found that a history of panic attacks was one of the best predictors of good response (12).

A recent study (28) documented that two-thirds of panic disorder/agoraphobic patients have had an episode of major depression at some time in their lives; about half the time the first depressive episode preceded the development of the anxiety disorder, and about half the time it followed it. In most of those with preceding MDEs, there was a long interval before the onset of the first panic attack (mean, three years). Patients with anxiety disorder with a history of MD had more severe anxiety symptoms and more resulting impairment, even if they were not currently depressed. A review of the literature (29) indicates that panic disorder and major depression co-occur frequently in the same patient, but are often temporally separate and therefore not symptomatic of each other.

The "not due to" criteria in DSM-III technically would allow for the diagnosis of both an anxiety disorder and an affective disorder if the anxiety disorder occurred first or the two syndromes were clearly temporally distinct. Most of the available research, however, concludes that the primary-secondary distinction and temporal separateness are not important—the findings remain the same. Therefore, it was decided by the Anxiety Disorders Advisory Committee on DSM-III-R to suspend the hierarchies between mood and anxiety disorders with one exception: generalized anxiety disorder is not diagnosed if it occurs only during the course of a mood disorder. The validity data were considered weaker in the case of GAD, and at least one reliability study (10) concluded that it was difficult to diagnose GAD reliably when other disorders were present. A diagnosis of panic disorder was also excluded in DSM-III if schizophrenia, somatization disorder, or another nonorganic mental disorder was the cause. These exclusions have been eliminated from DSM-III-R, although empirical evidence of the usefulness of this change is not available. It is now possible, therefore, to make joint diagnoses of panic disorder and virtually any other nonorganic, nonsubstance-induced disorder.

AGORAPHOBIA

The broad definition of agoraphobia in DSM-III caused some adjustment problems for clinicians. Agoraphobia has come to mean not just fear of open spaces but a fear of going out of the house alone and being in crowds or in certain public places such as tunnels, bridges, buses, or trains from which escape might not be possible.

Agoraphobia as Matter of Degree

The DSM-III conceptualization of agoraphobia made it difficult to classify a large group of patients who had some travel restrictions or avoidance behavior, but not the full-blown syndrome. A typical patient of this type may have panic attacks that lead to some avoidance, some reluctance to remain for long periods in certain places, or anxiety that is tolerated because avoidance or quick escape is not possible. The following case description illustrates the problem.

New York Cowboy

A 27-year-old, single, former cowboy moved from Wyoming to New York to study acting. One day, while driving on the New Jersey Turnpike, he suddenly felt very weak, as if he were going to pass out. Within a minute he felt his heart pounding rapidly, experienced chest pain and shortness of breath, and became very frightened that he was having a heart attack. With the assistance of a state trooper, he made his way to a motel for the night. The next day a friend came and drove him home.

A visit to his internist failed to reveal any signs of physical illness; laboratory tests, including an EKG, were within normal limits. Over the ensuing six months, he had only one other severe attack, in which he felt as if he were going to die. He did, however, have about two milder anxiety attacks (which he terms "twinges") a week, accompanied by tachycardia, lightheadedness, chest discomfort, and a fear that he would pass out or act inappropriately.

As a result of his major attack, the patient is afraid to drive his car. He reports, however, that since he is living in New York City, it hasn't really been necessary. Mild attacks have occurred a few times in the subway, at which times he reports "I want to get away." Nevertheless, he rides the subway most of the time, though once he fled from a crowded station and walked the 50 blocks to his home. He admits to passing up a couple of movies when the line appeared too long and to choosing his run in the park along paths that seem less crowded. He describes, since the first attack, becoming more "vigilant," "scanning" new situations or particular places or circumstances, and wondering "Is this going to be a time when my legs get weak?"

The man in this vignette (who, incidentally, also has mostly "minor" attacks that do, however, meet criteria for panic attacks) has developed discomfort in certain situations and occasionally has avoided certain places, but certainly does not have generalized travel restriction.

DSM-III-R has revamped the subclassification of panic disorder in order to deal with a continuum of agoraphobic avoidance. In DSM-III there were categories of agoraphobia with and agoraphobia without panic attacks. Table 7.4 shows the new subclassification and definitions. Panic disorder without agoraphobia is for the patient with panic attacks only. In panic disorder with agoraphobia, the severity of the agoraphobic avoidance can be specified as mild, moderate, severe, in partial remission, or in full remission.

Table 7.4 DSM-III-R Diagnostic Criteria for Panic Disorder with Agoraphobia

A. Meets the criteria for panic disorder.

B. Agoraphobia: Fear of being in places or situations from which escape might be difficult (or embarrassing) or in which help might not be available in the event of a panic attack. (Include cases in which persistent avoidance behavior originated during an active phase of panic disorder, even if the person does not attribute the avoidance behavior to fear of having a panic attack.) As a result of this fear, the person either restricts travel or needs a companion when away from home, or else endures agoraphobic situations despite intense anxiety. Common agoraphobic situations include being outside the home alone, being in a crowd or standing in a line, being on a bridge, and traveling in a bus, train, or car.

Specify current severity of agoraphobic avoidance:

Mild: Some avoidance (or endurance with distress), but relatively normal life-style, e.g., travels unaccompanied when necessary, such as to work or to shop; otherwise avoids traveling alone.

Moderate: Avoidance results in constricted life-style, e.g., the person is able to leave the house alone, but not to go more than a few miles unaccompanied.

Severe: Avoidance results in being nearly or completely housebound or unable to leave the house unaccompanied.

In partial remission: No current agoraphobic avoidance, but some agoraphobic avoidance during the past six months.

In full remission: No current agoraphobic avoidance and none during the past six months.

Specify current severity of panic attacks:

Mild: During the past month, either all attacks have been limited symptom attacks (i.e., fewer than four symptoms), or there has been no more than one panic attack.

Moderate: During the past month, attacks have been intermediate between mild and severe.

Severe: During the past month, there have been at least eight panic attacks.

In partial remission: The condition has been intermediate between in full remission and mild.

In full remission: During the past six months, there have been no panic or limited symptom attacks.

The specification "mild agoraphobic avoidance" would fit the patient described as the "New York Cowboy": there is some phobic avoidance, but a relatively normal life-style. This specification incorporates the concept of enduring the phobic situation with intense anxiety or dread. The diagnosis can therefore be made for the commuter who must cross a bridge to get to work or lose his job, but who arrives each morning in a sweat because of his fear of the experience.

In panic disorder with severe agoraphobia, the affected person is housebound, or nearly housebound, has generalized travel restrictions, or, in many cases, can leave home only with a companion. If a patient with panic attacks and agoraphobic avoidance does not attribute the avoidance to fear of having a panic attack, the diagnosis of panic disorder with agoraphobia can still be made if the avoidance behavior began during an active phase of panic disorder.

Agoraphobia Without Panic Attacks

The above subcategories apply to patients with clear panic disorder and avoidance behavior. What about the patient with agoraphobic symptoms, but no history of panic attacks?

The role of panic attacks in agoraphobia is somewhat controversial. In clinical settings, 95% of agoraphobic patients report spontaneous panic attacks preceding or during the course of the development of phobic avoidance. In fact, it is generally assumed that what the agoraphobic patient fears is the occurrence of a spontaneous panic attack in a place where he or she cannot escape or cannot get help. This reasoning led to a proposal to delete agoraphobia without panic attacks from the DSM-III-R classification and to substitute the category "limited symptom attacks with agoraphobia." This meant that every person with agoraphobia would be assumed to have had some panic attacks, if only of the "minor" variety.

Recently, however, the ECA study (30) indicated that in a nonpatient community population, agoraphobia occurred in a substantial proportion of people without a history of panic disorder or even panic symptoms (23%–53% of agoraphobic patients, depending on the study site). ECA diagnoses are made by trained lay interviewers using the NIMH Diagnostic Interview Schedule (DIS) (31), and such cases would therefore need validation by a clinician interview and other methods. Nonetheless, this finding illustrates how our concepts of disorders may be biased because of the treatment setting in which we encounter them. In the final DSM-III-R classification, agoraphobia without a history of panic *disorder* (emphasis added), has no subcategories for degrees of agoraphobia corresponding to the phobic avoidance associated with full-blown panic disorder; hence, a patient with limited symptom attacks and limited agoraphobic avoidance would receive the diagnosis anxiety disorder NOS.

SOCIAL PHOBIA

Social phobia is a new diagnosis, introduced in DSM-III. Its essential feature is "A persistent irrational fear of, and compelling desire to avoid, a situation in which the individual is exposed to possible scrutiny by others and fears that he or she may act in a way that will be humiliating or embarrassing" (8, p. 288). A number of problems in the differential diagnosis of social phobia from other phobias and from panic disorder have surfaced as increased attention has been paid to this anxiety disorder.

Nature and Limits of Social Phobia

Social anxiety appears to be distributed along a continuum ranging from general discomfort in social situations to fears of specific acts in the presence of other people. One question, therefore, is, What are the limits of the diagnosis of social phobia as applied to social anxiety?

Liebowitz (32) has pointed out that the DSM-III description of social phobia appears to be that of a broad concept; the examples given, however, are all of specific social fears. For instance, DSM-III mentions public speaking, eating or writing in public, and use of public restrooms when referring to social phobias. Furthermore, there is an exclusion criterion for social phobia that is due to avoidant personality disorder—a disorder that includes a wide variety of social discomfort and withdrawal; but there is no firm empirical basis for this exclusion.

Although there is no limitation to the number of social fears that a person with social phobia may have, DSM-III implies that there is usually only one. The presence of multiple social fears, which may in fact characterize many people with social phobia, broadens the scope of socially feared situations, again making the distinction between social phobia and an avoidant personality pattern more difficult.

DSM-III-R has attempted to eliminate some of these ambiguities. First, the criteria (see Table 7.5) state explicitly that there may be one or more situations the person fears. Second, there is no longer an exclusion for avoidant personality disorder. Since avoidant personality disorder involves fears of being rejected or criticized (see Chapter 9), as well as fears of being embarrassed, it does not necessarily indicate social phobia, in which the basic fear is of humiliation or embarrassment. When both syndromes are present, both diagnoses can be given.

Table 7.5 DSM-III-R Diagnostic Criteria for Social Phobia

A. A persistent fear of one or more situations (the social phobic situations) in which the person is exposed to possible scrutiny by others and fears that he or she may do something or act in a way that will be humiliating or embarrassing. Examples include: being unable to continue talking while speaking in public, choking on food when eating in front of others, being unable to urinate in a public lavatory, hand-trembling when writing in the presence of others, and saying foolish things or not being able to answer questions in social situations.

B. If an Axis III or another Axis I disorder is present, the fear in **A** is unrelated to it, e.g., the fear is not of having a panic attack (panic disorder), stuttering (stuttering), trembling (Parkinson's disease), or exhibiting abnormal eating behavior (anorexia nervosa or bulimia nervosa).

C. During some phase of the disturbance, exposure to the specific phobic stimulus (or stimuli) almost invariably provokes an immediate anxiety response.

D. The phobic situation(s) is avoided, or is endured with intense anxiety.

E. The avoidant behavior interferes with occupational functioning or with usual social activities or relationships with others, or there is marked distress about having the fear.

F. The person recognizes that his or her fear is excessive or unreasonable.

G. If the person is under 18, the disturbance does not meet the criteria for avoidant disorder of childhood or adolescence.

Specify generalized type if the phobic situation includes most social situations, and also consider the additional diagnosis of avoidant personality disorder.

Examples within a broader definition of social phobia would include fear of initiating a conversation and fear of dating. The social phobia diagnosis can be further specified as "generalized type" if the phobic situation includes most social situations, whether or not the criteria for avoidant personality disorder are met.

Differential Diagnosis of Social Phobia vs. Panic Disorder

Social phobia is differentiated from the avoidance behavior that accompanies panic disorder in both DSM-III and DSM-III-R. As noted previously, people with panic disorder develop phobic avoidance, often of places where other people may be, because of fear of having a panic attack. True (primary) social phobics without a history of panic attacks have been differentiated from (secondary) social phobics who are actually patients with panic disorder with avoidance of certain performance or social situations (2). People with primary social phobia fear only situations in which they may be the subject of public scrutiny or evaluation. Patients with panic disorder may come to fear a variety of nonsocial situations from which easy exit is not apparent.

Patients with panic disorder are often comforted by the presence of close others, whereas those with true social phobia feel better if alone. Amies and associates (33) found that people with social phobia were more often male, had an earlier age at onset, more somatic symptoms, and lower measures of extroversion than those with agoraphobia. Thus, DSM-III-R includes a criterion for social phobia that states: "If an Axis III or another Axis I disorder is present, the fear . . . is unrelated to it. . . ." This criterion eliminates panic attacks as the source of the fear as well as the symptoms of other mental disorders such as abnormal eating behavior exhibited by patients with eating disorders. It also eliminates the signs of physical illnesses.

The following case vignette is an illustration of an anxiety syndrome for which panic disorder, agoraphobia, social phobia, and avoidant personality disorder might be considered.

Anxious Accountant

An internist referred a 24-year-old single accountant for psychiatric consultation after a workup for gastrointestinal distress proved negative. The young man had consulted his family physician after months of feeling bloated and nauseated in anticipation of certain distressing events and circumstances.

In discussing his problems with the psychiatrist, the patient described three years of anxiety attacks accompanied by palpitations, shortness of breath, hot flushes, sweating, and paresthesias, in addition to his abdominal discomfort. Their onset was clearly traced to a blind date arranged by a close friend. On the way with his friend to pick up the girl, he suddenly felt extreme nausea, and was forced to pull the car off to the side of the road; he got out for a breath of fresh air and promptly vomited. Although his friend forced him to go through with the date, the young man was extremely nervous and preoccupied throughout, took his date home immediately after the movie was over, and sped away without even walking her to her door.

Although he had previously been shy around girls, following this incident the patient panicked at the thought of a date. There were girls to whom he felt attracted, but whenever he brought himself to even consider asking one out, he became symptomatic. The anticipation generalized so that he became anxious going to local basketball games, bars, and concerts with friends because he might see girls he was interested in meeting, talking to, or dating. He frequently felt like staying home, but forced himself, with the help of some peer pressure, to go out, at least "with the boys."

As he neared completion of his Master's program, he had to go for job interviews; these also began to cause anticipatory anxiety. He described feeling "trapped" in the interview, with "no way out." He then developed a fear of talking on the phone to people to arrange appointments for interviews or follow-up. He was hired by a small firm ("I guess because my grades were good"), and stayed mostly to himself on the job. His telephone fear extended to conversations with clients.

On closer questioning, the psychiatrist discovered that all the situations that provoked anxiety in the young man were social. In all such situations he was intensely concerned about what others thought of him. He said he felt physically awkward (he was actually quite athletic) and stupid, and that he would say things that were stupid and embarrassing. Although he knew that his problem was due to "nerves," it was all he could do to force himself into situations in which he felt he was being evaluated. Even during visits to his family doctor he was beset by feelings of weakness and humiliation. Finally, an incident convinced him to seek professional help.

On a Friday night a few weeks before consulting the psychiatrist, he and a friend were at their favorite neighborhood night spot. A girl he had been admiring for several months walked in with another girl and sat down at a nearby table. The patient openly debated with himself whether he should go over to speak with the girl. Despite his friend's encouragement, he felt increasingly nauseated. He made two trips to the lavatory and vomited and went outside for fresh air. One hour passed, then two. He watched the girl dance with several other young men and finally leave with one of them. The patient felt crushed. The next day he phoned the doctor.

The "Anxious Accountant" fears more than one social situation—meeting and dating girls, interviews, business phone calls—but he is not fearful of all or even most social situations. He panics only when confronted with social situations in which he anticipates embarrassment or humiliation. Although he meets some of the criteria for avoidant personality disorder (see Chapter 9), he has close friends, does not worry excessively about being liked, does not exaggerate the difficulties of ordinary tasks, and is not overly concerned about showing signs of anxiety.

Threshold and Severity Criteria

As is the case with all of the anxiety disorders, there is a need to distinguish pathological social fears from ordinary social anxiety that normal people may experience from time to time. In DSM-III, mention was made of a persistent fear, a compelling desire to avoid certain situations, feeling significant distress, and recognition by the person that his or her fear was excessive or unreasonable.

As in agoraphobia, once a pattern of avoidance has become extensive, actually experienced anxiety may be reduced. Obviously, this is a function of the evolution of the disorder, and a diagnosis is still warranted. This is made clearer in DSM-III-R by the inclusion of a new criterion, C, that states: "During some phase of the disturbance, exposure to the specific phobic stimulus (or stimuli) almost invariably provokes an immediate anxiety response" (18, p. 243).

There are some people who would like to avoid social situations because of the anxiety they create, but whose occupation may make this impossible for economic reasons. Examples include a musician with severe performance anxiety or a sales representative who is expected to make many anxiety-provoking presentations. For these people, there is a new criterion for the anxiety disorders that states that if the situation cannot be avoided, it is endured with intense anxiety. Finally, a social phobia that involves, for instance, public speaking is obviously more significant clinically if it occurs in someone whose livelihood depends on this ability as opposed to someone who is rarely, if ever, called on to make a speech. Therefore, a requirement for social or occupational functioning impairment has been added in case it is not clear that the phobia causes extreme distress.

Other Disorders to Be Excluded

Although neither depressive disorders nor avoidant personality disorder now preclude a diagnosis of social phobia, there are other common clinical situations that need to be differentiated. The first is the case of the patient with an obsessive compulsive disorder whose obsessions are the source of embarrassment, or would be if they became known to others. A common example would be an obsession with sexual content, such as frequent mental "undressing" of people encountered on the street. Such thoughts may lead a person to fear social situations and to avoid them. These, however, would not be considered manifestations of social phobia, and are excluded by DSM-III-R criterion B. Another situation, again sexual, would be that of a person's avoiding social contact because of a sexual dysfunction, such as inhibited male orgasm or premature ejaculation (see Chapter 8). These are also excluded from a diagnosis of social phobia.

Interest in social phobia is on the rise, as greater numbers of patients are being seen in anxiety disorders clinics. Socially phobic patients may have a mechanism of biological hyperactivity different from that of patients with panic disorder; more psychological factors may contribute to the problem, and the treatment response profile may be different. Beta-adrenergic blockers, cognitive and behavioral psychotherapies, and possibly MAO inhibitors appear to be of most benefit (2).

SIMPLE PHOBIAS

Fears of a circumscribed stimulus, object, or situation other than of having a panic attack or of humiliation or embarrassment in certain social situations are classified as simple phobias. Phobic objects include insects and animals, and phobic situations, heights and closed spaces. A very common simple phobia is the fear of seeing blood, having injections, the sight of needles, and other objects and situations that together make up a blood/injury/illness phobia (34,35).

The recent Epidemiologic Catchment Area study included some surprising data on the prevalence of simple phobias in the United States. The 6-month prevalence ranged from 4.5% to 11.8% of the general population of the areas, depending on the site (36). Psychiatrists, in follow-up clinical interviews (37,38), however, frequently disagreed with DIS estimates of which patients had clinically significant phobias, sometimes making more, and sometimes, fewer, diagnoses.

Fears of objects and situations may be common, but do they all constitute mental disorders? The main problem in diagnosing simple phobias is ensuring that they are indeed severe enough to warrant a diagnosis. DSM-III criteria are probably too weak in this regard. DSM-III-R criteria should help the clinician determine severity. The criteria for significance have already been discussed with reference to the other phobias in DSM-III-R, but it is worth mentioning one or two additional points that I think are particularly relevant to accurate assessment of simple phobias.

First, the anxiety response must have a close and immediate connection to the phobic stimulus. Many people report becoming uneasy when seeing a spider or finding themselves looking down from a height. But the anxiety response of a clinically phobic patient is both more severe and more immediate. The symptoms can mimic a panic attack. Second, many people report that they are phobic of a situation, but they neither go out of their way to avoid that situation nor experience very intense anxiety or dread upon being exposed to it. Finally, upon carefully questioning, one finds that many phobic fears are not a source of marked distress or functional impairment. The lesson to be learned is that through systematic probing concerning each of the threshold/severity components of phobic disorders, the clinician can reliably recognize many false-positive responses to screening questions about special fears.

Simple phobias are excluded only if the "stimulus" is related to the content of the obsessions of obsessive compulsive disorder or the trauma of posttraumatic stress disorder. Therefore, a patient who is preoccupied with dirt or thoughts or fears of being contaminated with germs will be properly diagnosed as having obsessive compulsive disorder, not simple phobia. Similarly, psychological distress and increased arousal associated with exposure to a stimulus resembling an aspect of a markedly traumatic event are common symptoms of posttraumatic stress disorder, not simple phobia.

OBSESSIVE COMPULSIVE DISORDER

Obsessive compulsive disorder (OCD) is one of the least well understood anxiety disorders. OCD is classified in DSM-III as an anxiety disorder because patients with this diagnostic class of disorders are said either to experience anxiety directly or to experience it if certain behaviors (avoidance, rituals) or thoughts are interfered with. Questions have been raised about whether OCD should be considered an anxiety disorder at all (39). Furthermore, it has been difficult to characterize the essence of obsessions and compulsions in a way that enables them to be distinguished from psychotic symptoms, depressive ruminations, and everyday superstitions.

Clarifying Characteristic Distinguishing Features

Obsessions are recurrent and persistent ideas, thoughts, impulses, or images that are intrusive and unwanted. They are usually senseless and in some way repugnant to the person harboring them. The most common obsessions are thoughts of violence, contamination, or doubt (40). The person attempts to suppress or ignore such thoughts, which DSM-III called "ego-dystonic" because they seemed to invade consciousness without volition on the part of the patient.

The fact that the person with obsessions experiences them as senseless and tries to suppress them or ignore them helps to distinguish obsessions from depressive ruminations. The patient with OCD may, however, also be depressed. Although the obsessive thoughts are perceived as unwanted and beyond the person's ability to control, the person with OCD does not believe the thoughts are coming from some outside source or person, which distinguishes them from the delusions of thought insertion sometimes observed in schizophrenia.

Compulsions are repetitive, purposeful, and intentional behaviors performed stereotypically or according to certain rules. The most common compulsions involve counting, checking, hand-washing, and touching. Since they are purposeful and intentional, they can usually be distinguished from the repetitive, stereotypic behavior of a regressed psychotic person, who may rock, pace, or bang objects. Compulsions are usually recognized as being not an end in themselves, but intended to neutralize or prevent some kind of discomfort. This is actually why OCD is considered an anxiety disorder, i.e., extreme anxiety is being controlled or warded off by the compulsive thoughts or rituals.

Some researchers, however, have questioned this relationship. Insel (33) observed that patients with obsessional doubts frequently became more, not less, uncertain when reassured. And, under conditions of stress, which would be expected to increase anxiety, some patients actually ritualize less. The observation that reducing rituals sometimes leads to less anxiety has become the basis for certain behavioral therapy techniques, such as response prevention, in which the person may be exposed to contamination, but prevented from washing (41). At one time in the deliberations on DSM-III-R, a proposal to make OCD a separate class of disorder was considered because it seemed unique, in a number of respects, from other anxiety disorders.

Problems in Differential Diagnosis

In addition to those already alluded to, there are several other difficulties in making a diagnosis of OCD. The DSM-III-R criteria for OCD help to distinguish obsessions from thought insertion and compulsions from stereotypic psychotic behavior. Yet, we may wonder why thoughts of being contaminated with germs, which are so firmly held that affected people will wash their hands raw, should not be considered delusions? Fixed, false beliefs that influence a person's behavior and cannot be changed even in the face of incontrovertible evidence of their lack of a basis in reality come very close to the definition of delusions presented in Chapter 5. This is a gray area in which the distinctions drawn can appear very arbitrary. Some clinicians argue that it is the focal and circumscribed nature of the false thought in OCD that distinguishes it from a delusional system, which is likely to be more elaborate. But there are many examples of delusions of limited scope in affective psychoses, such as a cancer delusion, or in delusional disorders, such as the Capgras delusion. In DSM-III-R the distinction boils down to whether the affected person can test reality at all about the reasonable or excessive aspects of his or her behavior: if the person is judged to be unable to do so, then he or she indeed has a psychotic disorder.

Since OCD has been found to respond to antidepressant drugs, the question has been raised about its relationship to mood disorder. Clinical observation has documented that depression is a frequent complication of OCD, occurring in as many as one-half of cases, although a family history of affective illness in these patients is considerably less frequent than in patients with primary affective disorder (42). Some believe that OCD is a variant of affective disorder; at the very least, OCD, with or without secondary depression, may be useful subtypes (39). There is no exclusion in DSM-III-R of OCD in the presence of major depression. It is possible for a patient to simultaneously meet criteria for both.

Oedipal Obsession

"Are you sure I'm not going crazy?" entreated a 22-year-old computer programmer after relating the persistent bizarre images he was "seeing" to the psychiatrist.

The patient complained that, for the past six months, he had been having intrusive images of murdering his father. Although only fleeting, the images were clear enough to depict to the patient an invariably gory scene in which he hacked at his victim with an ax, or ran over him while backing his car out of the garage. The patient would shake his head to clear the images and then would experience waves of anxiety as he worried about their significance. At their worst, the images caused the young man to check on the location and condition of his father by telephone, or drive around the block to make sure he wasn't lying mangled in the driveway.

Sometimes the patient was able to satisfy himself that this experience was just a "weird part of his imagination"; but the more reassured he felt, the more he was inclined to bring the image back to mind, just to prove it wasn't real. At other times he sat for an hour ruminating about whether or not he was having a "nervous breakdown."

The symptoms had begun just after the patient began a new job. He did not care for his boss or co-workers. As the images became more frequent and his concern about their significance intensified, he found himself becoming increasingly depressed. He felt less inclined to go out with friends, slept or ate during his free time, lacked energy, and wondered whether he would be better off dead. When the possibility of suicide became plausible to him, he asked his father, with whom he was, in fact, close, to arrange for him to see a psychiatrist.

The psychiatrist ascertained that the young man did not actually "see" the gruesome sights, but imagined them in his thoughts. Even when checking on the well-being of his father, the patient knew that nothing had actually happened to him. He spent considerable time distracting himself from the thoughts, but he had to struggle against the temptation to bring them back "to see if I really could control them."

The psychiatrist prescribed an MAO inhibitor, reassured the patient that the symptoms were not indicative of psychosis, and worked with him to understand the meaning of the obsessions.

Other Disorders and Conditions to Be Ruled Out

OCD can be confused with obsessive compulsive personality disorder, which is characterized by a pattern of perfectionism and inflexibility (see also Chapter 9, Personality Disturbances). The distinction to be made is that a person with OCD has the ego-dystonic *symptoms* of obsessions and compulsions as defined above, whereas the person with obsessive compulsive personality may be preoccupied with details, rules, and order and with doing everything in a particular way, but these behaviors do not have the stereotypic quality of OCD symptoms, and are usually designed for the purpose toward which they are explicitly directed. The two disorders may co-occur.

In a study by Insel (39), 7 of 20 patients with OCD had obsessional premorbid personality traits. The presence of these traits in his sample had an ominous connotation in that these patients tended to have severe "borderline" character pathology. This group of patients may be anomalous, though, since many people with obsessive personality traits are rather well integrated and sometimes are very successful.

The discussion of differential diagnosis in DSM-III-R suggests that OCD must be distinguished from behaviors in other mental disorders that might colloquially be called "compulsive," such as those observed in eating disorders, paraphilias, pathological gambling, or alcohol dependence. The criterion for distinguishing these behaviors from true compulsions is that the person derives pleasure from them and resists them only because of secondary deleterious consequences.

Many people have superstitious beliefs or rituals. Virtually every crapshooter, from Atlantic City to Las Vegas, must blow on the dice before the roll, or whisper secret good-luck incantations. Few people, if given a choice, would deliberately walk under a ladder. Superstitions have some, but not all, of the characteristics of obsessions and compulsions. They are especially designed either to bring good luck or to avoid misfortune. Some of them, like not stepping on a crack or tossing spilled salt over the shoulder, are performed according to ritual. Obviously, these are all not symptoms of OCD, although they could become a part of it.

The most useful distinguishing characteristics of the disorder are the repetitiveness and the excessiveness of the obsessive thoughts and behaviors and the marked distress or interference in a person's social or occupational functioning that results. Determining how often the person performs a ritual or how much time is spent in the relevant behavior each day may be required to make these distinctions. Severe compulsive rituals may last for hours at a time. Sometimes the person does not view the behavioral rituals as impairing his or her functioning, but they may involve family or friends to such a degree as to cause *them* distress and disability.

Subtypes of OCD?

OCD may not be a very homogeneous disorder. Although most studies indicate that the disorder has a rather chronic course, others suggest a less bleak prognosis, many patients improving over time. Treatment with various antidepressant drugs has seemed promising, but does not alleviate the disorder in all patients.

Rachman and Hodgson (43) have defined subtypes, according to predominant symptoms, as cleaners, checkers, ruminators, and a group characterized by primary obsessional slowness. Insel (39) found, on longitudinal follow-up, that symptom patterns changed over time. His subclassification of OCD with affective disorder or with narcissistic problems may have treatment-assigning potential since the former may do best on antidepressants (44), and the latter may require considerable individual and/or family psychotherapy.

POSTTRAUMATIC STRESS DISORDER

Although severe emotional responses to traumatic stress of exceptional proportions, such as war and natural disasters, have been recognized for many years, the introduction of posttraumatic stress disorder (PTSD) into DSM-III as an official category has stirred controversy. This is undoubtedly related to the fact that the largest single group to whom this diagnosis has been applied has been Vietnam veterans. Controversies about the Vietnam War and its aftermath, i.e., the readjustment of veterans to civilian life and their reassimilation into society, seem to have been played out among mental health professionals with PTSD as a focal point.

At the time of the preparation of DSM-III, certain groups sympathetic to the problems of the Vietnam veteran wanted the diagnosis to be called post-Vietnam syndrome. Similar desires to assist these veterans has led, in some instances, to designating any and all adjustment problems since the war as PTSD (45). On the other hand, some clinicians doubt the validity of the concept completely. Complicating matters are the facts that large numbers of Vietnam veterans undoubtedly need help because of emotional problems and that certain concrete aspects of this assistance, like medical care and disability payments, can be obtained only if the problems are judged to be directly connected to their war experiences.

The syndrome of PTSD, or traumatic neurosis, has been observed among combat soldiers in previous wars, in the survivors of concentration camp experiences, in victims of natural disasters and of violent crimes such as assault or rape, and among people exposed to other severe stressors. The symptoms of a "gross stress reaction" have generally been thought to be similar regardless of the nature of the stressor. As defined in DSM-III, therefore, posttraumatic stress disorder is a mental disorder that can result from a wide range of highly stressful experiences.

Clarifying Characteristic Features

The syndrome of PTSD, as described in DSM-III, is a relatively narrow one from a phenomenologic point of view; it is not meant to include all reactions to stress. According to the DSM-III multiaxial system (see Chapter 2), any Axis I disorder may be linked to a psychosocial stressor, which is listed and rated in terms of severity on Axis IV.

First of all, for the diagnosis of PTSD, the patient needs to have experienced a stressor of severe proportions. DSM-III described this as "a recognizable stressor that would evoke significant symptoms of distress in almost anyone." In the case of the Vietnam veteran, simply having been in the Armed Forces during the Vietnam era or in Southeast Asia during the war is not enough (under most circumstances) to warrant classifying a disorder as PTSD; usually, actual exposure to combat is necessary. Generally speaking, studies of war stress have found that PTSD and other mental symptoms are correlated with the severity of exposure to combat.

Reliance solely on the hypothetical "other person" as a referent in judging the severity of the stress was, however, too vague and difficult to be clinically practical. Therefore, in DSM-III-R, criterion A for PTSD (see Table 7.6) describes the experiencing of "an event that is outside the range of usual human experience and that would be markedly distressing to almost anyone." As examples, DSM-III-R lists "a serious threat to one's life or physical integrity; serious threat or harm to one's children, spouse, or other close relatives and friends; sudden destruction of one's home or community, or seeing another person who has recently been, or is being, seriously injured or killed as the result of an accident or physical violence."

Establishing the relationship of the stressor and the symptoms of PTSD can present problems. Does the patient need to be able to link the symptoms to the stressor, or is it the clinician's ability to do so that is diagnostic (46)? Since multiple stressors may have occurred during the time interval between the initial stressor and the patient's presen-

Table 7.6 DSM-III-R Diagnostic Criteria for Posttraumatic Stress Disorder

A. The person has experienced an event that is outside the range of usual human experience and that would be markedly distressing to almost anyone, e.g., serious threat to one's life or physical integrity; serious threat or harm to one's children, spouse, or other close relatives and friends; sudden destruction of one's home or community; or seeing another person who has recently been, or is being, seriously injured or killed as the result of an accident or physical violence.

B. The traumatic event is persistently reexperienced in at least one of the following ways:

(1) recurrent and intrusive distressing recollections of the event (in young children, repetitive play in which themes or aspects of the trauma are expressed)
(2) recurrent distressing dreams of the event
(3) sudden acting or feeling as if the traumatic event were recurring (includes a sense of reliving the experience, illusions, hallucinations, and dissociative [flashback] episodes, even those that occur upon awakening or when intoxicated)
(4) intense psychological distress at exposure to events that symbolize or resemble an aspect of the traumatic event, including anniversaries of the trauma

C. Persistent avoidance of stimuli associated with the trauma or numbing of general responsiveness (not present before the trauma), as indicated by at least three of the following:

(1) efforts to avoid thoughts or feelings associated with the trauma
(2) efforts to avoid activities or situations that arouse recollections of the trauma
(3) inability to recall an important aspect of the trauma (psychogenic amnesia)
(4) markedly diminished interest in significant activities (in young children, loss of recently acquired developmental skills such as toilet training or language skills)
(5) feeling of detachment or estrangement from others
(6) restricted range of affect, e.g., unable to have loving feelings
(7) sense of a foreshortened future, e.g., does not expect to have a career, marriage, or children, or a long life

D. Persistent symptoms of increased arousal (not present before the trauma), as indicated by at least two of the following:

(1) difficulty falling or staying asleep
(2) irritability or outbursts of anger
(3) difficulty concentrating
(4) hypervigilance
(5) exaggerated startle response
(6) physiologic reactivity upon exposure to events that symbolize or resemble an aspect of the traumatic event (e.g., a woman who was raped in an elevator breaks out in a sweat when entering any elevator)

E. Duration of the disturbance (symptoms in **B, C,** and **D**) of at least one month.

Specify delayed onset if the onset of symptoms was at least six months after the trauma.

---

tation of symptoms, how can a clinician know which stressor was prepotent (47)? There must be a discernable relationship between the symptoms and the stressor in that manifestations of the stressful experience must be present in the content of the intrusive images or in what is avoided. When PTSD precedes a particular stressor, it is usually easy to view the latter as simply exacerbating the already present disorder. This is helpful in military cases when stressors in civilian life occur after military stressors and the clinician needs to distinguish the source of the PTSD symptoms. Sometimes, however, in the case of a delayed onset, a later stressor may give rise to PTSD symptoms for the first time with images that are, at least in part, war related. The following case illustrates this point.

Delayed Reaction

Mr. B., a 57-year-old, married man with two children, was an apparently successful businessman with no significant medical history and no previous mental problems until he suffered an accident in June 1979. He was hit by a car while working at an automobile auction. He reports remembering being thrown in the air. This was followed by a brief period during which he was unaware of events until he realized that he was being taken to a hospital in an ambulance. At the hospital he was told that he had suffered neck and back injuries and had a broken rib.

For the first month after the accident, Mr. B. walked on crutches; thereafter he walked unaided. X-rays of his neck and back revealed no pathology. When he attempted to return to work, he was bothered by severe attacks of difficulty breathing and severe headaches. One day, he experienced tightness in his chest and shortness of breath in the presence of his brother-in-law, a retired internist. His brother-in-law remarked that Mr. B.'s difficulty breathing was not visible, and when he listened to his chest with a stethoscope, there were no audible wheezes or signs of difficulty with the passage of air in the bronchial tree. Mr. B. was advised to seek psychiatric help.

On questioning by the psychiatrist, Mr. B. denied nightmares, but reported frequent visual images during the day of himself being hit by the car. Apparently, a garage door was being raised as Mr. B. was hit. In his intrusive recollections of the accident, Mr. B. pictured the door not opening and himself being crushed between the car and the closed garage door. This, in turn, brought up images of his experiences in the Navy in World War II, in particular, of his role in the battle of Okinawa. As he described it, Mr. B. was in a ship that took medical personnel to the aid of injured sailors on other ships, and he frequently was confronted with gory sights of dead and maimed sailors, which he remembers looking like "mushed meat." These bloody scenes flashed through his mind whenever he pictured himself being hit by the car.

In addition, for the year preceding the psychiatric evaluation, Mr. B. had been very irritable and angry with his family, especially his wife of 35 years. He had been unable to give her emotional support during some difficult times when she had experienced physical illness. He had been unable to listen to her fears and shouted at her for talking about them. He avoided his place of work because of anxiety attacks.

Mr. B.'s mood was dejected. He was uninterested in seeing friends, children, or grandchildren. His dog had become his only companion. He awakened several times each night. He could not concentrate, and he frequently misplaced belongings in his house.

Before the accident he had had a very successful business, employing 15 people and paying a monthly rent of several thousand dollars. Afterward, the business was forced to move to smaller quarters, and the only employees became his son, a salesman, and a secretary. He had previously been very active socially, eating out in restaurants and vacationing frequently. For a period of 15 years he and his wife had gone to Miami twice a year, stayed at a hotel where they had many friends with whom they would visit and travel around. In recent years, before the accident, he and his wife had traveled extensively; but in the two years since the accident, Mr. B. had done virtually nothing except walk his dog.

The diagnosis of PTSD is not in question in this case: determining the relative contributions of the two traumatic stressors is not really feasible.

The second characteristic features of PTSD in DSM-III were two clusters of symptoms that entailed reexperiencing of the trauma and numbing of responsiveness to, or reduced involvement with, the external world. Horowitz and co-workers (48) had observed that these two groups of symptoms invariably occurred in stress responses. Reexperiencing phenomena were considered to include daytime intrusive recollections, dreams, and acting or feeling as if the traumatic event were reoccurring, and the numbing phenomena, loss of interest in activities, detachment from others, and constricted affect.

The third characteristic was the occurrence of some nonspecific symptoms, some of which indicated autonomic hyperarousal and others, such as survivor guilt, which were thought to be "classic" symptoms.

Problems in Differential Diagnosis

The symptom clusters of DSM-III PTSD have caused problems in differential diagnosis. Atkinson and his colleagues (47), working in the Veterans Administration system, identified a number of pitfalls in the assessment of veterans presenting to a VA center for disability benefits. These included: (*1*) professional bias against the diagnosis, (*2*) resistance to the use of full DSM-III diagnostic criteria in order to make the diagnosis, (*3*) adversarial interactions between claimants and staff, (*4*) lack of availability of third-party corroborative data, (*5*) silent claimants, (*6*) exaggeration and falsification of data, (*7*) presence of partial syndromes, (*8*) PTSD symptoms without stressors, (*9*) intercurrent civilian stress, (*10*) deviant social behavior, (*11*) either/or diagnostic judgments, and (*12*) negative impact on examiners. Some of these problems have to do with accurate recognition of the disorder itself, and others, with distinguishing the disorder from other mental disturbances.

Accurate recognition of PTSD. Problems in the recognition of PTSD stem from four sources: the kinds of symptoms included in the definition, the relative importance of the two main symptom clusters, the clinical course of the disorder, and difficulty in distinguishing real from false symptoms.

Brett and Ostroff (49), attaching primary importance to traumatic imagery in the recognition of PTSD, have pointed out that the manifestations of imagery experiences can be even broader than those included in DSM-III. Illusions, hallucinations, and dissociative (flashback) episodes, even those occurring upon awakening or when intoxicated, may be symptoms of the reexperiencing phenomena of PTSD. Affects, somatic states, and actions may also be evidence of reexperiencing traumatic events. Narrow concepts of "reexperiencing" may cause the clinician to miss the diagnosis or assign other, erroneous diagnoses (see below). Numbing symptoms may be viewed as defensive operations against the repetition phenomena, and may obscure the recognition of imagery experiences if they are successfully blocked out. Brett and Ostroff (49) recognized that some of the nonspecific D criterion symptoms were actually manifestations of either reexperiencing or numbing.

DSM-III-R has broadened the concept of the reexperiencing of symptoms in an effort to respond to observations such as these (50). Illusions, hallucinations, and dissociative episodes have been added, and physiologic reactivity or intense psychological distress upon exposure to events that symbolize or resemble an aspect of the traumatic event has been moved from criterion D to the reexperiencing criterion (B). Similarly, avoidance of trauma-associated thoughts, feelings, activities, or situations and psychogenic amnesia about the event have been moved from D to the numbing criterion (C).

Although most clinicians and researchers believe that both components of PTSD are necessary for the diagnosis, at least one researcher has found that requiring the aggregate symptom picture may cause the clinician to miss a number of significant stress reactions. Laufer and associates (51) found that if war stress in a Vietnam veteran population were divided into three types, these were related to different symptom patterns. Actual exposure to combat and witnessing abusive violence (atrocities) were both related to DSM-III PTSD and reexperiencing symptoms, but not to numbing or denial symptoms. Participating in abusive violence was related to denial, but not to reexperiencing traumatic events or the DSM-III disorder. Thus, DSM-III PTSD underestimated the prevalence of stress symptoms related to a particular kind of stressful circumstance. Similar patterns may be found in association with various nonmilitary stressors. Another view could be that the full-blown disorder includes both clusters of symptoms and that the presence of only one indicates a less severe reaction. Alternatively, the presence of one cluster may be a function of clinical course (see below) or may be related to the presence of another disorder. DSM-III-R continues to require symptoms from both the reexperiencing and the numbing categories.

When a patient is evaluated at different points during the course of PTSD, time sampling may influence recognition of the disorder. As has already been mentioned, some believe that numbing reactions may obscure observation of reexperiencing symptoms and lead the clinician to believe that they are absent. Green and colleagues (46) have pointed out that the course of PTSD can be variable, with alternating periods of intrusion, numbing, and relative symptom quiescence. Additional stressors or anniversaries may lead to exacerbations of symptoms. These authors hypothesize that patterns of behavior and attitudes toward self and others may fluctuate less than intrusive symptoms such as nightmares, which, in turn, would be more stable than symptoms of physiologic hyperarousal, which would not be expected to be very constant, even over short periods of time. Treatment would, of course, also be expected to influence expression of symptoms.

The clinician's job is to attempt to reconstruct the symptom picture at the height of the disorder (worst period) if the patient currently does not meet the full criteria for PTSD. There is no expectation that symptoms would be invariant. The initial draft of DSM-III-R made this more explicit by adding a criterion stating that symptoms from the three characteristic groups should have "all occurred during the same six-month period." It went on to add that "there may be other phases of the illness during which they do not coexist." This criterion was watered down in the subsequent draft and was deleted from the final version of DSM-III-R. It was thought that there were inadequate data, as yet, on the course of PTSD to warrant such a statement. The DSM-III-R criteria are ambiguous about when and how the symptoms co-occur; therefore, the clinician should keep in mind possible fluctuations in expressions of symptoms over the course of the disturbance.

An outgrowth of the apparent overdiagnosis of PTSD to refer to all reactions to stress has been a certain amount of skepticism about the veracity of those purporting to have symptoms of the disorder. Since considerable gain, in terms of benefits from government sources, can be derived from having PTSD, there is a need to rule out malingering. Malingering, in DSM-III, is defined as "voluntary production and presentation of false or grossly exaggerated physical or psychological symptoms . . . produced in pursuit of a goal that is obviously recognizable with an understanding of the individual's circumstances rather than of his or her individual psychology." To obtain medical or disability benefits would qualify as such a goal.

The Veterans Administration has been beset with claims for compensation for PTSD since its official recognition as a disorder in DSM-III. The fact that DSM-III includes a delayed subtype, which may have its onset after a prolonged symptom-free interval from the time of the stress, has made evaluation of these claims all the more difficult. Moreover, there are probably no more widely publicized criteria for a mental disorder than those of PTSD. Therefore, the possibility exists for someone to simply learn the cardinal features and to describe them when interviewed. Attempts should be made to obtain third party corroboration of symptoms when possible and to use clinicians with maximum experience and "second opinions" to guard against malingering (47).

Relationship of PTSD to other mental disorders. As has already been stated, some of the symptoms of PTSD may be confused with symptoms of other DSM-III disorders. Intrusive images may be difficult to distinguish from the hallucinations of schizophrenia, reenactments may resemble the acting-out of personality disorders, and numbing may look like major depression.

The initial task in differential diagnosis is to establish that the full PTSD syndrome is present. Partial syndromes (see above) may actually be mistaken diagnoses of other types of disorder, the most common being major depression. Certainly in DSM-III, and to a lesser extent in DSM-III-R, numbing symptoms plus several of the nonspecific symptoms such as sleep disturbance, concentration difficulties, and guilt could meet the criteria for major depression. The differential diagnosis would hinge on whether or not there were reexperiencing symptoms, apparently the most diagnosis-specific aspect of the syndrome. In DSM-III-R, elimination of guilt from criterion D may somewhat reduce the overlap with depression. The addition of irritability and anger to D may, however, increase confusion about distinguishing PTSD from acting-out or antisocial behavior. The violence associated with PTSD has been described as having a dissociative, stereotyped quality. The use of drugs or alcohol is usually an attempt to alleviate the symptoms and is rarely totally successful. In each case the clinician is forced to rely on his ability to detect the full criteria at some point in the clinical course of the disorder.

Data on the co-morbidity of PTSD and other mental disorders make differential diagnosis more complicated. There is no reason why PTSD must be the only diagnosis present; in fact, studies indicate that a rather high proportion of PTSD patients may have coexisting disorders. Green and her associates (40) report that the majority of PTSD inpatients have multiple diagnoses, most commonly alcoholism and drug dependence. In general, PTSD patients also have a high frequency of major affective disorder, anxiety disorder, or personality disorder. Davidson and colleagues (52) found 100% of chronic PTSD patients with additional diagnoses during their lifetime; more than half had more than one additional disorder. Again, alcohol abuse (41%) and major depression (41%) were most common; but bipolar disorder, anxiety disorders, substance abuse, and schizophrenia and related psychotic disorders were found. Most of these disorders developed subsequent to PTSD. In terms of family history, PTSD patients resembled probands with anxiety disorder more than probands with depression.

The high frequencies of additional disorders encountered in these groups may be a function of the treatment settings in which they were encountered (inpatients), the severity of the disorders, or their chronicity. The exact relationship of additional psychopathology to PTSD is not clear. Some forms of psychopathology may actually predispose to PTSD, but some may be viewed as complications or as co-occurring disorders that increase morbidity. It is important for the clinician to make additional diagnoses since they may ultimately influence treatment or outcome.

GENERALIZED ANXIETY DISORDER

The differentiation of panic attacks from heightened states of anxiety has already been discussed. Since panic disorder was separated from "anxiety neurosis," some controversy has arisen regarding what, exactly, remains. Because symptoms of anxiety were thought to be ubiquitous in the other anxiety disorders, in DSM-III generalized anxiety disorder was made a residual category. Thus, if patients had panic disorder, any of the phobic disorders, OCD, or PTSD, they were not likely to receive a DSM-III diagnosis of GAD unless this disorder clearly antedated the other anxiety disorder so that the clinician's impression was that the generalized anxiety was "not due to" the other anxiety disorder. Other, more pervasive, disorders higher in the DSM-III classification hierarchy, such as depressive disorders or schizophrenia, also specifically excluded a diagnosis of GAD. But in essence, all mental disorders could take diagnostic precedence over GAD if the anxiety were conceptualized as a manifestation of the other disorder.

Differential Diagnosis

Under the DSM-III scheme, generalized anxiety disorder disappeared, according to some clinicians and researchers. Some specialists in the treatment of panic disorder claimed that they had never seen a patient with GAD who had not had a panic attack. Even if this were the case, however, should such patients receive the dual diagnoses of GAD and panic disorder, since the GAD was temporally primary, or was the GAD just a prodrome of panic disorder, without independent diagnostic significance? And what about the patient who had a panic attack(s) in the past, but now had only symptoms of GAD? Under what circumstances might both diagnoses be given? Confusion over the boundaries of GAD and its relationship to other disorders has been found to be a source of relatively low reliability for the diagnosis (10).

GAD vs. other anxiety disorders. The defining feature of GAD is pervasive and excessive worry. Therefore, the worry associated with anticipation of a panic attack, encountering a phobic stimulus, or thoughts of being contaminated by germs should not be the extent of the anxiety in GAD. This principle has been incorporated in the definition of GAD in DSM-III-R by the addition of two criteria. The first describes worry or apprehension expectation "about two or more life circumstances." Thus, the clinician may discover that the patient with GAD worries frequently about whether he or she is doing a good job at work, will be accepted by peers, or be able to meet payments on a new car, and will shift the focus from one situation to another. The second criterion for DSM-III-R GAD states that if another Axis I disorder is present, "the focus of the worry is not related to it." Hence, in the above-described situation of the patient with past panic, even if panic attacks are no longer occurring, if the fear and apprehension are *limited* to the possibility of having another attack, then the anxiety is really best considered a residual of panic disorder. If a patient with diffuse anxiety happens also to experience panic attacks frequently enough to meet the criteria for PD, then both diagnoses may be given. These conventions have not been thoroughly studied, but it seems likely that the increased clinical heterogeneity in this area will have treatment implications.

Barlow and his associates (53) studied a group of patients with anxiety disorders and found the expected considerable overlap of GAD symptoms with the other anxiety disorders. They also found that if the duration of generalized anxiety symptoms was greater than the one month required by DSM-III, there was a reduction in the degree of overlap with other anxiety disorders. There was a smaller decrease in the proportion of patients meeting only GAD criteria, and this proportion remained stable with durations of up to three years. This study suggests that another problem of differentiating generalized anxiety disorder from the generalized type of anxiety that may be found in other anxiety disorders is that one month's duration does not constitute an anxiety syndrome of sufficient severity to be recognized independently. Therefore, a longer, six months' duration has been incorporated in the DSM-III-R criteria.

To further emphasize the pervasiveness and severity of the symptoms of GAD, the criteria in DSM-III-R require that the person be preoccupied with worry more days than not over the minimum six months' interval and that six, not three, generalized anxiety symptoms from the three main categories of motor tension, autonomic hyperactivity, and vigilance and scanning be present (see Table 7.7).

These stronger criteria have been tested in a community sample (54), in which it was found that the lifetime GAD prevalence rate decreased from 45% (by DSM-III) to 9%. The increased duration accounted for most of the decrease since even three-fourths of the DSM-III GAD respondents reported at least six symptoms. However, those with disorders of longer durations did have more symptoms, which suggests that the more chronic disorder was indeed symptomatically more severe (see below for discussion of overlap with major depression). It is hoped that the combination of distinguishing generalized anxiety as worry about multiple life situations, in contrast to the more limited focus of anticipatory anxiety, and requiring a more prolonged syndrome will lead to more accurate identification of GAD. The clinician will then be able to use GAD to indicate a coexisting, independent problem, as opposed to its more limited use as residual diagnosis, even in cases of mixed anxiety disorder. GAD will continue, however, not to be diagnosed when anxiety is considered an integral part of one of the other anxiety disorders.

GAD vs. other disorders. Many patients with symptoms of GAD

Table 7.7 Symptom Clusters in DSM-III-R Generalized Anxiety Disorder

Type	Symptoms
Motor tension	Trembling, twitching, shaking Muscle tension, aches, soreness Restlessness Easy fatigability
Autonomic hyperactivity	Dyspnea, smothering sensations Palpitations, tachycardia Sweating, cold clammy hands Dry mouth Dizziness, lightheadedness Nausea, diarrhea, abdominal distress Flushes, chills Urinary frequency Trouble swallowing, lump in throat
Vigilance/scanning	Feeling keyed up, on edge Exaggerated startle response Difficulty concentrating, mind going blank Insomnia Irritability

have other, coexisting, nonorganic Axis I disorders. The most common is probably major depression. Even with the revised, more stringent criteria described above, research indicates that almost three-fourths of the narrowly defined GAD patients have a lifetime history of major depression (54). This is much higher than the rate of major depression in patients with DSM-III GAD. Therefore, the more severe and chronic forms of GAD may result from interactions with major depression. Most patients with major depression plus GAD in a study by Breslau and Davis (55) reported that the first episode of each coincided.

The decision for the differential diagnosis between GAD and depressive disorders is based on the temporal overlap. Until such time as an additional diagnosis of GAD in the presence of major depression can be shown to have treatment or etiologic significance, as was found for panic disorder, it is a redundant diagnosis. Therefore, DSM-III-R criteria state that GAD does not occur (only) during the course of a major depressive episode. In excluding GAD, the situation with regard to schizophrenia is the same as that with respect to major depression.

Other disorders, particularly those with physical symptoms (see Chapter 8) have worry and apprehension as a common symptom. Patients with anorexia nervosa worry about being fat; those with hypochondriasis worry about being sick. Since these worries are relatively restricted, they do not correspond to the multiple worries of GAD, and are differentiated from it by DSM-III-R criteria.

ANXIETY DISORDERS WITH CHILDHOOD OR ADOLESCENT ONSET

There are several disorders from the class of disorders usually first evident in infancy, childhood, or adolescence that the general psychiatrist may need to consider when evaluating anxiety in a late adolescent or young adult: separation anxiety disorder, avoidant disorder of childhood or adolescence, and overanxious disorder. The distinguishing features of these disorders are listed in Table 7.8.

Separation anxiety disorder can be applied to a patient of any age if anxiety concerning separation from attachment figures had its onset before age 18. Avoidant disorder is the childhood or adolescent counterpart of social phobia, and is the diagnosis of choice if the disturbance is not so pervasive or persistent as to warrant a diagnosis of avoidant personality disorder, a diagnosis that can be made even if the adolescent is under 18. Overanxious disorder is comparable with generalized anxiety disorder; the latter diagnosis takes precedence if the patient is over 18.

ANXIETY IN RESPONSE TO STRESSORS

Any anxiety disorder can be considered "reactive" to psychosocial stressors. Maladaptive anxiety reactions to stressors that are not

Table 7.8 Features of DSM-III-R Anxiety Disorders of Childhood or Adolescence

Disorder	Key Identifying Feature
Separation anxiety disorder	Fear of separation from attachment figure; onset before age 18
Avoidant disorder of childhood	Fear of unfamiliar people; onset before age 18
Overanxious disorder	Excessive worry; onset before age 18

severe or persistent enough to meet the criteria for an anxiety disorder would be diagnosed as either adjustment disorder with anxious mood, adjustment disorder with mixed emotional features, or adjustment disorder with mixed disturbance of emotions and conduct.

SUMMARY

This chapter has discussed problems in differential diagnosis in the exciting and controversial area of the anxiety disorders. Studies of the course and treatment of anxiety disorders are rapidly growing in number, making this one of the new frontiers in psychiatry.

Since DSM-III took a single DSM-II category, anxiety neurosis, and split it into several distinct types—and added a new diagnosis, PTSD, as well—it was to be anticipated that many problems would be encountered in using the system. This chapter focuses on accurate recognition of the anxiety disorders and their relationships to other Axis I disorders. The boundaries between the various anxiety disorders have been shifted in DSM-III-R, new terminology has been introduced, and many hierarchical relationships to other disorders have been eliminated. These changes are expected to improve the accuracy of differential diagnosis in this area and to increase the usefulness of the relevant categories.

REFERENCES

1. Liebowitz MR, Fyer AJ, Gorman JM, Campeas R, Levin A: Phenelzine in social phobia. J Clin Psychopharmacol 6:93–98, 1986
2. Liebowitz MR, Gorman JM, Fyer AJ, Klein DF: Social phobia: review of a neglected anxiety disorder. Arch Gen Psychiatry 42:729–736, 1985
3. Insel TR, Murphy DSL: The psychopharmacological treatment of obsessive compulsive disorder: a review. J Clin Psychopharmacol 1:304–311, 1981
4. Insel TR, Murphy DL, Cohen RM, Alterman I, Kilts C, Linnoila M: Obsessive-compulsive disorder: a double-blind trial of clomipramine and clorgyline. Arch Gen Psychiatry 40:605–612, 1983
5. Perse TL, Greist JH, Jefferson JW, Rosenfeld R, Dar R: Fluvoxamine treatment of obsessive-compulsive disorder. Am J Psychiatry 144:1543–1548, 1987
6. Klerman GL: Overview of the Cross-National Collaborative Panic Study. Arch Gen Psychiatry 45:407–412, 1988
7. Ballenger JC, Burrows GD, DuPont RL Jr, Lesser IM, Noyes R Jr, Pecknold JC, Rifkin A, Swinson RP: Alprazolam in panic disorder and agoraphobia: results from a multicenter trial. I. Efficacy in short-term treatment. Arch Gen Psychiatry 45:413–422, 1988
8. American Psychiatric Association: Diagnostic and Statistical Manual of Mental Disorders, Third Edition. Washington, DC, American Psychiatric Association, 1980

9. Mackenzie TB, Popkin MK: Organic anxiety syndrome. Am J Psychiatry 140:342–344, 1983
10. Di Nardo PA, O'Brien GT, Barlow DH, Waddell MT, Blanchard EB: Reliability of DSM-III anxiety disorder categories using a new structured interview. Arch Gen Psychiatry 40:1070–1074, 1983
11. Aronson TA: A naturalistic study of imipramine in panic disorder and agoraphobia. Am J Psychiatry 144:1014–1019, 1987
12. Liebowitz MR, Quitkin FM, Stewart JW, McGrath PJ, Harrison W, Rabkin JG, Tricamo E, Markowitz JS, Klein DF: Psychopharmacologic validation of atypical depression. J Clin Psychiatry 45:22–25, 1984
13. Hoehn-Saric R: Comparison of general anxiety disorder with panic disorder patients. Psychopharmacol Bull 19:104–108, 1982
14. Anderson DJ, Noyes R Jr, Crowe RR: A comparison of panic disorder and generalized anxiety disorder. Am J Psychiatry 141:572–575, 1984
15. Barlow DH, Blanchard EB, Vermilyea JA, Vermilyea BB, Di Nardo PA: Generalized anxiety and generalized anxiety disorder: description and reconceptualization. Am J Psychiatry 143:41–44, 1986
16. Crowe RR, Noyes R, Pauls DL, Slymen D: A family study of panic disorder. Arch Gen Psychiatry 40:1065–1069, 1983
17. Noyes R Jr, Clarkson C, Crowe RR, Yates WR, McChesney CM: A family study of generalized anxiety disorder. Am J Psychiatry 144:1019–1024, 1987
18. American Psychiatric Association: Diagnostic and Statistical Manual of Mental Disorders, Third Edition, Revised. Washington, DC, American Psychiatric Association, 1987
19. Sheehan DV, Sheehan KH: The classification of anxiety and hysterical states. Part II: Toward a more heuristic classification. J Clin Psychopharmacol 386:393, 1982
20. Klein DF, Ross DC, Cohen P: Panic and avoidance in agoraphobia: application of a path analysis to treatment studies. Arch Gen Psychiatry 44:377–385, 1987
21. Liberthson R, Sheehan DV, King ME, Weyman AE: The prevalence of mitral valve prolapse in patients with panic disorders. Am J Psychiatry 143:511–515, 1986
22. Mazza DL, Martin D, Spacavento L, Jacobsen J, Gibbs H: Prevalence of anxiety disorders in patients with mitral valve prolapse. Am J Psychiatry 143:349–352, 1986
23. Von Korff MR, Eaton WW, Keyl PM: The epidemiology of panic attacks and panic disorder: results of three community surveys. Am J Epidemiol 122:970–981, 1985
24. Boyd JH, Burke JD Jr, Gruenberg E, Holzer CE 3d, Rae DS, George LK, Karno M, Stoltzman R, McEvoy L, Nestadt G: Exclusion criteria of DSM-III: a study of co-occurrence of hierarchy-free syndromes. Arch Gen Psychiatry 41:983–989, 1984
25. Leckman JF, Merikangas KR, Pauls DL, Prusoff BA, Weissman MM: Anxiety disorders and depression: contradictions between family study data and DSM-III conventions. Am J Psychiatry 140:880–882, 1983
26. Leckman JF, Weissman MM, Merikangas KR, Pauls DL, Prusoff BA: Panic disorder and major depression: increased risk of depression, alcoholism, panic, and phobic disorders in families of depressed probands with panic disorder. Arch Gen Psychiatry 40:1055–1060, 1983
27. Weissman MM, Merikangas KR, Wickramaratne P, Kidd KK, Prusoff BA, Leckman JF, Pauls DL: Understanding the clinical heterogeneity of major

depression using family data. Arch Gen Psychiatry 43:430–434, 1986
28. Breier A, Charney DS, Heninger GR: Major depression in patients with agoraphobia and panic disorder. Arch Gen Psychiatry 41:1129–1135, 1984
29. Breier A, Charney DS, Heninger GR: The diagnostic validity of anxiety disorders and their relationship to depressive illness. Am J Psychiatry 142:787–797, 1985
30. Weissman MM, Merikangas KR: The epidemiology of anxiety and panic disorders: an update. J Clin Psychiatry 47:11–17, 1986
31. Robins LN, Helzer JE, Croughan J, Ratcliff KS: National Institute of Mental Health Diagnostic Interview Schedule: its history, characteristics, and validity. Arch Gen Psychiatry 38:381–389, 1981
32. Liebowitz MR: Anxiety disorders, in An Annotated Bibliography of DSM-III. Edited by Skodol AE, Spitzer RL. Washington, DC, American Psychiatric Press, 1987, pp 111–117
33. Amies PL, Gelder, MG, Shaw PM: Social phobia: a comparative clinical study. Br J Psychiatry 142:174–179, 1983
34. Marks I: Blood-injury phobia: a review. Am J Psychiatry 1207–1213, 1988
35. Costello C: Fears and phobias in women: a community study. J Abnorm Psychol 91:280–286, 1982
36. Myers JK, Weissman MM, Tischler GL, Holzer CE 3d, Leaf PJ, Orvaschel H, Anthony JC, Boyd JH, Burke JD Jr, Kramer M, Stoltzman R: Six-month prevalence of psychiatric disorders in three communities: 1980 to 1982. Arch Gen Psychiatry 41:959–967, 1984
37. Anthony JC, Folstein M, Romanoski AJ, Von Korff MR, Nestadt GR, Chahal R, Merchant A, Brown CH, Shapiro S, Kramer M, Gruenberg EM: Comparison of the lay Diagnostic Interview Schedule and a standardized psychiatric diagnosis: experience in eastern Baltimore. Arch Gen Psychiatry 42:667–675, 1985
38. Helzer JE, Robins LN, McEvoy LT, Spitznagel EL, Stoltzman RK, Farmer A, Brockington IF: A comparison of clinical and diagnostic interview schedule diagnoses: physician reexamination of lay-interviewed cases in the general population. Arch Gen Psychiatry 42:657–666, 1985
39. Insel TR: Obsessive and compulsive disorder: five clinical questions and a suggested approach. Compr Psychiatry 23:241–251, 1982
40. Jenike MA: Obsessive compulsive disorder. Compr Psychiatry 24:99–115, 1983
41. Marks I: The care and cure of neurosis. Psychol Med 9:629–660, 1979
42. Coryell W: Obsessive compulsive disorder and primary unipolar depression. J Nerv Ment Dis 169:220–224, 1981
43. Rachman S, Hodgson R: Obsessions and Compulsions. Englewood Cliffs, NJ, Prentice-Hall, 1980
44. Marks IM, Stern RS, Mawson D, Cobb J, McDonald R: Clomipramine and exposure for obsessive compulsive rituals. Br J Psychiatry 136:1–25, 1980
45. Van Putten T, Yager J: Posttraumatic stress disorder: emerging from the rhetoric. Arch Gen Psychiatry 41:411–413, 1984
46. Green BL, Lindy JD, Grace MC: Posttraumatic stress disorder: toward DSM-IV. J Nerv Ment Dis 173:406–411, 1985
47. Atkinson RM, Henderson RG, Sparr LF, Deale S: Assessment of Viet Nam veterans for posttraumatic stress disorder in Veterans Administration disability claims. Am J Psychiatry 139:1118–1121, 1982
48. Horowitz MJ, Wilner N, Kaltreider N, Alvarez W: Signs and symptoms of posttraumatic stress disorder. Arch Gen Psychiatry 37:85–92, 1980
49. Brett EA, Ostroff R: Imagery and posttraumatic stress disorder: an overview. Am J Psychiatry 142:417–424, 1985

50. Brett EA, Spitzer RL, Williams JBW: DSM-III-R criteria for posttraumatic stress disorder. Am J Psychiatry 145:1232–1236, 1988
51. Laufer RS, Brett E, Gallops MS: Dimensions of posttraumatic stress disorder among Vietnam veterans. J Nerv Ment Dis 173:538–545, 1985
52. Davidson J, Swartz M, Storck M, Krishnan RR, Hammett E: A diagnostic and family study of posttraumatic stress disorder. Am J Psychiatry 142: 90–93, 1985
53. Barlow DH, Di Nardo PA, Vermilyea BB, Vermilyea J, Blanchard EB: Co–morbidity and depression among the anxiety disorders: issues in diagnosis and classification. J Nerv Ment Dis 174:63–72, 1986
54. Breslau N, Davis GC: DSM-III generalized anxiety disorder: an empirical investigation of more stringent criteria. Psychiatry Res 15:231–238, 1985
55. Breslau N, Davis GC: Further evidence on the doubtful validity of generalized anxiety disorder (letter). Psychiatry Res 16:177–179, 1985

CHAPTER 8

Physical Complaints

The interaction of physical symptoms and disorders with psychological factors challenges our understanding of the relationship between psyche and soma. Patients who present to physicians or mental health professionals with physical complaints or worry about physical illness have always posed difficult problems in differential diagnosis. Psychiatrists are most likely to encounter four types of physical illness in their patients: (*1*) disorders whose direct effects on the central nervous system (CNS) affect mental functioning, (*2*) disorders that influence the development of mental disorders through stress processes, (*3*) disorders that are adversely affected by psychological factors, and (*4*) physical illness that cannot be medically documented though the patient complains of various symptoms.

Disorders of the first type are classified as organic mental disorders, and are discussed in Chapter 3. Patients with the second type of disorder may have depressive disorders, anxiety disorders, adjustment disorder, or disorders from other major diagnostic classes; these are discussed in the corresponding chapters of this volume. The differentiation of these two groups, i.e., the physically ill whose coexisting psychological syndrome is a direct CNS effect versus those in whom the mental disorder is a reaction to the stress caused by the physical illness, is difficult; it will be discussed in detail in Chapter 11.

The latter two types of disorder mentioned above are the subjects of this chapter. The main point in differentiating between them is whether a physical illness can actually be diagnosed.

General Principles

The problems of patients with combined physical and psychologic symptoms or illnesses were traditionally labeled "psychosomatic." This term has become obsolete as understanding of the interrelationships of physical illnesses and psychological processes has grown. Few now would adhere to a reductionist theory of the disease process of illnesses historically considered psychosomatic, such as peptic ulcer or asthma, that would posit a unidirectional etiologic effect of psychological conflict on the physical illness: more sophisticated theories, based on bidirectional interactions between multiple emotional and physical factors that produce, exacerbate, and/or maintain illness, have replaced the old.

With the new concepts has come a need for new terminology, and with the terminology, a need for greater diagnostic rigor and the establishment of valid diagnostic categories. DSM-III represented a radical departure from traditional approaches to the diagnosis of the mental disorders of patients presenting with physical complaints and concerns about physical illness. The introduction of diagnostic criteria allowed for much greater specificity of diagnosis in this area, but the criteria themselves and the disorders they defined were largely unvalidated by empirical research. Since the publication of DSM-III, there has been some progress in investigating questions of validity, but not as much as one would hope, and far from what is necessary.

Before the advent of DSM-III, many of the patients with these problems were loosely lumped together under the rubric "hysteria." This term was meant to convey the notion that psychological conflict led to the development of physical illness through the defense mechanisms of repression and displacement. In accordance with the DSM-III practice, this murky area of psychodynamic inference was divided up into explicit categories based on observable clinical features. The approach to classification was described by Hyler and Spitzer (1) in an article entitled "Hysteria Split Asunder." The principles on which the differential diagnosis was based were: (*1*) establishing the presence or absence of a physical disorder by history, physical examination, and medical tests; (*2*) if a real physical illness were present, determining whether or not the symptoms were under voluntary control. Although this approach to classification answered some questions of differential diagnosis, it also raised many new problems, which will be discussed in what follows here.

One overriding note of caution should be kept in mind by all clinicians: failure to find a diagnosable physical illness in a patient with physical complaints does not necessarily mean that the person has a mental disorder. Too often, in an atmosphere of uncertainty when a medical diagnosis cannot be established, our medical colleagues define the disorder as "mental"; and too often as well, we accept this definition. Undiagnosed physical symptoms should not be equated with mental disorder. The early course of many physical illnesses is not clearly understood, and our methods of early detection are not so sensitive that we can be sure of no false-negative evaluations. Follow-up of undiagnosed physical symptoms may well reveal their evolution into a diagnosable disorder. The mental health clinician would do well, therefore, to require *positive* evidence of the role of psychological factors before regarding the problem as one within his or her domain.

Overview of Differential Diagnosis

Figure 8.1 is a decision tree for the differential diagnosis of mental disorders with physical complaints as prominent features. It is an expansion of the DSM-III-R decision tree for the differential diagnosis of somatoform disorders. Table 8.1 lists the disorders to be considered for the patient presenting with co-occurring physical and psychological complaints. This corresponds to the diagnostic decision tree for the differential diagnosis of physical complaints and irrational anxiety about physical illness in DSM-III, except that it includes a number of additional disorders, omitted from the DSM-III tree, that the clinician should consider.

As noted above, if a specific physical disorder is present that causes psychological symptoms through an effect on the CNS, a diagnosis of an organic mental disorder is relevant. The principal categories to be considered in the differential diagnosis are: psychological factors affecting physical condition; factitious disorders; the V code malingering; other major mental disorders either caused by stress or with physical symptoms as part of their manifestations; and the somatoform disorders—somatization disorder, psychogenic/idiopathic/somatoform pain disorder, conversion disorder, and hypochondriasis. Sexual dysfunctions are disturbances of physical functioning related to psychological problems, and should therefore be considered as well, as should eating disorders and the new DSM-III-R class sleep disorders, since they, too, are disturbances of physiologic functioning.

Psychological Factors Affecting Physical Condition

The diagnosis of psychological factors affecting physical condition (PFAPC) was introduced into DSM-III with great expectations that it would represent a breakthrough in the classification of what had been termed "psychophysiological disorders" in DSM-II. This DSM-II class had been criticized as rarely used, imprecise because of its implications of a unidirectional effect of the psychological on the physiological processes, and an obstacle to collaboration between psychiatrists and other physicians (2). Whereas the disorders that were usually considered "psychophysiological" were the traditional

Figure 8.1 Decision Tree for the Differential Diagnosis of Physical Complaints*

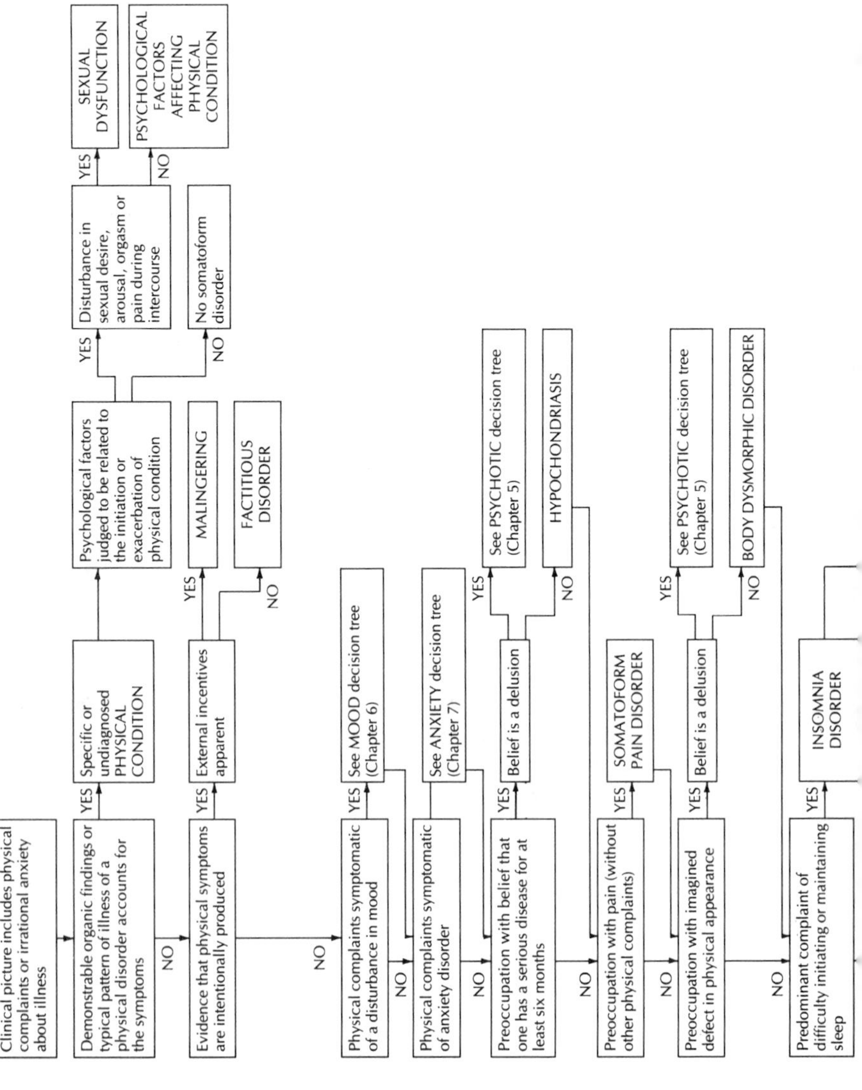

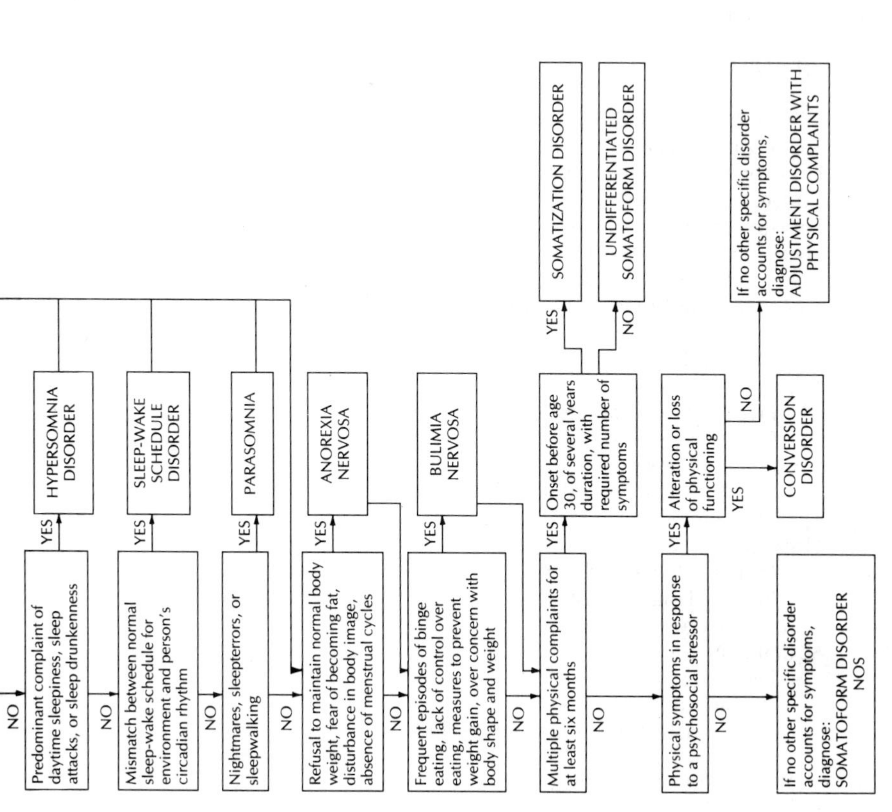

* Expanded version of the DSM-III-R decision tree for the differential diagnosis of somatoform disorders.

Table 8.1 Disorders in the Differential Diagnosis of Physical Complaints

SPECIFIC OR UNDIAGNOSED PHYSICAL CONDITION
- Psychological factors affecting physical condition

ORGANIC MENTAL DISORDERS

MALINGERING

FACTITIOUS DISORDERS
- Factitious disorder with physical symptoms

PSYCHOTIC DISORDERS

MOOD DISORDERS

ANXIETY DISORDERS

SOMATOFORM DISORDERS
- Somatization disorder
- Undifferentiated somatoform disorder
- Conversion disorder
- Somatoform pain disorder
- Hypochondriasis
- Body dysmorphic disorder
- Somatoform disorder not otherwise specified

SEXUAL DYSFUNCTIONS
- Sexual desire disorders
  - Hypoactive sexual desire disorder
  - Sexual aversion disorder
- Sexual arousal disorders
  - Female sexual arousal disorder
  - Male erectile disorder
- Orgasm disorders
  - Inhibited female orgasm
  - Inhibited male orgasm
  - Premature ejaculation
- Sexual pain disorders
  - Dyspareunia
  - Vaginismus
- Sexual dysfunction not otherwise specified

SLEEP DISORDERS (DYSSOMNIAS)
- Insomnia disorders
  - Primary insomnia
  - Insomnia related to another mental disorder (nonorganic)
  - Insomnia related to a known organic factor
- Hypersomnia disorders
  - Primary hypersomnia

Hypersomnia related to another mental disorder (nonorganic)
Hypersomnia related to a known organic factor
Sleep-wake schedule disorder
Dyssomnia not otherwise specified

EATING DISORDERS
Anorexia nervosa
Bulimia nervosa
Eating disorder not otherwise specified

ADJUSTMENT DISORDER
Adjustment disorder with physical complaints

---

psychosomatic illnesses, e.g., peptic ulcer, ulcerative colitis, asthma, rheumatoid arthritis, etc., the PFAPC diagnosis was intended to be used for any physical disorder or condition that the mental health clinician believed was adversely affected by psychological problems. The effect could, as a predisposition for the illness, contribute to its initiation, its exacerbation, or its maintenance. Type A personality characteristics as a risk factor for myocardial infarction would be an example of the appropriate use of PFAPC in an illness not considered psychophysiologic. "Nonillness" conditions, such as nausea and vomiting or frequent micturition, may also be appropriate for the diagnosis of PFAPC.

PFAPC has not lived up to the expectations held for it with respect to stimulating dialogue between psychiatrists and nonpsychiatric physicians (3). There have been no studies to date of use of the diagnosis; and from consultation-liaison services where the diagnosis would be expected to be used most frequently, problems with its use have been reported.

Problems Involving the Psychological Component

The question has been raised, "What may be considered psychological factors?" In DSM-III, something "psychological" was referred to as "the meaning ascribed to environmental stimuli by the individual" (4, p. 303). Examples given were stimuli arising from interpersonal relations, such as arguments or the loss of a loved one. The person himself or herself may or may not be aware of the meaning he or she ascribes to the stimuli, or the relationship of the stimuli to the initiation or exacerbation of the physical condition. When a judgment of such a high order of inference is involved in determining that psychological factors may be present, one might expect considerable unreliability in the use of the diagnosis. One clinician's interpretation of the meaning ascribed to the event or situation and its role in the illness process could easily disagree with the judgment of a second clinician. In the DSM-III Field Trials (5), one of the few sources of data on the PFAPC category, reliability was fair, with a kappa of 0.62 achieved in Phase I, and 0.44 in Phase II. Phase II reliability may have been poorer because a greater proportion of patients were interviewed separately, thus cutting down on the cues one clinician's line of questioning might provide the other about the diagnoses under consideration. In order to increase the potential value of this diagnosis, clinicians would do well to have solid evidence of the psychological factors involved in the illness.

Misinterpretation of the kinds of psychological factors that might be involved has been reported by Leigh and associates (6). They believed that an Axis I mental disorder could not be the psychological factor and erroneously went on to say that the criteria for PFAPC specifically exclude such Axis I disorders. In fact, there is no reason why another Axis I diagnosed disorder, such as major depression or generalized anxiety disorder, might not be diagnosed along with PFAPC when the former caused or adversely affected a physical illness. Leigh and colleagues' example of a patient with major depression scheduled for open-heart surgery who, they believed, was at greater risk for operative mortality or postoperative morbidity is a good one. Both Axis I conditions should be diagnosed since the major depression requires specific treatment.

Problems Involving the Relationship to Physical Illness

The DSM-III criteria for psychological factors affecting physical condition required establishing a temporal relationship between "psychologically meaningful environmental stimuli" and the initiation or exacerbation of the physical illness. As Leigh and associates (6) correctly point out, the psychological factors may occur (*a*) before the onset or exacerbation, (*b*) during the course and treatment of the illness and affecting one or the other, or (*c*) during the recovery or convalescent phases. They also argue, however, that an effect in the opposite direction, i.e., the occurrence of physical illness leading to the development of an Axis I mental disorder, should also be coded as a subtype of the 316.0 category and called "physical condition affecting mental disorder."

This would not be in accord with the DSM-III or the current DSM-III-R multiaxial conventions, which indicate this reversed relationship between physical and psychological syndromes in one of two different ways. If a physical illness, acting as a psychosocial stressor, leads to the development or exacerbation of a mental disorder, such as major depression or adjustment disorder with anxious mood, this relationship is represented by a diagnosis of the mental disorder on Axis I and the listing and rating of the severity of the psychosocial stressor on Axis IV. A serious illness should be rated 5 — Extreme on DSM-III-R Axis IV (an actual DSM-III-R Axis IV example of this scale point); a less serious illness might be rated 3 — Moderate or 4 — Severe, in keeping with Axis IV conventions (see Chapter 2, Multiaxial Diagnosis). If the physical illness is actually etiologically responsible for the development of the Axis I disorder, as in the case of the organic mental disorder delirium occurring in a patient hospitalized with renal failure, the mental disorder is, again, diagnosed on Axis I, and the physical illness is recorded on Axis III. If the presence of a physical disorder requires attention because it places some constraints on the management of the mental disorder, this illness also would be listed on Axis III. An example would be a patient with major depression who has a bundle branch block on electrocardiogram, or a bipolar disorder in a patient with kidney disease.

At one point in the deliberations on multiaxial diagnosis in the preparation of DSM-III-R, a system of notation that would indicate the "etiologic" versus the "management" significance of Axis III disorders was considered. The idea was abandoned because of concern about adding complexity to an already complex system.

A point on which DSM-III was ambiguous was whether an illness stressor should be listed on both Axis III and Axis IV. In my experience, illnesses that are listed on Axis III but not on Axis IV tend to be more chronic, and those noted on both axes, more acute. Also, the Axis I diagnostic distribution tends to be different; patients with schizophrenia who have illnesses more often have them listed exclusively on Axis III, whereas those with more acute disturbances such as major depression or adjustment disorder, have illnesses listed on both axes. This more limited conceptualization of the role of physical illness in schizophrenia may be a function of the Axis IV requirement that a stressor be related to a change in a patient's condition, or it may reflect a bias against considering social factors (i.e., physical illness as a stressor) important in schizophrenia.

The Special Case of Noncompliance with Medical Treatment

Noncompliance with medical treatment created a special problem for clinicians using DSM-III. Although such noncompliance clearly represents an instance in which psychological factors adversely affect the course and treatment of a physical illness, as Mackenzie and his colleagues (7) have pointed out, DSM-III is ambiguous, if not contradictory about how to designate this problem. In an article describing the new PFAPC category, Looney and associates (2) stated that the category would be used when the psychological factors acted indirectly, through behavior that adversely affected the disease process, and cited noncompliance as an example. In DSM-III itself, however, noncompliance is not given as an example of the PFAPC category: a V code, condition not attributable to a mental disorder, is listed for noncompliance with medical treatment. The V code description of noncompliance states that it should be used when a person has a religious belief that prohibits receiving medical treatment or has made a considered decision that the treatment is worse than the illness.

Mackenzie and his co-workers (7) propose a useful differential diagnosis when noncompliance is the result of a mental disorder. A personality disorder characterized by distrust, resistance to external demands, or self-defeating behavior is a possibility. A factitious disorder is also a possibility if the person is thought to be voluntarily refusing treatment in order to remain in the patient role. (If the person is purposely staying ill in order to win compensation or avoid an undesirable obligation such as military service, then malingering, another V code, would apply—see below.) I believe the PFAPC category should be used in cases of noncompliance in which the clinician's judgment is that the noncompliance is due to a mental disorder.

One important exclusion should be kept in mind. Since PFAPC requires that the illness have "a demonstrable organic pathology" or "a known pathophysiological process," it does not apply when a somatoform disorder is diagnosed. The physical symptoms in somatoform disorders, as will be discussed below, do not, by definition, meet these standards.

There have been no substantive changes in the PFAPC category in DSM-III-R—a reflection of the dearth of data on this category (8).

RECOGNIZING DISORDERS INVOLVING "VOLUNTARY" CONTROL

Another question that must be asked in approaching the diagnosis of the patient with physical complaints is, "If there is a disorder with demonstrable organic pathology or a known pathophysiologic mechanism, was it voluntarily or intentionally produced?" The motivation for intentional symptom production differentiates, in turn, between factitious disorder and malingering.

The judgment that the production of physical symptoms is under voluntary control or is intentional is by no means an easy one to make. For one thing, the patient's simulation of illness may be done in a surreptitious manner so as to escape discovery, and it therefore requires a skilled "detective-clinician" to suspect willful symptom production and then go on to prove it. In fact, it is the apparently purposeful way in which a patient goes about concealing his or her behavior that suggests that it is under some voluntary control. There is no doubt, however, that there is a driven quality to the behavior; the classic patient will engage in the deception over and over again, even when it is obviously dangerous or life-threatening. Therefore, the deliberate or voluntary nature of the behavior is more obvious than the person's actual ability to control it, i.e., to stop it.

The somatoform disorders involve physical symptoms that are judged not to be under voluntary control or intentional, though the hysterical seizures or paralyses of conversion disorder can appear to be under voluntary control in the sense that strong psychological conflict leads the person to the symptom production. The crucial distinction, according to DSM-III, is that the person does not experience the sense of producing the symptoms; the motivations are presumably at a less conscious level than in the case of factitious disorders or malingering. Actually, the clinical situation can be viewed in terms of the subject's awareness of motivation at various degrees of remoteness from the behavior. The person who is malingering (as we shall see below) knows very well exactly what he or she is doing and what the purpose is; the person with a factitious disorder apparently knows the more proximate motivation (i.e., I shall do such and such in order to induce symptoms), but does not really know why he or she chooses to be sick; the person with a conversion disorder is aware neither of "doing" anything nor of the more remote motivation for becoming symptomatic. The relevant criterion of conversion disorder in DSM-III-R now states: "The person is not conscious of intentionally producing the symptom" (9, p. 263).

As should be evident to the reader of this book, judgments made at such levels of inference are inherently unreliable. Factitious disorders are uncommon, and have had among the lowest levels of diagnostic reliability of any disorders in DSM-III. Further confusing the issue of voluntary control is the fact that for the factitious disorders, it is the judgment of observers that the behavior is voluntary that counts, whereas in the somatoform disorders, the subject's perception seems paramount.

Diagnosing Factitious Disorders

Once voluntary control (or intention) has been established, its motivation is assessed. If the person feigns illness for no obviously recognizable reason, then the diagnosis is factitious disorder. Such patients desire to be ill solely to assume the patient role. The motivation to be a patient may vary, however; it is usually based on deep-seated personality needs. Some writers have described an extreme desire to be taken care of as a motivation, a need to physically suffer, or a need to perplex and defeat the caregiver. If such patterns are observed, Axis II diagnoses of dependent, self-defeating, or sadistic personality disorders may also be warranted. The two types of factitious disorder relevant to the differential diagnosis of the patient with physical complaints are (*1*) factitious disorder with physical symptoms, and (2) atypical factitious disorder with physical symptoms. The former corresponds to the well-known Munchausen syndrome; the latter is a residual category.

Chronic factitious disorder with physical symptoms was the DSM-III diagnosis for an extensive pattern of self-induced physical symptoms. The criteria required that multiple hospitalizations result. The patient with classic Munchausen syndrome may spend his or her entire life inducing vomiting, blackouts, bleeding, infections, and fevers, which may result in admissions, needless diagnostic procedures, and unnecessary surgery. Substance abuse may develop as an associated diagnosis because of the frequent use of analgesics. Keys to distinguishing this disorder from true physical illness are: pseudologica fantastica (lying that creates a bizarre, exaggerated, and impossible medical history); disruptive ward behavior, including noncompliance; extensive medical knowledge; extensive use of analgesics; multiple surgical procedures; extensive history of traveling; few or no visitors; and a fluctuating clinical course, with new complications or new symptoms when an initial workup proves negative.

The residual atypical factitious disorder category of DSM-III was used for diagnosing a person with a more limited history. The word *chronic* was dropped from factitious disorder with physical symptoms in DSM-III-R, as was the requirement of multiple hospitalizations since the disorder is thought to have both a limited and a chronic (i.e., Munchausen) form.

Recognizing Malingering

In malingering, a V code, the goal for faking illness is readily apparent from the person's external circumstances rather than his or her psychopathology. Avoidance of work, being drafted into the army, or criminal prosecution; or obtaining drugs, workmen's compensation, or insurance benefits are the kinds of external incentives that might motivate a malingerer. DSM-III states that malingering should be carefully considered in all medicolegal presentations when a person's subjective distress or disability is grossly out of proportion to the objective findings, when a person does not fully cooperate with the diagnostic evaluation or fails to follow a prescribed regimen, or when the person has an antisocial personality disorder.

Malingering is also discussed in this book in the contexts of evaluations for injury compensation (see Chapter 12) and the assessment of the patient with psychotic symptoms (see Chapter 5).

Other Mental Disorders with Physical Symptoms

In the absence of a physical disorder to account for physical complaints and any suspicion of voluntary or intentional production or feigned illness, the clinician usually should next consider major mental disorders that might be responsible for the presenting symptoms. The somatoform disorders (see the next section) were all residual diagnoses to the major mental disorders above them in the DSM-III classification in that these more pervasive disorders took precedence over and excluded the somatoform disorders.

The exclusions are more limited in DSM-III-R. Even so, a patient with a fear of cancer may actually have a somatic delusion as part of a delusional disorder and, according to DSM-III-R, should receive only this latter diagnosis, not hypochondriasis. Other physical symptoms such as weight loss can be due to major depression or anorexia nervosa; in such cases, these diagnoses are sufficient. Shortness of breath, heart palpitations, and a fear of having a heart attack can be symptoms of panic disorder. These symptoms, if part of panic disorder, do not warrant a DSM-III-R diagnosis of undifferentiated somatoform disorder (see below); but if the symptoms lead to a persistent preoccupation with the fear of having heart disease, an additional diagnosis of hypochondriasis may be made, according to DSM-III-R, although DSM-III recommended no additional diagnosis.

Diagnosing Somatoform Disorders

Once other major disorders have been ruled out, the diagnostician considers the somatoform disorders. The members of this class include: somatization disorder, DSM-III psychogenic pain disorder (renamed somatoform pain disorder in DSM-III-R); conversion disorder; hypochondriasis; the two new DSM-III-R categories body dysmorphic disorder and undifferentiated somatoform disorder; and the ubiquitous, residual, atypical, or not otherwise specified (NOS) category. Somatoform disorders are disorders with physical complaints suggesting physical illness for which no physical disorder or pathophysiological mechanism can be found to explain the symptoms and for which there is positive evidence, or strong presumptive evidence, that the symptoms are linked to psychological factors or conflicts.

Somatization Disorder

Of the somatoform disorders, somatization disorder has the most extensive pattern of physical symptoms. Somatization disorder is described as a chronic syndrome of recurrent physical symptoms, from many different organ systems, that begins before the age of 30. No physical disorder can be found, but because of the distressing nature of the complaints, patients with the disorder use medical treatment facilities extensively.

Somatization criteria in DSM-III were an abridged version of the criteria, originally developed by Perley and Guze (10), for Briquet's syndrome. The parent syndrome consisted of at least 20 of 59 medically unexplained symptoms from 9 of 10 groups, occurring primarily in women. It has been extensively validated in that it has been demonstrated to be very stable over time and to show strong familial relationships, female relatives being affected with the disorder itself, and male relatives, with antisocial personality (10-13). The DSM-III criteria were shortened in an attempt to (*1*) make the diagnosis simpler, (*2*) reduce what some critics considered a bias in the sex ratio observed for Briquet's syndrome, and (*3*) reduce overlap with anxiety and depressive disorders, since the original list included symptoms of these disorders. The final DSM-III criteria required 14 of 37 symptoms for women and 12 for men (a lesser number because of the inapplicability of symptoms referring to menstruation); although the symptoms were divided into functional physical groups, no specific distribution was required.

Although all DSM-III somatization disorder symptoms occur in the Briquet's list, a patient may meet criteria for Briquet's syndrome, but not somatization disorder, because of the additional symptoms included in the Briquet's list, and may meet criteria for somatization disorder, but not Briquet's syndrome, because the smaller number of symptoms in DSM-III can be insufficient for the full Briquet's diagnosis. Cloninger and colleagues (14) recently compared the two sets of diagnostic criteria in a study of validity. They found that although the overlap between the two definitions was substantial among female outpatients, it was less so among relatives. Furthermore, familial aggregation was demonstrated for Briquet's syndrome, but not for DSM-III somatization disorder. By either set of criteria, the disorder was found to be extremely rare in men. Men with fewer somatic symptoms than twelve, the DSM-III threshold, were most often diagnosed as having an anxiety disorder.

It appears, then, that, paradoxically, there is considerably more evidence for the validity of Briquet's syndrome, a diagnosis not in DSM-III, than there is for DSM-III somatization disorder.

A continuum of somatizing patients. From a clinical point of view, a major problem in diagnosing patients with multiple physical complaints not associated with demonstrable disease is that such patients' complaints extend along a continuum. The extensiveness varies both in the number and distribution of the symptoms among organ systems and in the frequency and chronicity of the complaints. Kendell (15) has remarked that "no natural point of discontinuity between somatization disorder and other forms of somatic complaint has been demonstrated." DSM-III included some other specific somatoform disorder diagnoses to attempt to account for these other clinical presentations; but, as we shall see below, there are problems with both their application in clinical practice and their demonstrated usefulness. Furthermore, the most common group of patients with enough distress and disability from somatic complaints to seek or be referred for psychiatric treatment have complaints that are insufficient for a full diagnosis of somatization disorder (16). Some clinicians estimate that these patients may outnumber those who meet the full criteria by four or five to one. The existence of a syndrome of somatization that is less extensive than somatization disorder with respect to the number of symptoms reported and far more prevalent was recently confirmed in a community survey (17).

Cloninger offered a solution to this problem to the Somatoform Disorders Advisory Committee to the Work Group to Revise DSM-III. He suggested that the original, valid criteria for Briquet's syndrome be added to DSM-III-R and that DSM-III somatization disorder, perhaps with varying grades of severity based on numbers of symptoms, be used for patients who failed to meet full Briquet's criteria. Although there was considerable support for a "minor" or "partial" somatization syndrome, this solution was considered too radical. Instead, DSM-III-R somatization disorder (see Table 8.2) includes a list of 35 symptoms divided into 6 symptom types, 13 of which are required for the diagnosis in either men or women.

When the patient's symptoms are subthreshold for the full diagnosis, three options are available. A new, intermediate category called undifferentiated somatoform disorder has been introduced for a patient with one or more physical complaints (*1*) with either no organic pathology or pathophysiological mechanism to explain the complaints or social or occupational impairment grossly in excess of physical findings associated with real organic pathology, (*2*) of at least six months' duration, and (*3*) occurrence not just during the course of another somatoform disorder (e.g., somatization disorder), a sexual dysfunction, or a mood, anxiety, sleep, or psychotic disorder. If a patient has only a brief episode of non-stress-related complaints, clinicians are directed by DSM-III-R examples to the residual somato-

Table 8.2 DSM-III-R Diagnostic Criteria for Somatization Disorder

A. A history of many physical complaints or a belief that one is sickly, beginning before the age of 30 and persisting for several years.

B. At least 13 symptoms from the list below. To count a symptom as significant, the following criteria must be met:

(1) no organic pathology or pathophysiologic mechanism (e.g., a physical disorder or the effects of injury, medication, drugs, or alcohol) to account for the symptom or, when there is related organic pathology, the complaint or resulting social or occupational impairment is grossly in excess of what would be expected from the physical findings
(2) has not occurred only during a panic attack
(3) has caused the person to take medicine (other than over-the-counter pain medication), see a doctor, or alter life-style

Symptom list:

Gastrointestinal symptoms:

(1) **vomiting (other than during pregnancy)**
(2) abdominal pain (other than when menstruating)
(3) nausea (other than motion sickness)
(4) bloating (gassy)
(5) diarrhea
(6) intolerance of (gets sick from) several different foods

Pain symptoms:

(7) **pain in extremities**
(8) back pain
(9) joint pain
(10) pain during urination
(11) other pain (excluding headaches)

Cardiopulmonary symptoms:

(12) **shortness of breath when not exerting oneself**
(13) palpitations
(14) chest pain
(15) dizziness

Conversion or pseudoneurologic symptoms:

(16) **amnesia**
(17) **difficulty swallowing**
(18) loss of voice
(19) deafness
(20) double vision
(21) blurred vision
(22) blindness
(23) fainting or loss of consciousness

(24) seizure or convulsion
(25) trouble walking
(26) paralysis or muscle weakness
(27) urinary retention or difficulty urinating

Sexual symptoms for the major part of the person's life after opportunities for sexual activity:

(28) **burning sensation in sexual organs or rectum (other than during intercourse)**
(29) sexual indifference
(30) pain during intercourse
(31) impotence

Female reproductive symptoms judged by the person to occur more frequently or severely than in most women:

(32) **painful menustration**
(33) irregular menstrual periods
(34) excessive menstrual bleeding
(35) vomiting throughout pregnancy

Note: The seven items in boldface may be used to screen for the disorder. The presence of two or more of these items suggests a high likelihood of the disorder.

---

form disorder NOS. An episode of impairment or distress due to physical symptoms that is not a part of another major Axis I disorder, is in reaction to a psychosocial stressor, and lasts no longer than six months can be diagnosed as adjustment disorder with physical complaints, also a new DSM-III-R category.

Medically unexplained symptoms. One of the most important and difficult aspects of making a diagnosis of somatization disorder is the judgment that the symptoms are without an actual physical basis (18). In the Epidemiologic Catchment Area (ECA) study (19,20), which employed the Diagnostic Interview Schedule (DIS) administered by lay interviewers as a method of case ascertainment, the prevalence of somatization disorder was found to be only 0.1%, less than one-tenth the rate usually estimated for the disorder in the general population. Since the interviewers who administer the DIS are not medically trained, a probe flowchart, which relies essentially on the patient's subjective report, determines whether the symptom is medically explained or "psychiatric" in nature. Patients frequently attribute the symptoms to physical disorders that are not real, sometimes using the pseudomedical terminology of their physicians. Evaluators without medical training are unable to assess critically the symptom descriptions, the adequacy of the diagnostic evaluations, or the validity of the putative physical diagnoses. In the ECA study, follow-up interviews by psychiatrists (21) revealed that lay interviewers missed diagnoses of Briquet's syndrome. Although interviewers comparable with ECA survey personnel are not likely to practice clinically, social workers and psychologists *are* likely to have to make judgments about physical complaints.

Nonmedical mental health clinicians must be careful to explore a patient's medical explanations with his or her medical doctor. DSM-III-R has spelled out more explicitly, in criterion B, how to count a symptom as significant. The criterion allows that if there is organic pathology, the complaint or associated functional impairment is in excess of what would be expected on the basis of the physical findings and incorporates the DIS requirement that the symptom causes the person to take medicine (other than over-the-counter analgesics), see a doctor, or alter his or her life-style. As we have seen in the ECA survey, these guidelines may not be an adequate substitute for medical training.

Relationship to other somatoform disorders. Another confusing aspect of the diagnosis of somatization disorder is its relationship to the other somatoform disorders—hypochondriasis, somatoform pain disorder (psychogenic pain disorder), and conversion disorder. Worry about physical health, medically unexplained pain, and conversion symptoms can all be observed in somatization disorder. In DSM-III the diagnostic criteria for the other somatoform disorders all required that the clinician rule out somatization disorder, which took precedence because of its pervasiveness. DSM-III-R is less consistent in its guidelines.

The most complicated differential is between hypochondriasis and somatization disorder. Patients with somatization disorder usually are preoccupied with symptoms rather than the fear of specific diseases. In addition, the somatization patient, by definition, has a wide array of symptoms; the patient with hypochondriasis typically is focused on a particular disease or body system, such as fear of having cancer of the bowel. According to DSM-III-R, hypochondriasis and somatization disorder can be diagnosed together.

Recently, a series of studies conducted in Sweden (22,23) have provided some evidence for the validity of separating a type of hypochondriasis from somatization disorder. Women who had occupational disability (sick days) due to physical symptoms were found to fall into two groups: a group with more diverse somatic complaints and fewer sick days, and a somewhat smaller group, with symptoms focused on abdominal systems, that had very high rates of disability. The former "diversiform" somatizers and the latter "high-frequency" somatizers were shown not only to be clinically distinct, with little overlap in phenomenology between the groups, but also to have a distinct pattern of mental disorders among their relatives. The diversiform somatizers clinically resemble patients with somatization disorder, whereas the high-frequency patients fit definitions of hypochondriasis. It is also interesting to note that the high-frequency patients had mostly abdominal complaints, which historically have been an essential part of the definition of hypochondriasis, but which are no longer required by modern criteria.

Although there is no criterion excluding it, conversion disorder is not intended to be diagnosed in the presence of somatization disorder, according to the DSM-III-R guidelines for differential diagnosis. Somatoform pain disorder can, however, be an additional diagnosis. At present, I fail to see the advantage of the approach of diagnosing less pervasive disorders in the presence of a more pervasive disorder, a practice that violates the general principle of diagnostic exclusions, i.e., when the symptoms of one disorder are part of the *essential* features of another disorder, only the more pervasive diagnosis is needed. Perhaps the ability to characterize the heterogeneity of these disorders through use of DSM-III-R will prove useful.

Relationship to anxiety disorders. Many of the symptoms of somatization disorder are those common to anxiety, including the cardiopulmonary and pseudoneurological symptoms. Here DSM-III guidelines for differential diagnosis were contradictory. The DSM-III discussion of the differential diagnosis of panic disorder stated that panic disorder was not diagnosed if the panic attacks were due to somatization disorder. Later, however, under the discussion of somatization disorder, DSM-III stated that panic might "coexist with somatization disorder, in which case both diagnoses should be made" (4, p. 243). The intention was to exclude cardiopulmonary and other symptoms of panic disorder from the somatization disorder diagnosis if these symptoms occurred only during panic attacks. It is conceivable, however, that a patient might have such symptoms both during panic attacks and at other times as well, in which case both panic criteria and somatization criteria might be met. DSM-III-R criteria make it explicit that for the physical symptoms to "count" toward a diagnosis of somatization disorder, they should not occur only during a panic attack.

The following case illustrates the difficulties in assessing a patient with multiple somatic complaints.

Textbook Case

A 45-year-old, single woman musician was interviewed in the hospital where she was being evaluated for chronic depression. The patient said that she had been depressed since the age of ten. She had a very low opinion of herself, believed that she was not as good as everyone else, and was convinced that she would never feel happy. Until recently she had functioned adequately, despite her feelings of hopelessness and despair, although she described it as often "being a struggle." Lately, she had felt that she did not want to get out of bed, that she needed "a rest." She often thought about suicide, but said, "I know I don't have the guts."

The patient denied that she had ever been severely depressed for as sustained a period as two weeks; a week at a time appeared to be her maximum. At most other times, however, she was somewhat depressed. When she was severely depressed, she suffered from insomnia and fatigue, but no anorexia. She reported that she had had occasional anxiety attacks in the previous five years. During these attacks she experienced tachycardia, shortness of breath, nausea, and a feeling that she might lose control of herself in some way. She denied that she did not want to get up and leave the house because she was afraid of having panic attacks.

The woman also complained that there "must be something physically wrong." In the past several years, she reported, her health had not been good. She said that her body ached, "with pains all over," that she felt "sick every day," though no major diseases had been diagnosed.

The woman dated the onset of health problems also to age ten, when she began to have headaches. The psychiatrist, curious about the extent of the physical complaints, referred to a list of symptoms from a structured interview. In addition to being evaluated for migraines, over the years the woman had undergone medical workups for "an ulcer condition," cramps of two years' duration, diarrhea "over a four-year period," back pain, arthritis ten years previously that "went away," shortness of breath, heart fluttering "a few years back," faintness, difficulty swallowing "for a few years," blurred vision, trouble walking, and inability to move her right arm. She also described pain during sexual intercourse, painful menstruation of 5 years' duration, and excessive menstrual bleeding about 15 years previously. A year ago, she had become convinced she had AIDS; an HIV test was negative.

The story of this woman's somatic difficulties unfolds gradually. Initially, she complains of depression. In the absence of a two-week sustained episode, the diagnosis of dysthymia is warranted; but her desire for hospitalization and the recent impairment in functioning seem too severe for a diagnosis of dysthymia alone. She goes on to describe panic attacks, which have been "occasional" and thus do not indicate panic disorder. Her impairment is also not due to agoraphobia.

The key to this patient's primary diagnosis is her report that she feels something is physically wrong and has felt in poor health for years. The psychiatrist could have stopped with the complaints of undiagnosed pain and settled on an additional diagnosis of somatoform pain disorder. He pushed on, however, and by asking about more and more symptom areas, uncovered a full-blown picture of somatization disorder.

The three diagnoses somatization disorder, somatoform pain disorder, and dysthymia can all be made, according to DSM-III-R. The two somatoform diagnoses may be redundant unless, perhaps, treatment at a pain clinic is indicated. Conversion disorder for the pseudoneurologic symptoms is not separately diagnosed. As will be discussed below, it is not entirely clear whether a DSM-III-R insomnia disorder or the sexual dysfunction dyspareunia should also be diagnosed. The clinician who suspects that an assessment of Axis II disorders may be indicated is undoubtedly on target. This case demonstrates that patients with somatization disorder can have one or more co-occurring mental disorders. Research indicates that mood, anxiety, and psychoactive substance use disorders are the most common (24).

Clinicians find the list of somatization disorder symptoms impossible to memorize and rarely carry structured interviews in their briefcases. The seven symptoms of DSM-III-R somatization disorder that are printed in boldfaced type (see Table 8.2) have been shown to function well as a diagnostic screening test for somatization disorder (25), two or more indicating a high likelihood of the disorder.

Conversion Disorder

Problems in the differential diagnosis of conversion disorder include differentiation of conversion symptoms from real physical illness and establishing the evidence of a psychological component.

Differentiation from physical illness. Distinguishing the signs of a physical illness early in its course from a conversion disorder can be extremely difficult, especially if psychological factors are evident. The criteria for DSM-III and DSM-III-R conversion disorder base this part of the diagnosis on whether the symptom picture follows a known pathophysiological mechanism. This may be especially difficult to determine in cases in which the physical signs or symptoms are vague or shifting in time or space, such as in multiple sclerosis or systemic lupus erythematosus. Frequently, patients with undiagnosed physical illnesses present with considerable distress, and may exaggerate their symptoms (18). Studies (26,27) have shown that significant proportions of patients initially diagnosed as conversion disorder eventually are observed to develop a physical disease that explains the original symptoms.

The only clinical feature that seems clearly to help separate conversion disorder from the early signs of undiagnosed physical illnesses is a prior history of conversion disorder. Cloninger (18) has suggested that the criteria for conversion disorder be revised to require a pattern of similar or different types of loss or alteration in functioning that is recurrent over a period of at least six months. This has the advantage of maximizing the predictive validity of the diagnosis, in that clinicians would have the best chance of prognosticating that the disorder will not evolve into a true physical illness. It has the disadvantage that clinicians are left without a diagnosis for first-episode cases.

The proposal has often been made that such patients simply be designated "undiagnosed." Although an undiagnosed group may easily be excluded from research studies, such a designation is of little value to the clinician who must plan or recommend an intervention or to the colleagues with whom he or she communicates. DSM-III-R has adopted a subclassification of single or recurrent episode as a compromise solution. Conversion disorder, single episode, is available for first-episode cases, and might be considered a type of provisional diagnosis for the conservative clinician; conversion disorder, recurrent episode, is the diagnosis when a pattern of repeated episodes is evident. The latter diagnosis can be made with more confidence.

Cloninger (18) has also recommended that conversion disorder be limited to neurological symptoms, such as paralysis, blindness, aphonia, ataxia, or anesthesia. DSM-III allowed that both autonomic disturbances, such as vomiting or fainting, and endocrine disturbances, such as pseudocyesis, be diagnosed as conversion disorder. Cloninger's recommendation was made because pseudoneurological symptoms are the only symptoms that conform to the anticipated transient pattern of conversion disorder. Other types of symptoms tend to be more chronic and, also, associated with a greater likelihood of evolution into physical illnesses. Thus, limiting the diagnosis would have greater influence on predicting outcome and treatment selection. DSM-III-R continues with a broader definition of conversion disorder, but the clinician would do well to keep in mind that nonneurologic syndromes might have to be diagnosed as conversion disorder with less certainty.

Positive evidence of psychological factors. Although most clinicans would agree that some positive evidence of the role of psychological factors is necessary in conversion disorder, in order to guard against indiscriminately attributing undiagnosable physical symptoms to psychological causes, there is disagreement about the nature of such evidence. DSM-III permitted three indications of the role of psychological factors: (*1*) a temporal relationship between an environmental stimulus that is apparently related to a psychological conflict or need and the initiation or exacerbation of the symptom, (*2*) the symptom's enabling the person to avoid some activity that is noxious to him or her, and (*3*) the symptom's enabling the person to get support from the environment that otherwise might not be forthcoming. Permitting evidence of secondary gain (points 2 and 3) can be shown to present serious problems since it has been demonstrated that secondary gain accrues as often to patients with known physical disorders as to those with documented conversion disorders (28). DSM-III-R has eliminated the secondary gain criteria.

The temporal relationship criterion is now the sole evidence of the relevance of psychological factors, despite the fact that many physical illnesses are preceded by stressful life events. It is the linking of the environmental stimulus related to the conflict or need and the physical symptom that is crucial. DSM-III stated that this judgment becomes more reliable when it can be observed repeatedly. This again suggests that recurrent conversion disorder is likely to be a more reliable and valid diagnosis than a first-episode diagnosis.

Some clinicians and investigators have argued that the new criteria will allow the diagnosis of conversion disorder to be made too easily. It was suggested to the Work Group to Revise DSM-III that the physical ability to perform the altered or lost function in conversion disorder be shown to be present nevertheless and that, after psychological exploration, the patient agree that the symptom served the purpose of providing a maladaptive solution to an emotional conflict. These suggestions were not followed because of the difficulty of operationalizing the first and because the second restricted the diagnosis to patients capable of developing insight.

Excluding disorders. Conversion disorder is not diagnosed if the symptom is limited to pain or if the disturbance in functioning is in sexual functioning. The former diagnosis would, according to DSM-III, be psychogenic pain disorder, or, according to DSM-III-R, somatoform pain disorder. This symptom is expected to have a more chronic course than typical conversion symptoms—for example, disturbances in neurological functioning. The sexual dysfunctions are diagnosed as such, instead of as conversion disorder, although many of the general features are the same, because of the specific treatment approaches that have been developed for them. Sexual dysfunctions will be discussed later in this chapter.

DSM-III diagnoses of somatization disorder and schizophrenia excluded conversion disorder. The former exclusion was made because conversion symptoms are so commonly a part of somatization disorder that joint diagnoses would seem redundant. The latter was intended to distinguish psychological conflict resulting in a physical change in functioning from psychotic processes resulting in such a physical change. These exclusions have been eliminated from DSM-III-R criteria in order to document clinical heterogeneity. The discussion of differential diagnosis belies the wisdom of this change, however: it is stated that conversion disorder should not be diagnosed when conversion symptoms are due to somatization disorder or schizophrenia. Few clinicians would use a diagnosis of conversion disorder to refer to catatonic behavior in schizophrenia.

Psychogenic/Idiopathic/Somatoform Pain Disorder

The DSM-III criteria for psychogenic pain disorder were very similar to those of conversion disorder except that the predominant disturbance was severe and prolonged pain. Other differences were that the evidence for the pain's not being explained by organic pathology or a known psychophysiologic mechanism included its nonanatomic distribution and the possibility that some organic pathology was present if the pain was grossly in excess of that expected from the physical findings.

Many of the problems associated with the diagnosis of conversion disorder applied to DSM-III psychogenic pain. Follow-up studies (27,29) have frequently demonstrated that patients with a diagnosis of psychogenic pain develop physical disorders over time, including diagnoses such as reflex sympathetic dystrophy, nerve-root irritation, and thoracic outlet syndrome. Determinations that the pain is inconsistent with anatomy are frequently unreliable; often there is no evidence of psychological etiologic factors in patients with chronic pain. Blumer and Heilbronn (30) believed that patients with idiopathic chronic pain had a variant of depressive disorder and proposed the term "pain-prone disorder." Based on the findings of Blumer and Heilbronn and their own experience with the category, Williams and Spitzer (31) proposed a revised category, idiopathic pain disorder, to replace psychogenic pain disorder in DSM-III-R. The term *idiopathic pain disorder* conveys the belief among clinicians that the evidence for either primary or secondary gain is often absent in patients with chronic medically unexplained pain.

All that really can be said is that there is no adequate explanation for the severe pain. In order to avoid the implication that the cause of the pain will never be determined, the final term for the disorder in

DSM-III-R is *somatoform pain disorder*. Since such complaints are, by definition, chronic; a six-month duration is required. It is preoccupation with pain, rather than the pain itself, that must be present for more than six months. The other changes in the criteria for somatoform pain disorder (Table 8.3) are that (*1*) inconsistency with anatomical distribution of the nervous system is no longer mentioned, and (*2*) when the pain is related to organic pathology, social and occupational impairment and the complaint of pain itself may be grossly in excess of the expected.

Relationship to other disorders. There are no exclusion criteria in DSM-III-R for somatoform pain disorder. This is unfortunate since their absence is likely to result in much diagnostic redundancy. Certainly, many patients with major depression are going to have somatic complaints, including aches and pains; this is especially likely to be true if the disorder is chronic or recurrent. A psychotic patient with schizophrenia or a delusional disorder may have a somatic delusion that could involve pain. Other disorders that might also be frequently accompanied by complaints of pain include dysthymia, panic and generalized anxiety disorders (both have pain as one of the symptoms), the sexual pain disorders (dyspareunia, vaginismus), and the two somatoform disorders—somatization disorder (ten symptoms refer to pain) and undifferentiated somatoform disorder. An exclusion criterion should be added that might read "The pain does not occur only during the course of, and is not judged to be a symptom of . . ." any of these other disorders.

Hypochondriasis

Until recently (see above) many questioned the validity of hypo-

Table 8.3 DSM-III-R Diagnostic Criteria for Somatoform Pain Disorder

A. Preoccupation with pain for at least six months.

B. Either (1) or (2):

   (1) appropriate evaluation uncovers no organic pathology or pathophysiologic mechanism (e.g., a physical disorder or the effects of injury) to account for the pain
   (2) when there is related organic pathology, the complaint of pain or resulting social or occupational impairment is grossly in excess of what would be expected from the physical findings.

chondriasis as an independent diagnostic category (32). Defined as the fear or the belief that one has a serious disease, hypochondriacal complaints have been shown to be related to other Axis I disorders such as major depression or the anxiety disorders, conviction that one has a disease being highly associated with the former diagnosis and fear of disease with the latter (33). Barsky and Klerman (34) and Kellner (35) have recently completed extensive literature reviews of hypochondriasis.

There are two substantive differences between DSM-III and DSM-III-R hypochondriasis. First, DSM-III-R requires a six-month duration. Patients who do not meet the six-month criterion will receive the diagnosis somatoform disorder NOS. Second, DSM-III-R lists fewer exclusions; therefore, psychotic disorders, mood disorders, somatization disorder, and anxiety disorders do not explicitly exclude hypochondriasis. Again, this may create diagnostic redundancy. For example, should a patient with severe panic disorder who experiences frequent attacks characterized by cardiovascular symptoms and who then develops the fear of having a heart attack be diagnosed as having hypochondriasis as well?

In the next vignette, "Mental Block," a man presents with symptoms suggestive of an anxiety disorder. He then goes on to describe a belief that he has a serious physical illness. The case illustrates the fine line between hypochondriacal beliefs and more malignant psychopathology.

Mental Block

A 32-year-old, single, unemployed man is hospitalized for "chronic anxiety." He describes a ten-year history of constant worry about himself and his future, which has made him almost totally nonfunctional and dependent on his parents. He reports that when anxious, he feels shaky, tense, restless, easily fatigued, short of breath, sweaty, on edge, irritable, and easily startled and has a rapid heartbeat, a dry mouth, and an inability to concentrate—in fact, virtually the gamut of symptoms of anxiety.

The major source of his worry is his physical health. He is convinced that he has a serious "problem with my brain," even though he has seen many physicians who have assured him that nothing is wrong with him physically. When he is asked to elaborate on what he feels that convinces him that he is physically ill, he says, "Everything is stuck in my head; everything is on top. I've got a blockage in the brain, like a petrified tree. My brain has stopped feeling; it froze; nothing comes in or out. It's shut down. I can't feel anything. I can't feel months or days. I can't feel the chair. I have no concept of August 16th. I can't handle anything, I find activities hard."

When asked about strange sensations or feelings in his head, the man replies, "My head feels disfigured. There's nothing in the back. Things feel twisted inside my head; it feels anatomically misshapen. There's nothing in the back; it's all up front."

When asked whether he is speaking figuratively, the man replies, "No, Doc, this is for real."

This man presents his problem as one of generalized anxiety. His fear of having a serious brain abnormality is sufficiently persistent to warrant an additional diagnosis of hypochondriasis. Hypochondriacal concerns about illness, needless to say, are to be distinguished from somatic delusions. This man's beliefs seem extremely well developed, and his explanations of the mechanisms involved are quite unusual. He denies intending his descriptions to be metaphoric.

When the belief of having a serious disease is of delusional intensity, a diagnosis of a delusional disorder, somatic type, might apply. A delusional disorder diagnosis requires, however, nonbizarre delusions (see Chapter 5) and no prominent hallucinations. If this man truly believes that his brain has stopped working, this would seem to me to meet the definition of bizarre. He also reports tactile sensations in and around the head that appear to be hallucinations. DSM-III-R delusional disorder criteria mention only auditory or visual hallucinations in the exclusion, however, since tactile and olfactory hallucinations may be present in somatic delusional disorder syndromes.

If a delusional disorder has been ruled out, then schizophrenia would apply, given the long duration of the symptoms and the associated functional impairment. Oddly, delusional disorder is the only psychotic disorder that explicitly precludes a diagnosis of hypochondriasis. The discussion of the differential diagnosis of hypochondriasis in DSM-III-R states that hypochondriasis and either a psychotic disorder or generalized anxiety disorder can be diagnosed together. Few clinicians would consider hypochondriasis a meaningful diagnosis in a patient with schizophrenia who has bizarre somatic delusions and hallucinations. Incidentally, a diagnosis of generalized anxiety disorder *is* ruled out in the above case by the diagnosis of schizophrenia.

Body Dysmorphic Disorder

A new category termed *body dysmorphic disorder* has been added to DSM-III-R. This corresponds to the diagnosis of monosymptomatic hypochondriacal neurosis described by Bishop (36). The essential features are a preoccupation with some imagined defect in one's physical appearance that is out of proportion to any actual physical abnormality that may exist. The main points of differential diagnosis are with psychotic disorders and with anorexia nervosa. In body dysmorphic disorder, the belief is not held with the conviction of a delusion, but rather as an overvalued idea (see discussions in Chapters 5 and 9). In anorexia nervosa, the patient has the powerful conviction that she is fat, even when emaciated. This diagnosis takes precedence over body dysmorphic disorder. The complaints in body dysmorphic disorder frequently involve the face, and may be associated with a personality disorder. The following case vignette depicts this new DSM-III-R category.

Nothing Less Than Perfect

"You're not going to believe me. I know you're not going to accept this." So began a 31-year-old, single woman—a former model for clothing catalogues. The woman was hospitalized for the eighth time at a small community hospital and was applying for long-term inpatient treatment at a hospital in New England.

One and a half years before she had noticed two small "cysts" under the skin of her face, one just below the right ear and the other along the line of her lower jaw on the same side. She felt that they were "noticeable" in her photographs; and although no prospective employer or photographer had complained, she consulted a plastic surgeon, who agreed to remove them.

In the surgeon's opinion, the operation was a success, leaving two small hairline scars that he said would fade with time. To the patient the scars were "a disaster." She could not stand the fact that the scars were visible at all. She became obsessed with having them treated or removed. She consulted several other plastic surgeons, most of whom said they would not recommend any further work at the moment. One gave her "silicone shots" that "just made them worse."

The patient became reclusive. She would not work even though, with makeup, the scars were not visible in photographs of the full-length poses in which she usually modeled. She stayed away from people in general because she was embarrassed "about the way I look." She then became severely depressed, and attempted suicide by overdosing on over-the-counter sleeping pills. She was hospitalized seven more times for depression, with agitation, suicidal ideation, and extreme preoccupation with her scars. She received trials of thioridizine, perphenazine, fluphenazine, haloperidol, thiothixine, desipramine, imipramine, nortriptyline, phenelzine, diazepam, and alprazolam. None relieved her "obsession."

The psychiatrist told the patient that as she sat before him, he could not see the scars. "I know," the woman said. "With makeup on, no one can. But every night when I go to bed, I see them. They're there. *I* know it. I can't stand it! I want to look perfect."

This patient is able to recognize that to others her scars are imperceptible; therefore, she does not have a delusional disorder. Although she has developed recurrent major depression, her preoccupation with the scars preceded the depression, and thus cannot simply be considered a symptom of depression. Although the patient refers to being "obsessed" with her scars, the thoughts are not intrusive and senseless, and she does not try to suppress them, as would be the case with the obsessions of obsessive compulsive disorder. This patient has also developed social avoidance; but since her fear of scrutiny and embarrassment is based on the symptom of a body dysmorphic disorder, a diagnosis of social phobia is ruled out (see also Chapter 6, Anxiety Syndromes). There are suggestions in the vignette of a possible histrionic personality disorder on Axis II.

Trichotillomania

Trichotillomania is an interesting syndrome with physical symptoms that presented a difficult differential diagnosis according to DSM-III. Trichotillomania is self-inflicted, irresistible hair-pulling that generally results in noticeable alopecia. As such it could conceivably be diagnosed as psychological factors affecting physical condition (PFAPC) (alopecia on Axis III), a factitious disorder, obsessive compulsive disorder (OCD), conversion disorder, or an impulse control disorder. The following case illustrates a less common form of trichotillomania that presents problems for the clinician attempting to make the best diagnosis.

Make a Wish

The psychiatrist listened as a 33-year-old, divorced, mother of two and owner of an art gallery described the development of her "nervous habit."

"It goes all the way back to when I was a child. I remember another little girl told me in the first grade that if an eyelash falls out, you should make a wish and blow it away. The next year, when I was about six, my brother, who was three, was hit by a car, and was in the hospital for a week. I remember that I was very worried, and so I started to pull out eyelashes and made wishes that he would be all right. Then about two years after that, we moved from Steubenville to Pittsburgh, and I changed schools. My first teacher was very tyrannical, and I got very nervous and started to pull them out all the time. It became very compulsive."

From then on, the woman said, she pulled out eyelashes whenever she was nervous about school, particularly at exam time, and at other anxiety-provoking times. Sometimes she was unaware of doing it, for instance, while she was reading; at other times she was very aware of it, felt a sense of increasing tension, and had "debates" with herself about whether or not to do it. Almost invariably she yielded to the temptation. Afterward she felt very guilty and engaged in much self-reproach.

The woman related her story in an articulate and animated fashion. She described herself as feeling very nervous during the interview, but was not noticeably so. She was very attractive and, "with the help of one of my many pairs of false eyelashes," had very beautiful eyes.

PFAPC is ruled out in this case because psychological factors are creating, not affecting, the physical condition. The loss of eyelashes would not occur except for the patient's behavior. Conversion disorder can be eliminated from consideration because the problem can be explained by a known pathophysiologic mechanism. An atypical factitious disorder would not apply: in this case the patient's behaviors are not deliberate and purposeful, she is not attempting to simulate illness, nor is she seeking medical attention or pulling hair to assume the role of a patient.

By DSM-III standards, trichotillomania seemed best to fit the general criteria for an impulse control disorder not elsewhere classified. The essential features of these disorders are (*1*) failure to resist an impulse, drive, or temptation to perform some act that is harmful to the person or others, (*2*) an increasing sense of tension before committing the act, and (*3*) an experience of either pleasure, gratification, or release at the time of committing the act. The woman depicted in "Make a Wish" displays the first two of these features. Instead of relief, however, she feels guilt. In addition, as a child, pulling out her eyelashes was associated with having wishes come true. Repetitive, purposeful, or intentional behaviors performed in a stereotyped fashion that are designed to neutralize discomfort or prevent a future event are indicative of obsessive compulsive disorder (OCD). As an adult the patient continues compulsively pulling out her eyelashes, but the hair pulling is no longer purposeful or closely connected to preventing or producing some future event. Thus, OCD, though a possible diagnosis, is not the best choice.

Trichotillomania has been added to DSM-III-R as a disorder of impulse control not elsewhere classified. The criteria are presented in Table 8.4.

SEXUAL DYSFUNCTIONS

The sexual dysfunctions are a subset of the sexual disorders in DSM-III-R; in DSM-III they were referred to as psychosexual dysfunc-

Table 8.4 DSM-III-R Diagnostic Criteria for Trichotillomania

A. Recurrent failure to resist impulses to pull out one's own hair, resulting in noticeable hair loss.

B. Increasing sense of tension immediately before pulling out the hair.

C. Gratification or a sense of relief when pulling out the hair.

D. No association with a preexisting inflammation of the skin, and not a response to a delusion or hallucination.

tions; the revision includes both biogenic and psychogenic etiologies. The sexual dysfunctions are a natural part of the differential diagnosis of the patient with physical complaints.

The sexual dysfunctions are distinguished from other gender and sexual disorders. In the gender identity disorders, the primary problem is persistent discomfort and a sense of inappropriateness about one's assigned sex. These disorders may occur in adults or children and may or may not be accompanied by a desire to change primary and secondary sex characteristics or by cross-dressing. Actual sexual performance may or may not be affected. In the paraphilias, the aberration is in the object toward which the person is sexually oriented. Sexual arousal and desire, acts, and fantasies may involve children (pedophilia), exposing one's genitals (exhibitionism), infliction of suffering (sexual sadism), nonliving objects (fetishism), etc.; but again, performance of the sexual act with the object may not be impaired.

The essential features of the sexual dysfunctions are disturbances at various points of the sexual response cycle: desire, arousal, intercourse, or orgasm. Some of the terminology of the DSM-III psychosexual dysfunctions has been changed in DSM-III-R for greater clarity, and a few new categories have been added. Since a decrease in sexual functioning is associated with a number of Axis I disorders, especially depressive disorders, the clinician must first rule out these more pervasive disturbances. Most of the sexual dysfunctions include an exclusion criterion requiring this procedure.

Among the disorders in sexual desire is inhibited sexual desire/hypoactive sexual desire, in which there are persistently or recurrently deficient or absent sexual fantasies and desire for sexual activity. A new category has been added to DSM-III-R, sexual aversion disorder, for classifying patients who have such an extreme lack of desire that it actually takes the form of aversion to and avoidance of genital contact with a sexual partner. Obsessive compulsive disorder must be ruled out since avoidance of sexual activity may result from the content of obsessions or a behavioral ritual.

There are now two sexual arousal disorders corresponding to DSM-III inhibited sexual excitement: a version for women called *female sexual arousal disorder*, and one for men called *male erectile disorder*. The differences in criteria simply refer to the anatomical and physiologic differences between the sexes in sexual arousal, women requiring adequate lubrication-swelling responses and men adequate erections. Decreased subjective sexual excitement and pleasure are a part of both diagnoses.

The disorders of intercourse are characterized by painful intercourse and in DSM-III-R are grouped as sexual pain disorders, the two being dyspareunia and vaginismus. The former refers to genital pain before, during, or after intercourse and can occur in either men or women. The pain is not exclusively the result of inadequate lubrication or vaginismus. Vaginismus is involuntary spasm of the vagina that interferes with intercourse, the disturbance not being caused exclusively by a physical disorder.

The orgasm disorders are inhibited female orgasm, inhibited male orgasm, and premature ejaculation. In all cases, the sexual activity must be judged adequate in focus, intensity, and duration. Women who are able to achieve orgasm only through noncoital, manual clitoral stimulation may or may not be given this diagnosis; the determination depends on whether the clinician judges that "psychological inhibition" of orgasm during intercourse is present. Delay or absence of ejaculation characterizes inhibited male orgasm. Ejaculation that occurs with minimal sexual stimulation or before, upon, or shortly after penetration, and before the person wishes it, is the essential feature of premature ejaculation.

Other disorders of sexual functioning may be diagnosed as sexual dysfunction NOS. DSM-III-R gives three specific examples: (*1*) no erotic sensation or complete anesthesia despite normal physiologic components of orgasm, (*2*) the female analogue of premature ejaculation, (*3*) genital pain occurring during masturbation.

Figure 8.2 summarizes the differential diagnosis of the sexual dysfunctions.

As mentioned at the outset of this section, in DSM-III, sexual dysfunctions that were caused by physical factors were not diagnosed, whereas in DSM-III-R, these may be diagnosed if both psychogenic and biogenic factors are involved. Included would be cases characterized by reduced arousal or performance contributed to by medications or physical illnesses. Commonly used drugs that may

Figure 8.2 Decision Tree for the Differential Diagnosis of Sexual Dysfunction

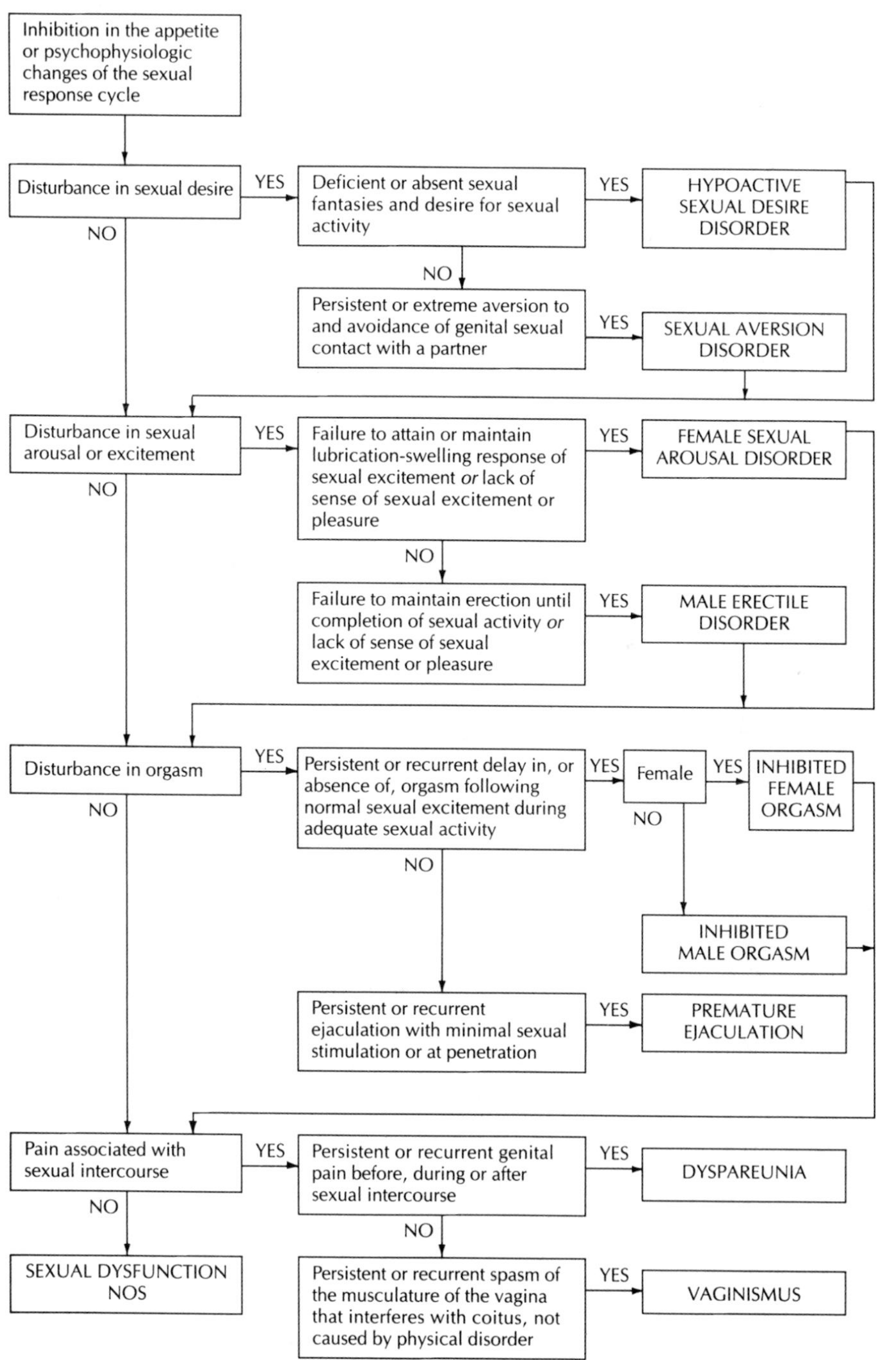

adversely affect sexual functioning include many antihypertensive agents, antipsychotic agents, antidepressants, oral contraceptives, opioids, and alcohol. Illnesses often associated with sexual dysfunction are multiple sclerosis, spinal cord injury, hypothyroidism, hyperthyroidism, Addison's disease, Cushing's syndrome, pituitary tumor, hemochromatosis, diabetes, renal failure, cirrhosis, chronic obstructive pulmonary disease, cancer, vascular disease, and myocardial infarction. In men, the measurement of nocturnal penile tumescence associated with rapid eye movement (REM) sleep is a useful diagnostic test in evaluating the role of a physical disorder in a sexual dysfunction such as male erectile disorder. Normal erections during sleep suggest that a failure during sexual activity is psychogenic.

The rationale for allowing biogenic contributions to sexual dysfunctions is that the etiology of the disorder in many patients has both an organic and a psychological component. The notation of both components, if present, ensures that adequate attention and treatment will be directed at each (37). After each relevant diagnosis in DSM-III-R, the clinican specifies whether the cause of the dysfunction is psychogenic only or psychogenic and biogenic, whether the dysfunction is lifelong or acquired, and whether it is generalized to all partners and situations or is situational. These subclassifications are thought to have treatment significance (38).

One of the sexual dysfunctions that does not include in its criteria an exclusion for its occurrence exclusively during the course of another Axis I disorder, such as major depression, is dyspareunia. This omission is unfortunate since, as we have seen in "Textbook Case" above, it may lead to a redundant diagnosis in patients with somatization disorder. The general principle of differential diagnosis followed by DSM-III-R in this area is that "If another Axis I mental disorder . . . is the primary cause of a disturbance in sexual functioning . . . a sexual dysfunction should not be diagnosed" (9, p. 293) unless it is unclear whether the disturbance in sexual functioning antedates the other mental disorder. In "Textbook Case," dyspareunia is a symptom of somatization disorder and, in my opinion, should not be diagnosed separately, even though it may have been present before the full picture of somatization disorder developed (which can take years).

SLEEP DISORDERS

Problems with sleep are another set of physical complaints frequently encountered in psychiatric patients (39). They may be especially prevalent among patients seen by consultation-liaison psychiatrists (40). Disorders in initiating or maintaining sleep (insomnia) or excessive daytime sleepiness (hypersomnia) were included only in a glossary in DSM-III, but have reached the status of recognized mental disorders in DSM-III-R. DSM-III-R terminology and definitions will be used here. The DSM-III-R classification of sleep disorders is a simplified version of the classification of sleep and arousal disorders used by many sleep investigators (41). It is intended for general clinical use.

Figure 8.3 presents a decision tree for the differential diagnosis of a predominant complaint of disturbance of sleep.

In DSM-III-R, insomnia is defined as a "predominant complaint of difficulty in initiating or maintaining sleep, or of not feeling rested after sleep that is apparently adequate in amount (nonrestorative sleep)" (9, p. 298), occurring at least three times a week for at least one month and being severe enough to cause the person to complain of daytime fatigue or lead others to observe some symptom or functional impairment that is attributable to the sleep disturbance. Hypersomnia is defined as "excessive daytime sleepiness or sleep attacks (not accounted for by an inadequate amount of sleep) or, more rarely, a prolonged transition to the fully awake state on awakening (sleep drunkenness)" (9, p. 302). To be considered a mental disorder, this disturbance should occur nearly every day for at least a month, or episodically over a longer period, and should result in impaired social or occupational functioning.

Sleep disorders are divided into two major groups: dyssomnias and parasomnias. The dyssomnias are characterized by a disturbance in the amount, quality, or timing of sleep. There are three groups of dyssomnias: insomnia disorders, hypersomnia disorders, and sleep-wake schedule disorder. In the parasomnias an abnormal event occurs, either during sleep or at the point between sleep and waking, that is itself the principal complaint of the patient rather than its effect on sleep.

To assess a patient for a sleep disorder, a clinician should take a comprehensive sleep history (42). The history may be obtained from the patient but should be corroborated by the patient's bed partner at home or by nursing staff in the case of a hospitalized patient. The sleep history should elicit data regarding (*1*) the customary sleep pattern; (*2*) the type of sleep problem, e.g., difficulty falling asleep, staying asleep, daytime sleepiness; (*3*) the clinical course, including age at onset, duration, frequency, severity, and precipitating and mitigating factors; (*4*) the 24-hour sleep-wake cycle; (*5*) a past history of sleep disturbances including childhood sleep pattern and pattern of sleep when under stress; (*6*) a family history of sleep disorders; (*7*) a personal history of sleep disorders; (*8*) a review of medication and psychoactive substance use; and (*9*) a psychiatric history.

In contrast to the sexual dysfunctions, the sleep disorders can be

Figure 8.3 Decision Tree for the Differential Diagnosis of Sleep Disturbance

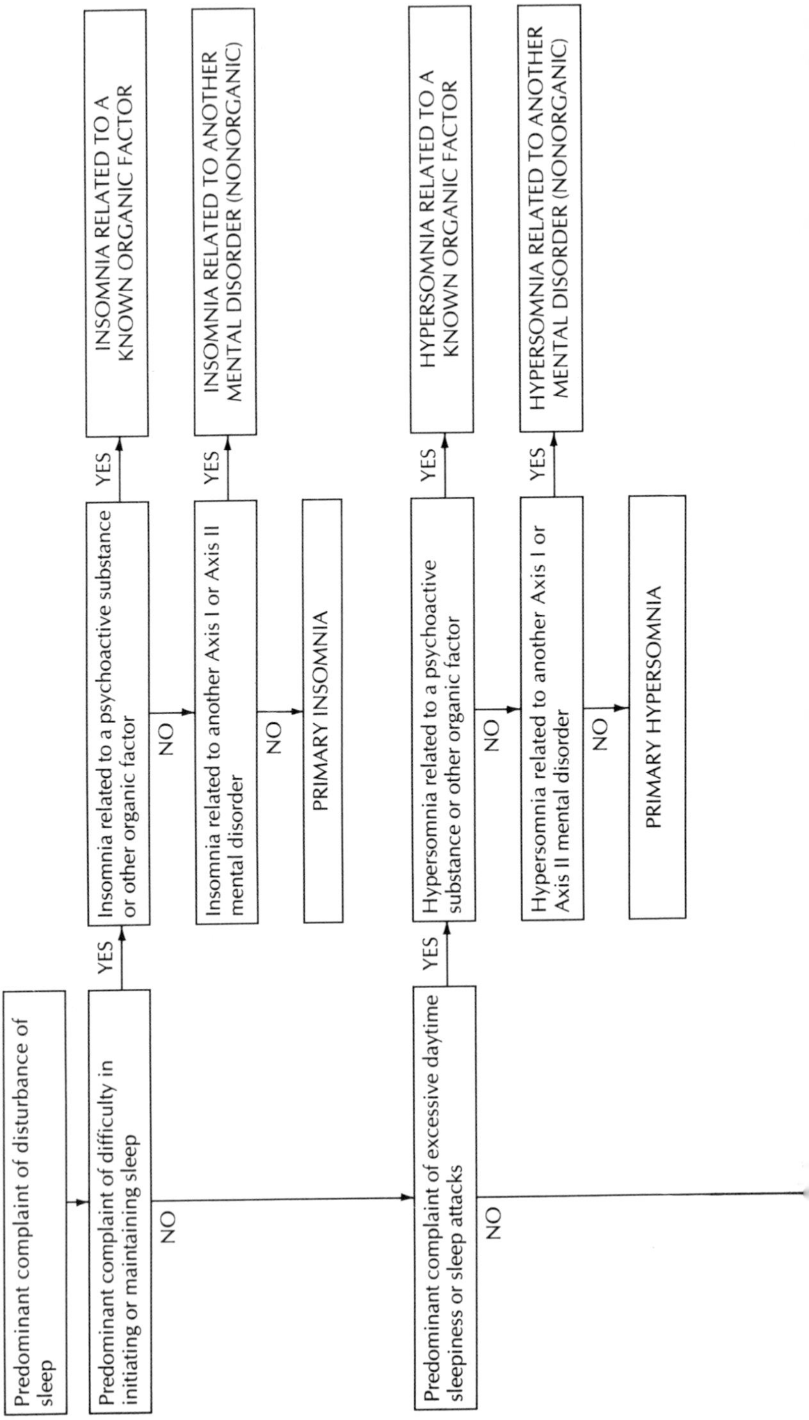

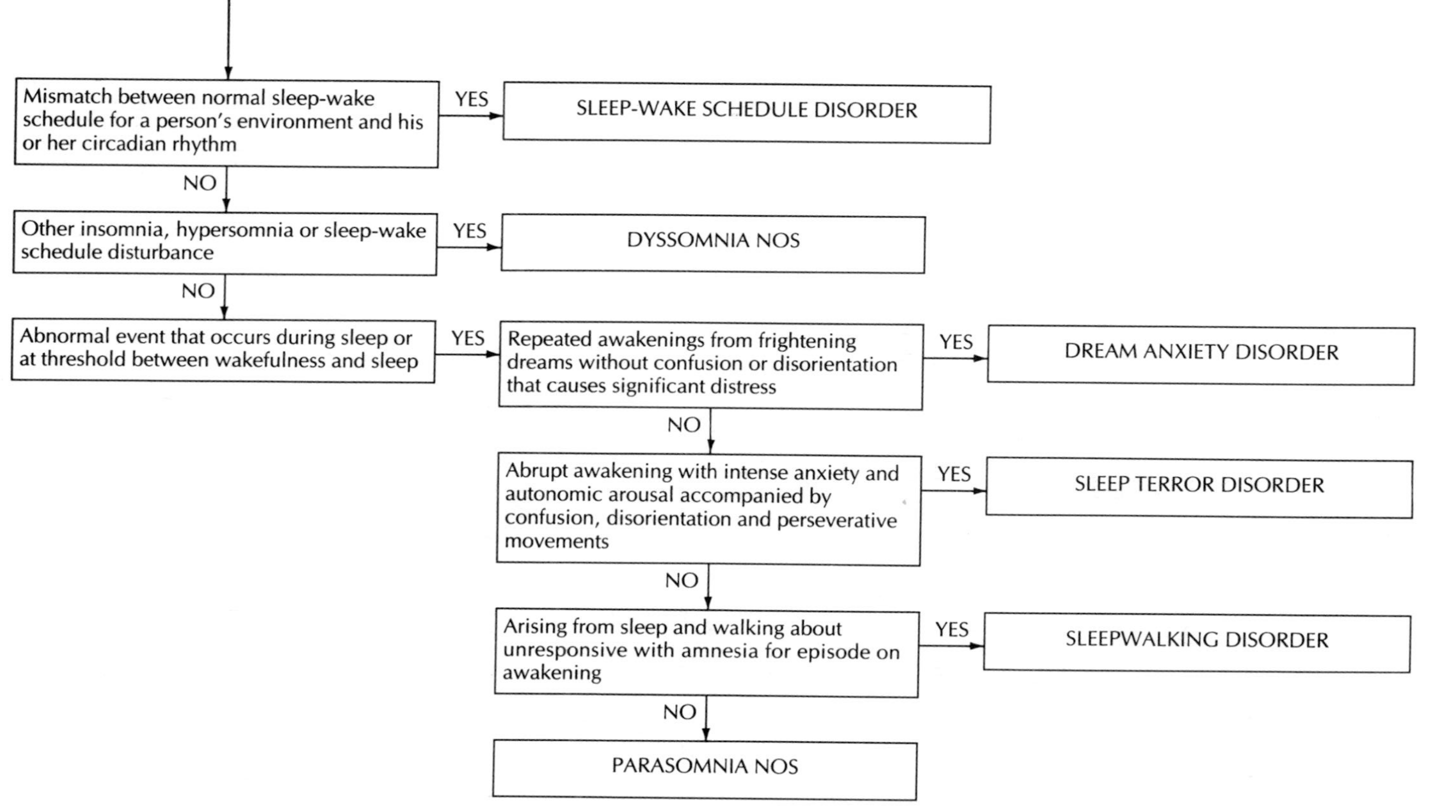
Mismatch between normal sleep-wake schedule for a person's environment and his or her circadian rhythm
YES
SLEEP-WAKE SCHEDULE DISORDER
NO
Other insomnia, hypersomnia or sleep-wake schedule disturbance
YES
DYSSOMNIA NOS
NO
Abnormal event that occurs during sleep or at threshold between wakefulness and sleep
YES
Repeated awakenings from frightening dreams without confusion or disorientation that causes significant distress
YES
DREAM ANXIETY DISORDER
NO
Abrupt awakening with intense anxiety and autonomic arousal accompanied by confusion, disorientation and perseverative movements
YES
SLEEP TERROR DISORDER
NO
Arising from sleep and walking about unresponsive with amnesia for episode on awakening
YES
SLEEPWALKING DISORDER
NO
PARASOMNIA NOS

diagnosed along with another Axis I disorder, even if symptomatic of that disorder, if the sleep disturbance is the predominant complaint.

Insomnia Disorders

The disorders in the insomnia cluster are primary insomnia, insomnia related to another mental disorder (nonorganic), and insomnia related to a known organic factor. In the first, the insomnia is unrelated to another mental disorder or to a known organic factor. The person constantly worries about not being able to fall asleep, makes intense efforts to fall asleep, and consequently gets into a pattern of apprehension and *increased* tension and arousal, falls asleep when not trying to, and sleeps well away from usual sleep environment. Sometimes the disturbance dates from early childhood, in other cases it begins when the person is under significant stress.

Insomnia related to another mental disorder (nonorganic) is the diagnosis to be used if the patient's chief complaint is insomnia and another mental disorder (except an organic mental disorder or a psychoactive substance use disorder) is the cause. Examples of the other mental disorders include depressive disorders, anxiety disorders, adjustment disorder, somatoform disorders, and personality disorders (43,44). Both the insomnia and the other mental disorder should be recorded on Axis I. (A personality disorder should be noted on Axis II.)

If insomnia is related to an organic factor, such as a physical illness, a psychoactive substance, or a medication, and it is the chief complaint, then insomnia related to a known organic factor is diagnosed. Examples of physical disorders that may cause insomnia are arthritis, angina, and Parkinson's disease. Insomnia-causing psychoactive substances include alcohol and amphetamines or other stimulants and examples of medications that may interfere with sleep are bronchodilators and decongestants. The physical disorder or medication should be noted on Axis III unless the medication use meets the criteria for a psychoactive substance use disorder or a psychoactive substance-induced organic mental disorder, in which cases the organic factor would be an additional Axis I diagnosis.

DSM-III-R was to include data obtainable from sleep laboratory procedures in its criteria for sleep disorders. In keeping with the convention of not referring to the results of specific laboratory tests in its diagnostic criteria, these data were deleted from the final DSM-III-R. Many diagnosticians of sleep disorders would require, for example, documentation of insomnia by polysomnographic evidence of sleep latency of more than 30 minutes or sleep efficiency of less than 85% in adults of average age (almost 10% of subjects complaining of insomnia have no significant objective evidence of sleep disturbance when studied). Furthermore, observations and testing in sleep laboratories have led to recognition of a number of precise sleep disturbance syndromes such as restless legs syndrome and sleep apnea, about which the patient may be unaware (45).

A recent study by Jacobs and associates (44) indicated that in nearly half of a consecutive series of 123 patients suffering from chronic insomnia who were evaluated with sleep laboratory studies, results of polysomnography led to some significant change in the clinical impression of the cause of the insomnia. The unexpected laboratory findings frequently were used to guide further diagnostic evaluation or to plan treatment. Several patients were unexpectedly found to have low REM density suggesting a central nervous system (CNS) illness and were referred for more comprehensive medical tests. In cases with depression, the failure to find shortened REM latency sometimes led to recommendations of nonpharmacologic treatment approaches. A number of patients were unexpectedly found to have nocturnal myoclonus suggesting treatment with benzodiazepines. A few cases of unsuspected sleep apnea were found, leading to pulmonary and ear, nose, and throat examinations and recommendation to avoid CNS-depressant drugs.

Currently, whether the added clinical utility of sleep laboratory studies justifies their great expense is a matter of controversy, except in the case of suspected sleep apnea (see below), which is associated with the greatest morbidity among the sleep disorders because of pulmonary and cardiovascular complications (46). Jacobs and her colleagues (44) suggest that polysomnography may also be indicated for patients whose insomnia has failed to respond to routine clinical interventions.

The following case is that of an elderly man with a variety of complaints, including insomnia.

Rx: Warm Milk

A 67-year-old, retired mailman was admitted to the hospital for evaluation of restlessness and agitation at night. His wife was at her wit's end because almost every night she was awakened by the patient's clumsily banging around their apartment. When she went to him, she described him as annoyed, restless, and agitated: "I can't sleep!" When she suggested that he try to get back into bed, he refused, "It won't do any good!" The wife was slowly becoming exhausted by these middle-of-the-night escapades. The man, on the other hand, took frequent daytime naps, which rested him somewhat.

The man had a 35-year history of bipolar disorder. When informed of the patient's insomnia, the psychiatrist added the drug Klonopin to the patient's lithium carbonate regimen, because he thought the man seemed to be becoming hypomanic. When the Klonopin did not effectively diminish the insomnia, the psychiatrist had the man admitted for a more complete evaluation. Prior to the sleep laboratory studies, a comprehensive mental status exam revealed a mild organic mental syndrome.

In the sleep laboratory, the man was observed to have periods of slow breathing during rapid eye movement (REM) sleep, but these did not always, or even frequently, coincide with his awakenings, which were more spontaneous. When he awoke, he appeared more confused than during the day. The laboratory technician encouraged him to go back to sleep. He said he "wasn't sleepy," but would promptly fall back to sleep. He dozed periodically during the day between the two nights of study. Some leg movements were observed during sleep, but were not regular enough to qualify as periodic movements in sleep (restless legs) or sufficient in number to be considered a significant contributing factor to the insomnia.

The diagnostic impression of the sleep disorders specialist was of a sleep/wake pattern associated with an organic mental syndrome that was worsened by medications and the pattern of irregular sleep habits the patient had developed.

Recommended treatment was to avoid hypnotics, institute a strict 12:00 midnight to 7:00 A.M. sleep (or in bed) schedule, increase daytime activities, and avoid daytime or evening dozing. It was recommended that if awake at night for more than 15-20 minutes, the patient get out of bed, have a glass of warm milk, read, and return to bed in half an hour. If not asleep within 15 minutes, he should again get out of bed and try sleeping after another half-hour. He was advised to sleep on his side to avoid the possible sleep disruption from REM hypoapneas he experienced when sleeping in a supine position.

Restless legs sleep disorder is characterized by a very unpleasant, deep sensation of "creeping" inside the calves when sitting or lying down. These dysesthesias are described as rarely painful, but agonizingly relentless, causing an irresistible urge to move the legs. The syndrome has been observed in association with diabetes, chronic venous insufficiency, uremic neuropathy, and other physical illnesses and occurs frequently among the elderly. The movements must be distinguished from the drug side effect akathisia in patients who are taking neuroleptic medications.

Table 8.5 presents the diagnostic criteria for the general subclass of insomnia disorders.

Hypersomnia Disorders

Among the hypersomnias are primary hypersomnia, hypersom-

Table 8.5 DSM-III-R Diagnostic Criteria for Insomnia Disorders

A. The predominant complaint is of difficulty in initiating or maintaining sleep, or of nonrestorative sleep (sleep that is apparently adequate in amount, but leaves the person feeling unrested).

B. The disturbance in A occurs at least three times a week for at least one month and is sufficiently severe to result in either a complaint of significant daytime fatigue or the observation by others of some symptom that is attributable to the sleep disturbance, e.g., irritability or impaired daytime functioning.

C. Occurrence not exclusively during the course of sleep-wake schedule disorder or a parasomnia.

nia related to another mental disorder, and hypersomnia related to a known organic factor.

In "Textbook Case," the woman complains of hypersomnia. An inability to get out of bed in the morning related to dysthymia seemed to be central to her functional impairment as she originally presented her complaints, and a diagnosis of hypersomnia related to another mental disorder may have been warranted. On the other hand, once viewed in the context of somatization disorder, I'm not sure that hypersomnia could be considered her predominant complaint. In such cases, no additional sleep disorder diagnosis should be made.

Narcolepsy is an example of an organic condition causing hypersomnia. It is characterized by daytime sleepiness, often with attacks of refreshing sleep. Clinical evidence of abnormal sleep is required, for example, cataplexy (episodic loss of muscle tone, triggered by strong emotions, that can result in falls), sleep paralysis (inability to move while falling asleep or upon sudden awakening), or hypnagogic or hypnopompic hallucinations. Sleep tests indicate repeated REM periods with very short latencies, usually within 10 minutes of sleep onset. Table 8.6 shows the general criteria for hypersomnia disorders.

Insomnia and hypersomnia disturbances. Some of the specific disturbances of sleep may actually cause insomnia and hypersomnia. For example, a syndrome known as myoclonic sleep disorder includes either insomnia or daytime sleepiness associated with polysomnographic evidence of repetitive and highly stereotyped leg muscle jerks that precede periods of arousal. The contractions have very specific characteristics in terms of frequency, duration, and periodicity. They may awaken the person either fully or partially. They may or may not occur in conjunction with sleep apnea.

Table 8.6 DSM-III-R Diagnostic Criteria for Hypersomnia Disorders

A. The predominant complaint is either (1) or (2):
   (1) excessive daytime sleepiness or sleep attacks not accounted for by an inadequate amount of sleep
   (2) prolonged transition to the fully awake state on awakening (sleep drunkenness)

B. The disturbance in A occurs nearly every day for at least one month, or episodically for longer periods of time, and is sufficiently severe to result in impaired occupational functioning or impairment in usual social activities or relationships with others.

C. Occurrence not exclusively during the course of sleep-wake schedule disorder.

Sleep apnea is another condition that disrupts sleep at night and then may lead to excessive sleepiness during the day. In sleep apnea, the polysomnograph reveals impaired air flow or arterial oxygen desaturation. The causes can be (*1*) cessation of air flow for 10 seconds or longer many times in spite of attempts to ventilate (obstructive sleep apnea), (*2*) cessation of air flow without ventilatory effort (nonobstructive or central sleep apnea), (*3*) multiple occurrences of reduced air flow with either partial obstruction or inadequate attempts to breathe (hypoventilation), (*4*) chronic obstructive pulmonary disease (COPD).

Insomnia and excessive daytime sleepiness can occur secondary to other physical disorders. The sleep disturbance is physiologically, not psychologically, related to the physical disorder — e.g., nocturnal dyspnea related to congestive heart failure causing insomnia and consequent daytime sleepiness.

DSM-III-R is not entirely clear about the correct diagnosis for a condition that causes both insomnia and hypersomnia. Presumably the diagnosis should be based on the patient's principal complaint. In its discussion of the differential diagnosis of insomnia disorders (9, p. 299), DSM-III-R appears to assume that daytime hypersomnia—related to sleep apnea or narcolepsy, for example—will bother the typical person more than nocturnal awakenings.

Sleep-Wake Schedule Disorders

There are three specific types of sleep-wake schedule disorder. People who suffer from insomnia or daytime sleepiness because of frequent changes in work shifts (i.e., daytime to night shift) or time zones (e.g., jet lag) are diagnosed as having sleep-wake schedule disorder, frequently changing type. People who do not follow a regular 24-hour sleep-wake schedule but take many naps and then do not sleep at night for any major length of time are diagnosed as having a sleep-wake schedule disorder, disorganized type. This diagnosis is not made if another disorder such as an insomnia disorder or a hypersomnia disorder causes the irregular sleep schedule. Advanced or delayed type sleep-wake schedule disorder is the diagnosis applied when the person's major daily sleep period has an onset and offset considerably advanced or delayed in relationship to what is desired. In these cases polysomnographs indicate no abnormality such as abnormal total sleep time or abnormal sleep architecture. Chronophysiologic measurements, such as body temperature and blood cortisol levels, reveal a phase delay or advance in the circadian rhythm that corresponds to the change in sleep pattern.

Parasomnias

Parasomnias are other disturbances of sleeping. Included in DSM-III-R are sleepwalking disorder and sleep terror disorder, both of which were in DSM-III, and a new diagnosis, dream anxiety disorder (nightmare disorder). The latter disorder is characterized by frequent nightmares from which the person awakens alert and oriented, in contrast to the confusion and disorientation of sleep terror disorder. Functional enuresis occurring at night is a parasomnia that is classified in DSM-III-R as a disorder of elimination in the major diagnostic class of disorders usually first evident in infancy, childhood, or adolescence.

Eating Disorders

Disturbances in eating are also included in the differential diagnosis of patients with psychological and physical complaints. Eating disorders are grouped in DSM-III and DSM-III-R in the large class of disorders usually first evident in infancy, childhood, or adolescence. The specific diagnostic categories of importance to the clinician who works with adult patients are anorexia nervosa, bulimia (now called bulimia nervosa), and a residual category, "eating disorder not otherwise specified." Problems in eating behavior often raise interesting and challenging issues of differential diagnosis, as the interview excerpts that make up the next clinical vignette illustrate.

Looking Good

"I'd been thinking about it for months," she said. "I haven't been happy since I was 12 years old. I just thought, 'Why bother with life, why go on?' My whole life was just going to work, going home, getting drunk, falling asleep. I thought about jumping off a bridge or out of a window; I tried to cut the arteries in my arms." She showed the scars to the doctor. "My parents didn't even notice them. Then I found the Dalmane. I took about 30 or 40 of them. My mother found me. I think I was awake, but I really didn't know what was happening. The next thing I knew, I was here."

"What made you so unhappy?" the doctor asked.

"Everything. I feel ugly. I think people are always making negative remarks—about my appearance. I sometimes get negative thoughts about them too—on a bus or the train—then I worry that they know it."

"Really?"

"Yes."

"Would you act differently on the basis of that?"

"Sometimes I go out of my way to be nice to someone that I had negative thoughts about or I avoid certain people."

"How often does this happen?"

"Oh, a few different times during the past year." She paused, then continued.

"I think people also think I'm fat. It's especially bad after I go on an eating binge."

"What's that like?"

"Sometimes I'll come home and I'll just start eating—cakes and pies, cookies, mostly sweets. I'll just keep eating until there's nothing left. It's like drinking. I guess you could say I have an addictive personality—once I start, I can't stop."

"Do you do anything to counteract the eating?"

"Oh yes, I've vomited. I've used laxatives."

"How much *do* you weigh?"

"Right now, 128."

"How tall are you?"

"Five-seven."

"Have you ever weighed much more?"

"Once I weighed 135."

"Do you consider yourself overweight now?"

"Yes."

"Have other people—boyfriends for instance, dates—told you that you're overweight?"

"The men I've been out with think I have a great body. That bothers me too. Then I think that's the only reason they go out with me."

"Have you ever weighed much less than you do now?"

"Three years ago. I weighed 103. I was in bad shape."

"At that time, were you afraid that you could become fat?"

"It's always been on my mind."

"But when you weighed 103, how do you think you looked? Did you still feel that you were too fat?"

"No, I was definitely too thin."
"What was going on then?"
"It was one of my depressed times. I was very depressed."
"How important is your physical appearance to you?"
"Very important. That's what's weird about it. I want to be attractive; I spend a lot of time trying to look good. I know I want people to notice me, but then when they do, I feel terrible."
"How often do you actually binge?"
"Maybe two or three times a month."

Anorexia Nervosa

The first task in the differential diagnosis of anorexia is to distinguish the anorexia that may be associated with a physical disorder or another mental disorder from anorexia nervosa. Patients with major depression may well respond positively to a screening question for anorexia nervosa such as the one included in the Structured Clinical Interview for DSM-III-R (47): "Have you ever had a time when you weighed much less than other people thought you ought to weigh?" Patients with psychotic disorders may also refuse to eat, and thus lose a great deal of weight. In these instances, obviously, weight loss is secondary to loss of appetite in the case of depression, or perhaps a delusion that food is poisoned in the case of a psychotic disorder (48), rather than due to the core disturbances in anorexia nervosa—an intense fear of becoming obese and a disturbance in body image, so that the person feels fat when underweight or even emaciated. The period of excessive weight loss described by the woman in "Looking Good" is undoubtedly related to her severe depressive episodes, not a symptom of anorexia nervosa.

The diagnostic criteria for anorexia nervosa do not exclude other mental disorders. In fact, coexisting major depression (49) and personality disorders, especially obsessive compulsive and borderline personality disorders, are common. It is necessary, however, that the core features of anorexia nervosa be present when these diagnoses are made jointly.

Several problems were encountered in the clinical application of DSM-III criteria for anorexia nervosa. For example, there is no consensus of opinion concerning the extent of weight loss necessary for the diagnosis. DSM-III required a weight loss of 25% of original body weight; but no studies have shown that patients with anorexia nervosa could be differentiated on any important clinical variables based on degree of weight loss. Many clinicians and investigators thought that 25% was too restrictive, so the DSM-III-R criteria (see Table 8.7) require only a 15% loss. In fact, the criteria now emphasize the more general requirement "Refusal to maintain body weight over a minimal normal weight for age and height. . . ."

Many investigators thought that a basic feature of anorexia nervosa was omitted from the DSM-III criteria—amenorrhea. Amenorrhea has been shown to precede significant weight loss in a substantial proportion of patients with anorexia nervosa. Similarly, after nutritional rehabilitation, weight returns to normal before the return of normal menstrual cycles (50,51). Anorexia nervosa patients whose weight is normal but who remain amenorrheic continue to show psychological disturbances compared with those with normal weight and menstruation (52).

All of these observations suggest that amenorrhea may be a primary disturbance in anorexia nervosa. The DSM-III-R criteria now require, in females, absence of at least three consecutive menstrual cycles that otherwise would be expected to occur. These can be missed after the onset of menstruation (secondary) or represent a delay in beginning menstruation (primary). Furthermore, DSM-III-R informs us that a woman is considered to have amenorrhea if her periods occur only following hormone (estrogen) administration. The requirement of amenorrhea will undoubtedly exclude a number of patients from receiving the diagnosis of anorexia nervosa. The diagnosis eating disorder NOS may still apply.

Another problem in diagnosis occurs when a particularly thin

Table 8.7 DSM-III-R Diagnostic Criteria for Anorexia Nervosa

A. Refusal to maintain body weight over a minimal normal weight for age and height, e.g., weight loss leading to maintenance of body weight 15% below that expected; or failure to make expected weight gain during period of growth, leading to body weight 15% below that expected.

B. Intense fear of gaining weight or becoming fat, even though underweight.

C. Disturbance in the way in which one's body weight, size, or shape is experienced, e.g., the person claims to "feel fat" even when emaciated, believes that one area of the body is "too fat" even when obviously underweight.

D. In females, absence of at least three consecutive menstrual cycles when otherwise expected to occur (primary or secondary amenorrhea). (A woman is considered to have amenorrhea if her periods occur only following hormone, e.g., estrogen, administration.)

young woman denies the behaviors and the classic ideas about her body and fatness that occur in anorexia nervosa. Expert clinicians such as Halmi (52) argue that a strong index of suspicion for anorexia nervosa should be raised when a thin young woman has leukopenia, a relative lymphocytosis, low fasting blood glucose, and elevated serum cholesterol.

Bulimia Nervosa

The major issues in differential diagnosis of bulimia are: (*1*) distinguishing the mental disorder bulimia from eating binges, (*2*) determining the relationship of bulimia nervosa to anorexia nervosa, and (*3*) recognizing commonly associated mental disorders.

Eating binges appear to be very common, especially in young women. Setting a lower diagnostic threshold for the mental disorder bulimia nervosa has not been a simple task. Some authors have argued (53) that specific eating and purging behaviors and frequency of binges may reduce the general population prevalence of persons with clinically significant bingeing by 15 times from the prevalence of people who simply report that they binge.

DSM-III criteria for bulimia included a number of descriptions of behaviors thought to characterize bulimic binge eating: consumption of high-caloric food, inconspicuous eating, particular ways in which binges ended, purging, and weight fluctuations as a result of binges and fasts. In addition, the criteria required that the food be consumed rapidly and that depressed mood follow the binge. Abraham and Beumont (54) reported that bingeing in the general population was not always rapid (could last over two hours), not always secretive, and sometimes was followed by relief rather than guilt or dysphoria. Several research groups (55-57) have indicated that the weight of bulimics is most often normal, but they have also pointed out that people with the disorder have a distorted belief or morbid sense of values about their weight. The patient in "Looking Good" is afraid that she is fat, even though she knows objectively that she is not.

The threshold for diagnosing an eating habit as an eating disorder should have clinical significance. One relevant question should be: "How much disruption or impairment does the behavior represent in the person's life?" Although follow-up studies of bulimia are rare, at least one study (58) points to the feeling of being out of control of one's eating behavior, the frequency of the binges, and the use of laxatives (and, secondarily, vomiting) for purging as predicting the most life impairment.

DSM-III-R criteria (see Table 8.8) now include a feeling of lack of control over eating as one of the requirements. A minimum of two

Table 8.8 DSM-III-R Diagnostic Criteria for Bulimia Nervosa

A. Recurrent episodes of binge eating (rapid consumption of a large amount of food in a discrete period of time).

B. A feeling of lack of control over eating behavior during the eating binges.

C. The person regularly engages in either self-induced vomiting, use of laxatives or diuretics, strict dieting or fasting, or vigorous exercise in order to prevent weight gain.

D. A minimum average of two binge eating episodes a week for at least three months.

E. Persistent overconcern with body shape and weight.

binge episodes per week for at least three months is also required. This frequency criterion is likely to have a dramatic effect in decreasing the applicability of the diagnosis of bulimia to binge eaters (59,60) and increasing the use of the residual category "eating disorder NOS." In "Looking Good," the woman clearly has bulimic-type eating binges, but they are too infrequent to meet the diagnostic criteria for bulimia nervosa. Finally, an "overconcern" with body shape and weight replaces actual weight fluctuations in the criteria, and depressed mood or self-deprecating thoughts are no longer required (see below for a discussion of the relationship of bulimia to mood disorders).

Bulimia nervosa vs. anorexia nervosa. In DSM-III, the diagnosis of bulimia was not made if the person had anorexia nervosa; binge eating was considered a possible associated symptom of the latter disorder. This distinction implied that there were two types of bulimia—one that occurred in normal-weight persons, and another that occurred in anorexic persons. The actual frequency with which bulimia and anorexia nervosa occur together is somewhat controversial, but most of the studies that have examined the subtype distinction (i.e., with or without anorexia nervosa) implied by DSM-III criteria have not found many significant differences between the types (55,61-63). More differences have been observed between persons with bulimia and those with so-called "restrictive" anorexia nervosa, who never binge. The DSM-III exclusion has been dropped so that, according to DSM-III-R, persons who meet the criteria for anorexia nervosa and bulimia nervosa can be given both diagnoses. Thus, the possibility exists for distinguishing three types of major eating disturbance:

anorexia nervosa alone (restrictive type), bulimia alone (normal weight), and the two syndromes occurring together (anorexia nervosa, bulimic type).

Bulimia nervosa and other disturbances. Many studies have pointed to a relationship between bulimia and mood disorders (64-68). In some cases the mood disorder precedes the eating disorder; in others, it co-occurs; and in still others, it follows, as if in reaction to the problems with eating. This association, plus the finding that mood disorders can be observed in the relatives of persons with eating disorders (69,70), especially if they themselves have a concurrent mood disorder (71), and the fact that bulimia appears responsive to antidepressant drugs (72), has led some investigators to postulate a causal relationship between the two types of disorder or a shared etiologic or pathogenic diathesis (73). Overeating secondary to depression does not warrant a diagnosis of bulimia nervosa; but in cases in which the full syndrome is present, the DSM-III and DSM-III-R convention of allowing more than one Axis I diagnosis to be made enables the clinician to track this potentially important clinical heterogeneity. In "Looking Good," the patient should receive diagnoses of both major depression and eating disorder NOS on Axis I. It may be that bulimia that responds to antidepressant drug therapy is the type associated with either a current or a lifetime mood disorder.

The second most common associated diagnosis in bulimia is a substance use disorder (64,65). Alcohol dependence seems very likely for the woman in "Looking Good." Kleptomania has also been reported (64), as have other, more general problems with adequate impulse control (63). These findings suggest that a careful assessment of the patient on Axis II is also warranted, and that borderline personality disorder might commonly be found. One research group (64,68) has also reported the co-occurrence of anxiety disorders and bulimia. Again, employing the DSM-III and DSM-III-R multiaxial systems, multiple diagnoses should be made.

Summary

In this chapter I have reviewed the differential diagnoses of mental disorders characterized by physical complaints. The numerous ways in which mental disorder and physical symptoms and illnesses can interact are discussed. The classes of disorders considered in detail are psychological factors affecting physical condition, factitious disorders or malingering, somatoform disorders, sexual dysfunctions, sleep disorders, and eating disorders.

This area of differential diagnosis is one of the most challenging to clinicians because of the ambiguities inherent in the diagnostic concepts and the limitations in our knowledge.

REFERENCES

1. Hyler SE, Spitzer RL: Hysteria split asunder. Am J Psychiatry 135:1500–1504, 1978
2. Looney JG, Lipp MR, Spitzer RL: A new method of classification for psychophysiologic disorders. Am J Psychiatry 135:304–308, 1978
3. Linn L, Spitzer RL: DSM-III. Implications for liaison psychiatry and psychosomatic medicine. JAMA 247:3207–3209, 1982
4. American Psychiatric Association: Diagnostic and Statistical Manual of Mental Disorders, Third Edition. Washington, DC, American Psychiatric Association, 1980
5. Willams JBW, Spitzer RL: DSM-III field trials: interrater reliability and list of project participants, in Diagnostic and Statistical Manual of Mental Disorders, Third Edition. Washington, DC, American Psychiatric Association, 1980
6. Leigh H, Price L, Ciarcia J, Mirassou MM: DSM-III and consultation-liaison psychiatry: toward a comprehensive medical model of the patient. Gen Hosp Psychiatry 4:283–289, 1982
7. Mackenzie TB, Popkin MK, Callies AL: Clinical applications of DSM-III in consultation-liaison psychiatry. Hosp Community Psychiatry 34:628–631, 1983
8. Popkin MK: Disorders with physical symptoms, in An Annotated Bibliography of DSM-III. Edited by Skodol AE, Spitzer RL. Washington, DC, American Psychiatric Press, 1987, pp 69–75
9. American Psychiatric Association: Diagnostic and Statistical Manual of Mental Disorders, Third Edition, Revised. Washington, DC, American Psychiatric Association, 1987
10. Perley M, Guze SB: Hysteria: the stability and usefulness of clinical criteria, a quantitative study based on a 6–8 year follow-up of 39 patients. N Engl J Med 266:421–426, 1962
11. Martin RL, Cloninger CR, Guze SB: The evaluation of diagnostic concordance in follow-up studies. II. A blind follow-up of female criminals. J Psychiatr Res 15:107–125, 1979
12. Cloninger CR, Reich T, Guze SB: The multifactorial model of disease transmission, III. Familial relationship between sociopathy and hysteria (Briquet's syndrome). Br J Psychiatry 127:23–32, 1975
13. Woerner PI, Guze SB: A family and marital study of hysteria. Br J Psychiatry 114:161–168, 1975
14. Cloninger CR, Martin RL, Guze SB, Clayton PJ: A prospective followup and family study of somatization in men and women. Am J Psychiatry 143:873–878, 1986.
15. Kendell RE: The choice of diagnostic criteria for biological research. Arch Gen Psychiatry 39:1334–1339, 1982
16. Katon W, Ries RK, Kleinman A: The prevalence of somatization in primary care. Compr Psychiatry 25:208–215, 1984
17. Escobar JI, Burnam MA, Karno M, Forsythe A, Golding JM: Somatization in the community. Arch Gen Psychiatry 44:713–718, 1987
18. Cloninger CR: Diagnosis of somatoform disorders: a critique of DSM-III,

in Diagnosis and Classification in Psychiatry. Edited by Tischler G. Cambridge, Cambridge University Press, 1987, pp 243–259
19. Robins LN, Helzer JE, Weissman MM, Orvaschel H, Gruenberg E, Burke JD Jr, Regier DA: Lifetime prevalence of specific psychiatric disorders in three sites. Arch Gen Psychiatry 41:949–958, 1984
20. Myers JK, Weissman MM, Tischler GL, Holzer CE 3d, Leaf PJ, Orvaschel H, Anthony JC, Boyd JH, Burke JD Jr, Kramer M, Stoltzman R: Six-month prevalence of psychiatric disorders in three communities: 1980 to 1982. Arch Gen Psychiatry 41:959–967, 1984
21. Helzer JE, Robins LN, McEvoy LT, Spitznagel EL, Stoltzman RK, Farmer A, Brockington IF: A comparison of clinical and diagnostic interview schedule diagnoses: physician reexamination of lay-interviewed cases in the general population. Arch Gen Psychiatry 42:657–666, 1985
22. Sigvardsson S, von Knorring AL, Bohman M, Cloninger CR: An adoption study of somatoform disorders. I. The relationship of somatization to psychiatric disability. Arch Gen Psychiatry 41:853–859, 1984
23. Cloninger CR, Sigvardsson S, von Knorring AL, Bohman M: An adoption study of somatoform disorders. II. Identification of two discrete somatoform disorders. Arch Gen Psychiatry 41:863–871, 1984
24. Liskow B, Othmer E, Penick EC, DeSouza C, Gabrielli W: Is Briquet's syndrome a heterogeneous disorder? Am J Psychiatry 143:626–629, 1986
25. Othmer E, DeSouza C: A screening test for somatization disorder (hysteria). Am J Psychiatry 142:1146–1149, 1985
26. Gatfield PD, Guze SB: Prognosis and differential diagnosis of conversion reactions (A follow-up study). Dist Nerv Syst 23:1–8, 1962
27. Slater E: Diagnosis of hysteria. Br Med J 1:1395–1399, 1965
28. Raskin M, Talbott JA, Meyerson AT: Diagnosis of conversion reactions: predictive value of psychiatric criteria. JAMA 197:102–106, 1966
29. Hendler N, Uematesu S, Long D: Thermographic validation of physical complaints in "psychogenic pain" patients. Psychosomatics 23:283–287, 1982
30. Blumer D, Heilbronn M: Chronic pain as a variant of depressive disease: the pain-prone disorder. J Nerv Ment Dis 170:381–406, 1982
31. Williams JBW, Spitzer RL: Idiopathic pain disorder: a critique of pain-prone disorder and a proposal for a revision of the DSM-III category psychogenic pain disorder. J Nerv Ment Dis 170:415–419, 1982
32. Kenyon FE: Hypochondriacal states. Br J Psychiatry 129:1–14, 1976
33. Bianchi GN: Patterns of hypochondriasis: a principal components analysis. Br J Psychiatry 122:541–548, 1973
34. Barsky AJ, Klerman GL: Overview: hypochondriasis, bodily complaints, and somatic styles. Am J Psychiatry 140:273–283, 1983
35. Kellner R: Functional somatic symptoms and hypochondriasis. A survey of empirical studies. Arch Gen Psychiatry 42:821–833, 1985
36. Bishop ER Jr: Monosymptomatic hypochondriasis. Psychosomatics 21:731–747, 1980
37. Benkert O, Maier W, Holsboer F: Multiaxial classification of male sexual dysfunction. Br J Psychiatry 142:342–345, 1985
38. Schover LR, Friedman JM, Weiler SJ, Heiman JR, LoPiccolo J: Multiaxial problem-oriented system for sexual dysfunctions: an alternative to DSM-III. Arch Gen Psychiatry 39:614–619, 1982
39. Bixler EO, Kales A, Soldatos CR: Sleep disorders encountered in medical practice: a national survey of physicians. Behav Med 6:1–6, 1979
40. Berlin RM, Litvovitz GL, Diaz MA: Sleep disorders on a psychiatric

consultation service. Am J Psychiatry 141:582–584, 1984
41. Sleep Disorders Classification Committee, Association of Sleep Disorders Centers: Diagnostic classification of sleep and arousal disorders. Sleep 2:5–137, 1979
42. Kales A, Soldatos CR, Kales JD: Taking a sleep history. Am Fam Physician 22:101–108, 1980
43. Tan TL, Kales JD, Kales A, Soldatos CR, Bixler EO: Biopsychobehavioral correlates of insomnia, IV: diagnosis based on DSM-III. Am J Psychiatry 141:357–362, 1984
44. Jacobs EA, Reynolds CF III, Kupfer DJ, Lovin PA, Ehrenpreis AB: The role of polysomnography in the differential diagnosis of chronic insomnia. Am J Psychiatry 145:346–349, 1988
45. Coleman RM, Roffwarg HP, Kennedy SJ, Guilleminault C, Cinque J, Cohn MA, Karacan I, Kupfer DJ, Lemmi H, Miles LE, Orr WC, Phillips ER, Roth T, Sassin JF, Schmidt HS, Weitzman ED, Dement WC: Sleep-wake disorders based on a polysomnographic diagnosis: a national collaborative study. JAMA 247:997–1003, 1982
46. Kales A, Vela-Bueno A, Kales JD: Sleep disorders: sleep apnea and narcolepsy. Ann Intern Med 106:434–443, 1987
47. Spitzer RL, Williams JBW, Gibbon M: Structured Clinical Interview for DSM-III-R—Patient Version (SCID-P). New York, Biometrics Research, NY State Psychiatric Institute, 1987
48. Lyketsos GC, Paterakis P, Beis A, Lyketsos CG: Eating disorders in schizophrenia. Br J Psychiatry 146:255–261, 1985
49. Herzog DB: Are anorexic and bulimic patients depressed? Am J Psychiatry 141:1594–1597, 1984
50. Hsu LKG: Outcome of anorexia nervosa: a review of the literature (1954-1978). Arch Gen Psychiatry 37:1041–1046, 1980
51. Hall A, Slim E, Hawker F, Salmond C: Anorexia nervosa: long-term outcome in 50 female patients. Br J Psychiatry 145:407–413, 1984
52. Halmi KA: The state of research in anorexia nervosa and bulimia. Psychiatr Dev 1:247–262, 1983
53. Healy K, Conroy RM, Walsh N: The prevalence of binge-eating and bulimia in 1063 college students. J Psychiatr Res 19:161–166, 1985
54. Abraham SF, Beumont PJV: How patients describe bulimia or binge eating. Psychol Med 12:625–635, 1982
55. Halmi KA, Falk JR, Schwartz E: Binge-eating and vomiting: a survey of a college population. Psychol Med 11:697–706, 1981
56. Fairburn CG, Cooper PJ: The clinical features of bulimia nervosa. Br J Psychiatry 144:238–246, 1984
57. Mitchell JE, Hatsukami D, Eckert ED, Pyle RL: Characteristics of 275 patients with bulimia. Am J Psychiatry 142:482–485, 1985
58. Johnson CL, Love SQ: Bulimia: multivariate predictors of life impairment. J Psychiatr Res 19:343–347, 1985.
59. Yager J, Landsverk J, Edelstein CK: A 20-month follow-up study of 628 women with eating disorders, I: course and severity. Am J Psychiatry 144:1172–1177, 1987
60. Drewnowski A, Yee DK, Krahn DD: Bulimia in college women: incidence and recovery rates. Am J Psychiatry 145:753–755, 1988
61. Herzog DB, Norman DK: Subtyping eating disorders. Compr Psychiatry 26:375–380, 1985
62. Garner DM, Olmsted MP, Garfinkel PE: Similarities among bulimic groups selected by different weights and weight histories. J Psychiatr Res 19:129–134, 1985

63. Garner DM, Garfinkel PE, O'Shaughnessy M: The validity of the distinction between bulimia with and without anorexia nervosa. Am J Psychiatry 142:581–587, 1985
64. Hudson JI, Pope HG Jr, Jonas JM, Yurgelun-Todd D: Phenomenologic relationship of eating disorders to major affective disorder. Psychiatry Res 9:345–354, 1983
65. Hatsukami D, Eckert E, Mitchell JE, Pyle R: Affective disorder and substance abuse in women with bulimia. Psychol Med 14:701–704, 1984
66. Swift WJ, Kalin NH, Wamboldt FS, Kaslow N, Ritholz M: Depression in bulimia at 2- to 5-year followup. Psychiatry Res 16:111–122, 1985
67. Walsh BT, Roose SP, Glassman AH, Gladis M, Sadik C: Bulimia and depression. Psychosom Med 47:123–131, 1985
68. Hudson JI, Pope HG Jr, Yurgelun-Todd D, Jonas JM, Frankenburg FR: A controlled study of lifetime prevalence of affective and other disorders in bulimic outpatients. Am J Psychiatry 144:1283–1287, 1987
69. Hudson JI, Pope HG Jr, Jonas JM, Yurgelun-Todd D: Family history study of anorexia nervosa and bulimia. Br J Psychiatry 142:133–138, 1983
70. Stern SL, Dixon KN, Nemzer E, Lake MD, Sansone RA, Smeltzer DJ, Lantz S, Schrier SS: Affective disorder in the famiiles of women with normal weight bulimia. Am J Psychiatry 141:1224–1227, 1984
71. Biederman J, Rivinus T, Kemper K, Hamilton D, Macfadyen J, Harmatz J: Depressive disorders in relatives of anorexia nervosa patients with and without a current episode of nonbipolar major depression. Am J Psychiatry 142:1495–1496, 1985
72. Walsh BT, Gladis M, Roose SP, Stewart JW, Stetner F, Glassman AH: Phenelzine vs placebo in 50 patients with bulimia. Arch Gen Psychiatry 45:471–475, 1988
73. Swift WJ, Andrews D, Barklage NE: The relationship between affective disorder and eating disorders: a review of literature. Am J Psychiatry 143:290–299, 1986

CHAPTER 9

Personality Disturbances

Personality disorders (PDs) were defined in DSM-III as "enduring patterns of perceiving, relating to, and thinking about the environment and oneself . . . exhibited in a wide range of important social and personal contexts" that were "inflexible and maladaptive and caused significant impairment in social or occupational functioning or subjective distress" (1, p. 305). Before the appearance of DSM-III, personality disorders were of interest primarily to certain groups of therapists involved in long-term, psychodynamic psychotherapy; since publication of DSM-III, however, personality disorders have become the focus of increased interest in a wide range of clinical and research settings. If affective disorders were the "disorders of the '70s" (see Chapter 6) and anxiety disorders are the "disorders of the '80s" (see Chapter 7), then personality disorders may well be the "disorders of the '90s."

Focus on personality disorders has been facilitated by DSM-III's multiaxial approach to evaluation (see Chapter 2), which places them on a separate axis, Axis II, from the majority of clinical syndromes. DSM-III listed personality disorders on Axis II specifically to ensure that "consideration is given to the possible presence of disorders that are frequently overlooked when attention is directed to the usually more florid Axis I disorder" (1, p. 23). Furthermore, there is a growing appreciation of the clinical importance of personality disorders in their own right. Interactions between Axis I and Axis II disorders have been observed, e.g., the presence of personality disorder may adversely affect the course of an Axis I disorder (2-6). Also, many people who use mental health services do not have any of the major Axis I disorders (7), which suggests the possibility that such patients seek treatment for problems stemming from personality disorders.

Although the multiaxial system has succeeded in bringing personality disorders into focus, the other major DSM-III innovation, diagnosis by specified criteria, has not had the same salutory effect on the reliability of diagnosis of personality disorder as it has had on that of many of the Axis I disorders. Diagnosis of personality disorder, even using DSM-III, continues to suffer from relatively low levels of reliability (8,9), a fault that has been traced to a number of specific problems, the majority of which will be discussed in this chapter.

GENERAL PROBLEMS IN DIFFERENTIAL DIAGNOSIS OF PERSONALITY DISORDERS

Many of the problems in the differential diagnosis of personality disorders apply to the entire class of disorders and thus can be discussed together. Problems specific to individual personality disorder categories will be described later in this chapter.

Interviewing Problems

One particular problem in evaluating a patient for a personality disorder arises from the fact that most people are not able to view their own personality characteristics objectively. Since personality is, by definition, the way the person sees, relates to, and thinks about himself or herself and the environment, a person's assessment of his or her own personality must be colored by it. This is not to say that the expression of Axis I psychopathology may not also be colored by Axis II personality style, e.g., symptoms exaggerated by the histrionic or minimized by the compulsive personality; but the symptoms of Axis I disorders are usually more clearly alien to the patient and more easily identified as problematic. People usually learn about their own problem behavior and patterns of interaction with others through the reactions or observations of other people in their environment.

Clinicians have traditionally not conducted the same kind of interview in assessing personality disturbance as they do with persons suspected of having a mood or an anxiety disorder. Rather than directly questioning the patient about characteristics of his or her personality, the clinician, assuming that the patient cannot accurately describe these traits, looks for patterns in the way the person describes social relations and work functioning. These two areas usually give the clearest picture of personality style in general, and personality problems specifically. Clinicians have also relied heavily on their observations of how patients interact with them during an evaluation interview or in treatment as manifestations of their patients' personalities.

These approaches have the advantage of circumventing the lack of objectivity patients might have about their personalities, but they also create differential diagnostic problems. The clinician usually comes away with a global impression of the patient's personality, but frequently is not aware of many of that patient's specific personality characteristics because he or she has not made a systematic assessment of symptoms of the wide range of personality disorders. I have found (10) that, in using DSM-III, clinicians limit their Axis II assessments to one, or at most two, diagnostic types when, in fact, clinical experience and research indicate that the overlapping nature of many of the personality disorders makes multiple Axis II diagnoses very common (11).

Reliance on interaction with the therapist for personality diagnosis runs the risk of assuming the generalizability of a mode of interpersonal relating that may be limited to a particular situation or context. Although the interaction of patient and therapist can be a useful and objective observation, caution should be used in interpreting its significance, and attempts must be made to integrate this bit of information into a broader, overall picture of patient functioning.

Structured assessment. In psychiatric research, a portion of the poor reliability of personality disorder diagnosis has been assumed to be due to the variance in information resulting from unsystematic assessment of personality traits. Therefore, efforts have been made to develop various structured methods for assessing PDs comparable with those, such as the Schedule for Affective Disorders and Schizophrenia (SADS), that have been successful in reducing information variance in assessing Axis I disorders. These methods include both self-report measures, such as the Personality Disorders Questionnaire (PDQ) (12) and the Millon Clinical Multiaxial Inventory (MCMI) (13), and clinical interviews, such as the Structured Interview for Disorders of Personality (SIDP) (14), the Personality Disorder Examination (PDE) (15), and the Structured Clinical Interview for DSM-III-R, Axis II (SCID-II) (16).

The interviews are all based on the general premise that the patient can be asked specific questions that will indicate the presence or absence of each of the criteria of each of the 11 DSM-III or DSM-III-R personality disorder types. The self-report instruments are generally considered to require more testing because of a very high rate of apparently false-positive responses, but initial data from studies comparing self-report measures with clinical interviews suggest that the former aid in identification of personality disturbances (17). What this means for the clinician is that patients do not necessarily deny negative personality attributes: in fact, the evidence suggests that they may even overreport traits that clinicians might not think are very important, and that they can, if asked, consistently describe a wide range of personality traits to multiple interviewers.

Consistency of personality disorder diagnoses (i.e., reliability findings) does not necessarily mean that people diagnosed as having personality disorders have clinically significant, i.e., valid, disturbances, however. Testing the validity of personality disorder diagnoses is in its infancy. I should, in any case, recommend careful and systematic questioning about the full range of DSM-III personality disorders in order to obtain the richest diagnostic description on Axis II (see also below the discussion of Personality Traits vs. Personality Disorders).

Assessing pervasiveness. As mentioned above, for a personality disorder to be significant, the disturbances have to be manifest frequently over a wide range of behaviors, feelings, and perceptions and in many different contexts. Pervasiveness is very difficult to determine, however. When the clinician inquires if a person "often" has a particular experience, the patient will frequently reply "sometimes," which then has to be judged for clinical significance. Some behaviors such as "self-mutilating behavior" (borderline personality disorder) may be significant at frequencies much lower than other behaviors such as "overconcern with physical attractiveness" (histrionic personality disorder). What constitutes a necessary frequency for a particular trait or behavior has not been well worked out, and clinicians are forced to rely on their own judgment, keeping in mind that maladaptivity and inflexibility are hallmarks of traits that are pathological (see also below).

In DSM-III-R, attempts have been made to stress the pervasiveness of the behaviors caused by personality disorders. Added to the basic definition of each personality disorder, serving as the "stem" to which individual features apply, is the phrase "present in a variety of contexts." For example, the criteria for paranoid personality disorder in DSM-III-R begin: "A pervasive and unwarranted tendency, beginning by early adulthood and present in a variety of contexts, to interpret the actions of people as deliberately demeaning or threatening, as indicated by at least four of the following:" (18, p. 339). Similarly, for passive aggressive personality disorder, the criteria start with: "A pervasive pattern of passive resistance to demands for adequate social and occupational performance, beginning by early adulthood and present in a variety of contexts, as indicated by at least five of the following:" (18, p. 357).

For the clinician interviewing a patient with a possible personality disorder, this means that data about many areas of functioning, interpersonal relationships with people interacting in different social roles with the patient, and the nature of the patient/therapist relationship should be integrated into a comprehensive assessment of pervasiveness. Too often clinicians place disproportionate importance on a patient's functioning on a particular job or with a particular boss or significant other person. The following case vignette illustrates role-specific behavior that, on close examination, does not correspond to a pervasive pattern.

The Fellow

A 29-year-old postdoctoral fellow in neurobiology requested a consultation with a psychiatrist because of problems he was having in his program. The professor under whom he was working had recently told him that he was unhappy with the fellow's work. The professor had complained that the fellow was "not making enough progress" and "seemed to lack initiative." He wondered whether the young man was "really sure he wanted to be a scientist."

The psychiatrist asked the man how the work seemed from his point of view. "First, I must tell you, this has me very upset. Nothing quite like this has ever happened to me. That's why I'm here." The fellow went on to describe a long-standing interest in biology and a fascination with the recent advances in neurobiology. His boss was a well-known senior scientist in the field, and the fellow felt fortunate to be selected to work in his lab, but the experience itself had been somewhat disappointing. Although the professor on many occasions asked for his assistance on a particular project that he was working on, it was very difficult for the fellow to get advice or direction from the professor on his own independent projects. "It's as if he can only get excited about what *he* is interested in; if it's not something that he cares about, then forget it. You'll be talking to him, and he'll look like he's falling asleep," the fellow said, obviously irritated.

The professor expected the fellow to do a certain amount of work on the lab's major projects, but also encouraged fellows to do their independent work. As the months went by, the fellow admitted that he was spending less time on the professor's projects and more time on his own, which were, according to the fellow, producing some interesting results. "I'm sure when he says I'm not making enough progress, he means on his things. Since he doesn't pay any attention to my stuff, it doesn't count as a sign of productivity in his eyes."

A past personal history taken by the psychiatrist indicated that the fellow had always been a successful student at prestigious schools. After gaining his doctorate, he had several fellowship positions from which to choose. He was happily married, and had a two-year-old child to whom he was very devoted and many friends. He was an avid runner, downhill skier, and tennis player. His only problems with people other than his boss that he was aware of were that his wife thought he "worked too hard" and several old friends had commented that he had become "too serious" since he was married.

The fellow has problems with his boss. He feels unjustly criticized for his lack of productivity at work and upset that his boss expects him to do more. He believes that his boss is not helping him, but rather is using him to further his own ends. He admits that he has been doing less of what the boss expects. He feels that the work he is doing is not being appreciated because it is not high on the professor's list of priorities.

The combination of not working up to the standards of his boss, feeling that the demands being made on him are unreasonable, becoming irritated by the expectations his boss has of him, feeling underrated, and criticizing the job the professor is doing as his mentor all may suggest a passive aggressive personality style or disorder (see also below). At the point of the evaluation, however, there is no clear evidence that this is a generalized pattern of behavior for the fellow. On the contrary, the young man appears to function more than adequately as a husband, father, and friend and has enjoyed academic success. His problems with his current boss are so out of the ordinary that they led him to seek help. They seem situation-specific, and therefore cannot be taken as evidence of a personality disorder.

Use of informants. Frequently, a patient with a personality disorder consults a mental health professional for evaluation or treatment because another person in his or her environment has found his or her behavior problematic. This may be a boss, spouse, boyfriend or girlfriend, teacher, parent, or representative of a social agency. Indeed, some people with personality disorders do not even recognize the problematic aspects of their manner of relating or perceiving except as it has a negative effect on someone with whom they interact.

Because of these "blind spots" that people with PD may have, the use of a third-party informant in the evaluation can be critical (19). In some treatment settings, such as a psychoanalytic clinic, it may be considered counterproductive or contraindicated to include a third party, but in most inpatient and outpatient settings, certainly during the evaluation process, it is appropriate and desirable to see some person close to the patient to corroborate both the patient's report and one's own clinical impressions. Of course, there is no reason to assume that the informant is bias-free or not coloring a report about the patient with his or her own personality style, so the clinician must make a judgment about the objectivity of the informant and use this as a part, but not a sufficient part, of the overall data on which to base a personality disorder diagnosis (20).

State vs. Trait

A major issue that cuts across all personality disorder diagnoses and presents considerable practical problems in differential diagnosis is the distinction between personality trait and clinical state. Personality is an enduring aspect of an individual, yet assessment of personality ordinarily takes place cross-sectionally, i.e., over a brief interval in time. Thus, the clinician is challenged to separate out certain long-term dispositions of the patient from other more immediate or situationally determined characteristics. This task is more often than not complicated by the fact that the patient comes for evaluation when there is some particularly acute problem, which may be a social or job-related crisis or may even be the onset of an Axis I disorder (see also below). In either case, the situation in which the patient is being evaluated is frequently a state that is not completely characteristic of the patient's life over the longer run.

DSM-III and DSM-III-R both indicate that personality disorders are characteristics of a person's long-term functioning and are not limited to episodes of illness. Determining these features in practice is not easy. First of all, an accurate assessment requires recognition of current state. This, in turn, includes knowledge of the circumstances that have prompted the person to seek treatment, their consequences in terms of his or her decision to seek treatment, the current level of stress, and any actual Axis I psychopathology, if present.

The DSM-III and DSM-III-R multiaxial systems (see also Chapter 2) are of considerable aid in the assessment of these problems because of their separation of Axis I disorders from Axis II disorders and their individual axes for physical disorders, psychosocial stressors, and adaptive functioning. A multiaxial system forces clinicians to think about the effects of aspects of patients' current state on long-term patterns of behavior, but it does not make the distinctions for them.

Assessing an enduring pattern. It was not clear from the diagnostic criteria of DSM-III how long a pattern of personality disturbance needed to be present, or when it should become evident, for a personality disorder to be diagnosed. DSM-III stated that patients were usually 18 years of age or older because it could be argued that, up to that age, a personality pattern could neither have been manifest long enough nor have become significantly entrenched to be considered a stable constellation of behavior; it also stated, however, that some manifestations of personality disorder were usually recognizable by adolescence or earlier.

When patients are under 18 and show signs of certain of the personality disorders, clinicians have the option of diagnosing one of several corresponding disorders from the DSM-III and DSM-III-R sections of disorders usually first evident in infancy, childhood, or adolescence. According to DSM-III, a teenager with no interest or pleasure in friends might have been diagnosed schizoid disorder of childhood or adolescence rather than schizoid personality disorder; a condition characterized by generalized resistance toward authority figures was called oppositional rather than passive aggressive personality disorder.

Schizoid disorder of childhood or adolescence was deleted from the DSM-III-R classification because it is now believed that a defect in the capacity to form social relationships among children or adolescents is seen only in association with more serious psychopathology, such as a pervasive developmental disorder. Although the oppositional/passive aggressive personality disorder connection is not listed in the DSM-III-R introduction to personality disorders, the discussion of the differential diagnosis on page 357 of the manual (18) indicates that DSM-III-R oppositional defiant disorder continues to preempt a diagnosis of passive aggressive personality disorder if the person is under 18.

Other childhood or adolescent disorders corresponding to Axis II disorders are avoidant disorder of childhood or adolescence (avoidant PD), conduct disorder (antisocial PD), and identity disorder (borderline PD). It is important to note that the clinician does have the option of diagnosing a personality disorder in an adolescent in those unusual instances in which particular maladaptive personality traits appear to be stable.

Regarding the course of a personality disorder, DSM-III and DSM-III-R state that they persist throughout most of adult life, although certain of them may become somewhat attenuated by middle or old age. This means that the features of personality disorders should be stable over time: in fact, stability has been used by research investigators to validate personality disorder categories (21,22).

To assess stability retrospectively, the clinician must ask questions about periods of a person's life that are of various degrees of remoteness from the current situation. Retrospective reporting is always subject to distortion, however, and the only sure way of demonstrating stability over time is therefore to do prospective, follow-up evaluations. From a practical, clinical, point of view, this would mean that personality disorder diagnoses made cross-sectionally and on the basis of retrospectively collected data would be tentative or provisional pending confirmation by longitudinal evaluation. On an inpatient service, three or four months of intense observation by many professionals from diverse perspectives may suffice to establish a pattern over time (23). In a typical outpatient setting, with much less frequent encounters with a patient, more time may be required. Ideally, features of a personality disorder should be evident over years, but it is not practical to delay inordinate amounts of time before coming to a diagnostic conclusion. A good retrospective history *confirmed* by a period of several months of prospective evaluation, should make the personality pattern evident.

One additional question that has been asked is whether DSM-III personality disorders were required to be present at the time of the evaluation. Considering the room for error inherent in an attempt to document a longitudinal pattern, one should certainly be able to discern current features.

Assessing the effect of Axis I disorder. There are several ways in which an Axis I disorder can complicate the diagnosis of a personality disorder. An Axis I disorder may cause changes in a person's behavior or attitudes that can appear to be signs of a personality disorder. Depression, for example, may cause a person to seem excessively dependent, avoidant, self-defeating, or resistant (as in passive aggressive personality disorder). Cyclothymia or bipolar disorder (NOS) (bipolar II) may lead to periods of grandiosity, impulsivity, poor judgment, and depression, which might be confused with manifestations of narcissistic or borderline personality disorders.

The clinician must be aware of the Axis I psychopathology and attempt to assess Axis II independently. This can be attempted in one of two ways. First, the clinician can ask about aspects of personality functioning at times when the patient is not experiencing Axis I symptoms. This is feasible when the Axis I disorder is of recent onset and short duration or, if more chronic, if the course of the disorder has been characterized by relatively clear-cut episodes with complete remission and symptom-free periods of long duration. When the Axis I disorder is chronic and unremitting, then the Axis I psychopathology and personality functioning blend together to an extent that makes differentiating between them clearly artificial.

A second approach to distinguishing signs of Axis I pathology from signs of Axis II personality is longitudinal, and would defer an Axis II diagnosis pending the outcome of a trial of treatment for the Axis I disorder. This may be the preferred approach in the case of a long-standing and chronic Axis I disorder, like cyclothymia, which has never been previously recognized or treated. Although one always runs the risk of a partial response to treatment and some residual symptoms, this tactic may bring the clinician as close, practically speaking, as he or she will get to observing the patient's baseline functioning.

The following case vignette demonstrates the difficulty of diagnosing Axis II personality disorders in a patient with a chronic mood disorder.

Taxi Driver

A 24-year-old, unemployed man sought psychiatric hospitalization because of a serious problem with depression. The man reported that he had felt mildly, but continuously, depressed since the age of 16. When he reached his twenties, he had begun to suffer from more severe bouts, which made him unable to function and suicidal.

During the most recent episode, beginning about six months previously, he had quit his job as a taxi driver and isolated himself from his friends. He spent his time "lying around and eating a lot" and, in fact, had gained 60 pounds. He had difficulty falling asleep, felt fatigued all day long, could not concentrate, felt worthless ("There's no purpose to my life") and guilty ("I missed my chances; I've put my family through hell") and had taken an overdose of sleeping pills.

The man received a structured assessment of Axis II psychopathology. In describing his personality, he said that he once thought of himself as lively and good-natured, but that over the past four or five years, he felt he had changed. He said that he was very sensitive to criticism, afraid to get involved with people, fearful of new places and experiences, convinced he was making a fool of himself, and afraid of losing control. He felt very dependent on others for decision making and for initiative. He said that he was so "needy" of others that they "could do anything" to him and he would "take it." He felt helpless when alone, was sure he would end up "alone and in the streets," and was constantly looking to others, especially family members, for comfort and reassurance.

The man also thought that people took advantage of him now, but also that he "let them" because he never stood up for his own self-interest. He felt like a total failure, with no redeeming virtues. He said he either deliberately passed up opportunities to improve his situation because he felt "I don't deserve any better" or else undermined himself "without thinking" by failing to follow through, for example, on a job interview. He believed that no one could really be trusted, that old friends probably talked about him behind his back ("They think I'm a slob"), that he could not open up with new people because they, too, would eventually turn on him and reject him, and that he now carried a chip on his shoulder because he had been "burned" by others so often. He admitted that he was not blame-free in relationships because he had also used people, especially members of his family.

The patient felt that he was not improving in his outpatient treatment of the last three years. His reason for seeking hospitalization, in addition to the fact that he continually thought of suicide and was frightened he might actually succeed in killing himself, was that he felt "totally lost" in his life, without direction, goals, or knowing what mattered to him. He said he felt "hollow." "If they cut me open after I was dead," he said, "they'd probably find out I was all shriveled up inside."

The "Taxi Driver's" description of his "personality," the ways in which he characteristically thought about himself, saw others and his relationships to them, and behaved, actually met DSM-III-R criteria for avoidant, dependent, paranoid, borderline, and self-defeating personality disorders. He was hospitalized for long-term treatment. In addition to receiving individual, psychoanalytically oriented psychotherapy sessions and participating in a variety of therapeutic groups, he was given phenelzine, up to 90 mg/day, for treatment of Axis I major depression and dysthymia.

Six months after admission, the patient reported that he felt significantly less depressed. Measured in terms of the Hamilton Rating Scale for Depression (HAM-D), his initial severity of depression score was 30 and his post-treatment score was 10. A repeat structured assessment of his personality functioning revealed that he no longer met DSM-III-R criteria for any personality disorder, although he continued to exhibit some dependent and self-defeating traits.

Another example of the way in which Axes I and II interact to obscure differential diagnosis is the case of apparent Axis II psychopathology that, in fact, represents the prodrome of an Axis I disorder. This is a particularly hard problem in terms of distinguishing personality disorders, such as paranoid, schizoid, and schizotypal from the early signs of Axis I disorders in the delusional, schizophrenic, and psychotic disorders NOS classes. If a clinician is evaluating a patient early in the course of the initial onset of a psychotic disorder, he or she may be confronted with *changes* in the person toward increasing suspiciousness, social withdrawal, eccentricity, or reduced functioning. Since, in DSM-III and DSM-III-R, the diagnosis of psychotic disorders, including schizophrenia, requires that the patient have an episode of active psychosis with delusions and hallucinations (see also Chapter 5), it is not possible to diagnose this prodrome as a psychotic disorder. In fact, until the full-blown disorder is present, the clinician cannot be certain if it is, indeed, a prodrome.

If a change in behavior is of recent onset, then it does not meet the stability criteria for a personality disorder. In such cases, the clinician is forced to diagnose an unspecified mental disorder, nonpsychotic, 300.90. If, however, the pattern of suspiciousness or social withdrawal with or without eccentricities has been well established, it may legitimately be a personality disorder and be diagnosed as such.

If the clinician follows such a patient over time and the patient develops a full-fledged psychotic disorder, the personality disturbance is no longer adequate for a complete diagnosis, since none of the Axis II disorders include frankly psychotic symptoms. This fairly obvious point is frequently overlooked in practice. All of the personality disorders that have counterpart psychotic disorders on Axis I have milder symptoms in which reality testing is, at least in part, intact. For instance, a patient with paranoid personality disorder may have referential ideas, but not frank delusions of reference, and a patient with schizotypal PD may have illusions, but not hallucinations. A possible exception is borderline personality disorder in which brief psychotic experiences (lasting minutes to an hour or two at most) are included as associated features. In all cases, however, when the patient becomes psychotic for even a day or two, an additional Axis I diagnosis is necessary. The Axis II personality disorder can now be listed as "premorbid." The same diagnosis applies if the clinician has retrospectively assessed a stable premorbid personality type in a patient who currently is being evaluated for a psychotic disorder.

The special relationship of schizotypal personality disorder (SPD) and schizophrenia deserves particular mention. There is some evidence, in family and biological studies (24-28), linking SPD to schizophrenia and some experts therefore think that SPD should be grouped with a class of schizophrenic disorders (see below, for limitations of research evidence, and Chapter 5). From the perspective of differential diagnosis, the symptoms of SPD very closely resembled the list of prodromal symptoms of schizophrenia in DSM-III, which, however, included symptoms of impaired functioning and peculiar behavior that were not symptoms of SPD. The symptoms of SPD, on the other hand, included ideas of reference, suspiciousness or paranoid ideation, and social anxiety, which were not considered to be part of the schizophrenic prodrome.

Peculiar behavior has been added to the symptoms of SPD in DSM-III-R, which makes the distinction between prodromal schizophrenia and SPD even more obscure. For the patient with a diagnosis of SPD, the occurrence of a psychotic episode almost certainly means the disturbance will meet the criteria for schizophrenia, the symptoms of SPD "counting" as prodromal symptoms toward the six-month duration requirement. This raises the question of whether the diagnosis of schizophrenia, with its pervasive effects on cognition, perception, functional ability, etc., is a sufficient diagnosis and SPD "premorbid" a redundancy. When the patient becomes nonpsychotic again, he or she would be be considered to have residual schizophrenia instead of SPD.

There is no single answer to this question. An individual clinician's conceptualization of schizophrenia as a chronic illness from which the patient rarely recovers (DSM-III) or as an illness with a much more variable course (29) may determine which alternative he or she chooses.

The state vs. trait distinction is also a clinically important one to make because of the ways in which Axis II psychopathology can affect the course and treatment of Axis I disorders. As has been previously discussed, in Chapter 6, the course and outcome of mood disorders appear to be made worse by the presence of borderline personality disorder, and most clinicians have experienced difficulty in managing even a relatively treatable Axis I disorder if noncompliance or control issues stemming from personality disorder interfere.

Personality Traits vs. Personality Disorders

Another distinction that is a source of difficulty is between personality traits or style and personality disorder. All patients — all people for that matter—can be described in terms of distinctive patterns of personality, but all do not necessarily warrant a diagnosis of personality disorder. This error is particularly common among inexperienced evaluators.

The important features that distinguish pathological personality traits from normal are their inflexibility and maladaptiveness. Inflexibility is indicated by a narrow repertoire of responses that are repeated even when the situation calls for an alternate behavior or in the face of clear evidence that a behavior is inappropriate or not working. For example, an obsessive compulsive person rigidly adheres to rules and organization even in recreation, and loses enjoyment as a consequence. An avoidant person is so sure that others are scrutinizing or finding fault with him or her, even in group situations in which he or she could hardly be the focus of such attention, that his or her life becomes painfully lonely. Maladaptiveness refers to the specific problems or difficulties caused by the personality traits. These may be functional problems in school, at work, as a parent, or in interpersonal relations. The patient is frequently unaware of the problems caused by his or her personality style until others call attention to them.

DSM-III recognized that it was important to describe personality style as well as to diagnose personality disorder on Axis II. Therefore, instructions were included to list significant traits on Axis II even when a personality disorder was absent or as a modifier of one or more diagnosed personality disorders (e.g., borderline personality disorder with histrionic features). In practice, however, this option was seldom utilized: in reviewing 200 multiaxial diagnostic evaluations (10), I found that fewer than 5% had personality traits listed on Axis II.

Several of my colleagues and I believed that personality traits play such a significant role in determining treatment approach, especially in psychotherapy, that we instituted a scaled system for rating DSM-III personality disorders in the outpatient clinic at the Columbia-Presbyterian Medical Center (30). According to this system, all patients were evaluated for features of each of the individual personality disorders and rated on a 4-point scale, with 1 corresponding to no or very few traits of the disorder, 2 equal to some traits present, 3 equal to almost meeting DSM-III criteria, and 4 meeting full DSM-III criteria for that disorder. Using this system, we found that, in addition to the approximately 50% of clinic patients who meet criteria for a personality disorder, another 35% warrant information descriptive of their personality styles on Axis II. The overlap among the features of personality disorders also became very evident when emphasis was placed on assessing for the traits of all personality disorders, even when one was predominant.

The following case vignette describes a patient with an Axis I disorder whose ongoing treatment was very much affected by Axis II personality traits, none of which met criteria for a personality disorder.

On the Outside Looking In

A 25-year-old, single, female receptionist was referred for outpatient therapy following hospitalization for her first manic episode. The patient had attended college for one year, but dropped out in order to "go into advertising." Over the next five years she had held a series of receptionist, secretarial, and sales jobs, each of which she quit because she wasn't "getting ahead in the world." She lived in an apartment on the North Side of Chicago, by herself, that her parents had furnished for her. She ate all of her meals, however, at her mother's house and claimed not even to have a box of crackers in her cupboard. Between jobs her rent was paid by her parents.

Her "career" problems stemmed from the fact that, although she felt quite ordinary and talentless for the most part, she fantasied having a career as a movie star or high fashion model. She took acting classes and singing lessons, but had never had even a small role in a play or show. What she desired was not so much the careers themselves, but the glamour associated with them. Although she wanted to move in the circles of the "beautiful people," she was certain that she had nothing to offer them. She sometimes referred to herself as nothing but a shell, and scorned herself because of it. She was unable to picture herself working her way up along any realistic career line, feeling both that it would take too long and that she would probably fail.

She had had three close relationships with men that were characterized by an intense interdependency that initially was agreeable to both parties. She craved affection and attention and fell deeply in love with these men. Eventually, however, she became overtly self-centered, demanding, and manipulative, so the man would break off the relationship. After breaking up, she would almost immediately start claiming that the particular man was "going nowhere," was not for her, and would not be missed. In between these relationships, she often had periods in which she engaged in a succession of one-night stands, having sex with a half-dozen partners in a month. Alternatively, she would frequent rock clubs and bars, "in spots," as she called them, merely on the chance of meeting someone who would introduce her to the glamour world she dreamed of.

The patient had no female friends other than her sister. She could see little use for such friendships. She preferred spending her time shopping for stylish clothes or at home watching T.V. alone. She liked to dress fashionably and seductively, but often felt too fat, or that her hair was the wrong color. She had trouble controlling her weight, and would periodically go on eating binges for a few days that might result in a ten-pound weight gain. She read popular novels, but had very few other interests. She admitted she was bored much of the time, but would not admit that cultural or athletic pursuits were other than a waste of time.

This patient was referred for outpatient follow-up without an Axis II personality disorder diagnosis. In fact, her long-term functioning failed to meet DSM-III criteria for any specific type of personality disorder. On the other hand, she almost met the criteria for several, especially borderline personality disorder: the patient showed signs of impulsivity (overeating, sexual promiscuity), intense interpersonal relationships (manipulative, overidealization/devaluation), identity disturbance, and feelings of emptiness or boredom. She did not, however, display intense anger, intolerance of being alone, physically self-damaging behavior, or affective instability independent of her mood disorder. Similarly, she had symptoms of histrionic personality disorder: she constantly drew attention to herself and craved excitement, but was not emotionally overdramatic, did not overreact to minor events, or have temper tantrums. She appeared to others as shallow; she was egocentric, vain, demanding, and dependent, but did not make manipulative suicide threats or attempts. She also had some features of narcissistic, avoidant, and dependent personality disorders. The attention paid to personality traits in her outpatient clinic evaluation conveyed a vivid picture of the patient's complicated personality pathology, which became the focus of her subsequent therapy.

Other features of personality. Axis II in DSM-III-R can also be used to indicate the habitual use of particular defense mechanisms. A separate axis for defense mechanisms was considered for DSM-III-R, in part because of the dissatisfaction of psychodynamically oriented clinicians with the DSM-III system of axes, which failed to discriminate between patients according to clinical variables important for planning treatment with psychotherapy (31). Several groups of researchers (32,33) have been able to document empirically the clinical utility of categorizing a patient's defensive functioning. Although this work was considered too early in its development to justify including a separate axis based on it, the glossary of technical terms in DSM-III-R includes a general definition of defense mechanisms and definitions of 18 specific defense mechanisms.

The general definition is as follows:

> Patterns of feelings, thoughts, or behaviors that are relatively involuntary and arise in response to perceptions of psychic danger. They are designed to hide or to alleviate the conflicts or stressors that give rise to anxiety. Some defense mechanisms, such as projection, splitting, and acting-out, are almost invariably maladaptive. Others, such as suppression and denial, may be either maladaptive or adaptive, depending on their severity, their inflexibility, and the context in which they occur (18, pp. 393–394).

The 18 defense mechanisms that are defined are acting-out, autistic fantasy, denial, devaluation, displacement, dissociation, idealization, intellectualization, isolation, passive aggression, projection, rationalization, reaction formation, repression, somatization, splitting, suppression, and undoing. All are considered at least potentially maladaptive. Defense mechanisms that are usually adaptive, such as sublimation and humor, are not defined.

Clinicians may note the description of defensive functioning on Axis II to supplement a personality disorder diagnosis, or when there is no personality disorder, to modify personality trait description, or even simply alone.

Multiple, Overlapping Personality Syndromes

Another difficulty in diagnosing personality disorders in general has been appropriate application of DSM-III categories to phenomenology that rarely appears to have discrete boundaries. Although DSM-III clearly stipulated that for many patients, personality disturbance would frequently meet criteria for more than one disorder, clinicians have found the practice of diagnosing multiple disorders conceptually difficult, and therefore seldom attempt such diagnoses.

Part of the problem has been that most of the DSM-III personality disorders are defined as classical categories (34), i.e., ones in which all members clearly share certain identifying features. Classical categories imply a clear demarcation between members and nonmembers, but natural phenomena rarely fit neatly into such categories.

Categories vs. dimensions of personality. Traditionally, in much of the psychological literature, personality has been described and measured along certain dimensions (35). Dimensions of personality frequently are continuous with opposite traits at either end of a spectrum, such as dominant-submissive or hostile-friendly. People can then vary in the extent to which each of the traits describes them. Dimensional models of personality diagnosis appear to be more flexible and specific than categorical models when the phenomenology lacks clear-cut boundaries between normal and abnormal and between different constellations of maladaptive traits, as seems true of personality disturbance (36). The scaled rating system described above was an attempt to transform Axis II disorders into dimensions, but it is not representative of dimensional approaches currently in use.

The most prominent dimensional model for personality assessment today is the interpersonal circle (IPC) or circumplex. There are several such systems (37,38), but they have in common the characteristic that types that are the opposite of each other reflect opposite poles of a bipolar dimension and have negative correlations, whereas types perpendicular to each other are poles of an orthogonal dimension with no correlations. Features close to each other on the circle are positively correlated; these correlations decrease as the traits become perpendicular. The distance from the center of the circle reflects the degree to which a particular trait is manifest. The major axes of the circumplex are usually considered to be (*1*) affiliation, the degree of involvement with others, and (*2*) power, the degree of status or control. Abnormality is represented by extreme, limited, and rigid positions on dimensions of the circumplex.

Currently, attempts are being made to relate Axis II to the IPC. The limitations of such systems are the unfamiliarity of the approach, the use of only interpersonal behaviors for classification, and the lack of evidence of validity that would lend the IPC to treatment applications (39). An IPC might be considered for a DSM-IV appendix or optional axis.

Classical vs. prototypal categories. If it is premature to use a dimensional model for PD diagnosis, there is another approach that can facilitate more reliable Axis II diagnosis and that has been incorporated into DSM-III-R. This approach defines PDs as prototypal categories.

Prototypal models have been shown to be more accurate than classical models in categorizing various natural phenomena. In the prototypal model, no defining feature is considered to be absolutely necessary, nor is any combination sufficient. Membership is heterogeneous, and boundaries overlap. There are few, if any, pathognomonic signs. The diagnostic criteria for a prototypal model are polythetic rather than monothetic. Monothetic classifications are those in which categories differ by at least one feature that is shared by each of its members. In contrast, in polythetic classifications, members share a large proportion of features, but do not necessarily share any particular feature (40,41). In the prototypal model, polythetic criteria would vary in their diagnostic value, and members would differ in terms of their prototypicality.

A prototypal approach to personality disorder classification is conceptually satisfying because of its flexibility, the inherent heterogeneity of the categories, and the acceptance of overlapping boundaries and many borderline cases. From a conceptual point of view, some of the diagnostic problems alluded to earlier would be lessened with a prototypal approach. Multiple diagnoses and variability within diagnostic groups would be expected, for example.

DSM-III personality disorders were defined in some cases by monothetic criteria sets, in other cases, by polythetic criteria, and in still other cases, by mixtures of the two approaches. Schizoid, avoidant, and dependent personality disorders were strictly monothetic. Each of the diagnostic criteria was required for a diagnosis. Borderline, schizotypal, and compulsive personality disorders were polythetic, in that of the defining criteria, some minimum number, but no single feature, was required. (BPD and SPD are better examples than compulsive personality disorder, since the latter requires virtually all—four of five—of the list of features.) Paranoid, histrionic, narcissistic, antisocial, and passive aggressive personality disorders in DSM-III were mixed categories because, although the A, B, C, D, etc., criteria were required, there was one or more lists of signs or symptoms within the larger criteria that defined the item polythetically.

Monothetic categories are inherently more difficult to recognize or diagnose because disagreement on any one of the required defining features results in disagreement on the diagnosis. With polythetic criteria, since no single symptom is required for a diagnosis, clinicians can disagree about an individual symptom and still agree on the diagnosis, provided the particular symptom was not the one that met the minimum threshold for the number of symptoms required for the diagnosis.

DSM-III-R has shifted to a prototypal model for all personality disorders defined by polythetic criteria sets. The number of features listed varies from seven to nine, with cut points for the diagnosis at four or five required symptoms. Antisocial personality disorder is an exception in that it is still a mixed category. A current age of 18, a childhood history of conduct disturbance, and irresponsible and antisocial behavior as an adult are necessary for the diagnosis. Tables 9.1

and 9.2 compare the criteria for histrionic personality disorder, a mixed category in DSM-III, and dependent personality disorder, a monothetic DSM-III category, with their polythetic definitions in DSM-III-R.

TABLE 9.1 DSM-III vs. DSM-III-R Criteria for Histrionic Personality Disorder

DSM-III Diagnostic Criteria for Histrionic Personality Disorder

The following are characteristic of the individual's current and long-term functioning, are not limited to episodes of illness, and cause either significant impairment in social or occupational functioning or subjective distress.

A. Behavior that is overly dramatic, reactive, and intensely expressed, as indicated by at least *three* of the following:

 (1) self-dramatization, e.g., exaggerated expression of emotions
 (2) incessant drawing of attention to oneself
 (3) craving for activity and excitement
 (4) overreaction to minor events
 (5) irrational, angry outbursts or tantrums

B. Characteristic disturbances in interpersonal relationships as indicated by at least *two* of the following:

 (1) perceived by others as shallow and lacking genuineness, even if superficially warm and charming
 (2) egocentric, self-indulgent, and inconsiderate of others
 (3) vain and demanding
 (4) dependent, helpless, constantly seeking reassurance
 (5) prone to manipulative suicidal threats, gestures, or attempts

DSM-III-R Diagnostic Criteria for Histrionic Personality Disorder

A pervasive pattern of excessive emotionality and attention-seeking, beginning by early adulthood and present in a variety of contexts, as indicated by at least *four* of the following:

 (1) constantly seeks or demands reassurance, approval, or praise
 (2) is inappropriately sexually seductive in appearance or behavior
 (3) is overly concerned with physical attractiveness
 (4) expresses emotion with inappropriate exaggeration, e.g., embraces casual acquaintances with excessive ardor, uncontrollable sobbing on minor sentimental occasions, has temper tantrums
 (5) is uncomfortable in situations in which he or she is not the center of attention
 (6) displays rapidly shifting and shallow expression of emotions
 (7) is self-centered, actions being directed toward obtaining immediate satisfaction; has no tolerance for the frustration of delayed gratification
 (8) has a style of speech that is excessively impressionistic and lacking in detail, e.g., when asked to describe mother, can be no more specific than, "She was a beautiful person."

TABLE 9.2 DSM-III vs. DSM-III-R Criteria for Dependent Personality Disorder

DSM-III Diagnostic Criteria for Dependent Personality Disorder

The following are characteristic of the individual's current and long-term functioning, are not limited to episodes of illness, and cause either significant impairment in social or occupational functioning or subjective distress.

A. Passively allows others to assume responsibility for major areas of life because of inability to function independently (e.g., lets spouse decide what kind of job he or she should have).

B. Subordinates own needs to those of persons on whom he or she depends in order to avoid any possibility of having to rely on self, e.g., tolerates abusive spouse.

C. Lacks self-confidence, e.g., sees self as helpless, stupid.

DSM-III-R Diagnostic Criteria for Dependent Personality Disorder

A pervasive pattern of dependent and submissive behavior, beginning by early adulthood and present in a variety of contexts, as indicated by at least *five* of the following:

(1) is unable to make everyday decisions without an excessive amount of advice or reassurance from others
(2) allows others to make most of his or her important decisions, e.g., where to live, what job to take
(3) agrees with people even when he or she believes they are wrong, because of fear of being rejected
(4) has difficulty initiating projects or doing things on his or her own
(5) volunteers to do things that are unpleasant or demeaning in order to get other people to like him or her
(6) feels uncomfortable or helpless when alone, or goes to great lengths to avoid being alone
(7) feels devastated or helpless when close relationships end
(8) is frequently preoccupied with fears of being abandoned
(9) is easily hurt by criticism or disapproval

Several problems remain to be solved before DSM-IV is prepared, however. All DSM-III-R criteria carry equal weight; in a true prototypal model, certain criteria would have more diagnostic significance. Research studies have demonstrated that for borderline personality disorder, certain individual symptoms, such as chronic feelings of emptiness and boredom, have a higher value in predicting a diagnosis than other symptoms, such as impulsivity, which may be even more common in BPD (42). Certain combinations of two symptoms, such as impulsivity and unstable-intense interpersonal relations, impulsivity and identity disturbance, or affective instability and chronic emptiness-boredom, prove to be very accurate predictors of the BPD diagnosis. Similar significant individual symptoms and combinations need to be determined for all of the personality disorders and an appropriate weighting system for them devised.

The currently required numbers of symptoms for each of the PDs is arbitrary. There have been arguments made that fixed cut points for diagnosis are inappropriate and inefficient. Appropriate cut points are actually dependent on the base rate of the syndrome, i.e., how common it is in the population. For a particular symptom to be more likely to indicate the presence of a syndrome rather than its absence, the ratio of the base rate to one minus the base rate must exceed the ratio of the false-positive rate to the true-positive rate (43). If a symptom correctly identifies 80% of patients with the disorder and misidentifies only 25% without the disorder, then at least 24% of the patients must have the disorder or the symptom will misclassify more patients than it correctly classifies. Therefore, if the disorder occurred less often, given the presence of any one symptom with the above diagnostic value, it would be more efficient never to diagnose the disorder since the clinician would then be wrong less often!

As the base rate of a syndrome changes, the efficiency of any cut point also changes. If the base rate is high, it is more efficient to move the cut point down because, with a high base rate, there is less chance of missing the diagnosis and more chance of correctly identifying the cases. If the base rate is low, the cut point should be increased because it is increasingly likely to incorrectly identify a noncase as a case. A higher threshold for the symptoms would guard against this error. Finally, the relative costs and gains of correctly or incorrectly diagnosing cases could be factored into establishing cut points (43). This depends on how the diagnosis is used or the implications of a missed diagnosis, and is referred to as the "utility." Studies need to be done to determine cut points for the various PDs that would be optimal in a variety of clinical settings and that might take into account the utilities of the diagnostic decisions.

Objective Behavior vs. Inference

Another major source of diagnostic unreliability with regard to the personality disorders stems from the degree of inference and judgment necessary to make many of the diagnoses. Numerous critics have noted that it is easy to disagree about symptoms such as affective instability, self-dramatization, exhibitionism, desire for affection and acceptance—all symptoms of DSM-III personality disorders. Only the antisocial criteria, among the personality disorders of DSM-III, have achieved acceptable levels of reliability, and those criteria emphasize overtly criminal and delinquent *acts*.

These observations have led several investigators to attempt to determine sets of *behaviors* that might serve to identify types of personality disorder. Although any one behavior might not be sufficient to indicate a particular personality trait, multiple behavioral indicators considered together would increase confidence in recognizing the trait.

Behaviors that typify a particular personality style have been referred to as prototypical. Recently, Livesley (44) has developed a set of prototypical behaviors for the DSM-III personality disorders and compared them to prototypical traits. He found that highly prototypical behaviors could be derived from corresponding traits. For example, with regard to the concepts of social awkwardness and withdrawal of the schizoid personality disorder, Livesley found that behaviors such as "does not speak unless spoken to," "does not initiate social contacts," and "rarely reveals self to others" were uniformly rated as highly prototypic. Corresponding to the overly dramatic and emotional traits of the histrionic personality disorder were behaviors such as "expressed feelings in an exaggerated way," "considered a minor problem catastrophic," and "flirted with several members of the opposite sex." Behaviors such as "has routine schedules and is upset by deviations," "overreacted to criticism," and "spent considerable time on the minutest details" corresponded to the controlled, perfectionist traits of compulsive personality disorder.

DSM-III-R makes strides in translating the characteristic traits of the personality disorders into explicit behaviors (45). The criteria for each personality disorder begin with the definition of the overall style or set of traits, followed by the listing of ways this might be expressed. In some instances, for example, for dependent personality disorder, the criteria are quite behavioral. For dependent PD, a pattern of dependent and submissive behavior is indicated by such items as "allows others to make most of his or her important decisions" and "volunteers to do things that are unpleasant or demeaning in order to get other people to like him or her" (18, p. 354). For other disorders, such as obsessive compulsive personality disorder, an example of the behavior is given along with the trait. For obsessive compulsive PD, perfectionism is indicated by the criterion: "perfectionism that interferes with task completion, e.g., inability to complete a project because own overly strict standards are not met" (18, p. 356).

Not all of the DSM-III-R personality disorders are equally well defined or illustrated by prototypical behaviors. But since it seems likely that such behaviors are much more reliably recognized than more abstract and inferential traits, the clinician should make special efforts to elicit examples of behaviors, from patients or other informants, that would constitute objective evidence of the presence of particular personality traits. Such an approach to assessment is likely to result in more accurate diagnosis.

Research into prototypical traits and behaviors indicates that these characteristics vary in their prototypicality (46). Currently, however, all the items in the polythetic lists are considered equally significant. Eventually, indicators of the degree to which patients are prototypic of the personality disorder might be incorporated. Such measures might help to clarify the distinctiveness of the disorders and their manner and degree of overlap.

SPECIFIC PROBLEMS IN DIFFERENTIAL DIAGNOSIS

In this section, the individual personality disorders are grouped according to the three descriptive clusters in DSM-III and DSM-III-R: (*1*) the odd or eccentric, (*2*) the dramatic, emotional, or erratic, and (*3*) the anxious or fearful (Table 9.3). Although these clusters were mentioned in DSM-III solely because of the descriptive similarities among the disorders grouped together, there has been some empirical evidence of the validity of the clusters generated since DSM-III's publication (30,36).

The Odd or Eccentric Cluster

Paranoid, schizoid, and schizotypal personality disorders constitute the odd or eccentric cluster. Disorders in this cluster share traits of social awkwardness, being ill at ease in social situations, and social withdrawal (47).

Schizoid personality disorder. There is some question of the validity of schizoid personality disorder as defined in DSM-III as a distinct personality disorder. People who would have received the diagnosis of schizoid personality according to DSM-II might be diagnosed as either schizoid, schizotypal, or avoidant by DSM-III criteria. In the few studies looking at the full range of DSM-III personality disorders (48), schizoid PD was rarely diagnosed. It must be remembered, however, that subjects in clinical studies are selected by virtue of their seeking treatment; schizoid people, by their very nature, are less likely to seek treatment because subjective distress about their attitudes and behavior is apt to be low, and impairment would be evident only in the eyes of others, whom they typically avoid. To assess the true prevalence of the various personality disorders, epidemiologic studies are needed. This is especially true for schizoid personality disorder.

The crucial distinguishing features of schizoid personality, ac-

TABLE 9.3 DSM-III-R Personality Disorder Clusters, Specific Types, and Their Defining Clinical Features

Cluster	Type	Characteristic features
A		**Odd or eccentric**
	Paranoid	Pervasive and unwarranted tendency to interpret the actions of people as deliberately demeaning or threatening.
	Schizoid	Pervasive indifference to social relationships and restricted range of emotional experience and expression.
	Schizotypal	Pervasive deficits in interpersonal relatedness and peculiarities of ideation, appearance, and behavior.
B		**Dramatic, emotional, or erratic**
	Antisocial	History of conduct disorder with onset before age 15; pattern of irresponsible and antisocial behavior; current age at least 18.
	Borderline	Pervasive instability of mood, interpersonal relationships, and self-image.
	Histrionic	Pervasive excessive emotionality and attention-seeking.
	Narcissistic	Pervasive grandiosity in fantasy or behavior, lack of empathy, and hypersensitivity to the evaluation of others.
C		**Anxious or fearful**
	Avoidant	Pervasive discomfort, fear of negative evaluation, and timidity.
	Dependent	Pervasive dependent and submissive behavior.
	Obsessive compulsive	Pervasive perfectionism and inflexibility.
	Passive aggressive	Pervasive passive resistance to demands for adequate social and occupational performance.

cording to DSM-III, were (*1*) that the person appeared to have a defect in the capacity to form social relationships and, consequently, was emotionally cold, aloof, and indifferent to the reactions and feelings of others; and (*2*) the person had none of the more unusual eccentricities of thought, behavior, or speech that are seen in schizotypal PD. The defect in the capacity to form relationships serves to distinguish schizoid persons from avoidant persons, who are also socially isolated, but who greatly desire relationships, but are petrified by them. This distinction, which has been attributed to the work of Millon, who served on the DSM-III Personality Disorders Advisory Committee, has recently been called into question by Livesley and colleagues (47).

Livesley and his colleagues argue that the historical concepts of schizoid personality disorder do not describe a dichotomous distinction between the capacity and the incapacity to form, or desire, relationships, but rather a tension that exists in such people between wanting and not wanting relationships. At times they appear indifferent, and at other times, more interested, but still unable, to form personal attachments. This characteristic, these authors maintain, is at the heart of schizoid personality disorder and illustrates, again, how a dimensional model of personality disturbance is more accurate. The category of schizoid personality disorder has at its core the dimension of desire for affiliation or attachment to others, and people vary on this dimension, from one extreme to the other, while not actually being able to establish relationships. An alternative view has been expressed by Frances (49), who believes that schizoid patients, as defined in DSM-III, are likely to differ in important ways from those with avoidant personality in their family history, predisposition to schizophrenia, ability to form therapeutic and other relationships, and need for and response to treatment.

Although during advisory committee meetings there was some brief discussion of the possibility of eliminating schizoid PD from DSM-III-R, the disorder remains. The essential features of indifference to social relationships and restricted expression of emotion are defined by a set of seven polythetic criteria, in keeping with the major overhaul of the approach to diagnosing personality disorders described above. The revised criteria permit the diagnosis of schizoid and schizotypal PDs together. In one recent study the revised criteria resulted in an eightfold increase in the diagnosis of schizoid PD (50).

Paranoid personality disorder. People with paranoid personality disorder were, according to DSM-III, characterized by (*1*) pervasive, unwarranted suspiciousness and mistrust, (2) hypersensitivity to others, and (3) restricted affectivity. Because of their intense expectation that others will trick or harm them in some way, they become very guarded and hypervigilant, and therefore may seem distant and removed from others. This social discomfort or withdrawal is distinguishable from that of the schizoid because the latter appears not to care whereas the former cares a great deal. People with paranoid personality disorder are therefore the opposite of those with schizoid PD in their responses to the praise or criticism of others. Whereas schizoid people are indifferent, paranoid people are extremely sensitive, very easily slighted, quick to take offense, ready to counterattack, and prone to bear grudges. In DSM-III, both paranoid personality disorder and schizoid personality disorder were characterized by emotional coldness.

The overlap between paranoid PD and schizoid PD has been

reduced in DSM-III-R by narrowing the definition of paranoid PD. The central concept of paranoid PD is an unwarranted tendency to interpret the actions of people and events as deliberately demeaning or threatening, and the restricted emotionality component present in the DSM-III criteria has been removed. Certain items have been identified more behaviorally, in keeping with the goal to reduce inference and improve reliability. "Pathological jealousy" in the DSM-III criteria, for example, has been defined in DSM-III-R as "questions, without justification, fidelity of spouse or sexual partner." "Guardedness or secretiveness" has been redefined as reluctance "to confide in others because of unwarranted fear that the information will be used against him or her" (18, p. 339).

Another point relevant to the differential diagnosis of paranoid personality disorder is the relationship of nonpsychotic suspiciousness and ideas of reference to the delusions characteristic of a delusional disorder or paranoid schizophrenia. The distinction, which is discussed in detail in Chapter 5, Psychotic Features, rests on the degree to which reality testing is impaired. In brief, in paranoid personality disorder, the person can at least entertain the possibility that his or her suspicions are unfounded or that he or she is overreacting. Also, the perceived threats of the person with a paranoid PD are more likely to come from known other people in the environment, a neighbor or a co-worker, for instance, or from common institutions such as the government or the utility company, rather than from bizarre sources.

In cases in which beliefs of expected harm or persecution are firmly held and result in extensive effects on behavior, paranoid personality disorder is not a sufficient diagnosis: diagnosis of a psychotic disorder is warranted. Since it is likely that people with paranoid personality disorder are predisposed to developing episodes of delusional disorder (or schizophrenia), a double diagnosis may be called for, the paranoid personality disorder being noted as a premorbid or interepisode type.

Schizotypal personality disorder. Schizotypal personality disorder (SPD) was a new category introduced in DSM-III. The criteria for schizotypal PD were developed in a study conducted by Spitzer and associates (51). The criteria were developed from the case records of the "borderline schizophrenic" relatives of people genetically related to probands with schizophrenia in the Danish Adoption Studies of Schizophrenia (52,53). They were intended to help clarify the murky diagnostic area of "borderline" patients.

SPD criteria have generated a great deal of research interest because of the possibility that the disorder was an additional phenotypic expression of the genotype for schizophrenia. Until recently, however, no study has been made of the frequency of occurrence of SPD in relatives, using comparison groups of patients with other major mental disorders, but not schizophrenia. Thus, it has not been known whether SPD is "specific" in its ability to discriminate relatives of patients with schizophrenia from controls or whether it identifies relatives of probands with a wider range of serious psychopathology, such as mood disorders. Two recent reports have found that SPD characteristics as defined by DSM-III may not have discriminant validity (54,55).

The key defining features of SPD are the soft, nonpsychotic symptoms that resemble those seen in more florid form in schizophrenia (11) and make SPD patients appear eccentric. These include magical thinking, ideas of reference, recurrent illusions, odd speech, and paranoid ideation. Among the problems in differential diagnosis are how to distinguish these features from their psychotic counterparts, how to distinguish SPD patients from others in the odd, eccentric cluster, and how best to define SPD for clinical and research purposes.

The distinction between the soft, suggestive signs and the full-blown psychotic symptoms rests on the conviction regarding the beliefs, the vividness of the illusions, and the degree of disorganization of speech. Since the evaluation of overvalued ideas vs. delusions has been discussed several times before in this volume, it will not be repeated again. Illusions are misperceptions of real external stimuli and are thus distinct from hallucinations, in which there is a sensory perception without external stimulation of the sense organs. An example of a visual illusion might be mistaking a shadow for a real person or seeing one's face change in a mirror. An auditory illusion might be hearing derogatory remarks made in muffled conversation heard from a distance. In the case of an illusion, the person can usually consider the possibility that his or her perception was mistaken.

Odd speech may be tangential, circumstantial, stilted, vague, or overly metaphorical. It differs from loosening of associations in that it is generally more understandable, although coherence is obviously along a continuum. If a person with SPD develops full-blown delusions or hallucinations, then the diagnosis becomes schizophrenia, because the premorbid symptoms of SPD almost invariably would meet the six-month duration requirement for schizophrenia as prodromal symptoms.

The likelihood of schizotypal personality disorder's evolving into schizophrenia is not fully established. What is known about the forerunners of SPD, simple and latent schizophrenia, suggests that only a limited proportion actually develops schizophrenia on follow-up. The only long-term follow-up study of DSM-III-defined SPD was recently completed by McGlashan (21). He found that pure SPD had a better prognosis than schizophrenia, but worse than borderline personality disorder. The frequency with which SPD became schizophrenia over the 15-year follow-up was not reported, but even "pure" SPD patients required frequent, short hospitalizations. If a patient with a past history of DSM-III schizophrenia currently displays symptoms of schizotypal personality disorder, the latter is usually referred to instead as residual schizophrenia.

Because SPD possibly has a genetic relationship to schizophrenia and has symptoms on a continuum of severity with schizophrenia, some theorists and researchers have questioned why this spectrum disorder is not classified with schizophrenia in a broader group of schizophrenic disorders. In a sense, this would be parallel to the DSM-II classification, which included nonpsychotic forms of schizophrenia as schizophrenia. This question raises very fundamental nosological considerations: On what basis should the classification be organized—according to familial patterns, symptoms, course and outcome, or treatment response? At present, and in DSM-III-R, classification is primarily by phenomenology. Thus, the organizing principle of the classification of schizophrenia and related psychotic disorders is the presence of criterion A, psychotic symptoms, at some time in the course of the illness. According to this principle, SPD should not be considered a schizophrenic disorder. Moreover, although there are some early suggestions that SPD may benefit from low dose neuroleptics (56), the benefit is much less clear than for schizophrenia; and important aspects of the course and outcome, including deterioration and need for hospitalization, are different. Regrouping SPD with schizophrenia would therefore seem regressive. Familial relationships have not been sufficiently clarified to be the basis of classification.

The schizoid/schizotypal distinction is made on the basis of the presence of the psychoticlike symptoms. Frances (57) has found that the distinction is rarely made in clinical practice.

The final question about SPD, how best to define the concept, remains unsolved. The answer may depend, as is invariably the case in nosology, on the purpose of the diagnosis. From the perspective of family studies, the best definition might be one that maximized the familial relationship to schizophrenia, i.e., the number of first-degree relatives of schizophrenics who had SPD. For other clinical purposes, a different definition may be best.

There are three definitions for SPD in the literature (58) that have demonstrated reliability: those of DSM-III, Siever and Gunderson (59), and Perry and co-workers (60). Each was generated from a slightly different perspective. Gunderson and Siever (59) have recommended greater emphasis on the symptoms of social withdrawal and poor functioning, the addition of an item on somatic preoccupation (61), and a de-emphasis on strange beliefs and perceptions in order to maximize the familial relationship to schizophrenia and minimize the overlap with BPD. Eliminating these hallmark features, however, moves the diagnosis much closer to schizoid personality disorder. Perry and co-workers' criteria overlap with DSM-III but have additional items for flat or blunted affect, cognitive slippage, fluctuating psychotic symptoms, chronic anhedonia, and general lack of interest. In DSM-III-R, SPD criteria differ only slightly from those in DSM-III, with the addition of odd or eccentric behavior or appearance to bring the criteria closer to the symptoms of prodromal or residual schizophrenia. The ultimate best definition for SPD remains to be determined.

The following vignette illustrates the case of a socially isolated person that raises differential diagnostic questions.

Fantastic Face

A videotaped interview of a 30-year-old bachelor was shown to 133 American and 194 British psychiatrists in the late 1960s as part of the United States–United Kingdom comparative study of psychiatric diagnosis.

Problems began for the patient when he was 13 or 14 years old. He described himself as insecure and very dependent on his mother for emotional support. Although he claimed he sometimes did well in high school—played football, boxed, acted, and played the trumpet—at other times, he said, he was afraid to go to school and would stay home with his mother. He said he was afraid other kids would pick on him and he would get into a fight. He attended several colleges, but did not study, and accumulated only one and a half years of credit.

He then joined the army, but lasted only five months. He was hospitalized briefly, at age 19, at Walter Reed Hospital, but claims he was told that there was nothing wrong. He states that he felt like a little boy and wanted to go home to his mother. He said he broke down and screamed and cried like a baby.

His current hospitalization is his fifth. The longest has been for five months; the others, for a couple of days to a couple of weeks. In all cases and on other occasions, he requested hospitalization. He was often refused and told that he did not need hospitalization, but should go to work. He has been treated with a variety of medicines, including phenothiazines, and received 20 electroconvulsive treatments as an outpatient.

Other problems he describes are periodic abuse of drugs, including alcohol, barbiturates, opioids, and amphetamines. He reports periods of not being able to get out of bed, shave, or shower; he denies depressed mood or symptoms of a depressive syndrome. He also denies grandiosity or other symptoms of a manic syndrome. He has worked very sporadically, and states that he purposely fails at tasks. He says he makes friends, but quickly loses them. He has not seen any friend for the past six months.

The patient has just described an incident in which he developed a "paralyzed arm," which his psychiatrist called a hysterical symptom.

Interviewer: "What other sorts of things have happened to your body?"

Patient: "Well, one thing is that no matter how I look to you now, my facial appearance changes sometimes, unbelievably. Now, a lot of doctors thought I was exaggerating, but my own mother says it's true. Sometimes my face just blows up, my nose gets wider, my eyes close up, and (giving his cheek a twist), I can't feel nothin'—like this."

Interviewer: "What does this to you?"

Patient: "Simply, if it didn't . . . I'd have no reason to tell myself that I'm afraid to go out into the world."

Interviewer: "You mean that your face actually does swell up, or that you imagine it?"

Patient: "It actually does! I swear on my heart that I never imagined anything, or seen anything that wasn't there."

Interviewer: "How long has this been happening to you?"

Patient: "Ten years."

Interviewer: "What happens if you look in the mirror?"

Patient: "I don't."

Interviewer: "Why not?"

Patient: "To avoid it. I try to forget about it. I know that my basic problem isn't my face—I used to think it was. Now I know it'll change when the basic problem goes away."

Interviewer: "Does it frighten you that this happens?"

Patient: "It used to. I used to think that I was the owner of a fantastic symptom that was totally unbelievable, plus I couldn't get any medical man to believe me. Finally, I went to one or two psychiatrists who told me they'd seen it before, maybe not the face, but a physical change can take place."

Interviewer: "If you go out in public, do you feel self-conscious about this?"

Patient: "That's what's amazing. When I'm sick like this I don't feel self-conscious. I could be as ugly as the day is long. But when I'm well, and look my best, or get attention from people, I can't stand it."

Interviewer: "What do you do then?"

Patient: "I withdraw—into myself. This way nobody is going to come up to me. I won't be forced to react—'Hello; goodbye.' Converse. Talk. Walk. Work."

Interviewer: "I see you wear dark glasses."

Patient: "Yeah, well in the safety of my own house, I feel O.K. But, if I walk out onto the street, it hits me: 'Where? How? Who do I go to? There's 30 billion people. Who do I speak to? Where do I go?' Next thing I know, I'm paranoid."

Interviewer: "What do you mean, paranoid?"

Patient: "People look at me. They could be saying anything. 'He's good-looking' or 'He's ugly.' But all I feel is 'Oh, my God! I can't stand this! People looking at me!' You know, when I get looked at because I look terrible, it doesn't frighten me. But should I feel good and get some attention, you know, I get sick."

The patient depicted in this vignette was fascinating because there was more disagreement between American and British psychiatrists on the appropriate diagnosis than on any other case in the U.S.-U.K. study (62). Sixty-nine percent of American psychiatrists in the late 1960s diagnosed this man as having schizophrenia; only 2% of British psychiatrists did so. The most common British diagnosis was personality disorder, usually hysterical. The next most common diagnosis by British psychiatrists was neurosis.

Cases such as this led the way to a narrowing of the traditionally broad conceptualization of schizophrenia in American psychiatry during the 1970s, culminating in the very narrow DSM-III definition (see Chapter 5). The case is still not an easy one to diagnose correctly, even using modern diagnostic criteria. Most mental health clinicians to whom I have presented the videotape corresponding to this vignette agree that on Axis I, diagnoses of mixed substance abuse and conversion disorder are warranted. A factitious disorder is the second most frequently chosen diagnosis. On Axis II, using DSM-III criteria, most clinicians chose schizotypal personality disorder with histrionic features. With the expansion of the concept of avoidant personality disorder in DSM-III-R to include more prominent fearfulness, I suspect that clinicians using DSM-III-R would also note avoidant features.

The Dramatic, Emotional, or Erratic Cluster

The dramatic, emotional, or erratic cluster includes histrionic, narcissistic, borderline, and antisocial personality disorders. These highly overlapping disorders share the characteristics of reactive emotionality and poor impulse control.

Histrionic personality disorder. Histrionic personality disorder was defined in DSM-III by dramatic, reactive, and intensely expressed behavior and disturbed interpersonal relationships due to excessive vanity, egocentrism, dependency, and manipulativeness. In clinical and research settings, the features of histrionic personality disorder overlapped considerably with those of other disorders in this cluster, especially the narcissistic and borderline, and with dependent personality disorder. Although histrionic patients may make up a large proportion of psychotherapy patients, they have not been well studied in terms of DSM-III criteria.

The diagnostic overlap of histrionic with narcissistic personality disorder is virtually assured by the diagnostic criteria the two have in common. Histrionic PD includes incessant drawing of attention to oneself; narcissistic PD, exhibitionism, described as requiring "constant attention and admiration"; histrionic PD also involves egocentrism and self-indulgence; narcissistic PD, a grandiose sense of self-importance, entitlement, interpersonal exploitiveness, and lack of empathy. When criteria for both disorders are met, both diagnoses should be given.

Patients with BPD are frequently histrionic. Histrionic patients have angry outbursts, make suicidal gestures, and are demanding and manipulative. BPD patients display inappropriate, intense anger, perform physically self-damaging acts, and manipulate others. There are patients, however, who are histrionic, but lack the more malignant characteristics of BPD. These patients, referred to in the classic literature as hysterical, may be very vain and self-indulgent, always drawing attention to themselves or craving action and excitement, without having angry outbursts or making suicidal threats. The more "hysterical" the patient, the better functioning he or she is, and the more likely psychotherapy alone is likely to be a successful treatment; the more borderline features the patient displays, the greater is the likelihood that functioning is poor and that medications may be required (63). The overlap between histrionic PD and borderline PD has been reduced in DSM-III-R criteria by the elimination of the item referring to manipulative suicidal threats, gestures, or attempts (see Table 9.1).

Another problem in making a diagnosis of histrionic PD is that the symptoms are difficult for the patient to recognize. A patient who overreacts to minor events in most cases does not consider it an overreaction or the event minor. Few patients are aware that others consider them shallow or insincere, that they are inconsiderate or manipulative, or that their speech is overly impressionistic. Therefore, histrionic PD is a diagnosis that often requires the input of third-party informants. Fortunately, histrionic traits are usually displayed to the therapist (see "The Showgirl" in Chapter 4), and observation is therefore of great diagnostic value.

Patients with histrionic personality disorder may be especially prone to Axis I disorders in the somatoform disorders class. The clinician should therefore be alert to the possible *additional* diagnoses of somatization disorder, conversion disorder, somatoform pain disorder (psychogenic pain disorder), and hypochondriasis. (The reader should also consult Chapter 8, Physical Complaints.)

Narcissistic personality disorder. The hallmark features of narcissistic PD in DSM-III were a grandiose sense of self-importance or uniqueness, preoccupation with fantasies of success, an exhibitionistic need for attention and admiration, inability to react appropriately to threats to self-esteem, and interpersonal relationship problems, such as feeling entitled, exploiting others for personal gain, alternately idealizing then devaluing the same person, and failing to empathize with the feelings of others.

Overlap with other disorders in the cluster was high. Overlap with histrionic PD has been described previously. In DSM-III narcissistic PD shared virtually identical criteria with borderline PD in terms of disturbances in interpersonal relationships. In fact, the corresponding BPD criterion (number 2) covered two separate narcissistic criteria (E2 and E3). The two disorders did not always overlap, however, since narcissistic patients may not have the impulsivity, self-damaging behavior, or identity disturbance of BPD. BPD patients are frequently not preoccupied with their own importance, but actually suffer from very low self-esteem. In an effort to reduce overlap between these diagnoses in DSM-III-R, idealization/devaluation has been limited to the criteria set for BPD, and interpersonal exploitiveness describes only narcissistic personality disorder (Table 9.4).

The diagnosis of narcissistic personality disorder presents the difficult problem of translating concepts of psychological functioning derived largely from the psychoanalytic literature into descriptions of traits and behaviors that can be recognized by clinicians with diverse theoretical orientations. As Frances (40) has indicated, the psychoanalytic definition of narcissistic PD would include: (*1*) deficits in object constancy, (*2*) incomplete internalization and maturation of psychic structures and mechanisms regulating self-esteem, and (*3*) immature grandiosity. These are not easily recognized, especially by nonanalytic clinicians in one or two diagnostic interviews.

Deficits in object constancy translated, in DSM-III terms, into the characteristic interpersonal disturbances listed in criterion E. Self-esteem problems were made concrete by specifying indifference or rage, inferiority, shame, humiliation, or emptiness in response to criticism or defeat. Immature grandiosity was reflected by narcissistic PD criteria A and B in DSM-III and 3, 4, 5, and 6 in DSM-III-R. A number of other authors have also remarked that DSM-III narcissistic PD may not include the more subtle features of narcissism (64,65). Whether or not these features can be identified reliably and have significance outside the realm of psychoanalysis remains to be seen.

Borderline personality disorder. Borderline personality disorder (BPD) has generated by far the most extensive and intensive research of all of the DSM-III personality disorders. This research interest

TABLE 9.4 DSM-III-R Diagnostic Criteria for Narcissistic Personality Disorder

A pervasive pattern of grandiosity (in fantasy or behavior), lack of empathy, and hypersensitivity to the evaluation of others, beginning by early adulthood and present in a variety of contexts, as indicated by at least *five* of the following:

(1) reacts to criticism with feelings of rage, shame, or humiliation (even if not expressed)
(2) is interpersonally exploitative: takes advantage of others to achieve his or her own ends
(3) has a grandiose sense of self-importance, e.g., exaggerates achievements and talents, expects to be noticed as "special" without appropriate achievement
(4) believes that his or her problems are unique and can be understood only by other special people
(5) is preoccupied with fantasies of unlimited success, power, brilliance, beauty, or ideal love
(6) has a sense of entitlement: unreasonable expectation of especially favorable treatment, e.g., assumes that he or she does not have to wait in line when others must do so
(7) requires constant attention and admiration, e.g., keeps fishing for compliments
(8) lack of empathy: inability to recognize and experience how others feel, e.g., annoyance and surprise when a friend who is seriously ill cancels a date
(9) is preoccupied with feelings of envy

simply reflects the intense clinical interest in borderline patients, who seem to have swelled the ranks of inpatient hospitals and outpatient practices of the past 20 years. The two major questions that have been asked are: (*1*) What are the "borders" of borderline? and (2) What are the key clinical features of this disorder?

The criteria for BPD were originally defined by Spitzer and his colleagues (51) in an effort to delineate what patients clinicians referred to as "borderline." These investigators found two overlapping sets of descriptive items, a set reflecting instability of affect, identity, and impulse control, and another reflecting eccentricity of thought, speech, and behavior. The former became the criteria for BPD, and the latter for schizotypal PD, in DSM-III.

Although traditionally, and in psychoanalytic terms, borderline patients were thought to occupy a "border" between psychosis or schizophrenia and "neurotic" disorders, a great deal of evidence has accumulated, based on the modern validation techniques of family history, treatment response, and outcome on follow-up, that indicates that BPD bears much more of a relationship to major affective disorder than to schizophrenia (66-68). This has led many clinicians (and researchers) into the diagnostic dilemma of attempting to distinguish whether a particular patient has BPD *or* an affective disorder.

This dilemma is a product of asking the wrong question. The appropriate question is which patients with BPD *also* have a mood disorder. The relevancy of this question for clinical practice is supported by the most recent reviews of this area of differential diagnosis. Gunderson and Elliot (69) examined three existing hypotheses about the interface between BPD and affective disorder: (*1*) that affective disorder is primary and that borderline character traits such as drug use and sexual promiscuity arise in an attempt to alleviate depression; (*2*) that BPD leads to affective disorder (depression) as a result of problems that result from primary deficits in impulse control, maintaining stable interpersonal relationships, and sense of self-esteem; and (*3*) that the two disorders are independent, but since both occur frequently in the population, they are often seen together. The data, Gunderson and Elliot argue, support none of the hypotheses as stated. They are most consistent with the independence hypothesis, but the two disorders co-occur more frequently than would be expected by chance. These authors offer a fourth hypothesis, which posits that both disorders start with a biological vulnerability that increases the chances of a person's being psychologically impaired. The vulnerability may manifest itself as either disorder or both in combination, depending on later physiological and psychological reactions to the environment and on temperament.

From a clinical perspective, the important distinctions to be made, therefore, are among BPD alone, BPD in association with a mood disorder in the depressive or bipolar spectra, and affective disorder alone. These distinctions are facilitated by the DSM-III and DSM-III-R multiaxial systems because Axes I and II are considered separately, and multiple diagnoses can be listed on each axis.

Studies of the drug treatment of patients with BPD (2,70,71) suggest that those with coexisting affective disorder respond better than those without a diagnosable affective disorder, but that such patients do not respond as well as depressed patients without a borderline personality disorder. Studies of clinical course have indicated that, although the course of patients with BPD resembles that of patients with affective disorders, in contrast to schizophrenia, certain interesting interactions with concurrent mood disorders occur. Pope and his group at McLean Hospital, in Boston (2), found that over four to seven years, patients with BPD who had a concurrent affective disorder did better than those with BPD alone, although not as well as those with an affective disorder alone. Similarly, McGlashan at Chestnut Lodge, in Rockville, Maryland (3), found a better overall course for BPD, but that coexisting BPD resulted in a poorer outcome in patients with affective disorders.

These findings are understandable if one considers that it is the effective treatment of the mood syndromes, when present, that ameliorates the course of BPD. These studies and others (21,22) have demonstrated considerable stability for the BPD diagnosis over time.

Thus, if he makes use of the multiaxial evaluation system, the clinician can gain valuable assistance in deciding whether antidepressants, for example, might be helpful in treating BPD, or why BPD might be the cause of a suboptimal treatment response in patients with affective disorders. The following case vignette is one in which Axis II disorders undermined the treatment of Axis I psychopathology and led to a chronic clinical course with severe morbidity.

Malignant Melancholy

A 37-year-old single woman, a bookkeeper for a building restoration and waterproofing company, was evaluated for long-term hospital treatment of personality disturbance. She described herself as chronically and severely depressed since the age of 18 and bulimic since her early 20s. She said, "I've cried every day for the past ten years." She had an extremely low opinion of herself: "You have never met anyone as bad as I am, I guarantee it."

She had had 14 years of therapy with a half-dozen therapists. She typically became very attached to them, then reacted extremely negatively, "sooner or later," when they let her down. Once, when a therapist would not allow her to extend a session beyond her time, she picked up an ashtray and threw it at him. Another time, she waited for one of her therapists after his day was over, lay down in front of his car, and would not let him go home before he talked more to her. On still another occasion when she was angry at a therapist, she took a razor blade from her purse and cut her wrist in the therapist's office.

Many medications had been tried for both the depression and the bulimia. She had been on Librium and Valium many years ago, then Elavil, Tofranil, Mellaril, and lithium, then Xanax, Parnate, and, most recently, Nardil. Occasionally, the depression abated slightly "for maybe one week." As far as her concern with her weight and her binge eating, she claimed nothing helped. Her weight had ranged from a low of 110 to a high of 130. She claimed that she had taken up to 70 Ex-Lax in a week, and had vomited every day for almost ten years. She also had panic attacks, and had abused alcohol, cannabis, and stimulants in the past.

The patient continued to work, although she did not get along well with her co-workers. "I know people don't like me. I'm just a lazy, nasty person. Some of them probably think I'm grotesque. I'm sure they're also laughing at me. Who wouldn't? I'm an absurdity." The patient had not had a date in eight years, and had only a few female "acquaintances."

A research interview indicated that the patient met DSM-III-R criteria for seven(!) personality disorders: avoidant, obsessive compulsive, passive aggressive, self-defeating, schizotypal, histrionic, and borderline. The borderline and self-defeating personality disorders were rated severe.

Standard treatments for major depression (or bulimia) are no match for this woman's personality psychopathology. It is not difficult to conceptualize her overall maladjustment as so severe that minor improvements in mood would be insignificant to her by contrast, or even unacceptable, given her self-defeating tendencies. A skeptical clinician might argue that given her tendencies to exaggerate, manipulate, and provoke, it would not be possible to accurately assess the state of her mood in response to treatment. This raises the question of which components of a mood disorder are most likely to be affected by Axis II psychopathology. Clearly, in work with patients with severe personality disorders, the subjective state of the patient is very resistant to change. Improvement may be evident only by objective criteria, from the perspective of either the clinician or of a significant other in the person's life.

Other Axis I disorders, such as anxiety disorders (see Chapter 7), substance use disorders (see Chapter 4), eating disorders and somatoform disorders (see Chapter 8), dissociative disorders (see Chapter 12), and psychotic disorders (see Chapter 5), may also complicate the course of BPD. Again, in these instances the clinician should not pose the differential diagnosis in terms of either/or, but instead as both/and.

There is some evidence to suggest that BPD patients with associated panic disorder may have a drug-responsive syndrome (72,73) and that such patients may have a poorer outcome than with uncomplicated anxiety disorder patients (74,75). Panic disorder may occur in combination with major depression in BPD (76). Although the exact nature of psychosis in BPD is debatable (see also below), it is well known that, when there are brief lapses in reality testing, BPD patients are often treated with some success with short courses of low-dose neuroleptic medications. Although there are no very effective treatments for the somatoform disorders, the clinician treating a patient with BPD might suspect that somatic complaints reflect a somatoform disorder and proceed cautiously with extensive or invasive diagnostic evaluations or potentially disfiguring or otherwise detrimental radical treatment.

BPD overlaps extensively with narcissistic, histrionic, and antisocial personality disorders. In the study at McLean Hospital, BPD, histrionic, and antisocial PDs were essentially indistinguishable. Recently, Perry (77) reported a study in which patients with both BPD and antisocial PD had less depression, on a lifetime basis, than borderline patients alone, which suggests that this combination may identify a special group with more problems in acting out than in maintaining self-esteem.

The occurrence of psychotic symptoms in BPD deserves separate mention. Whether brief psychotic episodes are characteristic of BPD is a matter of controversy. The Gunderson criteria for BPD make such breaks in reality testing essential for the diagnosis; DSM-III and DSM-III-R list them as possible associated features or complications. A recent review of the literature by Jonas and Pope (78) suggests that "narrowly defined" psychotic symptoms, meaning delusions and hallucinations, are rare in BPD, and that when they do occur, they are actually a manifestation of another coexistent disorder such as substance abuse or a major affective disorder. Broadly defined "psychotic" symptoms such as derealization, which would not be considered psychotic but rather dissociative by DSM-III and DSM-III-R definitions, are much more frequent, but are also frequent in many other nonpsychotic disorders and in normal subjects.

Pope and co-workers (79) went on to show that about one-third of a group of BPD patients had factitious psychotic symptoms, meeting DSM-III criteria for factitious disorder with psychological symptoms. Although many clinicians probably treat such symptoms with antipsychotics, the Pope study indicated that hardly any patients with these symptoms had a good response to such therapy.

The DSM-III-R Personality Disorders Advisory Committee debated whether to include brief psychotic symptoms in the revision's definition of BPD, but voted the proposal down.

Related to this discussion is a line of research designed to identify those features constituting the best definition of BPD. A study by Frances and colleagues (80) demonstrated that impulsivity was the most common characteristic of BPD in an outpatient population; affective instability was next, followed by inappropriate intense anger, unstable interpersonal relationships, chronic feelings of emptiness or boredom, identity disturbance, self-damaging acts, and intolerance of being alone. In terms of their ability to distinguish BPD from other personality disorders, however, unstable-intense relationships and chronic emptiness and boredom were the symptoms that best predicted a BPD diagnosis rather than diagnosis of another personality disorder. Intense anger and affective instability had the worst positive predictive value.

Certain combinations of two symptoms had very high predictive value, e.g., impulsivity and either unstable interpersonal relations or

TABLE 9.5 DSM-III-R Diagnostic Criteria for Borderline Personality Disorder

A pervasive pattern of instability of mood, interpersonal relationships, and self-image, beginning by early adulthood and present in a variety of contexts, as indicated by at least *five* of the following:

(1) a pattern of unstable and intense interpersonal relationships characterized by alternating between extremes of overidealization and devaluation
(2) impulsiveness in at least two areas that are potentially self-damaging, e.g., spending, sex, substance use, shoplifting, reckless driving, binge eating (Do not include suicidal or self-mutilating behavior covered in [5].)
(3) affective instability: marked shifts from baseline mood to depression, irritability, or anxiety, usually lasting a few hours and only rarely more than a few days
(4) inappropriate, intense anger or lack of control of anger, e.g., frequent displays of temper, constant anger, recurrent physical fights
(5) recurrent suicidal threats, gestures, or behavior, or self-mutilating behavior
(6) marked and persistent identity disturbance manifested by uncertainty about at least two of the following: self-image, sexual orientation, long-term goals or career choice, type of friends desired, preferred values
(7) chronic feelings of emptiness or boredom
(8) frantic efforts to avoid real or imagined abandonment (Do not include suicidal or self-mutilating behavior covered in [5].)

identity disturbance, and affective instability combined with chronic emptiness or boredom, although these were somewhat rare combinations. More common and also predictive combinations were physically self-damaging acts and either unstable-intense relations or chronic boredom, and unstable relations and identity disturbance. Therefore, it makes sense that the clinician can have a relatively high degree of confidence of a BPD diagnosis in the presence of one of these five symptom combinations, at least in an outpatient setting (Table 9.5). Which combinations of symptoms have the most clinical utility remains to be determined.

Antisocial personality disorder. The final diagnosis in the erratic cluster is antisocial personality disorder (ASPD). Antisocial PD is unique among DSM-III personality disorders in that it has been demonstrated to have reasonably high levels of interrater reliability. It is not so difficult to recognize because its characteristic pattern of behavior, which violates the rights of others, beginning in adolescence, is identified by very explicit lists of antisocial behaviors. Such an approach has also been demonstrated to have validity (81).

One major problem exists in DSM-III antisocial criteria: they do not include a criterion for the absence of loyalty, anxiety, or guilt, and therefore do not define sociopathy. This means that criminal behavior may become synonymous with antisocial PD by DSM-III criteria (82). It has been estimated that up to 80% of criminals could be diagnosed antisocial by DSM-III criteria, whereas with a requirement for an incapacity for feelings of loyalty and guilt, perhaps only 30% would meet the criteria (49). Certainly, distinguishing between criminals and true sociopaths would have relevance in deciding whether a person with criminal tendencies was likely to respond to treatment or rehabilitation that depended on the formation of interpersonal relationships. DSM-III-R criteria partially rectify this deficiency and sharpen the distinction between ASPD and criminality by adding the criterion "lacks remorse (feels justified in having hurt, mistreated, or stolen from another)" (18, p. 346).

Conditions to be considered in the differential diagnosis of antisocial personality disorder include conduct disorder, other mental disorders that may lead to antisocial behaviors (see also Chapter 10, Antisocial, Aggressive, or Violent Behavior), and the V code adult antisocial behavior. Conduct disorder is a diagnosis for a repetitive and persistent pattern of behavior in which the rights of others or societal norms are violated in children or adolescents under 18 years of age. The restriction of ASPD to persons over 18 means that the pattern has to have persisted into adult life, since many childhood conduct problems may remit or may lead to other mental disorders.

Other mental disorders such as psychotic disorders and mood disorders can lead to breaking of laws and antisocial acts. Schizophrenic or manic episodes preempt the diagnosis of ASPD. When antisocial behavior occurs that is not a part of the full pattern of ASPD or is not due to another mental disorder such as schizophrenia, then the V code category adult antisocial behavior is appropriate.

The Anxious and Fearful Cluster

Dependent, avoidant, obsessive compulsive, and passive aggressive personality disorders make up the anxious and fearful cluster. At least one study (30) has shown that compulsive PD may not fit as well into this group as the others.

Dependent personality disorder. Dependent personality disorder is characterized by dependent and submissive behavior. Dependent personality shares with histrionic personality disorder a covariation with gender, occurring far more frequently in women (83,84). It has been argued that this results because there is a sex bias in the diagnostic criteria (83), so that normal women conforming to their sex role stereotype will be labeled abnormal because of a masculine bias about what constitutes healthy behavior.

One of the real problems in the diagnosis of dependent personality disorder is its threshold for clinical significance. The earlier discussion in this chapter about personality traits vs. personality disorder is germane. For dependent personality traits to indicate a personality disorder, evidence of significant distress or social or occupational impairment is necessary. If a woman subordinates her needs to those of her husband in order to avoid losing him, then there would have to be clear evidence that this behavior is damaging to her in that there are other, equally viable options for her socially, and with respect to her family and living arrangements, that she does not choose because of her inability to make her own decisions or act according to her own needs. Another consideration is that a particular woman's needs may be very different from her husband's; she may desire greater affiliation and need less self-determination in traditional areas of living such as economic productivity. Keeping in mind the need for strong evidence of the pathological nature of the dependency may help guard against too many false-positive diagnoses of women.

The diagnostic criteria for dependent personality disorder in DSM-III-R are quite different from those in DSM-III. Many of the changes have resulted from a need to specify more explicitly the kinds of dependent behaviors indicative of the disorder and to emphasize their pathological nature. Therefore, DSM-III criterion A, "Passively allows others to assume responsibility for major areas of life . . ." has been separated into two items in the polythetic DSM-III-R model of DPD: (*1*) "allows others to make most of his or her important life decisions," and (2) "has difficulty initiating projects or doing things on his or her own" (18, p. 354). Subordination of needs (DSM-III criterion B) has been broken down into several items. Criterion C, "Lacks self-confidence," has been altered in an effort to reduce the overlap with depressive disorders. The difference in DPD is that the person stays in poor relationships, goes along with others even when thinking they are wrong, does demeaning things, and feels helpless when alone all because of an inability to see himself or herself as sufficiently competent. It is not the lack of confidence per se that is significant for the person with dependent personality disorder, but the pathological use of relationships to attempt to deal with the perceived deficiency. Patients with dependent personality disorder are still prone to having associated depressive or adjustment disorders because they are so vulnerable to disappointments and disruptions in relationships.

Dependent personality disorder co-occurs with other personality disorders (85). In using DSM-III, I have found the dependent-avoidant combination to be particularly common. This may be reduced somewhat by changes in the DSM-III-R criteria for avoidant PD (see next section). Another association, between dependent and histrionic disorders, may be increased in making DSM-III-R diagnoses, however, since both include an item referring to need for reassurance.

Avoidant personality disorder. Avoidant personality disorder is characterized by social discomfort due to a fear of being negatively evaluated by others. The limitations of the DSM-III distinction between the person with avoidant personality disorder, ambivalence in wanting social connection, but avoiding it because of fears of rejection, and the person with schizoid personality disorder, indifference toward others because of a defect in his or her capacity to form interpersonal relationships, has been discussed earlier in this chapter in the section on schizoid personality disorder.

The concept of avoidant PD has been altered somewhat in DSM-III-R. A new dimension of generalized timidity, not limited to just social situations, has been added. This is accomplished by three new criteria (numbers 5-7) shown in Table 9.6, DSM-III-R Criteria for Avoidant Personality Disorder. The addition of these items referring to exaggerating the difficulties or risks of new, but ordinary, activities and situations and embarrassment and social anxiety make avoidant personality disorder in DSM-III-R closer in concept to the "phobic character" style common in the psychoanalytic literature. Although this change may reduce the problem of an invalid distinction between

TABLE 9.6 DSM-III-R Diagnostic Criteria for Avoidant Personality Disorder

A pervasive pattern of social discomfort, fear of negative evaluation, and timidity, beginning by early adulthood and present in a variety of contexts, as indicated by at least *four* of the following:

(1) is easily hurt by criticism or disapproval
(2) has no close friends or confidants (or only one) other than first-degree relatives
(3) is unwilling to get involved with people unless certain of being liked
(4) avoids social or occupational activities that involve significant interpersonal contact, e.g., refuses a promotion that will increase social demands
(5) is reticent in social situations because of a fear of saying something inappropriate or foolish, or of being unable to answer a question
(6) fears being embarrassed by blushing, crying, or showing signs of anxiety in front of other people
(7) exaggerates the potential difficulties, physical dangers, or risks involved in doing something ordinary but outside his or her usual routine, e.g., may cancel social plans because she anticipates being exhausted by the effort of getting there

APD and schizoid personality disorder, it introduces another potential problem. Differentiating avoidant personality disorder from social phobia, especially generalized social phobia (see Chapter 7), becomes more difficult. In fact, DSM-III-R lists social phobia as a possible complication of avoidant personality disorder; when both are present, both diagnoses can be given.

Obsessive compulsive personality disorder. The essential features of obsessive compulsive personality disorder (OCPD) are perfectionism and inflexibility. Obsessive compulsive personality disorder does not overlap extensively with other personality disorders in this cluster. Obsessive compulsive personality disorder shares with dependent and histrionic the problem of being applied as a sex stereotype—only this time referring to stereotypic male behavior such as excessive devotion to work or insistence on getting one's way (86). The same caution applies, therefore, for the clinician to document the pathological nature of the behaviors and the impairment that results. This is somewhat easier in the case of obsessive compulsive PD than dependent PD because the disorder items in the former (somewhat in DSM-III, but especially in DSM-III-R), such as perfectionism, preoccupation with details, and indecisiveness, all explicitly refer to how these traits interfere with functioning. Indecisiveness, for example, results in decision making that is avoided or postponed so that "the person cannot get assignments done on time because of ruminating about priorities" (18, p. 356).

A significant distinction to be made is between obsessive compulsive personality disorder and obsessive compulsive anxiety disorder. The decision in DSM-III to call the personality disorder compulsive, rather than obsessive-compulsive as in DSM-II, was an effort to emphasize the distinction. Although estimates vary from 35% to 75% that patients with obsessive compulsive disorder may have compulsive personality traits (87), patients with obsessive compulsive personality disorder may not have true obsessions or compulsions, i.e., recurrent, senseless thoughts or repetitive, stereotypic behavior rituals. (See also Chapter 7, Anxiety Syndromes.) Occasionally, the OCPD person's preoccupation with details, lists, schedules, and the like may approach the threshold of definition of obsessions or compulsions, but usually these behaviors will "feel" ego-syntonic and purposeful to such a person.

Passive aggressive personality disorder. Passive aggressive (PA) personality disorder is identified by passive resistance to demands for adequate social and occupational performance. Passive aggressive personality disorder was seldom diagnosed when DSM-III was used.

As Frances (49) has pointed out, this may be because it was the only personality disorder that could not be diagnosed in the presence of another personality disorder. Another factor might have been its unidimensional nature. In DSM-III, all four criteria referred to a single trait, resistance to external demands (49,88). Although the exclusion of other personality disorders has been dropped from the DSM-III-R criteria, the item list is still rather narrow. Some attempt has been made to emphasize cognitive and affective aspects of the disorder. Thus, criteria refer to the person's believing "that he or she is doing a much better job than others think," resenting the suggestions of others, being critical or scornful of people in authority, and becoming "sulky, irritable, or argumentative when asked to do something that he or she does not want to do" (18, pp. 357-358).

The other major difficulty in the diagnosis of PA personality disorder is that the behavior must be evident even in situations in which more self-assertive behavior is possible. The military is usually given as the best example in which self-assertive behavior is frequently not permitted and compliance with the demands of others required. Passive resistance to demands in this situation would not necessarily indicate a personality disorder. Sometimes it is more difficult for the clinician to assess the rigidity of the demands imposed by the external circumstances. An example would be a job situation in which an employer indicated that there was much latitude for individual, independent initiative while subtly exerting almost total control of the employee's behavior.

Other or Mixed Personality Disorders

DSM-III had a residual category for atypical, mixed, or other personality disorders. Atypical personality disorder was used when the clinician judged that a personality disorder was present, but was unable, because of insufficient information, to make a specific diagnosis. The mixed category was to be used when a person with a personality disorder had features of several of the specific PD types, but did not meet the criteria for any one. "Other personality disorder" was used when the clinician wanted to diagnose a specific personality disorder type that was not included in DSM-III.

Personality disorder not otherwise specified (NOS). In DSM-III-R, both atypical and mixed personality disorders would be diagnosed personality disorder NOS. The clinician should be cautious in making a personality disorder diagnosis in the face of what he or she considers "insufficient information" to specify type. Usually personality style or traits are clearer than the evidence for social or occupational impairment needed for the diagnosis of a disorder. When personality traits are unclear, the clinician should be sure not to overlook some Axis I disorder that might be responsible for impairment.

A common error in the use of the personality disorders section of DSM-III was assigning a diagnosis of mixed personality disorder to a patient who met criteria for one disorder and had features of one or more other personality disorders, or to a patient who met full criteria for more than one personality disorder. In the first instance, the clinician should diagnose, for example, borderline personality disorder with narcissistic and histrionic traits; in the second instance, diagnoses of multiple individual personality disorders should be made.

Mixed personality disorder in DSM-III now corresponds to personality disorder NOS; but, again, the features of such a disorder should not meet the full criteria for any specific type, yet cause significant impairment or subjective distress. A diagnosis of "impulsive" or "immature" personality disorder, if a clinician wished to make it, would also be PD NOS.

Self-defeating personality disorder. The diagnosis of masochistic personality disorder was by far the most frequently made diagnosis under the rubric of other personality disorder in DSM-III. Therefore, a decision was made by the Personality Disorders Advisory Committee to the Work Group to Revise DSM-III to develop criteria for masochistic personality disorder for DSM-III-R. The process of developing these criteria is notable for having been based not only on the theoretical opinions of experts but also on empirical data. The process was initiated and directed through a series of revisions by Dr. Frederic Kass, with the assistance of Drs. Roger MacKinnon and Robert Spitzer (89). Initially, a representative item set was gleaned from the psychoanalytic literature. Then clinicians were asked to apply the criteria to a series of patients. The reliability of the items was established, and the wording of reliable items was improved even further. Next, a national mail survey was undertaken to test out the criteria as they appeared in the 10/5/85 Draft of DSM-III-R. Finally, analyses of sex ratios and the discriminatory value of the items were conducted.

Masochistic personality disorder is thought by many clinicians to be a useful concept. In the process of revising DSM-III, it quickly became a very controversial category, however, as especially feminist groups objected to what they viewed as its sexually discriminatory content. In part, in response to these objections, the diagnosis has been renamed "self-defeating personality disorder," and is included in Appendix A of DSM-III-R as a proposed diagnostic category needing further study. The final criteria describe a pattern of self-defeating behavior, as shown in Table 9.7.

TABLE 9.7 DSM-III-R Diagnostic Criteria for Self-defeating Personality Disorder

A. A pervasive pattern of self-defeating behavior, beginning by early adulthood and present in a variety of contexts. The person may often avoid or undermine pleasurable experiences, be drawn to situations or relationships in which he or she will suffer, and prevent others from helping him or her, as indicated by at least *five* of the following:

   (1) chooses people and situations that lead to disappointment, failure, or mistreatment even when better options are clearly available
   (2) rejects or renders ineffective the attempts of others to help him or her
   (3) following positive personal events (e.g., new achievement), responds with depression, guilt, or a behavior that produces pain (e.g., an accident)
   (4) incites angry or rejecting responses from others and then feels hurt, defeated, or humiliated (e.g., makes fun of spouse in public, provoking an angry retort, then feels devastated)
   (5) rejects opportunities for pleasure, or is reluctant to acknowledge enjoying himself or herself (despite having adequate social skills and the capacity for pleasure)
   (6) fails to accomplish tasks crucial to his or her personal objectives despite demonstrated ability to do so, e.g., helps fellow students write papers, but is unable to write his or her own
   (7) is uninterested in or rejects people who consistently treat him or her well, e.g., is unattracted to caring sexual partners
   (8) engages in excessive self-sacrifice that is unsolicited by the intended recipients of the sacrifice

B. The behaviors in A do not occur exclusively in response to, or in anticipation of, being physically, sexually, or psychologically abused.

C. The behaviors in A do not occur only when the person is depressed.

Note: For coding purposes, record: 301.90 Personality Disorder NOS (Self-defeating Personality Disorder).

Sadistic personality disorder. Some critics have also objected to the preoccupation of mental health professionals with classifying the "victim" and ignoring the "victimizer" in situations in which one person takes advantage of or abuses another. This mental set may be the result of the fact that victims are more likely than victimizers to seek help with emotional problems, but this does not justify trying to understand the nature of only the victims' troubles.

Therefore, included also in Appendix A of DSM-III-R are criteria for a new diagnosis that describes a pattern of behavior characterized by cruel, demeaning, and aggressive behavior for reasons other than

TABLE 9.8 DSM-III-R Diagnostic Criteria for Sadistic Personality Disorder

A. A pervasive pattern of cruel, demeaning, and aggressive behavior, beginning by early adulthood, as indicated by the repeated occurrence of at least *four* of the following:

   (1) has used physical cruelty or violence for the purpose of establishing dominance in a relationship (not merely to achieve some noninterpersonal goal, such as striking someone in order to rob him or her)
   (2) humiliates or demeans people in the presence of others
   (3) has treated or disciplined someone under his or her control unusually harshly, e.g., a child, student, prisoner, or patient
   (4) is amused by, or takes pleasure in, the psychological or physical suffering of others (including animals)
   (5) has lied for the purpose of harming or inflicting pain on others (not merely to achieve some other goal)
   (6) gets other people to do what he or she wants by frightening them (through intimidation or even terror)
   (7) restricts the autonomy of people with whom he or she has a close relationship, e.g., will not let spouse leave the house unaccompanied or permit teenage daughter to attend social functions
   (8) is fascinated by violence, weapons, martial arts, injury, or torture

B. The behavior in A has not been directed toward only one purpose (e.g., spouse, one child) and has not been solely for the purpose of sexual arousal (as in sexual sadism).

Note: For coding purposes, record: 301.90 Personality Disorder NOS (Sadistic Personality Disorder).

sexual arousal (the latter behavior falls under the rubric of the paraphilias, see Chapter 12). This disorder is called sadistic personality disorder. The criteria for this potential personality disorder subtype are presented in Table 9.8. The important points in the differential diagnosis will undoubtedly be to distinguish the behavior from that of the paraphilias and from that of other disorders in the differential diagnosis of violent behavior, such as antisocial PD (see also Chapter 10).

SUMMARY

This chapter considers problems in differential diagnosis in an area of rapidly growing clinical importance, the personality disorders. Included among a series of problems applying to diagnosis of personality disorders in general are discussions of problems in interviewing the patient with a suspected personality disorder, in state vs. trait discrimination, in trait vs. disorder distinctions, in categorical vs. alternative classificatory models, and in diagnosis based on inferential judgments. Problems in the diagnosis of each individual disorder are covered, grouped according to the three DSM-III clusters: the odd or eccentric group; the dramatic, emotional, or erratic group; and the anxious or fearful group. Improvements introduced by DSM-III-R in the diagnosis of personality disorders are highlighted. A description of the new proposed DSM-III-R personality types—self-defeating and sadistic personality disorders—concludes the chapter.

REFERENCES

1. American Psychiatric Association: Diagnostic and Statistical Manual of Mental Disorders, Third Edition. Washington, DC, American Psychiatric Association, 1980
2. Pope HG Jr, Jonas JM, Hudson JI, Cohen BM, Gunderson JG: The validity of DSM-III borderline personality disorder: a phenomenologic, family history, treatment response, and long-term follow-up study. Arch Gen Psychiatry 40:23–30, 1983
3. McGlashan TH: The borderline syndrome. II. Is it a variant of schizophrenia or affective disorder? Arch Gen Psychiatry 40:1319–1323, 1983
4. Zimmerman M, Coryell W, Pfohl B, Stangl D: ECT response in depressed patients with major depression. J Affective Disord 7:309–318, 1984
5. Pilkonis PA, Frank E: Personality pathology in recurrent depression: nature, prevalence, and relationship to treatment response. Am J Psychiatry 145:435–441, 1988
6. Reich JH: DSM-III personality disorders and the outcome of treated panic disorder. Am J Psychiatry 145:1149–1152, 1988
7. Shapiro S, Skinner EA, Kessler LH, Von Korff M, German PS, Tischler GL, Leaf PJ, Benham L, Cottler L, Regier DA: Utilization of health and mental health services: three Epidemiologic Catchment Area sites. Arch Gen Psychiatry 41:971–978, 1984
8. Spitzer RL, Forman JB, Nee J: DSM-III field trials: I. Initial interrater diagnostic reliability. Am J Psychiatry 136:815–817, 1979
9. Williams JBW, Spitzer RL: DSM-III field trials: interrater reliability and list of project staff and participants, in Diagnostic and Statistical Manual of Mental Disorders, Third Edition. Washington, DC, American Psychiatric Association, 1980
10. Skodol AE, Williams JBW, Spitzer RL, Gibbon M, Kass F: Identifying common errors in the use of DSM-III through diagnostic supervision. Hosp Community Psychiatry 35:251–255, 1984
11. Frances AJ, Widiger TA: Personality disorders, in An Annotated Bibliography of DSM-III. Edited by Skodol AE, Spitzer RL. Washington, DC, American Psychiatric Press, 1987, pp 125–133
12. Hyler SE, Rieder RO, Spitzer RL, Williams JBW: Personality Diagnostic Questionnaire (PDQ). New York, New York State Psychiatric Institute, 1982
13. Millon T: The MCMI provides a good assessment of DSM-III disorders:

the MCMI-II will prove even better. J Pers Assess 49:379–391, 1985
14. Stangl D, Pfohl B, Zimmerman M, Bowers W, Corenthal C: A structured interview for the DSM-III personality disorders: a preliminary report. Arch Gen Psychiatry 42:591–596, 1985
15. Loranger AW, Susman V, Oldham J, Russakoff L: The Personality Disorder Examination: a preliminary report. J Personality Disord 1:1–13, 1987
16. Spitzer RL, Williams JBW, Gibbon M: The Structured Clinical Interview for DSM-III-R Personality Disorders (SCID-II). New York, Biometrics Research, New York State Psychiatric Institute, 1987
17. Hurt SW, Hyler SE, Frances A, Clarkin JF, Brent R: Assessing borderline personality disorder with self-report, clinical interview, or semistructured interview. Am J Psychiatry 141:1228–1231, 1984
18. American Psychiatric Association: Diagnostic and Statistical Manual of Mental Disorders, Third Edition, Revised. Washington, DC, American Psychiatric Association, 1987
19. Zimmerman M, Pfohl B, Stangl D, Corenthal C: Assessment of DSM-III personality disorders: the importance of interviewing an informant. J Clin Psychiatry 47:261–263, 1986
20. Zimmerman M, Pfohl B, Coryell W, Stangl D, Corenthal C: Diagnosing personality disorder in depressed patients: a comparison of patient and informant interviews. Arch Gen Psychiatry 45:733–737, 1988
21. McGlashan TH: Schizotypal personality disorder. Chestnut Lodge follow-up study: VI. Long-term follow-up perspectives. Arch Gen Psychiatry 43:328–334, 1986
22. McGlashan TH: The Chestnut Lodge follow-up study: III. Long-term outcome of borderline personalities. Arch Gen Psychiatry 43:20–30, 1986
23. Skodol AE, Rosnick L, Kellman D, Oldham JM, Hyler SE: Validating structured DSM-III-R personality disorder assessments with longitudinal data. Am J Psychiatry 145:1297–1299, 1988
24. Kendler KS, Gruenberg AM, Strauss JS: An independent analysis of the Copenhagen sample of the Danish adoption study of schizophrenia. II. The relationship between schizotypal personality disorder and schizophrenia. Arch Gen Psychiatry 38:982–984, 1981
25. Baron M, Gruen R, Asnis L, Kane J: Familial relatedness of schizophrenia and schizotypal states. Am J Psychiatry 140:1437–1442, 1983
26. Baron M, Gruen R, Rainer JD, Kane J, Asnis L, Lord S: A family study of schizophrenic and normal control probands: implications for the spectrum concept of schizophrenia. Am J Psychiatry 142:447–455, 1985
27. Kendler KS: Diagnostic approaches to schizotypal personality disorder: a historical perspective. Schizophr Bull 11:538–553, 1985
28. Kety SS: Schizotypal personality disorder: an operational definition of Bleuler's latent schizophrenia? Schizophr Bull 11:590–594, 1985
29. Strauss JS, Hafez H, Lieberman P, Harding CM: The course of psychiatric disorder. III. Longitudinal principles. Am J Psychiatry 242:289–296, 1985
30. Kass F, Skodol AE, Charles E, Spitzer RL, Williams JBW: Scaled ratings of DSM-III personality disorders. Am J Psychiatry 142:627–630, 1985
31. Karasu TB, Skodol AE: VIth axis for DSM-III: psychodynamic evaluation. Am J Psychiatry 137:607–610, 1980
32. Bond MP, Vaillant JS: An empirical study of the relationship between diagnosis and defense style. Arch Gen Psychiatry 43:285–288, 1986
33. Vaillant GE, Bond M, Vaillant CO: An empirically validated hierarchy of defense mechanisms. Arch Gen Psychiatry 43:786–794, 1986
34. Cantor N, Smith EE, French RS, Mezzich J: Psychiatric diagnosis as

prototype categorization. J Abnorm Psychol 89:181–193, 1980
35. Frances A: Categorical and dimensional systems of personality diagnosis: a comparison. Compr Psychiatry 23:516–527, 1982
36. Widiger TA, Trull TJ, Hurt SW, Clarkin J, Frances A: A multidimensional scaling of the DSM-III personality disorders. Arch Gen Psychiatry 44:557–563, 1987
37. Lorr M, McNair DM: An interpersonal behavioral circle. J Abn Soc Psychology 67:68–75, 1963
38. Leary T: Interpersonal Diagnosis of Personality. New York, Ronald, 1957
39. Kendell RE: The Role of Diagnosis in Psychiatry. Oxford, Blackwell, 1975
40. Widiger TA, Kelso K: Psychodiagnosis of Axis II. Clin Psychol Rev 3:491–510, 1983
41. Widiger TA, Frances A: The DSM-III personality disorders: perspectives from psychology. Arch Gen Psychiatry 42:615–623, 1985
42. Widiger TA, Hurt SW, Frances A, Clarkin JF, Gilmore M: Diagnostic efficiency and DSM-III. Arch Gen Psychiatry 41:1005–1012, 1984
43. Finn SE: Base rates, utilities, and DSM-III: shortcomings of fixed rule systems of psychodiagnosis. J Abnorm Psychol 91:294–302, 1982
44. Livesley WJ: Trait and behavioral prototypes of personality disorder. Am J Psychiatry 143:728–732, 1986
45. Widiger TA, Frances A, Spitzer RL, Williams JBW: The DSM-III-R personality disorders: an overview. Am J Psychiatry 145:786–795, 1988
46. Livesley, WJ: A systematic approach to the delineation of personality disorders. Am J Psychiatry 144:772–777, 1987
47. Livesley WJ, West M, Tanney A: Historical comment on DSM-III schizoid and avoidant personality disorders. Am J Psychiatry 142:1344–1347, 1985
48. Pfohl B, Coryell W, Zimmerman M, Stangl D: DSM-III personality disorders: diagnostic overlap and internal consistency of individual DSM-III criteria. Compr Psychiatry 27:21–34, 1986
49. Frances A: The DSM-III personality disorders section: a commentary. Am J Psychiatry 137:1050–1054, 1980
50. Morey LC: Personality disorders in DSM-III and DSM-III-R: convergence, coverage, and internal consistency. Am J Psychiatry 145:573–577, 1988
51. Spitzer RL, Endicott J, Gibbon M: Crossing the border into borderline personality and borderline schizophrenia: the development of criteria. Arch Gen Psychiatry 36:17–24, 1979
52. Kety SS: Mental illness in the biological and adoptive relatives of schizophrenic adoptees: findings relevant to genetic and environmental factors in etiology. Am J Psychiatry 240: 720–727, 1983
53. Kety SS, Rosenthal D, Wender PH, Schulsinger F: The types and prevalences of mental illness in the biological and adoptive families of adopted schizophrenics, in The Transmission of Schizophrenia. Edited by Rosenthal D, Kety SS. Oxford, London, Pergamon Press, 1968, pp 345–362
54. Squires-Wheeler E, Skodol AE, Friedman D, Erlenmeyer-Kimling L: A preliminary report of the specificity of DSM-III schizotypal personality traits. Psychol Med 18:757–765, 1988
55. Coryell W, Zimmerman M: The heritability of schizophrenia and schizoaffective disorder: a family study. Arch Gen Psychiatry 45:323–327, 1988
56. Hymowitz P, Frances A, Jacobsberg L, Sickles M, Hoyt R: Neuroleptic treatment of schizotypal personality disorder. Compr Psychiatry 27:267–271, 1986
57. Frances A: Validating schizotypal personality disorders: problems with the schizophrenia connection. Schizophr Bull 1:595–597, 1985

58. Dahl AA: Diagnosis of the borderline disorders. Psychopathology 18:18–28, 1985
59. Siever LJ, Gunderson JG: The search for a schizotypal personality: historical origins and current status. Compr Psychiatry 24:199–212, 1983
60. Perry JC, O'Connell ME, Drake R: An assessment of the schedule for schizotypal personalities and the DSM-III criteria for diagnosing schizotypal personality disorder. J Nerv Ment Dis 172:674–680, 1984
61. Gunderson JG, Siever LJ, Spaulding E: The search for a schizotype: crossing the border again. Arch Gen Psychiatry 40:15–22, 1983
62. Kendell RE, Cooper JE, Gourlay AJ, Copeland JRM, Sharpe L, Gurland BJ: Diagnostic criteria of American and British psychiatrists. Arch Gen Psychiatry 25:123–130, 1971
63. Widiger TA, Frances A: Axis II personality disorders: diagnostic and treatment issues. Hosp Community Psychiatry 36:619–627, 1985
64. Akhtar S, Thompson JA Jr: Overview: narcissistic personality disorder. Am J Psychiatry 139:12–20, 1982
65. Goldstein WN: DSM-III and the narcissistic personality. Am J Psychother 39:4–16, 1985
66. Akiskal HS, Chen SE, Davis GC, Puzantian VR, Kashgarian M, Bolinger JM: Borderline: an adjective in search of a noun. J Clin Psychiatry 46:41–48, 1985
67. Snyder S, Sajadi C, Pitts WM Jr, Goodpaster WA: Identifying the depressive border of the borderline personality disorder. Am J Psychiatry 139:814–817, 1982
68. Docherty J, Fiester S, Shea T: Syndrome diagnosis and personality disorder, in Psychiatry Update: The American Psychiatric Association Annual Review (Vol 5). Edited by Francis A, Hales R. Washington, DC, American Psychiatric Press, 1986
69. Gunderson JG, Elliot GR: The interface between borderline personality disorder and affective disorder. Am J Psychiatry 142:277–288, 1985
70. Charney DS, Nelson JC, Quinlan DM: Personality traits and disorder in depression. Am J Psychiatry 138:1601–1604, 1981
71. Cole JO, Salomon M, Gunderson JG, Sunderland P III, Simmonds P: Drug therapy in borderline patients. Compr Psychiatry 25:249–262, 1984
72. Akiskal HS: Subaffective disorders: dysthymic, cyclothymic and bipolar II disorders in the "borderline" realm. Psychiatr Clin North Am 4:25–46, 1981
73. Stone MH: Borderline conditions: a consideration of subtypes and an overview: directions for research. Psychiatr Clin North Am 4:3– 24, 1981
74. Leckman JF, Weissman MM, Merikangas KR, Pauls DL, Prusoff BA: Panic disorder and major depression. Arch Gen Psychiatry 40:1055–1060, 1983
75. Van Valkenburg CH, Akiskal HS, Puzantian V, Rosenthal T: Anxious depressions: clinical, family history, and naturalistic outcome comparisons with panic and major depressive disorders. J Affective Disord 6:67–82, 1984
76. Grunhaus L, King D, Greden JF, Flegel P: Depression and panic in patients with borderline personality disorder. Biol Psychiatry 20:688–692, 1985
77. Perry JC: Depression in borderline personality disorder: lifetime prevalence at interview and longitudinal course of symptoms. Am J Psychiatry 142:15–21, 1985
78. Jonas JM, Pope HG Jr: Psychosis in borderline personality disorder. Psychiatr Dev 2:295–308, 1984

79. Pope HG Jr, Jonas JM, Hudson JI, Cohen BM, Tohen M: An empirical study of psychosis in borderline personality disorder. Am J Psychiatry 142:1285–1290, 1985
80. Frances A, Clarkin JF, Gilmore M, Hurt SW, Brown R: Reliability of criteria for borderline personality disorder: a comparison of DSM-III and the Diagnostic Interview for Borderline Patients. Am J Psychiatry 141:1080–1084, 1984
81. Robins L: Deviant Children Grown Up. Baltimore, MD, Williams & Wilkins, 1966
82. Wulach JS: Diagnosing the DSM-III antisocial personality disorder. Prof Psychol 14:330–340, 1983
83. Kaplan MA: A woman's view of DSM-III. Am Psychol 38:786–792, 1983
84. Kass F, Spitzer RL, Williams JBW: An empirical study of the issue of sex bias in the diagnostic criteria of DSM-III axis II personality disorders. Am Psychol 38:799–801, 1983
85. Trull TJ, Widiger TA, Frances A: Covariation of criteria sets for avoidant, schizoid, and dependent personality disorders. Am J Psychiatry 144:767–771, 1987
86. Reich J: Sex distribution of DSM-III personality disorders in psychiatric outpatients. Am J Psychiatry 144:485–488, 1987
87. Insel TR: Obsessive and compulsive disorder: five clinical questions and a suggested approach. Compr Psychiatry 23:241–251, 1982
88. Millon T: Disorders of Personality: DSM-III, Axis II. Somerset, NJ, Wiley, 1981
89. Kass F, MacKinnon RA, Spitzer RL: Masochistic personality: an empirical study. Am J Psychiatry 143:216–218, 1986

CHAPTER 10

Antisocial, Aggressive, or Violent Behavior

Aggressive or violent behavior takes many forms, and can be associated with a wide range of clinical conditions. The agitation of the acutely psychotic patient with schizophrenia, the attacks of rage of people with an explosive disorder, the chronic aggressive acting-out in antisocial personality disorder, and the disinhibited aggression associated with substance intoxication are a few of the clinical situations that may confront the mental health practitioner.

Recently there has been a resurgence of interest in methods for the clinical evaluation of violent behavior as new, more effective treatment approaches have been sought (1-3). An illustration is the development of the Overt Aggression Scale (OAS), by Yudofsky and associates (4), for objectively measuring aggressive acts. The OAS divides aggressive behavior into four categories: verbal aggression, physical aggression against objects, physical aggression against self, and physical aggression against other people. Each category has a four-point scale of severity, with examples of behavior for each scale point. For physical aggression against other people, for instance, "makes threatening gesture, swings at people, grabs at clothes" are behaviors at the least severe point on the scale, and "attacks others, causing several physical injury (broken bones, deep lacerations, internal injury)" are among the behaviors rated most severe. The Overt Aggression Scale demonstrates the heterogeneity of aggressive or violent behavior.

Evaluation of the violent patient is fraught with difficulties. Some of these were mentioned in the discussion of the uncooperative patient in Chapter 1. Briefly, violent patients, if they pose an acute threat, are frightening; they frequently obstruct the clinician in carrying out the evaluation, and are often assessed under emergency conditions, with inherent limitations in time, resources, and information. This is compounded by the problems of assessment created by the particular types of psychopathology that tend to be associated with violence, for example, the disorganized thinking of psychotic disorders, memory impairment of organic mental disorders, intellectual deficiency of mental retardation, or dishonesty of antisocial personality disorder.

Probably one of the greatest challenges to the psychiatrist, or other mental health professional, is to control his or her own fear sufficiently to think clearly and logically about the threatening patient while maintaining a sufficiently wary posture to ensure his or her own safety and that of the patient and of any other people involved. A complete discussion of the evaluation of the violent patient under acute circumstances is beyond the scope of this text. Readers are advised to consult textbooks on emergency psychiatry (5-7) for a more detailed treatment of the subject. In this chapter I am assuming, unless otherwise indicated, that the clinician can obtain the information necessary to make a DSM-III or DSM-III-R diagnosis and focus on the problems of differential diagnosis in light of that information.

A General Model for the Diagnosis of Violent Behavior

Violence occurs when the balance between impulse and control is disturbed. The imbalance may be a chronic problem or may occur acutely. Any psychological or physical process that either heightens the aggressive impulse or impairs the person's capacity to control himself or herself can result in violent thoughts, fears, wishes, or acts, depending on the degree of the disturbance. From a diagnostic viewpoint, factors that affect the impulse/control balance are commonly associated with organic or toxic disorders, functional mental disturbances, or compelling psychosocial stressors.

Predicting Violence

The prediction of violence is not, in my opinion, one of the goals of differential diagnosis; rational intervention and treatment, however, can follow from an accurate diagnosis (8). There have been many attempts to define dangerousness or develop a set of predictive criteria for identifying the patient who will become violent. Some factors that have been suggested to have predictive value include: the degree of intent to do violence, the presence of an identifiable victim, the frequency and openness of threats, the possession of a concrete plan, access to weapons, a demonstrated incapacity to maintain control (9), a prior history of inflicting or attempting to inflict serious physical injury on another person, chronic anger or hostility, enjoyment of witnessing or inflicting suffering, lack of compassion, self-image as victim, and resentment of authority (10). Various historical factors that have been suggested as reliable predictors of future violence are childhood brutality or deprivation; homes lacking warmth and affection; early loss of a parent; a so-called "violent triad" of fire-setting, bed-wetting, and cruelty to animals; prior violent acts; military history; and reckless driving (11-13). Probably the best predictor of future violence is past violence. But in the final analysis, all attempts to correlate future behavior with historical factors or personality traits have uniformly low predictive value (14).

Overview of Differential Diagnosis

Table 10.1 depicts the overall DSM-III-R classification of disorders of antisocial, aggressive, or violent behavior. The listed diagnoses correspond to those to which the diagnostician would be led by the DSM-III decision tree for differential diagnosis of antisocial, aggressive, defiant, or oppositional behavior, with a few significant additions. DSM-III-R no longer includes a decision tree for antisocial, aggressive, or violent behavior; Figure 10.1 is a modification of the DSM-III tree to reflect changes in the DSM-III-R classification and the somewhat broader list of diagnoses that I consider important in the differential.

Since full chapters are devoted to the differential diagnosis of psychotic features, mood disturbance, personality disturbance, and disorders with a specific organic etiology, disorders in these groups will be mentioned only briefly. The disorders that will be discussed in greater detail are mental retardation, the explosive disorders, conduct disorder, attention-deficit disorder, oppositional defiant disorder, adjustment disorder with distubance of conduct, and the V codes relevant to aggressive, violent, or antisocial behavior. In some instances, revisions in terminology or diagnostic concepts have been introduced by DSM-III-R. These will be mentioned or discussed in relation to the individual disorders.

General Principles of Differential Diagnosis

For diagnostic and treatment purposes, it is useful to answer a sequence of questions in order to establish a more narrow set of diagnostic possibilities for the patient who presents with violent behavior.

Figure 10.1 Decision Tree for the Differential Diagnosis of Antisocial, Aggressive, or Violent Behavior*

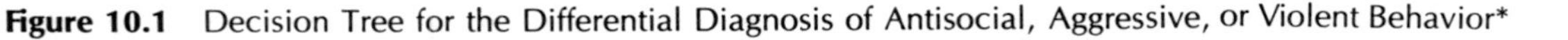

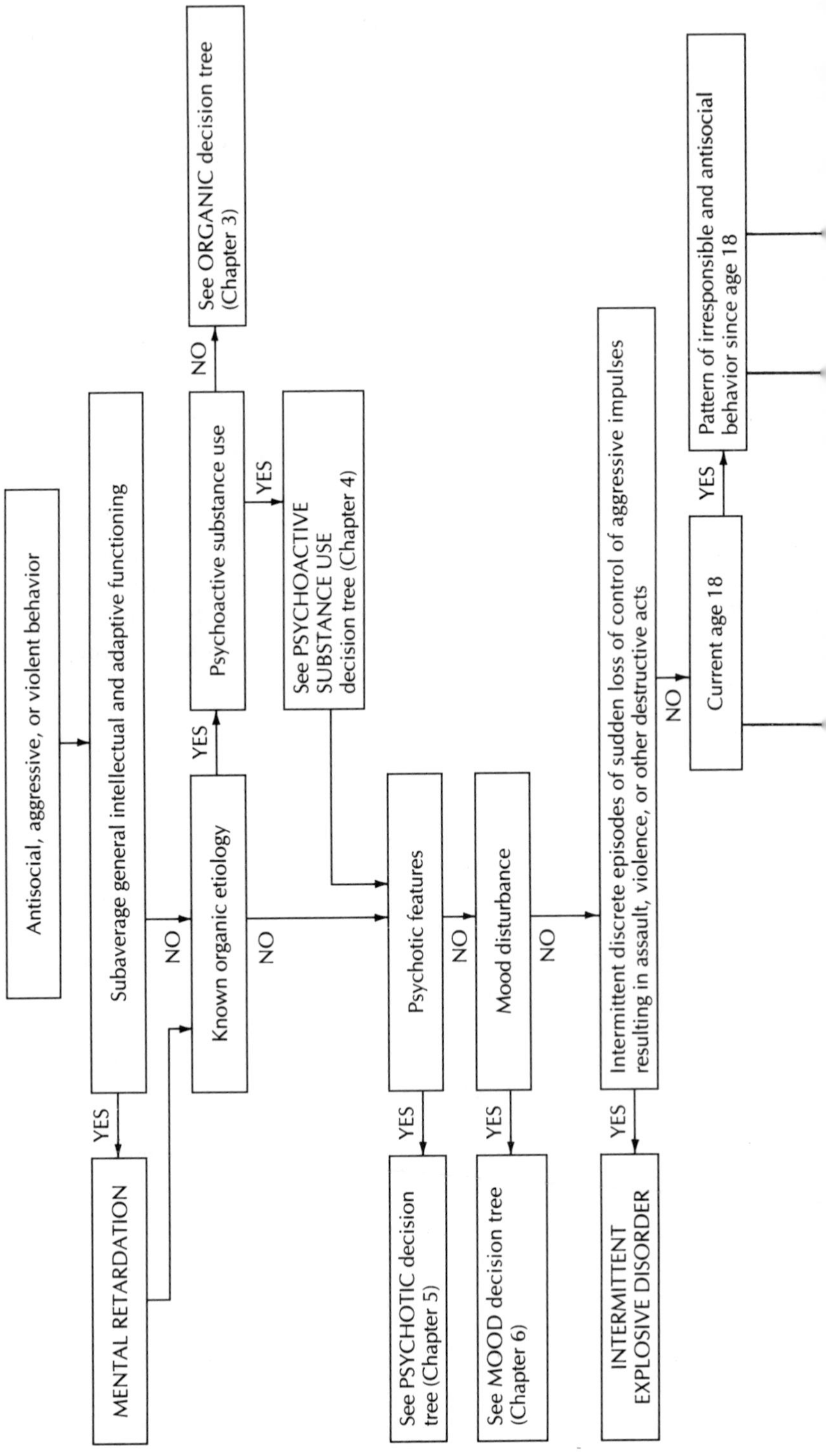

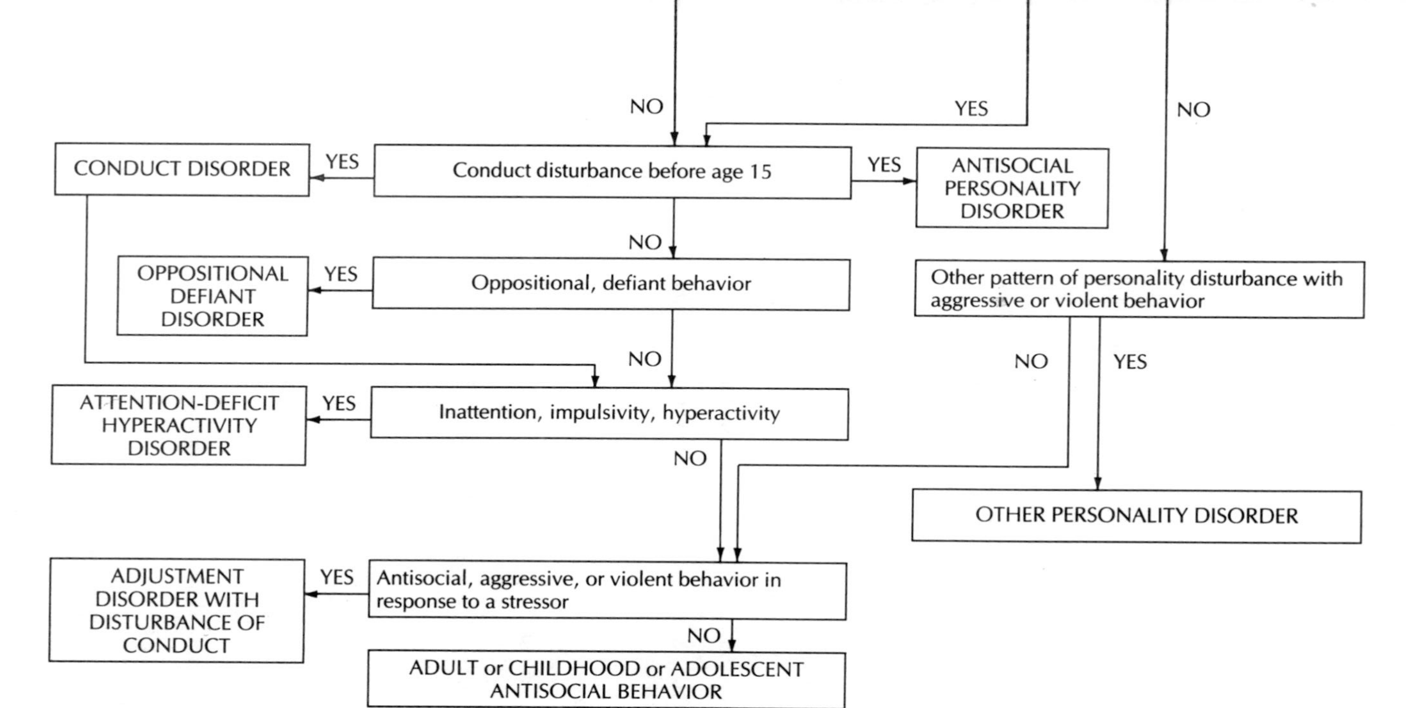

* Expanded version of the DSM-III decision tree for the differential diagnosis of antisocial, aggressive, defiant, or oppositional behavior.

1. Is the person of normal intelligence?
2. Is a known organic factor etiologically related to the behavior?
3. Is the behavior secondary to psychotic symptoms or a prominent mood abnormality?
4. Is the behavior an acute, discrete, or isolated episode, or is it a chronic, ongoing condition or pattern of behavior?
5. What is the patient's age?
6. What is the role, if any, of situational, stress-related factors?
7. Is the violence a sign of a mental disorder at all?

Table 10.1 Disorders in the Differential Diagnosis of Antisocial, Aggressive, or Violent Behavior

MENTAL RETARDATION

ORGANIC MENTAL DISORDERS
- Delirium and dementia
- Organic mood or delusional disorder
- Organic personality syndrome, explosive type
- Psychoactive substance-induced organic mental disorders

IMPULSE CONTROL DISORDERS NOT ELSEWHERE CLASSIFIED
- Intermittent explosive disorder

PSYCHOTIC DISORDERS
- Schizophrenia and psychotic disorders not otherwise specified
- Delusional (Paranoid) disorder
- Major mood disorders

PERSONALITY DISORDERS
- Antisocial
- Borderline
- Histrionic
- Narcissistic
- Paranoid
- Schizotypal

DISRUPTIVE BEHAVIOR DISORDERS
- Attention-deficit hyperactivity disorder
- Conduct disorder
- Oppositional defiant disorder

ADJUSTMENT DISORDER
- Adjustment disorder with disturbance of conduct
- Adjustment disorder with disturbance of emotions and conduct

V CODES
- Childhood, adolescent, or adult antisocial behavior

Assessing the Presence of Impaired Intellectual Functioning

In DSM-III, mental retardation (MR) was defined as significantly subaverage general intellectual functioning that results in, or is associated with, deficits or an impairment in adaptive functioning, and that begins before the age of 18. Significantly subaverage intellectual functioning was taken to be an IQ of 70, give or take 5 points, on an individually administered IQ test. Usually, major aspects of adaptive functioning such as self-sufficiency, personal independence, daily living skills, and social skills and responsibility were assumed to be impaired in people with IQs below 70, but both low IQ and functional impairment were deemed necessary for the diagnosis of MR. The clinician's judgment of adaptive functioning, based on considerations such as those discussed in the section on DSM-III Axis V in this book (see Chapter 2), was the sole standard for this requirement; no standardized test was required.

In DSM-III-R, scales useful in quantifying adaptive functioning are mentioned (the Vineland Adaptive Behavior Scales and the American Association of Mental Deficiency Adaptive Behavior Scale) but clinical judgment of general adaptation is still sufficient for making the diagnosis. In rating adaptive functioning, the clinician should remember to rate the mentally retarded person against the hypothetical population of all others in his or her age and cultural group, not simply against other people with mental retardation.

In DSM-III, mental retardation was divided into four subtypes based on severity, as measured by IQ level: mild (IQ, 50-70), moderate (35-49), severe (20-34), and profound (below 20). The IQ levels to be used in distinguishing the degrees of severity have been slightly modified in DSM-III-R: mild mental retardation (IQ, 50-55 to approximately 70), moderate (35-40 to 50-55), severe (20-25 to 35-40), and profound (below 20 or 25). These ranges reflect an error of measurement of IQ of about five points thought to characterize an IQ score obtained by any standardized test.

Mental retardation more severe than "mild" is rarely difficult to recognize clinically, even without formal testing or physical stigmata, such as in Down's syndrome or phenylketonuria. People with an IQ above 70 but under 85 may be given a V code, borderline intellectual functioning, if some clinical attention or services seem warranted. Adaptive functioning is very variable in this IQ range.

Behavior problems are prominent among the associated features of mental retardation. DSM-III specifically referred to irritability, aggressivity, and temper tantrums, which might bring the retarded person for diagnosis and treatment of aggressive behavior. DSM-III-R mentions low frustration tolerance, aggressiveness, and poor impulse control. When behavioral symptoms require intervention or treatment, their presence was noted in DSM-III by means of a 5th-digit subclassification of the level of mental retardation. This convention was dropped in DSM-III-R, which states: "At the present time there is no satisfactory subclassification of behavioral symptoms associated with mental retardation" (15, p. 29).

Problems in Differential Diagnosis

Mental retardation is discussed first in the differential diagnosis of aggressive behavior because many of the other DSM-III disorders with behavioral problems as prominent features had exclusion criteria to rule out mental retardation as a cause. The differential diagnosis between mental retardation and these other syndromes was problematic, however, because of the many different guidelines given.

Dementia, in DSM-III, was an organic mental syndrome characterized by general intellectual impairment. When intellectual impairment developed for the first time after the age of 18, dementia was the appropriate diagnosis according to DSM-III. Usually, there was a clear history of the development of a major physical illness or serious head injury, documented by laboratory tests and/or abnormal physical findings (see Chapter 3). When impaired intelligence was evident from birth, the diagnosis of mental retardation was sufficient. When the clinical picture developed before age 18 in a person who had previously had normal intelligence, then *both* a dementia and mental retardation should have been diagnosed.

Many of the other diagnoses found in the DSM-III section of disorders usually first evident in infancy, childhood, or adolescence describe symptom complexes that might be observed in mental retardation. Examples were the pervasive developmental disorders, infantile autism and childhood onset pervasive developmental disorders, attention deficit disorder with hyperactivity (ADDH), and stereotyped movement disorder. When these other Axis I disorders were present with mental retardation, DSM-III instructed that all diagnoses should be made. Attention deficit disorder, however, had an exclusion criterion for severe or profound mental retardation, which was a partial contradiction. Similarly, the specific developmental disorders were said to sometimes coexist with mental retardation, but several were specifically excluded by a diagnosis of mental retardation.

DSM-III also stated in its discussion of the differential diagnosis of mental retardation that a diagnosis of mental retardation "should be made regardless of the presence of another diagnosis." This should have been qualified, however, by the statement "providing the other diagnosis is not specifically excluded by MR." For example, DSM-III schizophrenia criterion F stated that the disturbance was "Not due to any Organic Mental Disorder or Mental Retardation" (16, p. 190). This was not always easy to determine. Poor social functioning, odd behavior, and limited emotional expressivity and cognitive capacity occur in mental retardation, and may suggest schizophrenia. In the discussion of differential diagnosis of schizophrenia, DSM-III said that the clinician could make both diagnoses if he or she was certain that delusions and hallucinations "are definitely present and are not the result of difficulties in communication" (16, p. 188). This statement that schizophrenia and mental retardation could be diagnosed together was in apparent contradiction to the diagnostic criteria for schizophrenia.

In the presence of a pervasive disturbance such as mental retardation, attribution of various symptoms to one process versus another is practically impossible and probably an example of a pseudoprecision in diagnosis that is neither reliable nor valid. Numerous critics of the DSM-III approach to mental retardation have argued that intellectual functioning is a domain of assessment that ought to be considered independently of Axis I symptomatology. As such, conceptually it fits more with Axis II pathology than Axis I. Consequently, in DSM-III-R mental retardation has been regrouped with specific and pervasive developmental disorders under the rubric of developmental disorders on Axis II. Developmental disorders and personality disorders usually have an onset in childhood or adolescence and persist in more or less stable form into adult life, thus unifying the Axis II concept (see also Chapter 2). When the etiology of mental retardation is evident, it is listed on Axis III.

The shift of mental retardation from Axis I to Axis II changes the relationship of MR to other disorders in differential diagnosis. Schizophrenia, for example, is no longer excluded by mental retardation. In fact, no other DSM-III-R disorder is specifically excluded by MR. Certain difficult clinical judgments must still be made before a diagnosis in addition to MR can be made. The statement suggesting that the clinician can attribute delusions or hallucinations to schizophrenia in a person with communication difficulties associated with MR remains in DSM-III-R. In the DSM-III-R discussion of the differential diagnosis of attention-deficit hyperactivity disorder (ADHD), it states that the additional diagnosis of ADHD is made for a child with mental retardation only if the "relevant symptoms are excessive for the child's mental age" (15, p. 52).

ASSESSING THE ROLE OF OTHER ORGANIC FACTORS

Finding that a person does not have subaverage or impaired general intellectual functioning does not rule out an organic cause for the violent behavior. Other structural, metabolic, or toxic conditions may give rise to either aggressive impulses or weaken controls. Organic etiologies may be either endogenous or exogenous. Structural abnormalities, such as a tumor, may result in an organic personality syndrome associated with aggressive behavior, or a subdural hematoma following head trauma may result in loss of behavioral control associated with a delirium. Examples of endogenous toxic/metabolic conditions would be deliria associated with uremia or anoxia, and of exogenous causes, psychoactive substance- or medication-induced disturbances. An organic etiology is highly presumptive when characteristic mental status findings of a delirium are present, including attentional difficulties, reduced level of consciousness, disorientation, and memory impairment. Perceptual disturbances, disorganized thinking or incoherent speech, disturbances of the sleep-wakefulness cycle (insomnia and daytime drowsiness), and psychomotor changes may be associated with either delirium or a functional mental disorder.

Sometimes, however, the symptoms of an organic brain syndrome are much softer, and are limited to a subtle change in personality or the abrupt occurrence of violent behavior itself. Evidence of the organic etiology comes through careful observation, questioning, physical examination, and laboratory tests. The reader is referred to Chapter 3, Disturbances with Specific Organic Etiologies, and Chapter 4, Disturbances Associated with the Use of Psychoactive Substances, for a complete discussion of the differential diagnosis of endogenous and substance-induced organic mental disorders. Several of the case vignettes in Chapter 4 illustrate the common role of substances in the etiology of aggressive or violent behavior.

Intermittent Explosive Disorder

DSM-III included intermittent explosive disorder as one of six disorders of impulse control not elsewhere classified. Intermittent explosive disorder was described as (*1*) discrete episodes of loss of control of aggressive impulses resulting in serious assault or destruction of property; (*2*) behavior that is grossly out of proportion to any precipitating stressor; (*3*) absence of signs of generalized impulsivity or aggressiveness between episodes; (*4*) behavior that was not due to schizophrenia, antisocial personality disorder, or conduct disorder. This diagnosis replaced the DSM-II diagnosis of explosive personality, with the rationale that the explosive behavior, although a pattern, was not characteristic of the person's overall functioning.

There have been a number of critics of the diagnosis of intermittent explosive disorder. In the only large-scale study of the diagnosis, Monopolis and Lion (17) collected data on 20 inpatients over a two-year period who received the diagnosis, documenting how many of the DSM-III criteria, the essential features described in the DSM-III text, the associated features, and the ancillary features each patient had. They found that the diagnostic criteria had not been applied rigorously; only 9 of the 20 patients met all of the DSM-III diagnostic criteria as they conceptualized them. In fact, none of the patients would have met the diagnostic criteria for intermittent explosive disorder as they actually appeared in the final DSM-III manual, since none of the 20 met the criterion of no generalized impulsivity/aggressiveness between episodes. What was significantly associated with the clinical diagnosis was a very high proportion of patients (17 of 20) with electroencephalographic (EEG) abnormalities.

The association of EEG abnormalities and other neurological parameters with episodic violence has been noted by researchers for a number of years. The term *episodic dyscontrol* has been used to describe these patients (18).

Frank epilepsy may be the most common neurological diagnosis associated with violent behavior. Violence may occur in conjunction with seizure discharge (rare) or, more commonly, as interictal or postictal phenomena (19,20). Patients report a sense of rising tension, which they liken to being flooded by a physical "wave of rage." Occasionally the patient can control the urge to strike out, but more often cannot. Afterward, if the patient remembers the behavior, he or she may experience remorse or guilt. These features are particularly characteristic of the temporal lobe attacks that occur in adolescent or young adult males. Not all patients with a history of epilepsy are prone to violent behavior, however; estimates in the literature range from 5% to 50% (21-24), with higher frequencies in temporal lobe epilepsy. Also, abnormal EEGs are not universal in patients with paroxysmal rage attacks (25).

Consistent with the EEG abnormalities, other investigators have pointed out that many patients with recurrent attacks of intermittent rage can eventually be shown to have an underlying developmental or acquired brain deficit. Elliott (26), in a study of 286 such patients, found evidence of organicity in 94%. Thirty percent had complex partial seizures. Yudofsky and Silver (personal communication) argued before the Organic Mental Syndromes and Disorders Advisory Committee working on DSM-III-R that it was not the exception, as DSM-III stated, but rather the rule that an underlying physical disorder or condition conducive to brain dysfunction, such as perinatal trauma, infantile seizures, head trauma, or encephalitis, predisposed to intermittent explosive disorder. They recommended a new diagnosis, organic aggressive syndrome, for DSM-III-R. The proposed criteria were to be (*1*) persistent or recurrent aggressive outbursts of either a verbal or a physical nature; (*2*) outbursts out of proportion to the precipitating stress or provocation; (*3*) evidence from history, physical examination, or laboratory tests of a specific organic factor judged to be etiologically related to the disturbance; and (*4*) evidence that the outbursts were not primarily related to personality features or disorders such as paranoia, bipolar disorder, conduct disorder, or antisocial, narcissistic, or borderline personality disorders. These investigators have found that such a syndrome is responsive to treatment with the beta blocker propranolol (27).

In response to these critiques, the diagnosis of intermittent explosive disorder was to be removed from DSM-III-R. Isolated explosive disorder, the diagnosis for a single, discrete episode of violence with catastrophic impact on others, was deleted, since this diagnosis might too readily be applied to anyone who committed a murder who was not generally impulsive or aggressive before the episode.

Intermittent explosive disorder was retained as a diagnosis in the final version of DSM-III-R. In addition to the disorders noted by DSM-III to exclude the diagnosis, DSM-III-R lists all other psychotic disorders (besides schizophrenia), borderline personality disorder, intoxication with a psychoactive substance, and organic personality syndrome. In DSM-III-R, the modified organic personality syndrome with an explosive subtype (see also Chapter 3) includes an item for "recurrent outbursts of aggression or rage that are grossly out of proportion to any precipitating psychosocial stressors" (15, p. 115) as one of the manifestations of the personality pattern or change in personality. The clinician is instructed by DSM-III-R to make the diagnosis of organic personality syndrome if the violent outbursts are judged to be the result of a specific organic factor. Intermittent explosive disorder would be diagnosed in those rare instances in which no organic factor is present and all other clinical syndromes that can cause episodic loss of control have been ruled out.

Attention-Deficit Disorder

The broadening of the criteria for the diagnosis of organic personality syndrome makes its differentiation from attention-deficit disorder important. Attention-deficit disorder is a behavioral disturbance that may cause violent behavior. It is associated with neurological soft signs and a history of perinatal or childhood trauma, anoxia, encephalitis, or febrile convulsions.

DSM-III included diagnoses of attention deficit disorder (ADD) with hyperactivity (ADDH) and without hyperactivity. The disturbance in children with the latter diagnosis was limited to signs of inattention and impulsivity. There was also a residual type, generally for adults who had ADDH as children. Although these people could be observed to be no longer hyperactive, they continued to show signs of attentional deficits and impulsivity in adult life, such as difficulties in organizing work and completing tasks, difficulty concentrating, being easily distracted, and making sudden decisions or acting without sufficient thought of the possible consequences. Diag-

Table 10.2 Symptoms of DSM-III-R Attention-Deficit Hyperactivity Disorder

1. Fidgets or squirms
2. Difficulty remaining seated
3. Easily distracted by extraneous stimuli
4. Difficulty waiting turn
5. Blurts out answers to questions
6. Difficulty following through on instructions
7. Difficulty sustaining attention to tasks or activities
8. Shifts from one uncompleted activity to another
9. Difficulty playing quietly
10. Talks excessively
11. Interrupts or intrudes on others
12. Does not listen
13. Often loses things
14. Engages in dangerous activities without considering consequences

Eight of 14 are required. The symptoms are frequently modified by the term "often." They are arranged in descending order of discriminating power based on data from a national field trial of the DSM-III-R criteria for disruptive behavior disorders. See DSM-III-R (p. 53) for the exact criteria.

nosis of ADD was not made if the symptoms were due to schizophrenia, affective disorder, or severe or profound mental retardation.

In a field trial of several hundred children, to revise the criteria for ADD, the clinical diagnosis of ADD without hyperactivity was hardly ever made. The diagnosis has therefore been eliminated from DSM-III-R. The new DSM-III-R diagnosis of attention-deficit hyperactivity disorder (ADHD) is defined by a broad index of 14 symptoms (see Table 10.2), 8 of which are required for a period of 6 months or more. The age at onset must be before seven. The diagnosis is not made if the disturbance meets the criteria for a pervasive developmental disorder (autistic disorder or pervasive developmental disorder NOS). The diagnostic criteria *do not* require neurological soft signs or typical childhood history, but these are discussed as associated features in DSM-III-R.

Differential diagnosis of organic personality syndrome and ADHD would be made according to the following logic. If the patient is still an adolescent, or younger, and has only the features of ADHD, then only this diagnosis applies. A child or adolescent with more severely out-of-control behavior and evidence of neurological impairment could receive the diagnosis of organic personality syndrome instead. If over 18, the person who displays aggression and neurological dysfunction receives a diagnosis of organic personality syndrome or, if the disturbance is milder, ADHD (residual state). Follow-up studies (28,29) have shown that hyperactivity can persist into adult life, making the DSM-III statement "signs of hyperactivity are no longer present" incorrect. Since any diagnosis can be listed as in a residual state in DSM-III-R, the need for a diagnosis of ADD, residual type, has been obviated.

The following case illustrates a tricky diagnostic discrimination between ADDH persisting into adulthood and personality disorder.

Temper, Temper

A 43-year-old director of a small public relations firm in Los Angeles and his wife sought counseling for marital problems. For the past four years the wife had been becoming increasingly dissatisfied with their relationship, which she claimed had been reduced to "bare minimums" because of the husband's ever-growing preoccupation with his work. In addition, they had been having major arguments about various commitments that he had made to their personal or family lives, such as taking a vacation or attending one of their children's school activities, and then reneged on. The fights began with her confronting him with his broken promise but then quickly escalated to shouting matches that culminated in his throwing books or potted plants across the room, breaking a shower door or a wooden chair, or even once turning over the dining-room table completely set for a dinner party. He had never actually hit his wife with an object or his hand, but he had on several occasions grabbed her arm and squeezed it hard enough to leave a mark.

Up until four years previously, the couple's relationship had been much better. Earlier in their marriage, the man had been employed by several large public relations concerns; he enjoyed his work, kept it "much more in perspective," and was able to socialize, relax, and have fun. It was just since he had ventured off on his own that he had begun to experience strain and pressure. He was now more serious about work, more anxious about whether he would be successful, and more driven to be productive, at the expense of everything else in his life. Although he had never before felt that he needed to be "the best," he now thought he was setting higher and higher standards and needed more and more financial success in order to feel fulfilled.

The man attributed his broken promises to "selfishness." He said, "I admit it; I never follow through. I say 'yes' to satisfy her, but I'm really thinking of other things. I don't know—I'm either not paying attention, or I forget. There's no question it's a sign of neglect, uncaring—if it's not for my immediate benefit, then forget it—but I don't seem to be able to do anything about it."

As the history of the problems unfolded, the man acknowledged that he continually started projects around the house or at work that he didn't finish. "I get distracted by the next thing," he said. "I'll get a phone call during a meeting, get interrupted in my train of thought, and not know what the meeting was about." Or else he would plan one agenda for a meeting, then, at the last minute, start talking about something quite different, without being aware of why he made the switch. He admitted that he generally was not a "feeling" person, didn't pay attention to the needs of others—only his own—and lacked concern and caring. He said he was very impatient, couldn't stand waiting in lines, and hated feeling responsible for anyone other than himself. On the other hand, he felt that his life was somehow now getting the better of him, "eating me up," and that he lacked a sense of where it was all heading. He claimed to want desperately to change.

A developmental history revealed that his mother thought that he had been hyperactive as a child. He had temper tantrums and cried when angry—"Everything had to go my way." He demanded lots of attention from his parents. He did well in school, however, was popular with his classmates, was in the Boy Scouts, and played the trumpet in the school band.

The man described his parents as extremely selfish people who also never did anything for others or cared about them. "They were children themselves, even after they had their own children." His father was usually very quiet, but occasionally had fits of screaming or shouting. His mother was undisciplined, spoiled, and pampered.

The man in "Temper, Temper" displays problems with inattention, difficulty completing tasks, impulsivity, low frustration tolerance, and a hot temper. Some investigators (30) believe that these signs (along with hyperactivity and affective lability) are diagnostic of attention-deficit disorder, residual type, in adults and predict a positive response to stimulant medication, such as methylphenidate or pemoline.

The man also shows signs of reacting to criticism with feelings of rage, interpersonal exploitativeness, preoccupation with success, entitlement, and lack of empathy that are suggestive of narcissistic personality disorder, and excessive devotion to work, restricted expression of affection, and lack of generosity that are obsessive compulsive personality traits.

There would be no reason not to give two diagnoses—ADHD, residual state, on Axis I and narcissistic personality disorder with obsessive compulsive traits on Axis II. The history of full-blown ADHD as a child (a requirement for the residual state designation), however, must be viewed with some skepticism, given the limitations of the man's parents and his lack of problems in school. Some clinicians might prefer to note the ADHD diagnosis as "provisional," pending the outcome of a trial of medication.

Other child and adolescent disorders with behavioral problems are conduct disorder and oppositional disorder. These have been grouped together with ADHD in DSM-III-R as disruptive behavior disorders. Since there are no, even subtle, signs of organicity in the patients with these disorders, they will be discussed below under aggressive patterns of behavior. DSM-III-R autistic disorder, which can clinically resemble an organic mental disorder in an adolescent or young adult, and which takes diagnostic precedence over ADHD, is discussed in the differential diagnosis of schizophrenia, childhood and adolescent onset, in Chapter 5.

ASSOCIATION WITH MAJOR FUNCTIONAL DISORDERS

Functional psychotic disorders frequently lead to reduced impulse control and violence (31,32). In my study (8) of patients presenting to an emergency room with violent behavior, the diagnosis of schizophrenia was frequently associated with aggressive acting-out that required hospitalization (33). The whole gamut of psychotic disorders, including psychotic affective disorders, must be considered, however. Schizophrenia and related psychotic disorders, including schizophreniform disorder, schizoaffective disorder, brief reactive psychosis, induced psychotic disorder (shared paranoid disorder), psychotic disorder NOS (atypical psychosis), and delusional (paranoid) disorder are discussed in Chapters 5 and 12. Mood disorders are discussed in Chapter 6.

PATTERNS OF AGGRESSIVE BEHAVIOR

When aggressive behavior seems to be a recurrent pattern rather than associated with episodic disruptions in reality testing or impulse control, then a personality disorder is a likely diagnosis. In DSM-III and DSM-III-R, the dramatic, emotional, or erratic cluster of personality disorders including histrionic, narcissistic, antisocial, and borderline personality disorder are most likely to be associated with a pattern of aggressive or violent behavior. The most common personality disturbance associated with violence would be antisocial personality disorder. The violent behavior of the antisocial personality is more organized and purposeful than that of the person with an organic mental syndrome or a psychotic disorder. Patients with borderline personality disorder may have frequent temper outbursts or recurrent physical fights. Occasionally, people with schizotypal or paranoid personality disorders "explode" with a very dramatic, violent outburst, as in a mass murder. The differential diagnosis of the individual personality disorders is the subject of Chapter 9.

A pattern of aggressive behavior in a person under the age of 18 suggests a conduct disorder. In DSM-III, conduct disorder, aggressive subtype, was defined as "a repetitive and persistent pattern of aggressive conduct in which the basic rights of others are violated" (16, p. 47). Aggressive conduct disorder was subdivided into an undersocialized subtype, with a "failure to establish a normal degree of affection, empathy, or bond with others" (16, p. 48), and a socialized subtype, with evidence of social attachment to others. The aggressive-nonaggressive distinction involved differentiating physical violence against persons or property, such as assault, mugging, rape, and breaking and entering, or theft involving confrontation with a victim, from behavior such as rule-breaking, running away from home, lying, and stealing that did not involve confrontation with a victim.

DSM-III subdivided conduct disorder on the basis of data that suggested that the undersocialized, aggressive subtype was most predictive of adult antisocial personality disorder (34). It was recognized that the subtyping was controversial. After experience with the categories, child psychiatrists and psychologists did not find them to be useful (35), and since the publication of DSM-III, the subtyping has not been in accordance with subsequent research findings. Conduct disorder is defined in DSM-III-R by an index of 13 symptoms, 3 of which are required over a 6-month period for the diagnosis. The criteria, outlined in Table 10.3, combine both aggressive and nonaggressive elements and many of the childhood symptoms of antisocial personality disorder (ASPD). Physical fights, use of weapons, forced sexual activity, fire-setting, and mugging are examples of violent behaviors. The new subtypes are solitary aggressive type and group type. A diagnosis of conduct disorder is not given to a person over 18 if the full criteria for ASPD are met.

The other disruptive behavior disorder of childhood and adolescence is oppositional defiant disorder. The criteria for oppositional defiant disorder in DSM-III-R have also been reformulated, using the prototype model of classification, into an index of nine symptoms, five of which are required over a period of at least six months. The criteria emphasize arguments, temper tantrums, and defiant, vindictive, or annoying behavior. The behavioral disturbances of oppositional behavior are milder than those of conduct disorder. If they occur in association with the more severe behaviors of conduct disorder, the

Table 10.3 Symptoms of DSM-III-R Conduct Disorder

1. Has stolen repeatedly without confrontation of victim
2. Runs away from home
3. Lies
4. Deliberately sets fires
5. Truant
6. Has broken into house, building, or car
7. Has deliberately destroyed others' property
8. Is physically cruel to animals
9. Has forced someone into sexual activity
10. Has used weapon in fights
11. Initiates physical fights
12. Has stolen with confrontation of victim
13. Is physically cruel to others

Three of 13 are required. The symptoms are frequently modified by the term "often" or "more than once." They are arranged in descending order of discriminating power based on data from a national field trial of the DSM-III-R criteria for disruptive behavior disorders. See DSM-III-R (p. 55) for exact criteria.

latter diagnosis takes precedence. Mood disorders, as a cause for oppositional behavior, also take precedence over a diagnosis of oppositional defiant disorder.

According to DSM-III criteria, attention deficit disorder, conduct disorder, and oppositional disorder frequently overlapped; the new criteria in DSM-III-R were designed to minimize overlap. Other than the previously mentioned exclusion of oppositional defiant disorder by conduct disorder, however, there are no exclusions. ADHD emphasizes symptoms of inattention, impulsivity, and hyperactivity that occur even when the child is alone and that do not necessarily involve others. It is conceivable, though, that patients may meet the criteria for ADHD and either oppositional defiant or conduct disorders if their behavior infringes on others, as in the case of excessive aggression or violence.

Assessing the Role of Psychosocial Stressors

Not all causes of heightened impulsiveness are organic, neurological, or related to functional mental disorders. Numerous studies have confirmed that violence commonly occurs in close or intimate social contexts (36). In assessing the nature and severity of psychosocial stressors associated with violent behavior, it is important to consider the source of the stress—e.g., parental, conjugal, financial, legal—and its course—Is it related to a single event, a recurring situation, or a persistent condition? Psychosocial stress may precipitate violent behavior in a person with a personality disorder or may lead to a transient conduct disturbance in an otherwise normal person.

A diagnosis of adjustment disorder with disturbance of conduct or with mixed disturbance of emotions and conduct may apply if the aggressive behavior occurs within three months of the onset of a stressor, is maladaptive, i.e., causes impairment in functioning, or is in excess of a normal and expectable reaction to the stressor and is not an instance of a pattern of overreaction to stress or an exacerbation of one of the other mental disorders. Adjustment disorder with disturbance of conduct diagnoses may be made in patients with personality disorders if aggression is not part of the maladaptive personality pattern.

The severity of psychosocial stressors are rated on DSM-III-R's Axis IV. The reader is referred to Chapter 2, on multiaxial diagnosis, for a complete discussion of the listing and rating of psychosocial stressors.

The following case vignette portrays a man who uncharacteristically threatened violence in response to stress.

Breaking Point

A defense counsel referred a 28-year-old, married, male employee of a large automobile-manufacturing company to a psychiatrist for evaluation following an incident in which the employee had held a factory foreman at bay with a gun for two hours.

The man had worked at the factory for five years. Previously, he had been known as a very reliable and conscientious worker. Two years before the incident, however, a new foreman had replaced his former boss. The new man had a reputation for "riding" his men in order to get them to be more productive; he had a sarcastic sense of humor that often bordered on the abusive. The foreman's biting remarks and attempts at humiliation visibly upset the patient; he would become tongue-tied, stammer a protest, become even more flustered, and sometimes embarrassingly have to leave his position in order to collect himself—all amidst the laughter of his co-workers and, especially, of the foreman himself. The sight of the patient's discomfort seemed to spur the foreman on to even more insults.

On the morning in question, the topic of the foreman's baiting was how satisfied each man's wife might be with her sex life. "Hey, Jack," he called to the patient. "How's your wife these days? I hear she used to be a tough one to please. Some of my boys here say she's the local expert on vibrators and dildos. Must be why you look so tired every morning, too!"

The patient's face flushed. He tried to suppress his anger. Fortunately, the lunch whistle blew, and he bolted out of the building. He went to the parking lot, as if on his way home. The next thing he remembered was being disarmed by police, approximately two and one-half hours later. In the interim, he had taken a rifle, which he used for hunting, out of the trunk of his car, reentered the factory during the lunch hour, found the foreman eating lunch alone in his office, fired one shot into the ceiling, and then threatened to shoot the foreman if he moved. The foreman reported that during this time he said very little, but looked "glassy-eyed" and sweated profusely.

Past history revealed that the patient was the product of a stable, working-class home. He had been married for four years and had two children. His upbringing had been strict, but discipline had been based on reasoning rather than on corporal punishment. He respected his father's authority—occasionally to the point of fear—but he had never been beaten. There was no childhood history of delinquent behavior, enuresis, fire-setting, or cruelty to animals. As an adult, the patient had no criminal history and no significant use of alcohol or other drugs. He had had a noncombatant role in military service and had been honorably discharged. He had been in two fistfights as a teenager. He owned several guns for target shooting and hunting; the gun used in the incident would not have been in his car except that he had been trying to find time to take it in for repair.

On mental status examination the patient showed no signs of psychosis, mood disturbance, or organicity, except, perhaps, for the reported lapse of memory concerning the brief period when he threatened the foreman. He also reported several *déjà vu* experiences, but no apparent instances of automatic behavior. He denied homicidal or suicidal ideation or intent. He was greatly concerned and embarrassed about the events that led to his arrest.

An EEG to rule out temporal lobe epilepsy was normal.

The best diagnosis in this case would appear to be an adjustment disorder with mixed disturbance of emotions and conduct. Some clinicians might argue for a diagnosis of a dissociative disorder, developing in the face of severe stress, because of the memory lapse and sudden onset of uncharacteristic behavior (see also Chapter 12). The patient's disorder would not seem pervasive enough to meet the criteria for one of the specific dissociative disorder diagnoses, but a dissociative disorder NOS is a plausible alternative choice.

Adjustment disorders in DSM-III-R do not persist for more than six months. Many clinicians and some researchers (37) believe that chronic adjustment disorders may occur if the environmental consequences of the stressor persist or the stressor is a chronic state of affairs.

Violence Not Due to a Mental Disorder

Society in general regards violence as closely linked to mental illness (38-40). Although violent behavior undoubtedly represents a societal breakdown, it cannot always be attributed to a diagnosable mental disorder. In some instances violence stems from intolerable social or political conditions. For some people, aggressive or violent behavior represents a way of life, but cannot be characterized as symptomatic of an antisocial personality disorder. If a clinician evaluates a person who has committed a violent or aggressive act and determines that the person does not have a mental disorder, he or she may, for administrative purposes, use the V codes adult antisocial behavior or child or adolescent antisocial behavior. The former might apply to a person involved in organized crime or an accused murderer. A boy involved in an isolated fight or mugging would exemplify the latter. Mental health professionals should not assume that all violence is the result of mental illness.

The Problem of Child Abuse

Child abuse is a form of violence that may be the result of any of the mental disorders discussed in this chapter. Unfortunately, some confusion was created when DSM-III used child abuse as an example of the V code parent-child problem. Since V codes were conditions not attributable to mental disorders, some clinicians strongly objected. What was overlooked was the crucial phrase "not attributable to a mental disorder of the parent" referring to the abuse. As with other forms of violence, some clinicians will have difficulty accepting the proposition that a parent who abuses a child is not, by definition, sick. DSM-III and DSM-III-R maintain the position, however, that such may be the case.

SUMMARY

In this chapter the differential diagnosis of antisocial, aggressive, and violent behavior is reviewed. A general model for the diagnosis of a person with violent behavior is presented in which any mental disorder associated with heightened aggressive impulses or impaired impulse control is to be considered. Organic mental and substance-induced disorders, psychotic disorders, and personality disorders can have violence as a major manifestation.

The chapter covers in greater detail differential diagnoses that have not been previously discussed in this volume. These include mental retardation, intermittent explosive disorder, the DSM-III-R disruptive behavior disorders of childhood and adolescence (attention-deficit hyperactivity disorder, conduct disorder, and oppositional defiant disorder), and adjustment disorder with disturbance of conduct.

REFERENCES

1. Sheard MH, Marini JI, Bridges CI, Wagner E: The effect of lithium on impulsive aggressive behavior in man. Am J Psychiatry 133:1409–1413, 1976
2. Yudofsky SC, Williams D, Gorman J: Propranolol in the treatment of rage and violent behavor in patients with chronic brain syndromes. Am J Psychiatry 138:218–220, 1981
3. Luchins DJ: Carbamazepine for the violent psychiatric patient (letter). Lancet 2:766, 1983
4. Yudofsky SC, Silver JM, Jackson W, Endicott J, Williams D: The Overt Aggression Scale for the objective rating of verbal and physical aggression. Am J Psychiatry 143:35–39, 1986
5. Bassuk EL, Skodol AE: The first few minutes: identifying and managing life-threatening emergencies, in Emergency Psychiatry: Concepts, Methods, and Practices. Edited by Bassuk EL, Birk AW. New York, Plenum Press, 1984, pp 21–36
6. Skodol AE: Emergency management of potentially violent patients, in Emergency Psychiatry: Concepts, Methods, and Practices. Edited by Bassuk EL, Birk AW. New York, Plenum Press, 1984, pp 83–96
7. Slaby AE, Lieb J, Tancredi LR: Handbook of Psychiatric Emergencies, Second Edition. New York, Medical Examination Publishing, 1981

8. Skodol AE, Karasu TB: Emergency psychiatry and the assaultive patient. Am J Psychiatry 135:202–205, 1978
9. Salamon I: Violent and aggressive behavior, in Psychiatric Emergencies. Edited by Glick RA, Meyerson AT, Robbins E, Talbott JA. New York, Grune and Stratton, 1976, pp 109–119
10. Kozol HL, Boucher RJ, Garofalo RF: The diagnosis and treatment of dangerousness. Crime and Delinquency 18:371–392, 1972
11. Hellman DS, Blackman N: Enuresis, firesetting and cruelty to animals: a triad predictive of adult crime. Am J Psychiatry 122:1431–1435, 1966
12. Silver JB, Dublin CC, Lourie RS: Does violence breed violence? Contributions from a study of the child abuse syndrome. Am J Psychiatry 126:404–407, 1969
13. Justice B, Kraft IA: Early warning signs of violence: is a triad enough? Am J Psychiatry 131:457–459, 1974
14. American Psychiatric Association: Clinical Aspects of the Violent Individual: A Report of the APA Task Force on Clinical Aspects of the Violent Individual. Washington, DC, American Psychiatric Association, 1974
15. American Psychiatric Association: Diagnostic and Statistical Manual of Mental Disorders, Third Edition, Revised. Washington, DC, American Psychiatric Association, 1987
16. American Psychiatric Association: Diagnostic and Statistical Manual of Mental Disorders, Third Edition. Washington, DC, American Psychiatric Association, 1980
17. Monopolis S, Lion JR: Problems in the diagnosis of intermittent explosive disorder. Am J Psychiatry 140:1200–1202, 1983
18. Bach-y-Rita, G, Lion JR, Climent CE, Ervin FR: Episodic dyscontrol: a study of 130 violent patients. Am J Psychiatry 127:1473–1478, 1971
19. Williams D: Neural factors related to habitual aggression. Brain 92:503–520, 1969
20. Stevens JR: Interictal clinical complications of complex partial seizures, in Advances in Neurology, Vol 2. Edited by Penry JK, Daly DD. New York, Raven Press, 1975
21. Bingley T: Mental symptoms in temporal lobe epilepsy and temporal lobe glioma. Acta Psychiatr Neurol Scand 33 (Supp 120):1–151, 1958
22. Curry S, Heathfield KWW, Henson RA, Scott DF: Clinical course and prognosis of temporal lobe epilepsy: a survey of 666 patients. Brain 94:173–190, 1971
23. Rodin EA: Psychomotor epilepsy and aggressive behavior. Arch Gen Psychiatry 28:210–213, 1973
24. Elliott FA: The neurology of explosive rage. Practitioner 217:51–60, 1976
25. Monroe RR: Episodic Behavioral Disorders: A Psychodynamic and Neurophysiologic Analysis. Cambridge, Harvard University Press, 1970
26. Elliott FA: Neurological factors in violent behavior: the dyscontrol syndrome. Bull Am Acad Psychiatr Law 4:297–315, 1976
27. Silver JM, Yudofsky SC: Propranolol for aggression: literature review and clinical guidelines. International Drug Therapy Newsletter 20:912, 1985
28. Wender PH, Reimherr W, Wood DR: Attention deficit disorder ("minimal brain dysfunction") in adults: a replication study of diagnosis and drug treatment. Arch Gen Psychiatry 38:449–456, 1981
29. Gittelman R, Mannuzza S, Shenker R, Bonagura N: Hyperactive boys almost grown up. I. Psychiatric status. Arch Gen Psychiatry 42:937–947, 1985

30. Wender PH, Reimherr FW, Wood D, Ward M: A controlled study of methylphenidate in the treatment of attention deficit disorder, residual type, in adults. Am J Psychiatry 142:547–552, 1985
31. Binder RL, McNiel DE: Effects of diagnosis and context on dangerousness. Am J Psychiatry 145:728–732, 1988
32. Segal SP, Watson MA, Goldfinger SM, Averbuck DS: Civil commitment in the psychiatric emergency room. II. Mental disorder indicators and three dangerousness criteria. Arch Gen Psychiatry 45:753–758, 1988
33. Skodol AE, Karasu TB: Toward hospitalization criteria for violent patients. Compr Psychiatry 21:162–166, 1980
34. Robins L: Sturdy childhood predictors of adult outcomes: replications from longitudinal studies. Psychol Med 8:611–622, 1978
35. Lewis DO, Lewis M, Unger L, Goldman C: Conduct disorder and its synonyms: diagnoses of dubious validity and usefulness. Am J Psychiatry 141:514–519, 1984
36. Field MH, Field HF: Marital violence and the criminal process: neither justice nor peace. Soc Sci Rev 47:221–240, 1973
37. Andreasen NC, Hoenk PR: The predictive value of adjustment disorders: a follow-up study. Am J Psychiatry 139:584–590, 1982
38. Grunberg F, Klinger BI, Gurmet B: Homicide and the deinstitutionalization of the mentally ill. Am J Psychiatry 134:685–687, 1977
39. Lagos JM, Perlmutter K, Saexinger H: Fear of the mentally ill: empirical support for the common man's response. Am J Psychiatry 134:1134–1137, 1977
40. Tardiff K, Sweilamm A: Assault, suicide and mental illness. Arch Gen Psychiatry 37:164–169, 1980

CHAPTER 11

Differential Diagnosis in the Elderly

The differential diagnosis of mental disorders in the elderly is becoming an increasingly important aspect of clinical practice. As a result of a steadily rising average life span, the proportion of people over 65 in the United States is progressively growing. Attention to the cognitive and emotional problems of the elderly has increased to the point where geriatric psychiatry has become a subspecialty. But more importantly, all mental health practitioners are encountering, and will continue to encounter, more elderly patients in the course of their work.

Some mental disorders, such as the organic mental disorders delirium and dementia, more commonly have their onset in the elderly than in any other age group. Others, such as the mood disorder major depression, although not necessarily more common in older people, are very prevalent. Still other disorders, such as personality disorders, may have an onset in early adult life, but persist into later life, and cause special problems in the elderly person's coping with the stress associated with advancing age.

Differential diagnosis in the elderly is problematic in a number of respects. The high frequency of physical and socioenvironmental problems that the elderly experience makes it difficult to tease apart the organic, functional, and situational aspects of emotional disturbances. The possibility of multiple, coexisting syndromes exists. Fortunately, the DSM-III and DSM-III-R approaches to diagnosis are especially suited to these complexities. A clear clinical history, however, may be difficult to obtain because of the memory deficits of the patient or his or her spouse co-informant; taking a history from an adult child who is involved with the parent may therefore be more productive.

OVERVIEW OF DIFFERENTIAL DIAGNOSIS

Table 11.1 lists the common DSM-III-R disorders in the differential diagnosis of mental disorders in the elderly (1). Virtually all of these diagnoses have been discussed previously in specific chapters; therefore, only their essential features will be mentioned here. Emphasis will be on the differential diagnostic issues that are particularly relevant to the elderly. These include: (*1*) distinguishing delirium from acute confusional states secondary to functional illnesses; (*2*) distinguishing the cognitive impairment of true organic dementia from the so-called "pseudodementia" occurring secondary to mood disorders; (*3*) evaluating delirium in the presence of dementia; (*4*) evaluating mood disturbance in the presence of physical illness; (*5*) identifying distinctive features of depression with initial onset during the involutional period; (*6*) distinguishing normal from pathological grief; and (*7*) differential diagnosis of late-onset psychotic disorders.

DIAGNOSTIC DILEMMAS

Disturbances of cognitive functioning (intellect and thought) and mood are the major sources of diagnostic dilemmas in the elderly.

Delirium vs. Acute Confusional States

Delirium is an organic mental syndrome characterized by reduced ability to maintain attention to external stimuli, and to shift attention appropriately to new external stimuli, that develops over a short period of time and fluctuates throughout the day. Delirium is accompanied by disturbances of thinking, perception, consciousness, psychomotor activity, the sleep-wake cycle, orientation, and memory. It has, by definition, an organic cause, and occurs frequently in the elderly because of the vulnerability of the central nervous system (CNS) to physical illness and drugs at advanced ages (see also Chapter 3). The presence of dementia may predispose to delirium, frequently with fatal consequences (2).

Various nonorganic, functional, mental disturbances can also present in the elderly with confusion, disorientation, memory impairment, inability to think coherently, and bewilderment that suggest the presence of delirium. These have been referred to as acute confusional states and have recently been termed, by Lipowski (3) "pseudodelirium," by analogy with pseudodementia, to emphasize that no specific organic etiologic factor can be demonstrated.

Common physical illnesses that cause delirium in the elderly include congestive heart failure, pneumonia, urinary tract infection,

Table 11.1 Differential Diagnosis of Mental Disorders in the Elderly

ORGANIC MENTAL DISORDERS (PHYSICAL DISORDERS LISTED ON AXIS III)
- Delirium
- Dementia
- Organic amnestic syndrome
- Organic mood syndrome
- Organic personality syndrome

DEMENTIAS ARISING IN SENIUM OR PRESENIUM
- Primary degenerative dementia of the Alzheimer type
- Multi-infarct dementia

SCHIZOPHRENIA

DELUSIONAL (PARANOID) DISORDER

PSYCHOTIC DISORDERS NOT ELSEWHERE CLASSIFIED
- Brief reactive psychosis
- Schizophreniform disorder
- Schizoaffective disorder
- Induced psychotic disorder

MOOD (AFFECTIVE) DISORDERS
- Major depression
- Dysthymic disorder
- Bipolar disorder

ADJUSTMENT DISORDER
- Adjustment disorder with depressed mood
- Adjustment disorder with withdrawal

PSYCHOLOGICAL FACTORS AFFECTING PHYSICAL CONDITION

V CODES
- Uncomplicated bereavement
- Phase of life problem or other life circumstance problem

cancer, uremia, malnutrition, hypokalemia, dehydration, sodium depletion, and cerebrovascular accidents. Systemic illnesses more frequently cause delirium than do primary diseases of the CNS. Intoxication with prescribed drugs is probably the most frequent cause of delirium in the elderly, the most frequently implicated drugs being diuretics, sedative-hypnotics, analgesics, antihistamines, antiparkinsonian agents, antidepressants, neuroleptics, cimetidine, and digitalis.

Evaluation of delirium in the elderly requires careful assessment of cognitive functioning and attention. DSM-III-R does not direct the clinician in this process, but the use of a standard clinical scale, such as the Mini-Mental State, can facilitate the task. A careful history of the medications used by the patient, physical and neurological examinations, and laboratory tests are required in the search for an organic factor. A standard test battery would include CBC, blood chemistry, urinalysis, serology, toxic drug screen, EKG, chest X-ray, lumbar puncture with CSF examination, EEG, and CT scan. Although the EEG finding of diffuse slowing is generally thought to be the most sensitive indicator of delirium, it is frequently less helpful in the elderly, according to Lipowski (3), because generalized slowing is also evident in primary degenerative dementia.

The frequency of pseudodelirium in the elderly has been estimated at 5%-20%. Functional mental disorders that may present with the symptoms of pseudodelirium include delusional disorders, mood disorders, schizophrenic disorder, and other psychotic disorders such as brief reactive psychosis. Signs of physical illness and laboratory evidence of systemic or cerebral illness should be absent. Past history of a major mental illness, flagrant signs of mania, depression, or psychosis, inconsistency in the mental status exam, and poor motivation in mental status testing are all more likely related to pseudodelirium. An amytal interview will result in improvement in the symptoms of pseudodelirium, but exacerbation of an organic delirium. Acutely stressful circumstances, such as bereavement, since they may result in significant mood alterations, may also present as pseudodelirium. Pseudodelirium should be reversible with adequate treatment of the underlying functional disorder.

Dementia vs. Pseudodementia

Dementia is characterized by impairment in short- and long-term memory severe enough to interfere with social or occupational functioning. Memory impairment, especially for recent events, occurs in a clear state of consciousness, unless delirium is superimposed thereon (see below). Since dementia reflects a global dysfunction of the cerebral cortex, other signs of cortical disturbance such as impaired abstract thinking, impaired judgment, and aphasia, apraxia, agnosia, or constructional difficulties should be present. Personality change consisting of alteration or accentuation of premorbid traits may also occur. These features, coupled with the requirement of evidence of an organic factor etiologically responsible for the disturbance, make up the diagnostic criteria for dementia in DSM-III-R.

Of 100 elderly patients seeking care at a geriatric center (4) for organic mental disorder, 69 had a dementia by DSM-III criteria. Of these, 43 had primary degenerative dementia, 10 had multi-infarct dementia, 7 had dementia associated with alcoholism, 6 had dementia associated with another neurological illness (including Huntington's chorea, pseudobulbar palsy, seizure disorder, and normal pressure hydrocephalus), and 3 had dementia associated with other systemic illnesses (including metastatic cancer, chronic arsenic ingestion, and hypothyroidism). In addition, 24 patients had a major depressive episode. The high frequency of patients with depression presenting with clinical signs of dementia illustrates the importance of distinguishing between these disorders.

The impairment in intellectual functioning that can accompany depression in the elderly is termed *pseudodementia* (see also Chapter 3, Disturbances with Specific Organic Etiologies). The differentiation of dementia from pseudodementia has been reviewed by Wells (5). Clinical assessment continues to offer the most reliable guidelines, even though a variety of neurologic, neuropsychological, and neuroradiologic procedures have been proposed. Wells divided clinical discriminators into (*1*) aspects of clinical course and history, (*2*) general symptoms and signs, and (*3*) features related to intellectual dysfunction.

Patients with pseudodementia usually have a more abrupt onset and more rapid progression of intellectual deterioration than patients with organic dementing illnesses. Therefore, the timing of the beginning of the memory deterioration, for example, is likely to be more clearly specified and more recent when the patient presents for clinical evaluation. The patient with pseudodementia is more apt to be depressed about the intellectual decline itself and the resulting functional impairment. The patient's range of activities is frequently more constricted than the level of cognitive impairment itself. In pseudodementia the patient's condition is less likely to worsen at night than is the case in true dementia. Organically demented patients, in contrast, are less concerned about their cognitive losses, often have a shallow affect, restrict their activities in line with the degree of impairment, and have more difficulties at night.

Patients with pseudodementia, according to Wells (5), have memory difficulties for both recent and remote events, with gaps for specific events or periods. The pseudodemented is less likely than the organically demented person to try to answer questions and performs unevenly on tasks, even though he or she appears to have better attention and concentration. In the organically demented patient, recent memory is more impaired than remote memory, and the person generally displays poor task performance, attention, and concentration. The presence of physical symptoms suggesting a physical disorder that may be the cause of the dementia can mask psychopathology and obscure the fact that a mental illness is responsible for the signs of dementia (6). The laboratory workup should be consistent with the suspected organic illness before a psychological etiology is ruled out.

As mentioned in Chapter 3, a positive family history for depression may alert the clinician to the possibility that the patient suffers from a depression (7). The importance of making the differential diagnosis between the pseudodementia of affective illness and the dementia of organic brain disease lies in the possibility of providing effective treatment, i.e., antidepressant drug therapy. Therefore, in most ambiguous cases, a trial of antidepressant medications is warranted, if there are no physical contraindications, both for diagnostic purposes and for potentially beneficial treatment (8-10). If the patient responds fully, then the diagnosis becomes conclusive. In the case of a partial response, the patient may still suffer from an underlying dementing illness, such as Alzheimer's, with a secondary, superimposed depression that exacerbated the cognitive deficits, but responded to the treatment.

The following case vignette illustrates the ambiguity of the admixture of depressive and cognitive symptoms and the use of a trial of antidepressant medications to attempt to clarify the diagnosis.

Overdue Bills

A 67-year-old retired schoolteacher presented to his internist with a six-month history of increasing inability to complete tasks, loss of interest, and feelings of general lassitude. He had not adapted well to his retirement two years previously, finding that he had too much time on his hands and too little to do.

In the past several months, he faced an ever-accumulating mound of unpaid bills and paperwork, but felt unable to sit down and sort it through. Periodically he made futile attempts that essentially consisted of moving items from one pile to another.

The internist found nothing positive following a comprehensive physical examination and a routine battery of laboratory tests. He referred the patient for psychiatric consultation. The psychiatrist was struck by the patient's anhedonia, loss of self-esteem, self-depreciating comments about the uselessness of his existence, and pessimism about the future and decided that a course of treatment with antidepressants should be undertaken.

Symptoms of depression improved over six weeks, but the patient "forgot" several appointments and finally, one day, got lost on his way to the psychiatrist's office. At this point the patient was given a CT scan, which revealed mild, beginning signs of cortical atrophy.

Episodes of bipolar illness may also occur among the elderly. Most patients will have a history of bipolar illness from earlier adult life, but in some, onset is after age 60. Manic episodes of bipolar illness presenting with the symptoms of dementia have also been described (11). Conversely, many neurological illnesses that occur among the elderly may produce mood syndromes. These include stroke (12), Parkinson's disease, and Huntington's disease (13,14). If signs of mood disturbance predominate over signs of dementia, the appropriate diagnoses in such cases are organic affective (DSM-III) or mood (DSM-III-R) syndrome and the neurological illness, which should he listed on Axis III (see Chapters 2 and 3). Many such patients are said to respond poorly to lithium carbonate treatment, and may develop neurotoxicity from the drug (15).

For patients with prominent symptoms of both dementia and organic mood syndrome, both diagnoses can be given, according to DSM-III-R. This represents a significant departure from the approach taken in DSM-III, in which many of the organic brain syndromes were considered mutually exclusive and were hierarchically arranged. Requiring that one set of features predominate over all others undoubtedly introduced an artificial element into the diagnosis of organic brain syndromes that made the categories less reliable and less useful.

Delirium Superimposed on Dementia

Since delirium frequently complicates chronic dementia in the elderly, with dramatically increased mortality rates, it is important for the clinician to recognize a superimposed delirium in the already cognitively impaired person. As many as one-third of hospitalized demented patients may suffer from a superimposed delirium. Lipowski (3) notes that in the case of an already demented patient, the signs of delirium are modified: Hallucinations and confabulation are less likely, the patient appears more apathetic, but has periods of restlessness and agitation; and memory deficits and thinking disturbance are variable. Certainly, if cognitive functioning in a patient with a known dementia worsens acutely or becomes fluctuating, a superimposed delirium should be suspected. Similarly, if a patient abruptly becomes less alert, arousable, and aware of his or her circumstances, a new condition is probable, and should be sought with appropriate history, examinations, and tests. Patients with dementia may also exhibit a pseudodelirium (see above) under stress. This should clear when the stressor ceases or the person adapts, and also should not be accompanied by any new physical findings or test abnormalities.

Sometimes the effects of treatment introduce even further complexity into differential diagnosis of the elderly. In the following case, an elderly man with a bipolar illness superimposed on mild cognitive loss became delirious because of self-medication with tranquilizers, then later showed signs of worsening dementia while receiving electroconvulsive therapy (ECT).

It Doesn't Feel Like It Wants to Cry

A 66-year-old greengrocer was admitted to the hospital with a two-week history of extreme agitation and anxiety. For the past two months he had been becoming increasingly preoccupied and worried about the future of his business. He had been told, shortly before, that he was going to lose the lease on his store, a fruit and vegetable market, which he had had for the past 20 years. Since receiving this news, he seemed to have lost interest in working. He came home early and sat, uncommunicative except for a few monosyllabic responses, in front of the television. Most recently, he had stopped going into work completely, and spent his time either pacing in the hall of his apartment or getting into bed and pulling the covers over his head. His wife became especially worried when she realized that various bottles of tranquilizers and sleeping pills kept in the medicine cabinet were empty.

The admitting psychiatrist found the grocer difficult to interview. Initially he lay in bed on his side, facing the wall, and sat up to talk only after considerable coaxing. He then faced straight ahead, barely acknowledging the doctor. He appeared to have trouble keeping his eyes open. When asked what had brought him to the hospital, he said, with slurred speech, "It started to bother me again." With repeated prompting to elaborate, he said "The angel . . . the anxiety . . . soreness, painful." When asked whether he was feeling sad or depressed, he said, "It doesn't feel like it wants to cry." The man did not know the date or the name of the hospital, although he knew he was in a hospital. Other questions on formal mental-status testing went unanswered.

The history obtained from the patient's wife and the referring psychiatrist indicated that the man had been first hospitalized for depression at age 34. He had had a manic episode at age 46. Since then, every two to three years he had required hospitalization for depression. Antidepressant medications were ineffective; ECT was the acute treatment of choice. During his manic episodes he worked very hard, became very excited about his business, had many ideas about expansion into new products, branches, restaurants, etc., and took out loans. During these periods he slept very little; he baked cakes and pies instead. During depressions he stopped working, stopped eating, lay in bed, avoided people, refused to talk, had no energy, expressed misery if anything, and took as many pills as he could get his hands on in order to stay asleep. Pills that were known to be in the house were Ativan, 5 mg; Dalmane, 30 mg; and Noludar. His wife said that just before she put him in the car for the trip to the hospital, she saw him put a handful of pills into his mouth. Lithium, 1800 mg/day, was the prescribed drug; but according to the referring psychiatrist, the patient was very noncompliant. On admission, his lithium level was 1.5 mEq/l.

Initially, the admitting psychiatrist interpreted the patient's cognitive impairment as resulting from intoxication with hypnotic and anxiolytic agents, compounded by some lithium toxicity. On the evening of the second hospital day, the nurses asked the psychiatrist to see the patient because he was agitated and repeatedly yelling, "I want to go home, I want to go home!" The psychiatrist observed the man to be diaphoretic, with a tremor of both hands. His pulse was 130. He seemed even more confused, uttering rambling and inconsistent complaints; and he was barely able to cooperate during the physical examination, let alone allow the psychiatrist to do any formal mental-status testing.

At this point the doctor feared sedative, hypnotic, or anxiolytic withdrawal delirium and instituted a detoxification schedule using chlordiazepoxide. The agitation and some confusion responded and the patient was much more cooperative as he was prepared for ECT. A neurologist suggested that the patient might have mild cognitive loss underlying his depression, but a decision was made to proceed with a course of ECT. After the first three treatments, the patient again became more agitated and confused beyond the posttreatment period. After six treatments, the ECT was interrupted. Within three days most of the confusion again cleared, and the patient's mood was noted to be somewhat improved. ECT was then administered at more widely spaced intervals. Although some confusion resulted from each treatment, it was short-lived. After ten treatments, the patient's mood was improved sufficiently for him to be discharged. Some difficulty with memory and abstract thinking persisted, and an early degenerative dementia was suspected.

Diagnosing Mood Disturbance in the Physically Ill

The diagnosis of depressive disorders among physically ill patients has recently been receiving increased attention (16-18). The relationship of physical illness to mood disturbance may be of several types. Most obviously, severe somatic illness is very stressful, and may therefore precipitate a depressive disorder or an adjustment disorder. Studies of risk factors (19) suggest that physical illness as a recent life event or as an ongoing burden or handicap may significantly increase the risk of major depression. The relationship, however, may not be through the life-stress process, but for certain diseases, at least, may be the result of organic factors that cause depression. This possibility has interested researchers studying stroke victims (20,21) and Parkinson's disease (22), not only for the treatment implications but also for light that may be shed on the biochemical and neuroanatomical implications of these diseases for "nonorganic" mood disorders. An additional question is whether episodes of mood disturbance in the physically ill occur because of preexisting vulnerability, such as a preexisting mood disorder, or simply appear in previously healthy people.

In terms of differential diagnosis, the possibilities for diagnosis of depression in the physically ill include organic mood disorder, major depression, dysthymia, depressive disorder NOS, adjustment disorder with depressed mood, or a V code such as "other life circumstance problem." The most important differential is between organic mood syndrome, discussed in Chapter 3, and major depression.

No completely clear-cut distinctions can be drawn among these disorders in certain physical illnesses, but a consensus has been developing concerning tentative guidelines (23). The differences can be in terms of phenomenology, clinical course, and past history. Organic mood disturbances associated with physical illness appear to present a preponderance of somatic symptoms, e.g., decreased energy and appetite and sleep and psychomotor changes, and fewer of the cognitive elements of depression, e.g., guilt, pessimism, and feelings of worthlessness. Therefore, the most useful discriminators of nonorganic major depressive episodes in patients with concomitant physical illness include a pervasive loss of pleasure, loss of interest in people, and loss of self-esteem. In contrast to the patient with adjustment disorder with depressed mood who feels badly about his or her situation, the physically ill person with major depression experiences feelings of worthlessness, self-reproach, excessive or inappropriate guilt, sense of failure, and a sense of being punished (24, 25). The clinical course of an organic mood disorder closely follows the clinical course of the underlying physical illness, with remissions and relapses corresponding to the effectiveness of the treatment of the underlying disorder. Patients with an organically caused depression are less likely to have a prior history of nonorganic mood disorder; in patients with an established positive past history, the physical illness is more likely to act as biological and/or psychological stressor in precipitating another episode.

In certain illnesses the phenomenology, history, course, and treatment response of the mood disturbance appear indistinguishable from those of functional major depression. An example is the occurrence of major depressive episodes following stroke, particularly of the left frontal lobe (26). These similarities suggest that certain physical illnesses may affect areas of the brain or neuronal mechanisms or pathways relevant to the occurrence of mood disorders in general.

Since the elderly frequently suffer from physical illnesses, differentiating a mood disturbance caused by such an illness (an organic mood syndrome in DSM-III-R) from major depression occurring in response to illness as a stressor is important. The reader is also referred to the discussion of organic mood (affective) syndrome on pages 97–99 of Chapter 3, Disturbances with Specific Organic Etiologies.

Diagnosing Involutional Melancholia

Before the development of DSM-III, depressions that occurred in the elderly were thought to have unique clinical pictures characterized by certain distinctive symptoms of the depressive syndrome. In DSM-II (27), the category involutional melancholia included, as characteristic symptoms, worry, anxiety, agitation, severe insomnia, guilt feelings, and somatic preoccupations, possibly of delusional proportions. DSM-II went on to state that the absence of previous episodes distinguished involutional melancholia from manic-depressive illness, and that the absence of the occurrence of relevant recent life events during the period preceding onset of the illness distinguished it from a psychotic depressive reaction.

During the development of DSM-III, a review of epidemiologic and clinical studies failed to demonstrate an increase in depression during the involutional period in comparison with other stages of adult life (28-31). Research by Weissman (32) on the symptom patterns of major depression in women did not reveal any age-related differences. Ratings on the Hamilton Rating Scale for Depression showed no significant differences in sleep disturbance, somatization, anxiety, depression, apathy, or overall severity of depression among three groups of women: subjects younger than 45, 45-55 years, and 56 years or older. The same study found no differences among the three groups in terms of absence of a history of previous episodes, the presence of stressful life circumstances, or the role of such circumstances in precipitating a depression. In fact, in light of changing life circumstances and accompanying stresses associated with aging, the findings might have been expected to be the reverse—i.e., the likelihood that stressful life events would be associated with the development of depression would be greater in the elderly than in other age groups. However, no such reversal was found.

The conclusion drawn was that there was insufficient evidence to suggest that depressions occurring at various ages could be distinguished on the basis of symptom profile. Therefore, the diagnosis of involutional melancholia was deleted from the classification. DSM-III assumes that the essential features of a major depressive episode are similar regardless of the patient's age. The diagnostic criteria are qualified, however, by the inclusion of certain age-specific associated features. For the elderly, these associated features, which are sometimes, but not invariably, present, include disorientation, memory loss, distractibility, apathy, and inattentiveness. These symptoms are suggestive of a dementia and make it difficult to distinguish between true organic dementia and depression-related pseudodementia, as discussed above.

Since the publication of DSM-III, several additional studies have reopened the issue of whether depressions with initial onset in the later years have distinctive clinical features. Pichot and Pull (33) pointed out that definitions of what might be taken to be an "involutional depression" have varied across studies. Their definition is a unipolar depression in which the first manifestation occurs after 50 years of age and which may either be chronic or recurrent. In comparing two groups of depressed patients of the same age, one with depression with initial onset before 50 and the other with onset after 50 years of age, they found only that, when limited to unipolar depressions, involutional patients displayed less suicidal ideation. These authors raise the possibility that the symptomatic expression of depression may change with increasing age. This so-called "pathoplastic" effect of age on symptoms is not the same phenomenon, however, as a distinct and different symptom picture between early- and late-onset depression.

In a similar vein, Dessonville and associates (34) studied samples of depressed persons and controls over 55 years of age with the aid of the Schedule for Affective Disorders and Schizophrenia (SADS) (35). Even in comparisons between the oldest and most physically unhealthy controls and the youngest, healthiest, depressed persons, the SADS revealed substantial differences in symptoms. Symptom patterns on the SADS subscales were similar to those previously obtained on younger populations in terms of depressed mood and ideation, endogenous features, and associated features; the elderly depressives were, however, less suicidal and more anxious. These findings indicate that standard definitions of depression are applicable to the elderly and are not in agreement with the opinion that the signs and symptoms of depression are difficult to distinguish from those of normal aging.

Although the symptom pattern of elderly persons with depression was similar, in most respects, to that of a more general sample of depressed persons, caution must be exercised in interpreting the report of symptoms of weight change, sleep disturbance, and the somatic manifestations of anxiety among the elderly, particularly physically ill older patients. A careful history of the developmental course of the symptoms and a comprehensive physical evaluation will help to determine when these symptoms are due primarily to health or age changes rather than to the onset of a depressive episode.

Brown and associates (36) have pointed out that Weissman's sample (see above) of depressed women consisted of all outpatients who had only moderately severe depressions (Hamilton Rating Scale average of 20) and who were relatively young, only 17 (4%) being over 55. They maintain that it was not surprising that she did not isolate a definable subset of women with a distinctive picture consistent with involutional melancholia. They subsequently conducted their own study of hospitalized depressed patients over 50 with initial episodes before and after this age. Patients whose first depressive episodes occurred when they were older than 50 had had fewer previous episodes (which was expected), had fewer relatives with a history of affective disorder, and suffered less guilt, less suicidal ideation, more anorexia and hypochondriasis, and fewer complaints about loss of libido. To control for the effects of age, current age- and sex-matched groups were compared. The findings relative to family history, guilt, anorexia, and hypochondriasis remained significant, and the group in which age at onset had been older reported more somatic anxiety. The authors conclude that although there were some symptomatic differences, they did not seem sufficient to justify an involutional melancholia subtype. Furthermore, the clinical picture of DSM-II involutional melancholia was not supported.

In addition, response to antidepressant medications was largely the same in the two groups of patients in this study except for those who experienced delusions; delusional depressives did poorly on tricyclic antidepressants, regardless of age (see also Chapter 6). Nondelusional patients responded well; those over 50, however, responded less well than those under 50. Patients responded well to ECT regardless of age or psychosis. The lesser family-history loading in the late-onset group confirmed earlier findings of Winokur (37), and suggests that genetic predisposition leads to earlier onset, or that a distinct pathophysiological mechanism associated with aging leads to neurotransmitter loss and increasing susceptibility to depression in the older age group.

Another study used the dexamethasone-suppression test (DST) to validate diagnosis in a treatment study of elderly major depressives in order to evaluate the adequacy of DSM-III criteria with respect to the elderly (38). The authors were responding to the comment by Blazer and Williams (39) that depression in the elderly might actually represent decreased life satisfaction and periodic episodes of grief secondary to the physical, social, and economic difficulties encountered by aging people (see also the discussion of depression vs. bereavement that follows). The findings of this study suggested that the majority of elderly patients meeting DSM-III criteria for major depression responded to antidepressant drug therapy, although those with nonsuppressor responses to the DST required more medication and generally did more poorly.

The data accumulated continues to support the DSM-III position that major depression in the elderly is symptomatically more similar to than different from major depression occurring at other ages.

DSM-III-R therefore continues to take the same approach. What is important for clinicians, however, is recognition of the possible pathoplastic effect of age on some of the symptoms of depression and the need to be alert to complicating factors such as coexisting physical illness in assessing symptoms.

Major Depression vs. Uncomplicated Bereavement

Because of the frequency of loss by death of important others experienced by the elderly, differential diagnosis of major depression vs. bereavement is most important in this age group. The DSM-III and DSM-III-R systems attempt to distinguish between major depression and normal grieving following the death of a loved one. The latter is called "uncomplicated bereavement," and is classified as one of the V codes, "conditions not attributable to a mental disorder that are a focus of attention or treatment." The DSM-III criterion for major depressive episode that directs the clinician to make this distinction states, "Not due to . . . Uncomplicated Bereavement" (40, p. 214).

Uncomplicated bereavement is described in the V codes section of DSM-III as a normal reaction to the death of a loved one that can be accompanied by a full depressive syndrome. The symptoms that are suggested to be atypical of a normal reaction and to signify a pathological state are morbid preoccupation with worthlessness, prolonged and marked functional impairment, and marked psychomotor retardation. The associated guilt is usually about things done or not done by the mourner at the time of the death, and thoughts of death should be limited to thinking that the survivor would also be better off dead or should have died as well. DSM-III-R, criterion B for major depressive episode, item (2), reads as follows: "The disturbance is not a normal reaction to the death of a loved one (Uncomplicated Bereavement). Note: Morbid preoccupation with worthlessness, suicidal ideation, marked functional impairment or psychomotor retardation, or prolonged duration suggest bereavement complicated by Major Depression" (41, p. 223). In fact, a reaction that is maladaptive, but insufficient in severity or duration for a major depressive episode, may also be considered a "complicated" grief reaction, and alternatively be diagnosed as an adjustment disorder with depressed mood.

There have been several recent studies relevant to assessment of grief, especially in the elderly. Gallagher and colleagues (42) studied groups of elderly bereaved persons, most of whom had lost a spouse; elderly depressed outpatients who had not had a recent loss; and elderly nondepressed, nonbereaved people in the community. Patients with major depression reported significantly higher symptom levels on the Beck Depression Inventory than either the bereaved subjects or the controls, but the bereaved were also significantly more symptomatic than the controls. The symptom that most distinguished the bereaved from other depressives was their relative lack of self-deprecatory thoughts and statements, not their general levels of affective distress.

The dexamethasone-suppression test was administered to 13 elderly bereaved people, 10 of whom met the criteria for a sustained major depression (43). Four of the subjects had at least one of the symptoms that DSM-III specifies indicates pathological grief; 6 of the 13 had a positive family history of depression; and 2 had both. All subjects suppressed on the DST, although those with the DSM-III symptoms of pathological grief had significantly higher post-DST cortisol levels. The DST was not useful in distinguishing normal from pathological grief; but the more severe the depression, the more likely it was to indicate a pathological reaction.

With respect to the outcome of bereavement, studies have failed to find strong symptomatic predictors of poor outcome. One report (44) indicated that sudden and unexpected loss was associated with a more pronounced grief reaction than that of persons whose relatives' deaths had been more or less anticipated. Another study (45) found, at a two-year follow-up evaluation, that poor outcome was associated with generally high symptom reports on the General Health Questionnaire (46) one month after the loss of a spouse, dissatisfaction with available help, a continued sense of the husband's presence, the presence of multiple other stressors before bereavement (low socioeconomic status, poor health, positive psychiatric history), lack of comfort in religion, short final illness of the husband, and absence of specific grief interventions. Thus, it appears that nonsymptomatic (especially social support), rather than symptomatic, factors may be more important in predicting and determining the outcome of bereavement. This is another indication of the potential clinical utility of the multiaxial approach to evaluation.

Diagnosing Late-Onset Psychoses

The differential diagnosis of nonorganic, nonaffective, late-onset psychotic disorders presents problems using DSM-III. Paranoid disorders (DSM-III-R delusional disorders) frequently have an onset in late life (see Chapter 5), and brief reactive psychosis may apply to cases precipitated by extreme stress. Schizophrenia, however, is restricted in DSM-III to cases with onset before age 45. Schizophreniform disorder (with duration less than six months) would similarly be excluded in elderly patients.

Roth (47) originally proposed the term *late paraphrenia* to describe an illness, occurring in patients over 60, that was characterized by delusions, hallucinations, relative preservation of personality, absence of signs of dementia or affective disorder, deafness (in one-third of patients), and premorbid schizoid traits and that affected predominantly women, who had low fertility rates. According to DSM-III (and DSM-III-R), delusions may characterize a paranoid (or delusional) disorder, but hallucinations are not prominent in such a disorder. Even though the range of delusions that may characterize a delusional disorder has been greatly expanded in DSM-III-R, prominent hallucinations would still rule out such disorders. Furthermore, the presence of bizarre delusions, such as the first-rank symptoms of Schneider, are inconsistent with the DSM-III-R diagnosis of a delusional disorder.

Several studies have appeared since DSM-III that characterize late-onset psychoses. In a study of 35 patients with psychotic disorders beginning after age 44, Rabins and associates (48) found that 21 met all DSM-III criteria for schizophrenia except for age at onset before 45; 11 met the criteria for schizophreniform disorder, and 3, for paranoia. Thirty-two of the patients were female; 24 had hallucinations, and 22, first-rank symptoms. Most of the patients responded to neuroleptic treatment. Grahame (49) studied 25 patients with onset of symptoms at age 60 or over, delusions, and absence of signs of dementia or affective disorder. They were predominantly female, and their mean age was actually 76 years. Fourteen of the 25 reported first-rank symptoms, and most had classically schizophrenic auditory hallucinations. Finally, Leuchter and Spar (50) studied a group of late-onset psychotic patients admitted to a geropsychiatric unit. Eight percent of all these patients could be classified as having had initial onset of a psychotic disorder after age 65. On admission, 25 (36%) patients were diagnosed as having major affective disorder; 23 (33%), organic mental disorder; and 22 (31%), a primary psychotic disorder that was neither affective nor organic. Seven of the last group were rediagnosed, after an extensive workup, as having affective disorders. Of the remaining 15 patients with a primary psychotic disorder, the following diagnoses were made: 5 patients with atypical paranoid disorder, 5 patients with atypical psychosis, 4 patients with paranoid disorder, and 1 patient with schizoaffective disorder. The atypical paranoid disorder diagnosis was necessitated by the presence of prominent auditory or visual hallucinations. Four of the five atypical psychosis diagnoses were made solely because of the late age at onset. The patients with primary psychotic disorders who could tolerate neuroleptic treatment improved following such treatment.

In response to these and other observations of the limitations of the DSM-III criteria for schizophrenia in relation to the late-onset psychoses, DSM-III-R now allows schizophrenia to be diagnosed at any age and provides for a subclassification according to age at onset. The clinician is now instructed to specify "late onset" if the disturbance develops after age 45. The broader criteria for delusional disorder, which allow for any nonbizarre delusion, continue to exclude patients with prominent hallucinations, however. Minor hallucinations, either auditory or visual, are allowed. This definition corresponds to the term *simple delusional disorder* in the literature (51). According to DSM-III-R, patients with prominent hallucinations and nonbizarre delusions, otherwise normal behavior, and no evident affective or organic etiologies should be diagnosed as having a psychotic disorder "not otherwise specified," because there is no category of delusional disorder NOS to take the place of atypical paranoid disorder.

The following vignette illustrates a case of a late-onset psychotic disorder and the comparative diagnostic approaches of DSM-III and DSM-III-R.

A Trip to See The Master

The patient is a 61-year-old divorced mother of two who was admitted for her fourth psychiatric hospitalization in four years. This admission was prompted by the patient's believing that the elderly male friend whom she had been taking care of was making passes at her. She called the police, was taken to a nearby emergency room, and was subsequently admitted.

The patient's mental problems had begun about six years earlier when, at age 54, she developed the belief that during her second pregnancy she had become the subject of an experiment in which a substance was surreptitiously put into her body, the instigator being a spiritual man from India, in conjunction with the CIA. The substance caused her to feel bodily changes—her eyes fluttering, increased heart rate, trembling, hot flashes, and a force pushing through her body. It also gave her special powers, such as being able to control the weather with her eyes. She also believed that she took "trips" to heaven to visit and make love to God—"The Master"—who called upon her when he wished to have pleasure. The FBI and CIA were after her; but rather than kill her, which she said would be like a second crucifixion of Christ, they now harassed her by getting her evicted from her apartment and trying to prove that she was crazy.

The patient had functioned well, until onset of her illness, as a homemaker, a mother, and an entertainer who sang in nightclubs and had had several small parts in movies. After separating from her husband, she had had a continuous relationship with a well-to-do businessman, who was the father of her second child, for 16 years before her first hospitalization.

Each hospitalization was preceded by a period in which the patient would not be able to care for her apartment or her younger son and would become argumentative and destructive of property. On each admission she would be mostly cooperative, congenial, coherent, expressive, and dramatic. Formal thought disorder was largely absent, and she was without prominent mood changes. Hallucinations were not conspicuous. She was always noted to be stylishly dressed and well-groomed, with attractive makeup and fresh nail polish.

The hospitalizations ranged in length from one week to four weeks. The patient was treated with moderate doses of antipsychotic medication, which reduced her agitation, but produced no change in her beliefs. She frequently had not complied with outpatient treatment or medication regimens, since she never felt that she was ill. In the past four years, she had not worked or maintained her own apartment; and she had withdrawn from many friends.

According to DSM-III, this woman's condition could be diagnosed only as atypical psychosis. Delusions other than of a persecutory or jealous content ruled out a paranoid disorder, and age at onset beyond 45 years ruled out schizophrenia. There was no manic syndrome evident, nor were there signs of an organic etiology. According to DSM-III-R, a diagnosis of a delusional disorder is still not warranted, even with the expanded definition (see Chapter 5). Certain of the patient's delusions would have to be considered bizarre, e.g., controlling the weather and taking trips to heaven. A diagnosis of schizophrenia with late onset is now possible, however, since the maximum age at onset limitation has been removed from the criteria.

SUMMARY

This chapter reviews the principles of differential diagnosis in the elderly, with emphasis on the special diagnostic problems likely to be encountered in an older age group. Differential diagnosis of organic and functional disorders that may present with similar symptoms, particular considerations in evaluating major depression in the elderly, and the question of late-onset psychoses are the central foci. Differential diagnosis in the elderly is likely to assume an increasingly important place in psychiatric assessment in the future.

REFERENCES

1. Skodol AE, Spitzer RL: Differential diagnosis in the elderly. Psychopharmacology Bull 17:94–96, 1981
2. Rabins PV, Folstein MF: Delirium and dementia: diagnostic criteria and fatality rates. Br J Psychiatry 140:149–153, 1982
3. Lipowski ZJ: Transient cognitive disorders (delirium, acute confusional states) in the elderly. Am J Psychiatry 140:1426–1436, 1983
4. Maletta GJ, Pirozzolo FJ, Thompson G, Mortimer JA: Organic mental

disorders in a geriatric population. Am J Psychiatry 139:521–523, 1982

5. Wells CE: Pseudodementia. Am J Psychiatry 136:895–900, 1979
6. Good MI: Pseudodementia and physical findings mask significant psychopathology. Am J Psychiatry 138:811–814, 1981
7. Hirschfeld RMA, Klerman GL: Treatment of depression in the elderly. Geriatrics 34:51–57, 1979
8. Schatzberg AF, Liptzin B, Satlin A, Cole JO: Diagnosis of affective disorders in the elderly. Psychosomatics 25:126–131, 1984
9. Janowsky DS: Pseudodementia in the elderly: differential diagnosis and treatment. J Clin Psychiatry 43(Suppl):19–25, 1982
10. Reynolds CF III, Hoch CC, Kupfer DJ, Buysse DJ, Houck PR, Stack JA, Campbell DW: Bedside differentiation of depressive pseudodementia from dementia. Am J Psychiatry 145:1099–1103, 1988
11. Thase ME, Reynolds CF III: Manic pseudodementia. Psychosomatics 25:256, 259–260, 1984
12. Robinson RG, Boston JD, Starkstein BE, Price TR: Comparison of mania and depression after brain injury: causal factors. Am J Psychiatry 145:172–178, 1988
13. Caine ED, Shoulson I: Psychiatric syndromes in Huntington's disease. Am J Psychiatry 140:728–733, 1983
14. Folstein SE, Folstein MF: Psychiatric features of Huntington's disease: recent approaches and findings. Psychiatr Dev 1:193–205, 1983
15. Himmelhoch JM, Neil JF, May SJ, Fuchs CZ, Licata SM: Age, dementia, dyskinesias, and lithium response. Am J Psychiatry 137:941–945, 1980
16. Schulberg HC, Saul M, McClelland M, Ganguli M, Christy W, Frank R: Assessing depression in primary medical and psychiatric practices. Arch Gen Psychiatry 42:1164–1170, 1985
17. Popkin MK, Callies AL, Colon E: A framework for the study of medical depression. Psychosomatics 28:27–33, 1987
18. Popkin MK, Callies AL, Lentz RD, Colon EA, Sutherland DE: Prevalence of major depression, simple phobia, and other psychiatric disorders in patients with long-standing type I diabetes mellitus. Arch Gen Psychiatry 45:64–68, 1988
19. Dohrenwend BP, Shrout PE, Link BG, Martin JL, Skodol AE: Overview and initial results from a risk-factor study of depression and schizophrenia, in Mental Disorders in the Community. Edited by Barrett JE, Rose RM. New York, Guilford Press, 1986, pp 184–215
20. Robinson RG, Lipsey JR, Price TR: Diagnosis and clinical management of post-stroke depression. Psychosomatics 26:769–772, 775–778, 1985
21. Robinson RG, Starr LB, Price TR: A two year longitudinal study of mood disorders following stroke: prevalence and duration at six months follow-up. Br J Psychiatry 144:256–262, 1984
22. Mayeux R, Stern Y, Williams JBW, Cote L, Frantz A, Dyrenfurth I: Clinical and biochemical features of depression in Parkinson's disease. Am J Psychiatry 143:756–759, 1986
23. Rodin G, Voshart K: Depression in the medically ill: an overview. Am J Psychiatry 143:696–705, 1986
24. Cavanaugh S, Clark DC, Gibbons RD: Diagnosing depression in the hospitalized medically ill. Psychosomatics 24:809–815, 1983
25. Cavanaugh SVA: Diagnosing depression in the hospitalized patient with chronic medical illness. J Clin Psychiatry 45:13–16, 1984
26. Lipsey JR, Spencer WC, Rabins PV, Robinson RG: Phenomenological

comparison of poststroke depression and functional depression. Am J Psychiatry 143:530–532, 1986
27. American Psychiatric Association: Diagnostic and Statistical Manual of Mental Disorders, Second Edition. Washington, DC, American Psychiatric Association, 1968
28. Adelstein AM, Downham DY, Stein Z, Susser MW: The epidemiology of mental illness in an English city. Soc Psychiatry 3:47–59, 1968
29. Myers JK, Lindenthal JJ, Pepper MP: Life events and mental status: a longitudinal study. J Health Soc Behav 13:398–406, 1972
30. Winokur G: Depression in the menopause. Am J Psychiatry 130:92–93, 1973
31. Weissman MM, Myers JK: Rates and risks of depressive symptoms in a United States urban community. Acta Psychiatr Scand 57:219–231, 1978
32. Weiesman MM: The myth of involutional melancholia. JAMA 242:742–744, 1979
33. Pichot P, Pull C: Is there an involutional melancholia? Compr Psychiatry 22:2–10, 1981
34. Dessonville C, Gallagher D, Thompson LW, Finnell K, Lewinsohn PM: Relation of age and health status on depressive symptoms in normal and depressed older adults. Essence 5:99–117, 1982
35. Endicott J, Spitzer RL: A diagnostic interview: the Schedule for Affective Disorders and Schizophrenia. Arch Gen Psychiatry 35:837–844, 1978
36. Brown RP, Sweeney J, Loutsch E, Kocsis J, Frances A: Involutional melancholia revisited. Am J Psychiatry 141:24–28, 1984
37. Winokur G: Unipolar depression: is it divisible into autonomous subtypes? Arch Gen Psychiatry 36:47–52, 1979
38. Spar JE, La Rue A: Major depression in the elderly: DSM-III criteria and the dexamethasone suppression test as predictors of treatment response. Am J Psychiatry 140:844–847, 1983
39. Blazer D, Williams CD: Epidemiology of dysphoria and depression in an elderly population. Am J Psychiatry 137:439–444, 1980
40. American Psychiatric Association: Diagnostic and Statistical Manual of Mental Disorders, Third Edition. Washington, DC, American Psychiatric Association, 1980
41. American Psychiatric Association: Diagnostic and Statistical Manual of Mental Disorders, Third Edition, Revised. Washington, DC, American Psychiatric Association, 1987
42. Gallagher D, Breckenridge JN, Thompson LW: Similarities and differences between normal grief and depression in older adults. Essence 5:127–139, 1982
43. Kosten TR, Jacobs S, Mason JW: The dexamethasone suppression test during bereavement. J Nerv Ment Dis 172:359–360, 1984
44. Lundin T: Long-term outcome of bereavement. Br J Psychiatry 145:424–428, 1984
45. Vachon M, Rogers J, Lyall A, Lancee W, Sheldon AR, Freeman SJJ: Predictors and correlates of adaptation to conjugal bereavement. Am J Psychiatry 139:998–1000, 1982
46. Goldberg D: The Detection of Psychiatric Illness by Questionnaire, a Technique for the Identification of Non-Psychotic Psychiatric Illness: Institute of Psychiatry Maudsley Monographs 21. London, Oxford University Press, 1972
47. Roth M: The natural history of mental disorder in old age. J Ment Sci 101:281–301, 1955

48. Rabins P, Pauker S, Thomas J: Can schizophrenia begin after age 44? Compr Psychiatry 25:290–293, 1984
49. Grahame PS: Schizophrenia in old age (late paraphrenia). Br J Psychiatry 145:493–495, 1984
50. Leuchter AF, Spar JE: The late-onset psychoses: clinical and diagnostic features. J Nerv Ment Dis 173:488–494, 1985
51. Kendler KS: The nosologic validity of paranoia (simple delusional disorder). Arch Gen Psychiatry 37:699–706, 1980

CHAPTER 12

Miscellaneous Syndromes: Common and Uncommon, New and Old

This chapter addresses a number of clinical syndromes that might be encountered by the clinician evaluating adult patients, but that do not fit meaningfully into the areas of differential diagnosis covered in the previous chapters. Some of these are DSM-III or DSM-III-R categories, whereas others reflect diagnostic concepts not explicitly included in the DSM-III systems. Some are quite common clinical problems and others, quite rare; the actual prevalence of a few of them is a subject of controversy. Such syndromes, though not included in DSM-III or DSM-III-R, are discussed here because clinicians frequently ask how to diagnose them according to these systems; and consideration of them here allows clinicians to judge the adequacy of DSM-III and DSM-III-R categories for conveying their salient features.

A brief section on culture bound syndromes is also included. DSM-III has achieved widespread international acceptance (1) and has been used in many cultures (2,3), but its relevance to some cultures, particularly of the Third World, has been challenged (4).

MISCELLANEOUS DSM-III DIAGNOSTIC CLASSES AND CATEGORIES

The diagnostic classes or subclasses in DSM-III that have not been discussed previously include the dissociative disorders, the sexual disorders (other than the sexual dysfunctions, which are discussed in Chapter 8), the impulse control disorders not elsewhere classified (other than trichotillomania, which is also discussed in Chapter 8), the gender identity disorders, and the V codes (other than malingering, borderline intellectual functioning, adult and childhood or adolescent antisocial behavior, and uncomplicated bereavement).

Dissociative Disorders

The dissociative disorders in DSM-III included psychogenic amnesia, psychogenic fugue, multiple personality, depersonalization disorder, and the residual atypical dissociative disorder. A new category, possession/trance disorder, was considered and rejected for DSM-III-R, so the same categories appear in the final version of the revision. Following DSM-III-R practice, however, the atypical category has been renamed "dissociative disorder not otherwise specified."

The core concepts of the dissociative disorders in DSM-III and DSM-III-R are quite different. According to DSM-III, the essential feature of all of the dissociative disorders was a "sudden, temporary alteration in the normally integrative functions of consciousness, identity, or motor behavior" (5, p. 253). In DSM-III-R, the essential feature of these disorders is described as "a disturbance or alteration in the normally integrative functions of identity, memory, or consciousness. The disturbance or alteration may be sudden or gradual, and transient or chronic" (6, p. 269).

The definition of the dissociative disorders by specific diagnostic criteria in DSM-III is generally regarded as a landmark in the study of these conditions (7). Although associated with long histories in clinical psychiatry, the dissociative disorders have rarely been studied systematically, and the literature is primarily clinical rather than empirical. Establishing the diagnosis of a dissociative disorder can be difficult, even with explicit criteria, and the usefulness of the categories for clinical purposes remains uncertain.

Psychogenic amnesia. In psychogenic amnesia there is a sudden inability to recall important personal information. The amount of information lost is too extensive to be explained by ordinary forgetfulness. The amnesia usually occurs as a reaction to conditions of extreme psychosocial stress. The stress may involve a threat of injury or death, such as may be experienced during combat or following a major natural disaster; unacceptable impulses or acts, such as having an affair or committing an act of violence; or an intolerable situation in life, such as being abandoned by a spouse.

The main differential, required by the diagnostic criteria, is with organic mental disorders (OMDs). Included would be physical conditions causing delirium, dementia, or organic amnestic syndromes (see Chapter 3) and syndromes associated with the use of certain psychoactive substances (see Chapter 4). The course of development of memory loss secondary to organic factors is usually gradual and not associated with psychosocial stressors. An exception would be an accident or other situation in which a severe head injury was sustained that resulted in memory loss. Amnesia following a concussion is typically retrograde, whereas psychogenic amnesia is almost always anterograde. Memory loss resulting from organic factors is frequently irreversible, whereas that of psychogenic amnesia is fully reversible. Memory impairment associated with epilepsy is sudden in onset, motor signs of seizures are evident, and the EEG is abnormal. Recovery of lost memories during an amobarbital interview or under hypnosis confirms a psychogenic etiology of the amnesia.

Intoxication, especially with alcohol, can cause memory loss. These "blackouts" can be distinguished from psychogenic amnesia by the history, physical signs, or laboratory results indicating alcohol ingestion and a failure to subsequently regain the memories. Long-term abuse of alcohol may lead to an alcohol amnestic disorder. The memory loss is for short-term, rather than immediate, memory, and is accompanied by other mental signs, such as confabulation, and the physical stigmata of chronic alcoholism.

DSM-III-R criteria differ from those in DSM-III in requiring that multiple personality disorder be ruled out before a diagnosis of psychogenic amnesia is made. In multiple personality disorder (see below), the personalities may be aware of "lost time" or experience amnesia in other ways. Multiple personality disorder also involves repeated shifts in identity, however, whereas psychogenic amnesia usually involves a single episode.

Since psychogenic amnesia typically follows extreme stress, it may be accompanied by the full syndrome of posttraumatic stress disorder (PTSD) (see Chapter 7). When this is the case, DSM-III and DSM-III-R allow for both diagnoses to be made, even though this violates the general DSM-III and DSM-III-R rules of parsimony, since memory impairment is one of the symptoms of PTSD (criterion D in DSM-III, and C in DSM-III-R).

Psychogenic fugue. Psychogenic fugue involves the sudden inability to recall one's identity, the assumption of a new identity, and unexpected travel away from home. This disorder typically occurs following severe psychosocial stress. Heavy alcohol use may be a predisposing factor.

The travel in psychogenic fugue is apparently purposeful, which helps to distinguish the condition from the confused or aimless wandering that may accompany an organic mental disorder or psychogenic amnesia. The loss of memory of one's identity is much more circumscribed than that observed in organic mental disorders. Knowledge of one's personal identity is rarely lost by patients with OMDs; when it is, it occurs only in the most grossly confused patient with prominent signs of reduced level of consciousness, general memory impairment, and inability to attend to external stimuli. These are not encountered in psychogenic fugue.

Some instances of temporal lobe epilepsy may involve travel, but only in a limited way, and without the assumption of a new identity or involvement in complex activities, such as taking on a new job.

Since fugue involves a new identity, it may be mistaken for multiple personality. In DSM-III, fugue was distinguished from multiple personality by its usually being limited to a single, brief episode, less complex social activities, and lack of awareness of the original personality. According to DSM-III-R, in multiple personality disorder (see below), the personalities, or personality states, do not have to be as complex, and awareness by one personality of the others is considered variable. The DSM-III-R criteria for psychogenic fugue now explicitly rule out this diagnosis if the disturbance meets the criteria for multiple personality.

Multiple personality disorder. Multiple personality disorder (MPD) is the dissociative disorder that has received the most attention since publication of DSM-III. As a consequence of the recent work, some inadequacies in the DSM-III criteria have been discovered. In addition, as a result of more extensive clinical experience with this dissociative disorder, more is known about problems in differential diagnosis.

The DSM-III criteria for multiple personality defined the condition by (*1*) the existence within the person of two or more distinct personalities, each of which was dominant at a particular time; (*2*) determination of the person's behavior by the personality that was dominant at the time; and (*3*) the existence of unique behavior patterns and social relationships that were complex and integrated for each individual personality.

Some clinicians with considerable experience in treating multiple personality have found that the requirement that the person's behavior be determined by the particular dominant personality at a given time is overly simplistic (8). Many personalities may influence behavior without completely emerging, or may contend with each other for control. Sometimes the patient experiences the control via a passive influence, which may appear to be a psychotic experience (see also below). The personalities may mimic one another or pass as one. In DSM-III-R, the relevant criterion, B, has been altered to read "At least two of these personalities or personality states recurrently take full control of the person's behavior" (6, p. 272). The emphasis is on control of behavior, rather than on the dominant personality at the time (Table 12.1).

Kluft (7) also believes that the personalities in multiple personality vary in their complexity, distinctness from each other, and degree of importance, dominance, and elaborateness over time. Therefore, the original DSM-III requirement that each personality be "complex and integrated was likely to result in too many atypical cases, or to confuse the diagnostician in recognizing the disorder. In DSM-III-R, criterion A now says that the personalities, or personality states, each has "its own relatively enduring pattern of perceiving, relating to, and thinking about the environment and self" (6, p. 272). A distinction is made between "personality" and "personality state": in the former, the "pattern" is exhibited in a wide range of important social and personal contexts; in the latter, it is not seen in as wide a range of contexts.

In my opinion, unless the disturbances meet the general definition of personality used in DSM-III or DSM-III-R, it does not make sense to refer to them as multiple personalities. They may simply be diverse aspects of a single, but inconsistent, personality style. Differences in views about how complex and how widely exhibited a personality state needs to be to qualify as "distinct" undoubtedly accounts for the extreme variability in the prevalence rate of multiple personality disorder reported from one site to another and for the unreliability of diagnosis in a given case.

Multiple personality disorder almost invariably involves a history of severe emotional trauma, usually child abuse. Its prevalence is a matter of debate, some clinicians arguing that it occurs as frequently as one in every seven hospital admissions, and others reporting that it

TABLE 12.1 DSM-III-R Diagnostic Criteria for Multiple Personality Disorder

A. The existence within the person of two or more distinct personalities or personality states (each with its own relatively enduring pattern of perceiving, relating to, and thinking about the environment and self).

B. At least two of these personalities or personality states recurrently take full control of the person's behavior.

occurs hardly at all. Those who contend that it is common argue that it is frequently misdiagnosed as another disorder; their opponents argue that the other disorders are the more valid diagnoses.

A recent study by Putnam and associates (9), from the National Institute of Mental Health, illustrates the source of the differential diagnostic confusion. From a survey of therapists treating 100 individual cases of multiple personality, data were gathered on the presenting mental and physical symptoms and the previous diagnoses received. The presenting mental symptoms reported in half or more of the cases included depression, mood swings, suicidality, insomnia, psychogenic amnesia, sexual dysfunctions, conversion symptoms, fugue episodes, panic attacks, depersonalization, and substance abuse. Other symptoms reported included phobias, compulsive rituals, hallucinations, delusions, thought disorder, anorexia, bulimia, and mania! The reader must conclude that mood disorders, somatoform and other disorders with physical complaints, anxiety disorders, psychoactive substance use disorders, schizophrenia and related psychotic disorders—essentially every group of mental disorders previously discussed—enter into the differential diagnosis of multiple personality. In fact, 50 percent or more of these cases had previously received diagnoses of depression, neurotic disorder, personality disorder, or schizophrenia.

Putnam and associates (9) found that patients being treated for multiple personality disorder also frequently presented with physical symptoms such as headache, unexplained pain, periods of unresponsiveness, gastrointestinal complaints, palpitations, paresthesias and analgesias, and weight loss, suggesting that, in addition to consideration for diagnoses of somatoform disorders, the patients were likely candidates for workups for a wide range of somatic, especially neurological, illnesses.

A major problem in deciding the "correct" diagnosis in such complex cases is the relative absence of external validity standards for the diagnosis of multiple personality. In the study by Putnam and co-workers (9), "the diagnosis was confirmed by the meeting of alternate personalities." Unfortunately, there is an inherent bias and circularity in such a process that does not meet current standards of validity.

Data are just now beginning to accumulate on familial patterns of multiple personality disorder (10,11). Hypnosis and the amytal interview show promise as specific procedures to which patients with multiple personality may respond in a characteristic way; these procedures currently are useful as aids in differential diagnosis, and may eventually be helpful as indicators of treatment response. They themselves, however, have yet to be subjected to blind (to patients' diagnoses) and controlled studies of their effects. Until external validity studies are conducted, it may be best to consider multiple personality a disorder that does not preclude a diagnosis of a mood disorder, an anxiety disorder, or a somatoform disorder.

The differential diagnosis of multiple personality disorder from borderline personality disorder (BPD) deserves special comment. In BPD, there is identity disturbance, which may be manifested by uncertainty about issues such as self-image, gender identity, or long-term goals or values. Patients with BPD are constantly changing their affiliations with people, groups, or causes and the direction of their lives, so that they can appear to be very different people in different circumstances or with different people. In addition, they experience affective instability and marked shifts in their attitudes toward others. These phenomena can readily be interpreted as symptoms of multiple personality, especially as the distinctiveness and complexity of the personalities become more blurred, as is likely to result from the changes in multiple personality criteria in DSM-III-R.

Obviously, some of the features of BPD may be absent in MPD, for example, the impulsivity or self-destructiveness. However, even these symptoms (see above) may be associated with the MPD diagnosis as it is made in clinical practice. Classic cases of MPD are likely to be distinguishable; but in ambiguous cases, since neither disorder has compelling evidence of its validity, the DSM-III multiaxial system, with MPD on Axis I and BPD on Axis II, may provide the only reasonable diagnostic approach.

The following case vignette illustrates the dilemma of choosing between a broadly defined concept of MPD and BPD.

Who Is in Control?

A 27-year-old, single, commercial artist started psychotherapy to work on "low self-esteem," "problems with anger," and "trouble with men."

The woman felt confused and disappointed about her life. She was not certain that she had any "real" artistic talent that would enable her to be a successful artist. She had worked for several different companies and freelanced as well, but never felt confident or secure. She frequently suffered depression for days at a time, during which she would not get out of bed.

The patient also reported that she was often overcome with feelings of intense rage that rose within her "like a tidal wave" and frequently resulted in her breaking objects, throwing things, or banging her fist against a table or a wall. This could happen whether she was alone or with someone. In fact, when she came for her initial visit, she was wearing a splint on the little finger of her right hand, which she had broken shortly before, during one of her tirades.

The young woman was intelligent, articulate, and attractive. Although she had many dates, men eventually broke off relationships with her "because they can't stand my tantrums." She tended initially to be very pleasant and warm with men she liked; but when they disappointed her in some way, she became increasingly scornful and ridiculed them. She reported that she was "afraid of sex; she never actively participated in love-making, but rather lay in bed passively and "let them do whatever they want."

During a session approximately two weeks into the treatment, the patient was describing intense and volatile relationships that she had had with her parents. The therapist asked the patient about early memories of her life. Suddenly, tears welled up in her eyes; she looked fearful, and began to tremble. She stared glassy-eyed and silently for several minutes. When the therapist spoke her name and asked her if she was all right, she said, in a higher-pitched voice than usual, "You're not going to hurt me, are you?" When the therapist reassured her, she said, "Please don't be mad at me; please don't hit me." With further reassurance and gentle suggestion that she try to calm down and talk about how she was feeling, the patient returned to her more usual self and, although upset, was able to converse. The entire episode lasted about fifteen minutes.

The patient told the therapist she had been aware, during the episode, of feeling extremely frightened and convinced that she was going to be beaten. She said that she was not sure who the therapist was at the time, and that she may have thought that he was her father. Later history revealed that her father had beaten her as a child, and that, throughout her life, whenever she had become emotionally close to a man, she had experienced extreme distrust and fear and felt that she needed to "get away" or drive the man away.

Over the first two years of the therapy, similar episodes occurred on a dozen occasions. They were usually precipitated by the patient's feeling that the therapist was being overly confrontational or pushing her too hard to remember details of stressful experiences, past or present. She occasionally had one when she did something she felt would make the therapist angry, e.g., was late for a session. It became apparent, over time, that these episodes occurred, also with some regularity, with men whom she dated more than a few times, when she felt "pushed" too quickly into sexual activities, or when the men threatened to stop seeing her.

In this case, the patient experienced episodes of dissociation in reaction to stress. Although she appeared to be distinctly childlike and vulnerable during an episode, it does not seem to me that there is enough of a pattern of behavior to warrant calling this a "personality state." Some clinicians might also point to the aggressive outbursts as distinct from the woman's usual personality functioning. But again, I view this more as evidence of the instability of affect and lack of self-control characteristic of BPD than of a personality state taking control of the woman's behavior. A clinician could make special note of the dissociative episodes by diagnosing dissociative disorder NOS on Axis I.

Depersonalization disorder. Depersonalization disorder was defined in DSM-III as an episode of depersonalization that was sufficient to produce significant impairment in social or occupational functioning and that was not due to any other mental or physical disorder, such as schizophrenia, affective disorder, organic mental disorder, anxiety disorder, or epilepsy. The question has been, and continues to be, whether depersonalization exists as a separate syndrome, or only as a symptom of another disorder.

In DSM-III-R, the criteria have been extensively revised.

1. A single episode is no longer sufficient for the diagnosis: persistent or recurrent experiences are required.
2. What is meant by *depersonalization* has been made explicit: (*a*) the experience of feeling detached from, and as if an outside observer of, one's mental processes or body, or (*b*) an experience of feeling like an automaton or as if in a dream.
3. During the depersonalization experience, reality testing is intact; this helps to distinguish the phenomenon from a psychotic experience.
4. The experience must be the predominant disturbance, not just a symptom of another disorder. This replaces the more vague "not due to" statement of the DSM-III criteria. New disorders to consider are mentioned, especially panic disorder and agoraphobia without a history of panic disorder, but with limited symptom attacks of depersonalization.
5. Social or occupational impairment is no longer required, but the disturbance must cause marked distress.

Dissociative disorder NOS. Expanded examples of the residual diagnostic category dissociative disorder NOS have been included in DSM-III-R. These now include Ganser's syndrome, which was formerly thought to be a factitious disorder; cases of multiple personality in which the personalities are not sufficiently complex or integrated to meet DSM-III-R criteria, or a second personality never actually assumes control; children experiencing repeated amnestic periods or trances following physical abuse; episodes of derealization; and dissociative states following periods of prolonged and intensive coercive persuasion, such as brainwashing or indoctrination while the captive of terrorists or cultists. In an area in which differential diagnosis is already difficult, the wary clinician will be alerted by atypical presentations of dissociative phenomena to look for other diagnostic explanations.

The Paraphilias

The paraphilias are classified with the sexual dysfunctions (see Chapter 8) as psychosexual disorders in DSM-III and as sexual disorders in DSM-III-R. They were formerly called sexual perversions or sexual deviations. Paraphilias involve sexual arousal in response to objects or situations that are not part of usual sexual activity and that may actually interfere with a person's capacity for reciprocal, affectionate sex. Paraphilias may involve sexual attraction to nonhuman objects, such as animals or articles of clothing. With humans they entail suffering or humiliation of either oneself or one's partner, or they may involve sexual arousal by children or other nonconsenting persons. A paraphilia may be diagnosed either if a person acts on these sexual urges or has recurrent urges, and is very distressed by them.

DSM-III and DSM-III-R both include diagnoses of fetishism, pedophilia, exhibitionism, voyeurism, sexual masochism, and sexual sadism. DSM-III transvestism is called transvestic fetishism in DSM-III-R, since the clothing involved in sexually arousing cross-dressing qualifies as the object of fetishism, i.e., a nonliving sexual object. Frotteurism, an example of an atypical paraphilia in DSM-III, has been elevated to a full-fledged diagnostic category in DSM-III-R. Zoophilia, a specific category in DSM-III, is now an example of a paraphilia NOS.

The severity of DSM-III-R paraphilias is noted as mild if there are recurrent, distressing urges, but the person never acts on them; moderate if the person occasionally acts on them; and severe if the person repeatedly acts on them.

Table 12.2 lists the DSM-III-R paraphilias and the objects or behaviors that are involved in the sexual arousal.

According to experts in the diagnosis and treatment of paraphilias (12), there are many more specific types of paraphilias than are included in DSM-III or DSM-III-R. Among them are acrotomophilia (amputee partner), antagonistophilia (on stage), mysophilia (filth), stigmatophilia (piercing; tattoo), and troilism (couple plus one). All of these would be classified in DSM-III as atypical and in DSM-III-R as paraphilia NOS.

Problems in the differential diagnosis of the paraphilias. In DSM-III an attempt was made to distinguish between an isolated paraphilic act and a repetitive pattern of behavior that might be more characteristic of a mental disorder by specifying that the paraphilic object or act

Table 12.2 DSM-III-R Paraphilias

Category	Object or behavior that is sexually arousing
Pedophilia	Child or children age 13 or younger
Exhibitionism	Exposure of genitals to unsuspecting stranger
Sexual sadism	Real (not simulated) psychological or physical suffering (including humiliation) of a victim
Sexual masochism	The act (real, not simulated) of being humiliated, beaten, bound, or otherwise made to suffer
Voyeurism	Observing an unsuspecting person who is naked, in the process of disrobing, or engaging in sexual activity
Fetishism	Nonliving objects other than female clothing used in cross-dressing or objects designed for sexual stimulation (e.g., vibrator)
Transvestic fetishism	Cross-dressing
Frotteurism	Touching and rubbing against a nonconsenting person
Paraphilia NOS	Feces (coprophilia) Corpse (necrophilia) Lewdness (telephone scatologia) Exclusive focus on part of the body (partialism) Animals (zoophilia) Enemas (klismaphilia) Urine (urophilia)

was "a repeatedly preferred or exclusive method of achieving sexual excitement." This proved unsatisfactory, however, because some people with paraphilias did not actually prefer the object or behavior but, in fact, suffered considerably from having to engage in the paraphilia. Furthermore, the paraphilia was often not the exclusive means of sexual excitement: people might engage in other paraphilias or in more ordinary sexual behavior as well.

In order to address these problems, the general format for the paraphilias in DSM-III-R has been changed. The criteria now emphasize a minimum duration of the disturbance of at least six months, and specify that the person acts on the sexual urges or recurrently experiences the urges and is markedly distressed by them. The new criteria also stress that it is the sexual urges and fantasies that constitute the abnormality, so that even if a person does not act on them, the diagnosis can be made if the urges and fantasies are sufficiently distressing. Table 12.3 compares the DSM-III and III-R criteria for voyeurism.

There are a number of specific differential diagnostic concerns involving the individual paraphilias. In diagnosing pedophilia, it is necessary to distinguish the disorder from an unusually young person's becoming sexually involved with another youth. As indicated in Table 12.2, the child or children who are the object of the paraphilia must be 13 years of age or younger. In addition, the diagnostic criteria of DSM-III-R require that the person diagnosed be at least 16 years old and at least 5 years older than the child who is the object. In DSM-III, the corresponding criteria referred to prepubertal children. As some children reach puberty at an increasingly early age, puberty seemed to be no valid indicator that they were no longer "children." In DSM-III, if the person was an adult, the age difference was stipulated as ten years, and if the person was a late adolescent, no age difference was required, leaving the determination of whether the acts constituted pedophilia up to the clinician.

DSM-III-R criteria explicitly include a note to the effect that a late adolescent involved in an ongoing sexual relationship with a 12- or

Table 12.3 A Comparison of DSM-III and DSM-III-R Criteria for Voyeurism

DSM-III Voyeurism

A. The individual repeatedly observes unsuspecting people who are either naked, in the act of disrobing, or engaging in sexual activity, and no sexual activity with the observed people is sought.

B. The observing is the repeatedly preferred or exclusive method of achieving sexual excitement.

DSM-III-R Voyeurism

A. Over a period of at least six months, recurrent intense sexual urges and sexually arousing fantasies involving the act of observing an unsuspecting person who is naked, in the process of disrobing, or engaging in sexual activity.

B. The person has acted on these urges, or is markedly distressed by them.

13-year-old should not receive a diagnosis of pedophilia. DSM-III-R criteria ask the clinician to specify whether the object of the patient's arousal is of the same sex, the opposite sex, or of either sex. Since this diagnosis would apply to some cases of incest, the clinician is also directed to specify if the disturbance is limited to incest. Finally, the clinician can note "exclusive type" if the patient is attracted only to children, or nonexclusive type if sometimes attracted to adults.

In making the diagnosis of sexual sadism, the clinician must distinguish the disorder from acts of rape or sexual assault that are not due to the disorder, i.e., are not committed because the inflicting of suffering is sexually exciting. A rapist may not have recurrent preoccupation with intense sexual urges to rape or sexually arousing fantasies about rape. Some rapists, especially repeat offenders, probably do meet the general criteria for a paraphilia (DSM-III-R states fewer than 10%). In a preliminary draft of DSM-III-R, a category for paraphilic rapism was proposed, the essential feature of which was a persistent association between intense sexual arousal or desire and acts, fantasies, or other stimuli involving coercing, or forcing a nonconsenting person to engage in oral, vaginal, or anal intercourse. The category met with considerable resistance from within and outside the mental health professions primarily because of its potential abuse as a legal defense for rapists standing trial. Sexual sadism is also to be distinguished from sadistic personality disorder (a new proposed diagnostic category needing further study in DSM-III-R Appendix A). Sadistic personality disorder is a pattern of cruel, demeaning, and aggressive behavior not solely for the purpose of sexual arousal.

Sexual masochism needs to be distinguished from "masochistic" personality traits. Persons who exhibit a pattern of self-defeating behavior, who avoid or undermine pleasurable experiences, or become involved in situations or relationships in which they will suffer, are commonly referred to as masochistic. DSM-III-R has a category in its Appendix A for self-defeating personality disorder (see also Chapter 9). This personality disorder is explicitly excluded if the typical behaviors occur only in response to, or in anticipation of, being physically, sexually, or psychologically abused. For a person to meet the criteria for sexual masochism, there must be intense sexual urges and sexually arousing fantasies involving acts of humiliation or being made to suffer. It is conceivable that a person could meet criteria for both diagnoses.

Voyeurism is not usually diagnosed in persons who enjoy watching pornographic movies or looking at pornographic magazines. Some people incorporate pornography into everyday sexual practices with their partners. Voyeurism is usually limited to cases involving secretive watching of unsuspecting people.

Many people incorporate nonhuman objects into their sexual activities, women's undergarments used in the course of sexual arousal and foreplay being an example. When the use of an object leads to normal, genital, sexual activity, a fetishism diagnosis is not indicated. Fetishism is also not diagnosed when the objects are limited to articles of female clothing used in cross-dressing; in such cases the diagnosis transvestic fetishism applies.

The main differential with transvestic fetishism is with gender identity disorder of adolescence or adulthood, nontranssexual type (GIDAANT), or transsexualism. These diagnoses, which are discussed below, take precedence over transvestic fetishism. Male homosexuals sometimes engage in cross-dressing. In DSM-III-R, transvestic fetishism is limited to heterosexual males.

Gender Identity Disorders

The gender identity disorders are characterized by a persistent discomfort and sense of inappropriateness about one's assigned sex. The prototype of this group of disorders is transsexualism, in which the person is preoccupied with getting rid of his or her own primary and secondary sex characteristics and acquiring the sexual characteristics of the opposite sex.

When a person has substantially changed his or her secondary sex characteristics, the disorder may not be immediately apparent. Once acknowledged, however, there are few conditions that can be mistaken for transsexualism. One is transvestic fetishism, in which the person (exclusively heterosexual men) merely cross-dresses for sexual stimulation, but is not actually uncomfortable with his sex or interested in becoming physically female. This disorder has been discussed above. When there are abnormalities affecting the sex chromosomes or evidence of physical intersex, DSM-III ruled out a transsexual diagnosis. This exclusion is no longer in the DSM-III-R criteria. In a disorder such as schizophrenia, a person may have the delusion that he or she is not really a man or woman, or is changing into a man or woman. Transsexualism is ruled out in such cases by DSM-III criteria, but not in DSM-III-R.

A problem with the revised criteria in DSM-III-R is the use of the term *preoccupation* with changes in sexual characteristics. The term is ambiguous and open to interpretation as to whether the person merely needs to be thinking constantly about changing or actually takes concrete steps to change, for example, by receiving hormone therapy or being evaluated for sex-change surgery. Conversely, if a person has had the surgery and is no longer preoccupied with changing, would he or she still be diagnosed transsexual? No doubt he or she would.

There also appears to be a milder version of gender identity disorder in which the person is uncomfortable about his or her gender and feels that it is inappropriate, but instead of actually pursuing change in primary and secondary sex characteristics, cross-dresses or fantasizes recurrently about cross-dressing. This condition is assigned a specific diagnostic category in DSM-III-R: gender identity disorder of adolescence or adulthood, nontranssexual type (GIDAANT).

There is also a gender identity disorder diagnosis for children who have not yet reached puberty. A recent follow-up study revealed that boys with gender identity problems in childhood frequently grew up to have homosexual orientation and behavior in adulthood (13).

In DSM-III-R, *adult* examples of gender identity disorder NOS include transient, stress-related, cross-dressing behavior; transsexualism of less than two years' duration; and persistent preoccupation with castration or penotomy without the wish to acquire the sex characteristics of the other sex. All the gender identity disorders are grouped together as disorders usually first evident in infancy, childhood, or adolescence in DSM-III-R since their initial manifestations are evident at an early age.

Impulse Control Disorders Not Elsewhere Classified

The impulse control disorders not elsewhere classified in DSM-III included pathological gambling, kleptomania, pyromania, intermittent explosive disorder, isolated explosive disorder, and atypical impulse control disorder. Isolated explosive disorder has been deleted from DSM-III-R for the reasons outlined in Chapter 10, Antisocial, Aggressive, or Violent Behavior. Trichotillomania has been added to this class of disorders in DSM-III-R, as discussed in Chapter 8, Physical Complaints.

In DSM-III the impulse control disorders that were not classified in other categories were grouped together on the basis of a cluster of features that were not, however, part of the diagnostic criteria for any of the individual disorders. An early draft of DSM-III-R was more explicit in listing these essential features (see Table 12.4) and requiring that persons meeting the individual criteria for a diagnosis also meet these general criteria, but the final version of DSM-III-R is as ambiguous as was DSM-III in this regard. For example, neither intermittent explosive disorder nor pathological gambling has a requirement for an increasing sense of tension or arousal before the act or pleasure, gratification, or release at the time of the act.

The most extensively revised of the categories is pathological gambling. The criteria have been recast using the prototypic model of classification originally proposed for the personality disorders (see Chapter 9), and the disorder has been defined so that it is an almost

Table 12.4 Essential Features of Impulse Control Disorders Not Elsewhere Classified in DSM-III-R

1. Repeated failure to resist an impulse, drive, or temptation to perform some act that is harmful to the person or others. There may or may not be conscious resistance to the impulse. The act may or may not be premeditated or planned.
2. An increasing sense of tension or arousal before committing the act.
3. An experience of either pleasure, gratification, or release at the time of committing the act. The act is ego-syntonic in that it is consonant with the person's immediate conscious wish. Immediately following the act there may or may not be genuine regret, self-reproach, or guilt.

Table 12.5 DSM-III-R Diagnostic Criteria for Pathological Gambling

Maladaptive gambling behavior, as indicated by at least four of the following:

(1) frequent preoccupation with gambling or with obtaining money to gamble
(2) frequent gambling of larger amounts of money or over a longer period of time than intended
(3) a need to increase the size or frequency of bets to achieve the desired excitement
(4) restlessness or irritability if unable to gamble
(5) repeated loss of money by gambling and returning another day to win back losses ("chasing")
(6) repeated efforts to reduce or stop gambling
(7) frequent gambling when expected to meet social or occupational obligations
(8) sacrifice of some important social, occupational, or recreational activity in order to gamble
(9) continuation of gambling despite inability to pay mounting debts, or despite other significant social, occupational, or legal problems that the person knows to be exacerbated by gambling

exact counterpart of psychoactive substance dependence. The DSM-III-R criteria are reproduced in Table 12.5. These revised criteria emphasize the compulsive nature of pathological gambling (14).

Pathological gambling could not be diagnosed along with Antisocial personality disorder in DSM-III; no such exclusion is made in DSM-III-R. Pathological gambling must be distinguished from gambling that may occur as part of a manic or a hypomanic episode, although there is no required exclusion. In describing the personality of the pathological gambler, Custer (14) lists superior intelligence, competitiveness, industriousness, high energy, and good athletic and scholastic ability; he claims that such people are at risk of becoming workaholics. Gamblers thrive on challenge and seek situations that are highly stimulating. This profile is strikingly reminiscent of the description, in Chapter 4, of cocaine dependent persons, some of whom actually have a mood disturbance in the bipolar spectrum. Social gambling should also be distinguished from pathological gambling, since most Americans probably engage in some form of gambling. Custer states that social gamblers, those who can easily quit, have that ability because their self-esteem is not tied to winning or losing, other aspects of their lives are more important and rewarding than gambling, and they rarely experience a "big win." Problem gambling has recently been found in 4.2% of a general population sample of New York State residents (15).

DSM-III-R criteria for kleptomania are very similar to those of DSM-III except for one change. Instead of a criterion stating that the stealing is done without long-term planning and assistance from, or collaboration with, others (DSM-III criterion D), DSM-III-R criterion D reads "the stealing is not committed to express anger or vengeance." Kleptomania is not to be diagnosed in a person who has a conduct disorder or an antisocial personality disorder.

The pyromania criteria in DSM-III-R have the added requirement that the person have a fascination with, interest in, curiosity about, or attraction to fires or their consequences. Instead of containing an exclusion criterion for organic mental disorders, schizophrenia, antisocial personality disorder, and conduct disorder, DSM-III-R criterion E for pyromania states: "The fire setting is not done for monetary gain, as an expression of sociopolitical ideology, to conceal criminal activity, to express anger or vengeance, to improve one's living circumstances, or in response to a delusion or hallucination" (6, p. 326).

Disorders of impulse control not elsewhere classified may frequently occur in association with a personality disorder. They should, however, be noted separately as an additional diagnosis, exclusion criteria permitting, because they will undoubtedly require specialized treatment approaches.

"Problems in Living"

DSM-III and DSM-III-R include codes that can be used by the clinician when evaluating or treating a client who, although presenting with a problem or difficulty, is judged not to have a diagnosable mental disorder. These are the V codes for "conditions not attributable to a mental disorder that are a focus of attention or treatment." A number of V codes have been discussed in previous chapters, in the clinical contexts in which they most commonly are encountered.

Malingering, the intentional production of false or grossly exaggerated physical or psychological symptoms motivated by external incentives, most commonly is considered when the clinician evaluates a patient with a psychotic syndrome (Chapter 5), physical complaints (Chapter 8), or, recently, symptoms of PTSD (Chapter 7). *Borderline intellectual functioning* (IQ in the 71-84 range) is a consideration in the evaluation of any patient who is suspected of being mentally retarded (Chapter 10). *Adult or childhood or adolescent antisocial behavior* is a possible designation for patients whose antisocial acts are not due to a mental disorder such as antisocial personality disorder (Chapters 9 and 10), an impulse control disorder (Chapter 10, and above), or a conduct disorder (Chapter 10). *Uncomplicated bereavement*—a normal grief reaction to the death of a loved one—must be considered in every patient who presents with a full depressive syndrome (Chapter 6), and is commonly encountered among the elderly (Chapter 11). *Noncompliance with medical treatment* is likely to be an issue for the consultant liaison psychiatrist in the case of a patient with physical problems (Chapter 8).

Other V codes cover additional problems of living. An *academic problem* may involve, for example, a pattern of significant academic underachievement in a person without a mental disorder such as a specific developmental disorder or mental retardation. An *occupational problem* is a parallel category that would include factors such as job dissatisfaction or career uncertainty—again, not due to a mental disorder such as a personality or a mood disorder. *Phase of life problem* or *other life circumstance problem* covers a wide range of situations that quite frequently crop up in the mental health clinician's practice. Included especially would be problems associated with developmental phases in the life cycle, e.g., beginning school, separating from parents, starting a new career, marriage, divorce, and retirement. The following vignette depicts a typical case in which the life circumstance V code would be appropriate.

Spread Too Thin

A 42-year-old surgeon was referred to a psychiatrist by a woman he was dating. The man had lost his wife three years earlier in an automobile accident.

Following a period of fairly intense grief, the surgeon had begun to put his life back together. He began to accept new patients in his practice; he settled on a live-in housekeeper (after a few false starts) to look after his three children, aged 12, 10, and 8, and his house; and, about 18 months earlier, had started to date occasionally. The woman he was dating currently was the first he had had any serious feelings for, and he tried to spend increasing amounts of time with her.

As his practice got busier and his dating more frequent, he spent less and less time at home. Then, one day his 12-year-old son brought home his first "mostly C's" report card of his life. The surgeon was angry and lectured the boy about the importance of doing well in school, to which the boy replied, "What do you care?" The boy sulked around the house for the next two weeks.

At work the surgeon began to "cut corners." He had always been extremely reliable in returning patient and house staff calls and in making rounds on his hospitalized patients, no matter how late. He found himself rushing through his routines in order to have more time to spend with his girlfriend.

His relationship with the woman was not easy, however. She complained of feeling like an "intruder" in his family life, and that she sensed that he was comparing her with his deceased wife. She also criticized him for not spending more time with his children, accusing him of neglect. Finally, he exploded at her one night over dinner, "Who do you think I am, Superman? I have a busy, difficult job; I'm trying to pay more attention to you, and the kids—well, I want to be there for them, but I don't know how I'm going to be the father they need and have a life for myself."

The woman suggested that he speak to someone professionally; and, feeling "pulled in all directions" and "spread too thin," the surgeon readily agreed.

Four other V codes are included in DSM-III and DSM-III-R: *marital problem,* for marital conflict not due to a mental disorder; *parent-child problem* and *other specified family circumstances,* for other intrafamilial difficulties; and *other interpersonal problem,* for problems between people who are not married or related, such as lovers or co-workers.

The major problems in differential diagnosis involving the V codes are the establishment of whether or not a mental disorder is present and, if so, whether or not the presenting problem is in fact due to the mental disorder. Some clinicians do not realize that it is possible to use a V code for a patient with a mental disorder when the problem appears unrelated to the mental disorder. The following vignette illustrates this possibility.

Spouse Abuse

A 22-year-old, unemployed, separated woman was referred to an outpatient psychiatric clinic by her neurosurgeon following a hospitalization for a brain abscess and meningitis.

Her marriage, of two years, was characterized by constant verbal and physical fights because her husband frequently and blatantly went out with other women. During these fights, he beat her. She sometimes exhibited dramatic behavior during the fights, e.g., she cut up her husband's clothes, and once poured alcohol over herself and threatened to set herself on fire.

Describing the fight that led to the hospitalization, the woman said, "He pushed me against the wall, then threw me down on the floor. He got on top of me and beat me in the face with his fists. He broke my nose, and my face got all black and blue." Shortly thereafter, complications set in.

The patient described lifelong feelings of self-consciousness and periods of derealization from adolescence on. Her only previous psychiatric contact had been once, as a teenager, when she was "giving (her) mother trouble." She complained of brief periods of depression.

Currently, the patient is living with her mother and stepfather. She is taking care of her only child, cooking and cleaning the house, and seeing a girlfriend. She wants help "in case he tries to come after me again."

Although the clinician may suspect a personality disorder in this case, the current reason for treatment, i.e., coping with the stressors of a serious illness and surgery, single parenthood, unemployment, and possible future abuse at the hands of her estranged husband, does not seem directly due to her personality problems.

NON-DSM-III DIAGNOSES

There are many diagnostic terms, categories, and concepts that do not appear in DSM-III or DSM-III-R. Their origins are historical (e.g., dementia praecox, hysterical psychosis, the neuroses, or the DSM-I "reactions"), national (e.g., the Scandinavian reactive psychoses or the French *bouffées délirantes*), or practical (e.g., compensation neurosis). A few of these have been discussed in previous chapters in the context of the differential diagnosis in which they arise. "Hysteroid dysphoria" is mentioned in Chapter 6, Mood Disturbances, under the discussion of atypical depression. "Cardiac neurosis" is mentioned in the discussion of panic disorder in Chapter 7, Anxiety Syndromes.

The non-DSM-III concepts and terms I shall be discussing in the remainder of this chapter are those that appear most frequently in the clinical literature or come up in case discussions, ones that often lead clinicians to ask, "How is that handled by DSM-III?" The list includes hysterical psychosis, deliberate self-harm syndrome, puerperal mental illness, premenstrual syndrome, compensation neurosis, and miscellaneous uncommon syndromes such as Capgras, de Clérambault's, and various culture-specific syndromes. As we shall see, in many cases besides those of hysteroid dysphoria or cardiac neurosis, DSM-

III and DSM-III-R concepts and categories adequately cover the non-DSM-III term. With regard to other categories, most frequently those of other national diagnostic traditions or cultures, the DSM-III systems are less adequate. The need for uniform international standards for diagnosis is underscored by these differences.

Hysterical Psychosis

The concept of hysterical psychosis has a long history in psychiatry. As formulated by Hollender and Hirsch (16), the characteristic features of hysterical psychosis are (*1*) sudden and dramatic onset, precipitated by extreme stress, (*2*) delusions and hallucinations, (*3*) depersonalization or bizarre behavior, (*4*) absence of prominent formal thought disorder, (*5*) volatile affect, (*6*) one to three weeks' duration, with little or no residual symptoms, (*7*) occurrence most frequently in persons with hysterical personalities.

These features of hysterical psychosis overlap with a number of other diagnostic concepts such as "reactive psychosis" and the culture-bound syndromes of *amok, latah, negi-negi,* and *wihtigo* (see below). In a Western psychiatric context, it is important to differentiate hysterical psychosis from "real" psychosis, because it may be a simulation, the parallel of a conversion disorder as a simulation of a neurologic illness. The usual treatment for psychotic disorders would be inappropriate and possibly harmful in simulated psychotic states. The simulated or "pseudopsychotic" nature of hysterical psychosis is implied by some (17), but not all, conceptualizations of the syndrome. The connection between hysterical psychosis and somatoform disorders has been reinforced by the observation that patients receiving the diagnosis frequently have histrionic personality traits or features of Briquet's syndrome.

Bishop and Holt (17) offer a somewhat different definition of what they term *pseudopsychosis.* The criteria resemble those for DSM-III conversion disorder and psychogenic pain disorder. They include (*1*) delusions and hallucinations; (*2*) absence of derailment of thought (looseness of associations) and blunted affect; (*3*) psychologic factors judged to be etiologically involved in the symptoms, such as a temporal relationship between psychologically meaningful environmental stimuli and initiation or exacerbation of the symptom, the symptoms enabling the person to avoid some activity that is noxious to him or her, or to gain support from the environment; (*4*) at least two other features not medically explained during the patient's lifetime, including visual hallucinations, pains or conversion symptoms, memory loss or amnesia, homosexual orientation or other sexual problems, or histrionic or antisocial personality; (*5*) absence of organic brain syndrome, schizophrenia, or affective disorder. The authors refer to a clinical triad of psychoticlike behavior, somatization, and histrionic or antisocial personality as a "red flag" for pseudopsychosis.

This definition differs from the Hollender and Hirsch (16) definition because it is not limited to brief psychotic states and it does not require precipitating events. The criterion that requires that schizophrenia be ruled out begs the issue, since a major problem is in deciding whether the psychotic symptoms indicate a true deficit in reality testing or not.

In an article entitled "The Heavenly Vision of a Poor Woman: A Down-to-Earth Discussion of the DSM-III Differential Diagnosis" (18), my colleagues and I in the Biometrics Research group at N.Y. State Psychiatric Institute discussed the DSM-III differential diagnosis of a patient many clinicians thought had a hysterical psychosis. The idea of hysterical psychosis was prompted by the highly stressful circumstances under which the woman had her episode, the bizarre and dramatic nature of her clinical presentation, and the impression that, somehow, her symptoms were "put on," i.e., to achieve an effect. A synopsis of the case, which also appeared in the *DSM-III Case Book* (19), is reproduced here.

Heavenly Vision

An obese, 34-year-old woman was brought to a local hospital by the police. She had removed her clothing and, standing naked beside her car in a gas station, had ostentatiously engaged in fellatio with her five-month-old son. She later claimed that she did this in response to a vision: "I felt I had been instructed to step out of the car, remove my clothes as a sort of shocking, attention-getting episode depicting the stripping that this nation is to be going through soon." She explained that the depiction of oral sex was in order to draw attention to the abuse of children in vile ways in this country, as in prostitution and pornography. She described her own behavior as a "bizarre act" and understood that it was viewed as evidence of a "mental aberration." But in her own words, "There's method to my madness."

The patient had apparently, for the past 20 years, been having "different levels of visionary states" during which she both saw and heard God. Recently she had been receiving religious and political messages from God and believed that "The Communist Party and the Nazi Party in America have joined hands and will be occupying the country . . . the strike of the invasion point will come over Canada down through the Midwest to the point of St. Louis."

The patient's description of her visionary experiences and her history was coherent and articulate and delivered in a matter-of-fact manner, although with many vivid and startling details.

Records from a previous hospitalization noted that the patient had a completely positive review of physical symptoms. Her presenting complaint at that time was migraine headaches; but as each physician examined her, the symptom list grew longer and longer. Records from a psychiatric outpatient evaluation nine years before the current admission noted that she complained of extreme shakiness, which had gone on for a number of years; of a painful "knot" growing at the lower part of the back of her head; and of blackout spells. After these spells, she said, she frequently went into a deep sleep. Several electroencephalograms (EEGs) were negative. A neurologist who examined her did not think she had epilepsy and recommended that she see a psychiatrist.

During her current hospitalization, the patient had some physical complaints, particularly back pain, which she attributed to a fall at age 18 and to arthritis of the lower spine. She had difficulty walking, and had consulted many doctors about this. She had a 100% disability rating for "nerves and arthritis."

On physical examination, the patient was noted to be overweight. She had several small lipomas on her back and arm. Palpation of her abdomen revealed a poorly localized right lower quadrant tenderness. She complained of polymenorrhea. A Pap smear and endometrial biopsy were normal. An electrocardiogram (EKG) showed a right bundle branch block and left ventricular hypertrophy. Radiological examination of her skull revealed microcephaly (greater than two standard deviations below the lower limits of normal) and osteosclerosis. A rheumatology consultant diagnosed mechanical low back pain exacerbated by obesity.

Her personal history was obtained from the patient alone. She reported that her father was a fundamentalist Christian minister, and she had been deeply involved in the church from an early age. She was baptized at 12, and was "speaking in tongues." At that age she "felt a call to the ministry." She completed high school with above-average grades. At 18, after a broken engagement (which she describes very dramatically, as she does every event in her history), she joined the WACs, against her parents' wishes; and she has been alienated from her family ever since. She claims to have been raped while in the service, and later to have fallen down, hit her head on concrete, and been "unconscious for nine days," after which she was "very weak" and had "bouts of amnesia." She left the WACs after 13 months and married a man who turned out to be a bigamist. She lived with him for 12 years, had 4 children, and separated from him when she discovered that he had molested her daughters. She has worked only sporadically since then.

After her marital separation, the patient left town with her children, because she was being "harassed" by gossiping neighbors. She moved to another town, but the harassment continued. At one point she took the children to Israel, with no money and no plans other than to settle there, claiming that she had traced a "Jewish bloodline" in her ancestry. She gives the impression of having been "on the road" a good deal of the time since her separation (four years earlier). For at least part of that time, she had placed her children in state foster homes.

Fourteen months before admission, she had slept with a stranger in a motel. She claims that this was her only sexual contact in four years; it resulted in the birth of her son, five months previously.

During her hospital stay the patient was quite verbal, and the staff noted her to be "hostile and histrionic." She held firmly to her religious beliefs, and referred to many prophecies that, she claimed, had come true. She produced tape cassettes from various people throughout the country who shared her religious beliefs. In these tapes she was generally praised for her steadfast faith and her gift of prophecy. In some tapes, "speaking in tongues" was prominent. The staff had the impression the patient experienced brief psychotic episodes, which centered on feelings of persecution by the government.

The patient was discharged after a month. She refused any follow-up care and told a few people that she was heading West in the hope of matriculating in an evangelistic training school. Her children remained in the custody of the appropriate state social service agency. Several days after her discharge she was sought by law-enforcement officials because she allegedly had written about $650 in bad checks and had apparently stolen the car she had been driving before admission. (19, pp. 201-206; Reprinted with permission)

In discussions of this case, the following DSM-III principles applied. First, the clinician had to decide whether or not the symptoms were under voluntary control. If so, then the DSM-III diagnoses of factitious disorder with psychological symptoms or the V code malingering would apply, depending upon whether the symptoms were feigned to achieve some obviously recognizable objective or to fulfill a psychological need, such as to assume the sick role. As noted in Chapter 8, the determination of voluntary control is by no means simple. The task is somewhat facilitated by the revised rewording in DSM-III-R with regard to factitious disorders, the emphasis now being on intentional production or feigning of symptoms rather than on voluntary control. Determining a person's intentions is still a matter of inference and judgment, however, especially when the person denies intentionality and is being purposely deceptive.

If a clinician believes that the psychotic symptoms are genuine, not feigned, then the next diagnosis that might apply is brief reactive psychosis. Brief reactive psychosis requires precipitation of a psychotic episode by extremely stressful circumstances, limited duration, and full, or virtual, recovery. Brief reactive psychosis, being a "true" psychotic disorder, is very similar to the Scandinavian concepts of reactive or psychogenic psychoses. The criteria for brief reactive psychosis have been revised somewhat in DSM-III-R (see Table 12.6); the changes are reviewed in Chapter 5.

If the psychotic period is preceded by prodromal symptoms or lasts longer than the maximum duration for brief reactive psychosis, then schizophreniform, schizophrenia, or a delusional disorder might apply. If there are any atypical features, then, as in the case above, in

Table 12.6 DSM-III-R Diagnostic Criteria for Brief Reactive Psychosis

A. Presence of at least *one* of the following symptoms indicating impaired reality testing (not culturally sanctioned):

(1) incoherence or marked loosening of associations
(2) delusions
(3) hallucinations
(4) catatonic or disorganized behavior

B. Emotional turmoil, i.e., rapid shifts from one intense affect to another, or overwhelming perplexity or confusion.

C. Appearance of the symptoms in A and B shortly after, and apparently in response to, one or more events that, singly or together, would be markedly stressful to almost anyone in similar circumstances in the person's culture.

D. Absence of the prodromal symptoms of schizophrenia, and failure to meet the criteria for schizotypal personality disorder before onset of the disturbance.

E. Duration of an episode of the disturbance of from a few hours to one month, with eventual full return to premorbid level of functioning. (When the diagnosis must be made without waiting for the expected recovery, it should be qualified as "provisional.")

F. Not due to a psychotic mood disorder (i.e., no full mood syndrome is present), and it cannot be established that an organic factor initiated and maintained the disturbance.

which the stressor was judged inadequate for brief reactive psychosis, the diagnosis of atypical psychosis (DSM-III) or psychotic disorder not otherwise specified (DSM-III-R) could apply. The phenomena of hysterical psychosis might sometimes better be captured by the diagnosis of a dissociative disorder (see above). In such cases, however, the clinician is judging that the symptoms are not, in fact, psychotic.

Although hysterical psychosis has traditionally been thought to be a common disorder, Gift and his colleagues (20) failed to find a single case among 217 first-admission patients with functional mental disorders, primarily because of the requirement that the psychosis be brief. Almost all the patients had a history of a protracted onset plus continuation of significant symptoms after admission, even though in 67% of those with a psychotic disorder onset was judged to have been precipitated by recognizable exogenous factors. The authors discuss the possibilities that changes in the manifestations of hysteria over time or different admission policies and emergency psychiatric practices may account for not finding such patients in hospitals.

Deliberate Self-Harm Syndrome

In 1983, Kahan and Pattison (21) proposed a new category for DSM-IV, the deliberate self-harm syndrome (DSH). Evidence from an analysis of 56 cases reported in the clinical literature was used to support the existence of an independent syndrome characterized by conscious and willful intent to deliberately perform apparently painful, destructive, and injurious acts upon one's own body without an apparent intent to commit suicide. The impulsive act of self-harm appears to produce psychic relief.

The authors proposed the category as an Axis I disorder under the diagnostic class of disorders of impulse control not elsewhere classified. They argued that the disturbance met the general criteria for this class of disorders (see above) i.e., (*1*) failure to resist an impulse, drive, or temptation to perform some act that is harmful to oneself or to others, (*2*) an increasing sense of tension before committing the act, (*3*) an experience of either pleasure, gratification, or release at the time of committing the act.

This proposal raises important questions about the requirements for a behavior or cluster of behaviors to constitute an independent syndrome. A syndrome is a cluster of signs and symptoms that have heuristic clinical value. The signs and symptoms covary and reflect a relationship to some underlying disease or group of diseases. Robins and Guze (22) have proposed five standards by which to validate a diagnostic category: (*1*) comprehensive description, (*2*) delimitation from other disorders, (*3*) demonstration of distinctive course or outcome, (*4*) demonstration of a familial pattern, (*5*) corroboration via distinctive laboratory findings. Many current DSM-III-R categories fail, as yet, to have adequate evidence supporting their validity.

How would DSM-III or DSM-III-R handle cases of deliberate self-harm? Kahan and Pattison's discussion of differential diagnosis requires some clarification. When self-harm is intentional, meeting psychological needs or external incentives, either a factitious disorder or malingering could apply. A factitious disorder with physical symptoms entails a psychological need to assume the sick role; malingering is the designation when the production of symptoms is motivated by external incentives. Kahan and Pattison's differential diagnosis allows for the additional diagnosis of DSH when schizophrenia, another psychotic disorder, or an affective or a personality disorder is present. According to DSM-III-R, certainly other diagnoses indicative of poor impulse control, such as psychoactive substance use disorders, can be made in association with an Axis II diagnosis or another Axis I disorder. An unofficial diagnostic principle, however, is that a separate, additional diagnosis would not be made for a symptom or set of symptoms that constituted the essential features of another disorder that was present *unless* the additional diagnosis had clear treatment significance over and above that of the primary disorder. A case could be made that DSH requires specific treatment approaches, which would justify its status as a secondary diagnosis.

The fact of the matter is that the DSM-III category "atypical impulse control disorder" or the DSM-III-R "impulse control disorder not otherwise specified" is a very appropriate designation for DSH as described by Kahan and Pattison. In keeping with the trend in DSM-III-R to reduce the use of diagnostic hierarchies (see Chapter 2) in favor of preserving diagnostic heterogeneity, the interested clinician is encouraged to use the residual impulse control disorder categories in cases in which DSH is a distinct management issue.

Puerperal Mental Illness

Studies have shown that women are more likely to be admitted to a psychiatric hospital following the delivery of a baby than at other times in their lives (23,24). Several diagnostic controversies surround this phenomenon. One is whether there is a mental illness specific to the period following childbirth or whether the usual mental illnesses have an increased incidence because of the psychological and physiological stressfulness of childbirth. Another possibility is that women with symptoms of emotional distress are more likely to be hospitalized for that condition following childbirth even though there is no actual increase in the incidence of episodes of mental illness (25). A second set of controversies related to the first concerns the treatment and outcome of mental disorders precipitated by childbirth.

A number of recent studies have attempted to describe the phenomenology of puerperal, or postpartum, mental illness, using rigorous diagnostic assessments and standardized diagnostic criteria sets, including DSM-III. The goal of these studies has been to determine whether the mental illnesses occurring in the puerperium can be adequately diagnosed using the general classifications of mental disorders, or whether the phenomenology is sufficiently distinct to constitute an independent syndrome or set of syndromes peculiar to this period or life event. DSM-III and DSM-III-R have no separate category for postpartum disorders; therefore, it is reasonable and useful to ask whether they adequately cover the disturbances likely to be observed.

Most of the recent studies have not used DSM-III criteria specifically: the Research Diagnostic Criteria (RDC) and the Present State Examination (PSE-CATEGO) systems have been employed. It is relatively easy to extrapolate from RDC to DSM-III since the criteria are similar; it is harder to extrapolate from the PSE-CATEGO, which does not emphasize, in differential diagnosis, the significance of the relationship of syndromes, e.g., schizophrenic or affective, to each other over time (see Chapters 5 and 6).

In a study by Dean and Kendell (25), the RDC were applied to all women admitted, within 90 days of delivery, to the Royal Edinburgh Hospital over a 6-year period and to a group of age- and diagnosis-matched controls also hospitalized for mental illness. Eighty-seven percent of the postpartum women were diagnosed as having an affective disorder, mostly a major or minor depressive disorder.

There was also an unusually high rate of manic disorder, constituting nearly 13% of all admissions. The peak period for admission was within the first two weeks after delivery. Patients with manic episodes were especially likely to be admitted during this period; those with major depression tended to be admitted later. Forty percent of the postpartum illnesses had their onset within the first week after delivery, the most common time of onset. Over half of the women with major depressive disorders had had symptoms at some time during their pregnancy, and many of them had sought professional help. This finding suggests that women who seek help for mental problems during pregnancy are at considerable risk for a psychiatric hospitalization after the pregnancy. In a comparison of the phenomenology of puerperal vs. nonpuerperal episodes of mania, no differences were found (the numbers were very small); but in major depression, the postpartum episodes were characterized by more psychotic features (delusions and hallucinations), more disorientation, more agitation, and more emotional lability. Signs of organicity, often considered characteristic of these disorders, were present in about 25% of patients, of whom only a very few had an infection or other physical difficulty other than the delivery itself. Many of the women, especially those with major depression, had had other, additional, stressful life events, especially losses, recently, or had long-term stressful life circumstances, such as being unmarried, having a poor marriage, or lacking social supports.

In a second study, by Brockington and colleagues (26), postpartum patients were selected if they had a "psychotic illness." Psychosis was defined broadly, as in DSM-II, to include patients with delusions and hallucinations or an alteration in mood severe enough to grossly impair their capacity to respond appropriately to the requirements of ordinary living. Again applying RDC, more of the puerperal patients had mania or hypomania, schizoaffective disorder (manic), and major or episodic minor depressive disorder than the controls, who received more diagnoses of schizoaffective (depressed) disorder and schizophrenia. Manic symptoms, such as elation, lability of mood, rambling speech, distractibility, observed euphoria and increased activity, and characteristics reflecting general incompetence were more common in the postpartum women; schizophrenic symptoms and poor sexual functioning were more common in the controls. A general factor of psychotic disorganization was slightly more frequent in the postpartum group, and mania was three times more common. The authors note that confusion, which is not so severe as to grossly disrupt cognitive testing or the mental status examination as in an acute organic brain syndrome, has often been associated with postpartum mental illnesses.

In a study that specifically employed DSM-III criteria (27), the two diagnostic categories that most often applied to women admitted within six months of childbirth were major depressive episode (48% of cases) and manic episode (21%); another 16% had probable depressive disorder. Control patients had more previous nonpuerperal admissions. Delay between onset of symptoms and admission was shorter for the puerperal patients with major depression than for controls with the same disorder. Comparison of the two groups in terms of individual symptoms revealed that the puerperal group had more delusions and more frequently had lability of mood.

Studies by Dean and Kendell (25) and Katona (27) uncovered few differences in response to treatment or outcome between disorders occurring postpartum compared with at other times. In the first study, puerperal women with major depression received phenothiazines more often than control women with major depression, and the latter group responded somewhat better to tricyclic antidepressants. Puerperal women with mania more often received electroconvulsive therapy (ECT). The length of stay in hospital did not differentiate the groups. The second study also disclosed no differences in length of hospitalization and more frequent use of ECT in the puerperal groups. Readmission rates within six months were no different, but the puerperal major depressed and manic groups had lower long-term readmission rates. One additional study (28) found a much poorer outcome for puerperal mental illness. This study differed from the others in that a much greater proportion of the puerperal group received diagnoses of schizophrenia.

Taken together, these studies indicate that puerperal mental illness can be diagnosed adequately with criterion-based systems like DSM-III or DSM-III-R. The affective or mood disorder categories, especially the subtypes with psychotic features, seem particularly appropriate. The inclusion in DSM-III-R of specific criteria for schizoaffective disorder, in combination with the allowance for mood-incongruent psychotic features in psychotic mania or depression, covers the schizoaffective presentations commonly encountered. There do seem to be some distinctive features in these disorders, however. Particularly problematic for differential diagnosis is the frequency of confusion, perplexity, and disorientation observed in the patients. The clinician might be led to consider a diagnosis of delirium. Another possibility might be DSM-III-R schizophreniform disorder with good prognostic features, if a mood syndrome is not prominent (see Chapter 5). The requirement that an etiologically related organic factor, such as infection, be identified, should determine cases in which an organic mental syndrome should be diagnosed.

Whether there is sufficient diagnostic heterogeneity to warrant a separate subclassification for puerperal mental illness remains to be seen. The treatment response and outcome data do not strongly support the distinctiveness of such illnesses occurring in postpartum women. One interesting question is whether personality disorder or style accounts for some of the observed heterogeneity. Alternatively, the puerperium itself may be a powerful pathoplastic factor that colors the clinical presentations of women liable to affective illness who tend to have episodes postpartum (26).

Premenstrual Syndrome (PMS)

Popular and scientific interest in the so-called "premenstrual syndrome" is on the rise. Actually, the term *premenstrual syndrome* is a misnomer, since most researchers have determined that there is a constellation of diversified subtypes within this broad categorization. Halbreich and associates (29) measured premenstrual changes (PMCs) on a variety of both negative and positive dimensions and as overlapping categories. Some of these included a full depressive syndrome, water retention, general discomfort, social impairment, decreased well-being, and organiclike changes (poor motor coordination, tendency to have accidents, forgetfulness, distractibility, difficulty concentrating).

Premenstrual dysphoric changes have been of particular interest. Although it is rare to find an "endogenous" type depression in the premenstrual period, a substantial number of women have dysphoria that is similar to so-called "atypical" depression (not in the DSM-III sense of atypical, see p. 245, Chapter 6), characterized by hypersomnia, increased appetite, and rapid mood changes; anxious or agitated depression, with anxiety, jitteriness, and restlessness; or hostile depression, with irritability, anger, and impatience. The similarities between premenstrual dysphoria and clinical depressive syndromes suggest that the premenstrual state may be useful as a model for the study of biological and psychosocial variables associated with depressive disorders.

Halbreich and Endicott (30) have reported that 57% of women

with a lifetime diagnosis of major depressive disorder (MDD), made by RDC and assessed independently of the menstrual cycle, also meet their research criteria for premenstrual depression, compared with only 14% of women who have never been mentally ill. Women with a lifetime diagnosis of MDD also reported more organic changes and more premenstrual impairment in social relations. Considered from a different perspective, 84% of the women who had a menstrual depressive syndrome also had a lifetime diagnosis of RDC major depressive disorder, whereas only 9% of those with the full syndrome were never mentally ill. These associations have been confirmed in most studies.

A couple of studies have prospectively demonstrated that premenstrual affective syndrome was also associated with an increased likelihood of developing major depression in the future (31, 32). This suggests that PMS may also be viewed as a risk factor for future disorder. These and many of the studies of premenstrual syndrome are imperfect in that they rely heavily on symptomatic volunteers for subjects, so that their findings cannot necessarily be generalized to the population at large. Also, ratings of premenstrual changes are often done retrospectively and depend on subjects' memory; these need to be confirmed by prospective daily "diary" reporting. Prospectively determined premenstrual syndrome appears to be less common than the syndrome diagnosed by retrospective self report (33) and less likely to be associated with a history of mental disorder (34).

In spite of these limitations, the Work Group to Revise DSM-III decided to propose a new diagnostic category for this condition. Originally, in DSM-III-R in Development (10/5/85 draft), the category was called "premenstrual dysphoric disorder," and was grouped with psychological factors affecting physical condition (316.00) in a class called "other disorders associated with physical condition." The inclusion of the category prompted immediate controversy, as opponents cited the inadequacy of research to support its validity. Women's groups believed that the category was discriminatory, in that it transformed physiological states into a mental disorder. The Work Group recommended including the category despite the protests, but was overruled by a vote of the American Psychiatric Association's Board of Trustees. The compromise was to include the category, under a new name, "late luteal phase dysphoric disorder," in an appendix to DSM-III-R, along with two other controversial categories, self-defeating and sadistic personality disorders (see above and Chapter 9).

The essential feature of late luteal phase dysphoric disorder is "a pattern of clinically significant emotional and behavioral symptoms that occur during the last week of the luteal phase and remit within a few days after the onset of the follicular phase" (6, p. 367) of the menstrual cycle. In most women this corresponds to the week before and the few days after the onset of menses. The diagnosis is to be given only if the symptoms are sufficiently severe to seriously interfere with work or with social activities or relationships and have occurred during a majority of menstrual cycles during the past year.

In the 10/5/85 draft of DSM-III-R, the diagnosis could also be given if the symptoms were severe enough to cause marked subjective distress, but this allowance was removed because it was considered an insufficient criterion of significance for the diagnosis of a mental disorder. The diagnosis is not to be made if the symptoms persist beyond the first few days after the onset of the follicular phase. Thus, patients who have a late luteal exacerbation of dysphoria associated with another mental disorder, such as major depression, dysthymia, an anxiety disorder, or a personality disorder, would not receive this diagnosis alone.

The shift from an emphasis on the relationship of the symptoms to the menses to the relationship of the symptoms to the luteal and follicular phases of the menstrual cycle enables the disorder to be diagnosed in nonmenstruating women, such as those who have had a hysterectomy, but still have ovarian function. The specific timing of the phases may require the measurement of circulating reproductive hormones. DSM-III-R takes note of one of the methodological weaknesses in existing data about premenstrual dysphoria by requiring that the symptoms be confirmed by prospective daily self-ratings of at least two symptomatic cycles (criterion E, see Table 12.7). On the basis of retrospective reports, the diagnosis can be made only provisionally.

The diagnostic criteria for late luteal phase dysphoric disorder in DSM-III-R are reproduced in Table 12.7. Of the list of symptoms in criterion B, the first four are considered most typical, and one of them is required. These are the symptoms directly referring to mood or affective disturbance; the diagnosis of late luteal phase dysphoric disorder cannot be made solely on the basis of physical symptoms that precede menses.

Criterion D notes that late luteal phase dysphoric disorder may be superimposed on another mental disorder, but is not a substitute diagnosis for it. In the discussion of differential diagnosis, DSM-III-R offers a guideline to the clinician considering an additional diagnosis of late luteal phase dysphoric disorder in a patient with a mood or anxiety disorder: both diagnoses can be given "if the person experiences characteristic periluteal phase dysphoric disorder symptoms that are markedly different from those . . . (experienced) as part of the coexisting disorder" (6, p. 368). In the case vignette "More Than PMS?," a woman with symptoms of depression is considered for the diagnosis of late luteal phase dysphoric disorder.

Table 12.7 DSM-III-R Diagnostic Criteria for Late Luteal Phase Dysphoric Disorder

A. In most menstrual cycles during the past year, symptoms in B occurred during the last week of the luteal phase and remitted within a few days after onset of the follicular phase. In menstruating females, these phases correspond to the week before, and a few days after, the onset of menses. (In nonmenstruating females who have had a hysterectomy, the timing of luteal and follicular phases may require measurement of circulating reproductive hormones.)

B. At least *five* of the following symptoms have been present for most of the time during each symptomatic late luteal phase, at least one of the symptoms being either (1), (2), (3), or (4):

(1) marked affective lability, e.g., feeling suddenly sad, tearful, irritable, or angry
(2) persistent and marked anger or irritability
(3) marked anxiety, tension, feelings of being "keyed up," or "on edge"
(4) markedly depressed mood, feelings of hopelessness, or self-deprecating thoughts
(5) decreased interest in usual activities, e.g., work, friends, hobbies
(6) easy fatigability or marked lack of energy
(7) subjective sense of difficulty in concentrating
(8) marked change in appetite, overeating, or specific food cravings
(9) hypersomnia or insomnia
(10) other physical symptoms, such as breast tenderness or swelling, headaches, joint or muscle pain, a sensation of "bloating," weight gain

C. The disturbance seriously interferes with work or with usual social activities or relationships with others.

D. The disturbance is not merely an exacerbation of the symptoms of another disorder, such as major depression, panic disorder, dysthymia, or a personality disorder (although it may be superimposed on any of these disorders).

E. Criteria A, B, C, and D are confirmed by prospective daily self-ratings during at least two symptomatic cycles. (The diagnosis may be made provisionally prior to this confirmation.)

Note: For coding purposes, record: 300.90 Unspecified Mental Disorder (Late Luteal Phase Dysphoric Disorder).

More Than PMS?

A 28-year-old single woman moved from Los Angeles to the Bay Area to attend graduate school in English. She had been seeing a therapist for six months for "depression related to PMS," and now was seeking follow-up care in her new city.

The woman described the depression as "particularly bad" over the past year. She had been having a "friendship" with a married man for three years. The relationship failed to progress beyond a platonic level, however—dinner, tennis, a day at the beach, "nothing physical" — and she finally gave up.

Her symptoms included loss of interest and pleasure, inability to concentrate at her job (copy editor), difficulty falling asleep, early morning awakening, overeating, decreased energy, and diurnal mood variation (worse in the morning). In addition, she sometimes felt that if she could not become involved in a more "positive" relationship with a man, she could not see a reason for living.

The patient related a past history of chronic depression since she was 15. She had had one severe episode, during which she was very depressed and nonfunctioning, while in college. She recovered from this episode over the course of several years, but felt that she had basically been "unhappy" since she was a teenager.

For several days before her menstrual period was expected, the symptoms of depression became more severe. "I can't seem to stop crying, I can't focus; it's like I don't have any control of my mind. All I do is think obsessively about Jack and the past—why it didn't work." There were no symptoms specific to the menstrual exacerbations.

The patient and the psychiatrist agreed that the depression was "more than PMS." Desipramine was prescribed and gradually increased to 250 mg/day. After about two months, the woman claimed she felt "better than I have in years."

There is little doubt in the case "More Than PMS?" that the depression cannot be explained on the basis of late luteal phase dysphoric disorder. Long-standing depression with superimposed severe episodes suggests DSM-III-R diagnoses of major depression, recurrent, and dysthymia (see Chapter 6). Since there are no distinctive symptoms specific to the premenstrual exacerbations, an additional diagnosis of late luteal phase dysphoric disorder is not warranted.

Compensation Neurosis

The term *compensation neurosis* has been applied to people with psychological or physical symptoms following an injury that seem out of proportion to the actual injury and are reinforced by claims for disability or other financial compensation. The DSM-III or DSM-III-R differential diagnosis of "compensation neurosis" has been outlined by Hyler and associates (35) and includes malingering, factitious disorder, somatoform pain disorder (DSM-III psychogenic pain disorder), psychological factors affecting physical condition (PFAPC), and posttraumatic stress disorder (PTSD). An understanding of this differential is important for the psychiatrist serving as expert witness.

The V code malingering is used when the clinician judges that the person has intentionally produced false or grossly exaggerated physical or psychological symptoms, motivated by external incentives. Obtaining financial compensation is listed in DSM-III-R as an example of an "external incentive."

Blatant malingering constitutes fraud. A person may stage a minor accident and feign unconsciousness or falsely claim malpractice against a physician. Clues to outright fraud include rapidity in obtaining legal assistance, instituting charges of injury, and requesting financial compensation as remedy, and the availability of witnesses, especially if known to the plaintiff. More commonly, malingering is a form of opportunism; the person does not stage or feign an injury but, once injured, takes advantage of the circumstances in order to maximize the financial award. Following an accident, this person may take no immediate steps to file a complaint. After discussing the situation with family or friends, he or she then visits an attorney and medical specialists known to testify frequently in injury or malpractice cases. Usually there is a marked discrepancy between the claimant's distress or disability and objective findings. The injured person often refuses to cooperate with evaluations by defense medical specialists or is resistant to treatment prescribed by a physician not directly involved in the case.

In factitious disorders, the physical or psychological symptoms are intentionally produced or feigned not for an obviously recognizable goal, but in order to assume the sick role. Persons with factitious disorders simulate illnesses in ways that are not likely to lead to discovery. This suggests a degree of voluntary control, meaning intentional or purposeful, but not in the sense that the acts themselves can necessarily be controlled (see also Chapter 8). The clinician may receive a clue to this diagnosis if the patient has a history of repeated, similar "accidents," with or without previous compensation. Factitious disorders are frequently related to personality disorders such as borderline, passive aggressive, or self-defeating.

If the complaint in a compensation case is limited to pain (as is frequently the case), there is no organic pathology or pathophysiologic mechanism to explain the pain, or the complaint of pain or resulting impairment grossly exceeds what would be expected from the physical findings, DSM-III-R somatoform pain disorder is the diagnosis. The reader is referred to Chapter 8, Physical Complaints, for a more complete discussion of somatoform pain disorder. In compensation cases with this disorder, financial payment is a form of secondary rather than primary gain, and settlement of the case may not, in itself, bring symptom relief.

Psychological factors affecting physical condition is the diagnosis if the course of real organic pathology is adversely affected by a person's emotions. A person may develop a stress-related illness or condition, such as peptic ulcer or angina pectoris, while working at a high-stress job as an air-traffic controller or stock options trader and seek disability pay from his or her employer. A regular relationship between stressful job-related events and a reappearance or worsening of symptoms is indicative of PFAPC. This diagnosis is also discussed in Chapter 8.

Finally, in a few compensation cases, the person may actually have posttraumatic stress disorder (PTSD). The man in "Delayed Reaction" (see Chapter 7) is an example. Serious accidents are common in many occupations; assaults in the workplace or other privately owned properties may also result in claims for compensation. For a PTSD diagnosis to be made, the full syndrome of reexperiencing the trauma, avoidance and numbing, and increased arousal should be present. The interesting twist in "Delayed Reaction" was that the recent trauma precipitated a syndrome that was contributed to by another unusually traumatic experience that had occurred more than thirty-five years before!

Culture-Bound Syndromes

Psychiatric diagnosis across cultures presents a number of problems. To what extent are diagnostic concepts or categories the same across cultures? To what extent may they overlap? To what extent are they unique to a particular culture? Can a diagnostician from one culture adequately assess and arrive at a diagnosis for a patient from another culture when the two may not even share the same language, let alone culture or world view? The twin problems of classification and of diagnostic method across cultures have recently been reviewed by Westermeyer (36).

A thorough discussion of cross-cultural diagnosis is beyond the scope of this book. In Chapter 5, Psychotic Features, I discussed the need to consider unusual ideas in the context of a shared belief system of a religious or subcultural group. This is no easy task, since clinicians can hardly be familiar with the beliefs of the wide range of religions and subcultures of the world. An opinion from or consultation with another member of the same cultural group may be the only way to assess whether a given person's beliefs are congruent with those of the larger group or are in some way deviant or idiosyncratic. In this section I shall discuss the correspondence of DSM-III and DSM-III-R categories and concepts to several culture-bound syndromes most likely to be familiar to Western mental health professionals: *latah, amok, koro, hwa-byung*, and *taijin-kyofu*.

Latah. *Latah* is a syndrome characterized by a startle reaction and subsequent imitative behavior, including echolalia, echopraxia, coprolalia, altered state of consciousness, and fear (37). It occurs in both sexes, but more commonly among women, primarily among the people of Malaysia and Indonesia. It is usually precipitated by stress. Loss of control of the self and hypersuggestibility have also been emphasized as important parts of the syndrome.

In terms of DSM-III and DSM-III-R diagnostic concepts, the symptoms of startle and fear suggest an anxiety disorder. However, *latah* seems to be characterized more by the altered consciousness and imitative behavior due to hypersuggestibility. These are akin to the processes observed in the dissociated states of hypnosis and the dissociative disorders. Kenny (38) has pointed out the analogy between hypnosis in Western cultures and *latah* and the relationship of the psychosocial mechanisms involved in the pathogenesis of *latah* to the processes thought to shape multiple personality phenomena (39). The dissociative disorders commonly occur in response to severe social stressors; therefore, a dissociative disorder NOS may be the best corresponding DSM-III-R diagnosis. Coprolalia and the stereotypic activity involved in mimicking others' behavior may suggest to some clinicians a diagnosis of Tourette's disorder; *latah,* however, though it may recur, does not have the persistence of Tourette's syndrome.

Amok. *Amok* refers to a syndrome in which a person emerges from a period of withdrawal and apathy with a sudden outburst of mania, agitation, and violent, homicidal attack on others, which frequently ends with the death of the perpetrator. The syndrome occurs almost exclusively in males, most commonly of Southeast Asia. In the "pre-*amok*" phase, people have also been described as experiencing depersonalization, derealization, paranoia, rage, and somatic symptoms. Amnesia accompanies the violence of the *amok* phase. If the person who "runs amok" is not killed, this phase ends in exhaustion and a return to normal consciousness.

Some of the symptoms of *amok* suggest a dissociative disorder; other aspects, a manic or an acute psychotic episode. Certainly, the occurrence of apparently random mass murders is not unknown in the United States (it is interesting to recall, for example, that, as in the McDonald's incident, of a few years ago in California, the mass murderer frequently is killed here as well). In Western cultures the mass murderer is often described as having a withdrawn, isolated, premorbid personality.

Attempts to determine the etiology of *amok* have pointed to factors that might result in an organic brain abnormality (febrile illnesses, other brain-damaging diseases such as syphilis). These bring *amok* closer in concept to the episodic dyscontrol syndromes described by Monroe (40). In Chapter 10, Antisocial, Aggressive, or Violent Behavior, I discussed the relationship of the DSM-III-R diagnosis intermittent explosive disorder and episodic dyscontrol. Another DSM-III-R equivalent of these disorders might be organic personality syndrome, explosive type. Actually, *amok* seems closest to DSM-III isolated explosive disorder, but this may merely be a result of the fact that the person who "runs amok" is often killed, and recurrences are, of course, therefore impossible.

Koro. The syndrome of *koro* occurs primarily among Chinese men of Southeast Asia and Hong Kong. It involves intense fear that one's penis will withdraw into the abdomen, possibly causing death. In women, in whom it is much less common, the fear is of the breasts' shrinking or the labia's withdrawing into the body. The intense fear has been likened to panic attacks. Although the fear and beliefs are irrational, they can be shared by many others in the subculture, and therefore may not actually be delusions.

It is not clear from published reports on *koro* whether reality testing is preserved. It is probable that the sensations of bodily change in *koro* are most like the fear of having a heart attack or of dying by some other means that is characteristic of DSM-III-R panic disorder, or like those accompanying the belief of having a serious disease that is essential to the diagnosis of hypochondriasis. Therefore, a diagnosis of panic disorder or hypochondriasis is probably the closest counterpart of *koro*.

Hwa-byung. A syndrome found mostly in Korea, *hwa-byung* is characterized by pent-up anger, depression, and multiple physical complaints, frequently associated with a feeling of an epigastric mass causing dyspnea, indigestion, bloating of the stomach, and pain. The presence of physical symptoms without a physical disease sufficient to explain them is reminiscent of a somatoform disorder in the DSM-III systems. The focus of symptoms in the epigastrium was part of the classic description of hypochondriasis, and has also recently received some empirical validation as part of a somatoform disorder that can be distinguished from somatization disorder (41) (see also Chapter 8).

Taijin-Kyofu. A common disorder in Japan, *taijin-kyofu*, or anthropophobia, is characterized by a fear of a situation in which the patient, without knowing exactly what he is doing, gives unpleasant feelings to people around him (42). The patient may worry about emitting rank body odors, unintentionally glancing at others and making them uncomfortable, having an ugly facial expression, or thinking aloud. Some of these symptoms sound like somatic delusions and thought broadcasting. Emotional contact, social functioning, and overall personality are intact in *taijin-kyofu,* however; pervasive deterioration such as that found in schizophrenia is also not evident.

Moreover, the patient fears that he is doing harm to others, not that others are harming him, i.e., persecuting him. If the beliefs are maintained with delusional intensity, however, the DSM-III-R expanded class of delusional disorders would cover the disorder.

Social phobia might come to mind; but again, the focus is on the harm to another, rather than to the self. Traditionally, Japanese psychiatrists have considered *taijin-kyofu* to be an obsessive-compulsive neurosis, although patients do not admit or recognize that their concerns are irrational or excessive. Similarities have also been drawn in Japan between *taijin-kyofu* and hypochondriasis, although, again, the worry is more about the effects on someone else, rather than on the self.

Adequacy of DSM-III or DSM-III-R across cultures. The foregoing discussions illustrate, I think, the limitations of applying DSM-III and DSM-III-R criteria to mental disturbances in cultures vastly different from our own. They certainly raise the question of whether it is possible to explain culture-bound syndromes in more general terms, or at least according to Western principles. At the very least, we must appreciate that culture exerts a powerful pathoplastic influence on the expression of symptoms.

In Japan, where the individual has traditionally deferred the good of the self for the good of society, *taijin-kyofu* is characterized by worry about how one adversely affects others. This would seem an unlikely affliction in the "me-oriented" society of the United States in the 1980s. Also in Japan, where I have lectured, Japanese psychiatrists found our psychosexual dysfunctions and personality disorders to be rather foreign to their experiences. And Westermeyer (36) has suggested that bulimia is predominantly a syndrome of North American Euroamerican females "bound" to our culture, which is perhaps uniquely preoccupied with physical appearance.

Difficult though it may be, psychiatric diagnosis across national and cultural boundaries is likely to become increasingly important: because of increased tourism, education abroad, economic migration, and refugee resettlement (36), clinicians will be faced more and more with patients from other cultures. Psychiatry will, in the future, need to focus on the development of more inclusive classification systems, applicable worldwide, and on better training of mental health professionals in cross-cultural diagnosis.

Uncommon Psychiatric Syndromes

This final section focuses on a number of distinctive, though uncommon, psychiatric syndromes that most clinicians have read about and been trained to recognize. Many clinicians, however, may never have actually evaluated patients with these disorders. The list that I shall discuss is taken from a book by Enoch and Trethowan (43); it includes the syndromes of Capgras, de Clérambault, Othello, Ganser, Couvade, Munchausen, Gilles de la Tourette, Cotard, folie à deux, and possession. I am not aware of a unified published discussion of all of these syndromes in terms of DSM-III or DSM-III-R criteria and concepts.

Capgras syndrome. A patient with Capgras syndrome believes that a person, usually someone closely related to him or her, has been replaced by an exact double, an impostor. The belief is firmly held in spite of obvious proof or evidence to the contrary; therefore it is a delusion. In the case "Miriam and Esther" in the *DSM-III Case Book* (19), the patient has, as one of her delusions, the idea that her real mother has been replaced by a family friend who is now masquerading as her mother. In the following vignette, a delusion about the identity of an intimate other leads the patient to question her own identity as well.

This Nice Man

A 32-year-old, married woman was brought to the hospital by her husband following a five-day period of sleepless nights and "compulsive" cleaning and straightening-up of their apartment. For the past two days she had been afraid to go out of her house to work for fear that someone would assault or rape her.

When she was asked what brought them to the hospital, the woman replied, "This nice man, Mr. Mathews (correct name) brought me. I don't know who he is—he says he's my husband. I'm afraid; I'm afraid of him. He's not my husband. I don't know who I am. I have a purse, a coat, a nice ring." She emptied her pocketbook on the desk. "I can feel my breathing. I'd like to be Debbie Mathews. I'm afraid I don't know who are . . ." her voice trailed off and her eyes darted to the ceiling, and corners of the room, as if she heard someone calling.

On the way to the admitting office, she sat down in the middle of the lobby, "I'm going to be a baby." With the help of a security guard, she was placed in a wheelchair and wheeled down the long corridors. She stopped the wheelchair several times by putting her feet on the ground and asked, "Why are we going in circles?" She walked the last 100 yards holding the resident's hand.

Historically, Capgras syndrome has generally not been considered an independent diagnostic entity, but rather a phenomenon that occurs as part of another psychotic illness. It has been described in association with schizophrenia, manic-depressive (bipolar) illness, and the sequelae of head trauma. Descriptions in the literature do not include prominent hallucinations; regarding visual hallucinations or illusions, most reports explicitly state that the patient does not distort what he or she sees, but in fact describes the impostor as exactly resembling the replaced person. Therefore, for a diagnosis of schizophrenia to apply, by either DSM-III or DSM-III-R criteria, the Capgras delusion would have to be regarded as bizarre or either a formal thought disorder, or flat or inappropriate affect would have to be present.

According to DSM-III-R, the diagnosis of a delusional disorder could apply, if the phenomenon did not qualify as bizarre. Given that it is possible to change one's appearance dramatically with plastic surgery and to use an alias or even to assume a new identity, complete with falsified birth certificate and other documents, I think that the Capgras delusion, though implausible, is not totally so. A prominent mood syndrome needs to be present, concurrent with the delusion, for a psychotic mood disorder to be diagnosed.

Capgras has usually been reported to occur in a clear state of consciousness, which causes some confusion when it is suggested that there is a potential organic etiology for the syndrome. In DSM-III and DSM-III-R, however, a reduced level of consciousness is seen only in a delirium. A focal organic lesion (e.g., from localized trauma to the brain) that caused the development of a delusion, but no global signs of organicity, is appropriately diagnosed organic delusional syndrome according to the DSM-III systems.

De Clérambault's syndrome. The typical patient with de Clérambault's syndrome is a woman who develops a delusion that a man with whom she has had very little previous contact is in love with her. The person selected is usually a public figure, such as a politician or an entertainer, but may also be a doctor or clergyman. The following case illustrates de Clérambault's syndrome.

In Love, Madly

A 38-year-old housewife was brought to a psychiatric emergency facility by police and an aide of her local congressman. The woman had appeared in the congressman's office for the third time in a week insisting that he stop trying to arrange a romantic liaison between the two of them. "I'm a married woman," she said, "my husband would be insane with jealousy if he knew."

When asked by the psychiatrist what evidence she had that the congressman was "after her," she replied that she had received numerous letters from his office that were "signs" of his interest and had seen his car "parked on the street where I usually shop." When asked whether this could he a product of her imagination, she replied angrily, "You men are all alike!"

Hallucinations are usually absent in de Clérambault's syndrome as in Capgras; there is no ambiguity, however, about whether the delusion in the former is implausible, i.e., bizarre—it clearly is not. An erotomanic delusion in the absence of prominent hallucinations (or a prominent mood syndrome) was assigned to the residual category of atypical psychosis in DSM-III. With the broadened definition of delusional disorder in DSM-III-R, a pure case of de Clérambault's syndrome is the prototypic example of the erotomanic subtype. De Clérambault's syndrome may also occur in the context of other signs of schizophrenia, in which case the latter diagnosis would apply.

The Othello syndrome. The Othello syndrome is characterized by the delusion of infidelity of the spouse. Delusions of jealousy in the absence of hallucinations or other signs of schizophrenia, mood symptoms, or signs of an organic etiology, which were diagnosed as paranoid disorders in DSM-III, are called delusional disorder, jealous type, in DSM-III-R. This delusion can also be seen as part of schizophrenia, paranoid type, bipolar illness or major depression with psychotic features, or an organic mental disorder, such as the organic delusional syndrome sometimes observed in chronic alcoholism.

The Ganser syndrome. The most prominent characteristic of the Ganser syndrome is the giving of approximate answers to simple and familiar questions, the person being in a state of disturbed or clouded consciousness. Historically, this condition was considered a "hysterical pseudodementia." Although pseudoneurological motor and sensory signs and symptoms may also be present, no organic etiology can be discovered.

Most clinicians have focused on the feigned nature of the symptoms in the Ganser syndrome. In DSM-III, feigned psychological symptoms were diagnosed as factitious disorder with psychological symptoms or as malingering, depending on whether the patient's motive was apparently to assume the role of a patient (factitious disorder) and was not otherwise understandable in light of the person's environmental circumstances (malingering). Some modern clinicians have focused more on the altered state of consciousness that accompanies Ganser syndrome and argued that it is a dissociative phenomenon.

DSM-III-R mentions Ganser syndrome as an example of a dissociative disorder not otherwise specified. It is defined as "the giving of 'approximate answers' to questions, commonly associated with other symptoms such as amnesia, disorientation, perceptual disturbances, fugue, and conversion symptoms" (6, p. 277). Factitious disorder with psychological symptoms applies only to cases in which the dissociative phenomena are absent.

The Couvade syndrome. The patient with the Couvade syndrome is usually the husband of a pregnant woman. He develops symptoms strikingly similar to those of pregnancy, including morning sickness, toothache, and abdominal pain and discomfort. Actual swelling of the abdomen is very rare. Since these physical symptoms have no demonstrable physical basis, they indicate a somatoform disorder. In its classic form, associated with a wife's pregnancy, the Couvade syndrome meets DSM-III-R criteria for a conversion disorder. The syndrome includes an alteration in physical functioning; etiologically related psychological factors, indicated by the temporal relationship between the course of the symptoms and the course of the wife's pregnancy; no conscious intentionality in producing the symptoms; no physical disorder to explain the symptoms; and more than simply a complaint of pain or a disturbance in sexual functioning.

The Munchausen syndrome. Patients with the Munchausen syndrome are repeatedly admitted to hospitals for acute physical illnesses that are self-induced; they recount a dramatic medical history, much of which is falsified. The key element is the intentional production or feigning of physical symptoms and illnesses to assume the sick role, but for no external reasons. Classically, abdominal, hemorrhagic, neurologic, cutaneous, cardiac, respiratory, and polysymptomatic subtypes have been described, based on the primary focus of the induced symptom(s). Munchausen syndrome is called factitious disorder with physical symptoms in DSM-III-R; it is also discussed in Chapter 8 of this book.

Gilles de la Tourette's syndrome. The patient with Tourette's syndrome is afflicted with multiple motor tics, accompanied by compulsive utterances, such as the forced shouting of obscenities (coprolalia), beginning in childhood. The patient may also repeat words or

Table 12.8 DSM-III-R Diagnostic Criteria for Tourette's Disorder

A. Both multiple motor and one or more vocal tics have been present at some time during the illness, although not necessarily concurrently.

B. The tics occur many times a day (usually in bouts), nearly every day or intermittently throughout a period of more than one year.

C. The anatomic location, number, frequency, complexity, and severity of the tics change over time.

D. Onset before age 21.

E. Occurrence not exclusively during psychoactive substance intoxication or known central nervous system disease, such as Huntington's chorea or postviral encephalitis.

phrases spoken to him (echolalia) or imitate, compulsively, movements and gestures of others around him (echokinesia or echopraxia).

DSM-III and DSM-III-R include Tourette's disorder, a tic disorder (stereotyped movement disorder in DSM-III), in the disorders usually first evident in infancy, childhood, or adolescence. An examination of the DSM-III-R criteria in Table 12.8 reveals an emphasis on the multiple motor and vocal tics rather than the imitative behavior. The criteria no longer require that the person be able to suppress the movements voluntarily.

Cotard's syndrome. The essential feature of Cotard's syndrome, a rare condition, is a nihilistic delusion that leads the patient to deny his own existence and that of the external world. There has been a debate about whether the syndrome ever exists in the absence of another major mental disorder, most commonly depression or an organic mental syndrome.

In DSM-III and DSM-III-R, nihilistic delusions are mentioned as examples of mood-congruent psychotic features in the subtyping of major depressive episodes. Therefore, in the presence of a full depressive syndrome, Cotard's syndrome would be diagnosed as major depression with mood-congruent psychotic features. Among the organic mental disorders, primary degenerative and multi-infarct dementias include a "with delusions" subtype, allowing for classification of nihilistic and other delusions occurring with dementias of the senium and presenium. Should a localized brain lesion (e.g., stroke) cause a Cotard-like delusion, but no more pervasive cognitive changes, an organic delusional disorder would apply.

Folie à deux. In *folie à deux,* delusions—usually persecutory—are transmitted from one person to another, closely associated person so that the second person comes to share the same delusional ideas. In DSM-III, *folie à deux* was called "shared paranoid disorder," and was listed as a category within the diagnostic class of paranoid disorders. In DSM-III-R, the syndrome has been renamed "induced psychotic disorder," and is listed as a psychotic disorder not elsewhere classified. The new term and the revised criteria (Table 12.9) reflect a more accurate description of the common form of the disorder *(folie imposée),* in which the person with the initial psychosis is a dominant individual who actively imposes the delusional beliefs on the other person, who is more passive, submissive, and suggestible.

Possession states. The common denominator in possession states is that the person believes that his or her symptoms, experiences, or behavior is due to some supernatural influence, commonly the devil. The beliefs may or may not be of delusional intensity.

In some cultures, beliefs in relatively concrete mechanisms of spiritual causality are quite common, even the norm. Subcultural relativity is important in evaluating patients speaking of possession. Patients with delusions of control have Schneiderian first-rank symptoms, which are bizarre, and would meet criterion A for schizophrenia or schizophreniform disorder. Nonpsychotic patients who felt possessed were difficult to classify by DSM-III. The Biometrics Research group at the N. Y. State Psychiatric Institute diagnosed such a case as an atypical dissociative disorder in the book *Psychopathology: A Case Book* (44). In DSM-III-R, a new category of possession-trace disorder was to be added to the dissociative disorders. The criteria from a preliminary draft of DSM-III-R are reproduced in Table 12.10. They require that the phenomena occur outside a culturally sanc-

Table 12.9 DSM-III-R Diagnostic Criteria for Induced Psychotic Disorder

A. A delusion develops (in a second person) in the context of a close relationship with another person, or persons, with an already established delusion (the primary case).

B. The delusion in the second person is similar in content to that in the primary case.

C. Immediately before onset of the induced delusion, the second person did not have a psychotic disorder or the prodromal symptoms of schizophrenia.

Table 12.10 Proposed Diagnostic Criteria for Possession/Trance Disorder

A. The predominant disturbance is either (1) or (2):

   (1) a trance, i.e., an altered state of consciousness with markedly diminished or selectively focused responsivity to environmental stimuli

   (2) possession, i.e., the belief that one has been taken over by some spirit or person (usually associated with trance)

B. The disturbance occurs outside a culturally sanctioned context, such as a religious ritual or ceremony.

C. The occurrence is not solely during the course of multiple personality disorder, brief reactive psychosis, or a psychotic disorder.

D. The disturbance is not due to a physical disorder, e.g., temporal lobe epilepsy, or a psychoactive substance-induced organic mental disorder, e.g., intoxication from peyote or mescaline.

tioned context, such as a religious ceremony, and that they be nonpsychotic and not substance-induced or of other organic etiology. In the final version of DSM-III-R, possession states are considered most commonly to be variants of multiple personality disorder (7).

SUMMARY

This chapter covers a broad range of differential diagnostic problems that could not be adequately addressed within the areas of psychopathology discussed in the previous chapters. Some of the syndromes, such as the premenstrual syndrome, are extremely common, while others, such as the Ganser syndrome, are so rare that many readers of this book may never actually see patients with them. Dissociative disorders, paraphilias, gender identity disorders, and impulse control disorders not elsewhere classified are DSM-III and DSM-III-R diagnostic groups with distinctive psychopathologies that set them apart from the more usual differential diagnostic concerns of disturbances in mood, anxiety states, psychotic features, etc. Non-DSM-III syndromes are included because many clinicians ask how the DSM-III systems would deal with these conditions.

The culture-bound syndromes tax the limits of our classification and underscore the pathoplastic influence of culture on all psychopathology. Uncommon psychiatric syndromes illustrate the coverage of the classifications and the historical continuity between modern systems and syndromes described in the past.

REFERENCES

1. Spitzer RL, Williams JBW, Skodol AE (eds): International Perspectives on DSM-III. Washington, DC, American Psychiatric Press, 1983
2. Mezzich JE, Fabrega H Jr, Mezzich AC, Coffman GA: International experience with DSM-III. J Nerv Ment Dis 173:738–741, 1985
3. Mezzich JE: International use and impact, in An Annotated Bibliography of DSM-III. Edited by Skodol AE, Spitzer RL. Washington, DC, American Psychiatric Press, 1987, pp 37–46
4. Wig NN: DSM-III: a perspective from the Third World, in International Perspectives on DSM-III. Edited by Spitzer RL, Williams JBW, Skodol AE. Washington, DC, American Psychiatric Press, 1983, pp 79–89
5. American Psychiatric Association: Diagnostic and Statistical Manual of Mental Disorders, Third Edition. Washington, DC, American Psychiatric Association, 1980
6. American Psychiatric Association: Diagnostic and Statistical Manual of Mental Disorders, Third Edition, Revised. Washington, DC, American Psychiatric Association, 1987
7. Kluft RP: Dissociative disorders, in An Annotated Bibliography of DSM-III. Edited by Skodol AE, Spitzer RL. Washington, DC, American Psychiatric Press, 1987, pp 119–124
8. Kluft RP: Aspects of the treatment of multiple personality disorder. Psychiatric Annals 14:51–57, 1984
9. Putnam FW, Guroff JJ, Silberman EK, Barban L, Post RM: The clinical phenomenology of multiple personality disorder: review of 100 recent cases. J Clin Psychiatry 47:285–293, 1986
10. Braun BG: The transgenerational incidence of dissociation and multiple personality disorder: a preliminary report, in Childhood Antecedents of Multiple Personality. Edited by Kluft RP. Washington, DC, American Psychiatric Press, 1985, pp 127–150
11. Coons PM: Children of parents with multiple personality disorder, in Childhood Antecedents of Multiple Personality. Edited by Kluft RP. Washington, DC, American Psychiatric Press, 1985, pp 151–165
12. Money J: Paraphilias: phenomenology and classification. Am J Psychother 38:164–179, 1984
13. Green R: Gender identity in childhood and later sexual orientation: follow-up of 78 males. Am J Psychiatry 142:339–341, 1985
14. Custer RL: Profile of the pathological gambler. J Clin Psychiatry 45:35–38, 1984
15. Volberg RA, Steadman HJ: Refining prevalence estimates of pathological gambling. Am J Psychiatry 145:502–505, 1988
16. Hollender MH, Hirsch SJ: Hysterical psychosis. Am J Psychiatry 120:1066–1074, 1964
17. Bishop ER Jr, Holt AR: Pseudopsychosis: a reexamination of the concept of hysterical psychosis. Compr Psychiatry 21:150–161, 1980
18. Spitzer RL, Gibbon M, Skodol A, Williams JBW, Hyler S: The heavenly vision of a poor woman: a down-to-earth discussion of the DSM-III differential diagnosis. J Operational Psychiatry 11:169–172, 1980
19. Spitzer RL, Skodol AE, Gibbon M, Williams JBW: DSM-III Case Book. Washington, DC, American Psychiatric Association, 1981
20. Gift TE, Strauss JS, Young Y: Hysterical psychosis: an empirical approach. Am J Psychiatry 142:345–347, 1985

21. Kahan J, Pattison EM: Proposal for a distinctive diagnosis: the deliberate self-harm syndrome (DSH). Suicide Life Threat Behav 14:17–35, 1984
22. Robins E, Guze S: Establishment of diagnostic validity in psychiatric illnesses: its application to schizophrenia. Am J Psychiatry 126:983–987, 1970
23. Paffenbarger RS Jr: Epidemiological aspects of postpartum mental illness. Br J Prevent Soc Med 18:189–195, 1964
24. Kendell RE, Wainwright S, Hailey A, Shannon B: The influence of childbirth on psychiatric morbidity. Psychol Med 6:297–302, 1976
25. Dean C, Kendell RE: The symptomatology of puerperal illness. Br J Psychiatry 139:128–133, 1981
26. Brockington IF, Cernik KF, Schofield EM, Downing AR, Francis AF, Keelan C: Puerperal psychosis: phenomena and diagnosis. Arch Gen Psychiatry 38:829–833, 1981
27. Katona CLE: Puerperal mental illness: comparisons with non-puerperal controls. Br J Psychiatry 141:447–452, 1982
28. Da Silva L, Johnstone EC: A follow-up study of severe puerperal psychiatric illness. Br J Psychiatry 139:346–354, 1981
29. Halbreich U, Endicott J, Nee J: Premenstrual depressive changes: value of differentiation. Arch Gen Psychiatry 40:535–542, 1983
30. Halbreich U, Endicott J: Relationship of dysphoric premenstrual changes to depressive disorders. Acta Psychiatr Scand 71:331–338, 1985
31. Schuckit MA, Daily V, Herman G, Hineman S: Premenstrual symptoms and depression in a university population. Dis Nerv Syst 36:516–517, 1975
32. Wetzel JN, Reich T, McClure JM, Wald I: Premenstrual affective syndrome and affective disorder. Br J Psychiatry 127:219–221, 1975
33. Schnurr PP: Some correlates of prospectively defined premenstrual syndrome. Am J Psychiatry 145:491–494, 1988
34. DeJong R, Rubinow DR, Roy-Byrne P, Hoban MC, Grover GN, Post RM: Premenstrual mood disorder and psychiatric illness. Am J Psychiatry 142:1359–1361, 1985
35. Hyler SE, Williams JBW, Spitzer RL: Where, in DSM-III-R, is "compensation neurosis"? Am J Forensic Psychiatry 9:3–12, 1988
36. Westermeyer J: Psychiatric diagnosis across cultural boundaries. Am J Psychiatry 142:798–805, 1985
37. Marsella AJ: Culture and mental health: an overview, in Cultural Conceptions of Mental Health and Therapy. Edited by Marsella AJ, White GM. Boston, Reidel Publishing Company, 1982, pp 359–388
38. Kenny MG: Paradox lost: the latah problem revisited. J Nerv Ment Dis 171:159–167, 1983
39. Kenny MG: Multiple personality and spirit possession. Psychiatry 44:337–358, 1981
40. Monroe RR: DSM-III style diagnoses of the episodic disorders. J Nerv Ment Dis 170:665–669, 1982
41. Cloninger CR, Sigvardsson S, von Knorring AL, Bohman M: An adoption study of somatoform disorders. II. Identification of two discrete somatoform disorders. Arch Gen Psychiatry 41:863–871, 1984
42. Honda, Y: DSM-III in Japan, in International Perspectives on DSM-III. Edited by Spitzer RL, Williams JBW, Skodol AE. Washington, DC, American Psychiatric Press, 1983, pp 185–201
43. Enoch MD, Trethowan WH: Some Uncommon Psychiatric Syndromes. Bristol, England, Wright, 1979
44. Spitzer RL, Skodol AE, Gibbon M, Williams JBW: Psychopathology: A Case Book. New York, McGraw-Hill, 1983

Index

Acrotomophilia, 480
Acute confusional states, 86, 450–452
Adaptive functioning, 15–16, 379
  assessing occupational functioning, 66–67, 70–71
  assessing social functioning, 65–66, 70–71
  assessing use of leisure time, 67–68
  as Axis V diagnosis, 54–72
  diagnostic interviewing, 3
  and psychosocial stress, 63
Addison's disease, 105
  and sexual dysfunction, 352
Adjustment disorder, 221, 315
  duration, 233–234
  geriatric patients, 457, 458
  and insomnia, 356
  with physical complaints, 335
  and physical illness, 219
  and psychological factors affecting physical illness, 326, 327
  psychosocial stressors, 57
  violent or aggressive behavior, 427, 443, 445
  vs. major depression, 232
  vs. personality disorders, 232, 413
Adolescent antisocial behavior, 488
Adult antisocial behavior, 488
Affect, definition, 31, 172, 221–222
Affective disorders. *See* Mood disorders
Age at onset
  distinguishing dementia subtypes, 108–109
  organic delusional syndrome, 94
  psychosis diagnosis, 162
Aging. *See* Geriatric psychiatry
Agoraphobia, 288–292, 338
  with secondary depression, 245
  severity ratings, 50
  vs. depressive disorders, 254
  vs. panic disorder, 286, 287
Alcohol amnestic disorder, 473
Alcohol dependence. *See* Alcoholism
Alcohol hallucinosis, 97, 155
Alcoholism, 135, 136–138, 140, 142, 473
  and bulimia nervosa, 367
  classification, 127
  and dementia, 452
  and depressive disorders, 236
  multiaxial diagnosis, 45
  and multiple substance dependence, 145
  and organic amnestic syndrome, 93
  and Othello syndrome, 512
  and personality disorders, 143–145
  and posttraumatic stress disorder, 310
  and psychosocial stressors, 60
  risk factors, 63
  vs. obsessive compulsive disorder, 301
Alcohol use, 139
  classification, 127
  and organic hallucinosis, 177
  and sexual dysfunction, 352
  vs. mood disorders, 153
Alcohol withdrawal, 132, 138, 147
  classification, 79
  exclusion criteria, 47
  multiaxial diagnosis, 45
  vs. anxiety disorder, 155
Alzheimer's disease, 85, 87, 105, 454

See also Primary degenerative dementia of the Alzheimer type
American Association of Mental Deficiency Adaptive Behavior Scale, 431
Amok, 491, 506, 507–508
Amphetamine delusional disorder, 155
Amphetamine dependence, 127, 128, 135
Amphetamine use
  classification, 127
  diagnostic hierarchies, 46
  and organic delusional syndrome, 177
  and psychotic disorders, 176
  substance-induced disorders, 149
  vs. mood disorders, 153
Anorexia nervosa, 346, 361, 363–365
  and other disorders, 363
  vs. bulimia nervosa, 366–367
  vs. generalized anxiety disorder, 314
  vs. major depression, 331
Antagonistophilia, 480
Anthropophobia, 508
Anticipatory anxiety, 282
Antisocial behavior, 472, 488
Antisocial personality disorder, 403, 409–410, 411–412, 426
  classification, 390
  diagnostic interviewing, 23
  incidence in criminals, 412
  and kleptomania, 487
  and pathological gambling, 486
  and substance use disorders, 141
  violent or aggressive behavior, 434, 436, 441
  vs. antisocial behavior, 488
  vs. substance-induced disorders, 156
Anxiety disorder NOS, 291–292
Anxiety disorders
  and bulimia nervosa, 367
  childhood or adolescent onset, 314
  diagnostic hierarchies, 46
  diagnostic interviewing, 12
  early indications, 17
  family history, 99–100
  and hypochondriasis, 344
  and insomnia, 356
  and mood disorders, 242, 246, 247, 254, 287
  multiaxial diagnosis, 45
  overview, 275–278
  and personality disorders, 409
  and physical illness, 219, 279
  and posttraumatic stress disorder, 310
  and premenstrual syndrome, 502
  and psychoactive substance use, 140, 141, 279
  psychosocial stressors, 314–315
  revised criteria and terminology, 279–280
  and somatization disorder, 332, 339
  vs. depressive disorders, 228, 244, 254
  vs. multiple personality disorder, 476, 477
  vs. schizophrenia, 279
  vs. substance-induced disorders, 149, 155–156
Attention-deficit disorder, 443
  residual type, 438, 439
  violent or aggressive behavior, 427, 436–440
Attention-deficit disorder with hyperactivity (ADDH), 432, 437
Attention-deficit hyperactivity disorder (ADHD), 433
  severity ratings, 50
  violent or aggressive behavior, 438, 440, 443
  vs. organic personality syndrome, 102, 103
Atypical affective disorder, 206, 222
Atypical depression, 222, 287, 490
  vs. typical depression, 244, 245–247
Atypical impulse control disorder, 485
Atypical organic brain syndrome, 92
Atypical organic mental syndrome. *See* Organic mental syndrome NOS
Atypical paranoid disorder, 465
Atypical personality disorder, 416
Atypical pervasive developmental disorder, 213

Atypical psychosis, 168, 196–197, 199, 212, 495
Autistic disorder, 438, 440
  severity ratings, 50
  vs. schizophrenia, 214
Avoidant disorder of childhood or adolescence, 314, 380
Avoidant personality disorder, 387, 395, 397, 403, 412, 414–415
  classification, 390
  and other personality disorders, 413
  and social phobia, 292, 294–295, 296
  vs. mood disorders, 256

Barbiturates
  dependence, 126, 127, 132, 146. *See also* Substance dependence
  use, 127, 153
  withdrawal, 155
Beck Depression Inventory, 462
Benign senescent forgetfulness, 109
Bipolar disorder, 228, 257–267
  and Capgras syndrome, 511
  classification, 222, 223, 257
  family history, 16
  geriatric patients, 455, 456, 459
  and Othello syndrome, 512
  and posttraumatic stress disorder, 310
  and schizophreniform disorder, 202
  and substance use disorders, 142
  subtypes, 261
  threshold for clinical significance, 257–261
  violent or aggressive behavior, 436
  vs. cyclothymia, 265
  vs. major depression, 244, 247–248
  vs. schizoaffective disorder, 210, 267
  vs. substance-induced disorders, 151
Bipolar disorder NOS, 208, 264
  classification, 223, 257
  and personality disorders, 381
Bipolar II, 16, 248, 264, 381
Bizarre delusions, 169, 184, 185
Blindness and organic hallucinosis, 97, 178
Body dysmorphic disorder, 331, 345–347
Borderline intellectual functioning, 431, 472, 488
  See also Mental retardation
Borderline personality disorder, 246, 387, 400, 401, 403, 405–411, 417
  and anorexia nervosa, 363
  and bulimia nervosa, 367
  classification, 390, 392
  duration of symptoms, 199
  and factitious disorder, 505
  and mood disorders, 381, 385
  personality functioning, 14
  self-mutilating behavior, 376
  and substance dependence, 141
  violent or aggressive behavior, 436, 441
  vs. adjustment disorder, 232
  vs. mood disorders, 255, 256
  vs. multiple personality disorder, 477–478
  vs. substance-induced disorders, 156
Bouffees delirantes, 490
Brain injury, 100, 102, 432, 511
Brain tumor, 100, 106, 110, 178
Brief reactive psychosis, 167, 197, 494
  and delirium, 452
  geriatric patients, 463
Briquet's syndrome, 332, 333, 336, 491
Bulimia nervosa, 361, 365–367, 509
  vs. anorexia nervosa, 366–367

Caffeine, 145, 146
  vs. anxiety disorder, 155
Cannabis dependence, 126, 127, 128, 135, 136, 140
  See also Substance dependence
Cannabis use
  classification, 127
  and organic delusional syndrome, 177
  substance-induced disorders, 149
  vs. mood disorders, 153
Capgras syndrome, 299, 490, 510–511, 512

Cardiac neurosis, 282, 490
Child abuse, 12, 445–446, 475
Childhood antisocial behavior, 472, 488
Children's Global Assessment Scale, 43, 68
Clouding of consciousness, 81–84
Cocaine delusional disorder, 155
Cocaine dependence, 128–129, 135, 138, 140, 487
  and mood disorders, 142, 143
Cocaine use
  exclusion criteria, 47, 49
  and substance-induced organic mental disorders, 147–148
  vs. cyclothymia, 264–265
  vs. mood disorders, 153–155
  withdrawal, 49, 138
Columbia University Social Psychiatry Research Unit, 64
Compensation neurosis, 490, 504–506
Compulsive personality disorder, 412, 415
  and anorexia nervosa, 363
  classification, 390
  and major depression, 57
  prototypical behavior, 394
  vs. obsessive compulsive disorder, 301
Conduct disorders, 380, 412
  and kleptomania, 487
  severity ratings, 50
  violent or aggressive behavior, 427, 434, 436, 440, 441, 442, 443
Conversion disorder, 329, 331, 337, 339, 403, 491
  classification, 321
  and dementia, 89
  exclusions, 341–342
  and personality disorders, 404
  positive evidence of psychological factors, 340–341
  vs. Couvade syndrome, 513
  vs. physical illness, 339–340
  vs. trichotillomania, 347, 348
Cotard's syndrome, 510, 514
Couvade syndrome, 510, 513
Cushing's disease
  and organic affective syndrome, 99
  and organic anxiety syndrome, 100
  and sexual dysfunction, 352
Cyclothymia, 263–265
  classification, 222, 223, 257
  exclusion criteria, 49
  and personality disorders, 381
  and substance use disorders, 142
  vs. bipolar disorder, 265
  vs. dysthymia, 265
  vs. personality disorders, 265–267

Danish Adoption Studies of Schizophrenia, 16, 398
Deafness and organic hallucinosis, 97, 178
de Clerambault's syndrome, 490, 510, 511–512
Defense mechanisms, 387–388
Deficit state, 173
Deliberate self-harm syndrome, 490, 496–497
Delirium, 81–87
  age factor, 449
  classification, 79
  and dementia, 87–89
  diagnostic interviewing, 7–8
  and physical illness, 450–451
  and pregnancy, 500
  and psychological factors affecting physical illness, 327
  and substance use disorder, 149
  vs. acute confusional states, 450–452
  vs. functional disorder, 84–86
  vs. other organic mental disorders, 87
Delirium tremens, 147
Delusional disorders, 494, 509
  and delirium, 452
  geriatric patients, 463, 464, 465, 466
  and pain disorders, 343
  and somatoform disorders, 331
  vs. Capgras syndrome, 511
  vs. obsessive compulsive disorder, 299
  vs. Othello syndrome, 512
  vs. paranoid personality disorder, 398
Delusional (paranoid) disorders, 184–185, 188–190

Dementia
acute vs. chronic, 80
age factor, 449
as Axis III diagnosis, 41
classification, 79
and conversion disorder, 89
and delirium, 86, 87–89
diagnostic interviewing, 2, 7–8
and histrionic personality disorder, 89
and hypothyroidism, 78
loss of orientation, 32
and mood disorders, 89, 90
and organic delusional syndrome, 94
problems with multiaxial diagnosis, 43
psychotic vs. nonpsychotic, 79
recognizing mild cases, 91–92
severity ratings, 50
violent behavior, 432
vs. organic amnestic syndrome, 93
vs. organic personality syndrome, 102
vs. pseudodementia, 89–91, 452–455, 459
Dementia praecox, 151, 490
Dementias arising in the senium and presenium, 78, 105–111
classification, 80
distinguishing subtypes, 108–109
Dementia syndrome of depression, 90
Dependent personality disorder, 387, 412–414, 415
classification, 390, 391
prototypical behavior, 394
vs. mood disorders, 256
Depersonalization disorder, 472, 479
Depressive dementia, 90
Depressive disorder NOS, 208, 235
classification, 223
geriatric patients, 458
Depressive disorders
and alcoholism, 236
classification, 223
geriatric patients, 457
and insomnia, 356
pain-prone disorder, 342
and personality disorders, 413
and physical illness, 219
and pregnancy, 498
with psychotic features, 204–212
and social phobia, 296
and somatization disorder, 332
and substance use disorders, 141
typical vs. atypical depression, 244, 245–247
vs. anxiety disorders, 244, 254
vs. personality disorders, 244, 254–257
Depressive stupor, 239
Derailment, 172
Developmental disorders as Axis II diagnosis, 41
Dexamethasone suppression test (DST), 17, 63, 237, 257, 461, 463
Diagnostic interviewing
basic assumptions, 2–3
canine approach, 4–5
checklist approach, 4, 27
data gathering, 10–18
eliciting the chief complaint, 7–10
history of present illness, 12–13
hypothesis-testing strategies, 3–5
mental status examination, 30–33
past psychiatric history, 13–14
personality functioning, 14–15
physical status, 15
potential problems, 18–30
psychosocial stressors, 15
purposes, 2–3
smorgasbord approach, 4
sources of diagnostic unreliability, 25–26
structure of interview, 5–18
time limit, 1
Diagnostic Interview Schedule (DIS), 25, 175, 291, 297, 335, 336
Diazepam abuse. *See* Substance use disorders
Disruptive behavior disorders, 440
Dissociative disorder NOS, 472, 479, 479–480, 513
vs. possession state, 515
Dissociative disorders, 445, 471, 472–480, 507
and personality disorders, 409
vs. substance-induced disorders, 149
Double depression, 242, 248
Down's syndrome, 431

Dream anxiety disorder, 361
Drug abuse. *See* specific substances; Substance use
Drug addiction. *See* specific substances; Substance dependence
Drug-induced psychotic syndrome, 177–178
Dyspareunia, 339, 350, 352
Dyssomnias, 353
Dysthymia, 242–244, 338, 339
  and anxiety disorders, 247, 254
  classification, 222, 223
  diagnostic hierarchies, 46
  geriatric patients, 458
  and pain disorders, 343
  and premenstrual syndrome, 502, 504
  and substance use disorders, 142
  subtypes, 242–244
  vs. cyclothymia, 265
  vs. major depression, 244, 248–252
Dysthymic disorder. *See* Dysthymia

Eating disorder NOS, 361, 364, 366
Eating disorders, 361–367
  classification, 321
  and personality disorders, 409
  vs. obsessive compulsive disorder, 301
Eidetic imagery, 167
Elderly, mental disorders in. *See* Geriatric psychiatry
Elimination disorders, 361
Encephalitis
  and primary degenerative dementia, 106
Epidemiologic Catchment Area (ECA) Study, 254, 286, 291, 297, 335–336
Epilepsy
  and dissociative disorders, 473, 474
  and organic delusional syndrome, 178
  and organic mental syndrome NOS, 105
  and organic personality syndrome, 100
  violent behavior, 435

Episodic dyscontrol, 435, 508
Exhibitionism, 349, 480

Factitious disorders, 479, 494, 496, 504, 505
  classification, 321
  diagnostic interviewing, 23
  making the diagnosis, 329–330
  noncompliance with medical treatment, 328, 330
  and personality disorders, 410
  vs. Ganser syndrome, 512, 513
  vs. Munchausen syndrome, 513
  vs. psychotic disorders, 178–180
  vs. trichotillomania, 347, 348
Feighner criteria, 191, 235–236
Female sexual arousal disorder, 350
Fetishism, 349, 480, 484
Folie à deux, 510, 515
Folie imposee, 515
Frotteurism, 480
Frumkin, Sylvia, 210–212
Functional enuresis, 361
Fundamentalism, 167

Gambling. *See* Pathological gambling
Ganser syndrome, 479, 510, 512–513
Gender identity disorder of adolescence or adulthood, nontranssexual type (GIDAANT), 484, 485
Gender identity disorders, 349, 472, 484–485
General Health Questionnaire, 463
Generalized anxiety disorder (GAD), 279, 310–314, 326
  diagnostic hierarchies, 46
  and hypochondriasis, 345
  and mood disorders, 247, 313
  and obsessive compulsive disorder, 311
  and pain disorders, 343
  and panic disorder, 311
  and posttraumatic stress disorder, 311
  risk factors, 287
  and schizophrenia, 45
  vs. depressive disorders, 254

vs. other anxiety disorders, 311–312
vs. other disorders, 312–314
vs. panic disorder, 275, 280, 282
Geriatric psychiatry
acute functional confusional states, 86
delirium vs. acute confusional states, 450–452
delirium with dementia, 455–457
dementia vs. pseudodementia, 90, 452–455, 459
incidence of dementia, 87
late-onset psychoses, 463–466
major depression vs. uncomplicated bereavement, 462–463
mood disorders with physical illness, 457–458
Global Assessment of Functioning (GAF) Scale, 43, 68, 72
Global Assessment Scale, 43, 68

Hallucinations as psychotic feature, 163, 167, 173, 180, 181
diagnostic significance, 185–188
Hallucinogen dependence, 135, 138, 139
Hallucinogen use
classification, 127
and organic delusional syndrome, 177
and organic hallucinosis, 177
substance-induced disorders, 149
vs. psychotic disorders, 175
withdrawal, 138
Hamilton Rating Scale for Depression, 383, 459, 460
Heroin dependence, 122
Histrionic personality disorder, 246, 347, 376, 387, 403–404
classification, 390, 391
and dementia, 89
and other personality disorders, 405, 409–410, 414, 415
prototypical behavior, 394
and substance dependence, 143–145
violent and aggressive behavior, 441
vs. adjustment disorder, 232
Huntington's disease
and dementia, 92, 452
and mood disorders, 455
and organic delusional syndrome, 178
and organic personality syndrome, 100
Hwa-byung, 506, 508
Hydrocephalus and primary degenerative dementia, 106
Hypersomnia, 352, 358–360, 361
and insomnia, 359–360
Hypoactive sexual desire disorder, 349
exclusion criteria, 48, 49
Hypochondriasis, 331, 343–345, 508, 509
classification, 321
and depression, 245, 246, 247
and personality disorders, 404
vs. generalized anxiety disorder, 314
vs. somatization disorder, 336–337
Hysterical pseudodementia, 512
Hysterical psychosis, 490, 491–495
Hysteroid dysphoria, 246, 490

Iatrogenic psychoactive substance dependence syndrome, 144
Identity disorders, 380
See also Gender identity disorders
Idiopathic pain disorder, 342–343
classification, 321
relationship to other disorders, 343
Immature personality disorder, 417
Impulse control disorder NOS, 485–487, 496, 497
Impulse control disorders, 472
trichotillomania, 347
violent or aggressive behavior, 434
Impulsive personality disorder, 417
Inadvertent psychoactive substance dependence syndrome, 144
Induced psychotic disorder, 185, 515
Infantile autism, 432
vs. schizophrenia, 213, 214

Inhalant dependence, 135
Inhibited female orgasm, 350
Inhibited male orgasm, 350
Inhibited sexual desire, 349
Insomnia, 356–358, 361
  and cocaine abuse, 154
  definition, 352, 353
  and delirium, 84
  and hypersomnia, 359–360
  and major depressive episode, 229
  and posttraumatic stress disorder, 156
Intermittent explosive disorder, 485, 508
  violent or aggressive behavior, 434–436
  vs. organic personality syndrome, 102, 103
International Classification of Diseases, 9th Revision, Clinical Modification (ICD-9-CM), 77–78, 116, 196
International Pilot Study of Schizophrenia, 191
Isolated explosive disorder, 436, 485, 508

Jakob-Creutzfeldt disease, 109

Kleptomania, 485, 487
Koro, 506, 508
Korsakoff's syndrome, 93

Labile affect, 31
Latah, 491, 506, 507
Late luteal phase dysphoric disorder, 501
Late paraphrenia, 213, 463–464
Learning disabilities as Axis II diagnosis, 41
LSD-induced hallucinosis. *See* Substance use disorders
Luria-Nebraska neuropsychological battery, 87

Major depression, 227–242, 228, 326
  age factor, 449
  and anorexia nervosa, 363
  and anxiety disorders, 254
  associated symptoms, 5
  and body dysmorphic disorder, 347
  classification, 222
  and Cushing's disease, 99
  and dementia, 90
  diagnostic hierarchies, 46
  diagnostic interviewing, 5
  exclusion criteria, 47, 48, 49
  family history, 16, 99
  and generalized anxiety disorder, 313
  geriatric patients, 457, 458, 459
  and hypochondriasis, 344
  with melancholia, 236–239, 244
  and menopause, 52
  and organic personality syndrome, 104
  and Othello syndrome, 512
  and pain disorders, 343
  and panic disorder, 287
  and physical illness, 52, 54
  and pregnancy, 52, 499
  and premenstrual syndrome, 501, 502, 504
  and psychological factors affecting physical illness, 327
  and psychosocial stressors, 56, 57, 59–60, 61
  with psychotic features, 236, 239–241
  remission, 201
  and schizophrenia, 206
  with seasonal pattern, 241–242
  severity ratings, 50
  and sexual dysfunction, 352
  and substance use disorders, 142
  vs. adjustment disorder, 232–235
  vs. anorexia nervosa, 331
  vs. bipolar disorder, 244, 247–248
  vs. Cotard's syndrome, 514
  vs. dysthymia, 244, 248–252
  vs. physical illness, 244
  vs. posttraumatic stress disorder, 309
  vs. schizoaffective disorder, 210, 244, 252–254
  vs. uncomplicated bereavement, 244, 462–463
Male erectile disorder, 352

Male sexual arousal disorder, 350
Malingering, 178–180, 496, 504
  and antisocial personality disorder, 331
  as Axis V diagnosis, 488, 494, 505
  classification, 321
  diagnostic interviewing, 23
  making the diagnosis, 329, 330–331
  noncompliance with medical treatment, 328, 331
  vs. Ganser syndrome, 512–513
  vs. posttraumatic stress disorder, 309
Masochistic personality disorder, 417
Melancholia, 236–239, 244
  geriatric patients, 459–462
Memory impairment, 32–33
  and delirium, 84, 86
  and dementia, 452
  and organic amnestic syndrome, 93
  and organic personality syndrome, 102
  and other organic mental disorders, 426
  and pseudodementia, 453
  psychotic vs. substance-induced disorders, 151
Mental retardation, 426
  adaptive functioning, 64
  as Axis II diagnosis, 41
  diagnostic problems, 432–433
  organic factors, 434
  violent behavior, 427, 431–432, 438
Methadone maintenance, 122
Millon Clinical Multiaxial Inventory (MCMI), 375
Mini-Mental State Examination, 33, 87, 452
Mixed organic brain syndrome, 92
Monosymptomatic hypochondriacal neurosis, 345
Mood, definition, 31, 172, 221–222
Mood disorders, 172, 492
  age factor, 449
  and anxiety disorders, 287
  and borderline personality disorder, 385, 407
  and bulimia nervosa, 367
  and delirium, 452
  and dementia, 89
  diagnostic hierarchies, 46
  diagnostic interviewing, 12
  DSM vs. other diagnostic systems, 235–236
  exclusion criteria, 47
  family history, 16
  geriatric patients, 457–458, 466
  and hypochondriasis, 344
  and obsessive compulsive disorder, 299–300
  organic causes, 77
  and pathological gambling, 486, 487
  and personality disorders, 410
  and physical illness, 223, 229
  and posttraumatic stress disorder, 310
  and pregnancy, 498, 500
  and psychoactive substance use, 121
  with psychotic features, 161, 174, 204–212
  remission, 201
  revised terminology and reorganization, 221–223
  and schizophreniform disorder, 202
  and somatization disorder, 339
  and substance dependence, 141–143
  suspension of hierarchies, 287–288
  typical vs. atypical depression, 244, 245–247
  violent or aggressive behavior, 438, 440, 443
  vs. multiple personality disorder, 476, 477
  vs. other psychotic disorders, 226
  vs. personality disorders, 407
  vs. schizoaffective disorder, 209, 212
  vs. substance-induced disorders, 149, 152–155
  See also specific disorders
Multiaxial diagnosis
  Axis I conventions, 40–41, 42, 44–51
  Axis II conventions, 40–41, 43, 51
  Axis III conventions, 40, 41–42, 51–54

Axis IV conventions, 40, 42, 53–64
Axis V conventions, 40, 43–44, 64–72
changes in Axis V, 16
conceptual problems with DMS-III, 40–44
diagnostic hierarchies, 45–47
exclusion criteria, 47–50
rationale, 40
severity ratings, 50
Multi-infarct dementia (MID), 92, 111
classification, 105, 108, 109
incidence in elderly, 452
psychotic delusions, 178
vs. Cotard's syndrome, 514
vs. primary degenerative dementia of the Alzheimer type, 106–108
Multiple personality disorder, 472, 473, 474–479, 516
Munchausen syndrome, 330, 510, 513
Myoclonic sleep disorder, 359
Mysophilia, 480

Narcissistic personality disorder, 387, 403, 404–405, 409
classification, 390
and mood disorders, 381
violent or aggressive behavior, 436, 440, 441
Narcolepsy, 360
National Board of Medical Examiners, 1
Negative symptoms, 171, 173
Negi-negi, 491
Neurotic depression, 228, 235, 256–257
Newcastle scale for endogenous depression, 238
New York State Psychiatric Institute, 65
Nicotine dependence. *See* Tobacco dependence
Nightmare disorder, 361
NIMH Collaborative Study of the Psychobiology of Depression, 235, 240, 248
Noncompliance with medical treatment, 328, 330, 488

Obsessive compulsive disorder, 298–302
and antidepressant medication, 275
compulsions, definition, 298–299
diagnostic problems, 299–302
and generalized anxiety disorder, 311
and major depression, 246
obsessions, definition, 298
subtypes, 302
vs. compulsive personality disorder, 415
vs. depressive disorders, 254
vs. other disorders, 301–302
vs. sexual aversion disorder, 350
vs. simple phobia, 298
vs. trichotillomania, 347, 348
Opioid dependence, 127, 135
Opioid use, 127, 153, 352
Oppositional defiant disorder, 442, 443
severity ratings, 50
violent or aggressive behavior, 427
Oppositional disorder, 440
Oppositional personality disorder, 380
Organic affective syndrome, 97–99, 221
classification, 79, 92
geriatric patients, 458
vs. organic personality syndrome, 104
Organic aggressive syndrome, 436
Organic amnestic syndrome, 93–94
classification, 79, 92
vs. dissociative disorders, 473
Organic anxiety syndrome, 99–100
classification, 92
vs. functional anxiety disorder, 99–100
Organic brain syndromes, 491
diagnostic interviewing, 18, 21
geriatric patients, 455
organization of diagnostic criteria, 78
and pregnancy, 499
psychotic vs. nonpsychotic, 79–80
terminology, 78–79
vs. psychotic disorders, 176
See also Organic mental disorders

Organic delusional syndrome, 94–97
classification, 79, 80, 92
and Othello syndrome, 512
vs. Cotard's syndrome, 514
vs. psychotic disorders, 94–97, 177–178
Organic hallucinosis, 97
classification, 79, 80, 92
vs. psychotic disorders, 177–178
Organic mental disorders, 221, 226
acute vs. chronic, 80
age factor, 449
classification, 319
dementias arising in the senium and presenium, 105–111
diagnostic hierarchies, 45, 46
global, 80–92
incidence in elderly, 452
and insomnia, 356
organization of diagnostic criteria, 77–78
and Othello syndrome, 512
partial, 80–81, 92–105
and pregnancy, 500
and psychological factors affecting physical condition, 327
psychotic vs. nonpsychotic, 79–80
substance-induced, 121–156
substance-specific, 124
terminology, 78–79
violent or aggressive behavior, 432, 441
vs. Cotard's syndrome, 514
vs. dissociative disorders, 473, 474
vs. kleptomania, 487
vs. major depression, 228
See also specific disorders
Organic mental syndrome NOS, 104–105
Organic personality syndrome, 100–104
classification, 79, 92
explosive type, 102
violent or aggressive behavior, 102, 434, 436
vs. attention-deficit hyperactivity disorder, 438
vs. other mental disorders, 102–104
Othello syndrome, 510, 512
Overanxious disorder, 314
Overt Aggression Scale (OAS), 425

Pain-prone disorder, 342
Panic disorder, 279–288, 331, 338, 508
and antidepressant medication, 275
clinical significance of frequency, 284–285
diagnosis of subthreshold cases, 286–287
diagnostic hierarchies, 46
exclusion criteria, 49
and generalized anxiety disorder, 311
and major depression, 287
and pain disorders, 343
and personality disorders, 409
and physical illness, 286
severity ratings, 50
and social phobia, 296
vs. agoraphobia, 287
vs. dissociative disorders, 480
vs. generalized anxiety disorder, 275, 280, 282, 313
vs. heightened anxiety, 280–283
vs. phobias, 285–286, 293–295
Paranoid disorders, 213
acute, 185
diagnostic interviewing, 2
geriatric patients, 463, 464
ruling out organic factors, 175–178
Paranoid ideation, 185
and cocaine abuse, 154
and organic personality syndrome, 101
Paranoid personality disorder, 395, 397–398
classification, 390
definition, 376
violent behavior, 441
vs. paranoid schizophrenia, 398
Paraphilia NOS, 480
Paraphilias, 349, 419, 480–484
severity ratings, 50
vs. obsessive compulsive disorder, 301
Paraphrenia, 213
Parasomnias, 353, 361

Parinaud's syndrome, 95–96
Parkinson's disease, 457
  and insomnia, 356
  and mood disorders, 455
  and organic mental disorders, 111
  and primary degenerative dementia, 106
Passive aggressive personality disorder, 378, 380, 412, 415–416
  classification, 390
  definition, 376
  and factitious disorder, 505
  and mood disorders, 381
Pathological gambling, 485–487
  vs. obsessive compulsive disorder, 301
Pedophilia, 349, 480, 482–483
Personality Disorder Examination (PDE), 375
Personality disorder NOS, 416–417
Personality disorders
  age factor, 433, 449
  assessing pervasiveness, 376–378
  and body dysmorphic disorder, 346
  cross-cultural relevance, 509
  descriptive clusters, 305
  diagnostic interviewing, 2
  diagnostic problems, 25, 374–395
  and impulse control disorders, 487
  and insomnia, 356
  mixed personality disorders, 416
  multiaxial conventions, 40, 41, 51, 373–374, 381–385
  multiple, overlapping syndromes, 388–393
  noncompliance with medical treatment, 328
  objective behavior vs. inference, 393–395
  personality functioning, 14–15
  and posttraumatic stress disorder, 310
  and pregnancy, 500
  and premenstrual syndrome, 502
  psychotic features, 161
  risk factors, 63
  state vs. trait, 15, 378–385
  and substance use, 140, 143–145
  vs. adjustment disorder, 232
  vs. cyclothymia, 265–267
  vs. depressive disorders, 228, 244, 254–257
  vs. personality traits, 385–388, 413
  vs. posttraumatic stress disorder, 309
  vs. substance-induced disorders, 149, 156
Personality Disorders Questionnaire (PDQ), 375
Personality functioning, 14–15, 51
Pervasive developmental disorder NOS, 438
  vs. schizophrenia, 214
Pervasive developmental disorders, 380, 432, 433
  as Axis II diagnosis, 41
  early indications, 17
  vs. schizophrenia, 213
Phencyclidine or similarly acting arylcyclohexylamine abuse, 127
Phencyclidine or similarly acting arylcyclohexylamine dependence, 135
Phencyclidine use
  and psychotic disorders, 176
  vs. anxiety disorder, 155
Phenylketonuria, 431
Phobias, 32
  multiaxial diagnosis, 45
  vs. depressive disorders, 254
  vs. panic disorder, 285–286
Physical illness, 457
  and anxiety disorders, 279
  as Axis III diagnosis, 52–53
  conversion disorder, 339
  and delirium, 86, 450–451
  and dementia, 87, 92, 110, 452
  and mood disorders, 223, 229, 244, 455
  and organic amnestic syndrome, 93
  and organic anxiety syndrome, 99, 100
  and organic delusional syndrome, 96–97
  and organic mental syndrome, 107
  and organic mood syndrome, 97–98, 98
  and organic personality syndrome, 100, 104
  and panic disorder, 286

and primary degenerative dementia, 106, 107
as psychosocial stressor, 53–54, 58–59
and sexual dysfunction, 352
and violent or aggressive behavior, 432, 434
vs. major depression, 244
Pick's disease, 109
Polysubstance dependence, 145–146
Possession/trance disorder, 167, 472, 510, 515–516
Posthallucinogen perception disorder (PHPD), 152, 155
Postpartum mental illness. *See* Puerperal mental illness
Posttraumatic stress disorder (PTSD), 302–310, 473, 504, 506
diagnostic problems, 306–310
and generalized anxiety disorder, 311
vs. other mental disorders, 309–310
vs. simple phobia, 298
vs. substance-induced disorders, 155
Poverty of speech, 181
Premature ejaculation, 350
Premenstrual dysphoric disorder, 501
Premenstrual syndrome (PMS), 490, 500–504
Presenile dementia NOS, 109–111, 111
classification, 105
Present State Examination (PSE), 25, 497
Primary degenerative dementia of the Alzheimer type (PDDAT)
classification, 105, 108
etiology, 89
incidence, 87
vs. multi-infarct dementia, 106–108
vs. other causes of dementia, 105–106
Primary degenerative dementia (PDD), 111
adaptive functioning, 64
classification, 79, 105, 108–109
and delirium, 84–85
etiology, 89
incidence in elderly, 452
and organic amnestic syndrome, 93–94
and organic delusional syndrome, 94
psychotic delusions, 178
with secondary depression, 109
vs. Cotard's syndrome, 514
vs. delirium, 452
vs. multi-infarct dementia, 107–108
vs. other causes of dementia, 106
vs. other organic mental disorders, 111
Pseudodelirium, 450, 452, 455
Pseudodementia, 450
secondary to a mood disorder, 109
vs. dementia, 452–455, 459
Pseudologica fantastica, 179, 330
Pseudopsychosis, 491
Psychiatric Epidemiology Research Interview (PERI)
Life-Events Inventory, 58
Psychoactive substance dependence, 486
severity ratings, 50
See also specific substances
Psychoactive substance dependence NOS, 145–146
Psychoactive substance use
and anxiety disorders, 279
and cyclothymia, 264
and insomnia, 356
and mood disorders, 223, 226
and organic personality syndrome, 104
violent or aggressive behavior, 434, 436
vs. dissociative disorders, 473
See also specific substances
Psychoactive substance use disorder, 496
abuse vs. dependence, 139–140
classification and terminology, 121–123
degree of severity, 135–139
dependence on multiple substances, 145–146
diagnostic problems, 131–133
expanded categories, 149

and insomnia, 356
remission, 201
and somatization disorder, 339
substance-induced OMD vs. functional disorders, 149–156
vs. dissociative disorders, 476
vs. other mental disorders, 140–146
Psychogenic amnesia, 472–473
Psychogenic fugue, 472, 473–474
Psychogenic pain disorder, 331, 336, 342–343, 491, 504
and atypical depression, 246, 247
classification, 321
and personality disorders, 404
relationship to other disorders, 343
Psychological factors affecting physical condition (PFAPC), 321–328, 504, 506
multiaxial conventions, 326–327
noncompliance with medical treatment, 327–328
vs. trichotillomania, 347
Psychosexual dysfunctions. *See* Sexual dysfunctions
Psychosocial stressors
acute vs. chronic, 61–63
assessing multiple stressors, 58–59
as Axis IV diagnosis, 42, 54–64
diagnostic interviewing, 3, 5–6, 15
and major depression, 228
and mood disorders, 232
and psychotic symptoms, 197–199
and schizophrenia, 191
and violent or aggressive behavior, 443–445
Psychosomatic illness, 219–220, 325
Psychotic disorder NOS, 196–197, 208, 209, 210, 253, 465, 495
ruling out organic factors, 175–178
Psychotic disorders
and hypochondriasis, 344
and personality disorders, 409
vs. major depression, 228
Psychotic features
determining tenacity of false beliefs, 169–171
duration of symptoms, 190–204
mood congruency, 207–208, 239
and mood disorders, 204–212, 261
overview, 161–163
reality testing, 163, 168–169
ruling out factitious symptomatology and malingering, 178–180
ruling out organic factors, 175–178
special assessment problems, 173–175
subcultural relativity, 163–168
Puerperal mental illness, 490, 497–500
Pyromania, 485, 487

Reactive depression, 235, 256
Restless leg syndrome, 357, 358

Sadistic personality disorder, 418–419, 483, 501
Scandinavian reactive psychoses, 490
Schedule for Affective Disorders and Schizophrenia (SADS), 25, 235, 375, 460
Schizoaffective disorder
DSM-III criteria, 207–208
DSM-III-R criteria, 208–212
family history, 16
and pregnancy, 498
vs. bipolar disorder, 260, 267
vs. major depression, 240, 241, 244, 252–254
vs. schizophrenia, 174
Schizodepressive, 241
Schizoid disorder of childhood or adolescence, 379–380
Schizoid personality disorder, 395–397, 414, 415
classification, 390
diagnostic hierarchies, 47
prototypical behavior, 394
vs. schizoid disorder of childhood or adolescence, 379–380
vs. schizotypal personality disorder, 400–401

Schizophrenia, 342, 492
  age of onset, diagnostic significance, 212–214
  and atypical affective disorder, 206
  bizarre delusions, 169
  and Capgras syndrome, 511
  catatonic, 18
  and delirium, 452
  diagnostic difficulties, 43, 175
  diagnostic hierarchies, 46, 47
  duration of symptoms, 190–204
  exclusion criteria, 47
  family history, 16
  formal thought disorder, 172, 173
  and generalized anxiety disorder, 45
  geriatric patients, 463, 464, 466
  and hypochondriasis, 345
  identifying patterns, 192–204
  making the diagnosis, 180–190
  and menopause, 52
  and mental retardation, 433
  and multiaxial diagnosis, 71
  negative symptoms, 173
  organic causes, 77, 95, 97
  and organic delusional syndrome, 95–96
  and Othello syndrome, 512
  and pain disorders, 343
  and panic disorder, 288
  and personality disorders, 412
  and physical illness, 52, 54
  and posttraumatic stress disorder, 310
  and pregnancy, 52, 498, 499
  and psychoactive substance use, 121, 140, 141
  and psychological factors affecting physical illness, 327
  and psychosocial stressors, 55, 56
  psychotic features, 161, 162
  residual state, 173
  ruling out factitious symptoms and malingering, 180
  ruling out organic factors, 175–178
  subtyping, 199–204
  violent behavior, 434, 438, 440
  vs. anxiety disorders, 279
  vs. bipolar disorder, 258, 260, 262
  vs. gender identity disorder, 484
  vs. generalized anxiety disorder, 313
  vs. major depression, 240
  vs. mood disorder with psychotic features, 174
  vs. multiple personality disorder, 476
  vs. organic mental disorders, 177
  vs. organic personality syndrome, 102, 103
  vs. paranoid personality disorder, 398
  vs. possession state, 515
  vs. posttraumatic stress disorder, 309
  vs. schizoaffective disorder, 174, 204–212
  vs. schizotypal personality disorder, 174, 384, 399, 400, 402–403
  vs. substance-induced disorders, 151
Schizophreniform disorder, 26, 494
  classification, 201–202
  duration of symptoms, 199, 203, 204
  geriatric patients, 463, 464
  identifying patterns, 196–197
  and mood disorders, 253
  organic etiology, 97
  and pregnancy, 500
  remission, 202
  validity of diagnosis, 201
  vs. possession state, 515
  vs. substance-induced disorders, 151
Schizotypal personality disorder, 395, 396, 398–403, 405
  classification, 390
  identifying patterns, 192–194, 198
  violent behavior, 441
  vs. schizoid personality disorder, 400–401
  vs. schizophrenia, 174, 384
Schneiderian first-rank symptoms, 151, 169, 181, 187, 239, 241, 262, 464, 515
Seasonal affective disorder, 241–242
Self-defeating personality disorder, 409, 417–418, 501
  and factitious disorder, 505
Senile dementia NOS, 109–111, 111

classification, 105
Senile dementia of the Alzheimer type (SDAT), 92
classification, 105
Separation anxiety disorder, 314
Sexual arousal disorder, 350
Sexual aversion disorder, 349–350
Sexual deviations. *See* Paraphilias
Sexual dysfunction NOS, 350
Sexual dysfunctions, 339, 341, 348–352, 353, 480
classification, 321
cross-cultural relevance, 509
exclusion criteria, 48
Sexual masochism, 480, 483
Sexual pain disorders, 350
Sexual perversions. *See* Paraphilias
Sexual sadism, 349, 480, 483
Shared paranoid disorder, 185, 515
Simple delusional disorder, 465
Simple phobias, 297–298
Situational depression, 234–235
Sleep apnea, 357, 359, 360
Sleep disorders, 339, 352–361
classification, 321
and delirium, 84, 86
and depressive disorders, 27
exclusion criteria, 49
and major depressive syndrome, 5
Sleep terror disorder, 361
Sleep-wake schedule disorder, 353, 360–361
Sleepwalking disorder, 361
Social phobia, 347
and antidepressant medication, 275
exclusions, 296–297
nature and limits, 292–293
threshold and severity criteria, 295–296
vs. avoidant personality disorder, 415
vs. depressive disorders, 254
vs. panic disorder, 286, 293–295
Soft neurological signs, 176, 436, 438
and organic personality syndrome, 102
Somatization disorder, 331, 332–339, 342, 492, 508
and anxiety disorders, 332
classification, 321
and depressive disorder, 332
and hypersomnia, 359
and hypochondriasis, 344
and major depression, 246
and panic disorder, 288
and personality disorders, 404
relationship to anxiety disorders, 337–339
relationship to other somatoform disorders, 336–337
and sexual dysfunction, 352
Somatoform disorder NOS, 331, 335, 344
Somatoform disorders, 329, 331–348, 491, 508
and atypical depression, 246, 247
diagnostic hierarchies, 46
general principles, 319–321
and insomnia, 356
and mood disorders, 244
noncompliance with medical treatment, 328
and personality disorders, 409
vs. Couvade syndrome, 513
vs. multiple personality disorder, 476, 477
Somatoform pain disorder, 331, 336, 337, 339, 341, 342–343, 504
classification, 321
and personality disorders, 404
relationship to other disorders, 343
Specialty examination for certification in psychiatry, 1
Stereotyped movement disorder, 432, 514
Stigmatophilia, 480
Structured Clinical Interview for DSM-III-R (SCID), 25, 375
Structured Interview for Disorders of Personality (SIDP), 375
Subcultural syndromes, 506–509
Subdural hematoma and primary degenerative dementia, 106
Substance dependence, 78
definition, 124, 124–127
and posttraumatic stress disorder, 310
Substance-induced organic mental disorders, 78, 147–156
See also Substance use disorders

Substance use
  classification, 79
  definition, 124–127
  and delirium, 86
  and dementia, 110
  and mood disorders, 244
  multiaxial diagnosis, 45
  and organic anxiety syndrome, 99
  and organic hallucinosis, 97
  and organic mental disorders, 78
  and primary degenerative dementia, 106
  and psychosis, 13
  and psychotic disorders, 176
  and voluntary control disorders, 330
Substance use disorders, 403
  abuse vs. dependence, 123–127, 139–140
  and bulimia nervosa, 367
  classification, 121–123
  conceptual problems in DMS-III, 123–129
  degree of severity, 135–139
  dependence on multiple substances, 145–146
  diagnostic problems, 131–133
  duration of symptoms, 191
  expanded categories, 149
  and personality disorders, 410
  substance-induced OMD vs. functional disorders, 149–156
  tolerance, 124
  vs. other mental disorders, 140–146
Substance withdrawal, 124–125
  classification, 79
  and delirium, 86
  treatment, 78
Suicidal ideation, 32
  and cocaine abuse, 154
  with major depression, 57, 228
Superstitions vs. obsessive compulsive disorder, 301

Taijin-kyofu, 506, 508–509
Tangentiality, 172
Taylor and Abrams's Scale for Emotional Blunting, 172
Temporal lobe epilepsy and organic anxiety syndrome, 99
Tobacco dependence, 126–127, 128, 135, 145
Tourette's syndrome, 507, 510, 513–514
Transsexualism, 484
Transvestic fetishism, 480, 484
Trichotillomania, 347–348, 485
Troilism, 480
Tuberculosis and primary degenerative dementia, 106

Uncomplicated bereavement, 221, 472, 488
  exclusion criteria, 49
  vs. major depression, 244, 462–463
Undifferentiated somatoform disorder, 331
United States-United Kingdom Diagnostic Study, 240

Vaginismus, 350
Valium abuse. *See* Substance use disorders
Vineland Adaptive Behavior Scales, 431
Voluntary control disorders, 328–329
Voyeurism, 480, 483

Wechsler Memory Scale, 87
Wihtigo, 491
Winokur system, 235–236
Withdrawal. *See* Substance withdrawal
World Health Organization memorandum on nomenclature and classification of substance problems, 133

Zoophilia, 480